£11·65

A2-Level

Mathematics

ue for return on or before the la~

A2 Maths is seriously tricky — no question about that.
To do well, you're going to need to revise properly and practise hard.

This book has thorough notes on everything in modules C3, C4, S2 and M2.
It'll help you learn the stuff you need and take you step-by-step through loads of examples.

It's got practice questions... lots of them. For every topic there are warm-up and exam-style
questions. Plus there are two full practice exams at the end of each module.

And of course, we've done our best to make the whole thing vaguely entertaining for you.

Complete Revision and Practice

Exam Board: AQA

Contents

Contents

Contributors:

Andy Ballard, Mary Falkner, Paul Jordin, Sharon Keeley-Holden, Claire Jackson, Simon Little, Sam Norman, Ali Palin, Andy Park, David Ryan, Lyn Setchell, Caley Simpson, Jane Towle, Jonathan Wray, Dawn Wright

Proofreaders:

Mona Allen, Alastair Duncombe, Helen Greaves, Glenn Rogers

Published by CGP

ISBN: 978 1 84762 585 4

Groovy Website: www.cgpbooks.co.uk

Printed by Elanders Ltd, Newcastle upon Tyne.

Based on the classic CGP style created by Richard Parsons.

Functions and Mappings

In A2 maths, your teacher might ask you to draw a mapping diagram. Sadly, they don't want you to draw an exciting map with rivers, mountains, caves and secret tunnels on it — they want you to draw a boring diagram. Shame.

Values in the **Domain** are **Mapped** to values in the **Range**

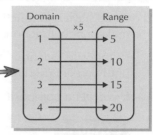

1) A mapping is an operation that takes one number and transforms it into another. E.g. 'multiply by 5', 'square root' and 'divide by 7' are all mappings.

2) The set of numbers you can start with is called the domain, and the set of numbers they can become is called the range. Mappings can be drawn as diagrams like this: You can also draw mappings as graphs (see below).

3) The domain and / or range will often be the set of real numbers, $\mathbb{R}$ (a real number is any positive or negative number (or 0) — fractions, decimals, integers, surds). If x can take any real value, it's usually written as $x \in \mathbb{R}$.

4) You might have to work out the range of a mapping from the domain you're given. For example, $f(x) = x^2$, $x \in \mathbb{R}$ has the range $f(x) \geq 0$, as all square real numbers are positive (or zero).

Other sets of numbers include $\mathbb{Z}$, the set of integers, $\mathbb{N}$, the set of natural numbers (positive integers, not including O) and $\mathbb{C}$, the complex numbers (made up of 'imaginary' numbers — you don't meet these in C3 or C4).

A **Function** is a type of **Mapping**

1) Some mappings take each number in the domain to only one number in the range. These mappings are called functions. If a mapping takes a number from the domain to more than one number in the range (or if it isn't mapped to any number in the range), it's not a function.

Functions (e.g. x^2) are usually written as $f(x) = x^2$.

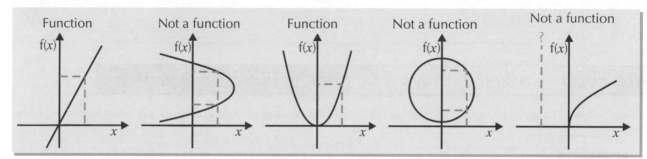

2) For the graphs above, the first and third are functions because each value of x is mapped to a single value of $f(x)$. The second and fourth aren't functions because the values of x are mapped to two different values of $f(x)$. The fifth also isn't a function, this time because $f(x)$ is not defined for $x < 0$.

3) Some mappings that aren't functions can be turned into functions by restricting their domain. For example, the mapping $y = \dfrac{1}{x-1}$ for $x \in \mathbb{R}$ is not a function, because it's not defined at $x = 1$ (draw the graph if you're not convinced). But if you change the domain to $x > 1$, the mapping is now a function.

Functions can be **One-to-One** or **Many-to-One**

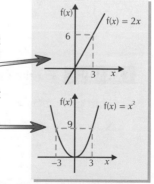

1) A one-to-one function maps one element in the domain to one element in the range — e.g. $f(x) = 2x$, $x \in \mathbb{R}$ is one-to-one, as every x is mapped to a unique value in the range (the range is also $\mathbb{R}$). So only 3 in the domain is mapped to 6 in the range.

2) A many-to-one function maps more than one element in the domain to one element in the range (remember that no element in the domain can map to more than one element in the range, otherwise it wouldn't be a function). $f(x) = x^2$, $x \in \mathbb{R}$ is a many-to-one function, as two elements in the domain map to the same element in the range — e.g. both 3 and −3 map to 9.

Welcome to my domain...

When you're drawing a function or a mapping, you should draw a mapping diagram if you're given a discrete set of numbers (e.g. $x \in \{0,1,2,3\}$), but you should draw a graph if the domain is continuous (e.g. $x \in \mathbb{R}$).

Composite Functions

You're not done with functions yet. Oh no. You need to know what happens if you put <u>two (or more) functions</u> together. There's only one way to find out...

Functions can be **Combined** to make a **Composite Function**

1) If you have two functions f and g, you can <u>combine</u> them (do one followed by the other) to make a new function. This is called a <u>composite function</u>.

2) Composite functions are written fg(x) — this means do g first, then f. If it helps, put <u>brackets</u> in until you get used to it, so fg(x) = f(g(x)). The <u>order</u> is really important — usually fg(x) ≠ gf(x).

3) If you get a composite function that's written f²(x), it means ff(x) — you do f <u>twice</u>.

Composite functions made up of three or more functions work in exactly the same way.

EXAMPLE For the functions $f(x) = 2x^3$ {$x \in \mathbb{R}$} and $g(x) = x - 3$ {$x \in \mathbb{R}$}, find:

> a) fg(4) b) fg(0) c) gf(0) d) fg(x) e) gf(x) f) f²(x).

a) $fg(4) = f(g(4))$
$= f(4 - 3) = f(1)$
$= 2 \times 1^3 = \boxed{2}$

b) $fg(0) = f(g(0))$
$= f(0 - 3) = f(-3)$
$= 2 \times (-3)^3 = 2 \times -27$
$= \boxed{-54}$

c) $gf(0) = g(f(0))$
$= g(2 \times 0^3) = g(0)$
$= 0 - 3 = \boxed{-3}$

From parts b) and c) you can see that fg(x) ≠ gf(x).

d) $fg(x) = f(g(x))$
$= f(x - 3)$
$= \boxed{2(x - 3)^3}$

e) $gf(x) = g(f(x))$
$= g(2x^3)$
$= \boxed{2x^3 - 3}$

f) $f^2(x) = f(f(x))$
$= f(2x^3)$
$= 2(2x^3)^3 = \boxed{16x^9}$

You could be asked to **Solve** a **Composite Function Equation**

If you're asked to <u>solve</u> an equation such as fg(x) = 8, the best way to do it is to <u>work out</u> what fg(x) is, then <u>rearrange</u> fg(x) = 8 to make <u>x</u> the subject.

EXAMPLE For the functions $f(x) = \sqrt{x}$ with domain {$x \geq 0$} and $g(x) = \dfrac{1}{x - 1}$ with domain {$x > 1$}, solve the equation fg(x) = ½. Also, state the range of fg(x).

First, find fg(x): $fg(x) = f\left(\dfrac{1}{x - 1}\right) = \sqrt{\dfrac{1}{x - 1}} = \dfrac{1}{\sqrt{x - 1}}$

So $\dfrac{1}{\sqrt{x - 1}} = \dfrac{1}{2}$

Rearrange this equation to find x:

$\dfrac{1}{\sqrt{x - 1}} = \dfrac{1}{2} \Rightarrow \sqrt{x - 1} = 2 \Rightarrow x - 1 = 4 \Rightarrow \boxed{x = 5}$

To find the range, it's often helpful to draw the graph of fg(x):

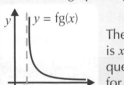

Be careful with the domains and ranges of composite functions.

The domain of fg(x) is $x > 1$ (though the question doesn't ask for this) and the range is $fg(x) > 0$.

EXAMPLE For the functions $f(x) = 2x + 1$ {$x \in \mathbb{R}$} and $g(x) = x^2$ {$x \in \mathbb{R}$}, solve gf(x) = 16.

Find gf(x): $gf(x) = g(2x + 1) = (2x + 1)^2$.

Now solve gf(x) = 16: $(2x + 1)^2 = 16 \Rightarrow 4x^2 + 4x + 1 = 16$
$\Rightarrow 4x^2 + 4x - 15 = 0$
$\Rightarrow (2x - 3)(2x + 5) = 0$ so $x = \dfrac{3}{2}$ or $x = -\dfrac{5}{2}$

Compose a concerto for f(x) and orchestra...

The most important thing to remember on this page is the order you do the functions in — for fg(x) you always do g first as g is next to x. It's like getting dressed — you wouldn't put your shoes on before your socks, as your socks go next to your feet.

Inverse Functions

Just when you'd got your head around <u>functions</u>, <u>ranges</u>, <u>domains</u> and <u>composite functions</u>, they go and turn it all back to front by introducing <u>inverses</u>.

Only **One-to-One Functions** have **Inverses**

1) An <u>inverse function</u> does the <u>opposite</u> to the function. So if the function was '+ 1', the inverse would be '− 1', if the function was '× 2', the inverse would be '÷ 2' etc. The inverse for a function f(x) is written f^{-1}(x).

2) An inverse function <u>maps</u> an element in the <u>range</u> to an element in the <u>domain</u> — the opposite of a function. This means that only <u>one-to-one functions</u> have inverses, as the inverse of a many-to-one function would be one-to-many, which isn't a function (see p.1).

3) For <u>any</u> inverse f^{-1}(x),

~ Doing the function and then the inverse... ~

$$f^{-1}f(x) = x = ff^{-1}(x)$$

...is the same as doing the inverse then doing the function — both just give you x.

4) The <u>domain</u> of the <u>inverse</u> is the <u>range</u> of the <u>function</u>, and the <u>range</u> of the <u>inverse</u> is the <u>domain</u> of the <u>function</u>.

EXAMPLE The function f(x) = x + 7 with domain $x \geq 0$ and range f(x) ≥ 7 is one-to-one, so it has an inverse.

The inverse of + 7 is − 7, so f^{-1}(x) = x − 7. f^{-1}(x) has domain $x \geq 7$ and range f^{-1}(x) ≥ 0.

Work out the **Inverse** using **Algebra**

For <u>simple</u> functions (like the one in the example above), it's easy to work out what the inverse is just by <u>looking</u> at it. But for more <u>complex</u> functions, you need to <u>rearrange</u> the original function to <u>change</u> the <u>subject</u>.

Finding the Inverse

1) **<u>Replace</u> f(x) with y to get an equation for y in terms of x.**

2) **<u>Rearrange</u> the equation to make x the subject.**

3) **<u>Replace</u> x with f^{-1}(x) and y with x — this is the <u>inverse function</u>.**

4) **<u>Swap round</u> the <u>domain</u> and <u>range</u> of the <u>function</u>.**

EXAMPLE Find the inverse of the function f(x) = $3x^2$ + 2 with domain $x \geq 0$, and state its domain and range.

1) First, replace f(x) with y: $y = 3x^2 + 2$.

2) Rearrange the equation to make x the subject:

$$y - 2 = 3x^2 \Rightarrow \frac{y-2}{3} = x^2 \Rightarrow \sqrt{\frac{y-2}{3}} = x$$

$x \geq 0$ so you don't need the negative square root.

~ It's easier to work with y than f(x). ~

3) Replace x with f^{-1}(x) and y with x:

$$f^{-1}(x) = \sqrt{\frac{x-2}{3}}$$

4) Swap the domain and range: the range of f(x) is f(x) ≥ 2, so f^{-1}(x) has domain $x \geq 2$ and range f^{-1}(x) ≥ 0.

You might have to **Draw the Graph** of the Inverse

The inverse of a function is its <u>reflection</u> in the line $y = x$.

EXAMPLE Sketch the graph of the inverse of the function f(x) = x^2 − 8 with domain $x \geq 0$.

It's easy to see what the domains and ranges are from the graph — f(x) has domain $x \geq 0$ and range f(x) ≥ -8, and f^{-1}(x) has domain $x \geq -8$ and range f^{-1}(x) ≥ 0.

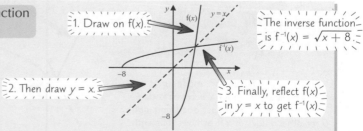

1. Draw on f(x).

2. Then draw $y = x$.

The inverse function is f^{-1}(x) = $\sqrt{x + 8}$.

3. Finally, reflect f(x) in $y = x$ to get f^{-1}(x).

Line y = x on the wall — who is the fairest of them all...

I think I've got the hang of this inverse stuff now — so the inverse of walking to the shops and buying some milk would be taking the money out of the till, putting the milk back on the shelf, leaving the shop and walking home backwards. Sorted.

Modulus

The <u>modulus</u> of a number is really useful if you don't care whether something's positive or negative — like if you were finding the difference between two numbers (e.g. 7 and 12). It doesn't matter which way round you do the subtraction (i.e. 12 − 7 or 7 − 12) — the difference between them is still 5.

Modulus is the *Size* of a number

1) The <u>modulus</u> of a number is its <u>size</u> — it doesn't matter if it's <u>positive</u> or <u>negative</u>. So for a <u>positive</u> number, the modulus is just the <u>same</u> as the number itself, but for a <u>negative</u> number, the modulus is its <u>positive value</u>. For example, the modulus of 8 is 8, and the modulus of −8 is also 8.

The modulus is sometimes called the absolute value.

2) The modulus of a number, x, is written $|x|$. So the example above would be written $|8| = |-8| = 8$.

3) In <u>general</u> terms, for $x \geq 0$, $|x| = x$ and for $x < 0$, $|x| = -x$.

4) <u>Functions</u> can have a modulus too — the modulus of a function f(x) is its <u>positive value</u>. Suppose f(x) = −6, then $|f(x)| = 6$. In general terms,

> $|f(x)| = f(x)$ when $f(x) \geq 0$ and
> $|f(x)| = -f(x)$ when $f(x) < 0$.

5) If the modulus is <u>inside</u> the brackets in the form f($|x|$), then you make the x-value positive <u>before</u> applying the function. So f($|-2|$) = f(2).

The *Graphs* of *|f(x)|* and *f(|x|)* are *Different*

You'll probably have to draw the <u>graph</u> of a modulus function — and there are <u>two different types</u>.

1) For the graph of $y = |f(x)|$, any <u>negative</u> values of f(x) are made <u>positive</u> by <u>reflecting</u> them in the <u>x-axis</u>. This <u>restricts</u> the <u>range</u> of the modulus function to $|f(x)| \geq 0$ (or some subset <u>within</u> $|f(x)| \geq 0$, e.g. $|f(x)| \geq 1$).

2) For the graph of $y = f(|x|)$, the <u>negative</u> x-values produce the <u>same result</u> as the corresponding <u>positive</u> x-values. So the graph of f(x) for $x \geq 0$ is <u>reflected</u> in the <u>y-axis</u> for the negative x-values.

3) The easiest way to draw these graphs is to draw f(x) (<u>ignoring</u> the modulus for now), then <u>reflect</u> it in the <u>appropriate axis</u>. This will probably make more sense when you've had a look at a couple of <u>examples</u>:

EXAMPLE Draw the graphs of $y = |f(x)|$ and $y = f(|x|)$ for the functions f(x) = 5x − 5 and f(x) = x^2 − 4x.

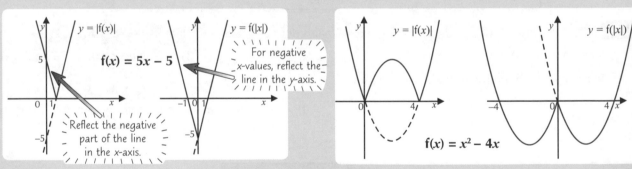

$y = |f(x)|$ $f(x) = 5x − 5$ Reflect the negative part of the line in the x-axis.

$y = f(|x|)$ For negative x-values, reflect the line in the y-axis.

$y = |f(x)|$ $f(x) = x^2 − 4x$ $y = f(|x|)$

EXAMPLE

Draw the graph of the function
$$f(x) = \begin{cases} |2x + 1| & x < 0 \\ \sqrt{x} & x \geq 0 \end{cases}.$$

Sometimes functions are made up of two or more parts — for x between certain values, the function does one thing, but for other values of x it behaves differently.

$y = |2x + 1|$ Draw on each part of the graph separately. $y = \sqrt{x}$

At $x = 0$, $y = |2(0) + 1| = 1$ for the first part of the function and $y = \sqrt{0} = 0$ for the second part of the function — so there'll be a gap in the graph.

Modulus built the city of Mode...

You might have to draw modulus graphs for functions like f(x) = ax + b from scratch. You could be asked for trig graphs and exponentials too. For harder graphs, you'll often be given a graph which you can use as a starting point for the modulus.

Modulus

An exam question might ask you to <u>solve</u> an equation like '$|f(x)| = n$' (for a constant n) or '$|f(x)| = g(x)$' for a function g. I admit, it would be more exciting to solve a <u>crime</u>, but I'm afraid modulus functions must come first...

Solving modulus functions usually produces More Than One solution

Here comes the method for solving '$|f(x)| = n$'. Solving '$|f(x)| = g(x)$' is <u>exactly the same</u> — just replace n with g(x).

Solving Modulus Equations of the form $|f(x)| = n$

1) First, <u>sketch</u> the functions $y = |f(x)|$ and $y = n$, on the <u>same axes</u>. ◄──── The <u>solutions</u> you're trying to find are where they <u>intersect</u>.

2) From the graph, work out the <u>ranges of x</u> for which $f(x) \geq 0$ and $f(x) < 0$:
   E.g. $f(x) \geq 0$ for $x \leq a$ or $x \geq b$ and $f(x) < 0$ for $a < x < b$ ◄──── These ranges should 'fit together' to cover all possible x values.

3) Use this to write <u>two new equations</u>, one true for each range of x...
   (1) $f(x) = n$ for $x \leq a$ or $x \geq b$ ◄──── The original equation '$|f(x)| = n$' becomes '$f(x) = n$' in the range where $f(x) \geq 0$...
   (2) $-f(x) = n$ for $a < x < b$ ◄──── ...and it becomes '$-f(x) = n$' in the range where $f(x) < 0$.

4) Now just <u>solve each equation</u> and check that any solutions are <u>valid</u>
   — get rid of any solutions <u>outside the range</u> of x you've got for that equation.

5) Look at the graph and <u>check</u> that your solutions look right.

Sketch the Graph to see How Many Solutions there are

EXAMPLE   Solve $|x^2 - 9| = 7$.

1) First off, <u>sketch the graphs</u> of $y = |x^2 - 9|$ and $y = 7$. ──────►
   They cross at 4 different points, so there should be <u>4 solutions</u>.

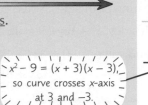

2) Now find out <u>where $f(x) \geq 0$ and $f(x) < 0$</u>:
   $x^2 - 9 \geq 0$ for $x \leq -3$ or $x \geq 3$, and $x^2 - 9 < 0$ for $-3 < x < 3$

$x^2 - 9 = (x + 3)(x - 3)$, so curve crosses x-axis at 3 and -3.

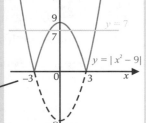

3) Form two equations for the different ranges of x:
   (1) $x^2 - 9 = 7$ for $x \leq -3$ or $x \geq 3$
   (2) $-(x^2 - 9) = 7$ for $-3 < x < 3$

4) Solving (1) gives: $x^2 = 16 \Rightarrow x = 4, x = -4$
   Check they're valid: $x = -4$ is in '$x \leq -3$' and $x = 4$ is in '$x \geq 3$' — so they're both valid.

   Solving (2) gives: $x^2 - 2 = 0 \Rightarrow x^2 = 2$ so $x = \sqrt{2}, x = -\sqrt{2}$.
   Check they're valid: $x = \sqrt{2}$ and $x = -\sqrt{2}$ are both within $-3 < x < 3$ — so they're also both valid.

5) Check back against <u>the graphs</u> — we've found <u>four solutions</u> and they're <u>in the right places</u>. Nice.

EXAMPLE   Solve $|x^2 - 2x - 3| = 1 - x$.

1) <u>Sketch</u> $y = |x^2 - 2x - 3|$ and $y = 1 - x$. The graphs <u>cross twice</u>. ──────►

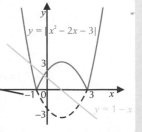

2) Looking at <u>where $f(x) \geq 0$</u> and <u>where $f(x) < 0$</u> gives...

$x^2 - 2x - 3 = (x + 1)(x - 3)$, so it crosses axis at -1 and 3.

3) (1) $x^2 - 2x - 3 = 1 - x$ for $x \leq -1$ or $x \geq 3$
   (2) $-(x^2 - 2x - 3) = 1 - x$ for $-1 < x < 3$.

4) <u>Solving (1)</u> using the quadratic formula gives $x = 2.562, x = -1.562.$
   $x \leq -1$ or $x \geq 3$, so this solution is not valid...   ...but this one is.
   <u>Solving (2)</u> using the quadratic formula gives $x = 3.562, x = -0.562.$
   $-1 < x < 3$, so this solution is not valid...   ...but this one is.

5) Checking against the <u>graph</u>, there are <u>two solutions</u> and they're <u>where we expected</u>. El coolio.

How very interesting...

So if the effect of the modulus is to make a negative positive, I guess that means that |exam followed by detention followed by getting splashed by a car on the way home| = sleep-in followed by picnic followed by date with Hugh Jackman. I wish.

Modulus

Three whole pages on modulus might seem a bit excessive, but it's a tricky little topic that can easily trip you up if you're not careful. It's better to be safe than sorry, as my Auntie Marjorie would say — and believe me, she would know.

You might come across a modulus in an **Equation** or an **Inequality**

You saw how to <u>solve</u> modulus equations on the previous page, but there are a few more useful <u>relations</u> you can use.

1) If you have $|a| = |b|$, this means that $a^2 = b^2$ (as $-a$ and a are the <u>same</u> when squared). This comes in really handy when you have to solve equations of the form $|f(x)| = |g(x)|$ (see below).

> This is because $|x| < 5$ means that $x < 5$ and $-x < 5$, and $-x < 5$ is the same as $x > -5$. You can then put the two inequalities together to get $-5 < x < 5$.

2) <u>Inequalities</u> that have a modulus in them can be really <u>nasty</u> — unfortunately you can't just leave the modulus in there. $|x| < 5$ means that $-5 < x < 5$.

3) Using this, you can <u>rearrange</u> more <u>complicated</u> inequalities like $|x - a| \leq b$. From the method above, this means that $-b \leq x - a \leq b$, so <u>adding a</u> to <u>each bit</u> of the inequality gives $a - b \leq x \leq a + b$.

> **EXAMPLE** Solve $|x - 4| < 7$.
>
> As $|x - 4| < 7$, this means that $-7 < x - 4 < 7$. Adding 4 to each bit gives $-3 < x < 11$.

Solve a modulus equation by **Squaring Both Sides**

If you have an equation of the form $|f(x)| = |g(x)|$, you can solve it using the method on the <u>previous page</u>, but it can get a bit <u>messy</u> with all the modulus signs flying all over the place. Instead, you can use the fact that if $|a| = |b|$ then $a^2 = b^2$ and <u>square both sides</u> of the equation. You'll end up with a <u>quadratic</u> to solve, but that should be a <u>doddle</u>.

> **EXAMPLE** By squaring both sides, solve $|x + 3| = |2x + 5|$.
>
> First, square both sides: $x^2 + 6x + 9 = 4x^2 + 20x + 25$
>
> Then rearrange and solve: $0 = 3x^2 + 14x + 16$
>
> $\qquad\qquad\qquad = (3x + 8)(x + 2)$ So $x = -\frac{8}{3}$ or $x = -2$.

> You can solve equations like $|2x + 3| = 5|x|$ in exactly the same way — just square both sides.

You could also have solved it by sketching the graphs like you did on the previous page:

> **EXAMPLE**
> a) By sketching the graphs, solve $|x + 3| = |2x + 5|$.
> b) Hence solve the inequality $|x + 3| < |2x + 5|$.
>
> a) Sketch $y = |x + 3|$ and $y = |2x + 5|$. The graphs cross twice.
>
> From the graph, you can see that there's one solution where $x + 3 = 2x + 5$, and another where $x + 3 = -(2x + 5) = -2x - 5$.
>
> Solving $x + 3 = 2x + 5$ gives $x = -2$ and solving $x + 3 = -2x - 5$ gives $x = -\frac{8}{3}$ (these are the solutions you found above — and you can see from the graph that they're in the right places).
>
> b) To solve the inequality $|x + 3| < |2x + 5|$, you have to look at the graphs and work out where the graph of $|x + 3|$ is underneath the graph of $|2x + 5|$: you can see from the sketch that this is true when $x < -\frac{8}{3}$ and when $x > -2$.

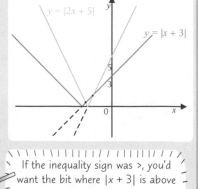

> If the inequality sign was >, you'd want the bit where $|x + 3|$ is above $|2x + 5|$ — where $-\frac{8}{3} < x < -2$.

If you'd tried to solve $-(x + 3) = -(2x + 5)$ and $-(x + 3) = 2x + 5$, you would have just got the <u>same pair of solutions</u>. This is true for <u>any</u> equation of the form $|f(x)| = |g(x)|$ — it might look <u>more complicated</u> than $|f(x)| = n$ or $|f(x)| = g(x)$, but it's actually a bit easier. You can either <u>square both sides</u> or, if you don't want to, you only have to <u>solve two equations</u>: $f(x) = g(x)$ and $-f(x) = g(x)$.

Be there or b^2...

Personally, I think squaring both sides is a bit easier (but then again, I'm a sucker for a quadratic equation). You'll get the same answer whichever way you do it, so it's up to you. By the way, please don't mention penguins to Auntie Marjorie.

Transformations of Graphs

Back in C1, you came across <u>transformations</u> of graphs — vertical and horizontal <u>translations</u>, <u>stretches</u> and <u>reflections</u>. In C2, you saw the same transformations on <u>trig</u> graphs. As if that wasn't enough for you, you now need to be able to do <u>combinations</u> of transformations — more than one applied to the same graph.

There are **Four** main **Transformations**

The transformations you met in C1 and C2 are <u>translations</u> (adding things — a vertical or horizontal <u>shift</u>), <u>stretches</u> or <u>squeezes</u> (either vertical or horizontal) and <u>reflections</u> in the x- or y- axis. Here's a quick reminder of what each one does:

$y = f(x + c)$

For c > 0, the graph is shifted along the x-axis.
f(x + c) is f(x) <u>translated c to the left</u>, and f(x − c) is f(x) <u>translated c to the right</u>.

$y = f(x) + c$

For c > 0, the graph is shifted along the y-axis.
f(x) + c is f(x) <u>translated c upwards</u>, and f(x) − c is f(x) <u>translated c downwards</u>.

All these graphs use f(x) = sin x.

$y = f(ax)$

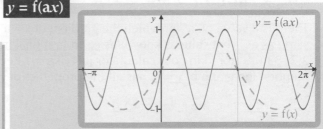

If a > 1, the graph of f(ax) is f(x) <u>squashed horizontally</u> (along the x-axis) by a factor of a.

If 0 < a < 1, the graph is <u>stretched horizontally</u>.

And if a < 0, the graph is also <u>reflected</u> in the <u>y-axis</u>.

$y = af(x)$

If a > 1, the graph of af(x) is f(x) <u>stretched vertically</u> (along the y-axis) by a factor of a.

If 0 < a < 1, the graph is <u>squashed</u>.

And if a < 0, the graph is also <u>reflected</u> in the <u>x-axis</u>.

Remember that a <u>squash</u> by a factor of a is really a <u>stretch</u> by a factor of $1/a$.

Do **Combinations** of Transformations **One at a Time**

<u>Combinations</u> of transformations can look a bit tricky, but if you take them <u>one step</u> at a time they're not too bad. Don't try and do <u>all</u> the transformations at once — break it up into <u>separate bits</u> (as above) and draw a <u>graph</u> for <u>each stage</u>.

EXAMPLE The graph shows the function y = f(x). Draw the graph of y = 3f(x + 2), showing the coordinates of the turning points.

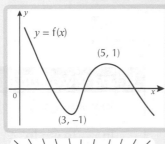

Make sure you do the transformations the right way round — you should do the bit in the brackets first.

Don't try to do everything at once. First draw the graph of y = f(x + 2) and work out the coordinates of the turning points.

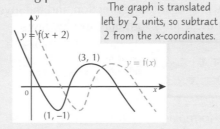

The graph is translated left by 2 units, so subtract 2 from the x-coordinates.

Now use your graph of y = f(x + 2) to draw the graph of y = 3f(x + 2).

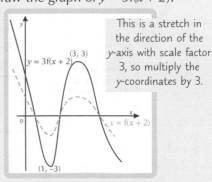

This is a stretch in the direction of the y-axis with scale factor 3, so multiply the y-coordinates by 3.

Tea and cake — the perfect combination...

Working out coordinates can be a bit tricky. The easiest way to do it is to work out what you're doing to the graph, then think about what that does to each point. Have a look at your transformed graph and check that the new coordinates make sense. You might have to apply these transformations to graphs like y = sec x (see p.14) and y = ln x (see p.8).

e^x, ln x and Graphs

This page is useful 'cos lots of 'real' things increase (or decrease) exponentially — <u>student debts</u>, <u>horrible diseases</u>... We'll start off with a <u>quick recap</u> of some things from C2, then I'll introduce you to some <u>very special functions</u>...

Graphs of $y = a^x$ and $y = a^{-x}$ show *Exponential Growth* and *Decay*

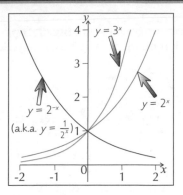

You should be familiar with these graphs from C2.
The main feature of <u>exponential growth / decay</u> is that the <u>rate of increase / decrease</u> of the function is <u>proportional to the function itself</u>.
So if we plotted the <u>gradient</u> of $y = a^x$, it would have the <u>same shape</u> as $y = a^x$.

The main points to remember for <u>$y = a^x$</u> functions (a > 0) are:

1) As $x \to \infty$, $y \to \infty$ (and the gradient also $\to \infty$).

2) As $x \to -\infty$, $y \to 0$ (which means that a^x is <u>always positive</u>).

3) When $x = 0$, $y = 1$ (so they all pass through <u>(0, 1)</u> on the y-axis).

> $\to$ means 'tends to'.

The *Gradient* of the *Exponential Function* $y = e^x$ *is* e^x

There is a value of 'a' for which the <u>gradient</u> of $y = a^x$ is <u>exactly the same as a^x</u>. That value is known as <u>e</u>, an <u>irrational number</u> around <u>2.7183</u> (it's stored in your calculator just like π). Because e is just a number, the graph of <u>$y = e^x$</u> has all the properties of <u>$y = a^x$</u>...

1) <u>$y = e^x$</u> cuts the y-axis at <u>(0, 1)</u>.

2) As $x \to \underline{\infty}$, $e^x \to \underline{\infty}$ and as $x \to \underline{-\infty}$, $e^x \to \underline{0}$.

3) $y = e^x$ <u>does not exist</u> for $y \le 0$ (i.e. e^x <u>can't be zero or –ve</u>).

The <u>disturbingly interesting</u> fact that e^x doesn't change when you differentiate is used lots in the differentiation section — see p.18.

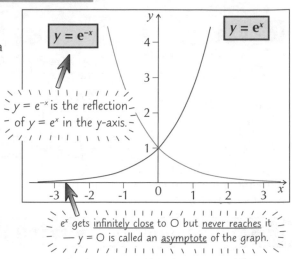

> $y = e^{-x}$ is the reflection of $y = e^x$ in the y-axis.

> e^x gets <u>infinitely close</u> to O but <u>never reaches</u> it — $y = O$ is called an <u>asymptote</u> of the graph.

ln x is the *Inverse Function* of e^x

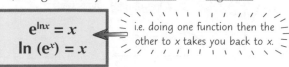

> $y = \ln x$ has an <u>asymptote</u> at $x = O$.

ln x (also known as $\log_e x$, or 'natural log'*) is the <u>inverse function</u> of $\underline{e^x}$ (see p.3):

1) $y = \ln x$ is the <u>reflection</u> of $y = e^x$ in the line <u>$y = x$</u>.

2) It cuts the x-axis at <u>(1, 0)</u> (so <u>ln 1 = 0</u>).

3) As $x \to \underline{\infty}$, ln $x \to \underline{\infty}$ (but 'slowly'), and as $x \to \underline{0}$, ln $x \to \underline{-\infty}$.

4) ln x <u>does not exist</u> for $x \le 0$ (i.e. x <u>can't be zero or negative</u>).

Because ln x is a logarithmic function and the inverse of e^x, we get these juicy <u>formulas</u> and <u>log laws</u>...

$$e^{\ln x} = x$$
$$\ln (e^x) = x$$

> i.e. doing one function then the other to x takes you back to x.

These formulas are <u>extremely useful</u> for dealing with <u>equations</u> containing '<u>e</u>'s or '<u>ln x</u>'s, as you'll see on the next page...

'Log laws' for ln x

$$\ln x + \ln y = \ln (xy)$$

$$\ln x - \ln y = \ln \left(\frac{x}{y}\right)$$

$$\ln x^k = k \ln x$$

> These are the same old log laws you saw in C2, applied to ln x.

*Certified organic

'e' is for *exponential*, but also for *easy exam* questions — no *excuses*...

When it comes to logs, I prefer the natural look. Remember the limits of $y = e^x$, $y = e^{-x}$ and $y = \ln x$ from the graphs, and polish up your skills with the log laws from C2, and the rest of the section should be a breeze. Naturally.

Using eˣ and ln x — Solving Equations

Now what makes e^x and $\ln x$ so clever is that you can use one to <u>cancel out</u> the other, which comes in <u>very handy</u> for <u>solving equations</u>. You'll need all those fruity <u>formulas</u> from the previous page to get through this one...

Use the *Inverse Functions* and *Log Laws* to *Solve Equations*

EXAMPLES   a) Solve the equation $2\ln x - \ln 2x = 6$, giving your answer as an <u>exact value</u> of x.

1) Use the <u>log laws</u> (see previous page) to simplify $2\ln x - \ln 2x = 6$ into:
$\ln x^2 - \ln 2x = 6 \Rightarrow \ln (x^2 \div 2x) = 6 \Rightarrow \ln (\frac{x}{2}) = 6$.

Using $e^{\ln x} = x$ from the last page

2) Now apply the <u>inverse function</u> e^x to both sides — this will remove the $\ln (\frac{x}{2})$:
$e^{\ln (\frac{x}{2})} = e^6 \Rightarrow \frac{x}{2} = e^6 \Rightarrow x = 2e^6$. And since we need an <u>exact</u> value, leave it as that.

b) Find the <u>exact solutions</u> of the equation $e^x + 5e^{-x} = 6$.

1) A big clue here is that you're asked for <u>more than one</u> solution. Think <u>quadratics</u>...

2) Multiply each part of the equation by e^x to get rid of that e^{-x}:
$e^x + 5e^{-x} = 6 \Rightarrow e^{2x} + 5 = 6e^x \Rightarrow e^{2x} - 6e^x + 5 = 0$.

Basic power laws — $(e^x)^2 = e^{2x}$ and $e^{-x} \times e^x = e^0 = 1$.

3) It starts to look a bit nicer if you <u>substitute</u> y for e^x: $y^2 - 6y + 5 = 0$.

4) Since we're asked for exact solutions, it will probably <u>factorise</u>:
$(y - 1)(y - 5) = 0 \Rightarrow y = 1$ and $y = 5$.

Using $\ln e^x = x$

5) Put e^x back in: $e^x = 1$ and $e^x = 5$.

6) Take 'ln' of both sides to solve: $\ln e^x = \ln 1 \Rightarrow x = \ln 1 = 0$ and $\ln e^x = \ln 5 \Rightarrow x = \ln 5$.

Real-Life functions look like **y = eᵃˣ⁺ᵇ + c** and **y = ln (ax + b)**

You should be familiar with the shape of the bog-standard exponential graphs, but most exponential functions will be <u>transformed</u> in some way. You need to know how the <u>key features</u> of the graph change depending on the function.

EXAMPLES   Sketch the <u>graphs</u> of the following functions, labelling any <u>key points</u> and stating the value of '<u>a</u>':
a) $y = e^{-7x+1} - 5$ $(x \in \mathbb{R}, y > a)$ and   b) $y = \ln (2x + 4)$ $(x \in \mathbb{R}, x > a)$.

$y = e^{-7x+1} - 5$

1) '<u>Key points</u>' usually means where the graph crosses the axes, i.e. where x and y are 0:
When $x = 0$, $y = e^1 - 5 = \underline{-2.28}$. When $y = 0$, $e^{-7x+1} = 5 \Rightarrow -7x + 1 = \ln 5 \Rightarrow x = \underline{-0.0871}$.

2) Next see what happens as x goes to $\pm\infty$ to find any <u>asymptotes</u>:
As $x \to \infty$, $e^{-7x+1} \to 0$, so $y \to -5$. As $x \to -\infty$, $e^{-7x+1} \to \infty$, so $y \to \infty$.

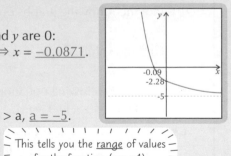

3) Now use this information to sketch out a graph. y can't go below -5, so if $y > a$, $\underline{a = -5}$.

This tells you the <u>range</u> of values for the function (see p.1).

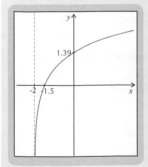

$y = \ln (2x + 4)$

1) First the intercepts: When $x = 0$, $y = \ln 4 = \underline{1.39}$. When $y = 0$, $2x + 4 = e^0 = 1 \Rightarrow x = \underline{-1.5}$.

2) As $x \to \infty$, $y \to \infty$ (gradually).

3) As $x \to -\infty$, y decreases up to the point where $2x + 4 = 0$, at which it can no longer exist (since $\ln x$ can only exist for $x > 0$). This gives an <u>asymptote</u> at $2x + 4 = 0$, i.e. $\underline{x = -2}$.

4) Sketch the graph using this information. x can't go below -2, so if $x > a$, $\underline{a = -2}$.

This tells you the <u>domain</u> (see p.1).

No problems — only solutions...

All the individual steps to solving these equations are easy — the hard bit is spotting what combination of things to try. A good thing to look for is hidden quadratics, so try and substitute for e^x or $\ln x$ to make things look a bit nicer.

C3 Section 1 — Practice Questions

Well, that's the first section over and done with, and what better way to round it off than with some <u>lovely questions</u>. Have a go at these warm-up questions to get you <u>in the mood</u>.

Warm-up Questions

1) For the following mappings, state the range and say whether or not the mapping is a function. If not, explain why, and if so, say whether the function is one-to-one or many-to-one.
   a) $f(x) = x^2 - 16,\ x \geq 0$
   b) $f(x) = x^2 - 7x + 10,\ x \in \mathbb{R}$
   c) $f(x) = \sqrt{x},\ x \in \mathbb{R}$
   d) $f(x) = \dfrac{1}{x-2},\ x \in \mathbb{R}$

2) For each pair of functions f and g, find fg(2), gf(1) and fg(x).
   a) $f(x) = \dfrac{3}{x},\ x > 0$ and $g(x) = 2x + 3,\ x \in \mathbb{R}$
   b) $f(x) = 3x^2,\ x \geq 0$ and $g(x) = x + 4,\ x \in \mathbb{R}$

3) A one-to-one function f has domain $x \in \mathbb{R}$ and range $f(x) \geq 3$. Does this function have an inverse? If so, state its domain and range.

4) Using algebra, find the inverse of the function $f(x) = \sqrt{2x - 4},\ x \geq 2$. State the domain and range of the inverse.

5) For the function $f(x) = 2x - 1\ \{x \in \mathbb{R}\}$, sketch the graphs of:
   a) $|f(x)|$
   b) $f(|x|)$

6) Use your graph from part 5) a) to help you solve the equation $|2x - 1| = 5$.

7) Solve the equation $|2x + 1| = |x + 4|$.

8) The function $y = f(x)$ is shown on the graph on the right. Sketch the graph of $y = 2f(x) + 1$.

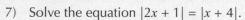
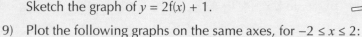

9) Plot the following graphs on the same axes, for $-2 \leq x \leq 2$:
   a) $y = 4e^x$ b) $y = 4e^{-x}$ c) $y = 4 \ln x$ d) $y = \ln 4x$.

10) Find the value of x, to 4 decimal places, when:
    a) $e^{2x} = 6$ b) $\ln (x + 3) = 0.75$ c) $3e^{-4x+1} = 5$ d) $\ln x + \ln 5 = \ln 4$.

11) Solve the following equations, giving your solutions as exact values:
    a) $\ln (2x - 7) + \ln 4 = -3$ b) $2e^{2x} + e^x = 3$.

12) Sketch graphs of the following, labelling key points and asymptotes:
    a) $y = 2 - e^{x+1}$ b) $y = 5e^{0.5x} + 5$ c) $y = \ln (2x) + 1$ d) $y = \ln (x + 5)$

Now that you're in the <u>functions zone</u> (not to be confused with the twilight zone or the phantom zone), I think you're ready to have a go at some <u>exam-style questions</u>.

Exam Questions

1   In words, describe what happens to the curve $y = x^3$ to transform it into the curve $y = 2(x - 1)^3 + 4$.

(6 marks)

C3 Section 1 — Practice Questions

They were nice questions to ease you in gently. I have to warn you, they get a bit harder on this page. It's nothing you can't handle though. Just arm yourself with a <u>mosquito net</u>, an <u>invisibility cloak</u> and some <u>Maths knowledge</u> and you'll be fine.

2   The functions f and g are given by: $f(x) = x^2 - 3$, $x \in \mathbb{R}$ and $g(x) = \frac{1}{x}$, $x \in \mathbb{R}$, $x \neq 0$.

   a)   Find an expression for gf(x).

(2 marks)

   b)   Solve $gf(x) = \frac{1}{6}$.

(3 marks)

3   For the functions f and g, where

$$f(x) = 2^x, \ x \in \mathbb{R} \qquad \text{and} \qquad g(x) = \sqrt{3x - 2}, \ x \geq \tfrac{2}{3},$$

   find:

   a)   fg(6)

(2 marks)

   b)   gf(2)

(2 marks)

   c)   (i) $g^{-1}(x)$

(2 marks)

        (ii) $fg^{-1}(x)$

(2 marks)

4   The function f(x) is defined as follows: $f(x) = \dfrac{1}{x + 5}$, domain $x > -5$.

   a)   State the range of f(x).

(1 mark)

   b)   (i)   Find the inverse function, $f^{-1}(x)$.

(3 marks)

        (ii)   State the domain and range of $f^{-1}(x)$.

(2 marks)

   c)   On the same axes, sketch the graphs of $y = f(x)$ and $y = f^{-1}(x)$.

(2 marks)

5   The graph below shows the curve $y = f(x)$, and the intercepts of the curve with the x- and y-axes.

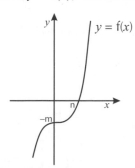

   Sketch the graphs of the following transformations on separate axes, clearly labelling the points of intersection with the x- and y-axes in terms of m and n.

   a) $y = |f(x)|$

(2 marks)

   b) $y = -3f(x)$

(2 marks)

   c) $y = f(|x|)$

(2 marks)

C3 Section 1 — Practice Questions

If your brain's still <u>functioning</u>, have a go at these <u>last few questions</u>. If it's not, it's just <u>tough</u>, you still have to do them anyway.

6   a)   Given that $6e^x = 3$, find the exact value of x.

(2 marks)

     b)   Find the exact solutions to the equation:

$$e^{2x} - 8e^x + 7 = 0.$$

(4 marks)

     c)   Given that $4 \ln x = 3$, find the exact value of x.

(2 marks)

     d)   Solve the equation:

$$\ln x + \frac{24}{\ln x} = 10$$

        giving your answers as exact values of x.

(4 marks)

7   The sketch below shows the function $y = e^{ax} + b$, where a and b are constants.

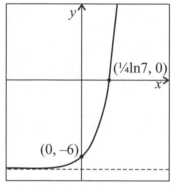

Find the values of a and b, and the equation of the asymptote shown on the sketch.

(5 marks)

8   A curve has the equation $y = \ln (4x - 3)$.

     a)   The point A with coordinate $(a, 1)$ lies on the curve. Find a to 2 decimal places.

(2 marks)

     b)   The curve is only defined for $x > b$. State the value of b.

(2 marks)

     c)   Sketch the curve, labelling any important points.

(2 marks)

9   Solve the following equations, giving your answers as exact values of x.

     a) $2e^x + 18e^{-x} = 20$

(4 marks)

     b) $2 \ln x - \ln 3 = \ln 12$

(3 marks)

Sin⁻¹, Cos⁻¹ and Tan⁻¹

I bet you started panicking when you saw the trig section — <u>trigonometry</u> has been known to bring people out in a <u>nasty rash</u>, or even make them <u>sneeze unstoppably</u>. Don't worry though — this section is short and sweet.

Sin⁻¹, Cos⁻¹ and *Tan⁻¹* are the *Inverses* of *Sin, Cos and Tan*

In Section 1 you saw that some functions have <u>inverses</u>, which reverse the effect of the function. The <u>trig functions</u> have inverses too.

<u>SIN⁻¹</u> is the <u>inverse of sine</u>. It's also known as <u>arcsine</u> (or <u>arcsin</u>).

<u>COS⁻¹</u> is the <u>inverse of cosine</u>. It's also known as <u>arccosine</u> (or <u>arccos</u>).

<u>TAN⁻¹</u> is the <u>inverse of tangent</u>. It's also known as <u>arctangent</u> (or <u>arctan</u>).

The inverse trig functions <u>reverse</u> the effect of sin, cos and tan.
For example, $\sin 30° = 0.5$, so $\sin^{-1} 0.5 = 30°$.

You should have buttons for doing sin⁻¹, cos⁻¹ and tan⁻¹ on your calculator.

To *Graph* the *Inverse Functions* you need to *Restrict their Domains*

1) The functions sine, cosine and tangent are NOT <u>one-to-one mappings</u> (see p.1) — lots of values of x give the same value for $\sin x$, $\cos x$ or $\tan x$. For example: $\cos 0 = \cos 2\pi = \cos 4\pi = 1$, and $\tan 0 = \tan \pi = \tan 2\pi = 0$.

2) Only <u>one-to-one functions</u> have inverses, so for the inverse to be a function you have to <u>restrict the domain</u> of the trig function to make it one-to-one (see graphs below). This means that you only plot the graphs between certain x values, so that for <u>each x value</u>, you end up with <u>one y value</u>.

3) As the graphs are inverse functions, they're also <u>reflections</u> of the sin, cos and tan functions in the line <u>$y = x$</u>.

SIN⁻¹

For $\sin^{-1}$, limit the domain of $\sin x$ to $-\frac{\pi}{2} \le x \le \frac{\pi}{2}$ (the range of $\sin x$ is still $-1 \le \sin x \le 1$).

This means the domain of $\sin^{-1} x$ is $-1 \le x \le 1$ and its range is $-\frac{\pi}{2} \le \sin^{-1} x \le \frac{\pi}{2}$.

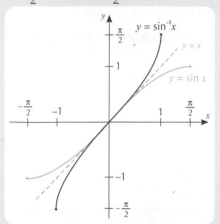

This graph goes through the origin.

The coordinates of its endpoints are $(1, \frac{\pi}{2})$ and $(-1, -\frac{\pi}{2})$.

COS⁻¹

For $\cos^{-1}$, limit the domain of $\cos x$ to $0 \le x \le \pi$ (the range of $\cos x$ is still $-1 \le \cos x \le 1$).

This means the domain of $\cos^{-1} x$ is $-1 \le x \le 1$ and its range is $0 \le \cos^{-1} x \le \pi$.

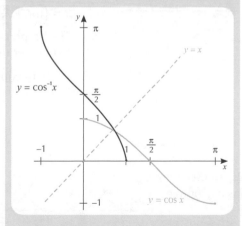

This graph crosses the y-axis at $(0, \frac{\pi}{2})$.

The coordinates of its endpoints are $(-1, \pi)$ and $(1, 0)$.

TAN⁻¹

For $\tan^{-1}$, limit the domain of $\tan x$ to $-\frac{\pi}{2} \le x \le \frac{\pi}{2}$ (this doesn't limit the range of $\tan x$).

This means that the domain of $\tan^{-1} x$ isn't limited, but the range of $\tan^{-1} x$ is limited to $-\frac{\pi}{2} \le \tan^{-1} x \le \frac{\pi}{2}$.

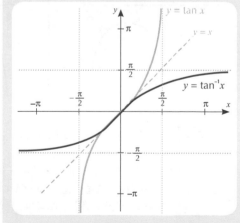

This graph goes through the origin.

It has asymptotes at $y = \frac{\pi}{2}$ and $y = -\frac{\pi}{2}$.

So applying the inverse function reverses everything...

It's really important that you can recognise the graphs of the inverse trig functions — you need to know what <u>shape</u> they are, what <u>restricted domains</u> you need to use to draw them, and any <u>significant points</u>, like where they end or where they cross the axes. You can check the graph by reflecting the curve in the line $y = x$ and seeing if you get the trig function you want.

Secant, Cosecant and Cotangent

Just when you thought you'd seen all the functions that trigonometry could throw at you, here come <u>three more</u>. These ones are <u>pretty important</u> — they'll come in really handy when you're <u>solving trig equations</u>.

Cosec, Sec and Cot are the Reciprocals of Sin, Cos and Tan

When you take the <u>reciprocal</u> of the three main trig functions, sin, cos and tan, you get three new trig functions — <u>cosecant</u> (or <u>cosec</u>), <u>secant</u> (or <u>sec</u>) and <u>cotangent</u> (or <u>cot</u>).

$$\operatorname{cosec} \theta \equiv \frac{1}{\sin \theta}$$

$$\sec \theta \equiv \frac{1}{\cos \theta}$$

$$\cot \theta \equiv \frac{1}{\tan \theta}$$

> The trick for remembering which is which is to look at the third letter — co<u>s</u>ec (1/<u>s</u>in), se<u>c</u> (1/<u>c</u>os) and co<u>t</u> (1/<u>t</u>an).

Since $\tan \theta = \frac{\sin \theta}{\cos \theta}$, you can also think of <u>cot θ</u> as being $\frac{\cos \theta}{\sin \theta}$.

Graphing Cosec, Sec and Cot

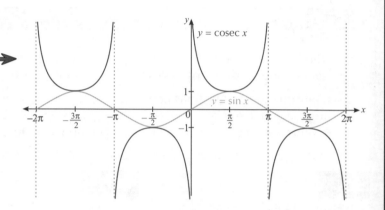

COSEC This is the graph of $y = \operatorname{cosec} x$.

1) Since $\operatorname{cosec} x = \frac{1}{\sin x}$, $y = \operatorname{cosec} x$ is <u>undefined</u> at any point where <u>sin $x = 0$</u>. So cosec x has <u>asymptotes</u> at $x = n\pi$ (where n is any integer).

2) The graph of cosec x has <u>minimum</u> points at $y = 1$ (wherever the graph of sin x has a maximum).

3) It has <u>maximum</u> points at $y = -1$ (wherever sin x has a minimum).

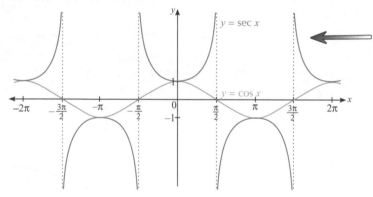

SEC This is the graph of $y = \sec x$.

1) As $\sec x = \frac{1}{\cos x}$, $y = \sec x$ is <u>undefined</u> at any point where <u>cos $x = 0$</u>. So sec x has <u>asymptotes</u> at $x = \left(n\pi + \frac{\pi}{2}\right)$ (where n is any integer).

2) The graph of sec x has <u>minimum</u> points at $y = 1$ (wherever the graph of cos x has a maximum).

3) It has <u>maximum</u> points at $y = -1$ (wherever cos x has a minimum).

COT This is the graph of $y = \cot x$.

1) Since $\cot x = \frac{1}{\tan x}$, $y = \cot x$ is <u>undefined</u> at any point where <u>tan $x = 0$</u>. So cot x has <u>asymptotes</u> at $x = n\pi$ (where n is any integer).

2) $y = \cot x$ <u>crosses the x-axis</u> at every place where the graph of tan x has an <u>asymptote</u> — this is any point with the coordinates $\left(\left(n\pi + \frac{\pi}{2}\right), 0\right)$.

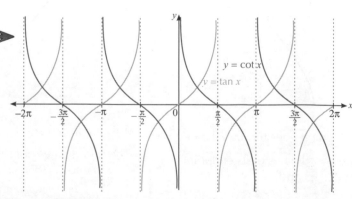

Why did I multiply cot x by sin x? Just 'cos...

Remember to look at the third letter to work out which trig function it's the reciprocal of. I'm afraid you do need to be able to sketch the three graphs from memory. Someone in examiner world clearly has a bit of a graph-sketching obsession. You might have to transform a trig graph too — you use the same method as you would for other graphs (see p.7).

Using Trigonometric Identities

Ahh, trig identities. More useful than a monkey wrench, and more fun than rice pudding. Probably.

Learn these Three Trig Identities

Hopefully you remember using this handy little trig identity before:

IDENTITY 1: $\cos^2\theta + \sin^2\theta \equiv 1$

> The ≡ sign tells you that this is true for all values of θ, rather than just certain values.

You can use it to produce a couple of other identities that you need to know about...

IDENTITY 2: $\sec^2\theta \equiv 1 + \tan^2\theta$

To get this, you just take everything in Identity 1, and divide it by $\cos^2\theta$:

$$\frac{\cos^2\theta}{\cos^2\theta} + \frac{\sin^2\theta}{\cos^2\theta} \equiv \frac{1}{\cos^2\theta}$$
$$1 + \tan^2\theta \equiv \sec^2\theta$$

> Remember that $\cos^2\theta = (\cos\theta)^2$.

IDENTITY 3: $\operatorname{cosec}^2\theta \equiv 1 + \cot^2\theta$

You get this one by dividing everything in Identity 1 by $\sin^2\theta$:

$$\frac{\cos^2\theta}{\sin^2\theta} + \frac{\sin^2\theta}{\sin^2\theta} \equiv \frac{1}{\sin^2\theta}$$
$$\cot^2\theta + 1 \equiv \operatorname{cosec}^2\theta$$

Use the Trig Identities to Simplify Equations...

You can use identities to get rid of any trig functions that are making an equation difficult to solve.

EXAMPLE   Solve the equation $\cot^2 x + 5 = 4\operatorname{cosec} x$ in the interval $0° \leq x \leq 360°$.

You can't solve this while it has both cot and cosec in it, so use Identity 3 to swap $\cot^2 x$ for $\operatorname{cosec}^2 x - 1$.

$$\operatorname{cosec}^2 x - 1 + 5 = 4\operatorname{cosec} x$$

Now rearranging the equation gives:

$$\operatorname{cosec}^2 x + 4 = 4\operatorname{cosec} x \implies \operatorname{cosec}^2 x - 4\operatorname{cosec} x + 4 = 0$$

So you've got a quadratic in $\operatorname{cosec} x$ — factorise it like you would any other quadratic equation.

$$\operatorname{cosec}^2 x - 4\operatorname{cosec} x + 4 = 0$$
$$(\operatorname{cosec} x - 2)(\operatorname{cosec} x - 2) = 0$$

> If it helps, think of this as $y^2 - 4y + 4 = 0$. Factorise it, and then replace the y with cosec x.

One of the brackets must be equal to zero — here they're both the same, so you only get one equation:

$$(\operatorname{cosec} x - 2) = 0 \implies \operatorname{cosec} x = 2$$

Now you can convert this into $\sin x$, and solve it easily:

$$\operatorname{cosec} x = 2 \implies \sin x = \tfrac{1}{2}$$
$$x = 30° \text{ or } x = 150°$$

To find the other values of x, draw a quick sketch of the sin curve: From the graph, you can see that $\sin x$ takes the value of ½ twice in the given interval, once at $x = 30°$ and once at $x = 180 - 30 = 150°$.

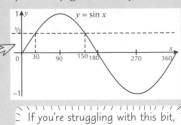

> If you're struggling with this bit, have a look back at C2.

...or to Prove that two things are The Same

You can also use identities to prove that two trig expressions are the same, like this:

EXAMPLE   Show that $\frac{\tan^2 x}{\sec x} \equiv \sec x - \cos x$.

You need to take one side of the identity and play about with it until you get the other side.   ⟹   Left-hand side: $\frac{\tan^2 x}{\sec x}$.

Try replacing $\tan^2 x$ with $\sec^2 x - 1$: $\equiv \dfrac{\sec^2 x - 1}{\sec x} \equiv \dfrac{\sec^2 x}{\sec x} - \dfrac{1}{\sec x} \equiv \sec x - \cos x$ ...which is the right-hand side.

C3 Section 2 — Practice Questions

See, I told you that wasn't too bad — just a few more <u>graphs</u> (and let's face it, when you've seen one trig graph you've seen them all) and a few new <u>identities</u>, both of which are based on one you already know. Nothing to worry about.

Warm-up Questions

1) Using your vast knowledge of trig values for common angles, evaluate these (in radians, between 0 and $\frac{\pi}{2}$):

    a) $\sin^{-1}\frac{1}{\sqrt{2}}$ b) $\cos^{-1}0$ c) $\tan^{-1}\sqrt{3}$

2) Sketch the graphs of $\sin^{-1}$, $\cos^{-1}$ and $\tan^{-1}$. Make sure you show their domains and ranges.

3) For $\theta = 30°$, find the exact values of: a) $\operatorname{cosec}\theta$ b) $\sec\theta$ c) $\cot\theta$

4) Sketch the graphs of cosecant, secant and cotangent for $-2\pi \leq x \leq 2\pi$.

5) Use the identity $\cos^2\theta + \sin^2\theta \equiv 1$ to produce the identity $\sec^2\theta \equiv 1 + \tan^2\theta$.

6) Use the trig identities to show that $\cot^2\theta + \sin^2\theta \equiv \operatorname{cosec}^2\theta - \cos^2\theta$.

Here is a selection of the <u>finest trigonometry exam questions</u> available, matured for 21 days and served with a delicious peppercorn sauce.

Exam Questions

1   a)   Sketch the graph of $y = \operatorname{cosec} x$ for $-\pi \leq x \leq \pi$.

> Don't forget to put your calculator in RAD mode when you're using radians (and DEG mode when you're using degrees)...

(3 marks)

     b)   Solve the equation $\operatorname{cosec} x = \frac{5}{4}$ for $-\pi \leq x \leq \pi$.
Give your answers correct to 3 significant figures.

(3 marks)

     c)   Solve the equation $\operatorname{cosec} x = 3\sec x$ for $-\pi \leq x \leq \pi$.
Give your answers correct to 3 significant figures.

(3 marks)

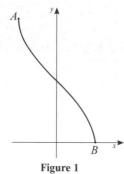

2   **Figure 1** shows the graph of $y = \cos^{-1}x$, where y is in radians. A and B are the end points of the graph.

     a)   Write down the coordinates of A and B.

(2 marks)

     b)   Express x in terms of y.

(1 mark)

     c)   Solve, to 3 significant figures, the equation $\cos^{-1}x = 2$ for the interval shown on the graph.

(2 marks)

Figure 1

3   a)   Show that $\dfrac{2\sin x}{1 - \cos x} - \dfrac{2\cos x}{\sin x} \equiv 2\operatorname{cosec} x$

(4 marks)

     b)   Use this result to find all the solutions for which

$$\frac{2\sin x}{1 - \cos x} - \frac{2\cos x}{\sin x} = 4 \qquad 0 < x < 2\pi.$$

(3 marks)

4   a)   (i)   Using an appropriate identity, show that $3\tan^2\theta - 2\sec\theta = 5$ can be written as $3\sec^2\theta - 2\sec\theta - 8 = 0$.

(2 marks)

        (ii)   Hence or otherwise show that $\cos\theta = -\frac{3}{4}$ or $\cos\theta = \frac{1}{2}$.

(3 marks)

     b)   Use your results from part a) above to solve the equation $3\tan^2 2x - 2\sec 2x = 5$ for $0 \leq x \leq 180°$. Give your answers to 2 decimal places.

(3 marks)

Chain Rule

That's right — our old friend <u>differentiation</u> is back again, this time with some <u>new exciting features</u>. Before you start panicking about how much you've already forgotten, all you need for now is: $\Longrightarrow$ $\boxed{\dfrac{d}{dx}(x^n) = nx^{n-1}}$

The **Chain Rule** is used for **Functions of Functions**

The <u>chain rule</u> is a nifty little tool that allows you to differentiate complicated functions by <u>splitting them up</u> into easier ones. The trick is spotting <u>how</u> to split them up, and choosing the right bit to <u>substitute</u>.

Chain Rule Method

- **Pick a suitable function of x for 'u' and rewrite y in terms of u.**

- **Differentiate u (with respect to x) to get $\dfrac{du}{dx}$, and differentiate y (with respect to u) to get $\dfrac{dy}{du}$.**

- **Stick it all in the formula.**

If $y = f(u)$ and $u = g(x)$
then:
$$\frac{dy}{dx} = \frac{dy}{du} \times \frac{du}{dx}$$

EXAMPLE Find the exact value of $\dfrac{dy}{dx}$ when $x = 1$ for $y = \dfrac{1}{\sqrt{x^2 + 4x}}$.

1)   First, write y in terms of powers to make it easier to differentiate: $y = (x^2 + 4x)^{-\frac{1}{2}}$.

2)   Pick a chunk of the equation to call 'u', and rewrite y in terms of u:
e.g. in this case let $u = x^2 + 4x$, so $y = u^{-\frac{1}{2}}$.

> Write down all the steps — it'll help you avoid small mistakes that could affect your final answer.

3)   Now differentiate both bits separately: $u = x^2 + 4x$, so $\dfrac{du}{dx} = 2x + 4$ and $y = u^{-\frac{1}{2}}$, so $\dfrac{dy}{du} = -\dfrac{1}{2}u^{-\frac{3}{2}}$.

4)   Use the chain rule to find $\dfrac{dy}{dx}$: $\dfrac{dy}{dx} = \dfrac{dy}{du} \times \dfrac{du}{dx} = -\dfrac{1}{2}u^{-\frac{3}{2}} \times (2x + 4)$.

5)   Substitute in for u and rearrange: $u = x^2 + 4x$, so $\dfrac{dy}{dx} = -\dfrac{1}{2}(x^2 + 4x)^{-\frac{3}{2}}(2x + 4) = -\dfrac{x + 2}{(\sqrt{x^2 + 4x})^3}$.

6)   Finally, put in $x = 1$ to answer the question: $\dfrac{dy}{dx} = -\dfrac{1 + 2}{(\sqrt{1^2 + (4 \times 1)})^3} = \dfrac{-3}{5\sqrt{5}} = \dfrac{-3\sqrt{5}}{25}$.

> 'Exact' means leave in surd form where necessary.

Use *dy/dx = 1 ÷ dx/dy* for *x = f(y)*

For $x = f(y)$, use
$$\frac{dy}{dx} = \frac{1}{\left(\frac{dx}{dy}\right)}$$

The <u>principle</u> of the chain rule can also be used where <u>x is given in terms of y</u> (i.e. $x = f(y)$). This comes from a bit of mathematical fiddling, but it's quite <u>useful</u>:

$\dfrac{dy}{dx} \times \dfrac{dx}{dy} = \dfrac{dy}{dy} = 1$, so rearranging gives $\dfrac{dy}{dx} = \dfrac{1}{\left(\frac{dx}{dy}\right)}$. Here's how to use it...

EXAMPLE A curve has the equation $x = y^3 + 2y - 7$. Find $\dfrac{dy}{dx}$ at the point $(-4, 1)$.

1)   Forget that the xs and ys are in the 'wrong' places and differentiate as usual:
$x = y^3 + 2y - 7$, so $\dfrac{dx}{dy} = 3y^2 + 2$.

2)   Use $\dfrac{dy}{dx} = \dfrac{1}{\left(\frac{dx}{dy}\right)}$ to find $\dfrac{dy}{dx}$: $\dfrac{dy}{dx} = \dfrac{1}{3y^2 + 2}$.

3) $y = 1$ at the point $(-4, 1)$, so put this in the equation:
$\dfrac{dy}{dx} = \dfrac{1}{3(1)^2 + 2} = \dfrac{1}{5} = 0.2$, so $\dfrac{dy}{dx} = 0.2$ at the point $(-4, 1)$.

> You'll be using this again on the next page so make sure you've learnt it now.

I'm in the middle of a chain rule differentiation...

You know, I'm not sure I've stressed enough just how important differentiation is. It's one of those bits of maths that examiners can tag on to almost any other A-Level topic. It's almost like they have a mantra: 'Give me ANY function and I will ask you to differentiate it, in a multitude of intricate ways'. To which you should respond: 'Bring. It. On.'

Differentiation of e^x and ln x

Remember those special little functions from Section 1? Well you're about to find out just how special they are as we take a look at how to differentiate them. I can tell you're overcome by excitement so I'll not keep you waiting...

The **Gradient** of **y = e^x** is **e^x** by **Definition**

$$y = e^x$$
$$\frac{dy}{dx} = e^x$$

OR

$$f(x) = e^x$$
$$f'(x) = e^x$$

Get used to using both types of function notation. You should remember from C2 that f'(x) means the same as dy/dx.

In Section 1 (see p.8) we saw that 'e' was just a number for which the <u>gradient of e^x</u> was <u>e^x</u>. Which makes it pretty simple to <u>differentiate</u>.

EXAMPLE   If $f(x) = e^{x^2} + 2e^x$, find f'(x) for $x = 0$.

1) Let's break down the function into its two bits and differentiate them separately:

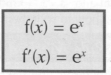 $y = e^{x^2}$ and $y = 2e^x$

2) This is the tricky bit.
   Use the <u>chain rule</u> from the last page:
   $u = x^2$ and $y = e^u$

3) Both u and y are now easy to differentiate:
   $\frac{du}{dx} = 2x$ and $\frac{dy}{du} = e^u$

4) $\frac{dy}{dx} = \frac{du}{dx} \times \frac{dy}{du} = 2x \cdot e^u = 2x \cdot e^{x^2}$

5) This bit's easy.
   If $y = 2e^x$ then $\frac{dy}{dx} = 2e^x$ too.

When $y = kf(x)$ where k is a constant, then dy/dx is just kf'(x).

6) Put the bits back together and you end up with $f'(x) = 2xe^{x^2} + 2e^x$.

7) So when $\underline{x = 0}$, $\underline{f'(x)} = 0 + 2e^0 \underline{= 2}$.

Turn **y = ln x** into **x = e^y** to **Differentiate**

$$y = \ln x$$
$$\frac{dy}{dx} = \frac{1}{x}$$

This result you can just <u>learn</u>, but it comes from another bit of mathematical fiddling:
If $y = \ln x$, then $x = e^y$ (see p.8).
Differentiating gives $\frac{dx}{dy} = e^y$, and $\frac{dy}{dx} = \frac{1}{\left(\frac{dx}{dy}\right)} = \frac{1}{e^y} = \frac{1}{x}$ (since $x = e^y$). Nice eh.

EXAMPLE   Find $\frac{dy}{dx}$ if $y = \ln (x^2 + 3)$.

1) Use the <u>chain rule</u> again for this one: $y = \ln u$ and $u = x^2 + 3$.

2) $\frac{dy}{du} = \frac{1}{u}$ (from above) and $\frac{du}{dx} = 2x$.

3) So $\frac{dy}{dx} = \frac{dy}{du} \times \frac{du}{dx} = \frac{1}{u} \times 2x = \frac{2x}{x^2 + 3}$.

Look again at your final answer. It comes out to $\frac{f'(x)}{f(x)}$.

This will <u>always be the case</u> for $y = \ln (f(x))$ so you can just <u>learn</u> this result:

$$y = \ln (f(x))$$
$$\frac{dy}{dx} = \frac{f'(x)}{f(x)}$$

These functions pop up everywhere in the e^xams...

There's nothing too tough on this page, so you have no excuse for not getting a good grasp of the basics while you can. The derivatives of e^x and ln x are just a couple more of those essential little things you've just got to learn. If you don't, you could get stumped by a fairly easy exam question. I know I'd gladly spend every waking hour learning this stuff if I could...

Differentiation of Sin, Cos and Tan

So you think you know all there is to know about <u>trigonometry</u>. Well think again, 'cos here it comes again.
(You see what I did there with the 'cos'? Pun #27 from 'Ye Olde Booke of Maths Punnes'...)

The **Rules** for **dy/dx** of **Sin**, **Cos** and **Tan** only work in **Radians**

For <u>trigonometric functions</u>, where the angle is measured in <u>radians</u>, the following rules apply:

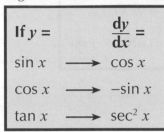

If $y =$	$\dfrac{dy}{dx} =$
$\sin x \longrightarrow$	$\cos x$
$\cos x \longrightarrow$	$-\sin x$
$\tan x \longrightarrow$	$\sec^2 x$

There's loads more about sec (and cosec and cot) on p.14.

Use the **Chain Rule** with **Sin/Cos/Tan (f(x))**

If you can't follow what's happening here, go back to p.1/ and brush up on the chain rule.

EXAMPLE: Differentiate $y = \cos 2x + \sin (x + 1)$ with respect to x.

It's the <u>chain rule</u> (again) for both parts of this equation:

1) Differentiate '$y = \cos 2x$': $y = \cos u$, $u = 2x$,

    so $\dfrac{dy}{du} = -\sin u$ (see above) and $\dfrac{du}{dx} = 2 \Rightarrow \dfrac{dy}{dx} = -2\sin 2x$.

2) Differentiate '$y = \sin (x + 1)$': $y = \sin u$, $u = x + 1$,

    so $\dfrac{dy}{du} = \cos u$ (see above) and $\dfrac{du}{dx} = 1 \Rightarrow \dfrac{dy}{dx} = \cos (x + 1)$.

3) Put it all together to get $\dfrac{dy}{dx} = -2\sin 2x + \cos (x + 1)$.

EXAMPLE: Find $\dfrac{dy}{dx}$ when $x = \tan 3y$.

1) First find $\dfrac{dx}{dy}$ using the <u>chain rule</u>: $x = \tan u$, $u = 3y$, $\dfrac{dx}{du} = \sec^2 u$, $\dfrac{du}{dy} = 3$, so $\dfrac{dx}{dy} = 3\sec^2 3y$.

See p.17 if you can't remember this.

2) Then use $\dfrac{dy}{dx} = \dfrac{1}{\left(\dfrac{dx}{dy}\right)}$ to get the final answer: $\dfrac{dy}{dx} = \dfrac{1}{3\sec^2 3y} = \dfrac{1}{3}\cos^2 3y$.

Remember to use **Trig Identities** where **Necessary**

EXAMPLE For $y = \frac{1}{2}\tan^2 x$, show that $\dfrac{dy}{dx} = \tan x + \tan^3 x$.

1) Writing out the equation in a <u>slightly different way</u> helps with the chain rule: $y = \frac{1}{2}(\tan x)^2$.

2) First, let $y = \frac{1}{2}u^2$, $u = \tan x$, so $\dfrac{dy}{du} = u$ and $\dfrac{du}{dx} = \sec^2 x$.

3) Putting it all in the chain rule formula gives $\dfrac{dy}{dx} = \tan x \sec^2 x$.

4) From the target answer in the question it looks like we need to get rid of the $\sec^2 x$, so use the identity $\sec^2 x \equiv 1 + \tan^2 x$ (see p.15):
$\dfrac{dy}{dx} = \tan x (1 + \tan^2 x)$ which <u>expands</u> nicely to give $\dfrac{dy}{dx} = \tan x + \tan^3 x$. Et voilà.

I'm having an identity crisis — I can't differentiate between sin and cos...

Don't get tied down by the chain rule (pun #28...). After a bit of practice you'll be able to do it a lot quicker in one step — just say in your working '<u>using the chain rule...</u>' so the examiner can see how clever you are.

Product Rule

In maths-speak, a 'product' is what you get when you <u>multiply</u> things together. So the 'product rule' is a rule about differentiating things that are multiplied together. And it's yet another rule you have to learn I'm afraid.

Use the **Product Rule** to differentiate **Two Functions Multiplied Together**

This is what it looks like:

$$\text{If } y = u(x)v(x)$$
$$\frac{dy}{dx} = u\frac{dv}{dx} + v\frac{du}{dx}$$

(*u* and *v* are functions of *x*.)

And here's how to use it:

EXAMPLES Differentiate the following with respect to x: a) $x^3 \tan x$ and b) $e^{2x}\sqrt{2x-3}$.

a) $x^3 \tan x$

1) The crucial thing is to write down everything in <u>steps</u>. Start with <u>identifying</u> '*u*' and '*v*':
$$u = x^3 \text{ and } v = \tan x.$$

2) Now differentiate these two <u>separately</u>, with respect to x:
$$\frac{du}{dx} = 3x^2 \text{ and } \frac{dv}{dx} = \sec^2 x.$$

3) Very <u>carefully</u> put all the bits into the <u>formula</u>:
$$\frac{dy}{dx} = u\frac{dv}{dx} + v\frac{du}{dx} = (x^3 \cdot \sec^2 x) + (\tan x \cdot 3x^2)$$

4) Finally, <u>rearrange</u> to make it look nicer:
$$\frac{dy}{dx} = x^3 \sec^2 x + 3x^2 \tan x.$$

b) $e^{2x}\sqrt{2x-3}$

1) Again, start with <u>identifying</u> '*u*' and '*v*':
$$u = e^{2x} \text{ and } v = \sqrt{2x-3}.$$

2) Each of these needs the <u>chain rule</u> to differentiate:
$$\frac{du}{dx} = 2e^{2x} \text{ and } \frac{dv}{dx} = \frac{1}{\sqrt{2x-3}} \text{ (do it in steps if you need to...)}$$

3) Put it all into the <u>product rule</u> formula:
$$\frac{dy}{dx} = u\frac{dv}{dx} + v\frac{du}{dx} = (e^{2x} \cdot \frac{1}{\sqrt{2x-3}}) + (\sqrt{2x-3} \cdot 2e^{2x})$$

4) Rearrange and simplify:
$$\frac{dy}{dx} = e^{2x}\left(\frac{1}{\sqrt{2x-3}} + 2\sqrt{2x-3}\right) = e^{2x}\left(\frac{1 + 2(2x-3)}{\sqrt{2x-3}}\right)$$
$$= \frac{e^{2x}(4x-5)}{\sqrt{2x-3}}.$$

Use the Rules **Together** to differentiate **Complicated Functions**

In the exam they <u>might</u> tell you <u>which rules</u> to use, but chances are they <u>won't</u>. And you'll probably have to throw a <u>whole load of rules</u> at any one question.

EXAMPLE <u>Solve</u> the equation $\frac{d}{dx}((x^3 + 3x^2)\ln x) = 2x^2 + 5x$, leaving your answer as an <u>exact value</u> of x.

1) The $\frac{d}{dx}$ just tells you to differentiate the bit in brackets first.

And since $(x^3 + 3x^2)\ln x$ is a product of two functions, use the <u>product rule</u>:
$$u = x^3 + 3x^2 \Rightarrow \frac{du}{dx} = 3x^2 + 6x \qquad \text{and} \qquad v = \ln x \Rightarrow \frac{dv}{dx} = \frac{1}{x} \text{ (see p.18)}$$

So $\frac{d}{dx}((x^3 + 3x^2)\ln x) = [(x^3 + 3x^2) \cdot \frac{1}{x}] + [\ln x \cdot (3x^2 + 6x)] = x^2 + 3x + (3x^2 + 6x)\ln x.$

> You should be well up on $\ln x$ and e^x after Section 1, but glance back at pages 8-9 if you need to.

2) Now put this into the <u>equation</u> from the question in place of $\frac{d}{dx}((x^3 + 3x^2)\ln x)$:
$$x^2 + 3x + (3x^2 + 6x)\ln x = 2x^2 + 5x$$

> You're asked for an exact value so leave in terms of e.

3) <u>Rearrange</u> and <u>solve</u> as follows:
$$(3x^2 + 6x)\ln x = 2x^2 + 5x - x^2 - 3x \Rightarrow (3x^2 + 6x)\ln x = x^2 + 2x \Rightarrow \ln x = \frac{x^2 + 2x}{3(x^2 + 2x)} = \frac{1}{3} \Rightarrow x = e^{\frac{1}{3}}.$$

The first rule of maths club is — you do not talk about maths club...

These rules are supposed to make your life <u>easier</u> when differentiating. Learning them means you don't have to do everything from first principles every time. Try not to get the product rule mixed up with the chain rule. Repeat after me: 'The chain rule is for functions of functions but the product rule is for products of functions'. Snappy, I know...

Quotient Rule

The world is a beautiful, harmonious place full of natural symmetry. So of course, if we have a 'product rule' to differentiate products, we must also have a 'quotient rule' to differentiate... er... quotients. Read on and learn.

Use the **Quotient Rule** for one function **Divided By** another

A quotient is one function divided by another one.
The rule for differentiating quotients looks like this:

$$\text{If } y = \frac{u(x)}{v(x)}$$

$$\frac{dy}{dx} = \frac{v\frac{du}{dx} - u\frac{dv}{dx}}{v^2}$$

You could, if you wanted to, just use the product rule on $y = uv^{-1}$
(try it — you'll get the same answer).
This way is so much quicker and easier though — and it's on the formula sheet.

EXAMPLE: Find the gradient of the tangent to the curve with equation $y = \frac{(2x^2 - 1)}{(3x^2 + 1)}$, at the point (1, 0.25).

1) 'Gradient of tangent' means differentiate.

This bit's just like the product rule from the last page.

2) First identify u and v for the quotient rule, and differentiate separately:

$$u = 2x^2 - 1 \Rightarrow \frac{du}{dx} = 4x \qquad \text{and} \qquad v = 3x^2 + 1 \Rightarrow \frac{dv}{dx} = 6x.$$

Don't try and simplify straight away or you'll get things mixed up.

3) It's very important that you get things in the right order, so concentrate on what's going where:

$$\frac{dy}{dx} = \frac{v\frac{du}{dx} - u\frac{dv}{dx}}{v^2} = \frac{(3x^2 + 1)(4x) - (2x^2 - 1)(6x)}{(3x^2 + 1)^2}$$

4) Now you can simplify things:

$$\frac{dy}{dx} = \frac{x[4(3x^2 + 1) - 6(2x^2 - 1)]}{(3x^2 + 1)^2} = \frac{x[12x^2 + 4 - 12x^2 + 6]}{(3x^2 + 1)^2} = \frac{10x}{(3x^2 + 1)^2}.$$

If it's a 'normal' rather than a 'tangent' do $-1 \div$ gradient.

5) Finally, put in $x = 1$ to find the gradient at (1, 0.25): $\frac{dy}{dx} = \frac{10}{(3 + 1)^2} = 0.625.$

Find **Further Rules** using the **Quotient Rule**

EXAMPLE Use the quotient rule to differentiate $y = \frac{\cos x}{\sin x}$, and hence show that for $y = \cot x$, $\frac{dy}{dx} = -\text{cosec}^2 x$.

1) Start off identifying $u = \cos x$ and $v = \sin x$.

2) Differentiating separately gives: $\frac{du}{dx} = -\sin x$, and $\frac{dv}{dx} = \cos x$ (see p.19).

3) Putting everything in the quotient rule formula gives:

$$\frac{dy}{dx} = \frac{(\sin x \times -\sin x) - (\cos x \times \cos x)}{(\sin x)^2} = \frac{-\sin^2 x - \cos^2 x}{\sin^2 x}.$$

Don't forget your easy C2 trig identities as well as the ones covered in Section 2.

4) Use a trig identity to simplify this ($\sin^2 x + \cos^2 x \equiv 1$ should do the trick...):

$$\frac{dy}{dx} = \frac{-(\sin^2 x + \cos^2 x)}{\sin^2 x} = \frac{-1}{\sin^2 x}.$$

5) Linking this back to the question, since $\tan x = \frac{\sin x}{\cos x}$, and $\cot x = \frac{1}{\tan x}$, then $y = \frac{\cos x}{\sin x} = \cot x$.

And since $\text{cosec } x = \frac{1}{\sin x}$, then $\frac{dy}{dx} = \frac{-1}{\sin^2 x} = -\text{cosec}^2 x.$ QED*

There's more of this trig stuff on the next page. This was just a taste of things to come...

*Quite Exciting Differentiation

The second rule of maths club is — *you do not talk about maths club...*

Confused yet? Yes I know, there are three very similar looking rules in this section, all using us and vs and xs and ys all over the shop. You won't remember them by reading them over and over again like some mystical code. You will remember them by using them lots and lots in practice questions. Plain and simple — just how I like my men...

More Trig Differentiation

After whetting your appetite with the little proof on the last page, let's have a gander at some more trig differentiation. Namely, the rules for differentiating cosec x, sec x and cot x, and the vast array of things you can do with them.

d/dx of Cosec, Sec and Cot come from the Quotient Rule

Since <u>cosec</u>, <u>sec</u> and <u>cot</u> are just the <u>reciprocals</u> of sin, cos and tan, the quotient rule can be used to differentiate them.

$$y = \operatorname{cosec} x = \frac{1}{\sin x}$$

1) For the quotient rule:
$$u = 1 \Rightarrow \frac{du}{dx} = 0 \quad \text{and} \quad v = \sin x \Rightarrow \frac{dv}{dx} = \cos x$$

2) $$\frac{dy}{dx} = \frac{v\frac{du}{dx} - u\frac{dv}{dx}}{v^2} = \frac{(\sin x \cdot 0) - (1 \cdot \cos x)}{\sin^2 x} = -\frac{\cos x}{\sin^2 x}$$

3) Since $\cot x = \frac{\cos x}{\sin x}$, and $\operatorname{cosec} x = \frac{1}{\sin x}$,
$$\frac{dy}{dx} = -\frac{\cos x}{\sin x} \times \frac{1}{\sin x} = -\operatorname{cosec} x \cot x.$$

$$y = \sec x = \frac{1}{\cos x}$$

1) For the quotient rule:
$$u = 1 \Rightarrow \frac{du}{dx} = 0 \quad \text{and} \quad v = \cos x \Rightarrow \frac{dv}{dx} = -\sin x$$

2) $$\frac{dy}{dx} = \frac{v\frac{du}{dx} - u\frac{dv}{dx}}{v^2} = \frac{(\cos x \cdot 0) - (1 \cdot -\sin x)}{\cos^2 x} = \frac{\sin x}{\cos^2 x}$$

3) Since $\tan x = \frac{\sin x}{\cos x}$, and $\sec x = \frac{1}{\cos x}$,
$$\frac{dy}{dx} = \frac{\sin x}{\cos x} \times \frac{1}{\cos x} = \sec x \tan x.$$

If $y =$	$\frac{dy}{dx} =$
$\operatorname{cosec} x \longrightarrow$	$-\operatorname{cosec} x \cot x$
$\sec x \longrightarrow$	$\sec x \tan x$
$\cot x \longrightarrow$	$-\operatorname{cosec}^2 x$

Go back a page for this one. Have a go at writing it out like the ones above, starting with $y = \cos x / \sin x$.

If you can't remember which trig functions give a negative result when you differentiate them, just remember it's all the ones that begin with c — cos, cosec and cot.

Use the Chain, Product and Quotient Rules with Cosec, Sec and Cot

So once you're familiar with the three rules in the box above you can use them with the <u>chain</u>, <u>product</u> and <u>quotient</u> rules and in combination with all the <u>other functions</u> we've seen so far.

EXAMPLES Find $\frac{dy}{dx}$ for the following functions: a) $y = \sec(2x^2)$ and b) $y = e^x \cot x$.

a) $y = \sec(2x^2)$

1) This is a <u>function of a function</u>, so think '<u>chain rule</u>':
$$y = \sec u \quad \text{and} \quad u = 2x^2$$

2) $$\frac{dy}{du} = \sec u \tan u \text{ (see above)} = \sec(2x^2) \tan(2x^2)$$

3) $$\frac{du}{dx} = 4x$$

4) So $\frac{dy}{dx} = \frac{dy}{du} \times \frac{du}{dx} = 4x \sec(2x^2) \tan(2x^2)$.

b) $y = e^x \cot x$

1) This is a <u>product of two functions</u>, so think '<u>product rule</u>':
$$u = e^x \quad \text{and} \quad v = \cot x$$

2) $$\frac{du}{dx} = e^x$$

3) $$\frac{dv}{dx} = -\operatorname{cosec}^2 x \text{ (see above)}$$

4) So $\frac{dy}{dx} = u\frac{dv}{dx} + v\frac{du}{dx} = (e^x \cdot -\operatorname{cosec}^2 x) + (\cot x \cdot e^x)$
$$= e^x(\cot x - \operatorname{cosec}^2 x).$$

Get it? Got it? <u>Good</u>.

I'm co-sec-sy for my shirt — co-sec-sy it hurts...

I have good news — the formulas above will be on the formula sheet in the exam, so you only need to know how to use them. So there's no excuse for anything less than <u>excellence</u>. Also acceptable: perfection, full marks and sheer brilliance.

More Differentiation

What?! More differentiation?! Surely not. This page is all about using what you know.

Finding the *Gradient*, *Tangent*, *dy/dx*, *f'(x)*, *d/dx(f(x))* — all mean '*Differentiate*'

Usually in exams, differentiation will be disguised as something else — either through different notation (f'(x), $\frac{dy}{dx}$ etc.) or by asking for the gradient or rate of change of something.
You could also be asked to find the equation of a tangent or normal to a curve at a given point:

EXAMPLE Find the equation of the tangent to the curve $y = \frac{5x + 2}{3x - 2}$ at the point (1, 7), in the form $y = mx + c$.

1) The gradient of the tangent is just the gradient of the curve at that point. So differentiate...

2) Use the quotient rule: $u = 5x + 2 \Rightarrow \frac{du}{dx} = 5$ and $v = 3x - 2 \Rightarrow \frac{dv}{dx} = 3$.
So $\frac{dy}{dx} = \frac{5(3x - 2) - 3(5x + 2)}{(3x - 2)^2} = -\frac{16}{(3x - 2)^2}$.

If you're asked for a 'normal', do −1 ÷ gradient of tangent here — then the rest is the same.

3) Gradient of tangent at (1, 7) is $\frac{dy}{dx}$ at $x = 1$, which is $-\frac{16}{(3 - 2)^2} = -16$.

4) Use the equation of a straight line $y - y_1 = m(x - x_1)$ with m = −16, $y_1 = 7$ and $x_1 = 1$, to give:
$y - 7 = -16(x - 1) \Rightarrow y = -16x + 23$ is the equation of the tangent.

The *Rules* might need to be used *Twice*

Some questions will really stretch your alphabet with a multitude of *u*s and *v*s:

EXAMPLE Differentiate $y = e^x \tan^2(3x)$

1) First off, this is product rule: $u = e^x$ (so $\frac{du}{dx} = e^x$) and $v = \tan^2(3x)$.

2) To find $\frac{dv}{dx}$ for the product rule, we need the chain rule twice:
$v = u_1{}^2$, where $u_1 = \tan(3x)$.
$\frac{dv}{du_1} = 2u_1 = 2\tan(3x)$, and $\frac{du_1}{dx} = 3\sec^2(3x)$ (which is an easy chain rule solution itself). So $\frac{dv}{dx} = 6\tan(3x)\sec^2(3x)$.

3) Now we can put this result in the product rule formula to get $\frac{dy}{dx}$:
$\frac{dy}{dx} = (e^x \cdot 6\tan(3x)\sec^2(3x)) + (\tan^2(3x) \cdot e^x) = e^x \tan(3x)[6\sec^2(3x) + \tan(3x)]$. Job done.
$\quad\quad u \quad\quad\quad \frac{dv}{dx} \quad\quad\quad v \quad\quad\quad \frac{du}{dx}$

Differentiate *Again* for *d²y/dx²*, *Turning Points*, *Stationary Points* etc.

Refresh your memory on C1, where you learnt all about maximums and minimums...

EXAMPLE Determine the nature of the stationary point of the curve $y = \frac{\ln x}{x^2}$ ($x > 0$).

1) First use the quotient rule to find $\frac{dy}{dx}$: $u = \ln x \Rightarrow \frac{du}{dx} = \frac{1}{x}$, $v = x^2 \Rightarrow \frac{dv}{dx} = 2x$. So $\frac{dy}{dx} = \frac{1 - 2\ln x}{x^3}$.

2) The stationary points occur where $\frac{dy}{dx} = 0$ (i.e. zero gradient) so this is when:
$\frac{1 - 2\ln x}{x^3} = 0 \Rightarrow \ln x = \frac{1}{2} \Rightarrow x = e^{\frac{1}{2}}$.

3) To find out whether it's a maximum or minimum, differentiate $\frac{dy}{dx}$ to get $\frac{d^2y}{dx^2}$:
$u = 1 - 2\ln x \Rightarrow \frac{du}{dx} = -\frac{2}{x}$, $v = x^3 \Rightarrow \frac{dv}{dx} = 3x^2$. So $\frac{d^2y}{dx^2} = \frac{6\ln x - 5}{x^4}$.

Positive means minimum, negative means maximum — it's all there in C1.

4) When $x = e^{\frac{1}{2}}$, $\frac{d^2y}{dx^2} < 0$ (i.e. negative), which means it's a maximum point.

Parlez vous exam?

It's often noted that mathematics has its own language — you need to make sure you're fluent or all your hard work will go to waste. Become an expert in deciphering exam questions so you do exactly what's expected with the minimum of fuss.

C3 Section 3 — Practice Questions

Those who know it, know they know it. Those who *think* they know it, need to <u>know</u> they know it.
So, you think you know it, no? Try these to <u>make sure</u>.

1) <u>Differentiate</u> with respect to x:
   a) $y = \sqrt{x^3 + 2x^2}$
   b) $y = \dfrac{1}{\sqrt{x^3 + 2x^2}}$
   c) $y = e^{5x^2}$
   d) $y = \ln(6 - x^2)$

2) Find $\dfrac{dy}{dx}$ when
   a) $x = 2e^y$
   b) $x = \ln(2y + 3)$

3) Find f$'(x)$ for the following functions:
   a) f$(x) = \sin^2(x + 2)$
   b) f$(x) = 2\cos 3x$
   c) f$(x) = \sqrt{\tan x}$

   Assume that questions involving trig are using radians unless stated otherwise.

4) Find the value of the <u>gradient</u> for:
   a) $y = e^{2x}(x^2 - 3)$ when $x = 0$
   b) $y = \ln x \sin x$ when $x = 1$

5) Find the <u>equation</u> of the <u>tangent</u> to the curve $y = \dfrac{6x^2 + 3}{4x^2 - 1}$ at the point $(1, 3)$.

6) Find $\dfrac{dy}{dx}$ when $x = 0$ for $y = \operatorname{cosec}(3x - 2)$.

And finally — a <u>megabeast</u> of a question. You probably won't get anything as involved as this in the exam, but if you think you're hard enough...

7) Find the <u>stationary point</u> on the curve $y = \dfrac{e^x}{\sqrt{x}}$, and say whether it is a <u>maximum or minimum</u>.

Well that's put some colour in your cheeks. Now to really excel yourself on the exam practice, but try not to pull a muscle — you need to be <u>match fit</u> for the real thing.

1 Find $\dfrac{dy}{dx}$ for each of the following functions. Simplify your answer where possible.

   a) $y = \ln(3x + 1)\sin(3x + 1)$.

   (4 marks)

   b) $y = \dfrac{\sqrt{x^2 + 3}}{\cos 3x}$.

   (4 marks)

   c) $y = \sin^3(2x^2)$

   (3 marks)

   d) $y = 2\operatorname{cosec}(3x)$

   (2 marks)

2 The curve shown below has the equation $x = \sqrt{y^2 + 3y}$.

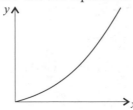

   a) Find $\dfrac{dy}{dx}$ at the point $(2, 1)$.

   (5 marks)

   b) Hence find the equation of the tangent to the curve at $(2, 1)$, in the form $y = ax + b$, where a and b are constants.

   (2 marks)

3 Use the quotient rule to show that, for the function f$(x) = \sec x$:

$$\text{f}'(x) = \sec x \tan x.$$

   (4 marks)

C3 Section 3 — Practice Questions

4   Differentiate the following with respect to x.

a) $\sqrt{(e^x + e^{2x})}$.

(3 marks)

b) $3e^{2x+1} - \ln(1 - x^2) + 2x^3$.

(3 marks)

5   A sketch of the function $f(x) = 4\ln 3x$ is shown in the diagram.

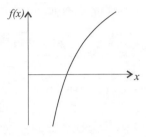

a)   Find $f'(x)$ at the point where $x = 1$.

(3 marks)

b)   Find the equation of the tangent to the curve at the point $x = 1$.

(3 marks)

6   Find the gradient of the tangent to the curve:
$$y = \sin^2 x - 2\cos 2x$$
at the point where $x = \frac{\pi}{12}$ radians.

(4 marks)

7   Given that $y = \dfrac{e^x + x}{e^x - x}$, find $\dfrac{dy}{dx}$ when $x = 0$.

(3 marks)

8   Find the equation of the normal to the curve $x = \sin 4y$ that passes through the point $\left(0, \frac{\pi}{4}\right)$.
Give your answer in the form $y = mx + c$, where m and c are constants to be found.

(6 marks)

9   A curve with equation $y = e^x \sin x$ has 2 turning points in the interval $-\pi \le x \le \pi$.

a)   Find the value of x at each of these turning points.

(6 marks)

b)   Determine the nature of each of the turning points.

(5 marks)

Integration of eˣ and 1/x

Integration is one of those pesky little topics that just won't go away. It already made an appearance in <u>C1</u> and <u>C2</u>, and now it's back again in <u>C3</u>. And yes, it does come up in <u>C4</u> as well — there's something to look forward to.

eˣ integrates to give eˣ (+ C)

As e^x <u>differentiates</u> to give e^x (see p.18), it makes sense that

$$\int e^x dx = e^x + C$$

Don't forget the constant of integration.

Once you're happy with that, you can use it to solve lots of integrations that have an e^x term in them.
If the <u>coefficient</u> of x isn't 1, you need to <u>divide</u> by that coefficient when you <u>integrate</u> — so $\int e^{kx} dx = \frac{1}{k} e^{kx} + C$

EXAMPLES   Integrate the following: a) e^{7x} b) $2e^{4-3x}$ c) $e^{\frac{x}{2}}$.

a) $\int e^{7x} dx = \frac{1}{7} e^{7x} + C$ If you differentiated e^{7x} using the chain rule, you'd get $7e^{7x}$. So when you integrate, you need to <u>divide</u> <u>by 7</u> (the coefficient of x). This is so that if you differentiated your answer you'd get back to e^{7x}.

b) $\int 2e^{4-3x} dx = -\frac{2}{3} e^{4-3x} + C$ This one isn't as bad as it looks — if you differentiated $2e^{4-3x}$, you'd get $-6e^{4-3x}$, so you need to <u>divide by −3</u> (the coefficient of x) when you integrate. Differentiating your answer gives you $2e^{4-3x}$.

c) $\int e^{\frac{x}{2}} dx = \int e^{\frac{1}{2}x} dx = 2e^{\frac{x}{2}} + C$ If you differentiated this one using the chain rule, you'd get $\frac{1}{2} e^{\frac{x}{2}}$, so you need to <u>multiply by 2</u> when you integrate.

Whenever you integrate,

ALWAYS DIFFERENTIATE YOUR ANSWER TO CHECK IT WORKS

— you should end up with the thing you <u>integrated</u> in the first place. It's the best way to check that you <u>divided</u> or <u>multiplied</u> by the right number.

1/x integrates to ln |x| (+ C)

When you first came across integration, you couldn't integrate $\frac{1}{x}$ $(= x^{-1})$ by <u>increasing</u> the <u>power</u> by 1 and <u>dividing</u> by it, as you ended up <u>dividing by 0</u> (which is baaaaad).

However, on p.18, you saw that $\ln x$ <u>differentiates</u> to give $\frac{1}{x}$, so

$$\int \frac{1}{x} dx = \ln|x| + C$$

Don't worry about where the modulus sign (see p.4) comes from — using $|x|$ just means that there isn't a problem when x is negative.

EXAMPLES   Integrate the following: a) $\frac{5}{x}$ b) $\frac{1}{3x}$ c) $\frac{1}{4x+5}$.

There are more examples like this one on p.28.

a) $\int \frac{5}{x} dx = 5\int \frac{1}{x} dx = 5\ln|x| + C$ 5 is a constant coefficient — you can take it outside the integral if you want. *You could also write $5\ln|x|$ as $\ln|x^5|$.*

b) $\int \frac{1}{3x} dx = \frac{1}{3}\int \frac{1}{x} dx = \frac{1}{3}\ln|x| + C$ Be careful with ones like this — 1/3 is just the coefficient, so it goes outside $\ln|x|$. Don't make the mistake of putting $\ln|3x|$ — this would differentiate to give $1/x$ (as $\ln 3x = \ln 3 + \ln x$, so when you differentiate, $\ln 3$ disappears).

c) $\int \frac{1}{4x+5} dx = \frac{1}{4}\ln|4x+5| + C$ However, for this one you have to leave the coefficient (4) inside $\ln$ because it's part of the function $4x + 5$. You still have to <u>divide by 4</u> though (again, try differentiating it to see why).

Integration feels pretty constant to me...

These integrations are pretty easy — the only thing you have to worry about is if x has a coefficient that isn't 1. When this happens, work out what you think the answer will look like (e.g. e^x, $\ln|x|$, etc.), then differentiate to see what you get. Then you might have to adjust your answer, usually by dividing or multiplying by the coefficient, to get back to what you started with.

Integration of Sin and Cos

If you thought you'd killed off the C3 <u>trig dragon</u>, you're sadly mistaken. It rears its ugly head again, and now you need to know how to <u>integrate trig functions</u>. Find your most trusty dragon-slaying sword and read on...

Sin and *Cos* are *Easy* to integrate

From Section 3, you know that <u>sin x</u> differentiates to give <u>cos x</u>, <u>cos x</u> differentiates to give <u>$-\sin x$</u> and <u>tan x</u> differentiates to give <u>sec$^2 x$</u> (where the angle x is in <u>radians</u>). So it's pretty obvious that:

$$\int \sin x \, dx = -\cos x + C$$
$$\int \cos x \, dx = \sin x + C$$
$$\int \sec^2 x \, dx = \tan x + C$$

Integrating tan x is a bit different — see p.28.

If x has a <u>coefficient</u> that <u>isn't 1</u> (e.g. sin $3x$), you just <u>divide</u> by the <u>coefficient</u> when you integrate — just like on the previous page.

EXAMPLE   Find $\int \cos 4x - 2\sin 2x + \sec^2 \tfrac{1}{2}x \, dx$.

Integrate each term separately using the results from above:

$$\int \cos 4x \, dx = \tfrac{1}{4}\sin 4x \qquad \int -2\sin 2x \, dx = -2\left(-\tfrac{1}{2}\cos 2x\right) = \cos 2x \qquad \int \sec^2 \tfrac{1}{2}x \, dx = \tfrac{1}{1/2}\tan \tfrac{1}{2}x = 2\tan \tfrac{1}{2}x$$

Putting these terms together and adding the constant gives:

$$\int \cos 4x - 2\sin 2x + \sec^2 \tfrac{1}{2}x \, dx = \tfrac{1}{4}\sin 4x + \cos 2x + 2\tan \tfrac{1}{2}x + C$$

There are some *Results* you can just *Use*

You've met these trig integrals before — they're the <u>results</u> of differentiating <u>cosec x</u>, <u>sec x</u> and <u>cot x</u> (see p.22).

$$\int \operatorname{cosec} x \cot x \, dx = -\operatorname{cosec} x + C$$
$$\int \sec x \tan x \, dx = \sec x + C$$
$$\int \operatorname{cosec}^2 x \, dx = -\cot x + C$$

There are some more trig integrals on page 28.

The coefficients of x have to be the same in each term — e.g. you couldn't integrate sec x tan $3x$.

As usual, you need to <u>divide</u> by the <u>coefficient of x</u> when you integrate.

EXAMPLE   Find $\int 10\sec 5x \tan 5x + \tfrac{1}{2}\operatorname{cosec} 3x \cot 3x - \operatorname{cosec}^2(6x+1) \, dx$.

This one looks a bit scary, but take it one step at a time. Integrate each bit in turn to get:

1. $\int 10\sec 5x \tan 5x \, dx = \tfrac{1}{5} \cdot 10\sec 5x$
   $$= 2\sec 5x$$

2. $\int \tfrac{1}{2}\operatorname{cosec} 3x \cot 3x \, dx = -\tfrac{1}{3} \cdot \tfrac{1}{2}\operatorname{cosec} 3x$
   $$= -\tfrac{1}{6}\operatorname{cosec} 3x$$

3. $\int -\operatorname{cosec}^2(6x+1) \, dx = -\tfrac{1}{6}(-\cot(6x+1))$

   The + 1 inside the brackets has no effect on the integration — differentiate to see why.

   $$= \tfrac{1}{6}\cot(6x+1)$$

Putting these terms together and adding the constant gives:

$$\int 10\sec 5x \tan 5x + \tfrac{1}{2}\operatorname{cosec} 3x \cot 3x - \operatorname{cosec}^2(6x+1) \, dx = 2\sec 5x - \tfrac{1}{6}\operatorname{cosec} 3x + \tfrac{1}{6}\cot(6x+1) + C$$

This is starting to grate on me now...

Although you're not given all of these integrals on the formula sheet, some of the trickier ones (e.g. sec x tan x and cosec^2x) are on the list of differentiation formulas. As long as you work backwards (i.e. from f'(x) to f(x)) you can just use these results without having to remember them all. Be careful with the coefficients — don't forget to divide by them when you integrate.

Integration of f´(x)/f(x)

Sometimes you get integrals that look really nasty — like <u>fractions</u>. However, there are a couple of clever <u>tricks</u> that can make them easy to integrate.

Some **Fractions** integrate to **ln**

If you have a fraction that has a <u>function of x</u> on the <u>numerator</u> and a <u>different function of x</u> on the <u>denominator</u> (e.g. $\frac{x-2}{x^3+1}$), you'll probably struggle to integrate it. However, if you have a fraction where the <u>numerator</u> is the <u>derivative</u> of the <u>denominator</u> (e.g. $\frac{3x^2}{x^3+1}$), it integrates to give <u>ln</u> of whatever the <u>denominator</u> is (in this case, $x^3 + 1$).

In general terms, this is written as:

$$\int \frac{f'(x)}{f(x)} \, dx = \ln|f(x)| + C$$

> This is another one that comes from the chain rule (p.17) — if you differentiated ln |f(x)|, you'd end up with the fraction on the left.

The hardest bit about questions like this is <u>recognising</u> that the denominator <u>differentiates</u> to give the numerator. Once you've spotted that, it's dead easy. They might make the numerator a <u>multiple</u> of the denominator just to confuse things, so watch out for that.

EXAMPLES

Find   a) $\int \frac{8x^3 - 4}{x^4 - 2x} \, dx$ and   b) $\int \frac{3\sin 3x}{\cos 3x + 2} \, dx$.

> Trig identities can even sneak into questions like this, but you probably won't get anything too nasty.

a) $\frac{d}{dx}(x^4 - 2x) = 4x^3 - 2$

and $8x^3 - 4 = 2(4x^3 - 2)$
The numerator is 2 × the derivative of the denominator, so

$\int \frac{8x^3 - 4}{x^4 - 2x} \, dx = 2\ln|x^4 - 2x| + C$

b) $\frac{d}{dx}(\cos 3x + 2) = -3\sin 3x$

The numerator is minus the derivative of the denominator, so

$\int \frac{3\sin 3x}{\cos 3x + 2} \, dx = -\ln|\cos 3x + 2| + C$

$= -\ln|\cos 3x + 2| + \ln k = -\ln|k(\cos 3x + 2)|$

> Using $C = \ln k$, you can combine all the terms into one using the laws of logs. ln k is just a constant.

You can get **ln** of **Trig Functions** too

You might have noticed from part (b) above that you can work out the integral of <u>tan x</u> using this method:

$\tan x = \frac{\sin x}{\cos x}$,

and $\frac{d}{dx}(\cos x) = -\sin x$

The numerator is minus the derivative of the denominator, so

$\int \tan x \, dx = \int \frac{\sin x}{\cos x} \, dx = -\ln|\cos x| + C$

> $-\ln|\cos x|$ is the same as ln $|\sec x|$ — this comes from the laws of logs on p.8.

There are some other <u>trig functions</u> that you can integrate in the same way:

$$\int \cot x \, dx = \ln|\sin x| + C$$

$$\int \operatorname{cosec} x \, dx = -\ln|\operatorname{cosec} x + \cot x| + C$$

$$\int \sec x \, dx = \ln|\sec x + \tan x| + C$$

This list is given in the <u>formula booklet</u> — so you don't need to <u>learn</u> them (just be able to <u>use</u> them).

EXAMPLE

Find $\int \frac{1}{2}\operatorname{cosec} 2x \, dx$.

You can just use the result above — so all you have to do is work out what happens to the coefficient. The coefficient is 2, so you need to divide by 2 when you integrate:

$\int \frac{1}{2}\operatorname{cosec} 2x \, dx = -\frac{1}{4}\ln|\operatorname{cosec} 2x + \cot 2x| + C$

> Check this by differentiating (using the chain rule with $u = \operatorname{cosec} 2x + \cot 2x$).

---

3 pages in and I've run out of jokes on integration. Please help...

If you come across an integration question with a fraction that doesn't seem to integrate easily, have a quick look and see if one bit is the derivative of the other. If it is, use the rule above and you'll be as happy as Larry (and Larry's always happy).

Integration Using the Chain Rule Backwards

Most integrations aren't as bad as they look — on the previous page, you saw how to integrate special <u>fractions</u>, and now it's time for certain <u>products</u>. There are some things you can look out for when you're integrating...

You can use the **Chain Rule** in **Reverse**

You came across the <u>chain rule</u> on p.17 — it's where you write the thing you're differentiating in terms of <u>u</u> (and u is a <u>function</u> of x). You end up with the <u>product</u> of <u>two derivatives</u> ($\frac{dy}{du}$ and $\frac{du}{dx}$).

When it comes to integrating, if you spot that your integral is a <u>product</u> where one bit is the <u>derivative</u> of part of the other bit, you can use this rule:

$$\int \frac{du}{dx} f'(u)\, dx = f(u) + C$$ where u is a function of x.

EXAMPLE

Find   a) $\int 6x^5 e^{x^6}\, dx$ and   b) $\int e^{\sin x} \cos x\, dx$.

a) $\int 6x^5 e^{x^6}\, dx = e^{x^6} + C$ If you differentiated $y = e^{x^6}$ using the chain rule, you'd get $6x^5 e^{x^6}$.
This is the function you had to integrate.

b) $\int e^{\sin x} \cos x\, dx = e^{\sin x} + C$ If you differentiated $y = e^{\sin x}$ using the chain rule, you'd get $e^{\sin x}\cos x$.
This is the function you had to integrate.

Some **Products** are made up of a **Function** and its **Derivative**

Similarly, if you spot that part of a <u>product</u> is the <u>derivative</u> of the other part of it (which is raised to a <u>power</u>), you can integrate it using this <u>rule</u>:

$$\int (n+1)f'(x)[f(x)]^n\, dx = [f(x)]^{n+1} + C$$

Remember that the <u>derivative</u> will be a <u>multiple</u> of <u>n + 1</u> (not n) — watch out for any other multiples too. This will probably make more sense if you have a look at an <u>example</u>:

EXAMPLE

Find   a) $\int 12x^3(2x^4 - 5)^2\, dx$ and   b) $\int 8\,\mathrm{cosec}^2 x\,\cot^3 x\, dx$.

a) Here, $f(x) = 2x^4 - 5$, so differentiating gives $f'(x) = 8x^3$. $n = 2$, so $n + 1 = 3$.
Putting all this into the rule above gives:
$$\int 3(8x^3)(2x^4 - 5)^2\, dx = \int 24x^3(2x^4 - 5)^2\, dx = (2x^4 - 5)^3 + C$$
Divide everything by 2 to match the original integral:
$$\int 12x^3(2x^4 - 5)^2\, dx = \tfrac{1}{2}(2x^4 - 5)^3 + C.$$

> This one looks pretty horrific, but it isn't too bad once you spot that $-\mathrm{cosec}^2 x$ is the derivative of $\cot x$.

b) For this one, $f(x) = \cot x$, so differentiating gives $f'(x) = -\mathrm{cosec}^2 x$. $n = 3$, so $n + 1 = 4$.
Putting all this into the rule gives:
$$\int -4\,\mathrm{cosec}^2 x\,\cot^3 x\, dx = \cot^4 x + C$$
Multiply everything by –2 to match the original integral:
$$\int 8\,\mathrm{cosec}^2 x\,\cot^3 x\, dx = -2\cot^4 x + C$$

To get rid of hiccups, drink a glass of water backwards...

It seems to me that most of this section is about reversing the things you learnt in Section 3. I don't know why they ask you to differentiate stuff if you're just going to have to integrate it again and end up where you started. At least it keeps you busy.

Integration by Substitution

In a <u>football match</u>, the correct substitution can mean the difference between <u>winning</u> and <u>losing</u>. In <u>C3 integration</u>, the correct substitution can mean the difference between being a <u>mathematical genius</u> and a <u>mathematical flop</u>.

Use **Integration by Substitution** on **Products** of **Two Functions**

On p.17, you saw how to <u>differentiate functions of functions</u> using the <u>chain rule</u>. <u>Integration by substitution</u> lets you <u>integrate functions of functions</u> by <u>simplifying</u> the <u>integral</u>. Like the chain rule, you have to write part of the function in terms of <u>u</u>, where <u>u</u> is some <u>function</u> of <u>x</u>.

Integration by Substitution

1) You'll be given an integral that's made up of <u>two functions of x</u> (one is often just <u>x</u>) — e.g. $x(3x + 2)^3$.

2) <u>Substitute</u> u for one of the functions of x (to give a function that's <u>easier to integrate</u>) — e.g. $u = 3x + 2$.

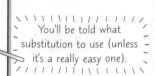 You'll be told what substitution to use (unless it's a really easy one).

$\frac{du}{dx}$ isn't really a fraction, but you can treat it as one for this bit.

3) Next, find $\frac{du}{dx}$, and <u>rewrite</u> it so that dx is on its own — e.g. $\frac{du}{dx} = 3$, so $dx = \frac{1}{3}du$.

4) <u>Rewrite</u> the original integral in terms of u and du — e.g. $\int x(3x+2)^3\, dx$ becomes $\int \left(\frac{u-2}{3}\right)u^3 \frac{1}{3}du = \int \frac{u^4 - 2u^3}{9}\, du$.

5) You should now be left with something that's <u>easier</u> to integrate — just <u>integrate</u> as normal, then at the last step <u>replace</u> u with the <u>original substitution</u> (so for this one, replace u with $3x + 2$).

EXAMPLE

Use the substitution $u = x^2 - 2$ to find $\int 4x(x^2 - 2)^4\, dx$.

As $u = x^2 - 2$, $\frac{du}{dx} = 2x$, so $dx = \frac{1}{2x}du$.

Substituting gives $\int 4x(x^2 - 2)^4\, dx = \int 4x u^4 \frac{1}{2x}du = \int 2u^4 du$.

The x's cancel, making it a lot easier to integrate — this often happens.

Integrate... $\int 2u^4 du = \frac{2}{5}u^5 + C$.

...and substitute x back in:

$= \frac{2}{5}(x^2 - 2)^5 + C$.

For **Definite Integrals**, you have to **Change** the **Limits**

If you're given a <u>definite integral</u>, it's really important that you remember to <u>change the limits</u> to u. Doing it this way means you <u>don't</u> have to <u>put x back in</u> at the last step — just put the numbers into the integration for u.

EXAMPLE

Use the substitution $u = \cos x$ to find $\int_{\frac{\pi}{2}}^{2\pi} -12 \sin x \cos^3 x\, dx$.

Trigonometry can pop up here as well.

As $u = \cos x$, $\frac{du}{dx} = -\sin x$, so $dx = -\frac{1}{\sin x}du$.

Find the limits of u:

when $x = \frac{\pi}{2}$, $u = \cos \frac{\pi}{2} = 0$,

when $x = 2\pi$, $u = \cos 2\pi = 1$.

So the limits of u are 0 and 1.

Substituting all this gives:

$\int_{\frac{\pi}{2}}^{2\pi} -12 \sin x \cos^3 x\, dx = \int_0^1 -12 \sin x\, u^3 \frac{-1}{\sin x}du = \int_0^1 12u^3 du$

Integrating and putting in the values of the limits gives:

$[3u^4]_0^1 = [3(1)^4] - [3(0)^4] = 3$

You could also have solved this one using the method on p.29.

Never substitute salt for sugar...

Life is full of limits — age limits, time limits, height limits, limits of how many times I can gaze at my Hugh Jackman poster while still getting my work done... But at least limits of integration will get you exam marks, so it's worth practising them.

Integration by Parts

Just like you can <u>differentiate products</u> using the <u>product rule</u> (see p.20), you can <u>integrate products</u> using the... er... <u>integration by parts</u>. Not quite as catchy I know, but just as thrilling.

Integration by Parts is the Reverse of the Product Rule

If you have to integrate a <u>product</u> but can't use integration by substitution (see previous page), you might be able to use <u>integration by parts</u>. The <u>formula</u> for integrating by parts is:

$$\int u\frac{dv}{dx}\,dx = uv - \int v\frac{du}{dx}\,dx$$

where u and v are both functions of x.

The hardest thing about integration by parts is <u>deciding</u> which bit of your product should be <u>u</u> and which bit should be $\frac{dv}{dx}$. There's no set rule for this — you just have to look at both parts and see which one <u>differentiates</u> to give something <u>nice</u>, then set that one as u. For example, if you have a product that has a <u>single x</u> as one part of it, choose this to be u. It differentiates to <u>1</u>, which makes <u>integrating</u> $v\frac{du}{dx}$ dead easy.

EXAMPLE   Find $\int 2xe^x\,dx$.

Let $u = 2x$ and let $\frac{dv}{dx} = e^x$. Then u differentiates to give $\frac{du}{dx} = 2$ and $\frac{dv}{dx}$ integrates to give $v = e^x$.

Putting these into the formula gives: $\int 2xe^x\,dx = 2xe^x - \int 2e^x\,dx$
$$= \boxed{2xe^x - 2e^x + C}$$

> If you have a product that has ln x as one of its factors, let $u =$ ln x, as ln x is easy to differentiate but quite tricky to integrate (see below).

You can integrate ln x using Integration by Parts

Up till now, you haven't been able to integrate <u>ln x</u>, but all that is about to change. There's a little trick you can use — write ln x as $1 \cdot \ln x$ then <u>integrate by parts</u>.

To find $\int \ln x\,dx$, write ln $x = 1 \cdot \ln x$.

Let $u =$ ln x and let $\frac{dv}{dx} = 1$. Then u differentiates to give $\frac{du}{dx} = \frac{1}{x}$ and $\frac{dv}{dx}$ integrates to give $v = x$.

$$\int \ln x\,dx = x\ln x - \int x\frac{1}{x}\,dx = x\ln x - \int 1\,dx = x\ln x - x + C$$

You might have to integrate by parts More Than Once

If you have an integral that <u>doesn't</u> produce a nice, easy-to-integrate function for $v\frac{du}{dx}$, you might have to carry out integration by parts <u>more than once</u>.

EXAMPLE   Find $\int x^2\sin x\,dx$.

Let $u = x^2$ and let $\frac{dv}{dx} = \sin x$.
Then u differentiates to give $\frac{du}{dx} = 2x$
and $\frac{dv}{dx}$ integrates to give $v = -\cos x$.
Putting these into the formula gives:
$$\int x^2\sin x\,dx = -x^2\cos x - \int -2x\cos x\,dx$$
$$= -x^2\cos x + \int 2x\cos x\,dx$$

$2x\cos x$ isn't very easy to integrate, so integrate by parts again (the $-x^2\cos x$ at the front just stays as it is):

Let $u = 2x$ and let $\frac{dv}{dx} = \cos x$. Then u differentiates to give $\frac{du}{dx} = 2$ and $\frac{dv}{dx}$ integrates to give $v = \sin x$.
Putting these into the formula gives:
$$\int 2x\cos x\,dx = 2x\sin x - \int 2\sin x\,dx = 2x\sin x + 2\cos x$$
So $\int x^2\sin x\,dx = \boxed{-x^2\cos x + 2x\sin x + 2\cos x + C}$.

Every now and then I fall apart...

After you've had a go at some examples, you'll probably realise that integrals with e^x, $\sin x$ or $\cos x$ in them are actually quite easy, as all three are really easy to integrate and differentiate. Fingers crossed you get one of them in the exam.

Volumes of Revolution

Volumes of revolution is a really exciting title for a fairly exciting subject. Sadly, it isn't to do with plotting your own revolution, but it does let you calculate the volumes of weird-shaped things.

You have to find the Volume of an area Rotated About the X-Axis...

If you're given a definite integral, the solution you come up with is the area under the graph between the two limits (you did this back in C1). If you now rotate that area 2π radians about the x-axis, you'll come up with a solid — and this is what you want to find the volume of. The formula for finding the volume of revolution is:

$$V = \pi \int_{x=x_1}^{x=x_2} y^2 \, dx$$

where y is a function of x (i.e. $y = f(x)$) and x_1 and x_2 are the limits of x.

EXAMPLE
Find the volume, V, of the solid formed when R, the area enclosed by the curve $y = \sqrt{6x^2 - 3x + 2}$, the x-axis and the lines $x = 1$ and $x = 2$ is rotated 2π radians about the x-axis.

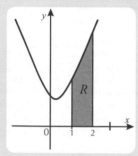

If $y = \sqrt{6x^2 - 3x + 2}$, then $y^2 = 6x^2 - 3x + 2$.

Don't forget to square y — you might think it's obvious, but it's easily done.

Putting this into the formula gives:

$$V = \pi \int_1^2 6x^2 - 3x + 2 \, dx = \pi\left[2x^3 - \tfrac{3}{2}x^2 + 2x\right]_1^2$$

$$= \pi\left(\left[2(2)^3 - \tfrac{3}{2}(2)^2 + 2(2)\right] - \left[2(1)^3 - \tfrac{3}{2}(1)^2 + 2(1)\right]\right)$$

$$= \pi\left([16 - 6 + 4] - \left[2 - \tfrac{3}{2} + 2\right]\right) = \pi\left(14 - 2\tfrac{1}{2}\right) = \boxed{11\tfrac{1}{2}\pi}$$

...or the Volume of an area Rotated About the Y-Axis

Instead of rotation about the x-axis, you might be asked to find the volume when an area is rotated about the y-axis instead. You do this using this formula:

$$V = \pi \int_{y=y_1}^{y=y_2} x^2 \, dy$$

This time, you need to rearrange the equations to get x^2 on its own (you'll often be given a function that already has x^2 in it). The limits are horizontal lines, e.g. $y = 1$ and $y = 2$.

EXAMPLE
Find the volume, V, of the solid formed when R, the area enclosed by the curve $y = \sqrt{x^2 + 5}$, the y-axis and the lines $y = 3$ and $y = 6$ is rotated 2π radians about the y-axis.

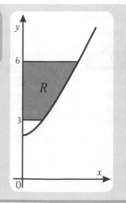

First, rearrange the equation to get x^2 on its own:

$$y = \sqrt{x^2 + 5} \Rightarrow y^2 = x^2 + 5 \quad \text{so } x^2 = y^2 - 5.$$

Now integrate: $V = \pi \int_3^6 y^2 - 5 \, dy = \pi\left[\tfrac{1}{3}y^3 - 5y\right]_3^6$

$$= \pi\left(\left[\tfrac{1}{3}(6)^3 - 5(6)\right] - \left[\tfrac{1}{3}(3)^3 - 5(3)\right]\right)$$

$$= \pi(42 - (-6)) = \boxed{48\pi}$$

Come the revolution, I will have to kill you all...

Not to be confused with the French Revolution, the Industrial Revolution or the lesser-known CGP Revolution, volumes of revolution is part of A2 Maths. So don't go getting any ideas about overthrowing your teachers and not letting them eat cake.

C3 Section 4 — Practice Questions

After all that excitement, I think you need some questions to help you relax a bit.
Have a go at these, and meditate on the wonders of integration.

Warm-up Questions

1) Find $\int 4e^{2x}\,dx$.

2) Find $\int e^{3x-5}\,dx$.

3) Find $\int \frac{2}{3x}\,dx$.

4) Find $\int \frac{2}{2x+1}\,dx$.

5) Find

    a) $\int \cos 4x - \sec^2 7x\,dx$,

    b) $\int 6\sec 3x \tan 3x - \operatorname{cosec}^2 \frac{x}{5}\,dx$.

6) Integrate $\int \frac{\cos x}{\sin x}\,dx$.

7) Integrate $\int 3x^2 e^{x^3}\,dx$.

8) Integrate $\int \frac{20x^4 + 12x^2 - 12}{x^5 + x^3 - 3x}\,dx$.

9) Use the substitution $u = e^x - 1$ to find $\int e^x(e^x + 1)(e^x - 1)^2\,dx$.

10) Find the exact value of $\int_{\frac{\pi}{4}}^{\frac{\pi}{3}} \sec^4 x \tan x\,dx$, using the substitution $u = \sec x$.

11) Use integration by parts to solve $\int 3x^2 \ln x\,dx$.

12) Use integration by parts to solve $\int 4x \cos 4x\,dx$.

13) Find the volume of the solid formed when the area bounded by the curve $y = \frac{1}{x}$, the x-axis and the lines $x = 2$ and $x = 4$ is rotated 2π radians about the x-axis.

14) Find the volume of the solid formed when the area bounded by the curve $y = x^2 + 1$, the y-axis and the lines $y = 1$ and $y = 3$ is rotated 2π radians about the y-axis.

A wise man* once said 'once you have mastered integration, you can master anything'.
With that in mind, have a go at these exam questions.

*my mate Steve

Exam Questions

1   Find $\int 3e^{(5-6x)}\,dx$.

(2 marks)

2   Find the volume of the solid formed when the region R, bounded by the curve $y = \operatorname{cosec} x$, the x-axis and the lines $x = \frac{\pi}{4}$ and $x = \frac{\pi}{3}$, is rotated 2π radians about the x-axis.
Give your answer to 3 decimal places.

(3 marks)

C3 Section 4 — Practice Questions

If I was feeling more <u>awake</u>, I'd think of something terribly <u>witty</u> and <u>amusing</u> to say about integration here. However, you'll have to just <u>pretend</u> that I did, or make something up for yourself. I'll take <u>full credit</u> for it of course.

3   Find the value of $\int_1^2 \frac{8}{x}(\ln x + 2)^3 \, dx$ using the substitution $u = \ln x$. Give your answer to 4 s.f.

(6 marks)

4

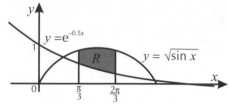

The region R above is formed by the curves $y = \sqrt{\sin x}$, $y = e^{-0.5x}$, $x = \frac{\pi}{3}$ and $x = \frac{2\pi}{3}$. Calculate the volume of the solid formed when R is rotated completely about the x-axis. Give your answer to 4 s.f.

(7 marks)

5   The diagram shows the graph of $y = x \sin x$. The region R is bounded by the curve and the x-axis ($0 \le x \le \pi$).

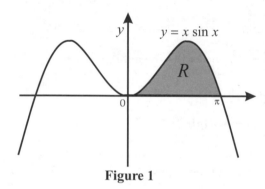

Figure 1

Find the exact area of R using integration by parts.

(4 marks)

6   The graph below shows the curve of $y = \frac{1}{x^2}$ for $x > 0$.

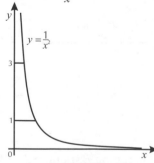

The region bounded by the curve, the y-axis and the lines $y = 1$ and $y = 3$ is rotated 2π radians about the y-axis. Calculate the exact volume of the solid formed.

(5 marks)

Location of Roots

And now to the final leg of the <u>magical mystery tour</u> known as C3. And what a finale. Small but perfectly formed, this section will tell you everything you need to know (for now) about finding <u>approximations of roots</u>. Oh the thrills.

A **Change of Sign** from **f(a) to f(b)** means a **Root Between a and b**

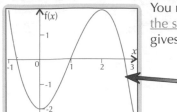

You may be asked to '<u>solve</u>' or '<u>find the roots of</u>' an equation (where <u>f(x) = 0</u>). This is <u>exactly the same</u> as finding the <u>value of x</u> where the graph <u>crosses the x-axis</u>. The <u>graph</u> of the function gives you a rough idea <u>how many</u> roots there are (<u>if any</u>) and <u>where</u>.

E.g. the function $f(x) = 3x^2 - x^3 - 2$ (shown here) has <u>3 roots</u> in the interval $-1 \leq x \leq 3$, since it crosses the x-axis <u>three times</u> (i.e. there are 3 solutions to the equation $3x^2 - x^3 - 2 = 0$). You can also see from the graph that <u>x = 1</u> is a root, and the other roots are <u>close to x = -1 and x = 3</u>.

Look at the graph above at the root $x = 1$. For x-values <u>just before</u> the root, f(x) is <u>negative</u>, and <u>just after</u> the root, f(x) is <u>positive</u>. It's the other way around for the other two roots, but either way:

> f(x) changes sign as it passes through a root.

This is only true for <u>continuous functions</u> — ones that are <u>joined up</u> all the way along with no 'jumps' or gaps.

> To show that a root lies in the <u>interval</u> between <u>two values</u> 'a' and 'b':
>
> 1) Find <u>f(a)</u> and <u>f(b)</u>.
>
> 2) If the two answers have <u>different signs</u>, and the function is <u>continuous</u>, there's a root somewhere between 'em.

f(x) = tan x is an example of a non-continuous function — it has gaps where f(x) changes sign even though there's no root.

> **EXAMPLE**   Show that $x^4 + 3x - 5 = 0$ has a root in the interval $1.1 \leq x \leq 1.2$.
>
> 1) Put both 1.1 and 1.2 into the expression:
> $f(1.1) = (1.1)^4 + (3 \times 1.1) - 5 = \underline{-0.2359}$. $f(1.2) = (1.2)^4 + (3 \times 1.2) - 5 = \underline{0.6736}$.
>
> 2) f(1.1) and f(1.2) have <u>different signs</u>, and f(x) is <u>continuous</u>, so there's a root in the interval $1.1 \leq x \leq 1.2$.

Use an **Iteration Formula** to find **Approximations** of Roots

Some equations are just too darn tricky to <u>solve properly</u>. For these, you need to find <u>approximations</u> to the roots, to a certain level of <u>accuracy</u>. You'll usually be told the value of x that a root is close to, and then <u>iteration</u> does the rest.

<u>Iteration</u> is like fancy trial and improvement. You put an approximate value of a root x into an <u>iteration formula</u>, and out pops a slightly more accurate value. Then <u>repeat</u> as necessary until you have an <u>accurate enough</u> answer.

> **EXAMPLE**   Use the <u>iteration formula</u> $x_{n+1} = \sqrt[3]{x_n + 4}$ to solve $x^3 - 4 - x = 0$, to 2 d.p. Start with $x_0 = 2$.
>
> 1) The notation x_n just means the approximation of x at the nth iteration.
> So putting x_0 in the formula for x_n, gives you x_{n+1}, which is x_1, the first iteration.
>
> 2) $x_0 = 2$, so $x_1 = \sqrt[3]{x_0 + 4} = \sqrt[3]{2 + 4} = 1.8171...$ *Leave this in your calculator for accuracy*
>
> 3) This value now gets put back into the formula to find x_2:
> $x_1 = 1.8171...$, so $x_2 = \sqrt[3]{x_1 + 4} = \sqrt[3]{1.8171... + 4} = 1.7984...$ *You should now just be able to type '3√(ANS + 4)' in your calculator and keep pressing enter for each iteration.*
>
> 4) Carry on until you get answers that are the same when rounded to 2 d.p:
> $x_2 = 1.7984...$, so $x_3 = \sqrt[3]{x_2 + 4} = \sqrt[3]{1.7984... + 4} = 1.7965...$
>
> 5) x_2, x_3, and all further iterations are the same when rounded to 2 d.p., so the root is $x = 1.80$ to 2 d.p.

The hat — an approximate solution to root problems...

Just to re-iterate (ho ho), the main ways to find those roots are sign changes and iteration formulas. It's a doddle. Don't get confused and go looking for tree roots — that involves a lot of digging, and you'll end up getting all muddy.

Iterative Methods

Now we come to the trickier bits. It's all well and good being able to plug numbers into a formula, but where do those formulas come from? And why don't they always work? Read on to find out...

Rearrange the Equation to get the Iteration Formula

The iteration formula is just a rearrangement of the equation, leaving a single 'x' on one side.

There are often lots of different ways to rearrange the equation, so in the exam you'll usually be asked to 'show that' it can be rearranged in a certain way, rather than starting from scratch.

You can also rearrange $x^3 - x^2 - 9 = 0$ into the iteration formula $x_{n+1} = \sqrt{x_n^3 - 9}$, which behaves differently, as shown below.

EXAMPLE Show that $x^3 - x^2 - 9 = 0$ can be rearranged into $x = \sqrt{\dfrac{9}{x-1}}$.

1) The '9' is on its own in the fraction so try:
   $x^3 - x^2 - 9 = 0 \Rightarrow x^3 - x^2 = 9$

2) The LHS can be factorised now: $x^2(x - 1) = 9$

3) Get the x^2 on its own by dividing by $x - 1$: $x^2 = \dfrac{9}{x-1}$

4) Finally square root both sides: $x = \sqrt{\dfrac{9}{x-1}}$

You can now use the iteration formula $x_{n+1} = \sqrt{\dfrac{9}{x_n-1}}$ to find approximations of the roots.

Sometimes an iteration formula just will not find a root. In these cases, no matter how close to the root you have x_0, the iteration sequence diverges — the numbers get further and further apart. The iteration also might stop working — e.g. if you have to take the square root of a negative number.

EXAMPLE The equation $x^3 - x^2 - 9 = 0$ has a root close to $x = 2.5$. What is the result of using $x_{n+1} = \sqrt{x_n^3 - 9}$ with $x_0 = 2.5$ to find this root?

1) Start with $x_1 = \sqrt{2.5^3 - 9} = 2.5739...$ (seems okay so far...)

2) Subsequent iterations give: $x_2 = 2.8376..., x_3 = 3.7214..., x_4 = 6.5221...$ — so the sequence diverges.

Usually though, in an exam question, you'll be given a formula that converges to a certain root — otherwise there's not much point in using it. If your formula diverges when it shouldn't, go back and check you've not made a mistake.

Use Upper and Lower Bounds to 'Show that' a root is correct

Quite often you'll be given an approximation to a root and be asked to show that it's correct to a certain accuracy. This is a lot like showing that the root lies in a certain interval (on the last page) — the trick is to work out the right interval.

EXAMPLE Show that $x = 2.472$ is a root of the equation $x^3 - x^2 - 9 = 0$ to 3 d.p.

1) If $x = 2.472$ is a root rounded to 3 decimal places, the exact root must lie between the upper and lower bounds of this value — 2.4715 and 2.4725. Any value in this interval would be rounded to 2.472 to 3 d.p.

```
      2.4715       2.4725
2.471        2.472        2.473
```

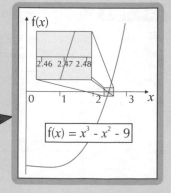

2) The function $f(x) = x^3 - x^2 - 9$ is continuous, so you know the root lies in the interval $2.4715 \le x \le 2.4725$ if f(2.4715) and f(2.4725) have different signs.

3) $f(2.4715) = 2.4715^3 - 2.4715^2 - 9 = -0.0116...$
   and $f(2.4725) = 2.4725^3 - 2.4725^2 - 9 = 0.0017...$

4) f(2.4715) and f(2.4725) have different signs, so the root must lie in between them. Since any value between would be rounded to 2.472 to 3 d.p. this answer must be correct.

You're bound to be asked questions on this...

There are usually several parts to an exam question on iteration, but it's all pretty standard stuff. I'd put good money on you having to rearrange an equation to get an iteration formula, or show that an approximation to a root is correct.

Iterative Methods

Whilst iterations are pretty thrilling on their own, put them into a <u>diagram</u> and the world's your lobster. Well, that might be a bit of an exaggeration, but you can show <u>convergence</u> or <u>divergence</u> easily on a diagram. And it looks pretty.

You can show *Iterations* on a *Diagram*

Once you've calculated a <u>sequence of iterations</u>, you can plot the points on a <u>diagram</u> and use it to show whether your sequence <u>converges</u> or <u>diverges</u>.

> ### Sketching Iterations
>
> 1) First, sketch the graphs of $y = x$ and $y = f(x)$ (where f(x) is the <u>iterative formula</u>). The point where the two graphs <u>meet</u> is the <u>root</u> you're aiming for.
> 2) Draw a <u>vertical line</u> from the x-value of your <u>starting point</u> (x_0) until it meets the <u>curve</u> y = f(x).
> 3) Now draw a <u>horizontal line</u> from this point to the <u>line</u> $y = x$. At this point, the x-value is x_1, the value of your <u>first iteration</u>. This is one <u>step</u>.
> 4) Draw <u>another step</u> — a <u>vertical line</u> from this point to the curve, and a <u>horizontal line</u> joining it to the line $y = x$.
> 5) Repeat step 4) for <u>each</u> of your <u>iterations</u>.
> 6) If your steps are getting <u>closer and closer</u> to the root, the sequence of iterations is <u>converging</u>. If the steps are moving <u>further and further away</u> from the root, the sequence is <u>diverging</u>.

This method produces two different types of diagrams — cobweb diagrams and staircase diagrams.

Convergent iterations *Home In* on the *Root*

It's probably easiest to follow the method by looking at a few <u>examples</u>:

EXAMPLES

This is an example of a <u>convergent staircase diagram</u>. Starting at x_0, the next iterations x_1, x_2 and x_3 are getting <u>closer</u> to the point where the two graphs intersect (the root).

This is an example of a <u>convergent cobweb diagram</u>. In this case, the iterations <u>alternate</u> between being <u>below</u> the root and <u>above</u> the root, but are still getting <u>closer</u> each time.

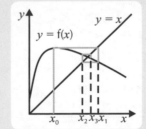

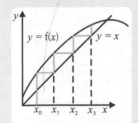

This is an example of a <u>divergent staircase diagram</u>. Starting at x_0, the iterations x_1 and x_2 are getting <u>further away</u> from the root.

In each case, the diagram will look different depending on where your starting point is.

There are cobwebs on my staircase...

Drawing diagrams is actually pretty easy — it's mainly just a case of drawing straight lines. If your iterative function is a bit nasty (which it probably will be), you'll be given the graph of it in the exam and you'll just have to add on the iteration steps.

Iterative Methods

So now that you know all you need to know to be able to tackle the exam questions, let's have a look at how it all fits together in a <u>worked example</u>. Brace yourself...

Questions on Locating Roots combine all the Different Methods

Obviously, the questions you come across in the exam won't be identical to the one below (if only...), but there are, after all, only a limited number of ways you can be asked to <u>find a root</u> using the numerical methods in this section. If you can <u>follow the steps</u> shown below you won't go far wrong.

EXAMPLE The graph below shows both roots of the continuous function $f(x) = 6x - x^2 + 13$.
a) Show that the positive root, α, lies in the interval $7 < x < 8$.
b) Show that $6x - x^2 + 13 = 0$ can be rearranged into the formula: $x = \sqrt{6x + 13}$.
c) Use the iteration formula $x_{n+1} = \sqrt{6x_n + 13}$ and $x_0 = 7$ to find α to 1 d.p.
d) Sketch a diagram to show the convergence of the sequence for x_1, x_2 and x_3.
e) Show that the negative root, β, is -1.690 to 3 d.p.

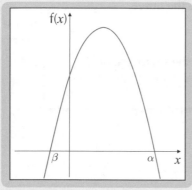

a) $f(x)$ is a <u>continuous function</u>, so if f(7) and f(8) have <u>different signs</u> then there is a root in the interval $7 < x < 8$:

$$f(7) = (6 \times 7) - 7^2 + 13 = 6.$$
$$f(8) = (6 \times 8) - 8^2 + 13 = -3.$$

There is a <u>change of sign</u> so $7 < \alpha < 8$.

b) Get the x^2 on its own to make: $6x + 13 = x^2$

Now take the (positive) square root to leave: $x = \sqrt{6x + 13}$.

c) Using $x_{n+1} = \sqrt{6x_n + 13}$ with $x_0 = 7$, gives $x_1 = \sqrt{6 \times 7 + 13} = 7.4161...$

Continuing the iterations:
$x_2 = \sqrt{6 \times 7.4161... + 13} = 7.5826...$ $x_3 = \sqrt{6 \times 7.5826... + 13} = 7.6482...$
$x_4 = \sqrt{6 \times 7.6482... + 13} = 7.6739...$ $x_5 = \sqrt{6 \times 7.6739... + 13} = 7.6839...$
$x_6 = \sqrt{6 \times 7.6839... + 13} = 7.6879...$ $x_7 = \sqrt{6 \times 7.6879... + 13} = 7.6894...$

The list of results from each iteration x_1, x_2, x_3... is called the iteration <u>sequence</u>.

x_4 to x_7 all round to 7.7 to 1 d.p., so to 1 d.p. $\alpha = 7.7$.

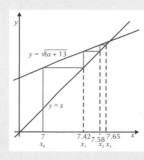

d) $y = \sqrt{6x + 13}$ and $y = x$ will be drawn for you, and the position of x_0 will be marked. All you have to do is draw on the <u>lines</u> and label the <u>values</u> of x_1, x_2 and x_3. You can see from the diagram that the sequence is a <u>convergent staircase</u>.

e) If $\beta = -1.690$ to 3 d.p. the <u>upper and lower bounds</u> are -1.6895 and -1.6905. The root must lie between these values in order to be rounded to -1.690.

As the function is <u>continuous</u>, if f(-1.6895) and f(-1.6905) have <u>different signs</u> then $-1.6905 \leq \beta \leq -1.6895$:

$$f(-1.6895) = (6 \times -1.6895) - (-1.6895)^2 + 13 = 0.00858...$$
$$f(-1.6905) = (6 \times -1.6905) - (-1.6905)^2 + 13 = -0.00079...$$

There is a <u>change of sign</u>, so $-1.6905 \leq \beta \leq -1.6895$, and so $\beta = -1.690$ to 3 d.p.

Trouble finding a root? Try sat-nav...

Nearly there now — just one more page of C3. OK, and then those practice questions you've come to know and love so well. And then there's a small matter of some practice exams. But apart from that, you're practically there.

Numerical Integration

There are a few ways of <u>estimating</u> areas under graphs that don't involve <u>integrating</u> — unfortunately looking at the picture and saying "I reckon that's about 5 cm²" isn't one of them. The ones you need are <u>Simpson's Rule</u> and the <u>Mid-Ordinate Rule</u>.

Simpson's Rule works for an Even Number of Strips

<u>Simpson's Rule</u> is a bit like the <u>Trapezium Rule</u> that you met back in C2 (have a look at your AS notes if you need a reminder) — it lets you <u>estimate</u> the area under a curve by <u>dividing it up</u> into smaller bits. It's given to you on the <u>formula sheet</u>, so you don't have to learn it. You do need to know <u>what it means</u>, and how to <u>use</u> it. It looks like this:

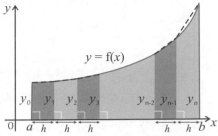

$$\int_a^b y \, dx \approx \tfrac{1}{3}h[(y_0 + y_n) + 4(y_1 + y_3 + \dots + y_{n-1}) + 2(y_2 + y_4 + \dots + y_{n-2})]$$

where $h = \frac{b-a}{n}$ (the width of each strip) and n (the number of strips) is even. $y_0, y_1, y_2, \dots, y_n$ are the heights of the sides of each strip — you get these by putting the x-values into the equation of the curve (like for the Trapezium Rule).

EXAMPLE

Use Simpson's Rule with 4 strips to approximate the area of $\int_0^1 e^{2x^2-1} \, dx$.

The width of each strip is $h = \frac{1-0}{4} = 0.25$,

so the x-values are 0, 0.25, 0.5, 0.75 and 1.

Using these, calculate the y-values (to 3 d.p.):

x	$y = e^{2x^2-1}$
$x_0 = 0$	$y_0 = 0.368$
$x_1 = 0.25$	$y_1 = 0.417$
$x_2 = 0.5$	$y_2 = 0.607$
$x_3 = 0.75$	$y_3 = 1.133$
$x_4 = 1$	$y_4 = 2.718$

Now put the y-values into the formula:

$$\int_0^1 e^{2x^2-1} \, dx$$
$$\approx \tfrac{1}{3}(0.25)[(0.368 + 2.718) + 4(0.417 + 1.133) + 2(0.607)]$$
$$= \tfrac{1}{12}[3.086 + 6.2 + 1.214] = 0.875 \quad \text{(3 d.p.)}$$

Using <u>more strips</u> will give you a <u>more accurate</u> approximation.

The Mid-Ordinate Rule adds up the Areas of lots of Rectangles

The <u>Mid-Ordinate Rule</u> works in a similar way to the <u>Trapezium Rule</u> — except that instead of adding up the areas of lots of <u>trapeziums</u> (or trapezia if you want to be fancy), it uses the areas of lots of <u>rectangles</u> (rectanglia?) instead. The <u>height</u> of the rectangle is given by the y-value at the <u>midpoint</u> of the strip.

Here's the Mid-Ordinate Rule:

$$\int_a^b y \, dx \approx h(y_{0.5} + y_{1.5} + \dots + y_{n-1.5} + y_{n-0.5})$$

where $h = \frac{b-a}{n}$.

This rule is also given on the formula sheet.

EXAMPLE

Use the Mid-Ordinate Rule to approximate the area of $\int_1^4 \ln(x^3 + 2x) \, dx$, where $n = 3$.

The width of each strip is $h = \frac{4-1}{3} = 1$, so the normal x-values would be $x_0 = 1$, $x_1 = 2$, $x_2 = 3$, and $x_3 = 4$. But for this rule, you want the midpoints of the strips, so instead you need to find the y-values at $x_{0.5} = 1.5$, $x_{1.5} = 2.5$ and $x_{2.5} = 3.5$:

x	$y = \ln(x^3 + 2x)$
$x_{0.5} = 1.5$	$y_{0.5} = 1.852$
$x_{1.5} = 2.5$	$y_{1.5} = 3.027$
$x_{2.5} = 3.5$	$y_{2.5} = 3.910$

(3 d.p.)

Putting these values into the formula gives:
$$\int_1^4 \ln(x^3 + 2x) \, dx \approx 1(1.852 + 3.027 + 3.910)$$
$$= 8.789 \quad \text{(3 d.p.)}$$

I'd rather have subordinates than mid-ordinates...

There's nothing too tricky here — and it helps that both rules are on the formula sheet. Just remember that you must have an even number of strips for Simpson's Rule, and you use the midpoint of the strip to find the y-value for the Mid-Ordinate Rule.

C3 Section 5 — Practice Questions

To make up for a <u>short section</u> I'm giving you lots of <u>lovely practice</u>. Stretch those thinking muscles with this <u>warm-up</u>:

Warm-up Questions

1) The graph shows the function $f(x) = e^x - x^3$ for $0 \le x \le 5$.
   How many roots does the equation $e^x - x^3 = 0$ have in the interval $0 \le x \le 5$?

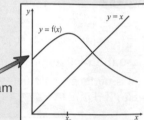

2) Show that there is a root in the interval:
   a) $3 < x < 4$ for $\sin(2x) = 0$,
   b) $2.1 < x < 2.2$ for $\ln(x - 2) + 2 = 0$,
   c) $4.3 < x < 4.5$ for $x^3 - 4x^2 = 7$.

   Don't forget to use radians when you're given trig functions.

3) By selecting an appropriate interval show that, to 1 d.p., $x = 1.2$ is a root of the equation $x^3 + x - 3 = 0$.

4) Use the formula $x_{n+1} = -\frac{1}{2}\cos x_n$, with $x_0 = -1$, to find a root of $\cos x + 2x = 0$ to 2 d.p.

5) Use the formula $x_{n+1} = \sqrt{\ln x_n + 4}$, with $x_0 = 2$, to find a root of $x^2 - \ln x - 4 = 0$ to 3 d.p.

6) a) Show that the equation $2x^2 - x^3 + 1 = 0$ can be written in the form:

   i) $x = \sqrt{\dfrac{-1}{2-x}}$ ii) $x = \sqrt[3]{2x^2 + 1}$ iii) $x = \sqrt{\dfrac{x^3 - 1}{2}}$

   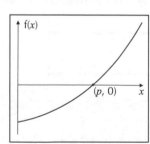

   b) Use iteration formulas based on each of the above rearrangements with $x_0 = 2.3$ to find a root of $2x^2 - x^3 + 1 = 0$ to 2 d.p. Which of the three formulas converge to a root?

7) Using the position of x_0 as given on the graph, draw a staircase or cobweb diagram showing how the sequence converges. Label x_1 and x_2 on the diagram.

8) a) Use <u>Simpson's Rule</u> with 6 strips to approximate the area of $\int_1^4 \ln(\sqrt{x} + 2)\,dx$.
   b) Why can't you use Simpson's Rule with <u>5 strips</u> to find an estimate?

   For extra practice, have a go at q8 using the Mid-Ordinate Rule and q9 using Simpson's Rule.

9) Use the <u>Mid-Ordinate Rule</u> to estimate the value of $\int_2^4 x^2 e^{x-2}\,dx$, using $n = 4$.

And for my next trick... Sadly no magic here, but all the right kinds of questions to prepare you for the exam.

Exam Questions

1   The sketch below shows part of the graph of the function $f(x) = 2xe^x - 3$.
    The curve crosses the x-axis at the point $P(p, 0)$, as shown, so p is a root of the equation $f(x) = 0$.

a) Show that $0.7 < p < 0.8$.

(3 marks)

b) Show that $f(x) = 0$ can be rewritten as:

$$x = \frac{3}{2}e^{-x}.$$

(2 marks)

c) Starting with $x_0 = 0.7$, use the iteration

$$x_{n+1} = \frac{3}{2}e^{-x_n}$$

to find x_1, x_2, x_3 and x_4 to 4 d.p.

(3 marks)

d) Show that $p = 0.726$, to 3 d.p.

(3 marks)

C3 Section 5 — Practice Questions

2   The graph of the function $y = \sin 3x + 3x$, $\;0 < x < \pi$, meets the line $y = 1$ when $x = a$.

    a)   Show that $0.1 < a < 0.2$.

(4 marks)

    b)   Show that the equation $\sin 3x + 3x = 1$ can be written as:

$$x = \tfrac{1}{3}(1 - \sin 3x).$$

(2 marks)

    c)   Starting with $x_0 = 0.2$, use the iteration:

$$x_{n+1} = \tfrac{1}{3}(1 - \sin 3x_n)$$

        to find x_4, to 3 d.p.

(2 marks)

3   The sequence given by:

$$x_{n+1} = \sqrt[3]{x_n^2 - 4}, \;\; x_0 = -1$$

converges to a number 'b'.

    a)   Find the values of x_1, x_2, x_3 and x_4 correct to 4 decimal places.

(3 marks)

    b)   Show that $x = b$ is a root of the equation:

$$x^3 - x^2 + 4 = 0$$

(2 marks)

    c)   Show that $b = -1.315$ to 3 decimal places, by choosing an appropriate interval.

(3 marks)

4   The function $\mathrm{f}(x) = \ln(x + 3) - x + 2$, $x > -3$ has a root at $x = m$.

    a)   Show that m lies between 3 and 4.

(3 marks)

    b)   Find, using iteration, the value of m correct to 2 decimal places.
        Use the iteration formula: $x_{n+1} = \ln(x_n + 3) + 2$ with $x_0 = 3$.

(3 marks)

    c)   Use a suitable interval to verify that your answer to part b) is correct to 2 decimal places.

(3 marks)

    d)   The graph below shows part of the curve $y = \ln(x + 3) + 2$, the line $y = x$ and the position of x_0.
        Complete the diagram showing the convergence of the iteration sequence, showing the
        locations of x_1 and x_2 on the graph.

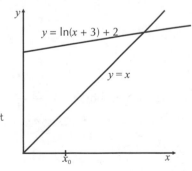

You can trace the graph if you don't
want to draw in your book.

(2 marks)

5   Using Simpson's Rule with 4 strips, approximate the area of $\displaystyle\int_1^5 \frac{1}{x^2 + 3x}\,\mathrm{d}x$.
    Give your answer to 3 s.f.

(4 marks)

6   Use the Mid-Ordinate Rule to approximate the area of $\displaystyle\int_1^3 2^x\,\mathrm{d}x$, with 4 strips.
    Give your answer to 4 s.f.

(3 marks)

General Certificate of Education
Advanced Subsidiary (AS) and Advanced Level

Core Mathematics C3 — Practice Exam One

Time Allowed: 1 hour 30 min

Graphical calculators may be used for this exam.

Give any non-exact numerical answers to an appropriate degree of accuracy.

There are 75 marks available for this paper.

1   For the function:

$$f(x) = 3 \ln x - \ln 3x, \qquad x > 0$$

find:

a)   the exact value of x when $f(x) = 0$.

(2 marks)

b) $f^{-1}(x)$.

(2 marks)

c)   the exact value of x when $f^{-1}(x) = 1$.

(2 marks)

d) $f'(x)$ when $x = 1$.

(2 marks)

2   The graph below shows the function $y = f(x)$, $x \in \mathbb{R}$, with turning points $A(-1, -2)$ and $B(3, 2)$.

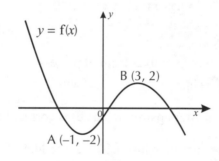

a)   On separate axes, sketch the graphs of the following, clearly showing the coordinates of A and B where possible.

(i) $y = f(|x|)$.

(3 marks)

(ii) $y = 3f(x + 2)$.

(3 marks)

b)   For the functions $g(x) = \sqrt{2x + 3}$, $x \geq -1.5$ and $h(x) = \dfrac{6}{x^2 - 4}$, $x > 2$, find:

(i)   gh(4)

(2 marks)

(ii)   hg(3)

(2 marks)

(iii)   hg(x)

(3 marks)

3   Find the exact value of

$$\int_0^{\frac{1}{2}} \frac{x}{1 - x^2} \, dx$$

using the substitution $x = \sin \theta$.

(6 marks)

4   Part of the curve

$$y = \frac{4x - 1}{\tan x}$$

is shown below.

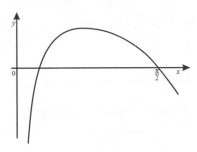

Show that:

$$4\cot x - (4x - 1)\operatorname{cosec}^2 x$$

is an expression for $\dfrac{dy}{dx}$.

(3 marks)

5   a)   On the same axes, draw the graphs of $f(x) = |2x + 3|$ and $g(x) = |5x - 4|$, showing clearly where each graph touches the coordinate axes.

(3 marks)

       b)   Hence or otherwise solve the equation $|2x + 3| = |5x - 4|$.

(4 marks)

       c)   Using your results to parts a) and b), solve the inequality $|2x + 3| \geq |5x - 4|$.

(2 marks)

6   The graph below shows the curve $y = \sqrt{\sin x}$, $0 \leq x \leq \pi$. The region R is bounded by the curve and the x-axis.

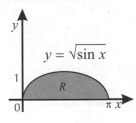

Find the volume of the solid formed when R is rotated 2π radians about the x-axis.

(4 marks)

7   a)   Find the values of θ in the range $0 \leq \theta \leq 2\pi$ for which $\operatorname{cosec} \theta = \frac{5}{3}$.
             Give your answers to 3 significant figures.

(2 marks)

       b)   (i)   Use an appropriate identity to show that $3 \operatorname{cosec} \theta = \cot^2\theta - 17$ can be written as
                    $18 + 3 \operatorname{cosec} \theta - \operatorname{cosec}^2\theta = 0$.

(2 marks)

            (ii)   Hence solve the equation $3 \operatorname{cosec} \theta = \cot^2\theta - 17$ for $0 \leq \theta \leq 2\pi$, giving your answers to 3 significant figures.

(4 marks)

8   The sketch below shows the intersection of the curve $y = 6^x$ with the line $y = x + 2$ at the point P.

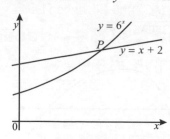

a)   Show that the equation $6^x = x + 2$ can be written in the form:

$$x = \frac{\ln(x + 2)}{\ln 6}.$$

(2 marks)

b)   Starting with $x_0 = 0.5$, use the iteration formula:

$$x_{n+1} = \frac{\ln(x_n + 2)}{\ln 6}$$

to find x_1, x_2 and x_3 correct to 4 decimal places.

(3 marks)

c)   By selecting an appropriate interval, show that $x = 0.515$ to 3 decimal places at point P.

(3 marks)

9   A curve has the equation $x = \dfrac{e^y + 2y}{e^y - 2y}$.

a)   Find $\dfrac{dy}{dx}$.

(3 marks)

b)   Find an equation of the normal to the curve at the point $(1, 0)$ in the form $y = ax + b$.

(3 marks)

10   The graph below shows the curve $y = \dfrac{3\ln x}{x^2}$, $x \geq 0$. The shaded region R is bounded by the curve, the x-axis and the line $x = 3$.

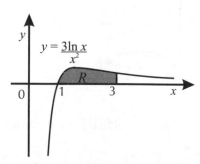

a)   Complete the table for the missing y-values. Give your answers to 5 decimal places.

x	1	1.5	2	2.5	3
y	0		0.51986	0.43982	

(2 marks)

b)   Hence find an approximation for the area of R, using Simpson's Rule with 4 strips.

(3 marks)

c)   Find the value of the integral $\displaystyle\int_1^3 \frac{3\ln x}{x^2}\, dx$ using integration by parts. Give your answer to 5 decimal places.

(5 marks)

General Certificate of Education
Advanced Subsidiary (AS) and Advanced Level

Core Mathematics C3 — Practice Exam Two

Time Allowed: 1 hour 30 min

Graphical calculators may be used for this exam.

Give any non-exact numerical answers to an appropriate degree of accuracy.

There are 75 marks available for this paper.

1   a)   Use integration by parts to find $\int 4xe^{-2x}\,dx$.

(4 marks)

     b)   Find $\int_{1}^{2}\left(\dfrac{\ln x}{\sqrt{x}}\right)^{2}dx$, using the substitution $u = \ln x$. Give your answer to 3 significant figures.

(5 marks)

2   The functions f and g are defined as follows:

$$f(x) = \frac{1}{x^2}, \quad x \in \mathbb{R}, \ x \neq 0$$
$$g(x) = x^2 - 9, \quad x \in \mathbb{R}$$

     a)   State the range of g.

(1 mark)

     b)   Neither f nor g have an inverse. Explain why.

(1 mark)

     c)   Find

         (i)   fg(4)

(2 marks)

         (ii) gf(1)

(2 marks)

     d)   (i)   Find fg(x), and write down the domain of the composite function fg.

(3 marks)

         (ii) Hence solve $fg(x) = \dfrac{1}{256}$.

(4 marks)

3   Given that $\cos x = \dfrac{8}{9}$ for the acute angle x, find the exact values of:

     a)   sec x.

(1 mark)

     b)   cosec x.

(2 marks)

     c) $\tan^2 x$.

(2 marks)

4 For the function:

$$f(x) = (\sqrt{x + 2})\ln(x + 2) \quad (x > 0)$$

a) Show that $f(x) = 6\ln 3$ when $x = 7$.

(2 marks)

b) Show that $f'(x) = \frac{1}{3}(1 + \ln 3)$ when $x = 7$.

(4 marks)

c) Hence show that the equation of the tangent to the curve:

$$y = (\sqrt{x + 2})\ln(x + 2).$$

at the point $x = 7$ can be written as:

$$3y = x + x\ln 3 + 11\ln 3 - 7.$$

(2 marks)

5 The curve $y = \ln (x^2 - 1)$, $(x > 1)$ is shown on the graph below.

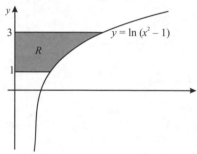

The shaded region R is bounded by the curve, the y-axis and the lines $y = 1$ and $y = 3$.

Find the volume formed when this region is rotated 2π radians about the y-axis.

Give your answer to 4 significant figures.

(5 marks)

6 a) (i) Using the Mid-Ordinate Rule with 4 strips, approximate the area of $\int_0^1 e^x \cos x \, dx$, where x is a measure in radians. Give your answer to 4 significant figures.

(4 marks)

(ii) How could you improve your approximation?

(1 mark)

b) Show that $\frac{d}{dx}\frac{1}{2}(e^x\sin x + e^x\cos x) = e^x\cos x$.

(4 marks)

c) Hence find the area of $\int_0^1 e^x \cos x \, dx$, giving your answer to 4 significant figures.

(2 marks)

7   A curve has the equation:

$$y = e^{2x} - 5e^x + 3x.$$

a)   Find $\dfrac{dy}{dx}$.

(2 marks)

b)   Find $\dfrac{d^2y}{dx^2}$.

(2 marks)

c)   Show that the stationary points on the curve occur when $x = 0$ and $x = \ln \frac{3}{2}$.

(4 marks)

d)   Determine the nature of each of the stationary points.

(4 marks)

8   The graph below shows the function:

$$f(x) = 4(x^2 - 1), \qquad x \geq 0,$$

and its inverse function $f^{-1}(x)$.

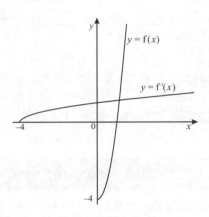

a)   By finding an expression for $f^{-1}(x)$, and by considering how the graphs are related, show that $x = \sqrt{\frac{x}{4} + 1}$ at the points where the graphs meet.

(4 marks)

b)   Show that the equation from part a) has a root in the interval $1 < x < 2$.

(3 marks)

c)   Starting with $x_0 = 0.5$, use the iteration formula:

$$x_{n+1} = \sqrt{\frac{x_n}{4} + 1}$$

to find the x coordinate of the point of intersection, correct to 3 significant figures.

(3 marks)

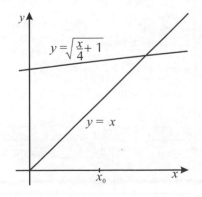

d)   The diagram on the left shows part of the curve $y = \sqrt{\frac{x}{4} + 1}$, the line $y = x$ and the position of x_0. Complete the diagram showing the convergence of the iteration sequence, clearly marking the positions of x_1 and x_2 on the graph.

(2 marks)

Simplifying Expressions

What a lovely way to start C4 — a page on <u>algebraic fractions</u>. Still, at least they're over with early on, so if they pop up later in C4 you'll know what to do. No, not run away and cower in a corner — use the things you learnt on this page.

Simplify algebraic fractions by *Factorising* and *Cancelling Factors*

<u>Algebraic fractions</u> are a lot like normal fractions — and you can treat them in the <u>same way</u>, whether you're <u>multiplying</u>, <u>dividing</u>, <u>adding</u> or <u>subtracting</u> them. All fractions are much <u>easier</u> to deal with when they're in their <u>simplest form</u>, so the first thing to do with algebraic fractions is to <u>simplify</u> them as much as possible.

A function you can write as a fraction where the top and bottom are both polynomials is called a <u>rational function</u>.

1) Look for <u>common factors</u> in the <u>numerator</u> and <u>denominator</u> — <u>factorise</u> top and bottom and see if there's anything you can <u>cancel</u>.

2) If there's a <u>fraction</u> in the numerator or denominator (e.g. $\frac{1}{x}$), <u>multiply</u> the <u>whole thing</u> (i.e. top and bottom) by the same factor to get rid of it (for $\frac{1}{x}$, you'd multiply through by x).

EXAMPLES Simplify the following:

a) $\dfrac{3x+6}{x^2-4} = \dfrac{3(x+2)}{(x+2)(x-2)} = \dfrac{3}{x-2}$

Watch out for the difference of two squares — see C1.

b) $\dfrac{2+\frac{1}{2x}}{4x^2+x} = \dfrac{\left(2+\frac{1}{2x}\right)\times 2x}{x(4x+1)\times 2x} = \dfrac{4x+1}{2x^2(4x+1)} = \dfrac{1}{2x^2}$

3) You <u>multiply</u> algebraic fractions in exactly the same way as normal fractions — multiply the <u>numerators</u> together, then multiply the <u>denominators</u>. It's a good idea to <u>cancel</u> any <u>common factors</u> before you multiply.

4) To <u>divide</u> by an algebraic fraction, you just <u>multiply</u> by its <u>reciprocal</u> (the reciprocal is 1 ÷ the original thing — for fractions you just turn the fraction <u>upside down</u>).

EXAMPLES Simplify the following:

a) $\dfrac{x^2-2x-15}{2x+8} \times \dfrac{x^2-16}{x^2+3x} = \dfrac{(x+3)(x-5)}{2(x+4)} \times \dfrac{(x+4)(x-4)}{x(x+3)}$

Factorise both fractions.

$= \dfrac{(x-5)(x-4)}{2x} \left(= \dfrac{x^2-9x+20}{2x}\right)$

b) $\dfrac{3x}{5} \div \dfrac{3x^2-9x}{20} = \dfrac{3x}{5} \times \dfrac{20}{3x(x-3)}$

Turn the second fraction upside down.

$= \dfrac{4}{x-3}$

Add and *Subtract* fractions by finding a *Common Denominator*

You'll have come across <u>adding</u> and <u>subtracting fractions</u> before, so here's a little reminder of how to do it:

EXAMPLE Simplify:

$\dfrac{2y}{x(x+3)} + \dfrac{1}{y^2(x+3)} - \dfrac{x}{y}$

① Find the Common Denominator

Take all the individual 'bits' from the bottom lines and multiply them together. Only use each bit once unless something on the bottom line is raised to a power.

The individual 'bits' here are x, $(x+3)$ and y...

$xy^2(x+3)$

...but you need to use y^2 because there's a y^2 in the second fraction's denominator.

The common denominator is the lowest common multiple (LCM) of all the denominators.

② Put Each Fraction over the Common Denominator

Make the denominator of each fraction into the common denominator.

$\dfrac{y^2 \times 2y}{y^2 x(x+3)} + \dfrac{x \times 1}{xy^2(x+3)} - \dfrac{xy(x+3) \times x}{xy(x+3)y}$

Multiply the top and bottom lines of each fraction by whatever makes the bottom line the same as the common denominator.

③ Combine into One Fraction

Once everything's over the common denominator you can just add the top lines together.

All the bottom lines are the same — so you can just add the top lines.

$= \dfrac{2y^3 + x - x^2y(x+3)}{xy^2(x+3)} = \dfrac{2y^3 + x - x^3y - 3x^2y}{xy^2(x+3)}$

Who are you calling common...

Nothing on this page should be a big shock to you — it's all stuff you've done before. You've been using normal fractions for years, and algebraic fractions work in just the same way. They look a bit scary, but they're all warm and fuzzy inside.

Algebraic Division

I'll be honest with you, <u>algebraic division</u> is a bit tricky. But as long as you take it <u>slowly</u> and don't rush, it'll all fall into place. And it's really quick and easy to <u>check your answer</u> if you're not sure. What more could you want?

There are some Terms you need to Know

There are a few words that keep popping up in <u>algebraic division</u>, so make sure you know what they all mean.

1) <u>DEGREE</u> — the highest power of x in the polynomial (e.g. the degree of $4x^5 + 6x^2 - 3x - 1$ is 5).

2) <u>DIVISOR</u> — this is the thing you're dividing by (e.g. if you divide $x^2 + 4x - 3$ by $x + 2$, the divisor is $x + 2$).

3) <u>QUOTIENT</u> — the bit that you get when you divide by the divisor (not including the remainder — see p.50).

Method 1 — Divide by Subtracting Multiples of the Divisor

Back in C1, you learnt how to do <u>algebraic division</u> by <u>subtracting</u> chunks of the <u>divisor</u>. Here's a quick reminder of how to divide a polynomial by $x - k$:

Algebraic Division

1) **<u>Subtract</u> a multiple of $(x - k)$ to get rid of the highest power of x.**

2) **<u>Repeat</u> step 1 until you've got rid of all the powers of x.**

3) **<u>Work out</u> how many lumps of $(x - k)$, you've subtracted, and read off the <u>remainder</u>.**

Have a look back at your C1 notes if you can't remember how to do this.

EXAMPLE Divide $2x^3 - 3x^2 - 3x + 7$ by $x - 2$.

① Start with $2x^3 - 3x^2 - 3x + 7$, and <u>subtract</u> $2x^2$ lots of $(x - 2)$ to get rid of the x^3 term. $\longrightarrow (2x^3 - 3x^2 - 3x + 7) - 2x^2(x - 2) = x^2 - 3x + 7$

② Now <u>start again</u> with $x^2 - 3x + 7$. The highest power of x is the x^2 term, so <u>subtract</u> x lots of $(x - 2)$ to get rid of that. $\longrightarrow (x^2 - 3x + 7) - x(x - 2) = -x + 7$

③ All that's left now is $-x + 7$. Get rid of $-x$ by <u>subtracting</u> $-1 \times (x - 2)$. $\longrightarrow (-x + 7) - (-1(x - 2)) = 5$

So $(2x^3 - 3x^2 - 3x + 7) \div (x - 2) = 2x^2 + x - 1$ remainder 5.

Method 2 — use Algebraic Long Division

To divide two <u>algebraic</u> expressions, you can use <u>long division</u> (using the same method you'd use for numbers).

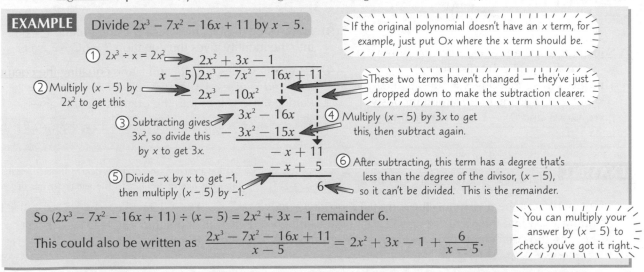

EXAMPLE Divide $2x^3 - 7x^2 - 16x + 11$ by $x - 5$.

If the original polynomial doesn't have an x term, for example, just put $0x$ where the x term should be.

① $2x^3 \div x = 2x^2$

$$x - 5 \overline{\smash{\big)}\,2x^3 - 7x^2 - 16x + 11}$$

quotient: $2x^2 + 3x - 1$

② Multiply $(x - 5)$ by $2x^2$ to get this $\longrightarrow -\ 2x^3 - 10x^2$

These two terms haven't changed — they've just dropped down to make the subtraction clearer.

③ Subtracting gives $3x^2$, so divide this by x to get $3x$.

$3x^2 - 16x$

$-\ 3x^2 - 15x$

④ Multiply $(x - 5)$ by $3x$ to get this, then subtract again.

$-x + 11$

$-\ -x + 5$

⑤ Divide $-x$ by x to get -1, then multiply $(x - 5)$ by -1.

6

⑥ After subtracting, this term has a degree that's less than the degree of the divisor, $(x - 5)$, so it can't be divided. This is the remainder.

So $(2x^3 - 7x^2 - 16x + 11) \div (x - 5) = 2x^2 + 3x - 1$ remainder 6.

This could also be written as $\dfrac{2x^3 - 7x^2 - 16x + 11}{x - 5} = 2x^2 + 3x - 1 + \dfrac{6}{x - 5}$.

You can multiply your answer by $(x - 5)$ to check you've got it right.

Just keep repeating — divide and conquer, divide and conquer...

For algebraic division to work, the degree of the divisor has to be less than (or equal to) the degree of the original polynomial (for example, you couldn't divide $x^2 + 2x + 3$ by $x^3 + 4$ as $3 > 2$, but you could do it the other way around). If you don't like either of these methods, you'll be pleased to know there's another way to divide coming up on the next page.

Algebraic Division

I really spoil you — as if two different methods for doing algebraic division weren't enough, I'm going to give you a third. If you're not sure about any of the terms, look back at the definitions on p.49.

Method 3 — use the Formula f(x) = q(x)d(x) + r(x)

There's a handy formula you can use to do algebraic division. It looks like this:

This comes from the Remainder Theorem that you met in C1. It's a good method for when you're dividing by a quadratic — long division can get a bit tricky when the divisor has 3 terms.

> A polynomial $f(x)$ can be written in the form $f(x) \equiv q(x)d(x) + r(x)$, where $q(x)$ is the quotient, $d(x)$ is the divisor and $r(x)$ is the remainder.

You'll be given $f(x)$ and $d(x)$ in the question, and it's down to you to work out $q(x)$ and $r(x)$. Here's how you do it:

Using the Formula

1) First, you have to work out the degrees of the quotient and remainder, which depend on the degrees of the polynomial and the divisor. The degree of the quotient is $\deg f(x) - \deg d(x)$, and the degree of the remainder has to be less than the degree of the divisor.

2) Write out the division using the formula above, but replace $q(x)$ and $r(x)$ with general polynomials (i.e. a general polynomial of degree 2 is $Ax^2 + Bx + C$, and a general polynomial of degree 1 is $Ax + B$, where A, B, C, etc. are constants to be found).

3) The next step is to work out the values of the constants — you do this by substituting in values for x to make bits disappear, and by equating coefficients.

Equating coefficients means comparing the coefficients of each power of x on the LHS and the RHS.

4) It's best to start with the constant term and work backwards from there.

5) Finally, write out the division again, replacing A, B, C, etc. with the values you've found.

The method looks a bit intense, but follow through the examples below to see how it works.

Start with the Remainder and Work Backwards

When you're using this method, you might have to use simultaneous equations to work out some of the coefficients. Have a look back at your C1 notes for a reminder of how to do this if you need to.

EXAMPLE Divide $x^4 - 3x^3 - 3x^2 + 10x + 5$ by $x^2 - 5x + 6$.

$f(x)$ has degree 4 and $d(x)$ has degree 2, which means that $q(x)$ has degree $4 - 2 = 2$. The remainder has degree 1 or 0 — put in $Dx + E$, as D can always be 0.

① First, write out the division in the form $f(x) \equiv q(x)d(x) + r(x)$:
$$x^4 - 3x^3 - 3x^2 + 10x + 5 \equiv (Ax^2 + Bx + C)(x^2 - 5x + 6) + Dx + E$$
$$\equiv (Ax^2 + Bx + C)(x - 2)(x - 3) + Dx + E.$$

$d(x)$ factorises to give $(x - 2)(x - 3)$.

② Substitute $x = 2$ and $x = 3$ into the identity to make the $q(x)d(x)$ bit disappear. This gives the equations $5 = 2D + E$ and $8 = 3D + E$. Solving these simultaneously gives $D = 3$ and $E = -1$, so the remainder is $3x - 1$.

③ Now, using these values of D & E and putting $x = 0$ into the identity gives the equation $5 = 6C + E$, so $C = 1$.

④ Using the values of C, D and E and equating the coefficients of x^4 and x^3 gives: $1 = A$ and $-3 = -5A + B$, so $B = 2$. Putting these values into the original identity gives:
$$x^4 - 3x^3 - 3x^2 + 10x + 5 \equiv (x^2 + 2x + 1)(x^2 - 5x + 6) + 3x - 1.$$

EXAMPLE Divide $x^3 + 5x^2 - 18x - 10$ by $x - 3$.

$f(x)$ has degree 3 and $d(x)$ has degree 1, which means that $q(x)$ has degree $3 - 1 = 2$. The remainder has degree 0.

First, write out the division in the form $f(x) \equiv q(x)d(x) + r(x)$: $x^3 + 5x^2 - 18x - 10 \equiv (Ax^2 + Bx + C)(x - 3) + D$.
Putting $x = 3$ into the identity gives $D = 8$. Now, setting $x = 0$ gives the equation $-3C + D = -10$, so $C = 6$.
Equating the coefficients of x^3 and x^2 gives $A = 1$ and $-3A + B = 5$, so $B = 8$.
So $x^3 + 5x^2 - 18x - 10 \equiv (x^2 + 8x + 6)(x - 3) + 8$.

A reminder about remainders...

The degree of the remainder has to be less than the degree of the divisor, otherwise it would be included in the quotient.
E.g. if $r(x) = (x + 1)$ and $d(x) = (x - 3)$, then $r(x)$ can be divided by $d(x)$, giving a remainder of 4 (so $(x + 1)$ wasn't the remainder).

Partial Fractions

Wait, wait — come back. You're not done with fractions yet. Not by a long way (well, 2 pages).

'Expressing in Partial Fractions' is the Opposite of Adding Fractions (sort of)

1) You can split a fraction with more than one linear factor in the denominator into partial fractions.

$\dfrac{7x - 7}{(2x + 1)(x - 3)}$ can be written as partial fractions of the form $\dfrac{A}{(2x + 1)} + \dfrac{B}{(x - 3)}$.

$\dfrac{9x^2 + x + 16}{(x + 2)(2x - 1)(x - 3)}$ can be written as partial fractions of the form $\dfrac{A}{(x + 2)} + \dfrac{B}{(2x - 1)} + \dfrac{C}{(x - 3)}$.

$\dfrac{x^2 + 17x + 16}{(x + 2)^2(3x - 1)}$ can be written as partial fractions of the form $\dfrac{A}{(x + 2)^2} + \dfrac{B}{(x + 2)} + \dfrac{C}{(3x - 1)}$.

← Watch out here — this one doesn't quite follow the pattern.

2) The tricky bit is figuring out what A, B and C are.
You can use the substitution method or the equating coefficients method:

EXAMPLE

Express $\dfrac{9x^2 + x + 16}{(x + 2)(2x - 1)(x - 3)}$ in partial fractions.

You know that $\dfrac{9x^2 + x + 16}{(x + 2)(2x - 1)(x - 3)} \equiv \dfrac{A}{(x + 2)} + \dfrac{B}{(2x - 1)} + \dfrac{C}{(x - 3)}$. Now to work out A, B and C.

1 Add the partial fractions and cancel the denominators from both sides

$$\dfrac{A}{(x + 2)} + \dfrac{B}{(2x - 1)} + \dfrac{C}{(x - 3)} \equiv \dfrac{A(2x - 1)(x - 3) + B(x + 2)(x - 3) + C(2x - 1)(x + 2)}{(x + 2)(2x - 1)(x - 3)}$$

So the numerators are equal: $9x^2 + x + 16 \equiv A(2x - 1)(x - 3) + B(x + 2)(x - 3) + C(2x - 1)(x + 2)$

2 Substitute x for values which get rid of all but one of A, B and C...

Substituting $x = 3$ gets rid of A and B: $(9 \times 3^2) + 3 + 16 = 0 + 0 + C((2 \times 3) - 1)(3 + 2)$
$$100 = 25C \Rightarrow \underline{C = 4}$$

Substituting $x = -2$ gets rid of B and C: $(9 \times (-2)^2) + (-2) + 16 = A((2 \times -2) - 1)(-2 - 3) + 0 + 0$
$$50 = 25A \Rightarrow \underline{A = 2}$$

Substituting $x = 0.5$ gets rid of A and C: $(9 \times (0.5^2)) + 0.5 + 16 = 0 + B(0.5 + 2)(0.5 - 3) + 0$
$$18.75 = -6.25B \Rightarrow \underline{B = -3}$$

...OR compare coefficients in the numerators

$9x^2 + x + 16 \equiv A(2x - 1)(x - 3) + B(x + 2)(x - 3) + C(2x - 1)(x + 2)$

x^2 coefficients: $9 = 2A + B + 2C$
x coefficients: $1 = -7A - B + 3C$
constant terms: $16 = 3A - 6B - 2C$

Solving these equations simultaneously gives $A = 2$, $B = -3$ and $C = 4$ — the same as the substitution method.

3 Write out the solution

$$\dfrac{9x^2 + x + 16}{(x + 2)(2x - 1)(x - 3)} \equiv \dfrac{2}{(x + 2)} - \dfrac{3}{(2x - 1)} + \dfrac{4}{(x - 3)}$$

Watch out for Difference of Two Squares Denominators

Just for added meanness, they might give you an expression like $\dfrac{4}{x^2 - 1}$ and tell you to express it as partial fractions.

You have to recognise that the denominator is a difference of two squares, write it as two linear factors, and then carry on as normal. E.g. $\dfrac{21x - 2}{9x^2 - 4} \equiv \dfrac{21x - 2}{(3x - 2)(3x + 2)} \equiv \dfrac{A}{(3x - 2)} + \dfrac{B}{(3x + 2)}$

Not all coefficients are created equal — but some are...

It's worth getting to grips with both methods for step 2. Sometimes one's easier to use than the other, and sometimes you might want to mix and match. It's just another crucial step on the path to going down in history as a mathematical great.

Partial Fractions

Now things are hotting up in the partial fractions department — here's an example involving a <u>repeated factor</u>.

Sometimes it's best to use **Substitution** AND **Equate Coefficients**

EXAMPLE   Express $\dfrac{x^2 + 17x + 16}{(x + 2)^2(3x - 1)}$ in partial fractions.

You know that $\dfrac{x^2 + 17x + 16}{(x + 2)^2(3x - 1)} \equiv \dfrac{A}{(x + 2)^2} + \dfrac{B}{(x + 2)} + \dfrac{C}{(3x - 1)}$. Now to work out A, B and C.

1 Add the partial fractions   You end up with an extra $(x + 2)$ factor in each term that can be cancelled.

$$\dfrac{A}{(x + 2)^2} + \dfrac{B}{(x + 2)} + \dfrac{C}{(3x - 1)} \equiv \dfrac{A(x + 2)(3x - 1) + B(x + 2)^2(3x - 1) + C(x + 2)(x + 2)^2}{(x + 2)^2(x + 2)(3x - 1)}$$

Cancel the denominators from both sides $x^2 + 17x + 16 \equiv A(3x - 1) + B(x + 2)(3x - 1) + C(x + 2)^2$

2 Substitute x for values which get rid of all but one of A, B and C

Substituting $x = -2$ gets rid of B and C: $(-2)^2 + (17 \times -2) + 16 = A((3 \times -2) - 1) + 0 + 0$
$$-14 = -7A \quad \Rightarrow \underline{A = 2}$$

Substituting $x = \frac{1}{3}$ gets rid of A and B: $\left(\frac{1}{3}\right)^2 + \left(17 \times \frac{1}{3}\right) + 16 = 0 + 0 + C\left(\frac{1}{3} + 2\right)^2$
$$\frac{196}{9} = \frac{49}{9}C \quad \Rightarrow \underline{C = 4}$$

The trouble is, there's <u>no value of x</u> you can substitute to get rid of A and C to just leave <u>B</u>.
So: Equate coefficients of x^2 From $x^2 + 17x + 16 \equiv A(3x - 1) + B(x + 2)(3x - 1) + C(x + 2)^2$
Coefficients of x^2 are: $1 = 3B + C$
You know $C = 4$, so: $1 = 3B + 4 \Rightarrow \underline{B = -1}$

3 Write out the solution   You now know A, B and C, so: $\dfrac{x^2 + 17x + 16}{(x + 2)^2(3x - 1)} \equiv \dfrac{2}{(x + 2)^2} - \dfrac{1}{(x + 2)} + \dfrac{4}{(3x - 1)}$

Divide Before Expressing **Improper Fractions** as Partial Fractions

The numerator of an <u>improper algebraic fraction</u> has a degree <u>equal to</u> or <u>greater than</u> the degree of the denominator.
E.g. $\dfrac{x^2 + 4 \leftarrow \text{degree 2}}{(x + 3)(x + 2) \leftarrow \text{degree 2}}$ $\dfrac{x^4 + 2x \leftarrow \text{degree 4}}{(x - 1)^2(x + 2) \leftarrow \text{degree 3}}$ The degree of a polynomial is the highest power of x.

There's an <u>extra step</u> involved in expressing an <u>improper fraction</u> as partial fractions:

1) <u>Divide</u> the numerator by the denominator to get the quotient ($q(x)$) + a <u>proper fraction</u> ($r(x) / d(x)$)
2) Express the <u>proper fraction</u> as partial fractions.   See pages 49-50 for algebraic division methods.

EXAMPLE   Express $\dfrac{x^4 - 3x^3 - 3x^2 + 10x + 5}{(x - 3)(x - 2)}$ as partial fractions.

This is $(x - 3)(x - 2)$ multiplied out.

1) First work out $(x^4 - 3x^3 - 3x^2 + 10x + 5) \div (x^2 - 5x + 6)$:
   Exactly as on page 50 — $q(x)$ = quotient, $d(x)$ = divisor and $r(x)$ = remainder.
   • Write out the result in the form $f(x) \equiv q(x)d(x) + r(x)$:
   $x^4 - 3x^3 - 3x^2 + 10x + 5 \equiv (x^2 + 2x + 1)(x^2 - 5x + 6) + 3x - 1$.
   • Divide through by $d(x)$: $\dfrac{x^4 - 3x^3 - 3x^2 + 10x + 5}{(x - 3)(x - 2)} \equiv (x^2 + 2x + 1) + \dfrac{3x - 1}{(x - 3)(x - 2)}$ $q(x) + \dfrac{r(x)}{d(x)}$

2) Now just express the proper fraction as partial fractions: $\dfrac{x^4 - 3x^3 - 3x^2 + 10x + 5}{(x - 3)(x - 2)} \equiv (x^2 + 2x + 1) + \dfrac{A}{(x - 3)} + \dfrac{B}{(x - 2)}$

Rid the partial fraction world of improperness — it's only proper...
After you've found the partial fractions, don't forget to go back to the <u>original fraction</u> and write out the <u>full solution</u>...

Modelling Using Exponential Functions

This page is all about <u>models</u>. Except they're modelling <u>exponential growth</u> and <u>decay</u> in <u>real-world applications</u> rather than the Chanel Autumn/Winter collection. Sorry. Have a look back at p.8-9 for a reminder about exponentials.

Use *Exponential Functions* to *Model* real-life *Growth and Decay*

In the exam you'll usually be given a background story to an exponential equation.
They may then ask you to find some values, work out a missing part of the equation, or even sketch a graph.
There's nothing here you haven't seen before — you just need to know how to deal with all the wordy bits.

EXAMPLE The exponential growth of a colony of bacteria can be modelled by the equation $B = 60e^{0.03t}$, where B is the number of bacteria, and t is the time in hours from the point at which the colony is first monitored ($t \geq 0$). Use the model to predict:

a) the number of bacteria after 4 hours.

You need to find B when $t = 4$,
so put the numbers into the equation:

$B = 60 \times e^{(0.03 \times 4)}$
$\quad = 60 \times 1.1274...$
$\quad = 67.6498...$
So $B = \underline{67 \text{ bacteria}}$.

> You shouldn't round up here — there are only 67 whole bacteria, not 68.

b) the time taken for the colony to grow to 1000 bacteria.

1) You need to find t when $B = 1000$,
so put the numbers into the equation:
$1000 = 60e^{0.03t} \Rightarrow e^{0.03t} = 1000 \div 60 = 16.6666...$

2) Now take 'ln' of both sides as usual:
$\ln e^{0.03t} = \ln(16.6666...) \Rightarrow 0.03t = 2.8134...$
$\Rightarrow t = 2.8134... \div 0.03 = \underline{93.8 \text{ hours}}$ to 3 s.f.

EXAMPLE The concentration (C) of a drug in the bloodstream, t hours after taking an initial dose, decreases exponentially according to $C = Ae^{-kt}$, where A and k are constants. If the initial concentration is 0.72, and this halves after 5 hours, find the values of A and k and sketch a graph of C against t.

1) The 'initial concentration' is 0.72 when $t = 0$, so put this information in the equation to find the missing constant A: $0.72 = A \times e^0 \Rightarrow 0.72 = A \times 1 \Rightarrow \underline{A = 0.72}$.

2) The question also says that when $t = 5$ hours, C is half of 0.72.
So using the value for A found above: $C = 0.72e^{-kt}$
$0.72 \div 2 = 0.72 \times e^{(-k \times 5)}$
$\Rightarrow 0.36 = 0.72 \times e^{-5k} \Rightarrow 0.36 = \dfrac{0.72}{e^{5k}} \Rightarrow e^{5k} = \dfrac{0.72}{0.36} = 2$.

3) Now take 'ln' of both sides to solve:
$\ln e^{5k} = \ln 2 \Rightarrow 5k = \ln 2 \Rightarrow k = \ln 2 \div 5 = \underline{0.139}$ to 3 s.f.

4) So the equation is $C = 0.72e^{-0.139t}$.
You still need to do a <u>sketch</u> though, so find the intercepts and asymptotes as you did on page 9:
When $t = 0$, $C = 0.72$. As $t \to \infty$, $e^{-0.139t} \to 0$, so $C \to 0$.

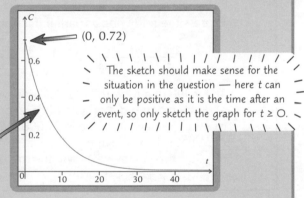

(0, 0.72)

> The sketch should make sense for the situation in the question — here t can only be positive as it is the time after an event, so only sketch the graph for $t \geq 0$.

It might not always be *e*

Sometimes the examiners will try to confuse you by giving you a model that <u>doesn't use e</u> (e.g. $Z = Ak^t$).
These are pretty much the same as the ones above, but they might ask you to <u>find k</u> as well.

EXAMPLE The value of a painting, V, is increasing according to the model $V = Ak^t$, where t is the time in years and A and k are constants. Its initial value is £300, and after 3 years it is worth £500. Find the values of A and k, and work out how long it will take for the value of the painting to triple (to the nearest year).

1) To find A, just put the values you're given into the equation (remembering that $t = 0$ at the initial value). So $300 = Ak^0 \Rightarrow \underline{A = 300}$ (as $k^0 = 1$).

2) Use your value of A to find k:
$500 = 300k^3 \Rightarrow \dfrac{5}{3} = k^3 \Rightarrow k = \sqrt[3]{\dfrac{5}{3}}$ or 1.185...

3) When the value has tripled, $V = 900$. Using this value and your values of A and k, find t:
$900 = 300(1.185...)^t \Rightarrow 3 = (1.185...)^t$.

Take ln of both sides:
$\ln 3 = \ln(1.185...)^t = t\ln(1.185...) \Rightarrow t = 6.45$ (3 s.f.).
So it will take 6 years for the value to triple.

Learn this and watch your knowledge grow exponentially...

For these wordy problems the key is just to extract the relevant information and solve them like you did in C3 (see p.8-9).
The more you practise, the more familiar they'll become — fortunately there's a fair bit of practice on the next two pages.

C4 Section 1 — Practice Questions

To successfully <u>infiltrate</u> the seedy world of algebraic division, partial fractions and exponentials, you need to be able to answer these <u>questions</u>.

Warm-up Questions

1) Simplify the following:

   a) $\dfrac{4x^2 - 25}{6x - 15}$ b) $\dfrac{2x + 3}{x - 2} \times \dfrac{4x - 8}{2x^2 - 3x - 9}$ c) $\dfrac{x^2 - 3x}{x + 1} \div \dfrac{x}{2}$

2) Write the following as a single fraction:

   a) $\dfrac{x}{2x + 1} + \dfrac{3}{x^2} + \dfrac{1}{x}$ b) $\dfrac{2}{x^2 - 1} - \dfrac{3x}{x - 1} + \dfrac{x}{x + 1}$

3) Use algebraic long division to divide $x^3 + 2x^2 - x + 19$ by $x + 4$.

4) Write $2x^3 + 8x^2 + 7x + 8$ in the form $(Ax^2 + Bx + C)(x + 3) + D$.
   Using your answer, state the result when $2x^3 + 8x^2 + 7x + 8$ is divided by $(x + 3)$.

You have to factorise the denominator in Q5 parts d, e and g, and in Q6, part d.

5) Express the following as <u>partial fractions</u>.

   a) $\dfrac{4x + 5}{(x + 4)(2x - 3)}$ b) $\dfrac{-7x - 7}{(3x + 1)(x - 2)}$ c) $\dfrac{x - 18}{(x + 4)(3x - 4)}$ d) $\dfrac{5x}{x^2 + x - 6}$

   e) $\dfrac{6 + 4y}{9 - y^2}$ f) $\dfrac{10x^2 + 32x + 16}{(x + 3)(2x + 4)(x - 2)}$ g) $\dfrac{4x^2 + 12x + 6}{x^3 + 3x^2 + 2x}$ h) $\dfrac{-11x^2 + 6x + 11}{(2x + 1)(3 - x)(x + 2)}$

6) Express the following as partial fractions — watch out for the <u>repeated factors</u>.

   a) $\dfrac{2x + 2}{(x + 3)^2}$ b) $\dfrac{6x^2 + 17x + 5}{x(x + 2)^2}$ c) $\dfrac{-18x + 14}{(2x - 1)^2(x + 2)}$ d) $\dfrac{8x^2 - x - 5}{x^3 - x}$

7) Express the following as partial fractions — they're all <u>improper</u>, so divide them first.

   a) $\dfrac{2x^2 + 18x + 26}{(x + 2)(x + 4)}$ b) $\dfrac{3x^2 + 9x + 2}{x(x + 1)}$ c) $\dfrac{24x^2 - 70x + 53}{(2x - 3)^2}$ d) $\dfrac{3x^3 - 2x^2 - 2x - 3}{(x + 1)(x - 2)}$

8) The value of a motorbike ($£V$) varies with age (in t years from new) according to $V = 7500k^{-0.2t}$.
   a) How much did it originally cost?
   b) After 5 years, its value is £3,000. What is the value of k?
   c) What is its value after 10 years?
   d) After how many years will the motorbike's value have fallen below £500?

That should have got the neurones nicely <u>warmed up</u>. Unless it made you very <u>sleepy</u> instead. Try these exam questions and make sure you can handle them.

Exam Questions

1   $f(x) = \dfrac{5x^2 + 3x + 6}{(3 - x)(2x - 1)^2}$

   Given that $f(x)$ can be expressed in the form $f(x) = \dfrac{A}{(3 - x)} + \dfrac{B}{(2x - 1)^2} + \dfrac{C}{(2x - 1)}$,
   find the values of A and B and C.

   (4 marks)

2   Write $x^3 + 15x^2 + 43x - 30$ in the form $(Ax^2 + Bx + C)(x + 6) + D$,
   where A, B, C and D are constants to be found.

   (3 marks)

3   Write $\dfrac{2x^2 - 9x - 35}{x^2 - 49}$ as a fraction in its simplest form.

   (3 marks)

C4 Section 1 — Practice Questions

All in all, I think this was a reasonably gentle start to C4. There was only a little bit of <u>algebra</u>, and everybody knows that its bark is worse than its bite. But I wouldn't recommend sticking your hand in the <u>jaws</u> of a <u>partial fraction</u> anytime soon.

4   Given that, for $x \neq -\dfrac{1}{3}$, $\dfrac{5 + 9x}{(1 + 3x)^2} \equiv \dfrac{A}{(1 + 3x)^2} + \dfrac{B}{(1 + 3x)}$, where A and B are integers, find the values of A and B.

(3 marks)

5   $\dfrac{18x^2 - 15x - 62}{(3x + 4)(x - 2)} \equiv A + \dfrac{B}{(3x + 4)} + \dfrac{C}{(x - 2)}$

Find the values of the integers A, B and C.

(4 marks)

6   A breed of mink is introduced to a new habitat.
The number of mink, M, after t years in the habitat, is modelled by:

$$M = 74e^{0.6t} \quad (t \geq 0)$$

a)   State the number of mink that were introduced to the new habitat originally.

(1 mark)

b)   Predict the number of mink after 3 years in the habitat.

(2 marks)

c)   Predict the number of complete years it would take for the population of mink to exceed 10 000.

(2 marks)

d)   Sketch a graph to show how the mink population varies with time in the new habitat.

(2 marks)

7   The algebraic fraction $\dfrac{-80x^2 + 49x - 9}{(5x - 1)(2 - 4x)}$ can be written in the form $4 + \dfrac{A}{(5x - 1)} + \dfrac{B}{(2 - 4x)}$,

where A and B are constants. Find the values of A and B.

(4 marks)

8   a)   Express the algebraic fraction $\dfrac{3x^2 + 12x - 11}{(x + 3)(x - 1)}$ in the form $A + \dfrac{B + Cx}{(x + 3)(x - 1)}$,

where A, B and C are constants.

(4 marks)

b)   Express $\dfrac{3x^2 + 12x - 11}{(x + 3)(x - 1)}$ as partial fractions.

(3 marks)

9   A radioactive substance decays exponentially so that its activity, A, can be modelled by

$$A = Be^{-kt}$$

where t is the time in days, and $t \geq 0$. Some experimental data is shown below.

t	0	5	10
A	50	42	

a)   State the value of B.

(1 mark)

b)   Find the value of k, to 3 significant figures.

(2 marks)

c)   Find the missing value from the table, to the nearest whole number.

(2 marks)

d)   The half-life of a substance is the time it takes for the activity to halve. Find the half-life of this substance, in days. Give your answer to the nearest day.

(3 marks)

The Addition Formulas

Like a persistent puppy, trigonometry just won't give up and leave you alone. It's back again in C4, and there are more identities to learn. The ones on this page are all about adding and subtracting angles...

You can use the Addition Formulas to find Sums of Angles

You can use the addition formulas to find the sin, cos or tan of the sum or difference of two angles.
When you have an expression like $\sin(x + 60°)$ or $\cos(n - \frac{\pi}{2})$, you can use these formulas to expand the brackets.

$$\sin(A \pm B) \equiv \sin A \cos B \pm \cos A \sin B$$

$$\cos(A \pm B) \equiv \cos A \cos B \mp \sin A \sin B$$

$$\tan(A \pm B) \equiv \frac{\tan A \pm \tan B}{1 \mp \tan A \tan B}$$

These formulas are given to you on the formula sheet.

Watch out for the $\pm$ and $\mp$ signs in the formulas — especially for cos and tan. If you use the sign on the top on the RHS, you have to use the sign on the top on the left-hand side too — so $\cos(A + B) = \cos A \cos B - \sin A \sin B$.

Use the Formulas to find the Exact Value of trig expressions

1) You should know the value of sin, cos and tan for common angles (in degrees and radians). These values come from using Pythagoras on right-angled triangles — you did it in C2.

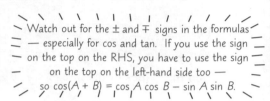

	0°	30°	45°	60°	90°
	0	$\frac{\pi}{6}$	$\frac{\pi}{4}$	$\frac{\pi}{3}$	$\frac{\pi}{2}$
sin	0	$\frac{1}{2}$	$\frac{1}{\sqrt{2}}$	$\frac{\sqrt{3}}{2}$	1
cos	1	$\frac{\sqrt{3}}{2}$	$\frac{1}{\sqrt{2}}$	$\frac{1}{2}$	0
tan	0	$\frac{1}{\sqrt{3}}$	1	$\sqrt{3}$	n/a

2) In the exam you might be asked to calculate the exact value of sin, cos or tan for another angle using your knowledge of those angles and the addition formulas.

3) Find a pair of angles from the table which add or subtract to give the angle you're after. Then plug them into the addition formula, and work it through.

EXAMPLE Using the addition formula for tangent, show that $\tan 15° = 2 - \sqrt{3}$.

Pick two angles that add or subtract to give 15°, and put them into the tan addition formula.
It's easiest to use $\tan 60°$ and $\tan 45°$ here, since neither of them are fractions.

$$\tan 15° = \tan(60° - 45°) = \frac{\tan 60° - \tan 45°}{1 + \tan 60° \tan 45°}$$

Using $\tan(A - B) \equiv \frac{\tan A - \tan B}{1 + \tan A \tan B}$

Substitute the values for tan 60° and tan 45° into the equation:

$$= \frac{\sqrt{3} - 1}{1 + (\sqrt{3} \times 1)} = \frac{\sqrt{3} - 1}{\sqrt{3} + 1}$$

Now rationalise the denominator of the fraction to get rid of the $\sqrt{3}$.

$$\frac{\sqrt{3} - 1}{\sqrt{3} + 1} \times \frac{\sqrt{3} - 1}{\sqrt{3} - 1} = \frac{3 - 2\sqrt{3} + 1}{3 - \sqrt{3} + \sqrt{3} - 1}$$

If you can't remember how to rationalise the denominator have a peek at your C1 notes.

Simplify the expression...

$$= \frac{4 - 2\sqrt{3}}{2} = 2 - \sqrt{3}$$

...and there's the right-hand side.

You can use these formulas to Prove Identities too

You might be asked to use the addition formulas to prove an identity. All you need to do is put the numbers and variables from the left-hand side into the addition formulas and simplify until you get the expression you're after.

EXAMPLE Prove that $\cos(a + 60°) + \sin(a + 30°) \equiv \cos a$

Be careful with the + and − signs here.

Put the numbers from the question into the addition formulas:

$$\cos(a + 60°) + \sin(a + 30°) \equiv (\cos a \cos 60° - \sin a \sin 60°) + (\sin a \cos 30° + \cos a \sin 30°)$$

Now substitute in any sin and cos values that you know...

$$= \frac{1}{2}\cos a - \frac{\sqrt{3}}{2}\sin a + \frac{\sqrt{3}}{2}\sin a + \frac{1}{2}\cos a$$

..and simplify:

$$= \frac{1}{2}\cos a + \frac{1}{2}\cos a = \cos a$$

This page has got more identities than Clark Kent...

I was devastated when my secret identity was revealed — I'd been masquerading as a mysterious caped criminal mastermind with an army of minions and a hidden underground lair. It was great fun, but I had to give it all up and write about trig.

The Double Angle Formulas

Whenever you see a trig expression with an <u>even</u> multiple of x in it, like sin $2x$, you can use one of the <u>double angle formulas</u> to prune it back to an expression just in terms of a single x.

There's a **Double Angle Formula** for **Each Trig Function**

<u>Double angle formulas</u> are just a slightly different kind of <u>identity</u>. They're called "double angle" formulas because they turn any <u>tricky 2x</u> type terms in trig equations back into <u>plain x terms</u>.

You need to know the double angle formulas for <u>sin</u>, <u>cos</u> and <u>tan</u>:

$$\sin 2A \equiv 2 \sin A \cos A$$

You can use the identity $\cos^2 A + \sin^2 A \equiv 1$ to get the other versions of the cos 2A formula.

$$\cos 2A \equiv \cos^2 A - \sin^2 A$$
$$\text{or} \qquad \equiv 2\cos^2 A - 1$$
$$\text{or} \qquad \equiv 1 - 2\sin^2 A$$

$$\tan 2A \equiv \frac{2 \tan A}{1 - \tan^2 A}$$

You get these formulas by writing $2A$ as $A + A$ and using the addition formulas from the previous page.

Use the **Double Angle Formulas** to **Simplify** and **Solve Equations**

If an equation has a <u>mixture</u> of <u>sin x</u> and <u>sin 2x</u> terms in it, there's not much that you can do with it. So that you can <u>simplify</u> it, and then <u>solve</u> it, you have to use one of the <u>double angle formulas</u>.

EXAMPLE Solve the equation $\cos 2x - 5 \cos x = 2$ in the interval $0 \le x \le 2\pi$.

First use the double angle formula $\cos 2A \equiv 2 \cos^2 A - 1$ to get rid of cos $2x$ (use this version so that you don't end up with a mix of sin and cos terms).

$$2\cos^2 x - 1 - 5 \cos x = 2$$

Simplify so you have zero on one side...
...then factorise and solve the quadratic that you've made:

$$2\cos^2 x - 5 \cos x - 3 = 0$$
$$(2 \cos x + 1)(\cos x - 3) = 0$$
$$\text{So } (2 \cos x + 1) = 0 \text{ or } (\cos x - 3) = 0$$

The second bracket gives you $\cos x = 3$, which has no solutions since $-1 \le \cos x \le 1$.

So all that's left is to solve the first bracket to find x:

$$2 \cos x + 1 = 0$$
$$\cos x = -\frac{1}{2} \Rightarrow x = \frac{2}{3}\pi \text{ or } x = \frac{4}{3}\pi.$$

Sketch the graph of cos x to find all values of x in the given interval:
$\cos x = -\frac{1}{2}$ twice, once at $\frac{2}{3}\pi$ and once at $2\pi - \frac{2}{3}\pi = \frac{4}{3}\pi$.

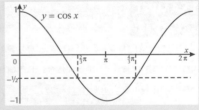

You can use a **Double Angle Formula** even when the x term **Isn't 2x**

Whenever you have an expression that contains any angle that's <u>twice the size</u> of another, you can use the double angle formulas — whether it's sin x and sin $2x$, cos $2x$ and cos $4x$ or tan x and tan $\frac{x}{2}$.

EXAMPLE Prove that $2 \cot \frac{x}{2}(1 - \cos^2 \frac{x}{2}) \equiv \sin x$

Use the identity $\sin^2 \theta + \cos^2 \theta \equiv 1$ to replace $1 - \cos^2 \frac{x}{2}$ on the left-hand side:

Left-hand side: $2 \cot \frac{x}{2} \sin^2 \frac{x}{2}$

Now write cot θ as $\frac{\cos \theta}{\sin \theta}$:

$$2 \frac{\cos \frac{x}{2}}{\sin \frac{x}{2}} \sin^2 \frac{x}{2} \equiv 2 \cos \frac{x}{2} \sin \frac{x}{2}$$

Now you can use the sin $2A$ double angle formula to write $\sin x \equiv 2 \sin \frac{x}{2} \cos \frac{x}{2}$ (using $A = \frac{x}{2}$).

So using the sin double angle formula... $\equiv \sin x$ ...you get the <u>right-hand side</u>.

You can work out <u>half-angle formulas</u> for <u>cos</u> and <u>tan</u> from the double angle formulas. This example uses the one for <u>sin</u>.

Double the angles, double the fun...

You definitely need to know the double angle formulas off by heart, because they won't be on the exam formula sheet. So it's a case of the old "learn 'em, write 'em out, and keep going until you can do all three perfectly" strategy. And don't forget to be on the lookout for sneaky questions that want you to use a double angle formula but don't contain a "2x" bit.

The R Addition Formulas

A different kind of addition formula this time — one that lets you go from an <u>expanded expression</u> to one with <u>brackets</u>...

Use the **R Formulas** when you've got a **Mix** of **Sin** and **Cos**

If you're solving an equation that contains <u>both</u> $\sin \theta$ and $\cos \theta$ terms, e.g. $3\sin \theta + 4\cos \theta = 1$, you need to <u>rewrite</u> it so that it only contains <u>one</u> trig function. The formulas that you use to do that are known as the <u>R formulas</u>:

One set for sine:
$$a\sin \theta \pm b\cos \theta \equiv R\sin (\theta \pm \alpha)$$

And one set for cosine:
$$a\cos \theta \pm b\sin \theta \equiv R\cos (\theta \mp \alpha)$$

where a and b are <u>positive</u>. Again, you need to be careful with the $+$ and $-$ signs here — see page 56.

Using the R Formulas

1) You'll start with an identity like $2\sin x + 5\cos x \equiv R\sin (x + \alpha)$, where <u>$R$ and α need to be found</u>.

2) First, <u>expand the RHS</u> using the <u>addition formulas</u> (see p.56):
$2\sin x + 5\cos x \equiv R\sin x \cos \alpha + R\cos x \sin \alpha$.

3) <u>Equate the coefficients</u> of $\sin x$ and $\cos x$. You'll get <u>two equations</u>:
① $R\cos \alpha = 2$ and ② $R\sin \alpha = 5$.

4) To find α, <u>divide</u> equation ② by equation ①, then take <u>$\tan^{-1}$</u> of the result.

5) To find R, <u>square</u> equations ① and ② and <u>add</u> them together, then take the <u>square root</u> of the answer.

$(R\sin\alpha)^2 + (R\cos\alpha)^2$
$\equiv R^2(\sin^2\alpha + \cos^2\alpha)$
$\equiv R^2$ (using the identity
$\sin^2\alpha + \cos^2\alpha \equiv 1$).

This is because $\dfrac{R\sin\alpha}{R\cos\alpha} = \tan\alpha$.

This method looks a bit scary, but follow the example below through and it should make more sense.

Solve the equation in Stages

You'll almost always be asked to solve equations like this in <u>different stages</u> — first <u>writing out</u> the equation in the form of one of the R formulas, then <u>solving</u> it. You might also have to find the <u>maximum</u> or <u>minimum</u> value.

EXAMPLE (Part 1): Express $2\sin x - 3\cos x$ in the form $R\sin (x - \alpha)$, given that $R > 0$ and $0 \leq \alpha \leq 90°$.

$2\sin x - 3\cos x \equiv R\sin (x - \alpha)$, so expand the RHS to get $2\sin x - 3\cos x \equiv R(\sin x \cos \alpha - \cos x \sin \alpha)$.

Equating coefficients gives the equations $R\cos \alpha = 2$ and $R\sin \alpha = 3$.

Solving for α: $\dfrac{R\sin\alpha}{R\cos\alpha} = \dfrac{3}{2} = \tan \alpha$

$\alpha = \tan^{-1} 1.5 = 56.31°$

This value fits into the correct range so you can leave it as it is.

Look at the coefficients of $\sin x$ on each side of the equation — on the LHS it's 2 and on the RHS it's $R\cos\alpha$, so $2 = R\cos\alpha$. You find the coefficient of $\cos x$ in the same way.

Solving for R: $(R\cos \alpha)^2 + (R\sin \alpha)^2 = 2^2 + 3^2 = R^2$

$R = \sqrt{2^2 + 3^2} = \sqrt{13}$

So $2\sin x - 3\cos x \equiv \sqrt{13} \sin (x - 56.31°)$

EXAMPLE (Part 2): Hence solve $2\sin x - 3\cos x = 1$ in the interval $0 \leq x \leq 360°$.

If $2\sin x - 3\cos x = 1$, that means $\sqrt{13} \sin (x - 56.31°) = 1$, so $\sin (x - 56.31°) = \dfrac{1}{\sqrt{13}}$.

$0 \leq x \leq 360°$, so $-56.31° \leq x - 56.31° \leq 303.69°$.

Solve the equation using $\sin^{-1}$:

$x - 56.31° = \sin^{-1}\left(\dfrac{1}{\sqrt{13}}\right) = 16.10°$ <u>or</u> $180 - 16.10 = 163.90°$.

So $x = 16.10 + 56.31 = \boxed{72.4°}$ <u>or</u> $x = 163.90 + 56.31 = \boxed{220.2°}$

Careful — you're looking for solutions between $-56.31°$ and $303.69°$ here.

EXAMPLE (Part 3): What are the max and min values of $2\sin x - 3\cos x$?

The maximum and minimum values of sin (and cos) are ± 1, so the maximum and minimum values of $R\sin (x - \alpha)$ are $\pm R$.

As $2\sin x - 3\cos x = \sqrt{13} \sin (x - 56.31°)$, $R = \sqrt{13}$, so the maximum and minimum values are $\pm\sqrt{13}$.

A pirate's favourite trigonometry formula...

The R formulas might look a bit scary, but they're OK really — just do lots of examples until you're happy with the method. Careful with the <u>adjusting the interval</u> bit that came up in part 2 above — it's pretty fiddly and easy to get muddled over.

More Trigonometry Stuff

And here we have the final trig page... a collection of random bits that didn't really fit on the other pages. That's one of the scary things about trig questions — you never know what you're going to get.

The **Factor Formulas** come from the **Addition Formulas**

As if there weren't enough <u>trig formulas</u> already, here come a few more. Don't worry though — these ones are given to you on the <u>exam formula sheet</u> so you don't need to learn them off by heart.

$$\sin A + \sin B \equiv 2\sin\left(\frac{A+B}{2}\right)\cos\left(\frac{A-B}{2}\right)$$

$$\sin A - \sin B \equiv 2\cos\left(\frac{A+B}{2}\right)\sin\left(\frac{A-B}{2}\right)$$

$$\cos A + \cos B \equiv 2\cos\left(\frac{A+B}{2}\right)\cos\left(\frac{A-B}{2}\right)$$

$$\cos A - \cos B \equiv -2\sin\left(\frac{A+B}{2}\right)\sin\left(\frac{A-B}{2}\right)$$

These are the <u>factor formulas</u>, and they come from the <u>addition formulas</u> (see below). They come in handy for some <u>integrations</u> — it's a bit tricky to integrate $2\cos 3\theta \cos \theta$, but integrating $\cos 4\theta + \cos 2\theta$ is much easier.

EXAMPLE Use the addition formulas to show that $\cos A + \cos B \equiv 2\cos\left(\frac{A+B}{2}\right)\cos\left(\frac{A-B}{2}\right)$

You can derive the other formulas using the same method.

Use the cos addition formulas: $\cos (x + y) \equiv \cos x \cos y - \sin x \sin y$
and $\cos (x - y) \equiv \cos x \cos y + \sin x \sin y$.
Add them together to get: $\cos (x + y) + \cos (x - y) \equiv \cos x \cos y - \sin x \sin y + \cos x \cos y + \sin x \sin y$
$$\equiv 2\cos x \cos y.$$
Now substitute in $A = x + y$ and $B = x - y$.
Subtracting these gives $A - B = x + y - (x - y) = 2y$, so $y = \frac{A-B}{2}$.
Adding gives $A + B = x + y + (x - y) = 2x$, so $x = \frac{A+B}{2}$.

So $\cos A + \cos B \equiv 2\cos\left(\frac{A+B}{2}\right)\cos\left(\frac{A-B}{2}\right)$.

You might have to use **Different Bits** of **Trig** in the **Same Question**

Some exam questions might try and catch you out by making you use <u>more than one</u> identity to show that two things are equal...

EXAMPLE Show that $\cos 3\theta \equiv 4\cos^3\theta - 3\cos \theta$.

You have to use both the addition formula and the double angle formulas in this question.

First, write $\cos 3\theta$ as $\cos(2\theta + \theta)$, then you can use the cos <u>addition formula</u>:
$\cos (3\theta) \equiv \cos (2\theta + \theta) \equiv \cos 2\theta \cos \theta - \sin 2\theta \sin \theta$.

Now you can use the cos and sin <u>double angle formulas</u> to get rid of the 2θ:
$\cos 2\theta \cos \theta - \sin 2\theta \sin \theta \equiv (2\cos^2\theta - 1)\cos \theta - (2\sin \theta \cos \theta)\sin \theta$

This uses the identity $\sin^2\theta + \cos^2\theta \equiv 1$ in the form $\sin^2\theta \equiv 1 - \cos^2\theta$.

$\equiv 2\cos^3\theta - \cos \theta - 2\sin^2\theta \cos \theta \equiv 2\cos^3\theta - \cos \theta - 2(1 - \cos^2\theta)\cos \theta$

$\equiv 2\cos^3\theta - \cos \theta - 2\cos \theta + 2\cos^3\theta \equiv \boxed{4\cos^3\theta - 3\cos \theta}$.

...or even drag up trig knowledge from <u>C2</u>, <u>C3</u> or even <u>GCSE</u>. This question looks short and sweet, but it's actually pretty nasty — you need to know a sneaky <u>conversion</u> between <u>sin</u> and <u>cos</u>.

EXAMPLE If $y = \sin^{-1}x$ for $-1 \leq x \leq 1$ and $-\frac{\pi}{2} \leq y \leq \frac{\pi}{2}$, show that $\cos^{-1}x = \frac{\pi}{2} - y$.

$y = \sin^{-1}x$, so $x = \sin y$.
Now the next bit isn't obvious — you need to use an identity
to switch from sin to cos. This gives... $x = \cos(\frac{\pi}{2} - y)$.
Now, taking inverses gives $\cos^{-1}x = \cos^{-1}(\cos(\frac{\pi}{2} - y))$, so $\boxed{\cos^{-1}x = \frac{\pi}{2} - y}$.

<u>Converting Sin to Cos (and back):</u>
$\sin t \equiv \cos(\frac{\pi}{2} - t)$
and $\cos t \equiv \sin(\frac{\pi}{2} - t)$.
Remember sin is just cos translated by $\frac{\pi}{2}$ and vice versa.

Trig is like a box of chocolates...

You'll be pleased to know that you've seen all the trig formulas you need for C4. I know there are about 1000 of them (N.B. exaggerations like this may lose you marks in the exam), but any of them could pop up. Examiners particularly like it when you have to use one identity or formula to prove or derive another, so get practising. Then go off and have a nice cup of tea.

C4 Section 2 — Practice Questions

There are a <u>lot of formulas</u> in this section — try writing them all out and <u>sticking them somewhere</u> so you can learn them. The best way to get to grips with them is to <u>practise using them</u> — so here are some questions for you to have a go at.

Warm-up Questions

1) State the three different versions of the double angle formula for cos.

2) Use the double angle formula to solve the equation: $\sin 2\theta = -\sqrt{3}\sin\theta$, $0 \le \theta \le 360°$.

3) Using the addition formula for cos, find the exact value of $\cos\frac{\pi}{12}$.

4) Find the exact value of $\sin(A + B)$, given that $\sin A = \frac{4}{5}$ and $\sin B = \frac{7}{25}$. You might find these triangles useful: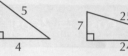

5) Which two R formulas could you use to write $a\cos\theta + b\sin\theta$ $(a, b > 0)$ in terms of just sin or just cos?

6) Write $5\sin\theta - 6\cos\theta$ in the form $R\sin(\theta - \alpha)$, where $R > 0$ and $0 \le \alpha \le 90°$.

7) Use the addition formulas to show that $\sin A - \sin B \equiv 2\cos\left(\frac{A + B}{2}\right)\sin\left(\frac{A - B}{2}\right)$.

8) Show that $\frac{\cos\theta}{\sin\theta} + \frac{\sin\theta}{\cos\theta} \equiv 2\operatorname{cosec} 2\theta$.

Have you got your breath back? Good. Here are some exam questions, so take a <u>deep breath</u> and get ready to <u>dive in</u> again.

Exam Questions

1   a)   Write $9\sin\theta + 12\cos\theta$ in the form $R\sin(\theta + \alpha)$, where $R > 0$ and $0 \le \alpha \le \frac{\pi}{2}$.

(3 marks)

   b)   Using the result from part (a) solve $9\sin\theta + 12\cos\theta = 3$, giving all solutions for θ in the range $0 \le \theta \le 2\pi$.

(5 marks)

2   Using the double angle and addition identities for sin and cos, find an expression for $\sin 3x$ in terms of $\sin x$ only.

(4 marks)

3   a)   Write $5\cos\theta + 12\sin\theta$ in the form $R\cos(\theta - \alpha)$, where $R > 0$ and $0 \le \alpha \le 90°$.

(4 marks)

   b)   Hence solve $5\cos\theta + 12\sin\theta = 2$ for $0 \le \theta \le 360°$, giving your answers to 2 decimal places.

(5 marks)

   c)   Use your results from part a) above to find the minimum value of $(5\cos\theta + 12\sin\theta)^3$.

(2 marks)

Parametric Equations of Curves

Parametric equations seem kinda weirdy to start with, but they're actually pretty clever.
You can use them to replace one horrifically complicated equation with two relatively normal-looking ones.
I bet that's just what you always wanted...

Parametric Equations split up x and y into Separate Equations

1) Normally, graphs in the (x, y) plane are described using a Cartesian equation — a single equation linking x and y.

2) Sometimes, particularly for more complicated graphs, it's easier to have
   two linked equations, called parametric equations.

3) In parametric equations x and y are each defined separately in terms of a third variable,
   called a parameter. The parameter is usually either t or θ.

 EXAMPLE

This graph is given by the parametric equations $y = t^2 - 1$ and $x = t + 1$:

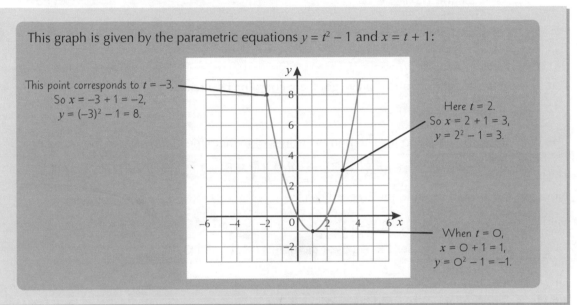

This point corresponds to $t = -3$.
So $x = -3 + 1 = -2$,
$y = (-3)^2 - 1 = 8$.

Here $t = 2$.
So $x = 2 + 1 = 3$,
$y = 2^2 - 1 = 3$.

When $t = 0$,
$x = 0 + 1 = 1$,
$y = 0^2 - 1 = -1$.

You can use the parametric equations of a graph to find coordinates of points on the
graph, and to find the value of the parameter for given x- or y-coordinates.

EXAMPLE

A curve is defined by the parametric equations $y = \dfrac{1}{3t}$ and $x = 2t - 3$, $t \neq 0$.

a) Find the x- and y- values of the point the curve passes through when $t = 4$.

b) What value of t corresponds to the point where $y = 9$?

c) What is the value of y when $x = -15$?

Nothing to this question — just sub the right values into the right equations and you're away:

a) When $t = 4$, $x = 8 - 3 = 5$, and $y = \dfrac{1}{12}$

Use the equation for x to find t first, then use that value of t in the other equation to find y.

b) $9 = \dfrac{1}{3t} \Rightarrow t = \dfrac{1}{27}$

c) $-15 = 2t - 3 \Rightarrow t = -6 \Rightarrow y = -\dfrac{1}{18}$

Time to make like x and y in a set of parametric equations, and split...

Well that was a painless introduction to a topic if ever there was one. Yes, I can tell this section's going to be plain sailing...
wait a minute... holy flip, would you look at the size of the example on the next page. And I think I see some trig functions
looming in the distance. And that's either Godzilla or a double angle formula on the horizon. Batten down the hatches...

Using Parametric Equations

There's plenty of <u>tinkering around</u> with equations to be done in this topic, so get your <u>rearranging</u> hat on. My rearranging hat is a jaunty straw boater.

Use **Parametric Equations** to find where graphs **Intersect**

A lot of parametric equations questions involve identifying points on the curve defined by the equations.

EXAMPLE

The curve shown in this sketch has the parametric equations $y = t^3 - t$ and $x = 4t^2 - 1$.

Find the coordinates of the points where the graph crosses:
a) the x-axis,
b) the y-axis,
c) the line $8y = 3x + 3$.

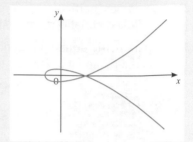

Part a) is pretty straightforward. You've got the <u>y-coordinates</u> already:

a) On the x-axis, $y = 0$.

Use the <u>parametric equation for y</u> to find the <u>values of t</u> where the graph crosses the x-axis:

So $0 = t^3 - t \implies t(t^2 - 1) = 0 \implies t(t + 1)(t - 1) = 0 \implies t = 0, t = -1, t = 1$

> $t = -1$ and $t = 1$ give the same coordinates — that's where the curve crosses over itself.

Now use those values to find the <u>x-coordinates</u>:

$t = 0 \implies x = 4(0)^2 - 1 = -1 \qquad t = -1 \implies x = 4(-1)^2 - 1 = 3 \qquad t = 1 \implies x = 4(1)^2 - 1 = 3$

So the graph crosses the x-axis at the points $(-1, 0)$ and $(3, 0)$.

> The sketch shows there are two points where the graph crosses each axis.

And b) is <u>very similar</u>:

b) On the y-axis, $x = 0$.

So $0 = 4t^2 - 1 \implies t^2 = \frac{1}{4} \implies t = \pm\frac{1}{2}$

$t = \frac{1}{2} \implies y = \left(\frac{1}{2}\right)^3 - \frac{1}{2} = -\frac{3}{8} \qquad\qquad t = -\frac{1}{2} \implies y = \left(-\frac{1}{2}\right)^3 - \left(-\frac{1}{2}\right) = \frac{3}{8}$

So the graph crosses the y-axis at the points $(0, -\frac{3}{8})$ and $(0, \frac{3}{8})$.

Part c) is just a little trickier. First, <u>sub the parametric equations into $8y = 3x + 3$</u>:

c) $8y = 3x + 3 \implies 8(t^3 - t) = 3(4t^2 - 1) + 3$

<u>Rearrange</u> and <u>factorise</u> to find the values of t you need:

$\implies 8t^3 - 8t = 12t^2 \implies 8t^3 - 12t^2 - 8t = 0 \implies t(2t + 1)(t - 2) = 0 \implies t = 0, t = -\frac{1}{2}, t = 2$

Go back to the <u>parametric equations</u> to find the x- and y-coordinates:

> You can check the answers by sticking these values back into $8y = 3x + 3$.

$t = 0 \implies x = -1, y = 0$
$t = -\frac{1}{2} \implies x = 4(\frac{1}{4}) - 1 = 0, y = (-\frac{1}{2})^3 + \frac{1}{2} = \frac{3}{8}$
$t = 2 \implies x = 4(4) - 1 = 15, y = 2^3 - 2 = 6$

So the graph crosses the line $4y = 3x + 3$ at the points $(-1, 0)$, $(0, \frac{3}{8})$, $(15, 6)$.

y-coordinates? y not...

You quite often get given a sketch of the curve that the parametric equations define. Don't forget that the sketch can be useful for checking your answers — if the curve crosses the x-axis twice, and you've only found one x-coordinate for when $y = 0$, you know something's gone a bit pear-shaped and you should go back and sort it out, sunshine.

Parametric and Cartesian Equations

If you've been dying for θ to put in an appearance since I mentioned it on page 61, then I've got good news. If, on the other hand, you're bored of parametric equations already... I'm sorry.

Rearrange Parametric Equations to get the Cartesian Equation

Some parametric equations can be converted into Cartesian equations. There are two main ways to do this:

To convert Parametric Equations to a Cartesian Equation:

① **Rearrange** one of the equations to make the parameter the subject, then substitute the result into the other equation.

or

② **If your equations involve trig functions, use trig identities (see C3 Section 2 and C4 Section 2) to eliminate the parameter.**

You can use the first method to combine the parametrics used in the examples on p.61:

EXAMPLE Give the Cartesian equations, in the form $y = f(x)$, of the curves represented by the following pairs of parametric equations:

a) $y = t^2 - 1$ and $x = t + 1$,

b) $y = \dfrac{1}{3t}$ and $x = 2t - 3$, $t \neq 0$.

You want the answer in the form $y = f(x)$, so leave y alone for now, and rearrange the equation for x to make t the subject:

a) $x = t + 1 \implies t = x - 1$

Now you can eliminate t from the equation for y:

$y = t^2 - 1 \implies y = (x-1)^2 - 1 = x^2 - 2x + 1 - 1$
$\implies y = x^2 - 2x$

b) $x = 2t - 3 \implies t = \dfrac{x+3}{2}$

So $y = \dfrac{1}{3t} \implies y = \dfrac{1}{3\left(\frac{x+3}{2}\right)} \implies y = \dfrac{1}{\frac{3(x+3)}{2}} \implies y = \dfrac{2}{3x+9}$

If there are Trig Functions... use Trig Identities

Things get a little trickier when the likes of sin and cos decide to put in an appearance:

EXAMPLE A curve has parametric equations

$x = 1 + \sin\theta, \quad y = 1 - \cos2\theta$

Give the Cartesian equation of the curve in the form $y = f(x)$.

If you try to make θ the subject of these equations, things will just get messy. The trick is to find a way to get both x and y in terms of the same trig function.

You can get $\sin\theta$ into the equation for y using the identity $\cos2\theta = 1 - 2\sin^2\theta$ (see p.57):

$y = 1 - \cos2\theta = 1 - (1 - 2\sin^2\theta) = 2\sin^2\theta$

Rearranging the equation for x gives:

$\sin\theta = x - 1, \quad \text{so} \quad y = 2\sin^2\theta$
$\implies y = 2(x-1)^2 = 2x^2 - 4x + 2$

> If one of the parametric equations includes $\cos2\theta$ or $\sin2\theta$, that's probably the one you need to substitute — so make sure you know the double angle formulas.

Cartesy peasy, lemon squeezy...

Sometimes you'll get a nasty question where it's really difficult to get the parameter on its own — in that case you might have to do something clever like think about multiplying x and y or dividing y by x. If something like that comes up in an exam, they'll usually give you a hint — but be aware that you might need to think outside the box.

C4 Section 3 — Practice Questions

Before it became famous in the world of maths, the word 'parametric' had several other jobs. For example, it once starred as the last name of a <u>Bond villain</u> from the <u>former Yugoslavia</u>. Here are some <u>questions</u>. Enjoy.

Warm-up Questions

1) A curve is defined by the parametric equations $y = 2t^2 + t + 4$ and $x = \frac{6-t}{2}$.
   a) Find the values of x and y when $t = 0$, 1, 2 and 3.
   b) What are the values of t when: (i) $x = -7$ (ii) $y = 19$?
   c) Find the Cartesian equation of the curve, in the form $y = f(x)$.

2) The parametric equations of a curve are $x = 2\sin\theta$ and $y = \cos^2\theta + 4$, $-\frac{\pi}{2} \le \theta \le \frac{\pi}{2}$.
   a) What are the coordinates of the points where: (i) $\theta = \frac{\pi}{4}$ (ii) $\theta = \frac{\pi}{6}$
   b) What is the Cartesian equation of the curve?
   c) What restrictions are there on the values of x for this curve?

3) The curve C is defined by the parametric equations $x = \frac{\sin\theta}{3}$ and $y = 3 + 2\cos2\theta$.
   Find the Cartesian equation of C.

4) A curve has parametric equations $y = 4 + \frac{3}{t}$ and $x = t^2 - 1$.
   What are the coordinates of the points where this curve crosses
        a)   the y-axis   b)   the line $x + 2y = 14$?

Former career of the word 'parametric' #2 — stand-in for the word '<u>hallelujah</u>' in an early draft of <u>Handel's Messiah</u>. Meanwhile, back at the <u>practice questions</u>...

Exam Questions

1   The curve C is defined by the parametric equations

$$x = 1 - \tan\theta, \qquad y = \tfrac{1}{2}\sin2\theta, \qquad -\frac{\pi}{2} < \theta < \frac{\pi}{2}.$$

   a) P is the point on curve C where $\theta = \frac{\pi}{3}$. Find the exact coordinates of P.

                                                              (2 marks)

   b)   Point Q on curve C has coordinates $(2, -\frac{1}{2})$. Find the value of θ at Q.

                                                              (2 marks)

   c)   Using the identity $\sin2\theta \equiv \dfrac{2\tan\theta}{1 + \tan^2\theta}$, show that the Cartesian equation of C is $y = \dfrac{1-x}{x^2 - 2x + 2}$.

                                                              (3 marks)

2

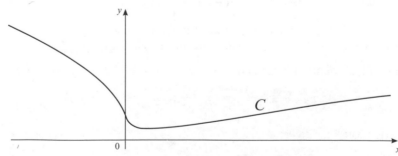

    Curve C has parametric equations $x = t^3 + t$, $y = t^2 - 2t + 2$.

   a) K is a point on C, and has the coordinates $(a, 1)$. Find the value of a.

                                                              (2 marks)

   b)   The line $8y = x + 6$ passes through C at points K, L and M.
         Find the coordinates of L and M, given that the x-coordinate of M is greater than the x-coordinate of L.

                                                              (6 marks)

C4 Section 3 — Practice Questions

Former career of the word 'parametric' #3 — proposed name for the next ocean to be discovered. Unfortunately it turned out all the oceans have already been discovered. Ooh look, more questions...

3

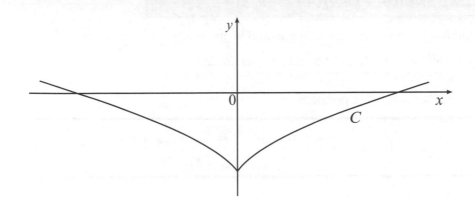

The curve C has parametric equations
$$x = t^3, \qquad y = t^2 - 4.$$

a) At the point F, t has the value 0.5. Find the coordinates of F.

(2 marks)

b) The line $3y = 2x - 11$ meets C twice. Find the coordinates of the points of intersection.

(6 marks)

4

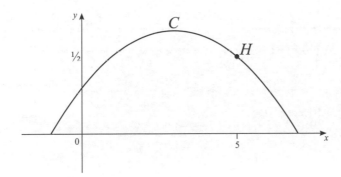

The parametric equations of curve C are
$$x = 3 + 4\sin\theta, \qquad y = \frac{1 + \cos 2\theta}{3}, \qquad -\frac{\pi}{2} \leq \theta \leq \frac{\pi}{2}.$$

Point H on C has coordinates $(5, \frac{1}{2})$.

a) Find the value of θ at point H.

(2 marks)

b) Show that the Cartesian equation of C can be written $y = \dfrac{-x^2 + 6x + 7}{24}$.

(4 marks)

c) Find the domain of values of x for the curve C.

(2 marks)

The Binomial Expansion

Yeah, I know the <u>binomial expansion</u>. We spent some time together back in C2. Thought I'd never see it again. And then, of all the sections in all the maths books in all the world, the binomial expansion walks into mine...

The *Binomial Expansion Formula* is pretty useful

The <u>binomial expansion</u> is a way to raise a given expression to <u>any power</u>.

For simpler cases it's basically a fancy way of <u>multiplying out brackets</u>.
You can also use it to <u>approximate</u> more complicated expressions (see p69).

This is the <u>general formula</u> for <u>binomial expansions</u>:

$$(1 + x)^n = 1 + nx + \frac{n(n-1)}{1 \times 2}x^2 + \dots + \frac{n(n-1)\dots(n-r+1)}{1 \times 2 \times \dots \times r}x^r + \dots$$

The *Binomial Expansion* sometimes gives a *Finite Expression*

From the general formula, it looks like the expansion always goes on forever.
But if *n* is a <u>positive integer</u>, the binomial expansion is <u>finite</u>.

EXAMPLE   Give the binomial expansion of $(1 + x)^5$.

You can use the <u>general formula</u> and plug in <u>*n* = 5</u>:

$n(n-1)$

$n = 5$

$$(1 + x)^5 = 1 + 5x + \frac{5(5-1)}{1 \times 2}x^2 + \frac{5(5-1)(5-2)}{1 \times 2 \times 3}x^3 + \frac{5(5-1)(5-2)(5-3)}{1 \times 2 \times 3 \times 4}x^4$$
$$+ \frac{5(5-1)(5-2)(5-3)(5-4)}{1 \times 2 \times 3 \times 4 \times 5}x^5 + \frac{5(5-1)(5-2)(5-3)(5-4)(5-5)}{1 \times 2 \times 3 \times 4 \times 5 \times 6}x^6 + \dots$$

$$= 1 + 5x + \frac{5 \times 4}{1 \times 2}x^2 + \frac{5 \times 4 \times 3}{1 \times 2 \times 3}x^3 + \frac{5 \times 4 \times 3 \times 2}{1 \times 2 \times 3 \times 4}x^4$$
$$+ \frac{5 \times 4 \times 3 \times 2 \times 1}{1 \times 2 \times 3 \times 4 \times 5}x^5 + \frac{5 \times 4 \times 3 \times 2 \times 1 \times 0}{1 \times 2 \times 3 \times 4 \times 5 \times 6}x^6 + \dots$$

> You can stop here — all the terms after this one are zero

$$= 1 + 5x + \frac{20}{2}x^2 + \frac{60}{6}x^3 + \frac{120}{24}x^4 + \frac{120}{120}x^5 + \frac{0}{720}x^6 + \dots$$

$$= 1 + 5x + 10x^2 + 10x^3 + 5x^4 + x^5$$

The formula still works if the coefficient of *x* isn't 1.

EXAMPLE   Give the binomial expansion of $(1 - 3x)^4$.

This time *n* = 4, but you also have to <u>replace every *x*</u> in the formula with <u>−3*x*</u>:

$(1 - 3x)^4$ ← Think of this as $(1 + (-3x))^4$ — you need to put the minus into the formula as well as the 3*x*.

$n = 4$ $n(n-1)$ Don't forget to square the −3 as well.   Stop here

$$= 1 + 4(-3x) + \frac{4 \times 3}{1 \times 2}(-3x)^2 + \frac{4 \times 3 \times 2}{1 \times 2 \times 3}(-3x)^3 + \frac{4 \times 3 \times 2 \times 1}{1 \times 2 \times 3 \times 4}(-3x)^4 + \frac{4 \times 3 \times 2 \times 1 \times 0}{1 \times 2 \times 3 \times 4 \times 5}(-3x)^5 + \dots$$

$$= 1 + 4(-3x) + \frac{12}{2}(9x^2) + \frac{4}{1}(-27x^3) + (81x^4) + \frac{0}{5}(-243x^5) + \dots$$

> Make life easier for yourself by cancelling down the fractions before you multiply.

$$= 1 - 12x + 54x^2 - 108x^3 + 81x^4$$

The Binomial Expansion

Unfortunately, you only get a nice, neat, <u>finite expansion</u> when you've got a <u>positive integer n</u>. But that pesky n sometimes likes to be a <u>negative number</u> or a <u>fraction</u>. n for nuisance. n for naughty.

If n is Negative the expansion gets more complicated...

EXAMPLE Find the binomial expansion of $\dfrac{1}{(1+x)^2}$ up to and including the term in x^3.

This is where things start to get a bit more interesting.

First, <u>rewrite the expression</u>: $\dfrac{1}{(1+x)^2} = (1+x)^{-2}$.

You can still use the <u>general formula</u>. This time <u>$n = -2$</u>:

$n = -2$ $n(n-1)$

$$(1+x)^{-2} = 1 + (-2)x + \frac{(-2) \times (-2-1)}{1 \times 2}x^2 + \frac{(-2) \times (-2-1) \times (-2-2)}{1 \times 2 \times 3}x^3 + \ldots$$

$$= 1 + (-2)x + \frac{(-2) \times (-3)}{1 \times 2}x^2 + \frac{(-2) \times (-3) \times (-4)}{1 \times 2 \times 3}x^3 + \ldots$$

$$= 1 + (-2)x + \frac{3}{1}x^2 + \frac{-4}{1}x^3 + \ldots$$

$$= 1 - 2x + 3x^2 - 4x^3 + \ldots$$

> With a negative n, you'll never get zero as a coefficient. If the question hadn't told you to stop, the expansion could go on forever.

> Again, you can cancel down before you multiply — but be careful with those minus signs.

We've left out all the terms after $-4x^3$, so the cubic expression you've ended up with is an <u>approximation</u> to the original expression. You could also write the answer like this:

$$\frac{1}{(1+x)^2} \approx 1 - 2x + 3x^2 - 4x^3$$

... and if n is a Fraction things can be tricky too

The binomial expansion formula doesn't just work for integer values of n.

EXAMPLE Find the binomial expansion of $\sqrt[3]{1+2x}$ up to and including the term in x^3.

This time we've got a <u>fractional power</u>: $\sqrt[3]{1+2x} = (1+2x)^{\frac{1}{3}}$

So this time $n = \frac{1}{3}$, and you also need to replace x with $2x$:

$n = \frac{1}{3}$ $n(n-1)$

$$(1+2x)^{\frac{1}{3}} = 1 + \frac{1}{3}(2x) + \frac{\frac{1}{3} \times \left(\frac{1}{3}-1\right)}{1 \times 2}(2x)^2 + \frac{\frac{1}{3} \times \left(\frac{1}{3}-1\right) \times \left(\frac{1}{3}-2\right)}{1 \times 2 \times 3}(2x)^3 + \ldots$$

$$= 1 + \frac{2}{3}x + \frac{\frac{1}{3} \times \left(-\frac{2}{3}\right)}{1 \times 2}4x^2 + \frac{\frac{1}{3} \times \left(-\frac{2}{3}\right) \times \left(-\frac{5}{3}\right)}{1 \times 2 \times 3}8x^3 + \ldots$$

$$= 1 + \frac{2}{3}x + \frac{\left(-\frac{2}{9}\right)}{2}4x^2 + \frac{\left(\frac{10}{27}\right)}{6}8x^3 + \ldots$$

$$= 1 + \frac{2}{3}x + \left(-\frac{2}{9} \times \frac{1}{2}\right)4x^2 + \left(\frac{10}{27} \times \frac{1}{6}\right)8x^3 + \ldots$$

$$= 1 + \frac{2}{3}x - \frac{4}{9}x^2 + \frac{40}{81}x^3 + \ldots$$

> Cancelling down is much trickier with this type of expansion — it's usually safer to multiply everything out fully.

> Exam questions often ask for the coefficients as simplified fractions.

The Binomial Expansion

More binomial goodness... this page is so jam-packed with the stuff, there's only room for a one-line intro...

If the **Constant** in the brackets isn't **1**, you have to **Factorise** first

So the general binomial expansion of $(1 + x)^n$ works fine for any n, and you can replace the x with other x-terms, but that 1 has to be a 1 before you can expand. That means you sometimes need to start with a sneaky bit of factorisation.

EXAMPLE   Give the binomial expansion of $(3 - x)^4$.

To use the <u>general formula</u>, you need the <u>constant term</u> in the brackets to be <u>1</u>.
You can take the 3 outside the brackets by <u>factorising</u>:

> The aim here is to get an expression in the form $c(1 + dx)^n$, where c and d are constants.

$$3 - x = 3(1 - \tfrac{1}{3}x)$$
$$\text{so} \quad (3 - x)^4 = [3(1 - \tfrac{1}{3}x)]^4$$
$$= 3^4(1 - \tfrac{1}{3}x)^4$$
$$= 81(1 - \tfrac{1}{3}x)^4$$

Now we can use the general formula, with $n = 4$, and $-\tfrac{1}{3}x$ instead of x:

$$\left(1 - \tfrac{1}{3}x\right)^4 = 1 + 4\left(-\tfrac{1}{3}x\right) + \tfrac{4 \times 3}{1 \times 2}\left(-\tfrac{1}{3}x\right)^2 + \tfrac{4 \times 3 \times 2}{1 \times 2 \times 3}\left(-\tfrac{1}{3}x\right)^3 + \tfrac{4 \times 3 \times 2 \times 1}{1 \times 2 \times 3 \times 4}\left(-\tfrac{1}{3}x\right)^4$$
$$= 1 - \tfrac{4}{3}x + 6\left(\tfrac{1}{9}x^2\right) + 4\left(-\tfrac{1}{27}x^3\right) + \tfrac{1}{81}x^4$$
$$= 1 - \tfrac{4x}{3} + \tfrac{2x^2}{3} - \tfrac{4x^3}{27} + \tfrac{x^4}{81}$$

So now we can expand the original expression:

$$(3 - x)^4 = 81\left(1 - \tfrac{1}{3}x\right)^4$$
$$= 81\left(1 - \tfrac{4x}{3} + \tfrac{2x^2}{3} - \tfrac{4x^3}{27} + \tfrac{x^4}{81}\right)$$
$$= 81 - 108x + 54x^2 - 12x^3 + x^4$$

Some **Binomial Expansions** are only **Valid** for **Certain Values** of x

When you find a binomial expansion, you usually have to state which values of x the expansion is valid for.

> If n is a <u>positive integer</u>, the binomial expansion of $(p + qx)^n$ is valid for <u>all values of x</u>.

If n is <u>not</u> a positive integer, the expansion would be <u>infinite</u>. Because you only write out a few terms, the binomial expansion you get is just an <u>approximation</u>. But the approximation is only valid if the sequence <u>converges</u> — this only happens if x is <u>small enough</u> (for larger values of x, the sequence will diverge)...

> If n is a <u>negative integer</u> or a <u>fraction</u>, the binomial expansion of $(p + qx)^n$ is valid when $\left|\tfrac{qx}{p}\right| < 1$.

> You can rewrite this as $|x| < \left|\tfrac{p}{q}\right|$ — just use the version you find easiest to remember.

This means there's a little bit more to do for the two examples on the previous page:

$$(1 + x)^{-2} = 1 - 2x + 3x^2 - 4x^3 + \dots \qquad \text{This expansion is valid for } |x| < 1.$$

$$(1 + 2x)^{\frac{1}{3}} = 1 + \tfrac{2}{3}x - \tfrac{4}{9}x^2 + \tfrac{40}{81}x^3 + \dots$$

This expansion is valid if $|2x| < 1 \Rightarrow 2|x| < 1 \Rightarrow |x| < \tfrac{1}{2}$.

> You might already know the rules $|ab| = |a||b|$ and $\left|\tfrac{a}{b}\right| = \tfrac{|a|}{|b|}$.
> If you don't, then get to know them — they're handy for rearranging these limits.

Lose weight and save money — buy no meals...

Two facts: 1) You can pretty much guarantee that there'll be a binomial expansion question on your C4 exam, and 2) any binomial expansion question they can throw at you will feature some combination of these adaptations of the general formula.

Approximating with Binomial Expansions

Binomial expansions can give you a handy way to estimate various roots.
OK, so it's not that handy... just go with it for now...

To find Approximations, substitute the right value of x

When you've done an expansion, you can use it to estimate the value of the original expression for given values of x.

EXAMPLE

The binomial expansion of $(1 + 3x)^{\frac{1}{3}}$ up to the term in x^3 is $(1 + 3x)^{\frac{1}{3}} \approx 1 + x - x^2 + \frac{5}{3}x^3$.

The expansion is valid for $|x| < \frac{1}{3}$.

Use this expansion to approximate $\sqrt[3]{1.3}$. Give your answer to 4 d.p.

For this type of question, you need to find the right value of x to make the expression you're expanding equal to the thing you're looking for.

In this case it's pretty straightforward: $\sqrt[3]{1.3} = (1 + 3x)^{\frac{1}{3}}$ when $x = 0.1$.

$$\sqrt[3]{1.3} = (1 + 3(0.1))^{\frac{1}{3}}$$
$$\approx 1 + 0.1 - (0.1)^2 + \frac{5}{3}(0.1)^3$$
$$= 1 + 0.1 - 0.01 + \frac{0.005}{3}$$
$$= 1.0917 \text{ (to 4 d.p.)}$$

This is the expansion given in the question, with $x = 0.1$.

Don't forget to use a "≈" here — the answer's an approximation because you're only using the expansion up to the x^3 term.

In trickier cases you have to do a spot of rearranging to get to the answer.

EXAMPLE

The binomial expansion of $(1 - 5x)^{\frac{1}{2}}$ up to the term in x^2 is $(1 - 5x)^{\frac{1}{2}} \approx 1 - \frac{5x}{2} - \frac{25}{8}x^2$.

The expansion is valid for $|x| < \frac{1}{5}$.

Use $x = \frac{1}{50}$ in this expansion to find an approximate value for $\sqrt{10}$.

Find the percentage error in your approximation, to 2 s.f.

First, sub $x = \frac{1}{50}$ into both sides of the expansion:

$$\sqrt{\left(1 - 5\left(\frac{1}{50}\right)\right)} \approx 1 - \frac{5}{2}\left(\frac{1}{50}\right) - \frac{25}{8}\left(\frac{1}{50}\right)^2$$
$$\sqrt{\left(1 - \frac{1}{10}\right)} \approx 1 - \frac{1}{20} - \frac{1}{800}$$
$$\sqrt{\frac{9}{10}} \approx \frac{759}{800}$$

Now simplify the square root and rearrange to find an estimate for $\sqrt{10}$:

$$\sqrt{\frac{9}{10}} = \frac{\sqrt{9}}{\sqrt{10}} = \frac{3}{\sqrt{10}} \approx \frac{759}{800} \quad \Rightarrow \quad \sqrt{10} \approx 3 \div \frac{759}{800} = \frac{800}{253}$$

The percentage error is
$$\left|\frac{\text{real value} - \text{estimate}}{\text{real value}}\right| \times 100 = \left|\frac{\sqrt{10} - \frac{800}{253}}{\sqrt{10}}\right| \times 100 = 0.0070\% \text{ (to 2 s.f.)}$$

You never know when you might need to estimate the cube root of 1.3...

That percentage error bit in the second example is one of those ways they might sneak a seemingly unrelated topic into an exam question. The examiners are allowed to stick a bit from any of the earlier Core modules into C4, so don't freak out if they ask you something slightly unexpected — remember, you **will** have seen it before and you **do** know how to do it.

Binomial Expansions and Partial Fractions

Binomial expansions on their own are pretty nifty, but when you combine them with <u>partial fractions</u> (see p.51-52) they become all-powerful. I'm sure there's some sort of message about friendship or something in there...

Split functions into *Partial Fractions*, then add the *Expansions*

You can find the binomial expansion of even more complicated functions by splitting them into partial fractions first.

EXAMPLE

$$f(x) = \frac{x-1}{(3+x)(1-5x)}$$

a) $f(x)$ can be expressed in the form $\frac{A}{(3+x)} + \frac{B}{(1-5x)}$. Find the values of A and B.

b) Use your answer to part a) to find the binomial expansion of $f(x)$ up to and including the term in x^2.

c) Find the range of values of x for which your answer to part b) is valid.

a) Convert $f(x)$ into <u>partial fractions</u>:

See C4 Section 1 if you need a reminder about how to do partial fractions.

$$\frac{x-1}{(3+x)(1-5x)} \equiv \frac{A}{(3+x)} + \frac{B}{(1-5x)} \quad \Rightarrow \quad x-1 \equiv A(1-5x) + B(3+x)$$

Let $x = -3$, then $-3 - 1 = A(1-(-15)) \Rightarrow -4 = 16A \Rightarrow A = -\frac{1}{4}$

Let $x = \frac{1}{5}$, then $\frac{1}{5} - 1 = B\left(3 + \frac{1}{5}\right) \Rightarrow -\frac{4}{5} = \frac{16}{5}B \Rightarrow B = -\frac{1}{4}$

b) Start by <u>rewriting</u> the partial fractions in $(a + bx)^n$ form:

$$f(x) = -\frac{1}{4}(3+x)^{-1} - \frac{1}{4}(1-5x)^{-1}$$

Now do the two <u>binomial expansions</u>:

$$(3+x)^{-1} = \left(3\left(1 + \frac{1}{3}x\right)\right)^{-1}$$
$$= \frac{1}{3}\left(1 + \frac{1}{3}x\right)^{-1}$$
$$= \frac{1}{3}\left(1 + (-1)\left(\frac{1}{3}x\right) + \frac{(-1)(-2)}{2}\left(\frac{1}{3}x\right)^2 + ...\right)$$
$$= \frac{1}{3}\left(1 - \frac{1}{3}x + \frac{1}{9}x^2 + ...\right)$$
$$= \frac{1}{3} - \frac{1}{9}x + \frac{1}{27}x^2 + ...$$

$$(1-5x)^{-1} = 1 + (-1)(-5x) + \frac{(-1)(-2)}{2}(-5x)^2 + ...$$
$$= 1 + 5x + 25x^2 + ...$$

And put <u>everything together</u>:

$$f(x) = -\frac{1}{4}(3+x)^{-1} - \frac{1}{4}(1-5x)^{-1} \approx -\frac{1}{4}\left(\frac{1}{3} - \frac{1}{9}x + \frac{1}{27}x^2\right) - \frac{1}{4}(1 + 5x + 25x^2)$$
$$= -\frac{1}{12} + \frac{1}{36}x - \frac{1}{108}x^2 - \frac{1}{4} - \frac{5}{4}x - \frac{25}{4}x^2$$
$$= -\frac{1}{3} - \frac{11}{9}x - \frac{169}{27}x^2$$

c) Each of the two expansions from part b) is valid for different values of x.
The combined expansion of $f(x)$ is valid where these two ranges <u>overlap</u>, i.e. over the <u>narrower of the two ranges</u>.

The expansion of $(3+x)^{-1}$ is valid when $\left|\frac{x}{3}\right| < 1 \Rightarrow \frac{|x|}{|3|} < 1 \Rightarrow |x| < 3$.

The expansion of $(1-5x)^{-1}$ is valid when $|-5x| < 1 \Rightarrow |-5||x| < 1 \Rightarrow |x| < \frac{1}{5}$.

Remember — the expansion of $(p + qx)^n$ is valid when $\left|\frac{qx}{p}\right| < 1$.

The expansion of $f(x)$ is valid for values of x in both ranges, so the expansion of $f(x)$ is valid for $|x| < \frac{1}{5}$.

Don't mess with me — I'm a partial arts expert...

Here's where it all comes together. This example looks pretty impressive, but if you know your stuff you'll sail through questions like this. I think that's all I've got to say for this page... hmm, looks like I've still got another line to fill... So, going anywhere nice on your holidays this year? Read any good books lately? (Answer: Yes, this one.)

C4 Section 4 — Practice Questions

Ah, here we are on another of these soothing green pages. Relax... this is your happy place... nothing to worry about here... enjoy this tranquil blue pool of shimmering warm-up questions.

Warm-up Questions

1) Give the binomial expansion of:

   a) $(1 + 2x)^3$ b) $(1 - x)^4$ c) $(1 - 4x)^4$

2) For what values of n does the binomial expansion of $(1 + x)^n$ result in a finite expression?

3) Find the binomial expansion of each of the following, up to and including the term in x^3:

   a) $\dfrac{1}{(1 + x)^4}$ b) $\dfrac{1}{(1 - 3x)^3}$ c) $\sqrt{1 - 5x}$

4) a) If the full binomial expansion of $(c + dx)^n$ is an infinite series, what values of x is the expansion valid for?

   b) What values of x are the expansions from question 3 valid for?

5) Give the binomial expansions of the following, up to and including the term in x^2. State which values of x each expansion is valid for.

   a) $\dfrac{1}{(3 + 2x)^2}$ b) $\sqrt[3]{8 - x}$

By now all your cares should have floated away on the binomial breeze.
Time for a bracing dip in an ice-cool bath of exam questions.

Exam Questions

1      $$f(x) = \frac{1}{\sqrt{(9 - 4x)}}, \text{ for } |x| < \frac{9}{4}.$$

   a) Find the binomial expansion of $f(x)$ up to and including the term in x^3.

   (5 marks)

   b) Hence find the first three terms in the expansion of $\dfrac{2 - x}{\sqrt{(9 - 4x)}}$.

   (4 marks)

2      $$f(x) = \frac{36x^2 + 3x - 10}{(4 + 3x)(1 - 3x)^2}$$

   a) Given that $f(x)$ can be expressed in the form

   $$f(x) = \frac{A}{(4 + 3x)} + \frac{B}{(1 - 3x)} + \frac{C}{(1 - 3x)^2}$$

   find the values of A, B and C.

   (4 marks)

   b) Find the binomial expansion of $f(x)$, up to and including the term in x^2.

   (6 marks)

   c) Find the range of values of x for which the binomial expansion of $f(x)$ is valid.

   (2 marks)

C4 Section 4 — Practice Questions

Congratulations, you've almost achieved <u>C4 Sequences and Series nirvana</u>.
Just a few more <u>exam question</u> steps and you'll be there...

3   a)   Find the binomial expansion of $(16 + 3x)^{\frac{1}{4}}$, for $|x| < \frac{16}{3}$, up to and including the term in x^2.

(5 marks)

    b)   (i)   Estimate $\sqrt[4]{12.4}$ by substituting a suitable value of x into your expansion from part (a). Give your answer to 6 decimal places.

(2 marks)

        (ii)   What is the percentage error in this estimate? Give your answer to 3 s.f.

(2 marks)

4   a)   Find the binomial expansion of $\left(1 - \frac{4}{3}x\right)^{-\frac{1}{2}}$, up to and including the term in x^3.

(4 marks)

    b)   Hence find the values of integer constants a, b and c, such that

$$\sqrt{\frac{27}{(3 - 4x)}} \approx a + bx + cx^2,$$

      and state the range of values of x for which this approximation is valid.

(3 marks)

5   a)   (i)   Show that $\sqrt{\dfrac{1 + 2x}{1 - 3x}} \approx 1 + \frac{5}{2}x + \frac{35}{8}x^2$.

(5 marks)

        (ii)   For what values of x is your expansion valid?

(2 marks)

    b)   Using the above expansion with $x = \frac{2}{15}$, show that $\sqrt{19} \approx \frac{127}{30}$.

(2 marks)

6   a)   Find the values of A and B such that $\dfrac{13x - 17}{(5 - 3x)(2x - 1)} \equiv \dfrac{A}{(5 - 3x)} + \dfrac{B}{(2x - 1)}$.

(3 marks)

    b)   (i)   Find the binomial expansion of $(2x - 1)^{-1}$, up to and including the term in x^2.

(2 marks)

        (ii)   Show that $\dfrac{1}{(5 - 3x)} \approx \frac{1}{5} + \frac{3}{25}x + \frac{9}{125}x^2$, for $|x| < \frac{5}{3}$.

(5 marks)

    c)   Using your answers to parts a) and b), find the first three terms of the binomial expansion of $\dfrac{13x - 17}{(5 - 3x)(2x - 1)}$.

(2 marks)

Differentiation with Parametric Equations

Another shiny new section — oh the joys of <u>calculus</u> (that's <u>differentiation</u> and <u>integration</u> to me and you). It starts with the return of an old friend. If you've forgotten what <u>parametric equations</u> are already, go back to Section 3. Go on, I'll wait for you... ... ...OK, are you back now? Ready? Right, on we go...

Differentiating Parametric Equations is a lot Simpler than you might expect

Just suppose you've got a <u>curve</u> defined by two <u>parametric equations</u>, with the parameter t: $y = f(t)$ and $x = g(t)$.

If you can't find the <u>Cartesian equation</u>, it seems like it would be a bit tricky to find the gradient, $\frac{dy}{dx}$.

Luckily the chain rule (see p17) is on hand to help out:

$$\frac{dy}{dx} = \frac{dy}{dt} \div \frac{dx}{dt}$$

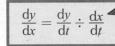 This is exactly the same as on p17, except we've replaced '$\times \frac{dt}{dx}$' with '$\div \frac{dx}{dt}$'

EXAMPLE The curve C is defined by the parametric equations $y = t^3 - 2t + 4$ and $x = t^2 - 1$.

Find: a) $\frac{dy}{dx}$ in terms of t, b) the gradient of C when $t = -1$.

Start by <u>differentiating</u> the two parametric equations <u>with respect to t</u>:

a) $\frac{dy}{dt} = 3t^2 - 2$, $\frac{dx}{dt} = 2t$

Now use the <u>chain rule</u> to combine them:

$$\frac{dy}{dx} = \frac{dy}{dt} \div \frac{dx}{dt} = \frac{3t^2 - 2}{2t}$$

Use the answer to a) to find the <u>gradient</u> for a <u>specific value</u> of t:

b) When $t = -1$, $\frac{dy}{dx} = \frac{3(-1)^2 - 2}{2(-1)} = \frac{3 - 2}{-2} = -\frac{1}{2}$

Use the Gradient to find Tangents and Normals

Of course, it's rarely as straightforward as just finding the gradient. A lot of the time, you'll then have to use it in the equation of a <u>tangent</u> or <u>normal</u> to the parametric curve.

EXAMPLE For the curve C in the example above, find:
a) the equation of the tangent to the curve when $t = 2$,
b) the equation of the normal to the curve when $t = 2$.

First you need the <u>coordinates</u> of the point where $t = 2$:

a) When $t = 2$, $x = (2)^2 - 1 = 3$ and $y = (2)^3 - 2(2) + 4 = 8 - 4 + 4 = 8$.

You also need the <u>gradient</u> at that point:

When $t = 2$, $\frac{dy}{dx} = \frac{3(2)^2 - 2}{2(2)} = \frac{10}{4} = \frac{5}{2}$

Now use that information to find the equation of the <u>tangent</u>:

The tangent to C at $(3, 8)$ has an equation of the form $y = mx + c$.

So $8 = \frac{5}{2}(3) + c \Rightarrow c = \frac{1}{2}$.

The tangent to curve C when $t = 2$ is $y = \frac{5}{2}x + \frac{1}{2}$.

> You could also use $y - y_1 = m(x - x_1)$ to get the equation.

You can find the <u>normal</u> in a similar way:

b) The normal to C at $(3, 8)$ has gradient $-\frac{1}{\left(\frac{5}{2}\right)} = -\frac{2}{5}$.

So $8 = -\frac{2}{5}(3) + c \Rightarrow c = \frac{46}{5}$.

The normal to curve C when $t = 2$ is $y = -\frac{2}{5}x + \frac{46}{5}$.

> If you're not quite following all this tangents and normals business, take a look back at C1 to refresh your memory.

And now, yet another chocolate biscuit reference...

To an examiner, adding a 'find the tangent' or 'find the normal' part to a parametric equations question is like adding chocolate to a digestive biscuit — it makes it at least 4 times better. In other words: this is very likely to show up in your C4 exam, so be ready for it. And in case you were wondering, tangent = milk chocolate, normal = dark chocolate.

Implicit Differentiation

This really isn't as complicated as it looks... in fact, I think you'll find that if something's implicit between x and y, it can be ximplicity itself. No, that's not a typo, it's a hilarious joke... 'implicit' between 'x' and 'y'... do you see?...

You need **Implicit Differentiation** if you can't write the **Equation** as $y = f(x)$

1) An 'implicit relation' is the maths name for any equation in x and y that's written in the form $f(x, y) = g(x, y)$ instead of $y = f(x)$.

> $f(x, y)$ and $g(x, y)$ don't actually both have to include x and y — one of them could even be a constant.

2) Some implicit relations are either awkward or impossible to rewrite in the form $y = f(x)$. This can happen, for example, if the equation contains a number of different powers of y, or terms where x is multiplied by y.

3) This can make implicit relations tricky to differentiate — the solution is implicit differentiation:

Implicit Differentiation

To find $\frac{dy}{dx}$ for an implicit relation between x and y:

1) **Differentiate terms in x^n only (and constant terms) with respect to x, as normal.**

2) **Use the chain rule to differentiate terms in y^m only:**

$$\frac{d}{dx}f(y) = \frac{d}{dy}f(y)\frac{dy}{dx}$$

> In other words, 'differentiate with respect to y, and stick a $\frac{dy}{dx}$ on the end'.

3) **Use the product rule to differentiate terms in both x and y:**

$$\frac{d}{dx}u(x)v(y) = u(x)\frac{d}{dx}v(y) + v(y)\frac{d}{dx}u(x)$$

> This version of the product rule is slightly different from the one on p20 — it's got v(y) instead of v(x).

4) **Rearrange the resulting equation in x, y and $\frac{dy}{dx}$ to make $\frac{dy}{dx}$ the subject.**

EXAMPLE Use implicit differentiation to find $\frac{dy}{dx}$ if $2x^2y + y^3 = 6x^2 + 5$.

We need to differentiate each term of the equation with respect to x.

Start by sticking '$\frac{d}{dx}$' in front of each term:

$$\frac{d}{dx}2x^2y + \frac{d}{dx}y^3 = \frac{d}{dx}6x^2 + \frac{d}{dx}5$$

First, deal with the terms in x and constant terms — in this case that's the two terms on the RHS:

$$\Rightarrow \frac{d}{dx}2x^2y + \frac{d}{dx}y^3 = 12x + 0$$

Now use the chain rule on the term in y:

$$\Rightarrow \frac{d}{dx}2x^2y + 3y^2\frac{dy}{dx} = 12x + 0$$

> Using the chain rule from the box above, $f(y) = y^3$.

> Leave this $\frac{dy}{dx}$ where it is for now.

And use the product rule on the term in x and y:

$$\Rightarrow 2x^2\frac{d}{dx}(y) + y\frac{d}{dx}(2x^2) + 3y^2\frac{dy}{dx} = 12x + 0$$

$$\Rightarrow 2x^2\frac{dy}{dx} + y4x + 3y^2\frac{dy}{dx} = 12x + 0$$

> So in terms of the box above, $u(x) = 2x^2$ and $v(y) = y$.

> You get a $\frac{dy}{dx}$ term here too (from the '$\frac{d}{dx}v(y)$' bit).

Finally, rearrange to make $\frac{dy}{dx}$ the subject:

$$\Rightarrow \frac{dy}{dx}(2x^2 + 3y^2) = 12x - 4xy$$

$$\Rightarrow \frac{dy}{dx} = \frac{12x - 4xy}{2x^2 + 3y^2}$$

If an imp asks to try your ice lolly, don't let the imp lick it...

Learn the versions of the chain rule and product rule from the box above. All the different bits of the method for implicit differentiation can make it confusing — read the example carefully and make sure you understand every little bit of it.

Implicit Differentiation

If you've gone to all the hard work of <u>differentiating</u> an <u>implicit relation</u>, it would be a shame not to use it. It'd be like a <u>shiny toy</u> that's been kept in its box and never played with. Don't make the maths sad — <u>play with it</u>.

Implicit Differentiation still gives you an expression for the *Gradient*

Most <u>implicit differentiation</u> questions aren't really that different at heart to any other <u>differentiation question</u>. Once you've got an expression for the <u>gradient</u>, you'll have to <u>use it</u> to do the sort of stuff you'd normally expect.

EXAMPLE Curve A has the equation $x^2 + 2xy - y^2 = 10x + 4y - 21$

a) Show that when $\frac{dy}{dx} = 0$, $y = 5 - x$.

b) Find the coordinates of the stationary points of A.

For starters, we're going to need to find $\frac{dy}{dx}$ by <u>implicit differentiation</u>:

a)
$$\frac{d}{dx}x^2 + \frac{d}{dx}2xy - \frac{d}{dx}y^2 = \frac{d}{dx}10x + \frac{d}{dx}4y - \frac{d}{dx}21$$

> Differentiate x^2, 10x and 21 with respect to x.

$$\Rightarrow 2x + \frac{d}{dx}2xy - \frac{d}{dx}y^2 = 10 + \frac{d}{dx}4y - 0$$

> Use the chain rule to differentiate y^2 and 4y.

$$\Rightarrow 2x + \frac{d}{dx}2xy - 2y\frac{dy}{dx} = 10 + 4\frac{dy}{dx}$$

> Use the product rule to differentiate 2xy.

$$\Rightarrow 2x + 2x\frac{dy}{dx} + y\frac{d}{dx}2x - 2y\frac{dy}{dx} = 10 + 4\frac{dy}{dx}$$

$$\Rightarrow 2x + 2x\frac{dy}{dx} + 2y - 2y\frac{dy}{dx} = 10 + 4\frac{dy}{dx}$$

> Collect '$\frac{dy}{dx}$' terms on one side, and everything else on the other side.

$$\Rightarrow 2x\frac{dy}{dx} - 2y\frac{dy}{dx} - 4\frac{dy}{dx} = 10 - 2x - 2y$$

$$\Rightarrow \frac{dy}{dx} = \frac{10 - 2x - 2y}{2x - 2y - 4}$$

So when $\frac{dy}{dx} = 0$, $\frac{10 - 2x - 2y}{2x - 2y - 4} = 0$ $\Rightarrow$ $10 - 2x - 2y = 0$ $\Rightarrow$ $y = 5 - x$

Now we can <u>use</u> the answer to part a) in the equation of the <u>curve</u> to find the points where $\frac{dy}{dx} = 0$.

b) When $\frac{dy}{dx} = 0$, $y = 5 - x$. So at the stationary points,

$$x^2 + 2xy - y^2 = 10x + 4y - 21$$

$$\Rightarrow x^2 + 2x(5 - x) - (5 - x)^2 = 10x + 4(5 - x) - 21$$

> Substitute y = 5 − x into the original equation to find the values of x at the stationary points.

$$\Rightarrow x^2 + 10x - 2x^2 - 25 + 10x - x^2 = 10x + 20 - 4x - 21$$

$$\Rightarrow -2x^2 + 20x - 25 = 6x - 1$$

$$\Rightarrow -2x^2 + 14x - 24 = 0$$

$$\Rightarrow x^2 - 7x + 12 = 0$$

$$\Rightarrow (x - 3)(x - 4) = 0$$

$$\Rightarrow x = 3 \text{ or } x = 4$$

$$x = 3 \Rightarrow y = 5 - 3 = 2 \qquad x = 4 \Rightarrow y = 5 - 4 = 1$$

So the stationary points of A are (3, 2) and (4, 1).

Pah, differentiation? They should have called it same-iation...

...you know, cos all the questions basically end up asking for the same thing. Other familiar faces that are likely to show up in implicit differentiation questions include finding tangents and normals to implicitly defined curves. All these differentiation questions set off in different ways to end up asking you the same thing, so make sure you know the basics.

Integrating Trig Things Using Trig Identities

Not only do you have to do <u>more integration</u>, you also have to do <u>more trigonometry</u>. How <u>unoriginal</u>.
I think the examiners are running out of ideas.

The **Double Angle Formulas** are useful for **Integration**

If you're given a tricky <u>trig function</u> to integrate, see if you can <u>simplify</u> it using one of the <u>double angle formulas</u>.
They're especially useful for things like <u>cos²x</u>, <u>sin²x</u> and <u>sin x cos x</u>. Here are the double angle formulas (see p.57):

$$\sin 2x \equiv 2 \sin x \cos x \qquad \cos 2x \equiv \cos^2 x - \sin^2 x$$

$$\tan 2x \equiv \frac{2\tan x}{1 - \tan^2 x} \qquad \cos 2x \equiv 2\cos^2 x - 1$$

$$\cos 2x \equiv 1 - 2\sin^2 x$$

You can <u>rearrange</u> the second two cos 2x formulas to get expressions for <u>cos²x</u> and <u>sin²x</u>: $\cos^2 x = \frac{1}{2}(\cos 2x + 1)$
$\sin^2 x = \frac{1}{2}(1 - \cos 2x)$

Once you've <u>replaced</u> the <u>original function</u> with one of the <u>double angle formulas</u>,
you can just <u>integrate</u> as normal.

Don't forget to double the coefficient of x here. You'll also need to divide by 10 when you integrate.

EXAMPLE   Find   a) $\int \sin^2 x \, dx$ b) $\int \cos^2 5x \, dx$ c) $\int \sin x \cos x \, dx$.

a)   Using the double angle formula above,
write $\sin^2 x$ as $\frac{1}{2}(1 - \cos 2x)$, then integrate.

$$\int \sin^2 x \, dx = \int \frac{1}{2}(1 - \cos 2x)dx$$
$$= \frac{1}{2}\left(x - \frac{1}{2}\sin 2x\right) + C = \frac{1}{2}x - \frac{1}{4}\sin 2x + C$$

b)   Using the double angle formula above,
write $\cos^2 5x$ as $\frac{1}{2}(\cos 10x + 1)$, then integrate.

$$\int \cos^2 5x \, dx = \int \frac{1}{2}(\cos 10x + 1)dx$$
$$= \frac{1}{2}\left(\frac{1}{10}\sin 10x + x\right) + C = \frac{1}{20}\sin 10x + \frac{1}{2}x + C$$

c)   Using the double angle formula above, write $\sin x \cos x$ as $\frac{1}{2}\sin 2x$, then integrate.

$$\int \sin x \cos x \, dx = \int \frac{1}{2}\sin 2x \, dx = \frac{1}{2}\left(-\frac{1}{2}\cos 2x\right) + C = -\frac{1}{4}\cos 2x + C$$

Use the **Identities** to get a function you **Know** how to **Integrate**

There are a couple of other <u>identities</u> you can use to <u>simplify trig functions</u> (see p.15):

$$\sec^2 \theta \equiv 1 + \tan^2 \theta \qquad \operatorname{cosec}^2 \theta \equiv 1 + \cot^2 \theta$$

These two identities are really useful if you have to integrate <u>tan²x</u> or <u>cot²x</u>, as you already know how to
integrate <u>sec²x</u> and <u>cosec²x</u> (see p.27). Don't forget the stray <u>1s</u> flying around — they'll just integrate to <u>x</u>.

EXAMPLE   Find   a) $\int \tan^2 x - 1 \, dx$

b) $\int \cot^2 3x \, dx$.

a)   Rewrite the function in terms of sec²x:
$\tan^2 x - 1 \equiv \sec^2 x - 1 - 1 \equiv \sec^2 x - 2$.
Now integrate:
$$\int \sec^2 x - 2 \, dx = \tan x - 2x + C$$

b)   Get the function in terms of cosec²x:
$\cot^2 3x \equiv \operatorname{cosec}^2 3x - 1$.
Now integrate:
$$\int \operatorname{cosec}^2 3x - 1 \, dx = -\frac{1}{3}\cot 3x - x + C$$

EXAMPLE   Evaluate $\int_0^{\frac{\pi}{3}} 6 \sin 3x \cos 3x + \tan^2 \frac{1}{2}x + 1 \, dx$.

Using the identities, $6 \sin 3x \cos 3x \equiv 3 \sin 6x$
and $\tan^2 \frac{1}{2}x + 1 \equiv \sec^2 \frac{1}{2}x$ gives:

$$\int_0^{\frac{\pi}{3}} 3 \sin 6x + \sec^2 \frac{1}{2}x \, dx = \left[-\frac{3}{6}\cos 6x + 2 \tan \frac{1}{2}x\right]_0^{\frac{\pi}{3}}$$

$$= \left[-\frac{1}{2}\cos 6\left(\frac{\pi}{3}\right) + 2\tan\frac{1}{2}\left(\frac{\pi}{3}\right)\right] - \left[-\frac{1}{2}\cos 6(0) + 2\tan\frac{1}{2}(0)\right]$$

$$= \left[-\frac{1}{2}\cos(2\pi) + 2\tan\left(\frac{\pi}{6}\right)\right] - \left[-\frac{1}{2}\cos(0) + 2\tan(0)\right]$$

$$= \left[-\frac{1}{2}(1) + 2\left(\frac{1}{\sqrt{3}}\right)\right] - \left[-\frac{1}{2}(1) + 2(0)\right] = -\frac{1}{2} + \frac{2}{\sqrt{3}} + \frac{1}{2} = \frac{2}{\sqrt{3}}$$

Use the table of common trig angles on p.56 to help you here.

Remember to divide by 3, the coefficient of x, when you integrate.

I can't help feeling I've seen these somewhere before...

If you're given a trig function that you don't know how to integrate, play around with these identities and see if you can
turn it into something you can integrate. Watch out for coefficients though — they can trip you up if you're not careful.

Tough Integrals

With a name like 'Tough Integrals', it doesn't sound like it's going to be a very nice page. However, names can be deceiving. Maybe not in this case, but they can be.

You can integrate Partial Fractions

In Section 1 (pages 51-52), you saw how to break down a scary-looking algebraic fraction into partial fractions. This comes in pretty handy when you're integrating — you could try integration by parts on the original fraction, but it would get messy and probably end in tears. Fortunately, once you've split it up into partial fractions, it's much easier to integrate, using the methods on p.26 and p.28.

EXAMPLE

Find $\int \dfrac{9x^2 + x + 16}{(x+2)(2x-1)(x-3)}\, dx$.

This is the example from p.51, and it can be written as partial fractions like this: $\dfrac{2}{(x+2)} - \dfrac{3}{(2x-1)} + \dfrac{4}{(x-3)}$

Don't forget the coefficients here. Have a look back at p.26 if you can't remember how to do this.

Integrating the partial fractions is much easier: $\int \dfrac{2}{(x+2)} - \dfrac{3}{(2x-1)} + \dfrac{4}{(x-3)}\, dx = 2\ln|x+2| - \dfrac{3}{2}\ln|2x-1| + 4\ln|x-3| + C$

$$= \ln\left|\dfrac{(x+2)^2(x-3)^4}{(2x-1)^{\frac{3}{2}}}\right| + C$$

Use the log laws from p.8 to combine all the ln terms.

EXAMPLE

Find $\int \dfrac{x^2 + 17x + 16}{(x+2)^2(3x-1)}\, dx$.

This is the example from p.52. It's a bit trickier because it has a repeated factor. Written in partial fractions, it looks like this: $\dfrac{2}{(x+2)^2} - \dfrac{1}{(x+2)} + \dfrac{4}{(3x-1)}$

You might find it easiest to use integration by substitution (p.30) on the first fraction:

Let $u = x + 2$, then $\dfrac{du}{dx} = 1$, so $du = dx$. Substituting gives:

$$\int \dfrac{2}{(x+2)^2}\, dx = \int \dfrac{2}{u^2}\, du = -\dfrac{2}{u} = -\dfrac{2}{(x+2)}$$

Putting it all together: $\int \dfrac{2}{(x+2)^2} - \dfrac{1}{(x+2)} + \dfrac{4}{(3x-1)}\, dx = -\dfrac{2}{x+2} - \ln|x+2| + \dfrac{4}{3}\ln|3x-1| + C$

$$= -\dfrac{2}{x+2} + \ln\left|\dfrac{(3x-1)^{\frac{4}{3}}}{x+2}\right| + C$$

Some Trig Integrals can be really Nasty

Unfortunately, the vast range of trig identities and formulas you've seen, as well as lots of different rules for integration, mean that there's no end of evil integration questions they can ask you. Here's a particularly nasty example:

EXAMPLE

Use the substitution $u = \tan x$ to find $\int \dfrac{\sec^4 x}{\sqrt{\tan x}}\, dx$.

Integration by substitution is covered on p.30.

First, work out what all the substitutions will be:

- If $u = \tan x$, then $\dfrac{du}{dx} = \sec^2 x$, so $dx = \dfrac{du}{\sec^2 x}$.

This will leave $\sec^2 x$ on the numerator — you need to find this in terms of u:
From the identity $\sec^2 x \equiv 1 + \tan^2 x$, you get $\sec^2 x \equiv 1 + u^2$,

Remember to stick $u = \tan x$ back into the equation.

Then substitute all these bits into the integral:

$$\int \dfrac{\sec^4 x}{\sqrt{\tan x}}\, dx = \int \dfrac{1 + u^2}{\sqrt{u}}\, du$$

$$= \int \dfrac{1}{\sqrt{u}} + \dfrac{u^2}{\sqrt{u}}\, du = \int u^{-\frac{1}{2}} + u^{\frac{3}{2}}\, du$$

$$= 2u^{\frac{1}{2}} + \dfrac{2}{5}u^{\frac{5}{2}} + C$$

$$= 2\sqrt{\tan x} + \dfrac{2}{5}\sqrt{\tan^5 x} + C$$

I'm partial to a cup of tea...

Partial fractions quite often pop up in a two-part question — for the first part, you'll have to write a tricky fraction in partial fractions, and in the second part you'll have to integrate it. It's a good job you're such a whizz at integrating.

Differential Equations

Differential equations are tricky little devils that have a lot to do with differentiation as well as integration. They're often about rates of change, so the variable t pops up quite a lot.

Differential Equations have a dy/dx Term

(or $\frac{dP}{dt}$, $\frac{ds}{dt}$, $\frac{dV}{dr}$, etc. — depending on the variables)

1) A differential equation is an equation that includes a derivative term (such as $\frac{dy}{dx}$), as well as other variables (like x and y).

2) Before you even think (or worry) about solving them, you have to be able to set up ('formulate') differential equations.

3) Differential equations tend to involve a rate of change (giving a derivative term) and a proportion relation. Remember — if $a \propto b$, then $a = kb$ for some constant k.

EXAMPLE The number of bacteria in a petri dish is increasing over time, t, at a rate directly proportional to the number of bacteria at a given time, b. Formulate a differential equation that shows this information.

The rate of change, $\frac{db}{dt}$, is proportional to b, so $\frac{db}{dt} \propto b$. This means that $\frac{db}{dt} = kb$ for some constant k, $k > 0$.

EXAMPLE The volume of interdimensional space jelly, V, in a container is decreasing over time, t, at a rate directly proportional to the square of its volume. Show this as a differential equation.

The rate of change, $\frac{dV}{dt}$, is proportional to V^2, so $\frac{dV}{dt} \propto V^2$. $\frac{dV}{dt} = -kV^2$ for some constant k, $k > 0$.

 V is decreasing, so don't forget the $-$.

Solve differential equations by Integrating

Now comes the really juicy bit — solving differential equations. It's not as bad as it looks (honest).

Solving Differential Equations

1) **You can only solve differential equations if they have separable variables — where x and y can be separated into functions $f(x)$ and $g(y)$.**

   Remember — it might not be in terms of x and y.

2) **Write the differential equation in the form $\frac{dy}{dx} = f(x)g(y)$.**

3) **Then rearrange the equation to get all the terms with y on the LHS and all the terms with x on the RHS. It'll look something like this: $\frac{1}{g(y)}dy = f(x)dx$.**

   Like in integration by substitution, you can treat dy/dx as a fraction here.

4) **Now integrate both sides: $\int \frac{1}{g(y)}dy = \int f(x)dx$.**

5) **Rearrange your answer to get it in a nice form — you might be asked to find it in the form $y = h(x)$. Don't forget the constant of integration (you only need one — not one on each side). It might be useful to write the constant as $\ln k$ rather than C (see p.28).**

6) **If you're asked for a general solution, leave C (or k) in your answer. If they want a particular solution, they'll give you x and y values for a certain point. All you do is put these values into your equation and use them to find C (or k).**

EXAMPLE Find the particular solution of $\frac{dy}{dx} = 2y(1 + x)^2$ when $x = -1$ and $y = 4$.

This equation has separable variables: $f(x) = 2(1 + x)^2$ and $g(y) = y$.

Rearranging this equation gives: $\frac{1}{y}dy = 2(1 + x)^2dx$

And integrating: $\int \frac{1}{y}dy = \int 2(1 + x)^2dx$

$\Rightarrow \ln|y| = \frac{2}{3}(1 + x)^3 + C$

If you were asked for a general solution, you could just leave it in this form.

Now put in the values of x and y to find the value of C:

$\ln 4 = \frac{2}{3}(1 + (-1))^3 + C \Rightarrow \ln 4 = C$

so $\ln|y| = \frac{2}{3}(1 + x)^3 + \ln 4$

I will formulate a plan to take over the world...

...starting with Cumbria. I've always liked Cumbria. You're welcome to join my army of minions, but first you'll have to become an expert on solving differential equations. Do that, and I'll give you Grasmere — or name a mountain after you.

Differential Equations

One of the most exciting things about differential equations is that you can apply them to real-life situations. Well, I say exciting, but perhaps I should say 'mildly interesting', or maybe just 'more stuff for you to learn'.

You might be given Extra Information

1) In the exam, you might be given a question that takes a real-life problem and uses differential equations to model it.

2) Population questions come up quite often — the population might be increasing or decreasing, and you have to find and solve differential equations to show it. In cases like this, one of your variables will usually be t, time.

3) You might be given a starting condition — e.g. the initial population. The important thing to remember is that:

> the starting condition occurs when $t = 0$.

This is pretty obvious, but it's really important.

4) You might also be given extra information — e.g. the population after a certain number of years (where you have to figure out what t is), or the number of years it takes to reach a certain population (where you have to work out what the population will be). Make sure you always link the numbers you get back to the situation.

Exam Questions are often Broken Down into lots of Parts

Questions like the one below can be a bit overwhelming, but follow it through step by step and it shouldn't be too bad.

EXAMPLE

> The population of rabbits in a park is decreasing as winter approaches.
> The rate of decrease is directly proportional to the current number of rabbits (P).
>
> a) Formulate a differential equation to model the rate of decrease in terms of the variables P, t (time in days) and k, a positive constant.
>
> b) If the initial population is P_0, solve your differential equation to find P in terms of P_0, k and t.
>
> c) Given that $k = 0.1$, find the time at which the population of rabbits will have halved, to the nearest day.

a) If the rate of decrease is proportional to the number of rabbits, then $\dfrac{dP}{dt} = -kP$ (it's negative because the population is decreasing).

b) First, solve the differential equation to find the general solution: $\dfrac{dP}{dt} = -kP \Rightarrow \dfrac{1}{P}\,dP = -k\,dt$

Integrating this gives: $\int \dfrac{1}{P}\,dP = \int -k\,dt$

$\Rightarrow \ln P = -kt + C$

You don't need modulus signs for $\ln P$ as $P \geq 0$ — you can't have a negative population.

At $t = 0$, $P = P_0$. Putting these values into the equation gives: $\ln P_0 = -k(0) + C$

$\Rightarrow \ln P_0 = C$

So the differential equation becomes: $\ln P = -kt + \ln P_0$

$\Rightarrow P = e^{(-kt + \ln P_0)} = e^{-kt}e^{\ln P_0}$

$\Rightarrow P = P_0 e^{-kt}$

Remember that $e^{\ln x} = x = \ln e^x$.

c) When the population of rabbits has halved, $P = \frac{1}{2}P_0$. You've been told that $k = 0.1$, so substitute these values into the equation above and solve for t:

$\dfrac{1}{2}P_0 = P_0 e^{-0.1t}$

$\dfrac{1}{2} = e^{-0.1t}$

$\ln \dfrac{1}{2} = -0.1t$

$-0.6931 = -0.1t \Rightarrow t = 6.931$

So, to the nearest day, $t = 7$. This means that it will take 7 days for the population of rabbits to halve.

At t = 10, we kill all the bunnies...

These questions can get a bit morbid — just how I like them. They might look a bit scary, as they throw a lot of information at you in one go, but once you know how to solve them, they're a walk in the park. Rabbit traps optional.

C4 Section 5 — Practice Questions

If you think that was a <u>lot of calculus</u>, be thankful you didn't live in Ancient Molgarahenia, where calculus was the only maths permitted. Try these tasty warm-up questions for an <u>authentic taste</u> of Molgarahenian life.

Warm-up Questions

1) A curve is defined by the <u>parametric equations</u> $x = t^2$, $y = 3t^3 - 4t$.

   a) Find $\dfrac{dy}{dx}$ for this curve.

   b) Find the coordinates of the <u>stationary points</u> of the curve.

2) Use <u>implicit differentiation</u> to find $\dfrac{dy}{dx}$ for each of the following equations:
   a) $4x^2 - 2y^2 = 7x^2y$
   b) $3x^4 - 2xy^2 = y$
   c) $\cos x \sin y = xy$

3) Using your answers to question 2, find:
   a) the gradient of the <u>tangent</u> to the graph of $4x^2 - 2y^2 = 7x^2y$ at $(1, -4)$,
   b) the gradient of the <u>normal</u> to the graph of $3x^4 - 2xy^2 = y$ at $(1, 1)$.

4) Use the appropriate <u>trig identity</u> to find $\int \dfrac{2\tan 3x}{1 - \tan^2 3x}\, dx$.

5) Use the <u>trig identity</u> $\sec^2 x \equiv 1 + \tan^2 x$ to find $\int 2\tan^2 3x + 2\, dx$.

6) Use $\dfrac{3x + 10}{(2x + 3)(x - 4)} \equiv \dfrac{A}{2x + 3} + \dfrac{B}{x - 4}$ to find $\int \dfrac{3x + 10}{(2x + 3)(x - 4)}\, dx$.

7) Find the <u>general solution</u> to the <u>differential equation</u> $\dfrac{dy}{dx} = \dfrac{1}{y}\cos x$. Give your answer in the form $y^2 = f(x)$.

8) The population of <u>squirrels</u> is increasing suspiciously quickly. The <u>rate of increase</u> is <u>directly proportional</u> to the current number of squirrels, S.

   a) Formulate a <u>differential equation</u> to model the rate of increase in terms of S, t (time in weeks) and k, a positive constant.

   b) The squirrels need a population of 150 to successfully <u>take over</u> the forest. If the <u>initial population</u> is 30 and the value of k is 0.2, how long (to the nearest week) will it take before they can overthrow the <u>evil hedgehogs</u>?

It is said that the Great Molgarahenian Plain was carpeted with calculus <u>as far as the eye could see</u>. The C4 exam won't be <u>quite</u> that bad, but there will be <u>some calculus</u> in there, so get practising...

Exam Questions

1   The curve C is defined by the parametric equations

$$x = 3\theta - \cos 3\theta, \quad y = 2\sin\theta, \quad -\pi \le \theta \le \pi.$$

   a)   Find an expression for $\dfrac{dy}{dx}$.

   (3 marks)

   b)   (i)   Show that the gradient of C at the point $(\pi + 1, \sqrt{3})$ is $\dfrac{1}{3}$.

   (3 marks)

   (ii)   Find the equation of the normal to C when $\theta = \dfrac{\pi}{6}$.

   (4 marks)

2   Use an appropriate identity to find $\int 2\cot^2 x\, dx$.

   (3 marks)

C4 Section 5 — Practice Questions

In 272 BC, the famous Molgarahenian philosopher, <u>Bobby the Wise</u>, was put to death for straying from the path of <u>calculus</u> and doing some simultaneous equations. Don't be like Bobby, stick with <u>these questions</u> (for now)...

3   The equation of curve C is $6x^2y - 7 = 5x - 4y^2 - x^2$.

    a)   The line T has the equation $y = c$ and passes through a point on C where $x = 2$.
        Find c, given that $c > 0$.

(2 marks)

    b) T also crosses C at point Q.

        (i)   Find the coordinates of Q.

(2 marks)

        (ii)   Find the gradient of C at Q.

(6 marks)

4   a)   Find the general solution to the differential equation

$$\frac{dy}{dx} = \frac{\cos x \cos^2 y \cdot}{\sin x}$$

(4 marks)

    b)   Given that $y = \pi$ when $x = \frac{\pi}{6}$, solve the differential equation above.

(2 marks)

5   The curve C has the equation $3e^x + 6y = 2x^2y$.

    a)   (i)   Use implicit differentiation to find an expression for $\frac{dy}{dx}$.

(3 marks)

        (ii)   Show that at the stationary points of C, $y = \frac{3e^x}{4x}$.

(2 marks)

    b)   Hence find the exact coordinates of the two stationary points of C.

(4 marks)

6   A company sets up an advertising campaign to increase sales of margarine. After the campaign, the number of tubs of margarine sold each week, m, increases over time, t weeks, at a rate that is directly proportional to the square root of the number of tubs sold.

    a)   Formulate a differential equation in terms of t, m and a constant k.

(2 marks)

    b)   At the start of the campaign, the company was selling 900 tubs of margarine a week.
        Use this information to solve the differential equation, giving m in terms of k and t.

(4 marks)

    c)   Hence calculate the number of tubs sold in the fifth week after the campaign, given that $k = 2$.

(3 marks)

Vectors

If you did M1, then you've probably seen some of this vector stuff before. If not, you've got lots to look forward to. In any case, we're going to start with the <u>basics</u> — like what vectors are.

Vectors have Magnitude and Direction — Scalars Don't

1) Vectors have both <u>size and direction</u> — e.g. a velocity of 2 m/s on a bearing of 050°, or a displacement of 3 m north. <u>Scalars</u> are just quantities <u>without a direction</u>, e.g. a speed of 2 m/s, a distance of 3 m.

2) Vectors are drawn as lines with arrowheads on them.
   - The <u>length</u> of the line represents the <u>magnitude</u> (size) of the vector (e.g. the speed component of velocity). Sometimes vectors are drawn <u>to scale</u>.
   - The <u>direction</u> of the arrowhead shows the <u>direction</u> of the vector.

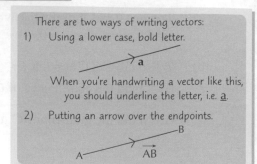

There are two ways of writing vectors:
1) Using a lower case, bold letter.

   When you're handwriting a vector like this, you should underline the letter, i.e. <u>a</u>.
2) Putting an arrow over the endpoints.

Find the Resultant by Drawing Vectors Nose to Tail

You can add vectors together by drawing the arrows <u>nose to tail</u>.
The single vector that goes from the start to the end of the vectors is called the <u>resultant</u> vector.

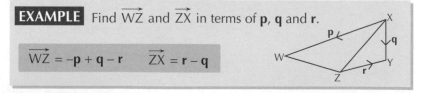

a + b

Resultant: **r = a + b**

a + b = b + a

Resultant: **r = a + b + c**

Subtracting a Vector is the Same as Adding a Negative Vector

1) The vector **–a** is in the <u>opposite direction</u> to the vector **a**. They're both exactly the <u>same size</u>.

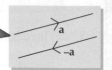

2) So <u>subtracting a vector</u> is the same as <u>adding the negative vector</u>:

$$\mathbf{b} - \mathbf{a} = \mathbf{b} + (-\mathbf{a})$$

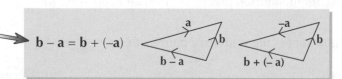

3) You can use the adding and subtracting rules to find a vector <u>in terms of other vectors</u>.

EXAMPLE Find $\overrightarrow{WZ}$ and $\overrightarrow{ZX}$ in terms of **p**, **q** and **r**.

$$\overrightarrow{WZ} = -\mathbf{p} + \mathbf{q} - \mathbf{r} \qquad \overrightarrow{ZX} = \mathbf{r} - \mathbf{q}$$

Vectors a, 2a and 3a are all Parallel

You can <u>multiply</u> a vector by a <u>scalar</u> (just a number, remember) — the <u>length changes</u> but the <u>direction stays the same</u>.

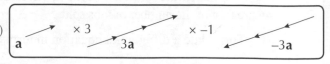

Multiplying a vector by a non-zero scalar always produces a <u>parallel vector</u>.

This is $\frac{2}{3}(9\mathbf{a} + 15\mathbf{b})$.

All these vectors are <u>parallel</u>: $9\mathbf{a} + 15\mathbf{b}$ $18\mathbf{a} + 30\mathbf{b}$ $6\mathbf{a} + 10\mathbf{b}$ $3\mathbf{a} + 5\mathbf{b}$ This is $\frac{1}{3}(9\mathbf{a} + 15\mathbf{b})$.

This is $2(9\mathbf{a} + 15\mathbf{b})$.

Eating pasta = buying anti-pasta?...

If an exam question asks you to show that two lines are <u>parallel</u>, you just have to show that one vector's a <u>multiple</u> of the other. By the way — exam papers often use λ and μ as scalars in vector questions (so you don't confuse them with vectors).

Vectors

There are a few more ways of representing vectors that you need to know about. Then it's off to the third dimension...

Position Vectors Describe Where a Point Lies

You can use a vector to describe the position of a point, in relation to the origin, O.

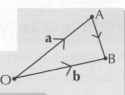

The position vector of point A is $\overrightarrow{OA}$. It's usually called vector **a**.
The position vector of point B is $\overrightarrow{OB}$. It's usually called vector **b**.

You can write other vectors in terms of position vectors: $\overrightarrow{AB} = -\overrightarrow{OA} + \overrightarrow{OB} = \overrightarrow{OB} - \overrightarrow{OA}$
$= -\mathbf{a} + \mathbf{b} = \mathbf{b} - \mathbf{a}$

Vectors can be described using i + j Units

1) A unit vector is any vector with a magnitude of 1 unit.

There's more on unit vectors on the next page.

2) The vectors **i** + **j** are standard unit vectors. **i** is in the direction of the x-axis, and **j** is in the direction of the y-axis. They each have a magnitude of 1 unit, of course.

3) They're a dead handy way of describing any vector. You use them to say how far horizontally and vertically you have to go to get from the start of the vector to the end.

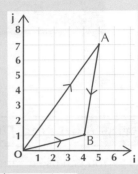

The position vector of point A = **a** = 5**i** + 7**j**
The position vector of point B = **b** = 4**i** + **j**

Vector $\overrightarrow{AB} = \mathbf{b} - \mathbf{a}$
$= (4\mathbf{i} + \mathbf{j}) - (5\mathbf{i} + 7\mathbf{j})$
$= -\mathbf{i} - 6\mathbf{j}$

This tells you that point B lies 4 units to the right and 1 unit above the origin — it's just like coordinates.

Add/subtract the **i** and **j** components separately.

To go from A to B, you go 1 unit left and 6 units down. It's just like a translation.

And then there are Column Vectors

1) If writing i's and j's gets a bit much for your wrists, you can use column vectors instead. $x\mathbf{i} + y\mathbf{j} = \begin{pmatrix} x \\ y \end{pmatrix}$

2) You can write unit vectors as column vectors too: $\mathbf{i} = \begin{pmatrix} 1 \\ 0 \end{pmatrix}$ and $\mathbf{j} = \begin{pmatrix} 0 \\ 1 \end{pmatrix}$.

3) Calculating with them is a breeze. Just add or subtract the top row, then add or subtract the bottom row separately.

4) When you're multiplying a column vector by a scalar, you multiply each number in the column vector by the scalar.

$\mathbf{a} = 5\mathbf{i} + 7\mathbf{j} = \begin{pmatrix} 5 \\ 7 \end{pmatrix}$ $\mathbf{b} = 4\mathbf{i} + \mathbf{j} = \begin{pmatrix} 4 \\ 1 \end{pmatrix}$

$\overrightarrow{AB} = \mathbf{b} - \mathbf{a} = \begin{pmatrix} 4 \\ 1 \end{pmatrix} - \begin{pmatrix} 5 \\ 7 \end{pmatrix} = \begin{pmatrix} -1 \\ -6 \end{pmatrix}$

$2\mathbf{b} - 3\mathbf{a} = 2\begin{pmatrix} 4 \\ 1 \end{pmatrix} - 3\begin{pmatrix} 5 \\ 7 \end{pmatrix} = \begin{pmatrix} 8 \\ 2 \end{pmatrix} - \begin{pmatrix} 15 \\ 21 \end{pmatrix} = \begin{pmatrix} -7 \\ -19 \end{pmatrix}$

You Can Have Vectors in Three Dimensions Too

1) Imagine that the x- and y-axes lie flat on the page. Then imagine a third axis sticking straight through the page at right angles to it — this is the z-axis.

2) The points in three dimensions are given (x, y, z) coordinates.

3) When you're talking vectors, **k** is the unit vector in the direction of the z-axis.

4) You can write three-dimensional vectors as column vectors like this: $x\mathbf{i} + y\mathbf{j} + z\mathbf{k} = \begin{pmatrix} x \\ y \\ z \end{pmatrix}$

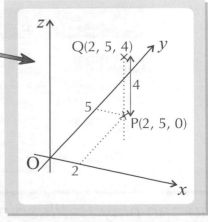

5) So the position vector of point Q is: $2\mathbf{i} + 5\mathbf{j} + 4\mathbf{k} = \begin{pmatrix} 2 \\ 5 \\ 4 \end{pmatrix}$

I've got B + Q units in my kitchen...

In the exam, you'll probably be given column vectors — you can use **i**, **j** and **k** notation if you prefer though.

Vectors

Pythagoras pops up all over the place, and here he is again. Fascinating fact — Pythagoras refused to say words containing the Greek equivalent of the letter c. I read it on the internet, so it has to be true.

Use Pythagoras' Theorem to Find Vector Magnitudes

1) The <u>magnitude</u> of vector **a** is written as $|\mathbf{a}|$, and the magnitude of $\overrightarrow{AB}$ is written as $|\overrightarrow{AB}|$.

> *A vector's magnitude is sometimes called its modulus.*

2) The x and y components of a vector form a convenient <u>right-angled triangle</u>, so just bung them into the <u>Pythagoras formula</u> to find the vector's magnitude.

3) You might be asked to find a <u>unit vector</u> in the direction of a particular vector. Remember — a unit vector has a <u>magnitude of 1</u> (see the previous page).

> A unit vector in the direction of vector $\mathbf{a} = \dfrac{\mathbf{a}}{|\mathbf{a}|}$

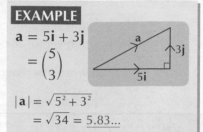

EXAMPLE

$\mathbf{a} = 5\mathbf{i} + 3\mathbf{j}$

$= \begin{pmatrix} 5 \\ 3 \end{pmatrix}$

$|\mathbf{a}| = \sqrt{5^2 + 3^2}$

$\quad = \sqrt{34} = \underline{5.83...}$

EXAMPLE If vector **p** has a magnitude of 12 units, find a unit vector parallel to **p**.

$$\frac{\mathbf{p}}{|\mathbf{p}|} = \frac{\mathbf{p}}{12} = \frac{1}{12}\mathbf{p}$$

You Can Use Pythagoras in Three Dimensions Too

1) You can use a variation of <u>Pythagoras' theorem</u> to find the distance of any point in 3 dimensions from the origin, O.

> The distance of point (x, y, z) from the origin is $\sqrt{x^2 + y^2 + z^2}$

EXAMPLE 1

Find $|\overrightarrow{OQ}|$.

$|\overrightarrow{OQ}| = \sqrt{x^2 + y^2 + z^2}$

$\quad = \sqrt{2^2 + 5^2 + 4^2}$

$\quad = \sqrt{45}$

$\quad = 6.7$ units

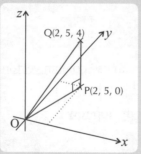

> Here's where this formula comes from:
> $OP = \sqrt{x^2 + y^2}$
> $OP^2 = x^2 + y^2$
> $OQ = \sqrt{OP^2 + z^2}$
> $OQ = \sqrt{x^2 + y^2 + z^2}$

EXAMPLE 2 Find the magnitude of the vector $\mathbf{r} = 5\mathbf{i} + 7\mathbf{j} + 3\mathbf{k}$.

$|\mathbf{r}| = \sqrt{5^2 + 7^2 + 3^2}$

$\quad = \sqrt{83} = 9.1$ units

2) There's also a Pythagoras-based formula for finding <u>the distance between any two points</u>.

> The distance between points (x_1, y_1, z_1) and (x_2, y_2, z_2) is $\sqrt{(x_1 - x_2)^2 + (y_1 - y_2)^2 + (z_1 - z_2)^2}$

EXAMPLE

The position vectors of points A and B are $\begin{pmatrix} 3 \\ 2 \\ 4 \end{pmatrix}$ and $\begin{pmatrix} 2 \\ 6 \\ -5 \end{pmatrix}$ respectively.

Find $|\overrightarrow{AB}|$.

A has the coordinates (3, 2, 4), B has the coordinates (2, 6, –5).

$|\overrightarrow{AB}| = \sqrt{(x_1 - x_2)^2 + (y_1 - y_2)^2 + (z_1 - z_2)^2}$

$\quad = \sqrt{(3 - 2)^2 + (2 - 6)^2 + (4 - (-5))^2}$

$\quad = \sqrt{1 + 16 + 81} = 9.9$ units

You can play Battleships with 3D coordinates too — but you don't have to...

The magnitude is just a <u>scalar</u>, so it doesn't have a direction — the magnitude of $\overrightarrow{AB}$ is the same as the magnitude of $\overrightarrow{BA}$. Squaring the numbers in the formulas gets rid of any minus signs, so you don't have to worry about which way round you subtract the coordinates (phew). There's not a lot new on this page, in fact, it's mostly just good old Pythagoras.

Vector Equations of Lines

At first glance, <u>vector equations of straight lines</u> don't look much like normal straight-line equations. But they're pretty similar if you look closely. In any case, just learn the formulas <u>really well</u> and you'll be fine.

Learn the Equation of the Line *Through a Point* and *Parallel to Another Vector*

A straight line which goes through point A, and is parallel to vector **b**, has the vector equation: $\mathbf{r} = \mathbf{a} + t\mathbf{b}$

a = position vector of point A
r = position vector of a point on the line, and t = a scalar.

A is a fixed point.

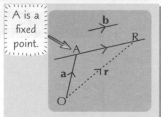

This is pretty much a 3D version of the old $y = mx + c$ equation. **b** is similar to the gradient, m, and **a** gives a point that the line passes through, just like c gives the y-axis intercept.

Each different value you stick in for $\underline{t}$ in the vector equation gives you the <u>position vector, **r**</u>, of a different point on the line.

EXAMPLE A straight line is parallel to the vector $\mathbf{i} + 3\mathbf{j} - 2\mathbf{k}$. It passes through a point with the position vector $3\mathbf{i} + 2\mathbf{j} + 6\mathbf{k}$. Find its vector equation.

$$\mathbf{r} = \mathbf{a} + t\mathbf{b} = (3\mathbf{i} + 2\mathbf{j} + 6\mathbf{k}) + t(\mathbf{i} + 3\mathbf{j} - 2\mathbf{k})$$

Alternative ways of writing this are:
$\mathbf{r} = (3 + t)\mathbf{i} + (2 + 3t)\mathbf{j} + (6 - 2t)\mathbf{k}$,
$$\mathbf{r} = \begin{pmatrix} 3 \\ 2 \\ 6 \end{pmatrix} + t\begin{pmatrix} 1 \\ 3 \\ -2 \end{pmatrix} \text{ and } \mathbf{r} = \begin{pmatrix} 3 + t \\ 2 + 3t \\ 6 - 2t \end{pmatrix}$$

And the Equation of the Line Passing *Through Two Known Points*

A straight line through points C and D, with position vectors **c** and **d**, has the vector equation:

$$\mathbf{r} = \mathbf{c} + t(\mathbf{d} - \mathbf{c})$$ **r** = position vector of a point on the line, t = a scalar.

This is basically the same as the vector equation above. You just have to find a vector in the direction of CD first (i.e. **d** − **c**).

EXAMPLE

A line passes through points with the coordinates (3, 2, 4) and (−1, 3, 0). Find a vector equation for this line.

If $\mathbf{c} = \begin{pmatrix} 3 \\ 2 \\ 4 \end{pmatrix}$, and $\mathbf{d} = \begin{pmatrix} -1 \\ 3 \\ 0 \end{pmatrix}$, then $\mathbf{r} = \begin{pmatrix} 3 \\ 2 \\ 4 \end{pmatrix} + t\left(\begin{pmatrix} -1 \\ 3 \\ 0 \end{pmatrix} - \begin{pmatrix} 3 \\ 2 \\ 4 \end{pmatrix}\right)$ $\Rightarrow$ $\mathbf{r} = \begin{pmatrix} 3 \\ 2 \\ 4 \end{pmatrix} + t\begin{pmatrix} -4 \\ 1 \\ -4 \end{pmatrix}$

Find the *Point of Intersection* of two Lines with *Simultaneous Equations*

If l_1, $\mathbf{r} = \begin{pmatrix} 5 \\ 2 \\ -1 \end{pmatrix} + \mu\begin{pmatrix} 1 \\ -2 \\ -3 \end{pmatrix}$, and l_2, $\mathbf{r} = \begin{pmatrix} 2 \\ 0 \\ 4 \end{pmatrix} + \lambda\begin{pmatrix} 1 \\ 2 \\ -1 \end{pmatrix}$, <u>intersect</u>, there'll be a value for μ and a

If you can't find values that work for both lines, it means the lines don't intersect. Two lines that aren't parallel and don't intersect are called <u>skew lines</u>.

value for λ that result in <u>the same point for both lines</u>. This is the <u>point of intersection</u>.

EXAMPLE Determine whether Line 1 and Line 2 (above) intersect. If they do, find the point of intersection.

At the point of intersection, $\begin{pmatrix} 5 \\ 2 \\ -1 \end{pmatrix} + \mu\begin{pmatrix} 1 \\ -2 \\ -3 \end{pmatrix} = \begin{pmatrix} 2 \\ 0 \\ 4 \end{pmatrix} + \lambda\begin{pmatrix} 1 \\ 2 \\ -1 \end{pmatrix}$. You can get 3 equations from this:
① $5 + \mu = 2 + \lambda$
② $2 - 2\mu = 0 + 2\lambda$
③ $-1 - 3\mu = 4 - \lambda$

Solve the first two <u>simultaneously</u>: $2 \times ①$: $10 + 2\mu = 4 + 2\lambda$ ④
④ − ②: $8 + 4\mu = 4 \Rightarrow \mu = -1$
sub. in ②: $2 - 2(-1) = 0 + 2\lambda \Rightarrow \lambda = 2$

Substitute the values for μ and λ into equation ③. If they make the equation <u>true</u>, then the lines <u>do</u> intersect:
$-1 - (3 \times -1) = 4 - 2 \Rightarrow 2 = 2$ — True, so they do intersect.

Now find the <u>intersection point</u>: $\mathbf{r} = \begin{pmatrix} 5 \\ 2 \\ -1 \end{pmatrix} + \mu\begin{pmatrix} 1 \\ -2 \\ -3 \end{pmatrix} = \begin{pmatrix} 5 \\ 2 \\ -1 \end{pmatrix} - 1\begin{pmatrix} 1 \\ -2 \\ -3 \end{pmatrix} \Rightarrow \mathbf{r} = \begin{pmatrix} 4 \\ 4 \\ 2 \end{pmatrix} = 4\mathbf{i} + 4\mathbf{j} + 2\mathbf{k}$

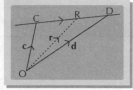

This is the <u>position vector</u> of the intersection point. The coordinates are (4, 4, 2).

Stardate 45283.5, position vector 20076*i* + 23485*j* + 48267*k*...

Ahhh, good old simultaneous equations. Have a look back over your AS notes if you need a reminder on how to do them.

Scalar Product

The <u>scalar product of two vectors</u> is kind of what it says on the tin — two vectors multiplied together to give a <u>scalar result</u>. But this is A2, so it's going to be <u>trickier than simple multiplying</u>. It even involves a bit of cos-ing.

Learn the Definition of the **Scalar Product of Two Vectors**

Scalar Product of Two Vectors

$$\mathbf{a}.\mathbf{b} = |\mathbf{a}||\mathbf{b}|\cos\theta$$

θ is the angle <u>between</u> position vectors $\mathbf{a}$ and $\mathbf{b}$.

<u>Both</u> vectors have to be <u>directed away</u> from the intersection point.

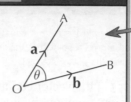

Watch out — the correct angle might not always be obvious.
θ is the angle in the definition.

Here you have to continue $\mathbf{b}$ on so that it's also directed away from the intersection point.

1) The scalar product of two vectors is always a <u>scalar quantity</u> — it's <u>never</u> a vector.

2) The <u>scalar product</u> can be used to calculate the <u>angle</u> between two lines (see the next page)
— $\mathbf{a}.\mathbf{b} = |\mathbf{a}||\mathbf{b}|\cos\theta$ rearranges to $\cos\theta = \dfrac{\mathbf{a}.\mathbf{b}}{|\mathbf{a}||\mathbf{b}|}$.

3) The scalar product $\mathbf{a}.\mathbf{b}$ is read '<u>a dot b</u>'. It's really, really important to put the dot in, as it shows you mean the <u>scalar product</u> (rather than a different sort of vector product that you don't have to worry about in C4).

A **Zero Scalar Product** Means the Vectors are **Perpendicular**

1) If the two vectors are <u>perpendicular</u>, they're at <u>90°</u> to each other.

2) <u>Cos 90° = 0</u>, so the scalar product of the two vectors is <u>0</u>.

Scalar Product of Two Perpendicular Vectors

$$\mathbf{a}.\mathbf{b} = |\mathbf{a}||\mathbf{b}|\cos 90° = 0$$

3) The unit vectors $\mathbf{i}$, $\mathbf{j}$ and $\mathbf{k}$ are all <u>perpendicular</u> to each other.

So, $\mathbf{i}.\mathbf{j} = 1 \times 1 \times 0 = 0$ and $3\mathbf{j}.4\mathbf{k} = 3 \times 4 \times 0 = 0$

4) This all assumes that the vectors are <u>non-zero</u>. Because if either vector was 0, you'd always get a scalar product of <u>0</u>, regardless of the angle between them.

The Scalar Product of **Parallel Vectors** is just the **Product of the Magnitudes**

1) If two vectors are <u>parallel</u>, the angle between them is <u>0°</u>. And <u>cos 0° = 1</u>, so...

Scalar Product of Two Parallel Vectors

$$\mathbf{a}.\mathbf{b} = |\mathbf{a}||\mathbf{b}|\cos 0° = |\mathbf{a}||\mathbf{b}|$$

2) Two $\mathbf{i}$ unit vectors are <u>parallel</u> to each other (as are two $\mathbf{j}$s or two $\mathbf{k}$s).

So, $\mathbf{j}.\mathbf{j} = 1 \times 1 \times 1 = 1$ and $3\mathbf{k}.4\mathbf{k} = 3 \times 4 \times 1 = 12$

3) Again, this all assumes that the vectors are <u>non-zero</u>.

Scaley product — a lizard-skin handbag...

The fact that two perpendicular vectors have a zero scalar product is the key to loads of vector exam questions. E.g. you might be asked to show two vectors are perpendicular, or told that two vectors are perpendicular and asked to find a missing vector. Whatever they ask, you'll definitely have to multiply the two vectors — and you're about to learn how.

Scalar Product

Finding the scalar product of two vectors is super quick and easy once you know how to do it.

Learn This Result for the **Scalar Product**

1) You can use this result to find the <u>scalar product</u> of two known vectors:

$$\text{If } \mathbf{a} = \begin{pmatrix} a_1 \\ a_2 \\ a_3 \end{pmatrix} \text{ and } \mathbf{b} = \begin{pmatrix} b_1 \\ b_2 \\ b_3 \end{pmatrix}, \text{ then } \mathbf{a.b} = a_1 b_1 + a_2 b_2 + a_3 b_3$$

In **i**, **j**, **k** vector form, this is: if $\mathbf{a} = a_1 \mathbf{i} + a_2 \mathbf{j} + a_3 \mathbf{k}$, and $\mathbf{b} = b_1 \mathbf{i} + b_2 \mathbf{j} + b_3 \mathbf{k}$, then $\mathbf{a.b} = a_1 b_1 + a_2 b_2 + a_3 b_3$.

2) The <u>normal laws</u> of multiplication apply to scalar products too — e.g. the <u>commutative law</u> ($\mathbf{a.b} = \mathbf{b.a}$) and the <u>distributive law</u> ($\mathbf{a.(b+c)} = \mathbf{a.b} + \mathbf{a.c}$).

3) By applying these laws, you can derive the result above...

Applying the normal rules for multiplying brackets gives this.

Now use the scalar product formulas on the previous page to work out each of these terms. Unit vectors **i**, **j** and **k** are all <u>perpendicular</u> to each other, so multiplying them together always gives a product of zero.

Using the scalar product definition...

$$\begin{aligned} \mathbf{a.b} &= (a_1 \mathbf{i} + a_2 \mathbf{j} + a_3 \mathbf{k}).(b_1 \mathbf{i} + b_2 \mathbf{j} + b_3 \mathbf{k}) \\ &= (a_1 \mathbf{i}).(b_1 \mathbf{i}) + (a_1 \mathbf{i}).(b_2 \mathbf{j}) + (a_1 \mathbf{i}).(b_3 \mathbf{k}) + (a_2 \mathbf{j}).(b_1 \mathbf{i}) + (a_2 \mathbf{j}).(b_2 \mathbf{j}) \\ &\quad + (a_2 \mathbf{j}).(b_3 \mathbf{k}) + (a_3 \mathbf{k}).(b_1 \mathbf{i}) + (a_3 \mathbf{k}).(b_2 \mathbf{j}) + (a_3 \mathbf{k}).(b_3 \mathbf{k}) \\ &= (a_1 \mathbf{i}).(b_1 \mathbf{i}) + 0 + 0 + 0 + (a_2 \mathbf{j}).(b_2 \mathbf{j}) + 0 + 0 + 0 + (a_3 \mathbf{k}).(b_3 \mathbf{k}) \\ &= (a_1 \mathbf{i}).(b_1 \mathbf{i}) + (a_2 \mathbf{j}).(b_2 \mathbf{j}) + (a_3 \mathbf{k}).(b_3 \mathbf{k}) \\ &= |a_1 \mathbf{i}||b_1 \mathbf{i}|\cos 0° + |a_2 \mathbf{j}||b_2 \mathbf{j}|\cos 0° + |a_3 \mathbf{k}||b_3 \mathbf{k}|\cos 0° \\ &= a_1 b_1 + a_2 b_2 + a_3 b_3 \end{aligned}$$

Cos 0° = 1

Use the **Scalar Product** to Find the **Angle** Between Two Vectors

Finding the <u>angle</u> between two vectors often crops up in vector exam questions.
It's just a matter of using the above result to find the <u>scalar product</u> of the two vectors,
then popping it into the <u>scalar product definition</u>, $\cos \theta = \dfrac{\mathbf{a.b}}{|\mathbf{a}||\mathbf{b}|}$, to find the <u>angle</u>.

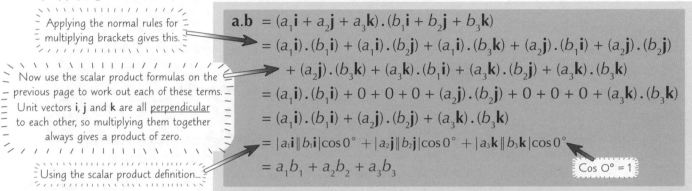

EXAMPLE

Find the angle between the vectors $\mathbf{a} = \begin{pmatrix} -1 \\ -6 \\ 0 \end{pmatrix}$ and $\mathbf{b} = \begin{pmatrix} 4 \\ 2 \\ 8 \end{pmatrix}$.

1) Find the <u>scalar product</u> of the vectors.

$$\mathbf{a.b} = (-1 \times 4) + (-6 \times 2) + (0 \times 8) = -4 - 12 + 0 = -16$$

This uses the result above.

2) Find the <u>magnitude</u> of each vector (see page 84).

$$|\mathbf{a}| = \sqrt{(-1)^2 + (-6)^2 + (0)^2} = \sqrt{37} \qquad |\mathbf{b}| = \sqrt{(4)^2 + (2)^2 + (8)^2} = \sqrt{84}$$

3) Now plug these values into the equation and find the <u>angle</u>.

$$\cos \theta = \frac{\mathbf{a.b}}{|\mathbf{a}||\mathbf{b}|} = \frac{-16}{\sqrt{37}\sqrt{84}} \quad \Rightarrow \quad \theta = \underline{106.7°}$$

Scalar product — Ooops. I'd best stop eating chips every day...

So when you scalar multiply two vectors, you basically multiply the **i** components together, multiply the **j** components together, multiply the **k** components together, then add up all the products. You end up with <u>just a number</u>, with no **i**s, **j**s or **k**s attached to it. You'll see this more in the examples on the next page, so don't worry if it seems a bit strange at the mo.

Scalar Product

Right, you've learnt the definitions and the facts. Now it's time to put them to good use.

You Might have to Find the Angle from *Vector Equations* or from *Two Points*

1) If you're given the <u>vector equations</u> for lines that you're finding the angle between, it's important to use the correct bits of the vector equations.

2) You use the **b** bit in $\mathbf{r} = \mathbf{a} + t\mathbf{b}$ (the '<u>parallel to</u>' or the '<u>direction</u>' bit).

> **EXAMPLE**   Line l has the equation $\mathbf{r} = \begin{pmatrix} 2 \\ 0 \\ 4 \end{pmatrix} + \lambda \begin{pmatrix} 1 \\ 2 \\ -1 \end{pmatrix}$.
>
> Point A and point B have the coordinates (4, 4, 2) and (1, 0, 3) respectively. Point A lies on l.
> Find the acute angle between l and line segment AB.

1) First draw a <u>diagram</u> — it'll make everything clearer.

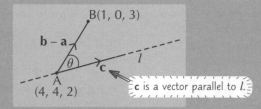

c is a vector parallel to l.

2) Find the vectors that you want to <u>know the angle</u> between.

$$\overrightarrow{AB} = \mathbf{b} - \mathbf{a} = \begin{pmatrix} 1 \\ 0 \\ 3 \end{pmatrix} - \begin{pmatrix} 4 \\ 4 \\ 2 \end{pmatrix} = \begin{pmatrix} -3 \\ -4 \\ 1 \end{pmatrix}$$ and the 'parallel to' bit of l (which we've called **c**): $\mathbf{c} = \begin{pmatrix} 1 \\ 2 \\ -1 \end{pmatrix}$

3) Find the <u>scalar product</u> of these vectors. $\overrightarrow{AB} \cdot \mathbf{c} = (-3 \times 1) + (-4 \times 2) + (1 \times -1) = -3 - 8 - 1 = -12$

4) Find the <u>magnitude</u> of each vector.

$$|\overrightarrow{AB}| = \sqrt{(-3)^2 + (-4)^2 + (1)^2} = \sqrt{26} \qquad |\mathbf{c}| = \sqrt{(1)^2 + (2)^2 + (-1)^2} = \sqrt{6}$$

5) Now plug these values into the equation and find the angle.

$$\cos\theta = \frac{\overrightarrow{AB} \cdot \mathbf{c}}{|\overrightarrow{AB}||\mathbf{c}|} = \frac{-12}{\sqrt{26}\sqrt{6}} \Rightarrow \theta = 164° \text{ (3 s.f.)}$$

6) Whoops. The formula gives the <u>non-acute angle</u> — the situation must have been more like this:

Remember — the vectors diverge on each side of the angle given by the formula.

Don't panic — just <u>subtract this angle from 180°</u> to get the acute angle, x, between the lines.

$$180° - 164° = 16°$$

Prove Lines are *Perpendicular* by Showing that the *Scalar Product = 0*

> **EXAMPLE**   Show that the lines $\mathbf{r}_1 = (\mathbf{i} + 6\mathbf{j} + 2\mathbf{k}) + \lambda(\mathbf{i} + 2\mathbf{j} + 2\mathbf{k})$ and $\mathbf{r}_2 = (3\mathbf{i} - \mathbf{j} + \mathbf{k}) + \mu(4\mathbf{i} - 3\mathbf{j} + \mathbf{k})$
> are perpendicular.

1) Make sure you've got the right bit of each vector equation — it's the <u>direction</u> you're interested in, so it's **b** in $\mathbf{r} = \mathbf{a} + t\mathbf{b}$. $\mathbf{i} + 2\mathbf{j} + 2\mathbf{k}$ and $4\mathbf{i} - 3\mathbf{j} + \mathbf{k}$

2) Find the <u>scalar product</u> of the vectors. $(\mathbf{i} + 2\mathbf{j} + 2\mathbf{k}).(4\mathbf{i} - 3\mathbf{j} + \mathbf{k}) = 4 - 6 + 2 = 0$

3) Draw the correct <u>conclusion</u>.   The scalar product is 0, so the vectors are <u>perpendicular</u>.

P...P...P... — prove perpendicularity using products...

They'll word these questions in a zillion different ways. Drawing a diagram can often help you figure out what's what.

C4 Section 6 — Practice Questions

Vectors might cause some mild vexation. It's not the simplest of topics, but <u>practising</u> does help.
Try these warm-up questions and see if you can remember what you've just read.

Warm-up Questions

1) Give two vectors that are <u>parallel</u> to each of the following: a) $2\mathbf{a}$ b) $3\mathbf{i} + 4\mathbf{j} - 2\mathbf{k}$ c) $\begin{pmatrix} 1 \\ 2 \\ -1 \end{pmatrix}$

2) Find these vectors in terms of vectors $\mathbf{a}$, $\mathbf{b}$ and $\mathbf{c}$.

   a) $\overrightarrow{AB}$ b) $\overrightarrow{BA}$ c) $\overrightarrow{CB}$ d) $\overrightarrow{AC}$

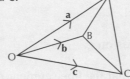

3) Give the <u>position vector</u> of point P,
    which has the coordinates $(2, -4, 5)$.
    Give your answer in <u>$\mathbf{i}$, $\mathbf{j}$ vector</u> form.

4) Find the <u>magnitudes</u> of these vectors:

   a) $3\mathbf{i} + 4\mathbf{j} - 2\mathbf{k}$ b) $\begin{pmatrix} 1 \\ 2 \\ -1 \end{pmatrix}$

5) If $A(1, 2, 3)$ and $B(3, -1, -2)$, find: a) $|\overrightarrow{AB}|$ b) $|\overrightarrow{OA}|$ c) $|\overrightarrow{OB}|$

6) Find <u>vector equations</u> for the following <u>lines</u>.
    Give your answer in $\mathbf{i}$, $\mathbf{j}$, $\mathbf{k}$ form and in <u>column vector</u> form.

   a) a straight line through $(4, 1, 2)$, parallel to vector $3\mathbf{i} + \mathbf{j} - \mathbf{k}$.

   b) a straight line through $(2, -1, 1)$ and $(0, 2, 3)$.

7) Find <u>three points</u> that lie on the line with <u>vector equation</u> $\mathbf{r} = \begin{pmatrix} 3 \\ 2 \\ 4 \end{pmatrix} + t\begin{pmatrix} -1 \\ 3 \\ 0 \end{pmatrix}$.

8) Find $\mathbf{a}.\mathbf{b}$ if: a) $\mathbf{a} = 3\mathbf{i} + 4\mathbf{j}$ and $\mathbf{b} = \mathbf{i} - 2\mathbf{j} + 3\mathbf{k}$ b) $\mathbf{a} = \begin{pmatrix} 4 \\ 2 \\ 1 \end{pmatrix}$ and $\mathbf{b} = \begin{pmatrix} 3 \\ -4 \\ -3 \end{pmatrix}$

9) $\mathbf{r}_1 = \begin{pmatrix} 2 \\ -1 \\ 2 \end{pmatrix} + t\begin{pmatrix} -4 \\ 6 \\ -2 \end{pmatrix}$ and $\mathbf{r}_2 = \begin{pmatrix} 3 \\ 2 \\ 4 \end{pmatrix} + u\begin{pmatrix} -1 \\ 3 \\ 0 \end{pmatrix}$

   a) Show that these lines <u>intersect</u> and find the <u>position vector</u> of their <u>intersection point</u>.
   b) Find the <u>angle</u> between these lines.

10) Find a vector that is <u>perpendicular</u> to $3\mathbf{i} + 4\mathbf{j} - 2\mathbf{k}$.

You might look at an exam question and think that it's complete <u>gobbledegook</u>. But chances are, when you look at
it carefully, you can <u>use what you know</u> to solve it. If you don't know what you need to, you can peek back while
doing these questions. You won't be able to in the proper exam, so all the more reason to practise on these.

Exam Questions

1   The quadrilateral ABCD has vertices $A(1, 5, 9)$, $B(3, 2, 1)$, $C(-2, 4, 3)$ and $D(5, -1, -7)$.

   a) Find the vector $\overrightarrow{AB}$.

   (2 marks)

   b) C and D lie on line l_1. Using the parameter μ, find the vector equation of l_1.

   (2 marks)

   c) Find the coordinates of the intersection point of l_1 and the line that passes through AB.

   (5 marks)

   d) (i) Find the acute angle between l_1 and AB. Give your answer to 1 decimal place.

   (4 marks)

   (ii) Find the shortest distance from point A to l_1.

   (4 marks)

C4 Section 6 — Practice Questions

And there's more, as Jimmy Cricket (not to be confused with Jiminy Cricket) used to say.

2   The lines l_1 and l_2 are given by the vector equations:

$$l_1: \quad \mathbf{r} = \begin{pmatrix} 3 \\ -3 \\ -2 \end{pmatrix} + \mu \begin{pmatrix} 1 \\ -4 \\ 2 \end{pmatrix} \qquad l_2: \quad \mathbf{r} = \begin{pmatrix} 10 \\ -21 \\ 11 \end{pmatrix} + \lambda \begin{pmatrix} -3 \\ 12 \\ -6 \end{pmatrix}$$

a)   Show that l_1 and l_2 are parallel.

(1 mark)

b)   Show that point A(2, 1, –4) lies on l_1.

(2 marks)

c)   Point B lies on l_2 and is such that the line segment AB is perpendicular to l_1 and l_2. Find the position vector of point B.

(6 marks)

d)   Find $|\overrightarrow{AB}|$.

(2 marks)

3   The lines l_1 and l_2 are given by the equations: $l_1: \mathbf{r} = \begin{pmatrix} 3 \\ 0 \\ -2 \end{pmatrix} + \lambda \begin{pmatrix} 1 \\ 3 \\ -2 \end{pmatrix} \qquad l_2: \mathbf{r} = \begin{pmatrix} 0 \\ 2 \\ 1 \end{pmatrix} + \mu \begin{pmatrix} 2 \\ -5 \\ -3 \end{pmatrix}$

a)   Show that l_1 and l_2 do not intersect.

(4 marks)

b)   Point P has position vector $\begin{pmatrix} 5 \\ 8 \\ -3 \end{pmatrix}$. Point Q is the image of point P after reflection in line l_1.

    Point P and Q both lie on the line with equation $\mathbf{r} = \begin{pmatrix} 5 \\ 4 \\ -9 \end{pmatrix} + t \begin{pmatrix} 0 \\ 2 \\ 3 \end{pmatrix}$.

    (i)   Find the intersection point of line segment PQ and line l_1.

(4 marks)

    (ii)   Show that the line segment PQ and line l_1 are perpendicular.

(2 marks)

    (iii)   Find the position vector of point Q.

(3 marks)

4   Point A has the position vector $\begin{pmatrix} 3 \\ 2 \\ 1 \end{pmatrix}$ and point B has position vector $\begin{pmatrix} 3 \\ -4 \\ -1 \end{pmatrix}$.

a)   Show that AOB is a right-angled triangle.

(3 marks)

b)   Find angle ABO in the triangle using the scalar product definition.

(5 marks)

c)   (i)   Point C has the position vector $\begin{pmatrix} 3 \\ -1 \\ 0 \end{pmatrix}$. Show that triangle OAC is isosceles.

(3 marks)

    (ii)   Calculate the area of triangle OAC.

(4 marks)

d)   (i)   Find a vector equation for line l, which passes through points A and B.

(2 marks)

    (ii)   The point D lies on line l and has the position vector $\begin{pmatrix} a \\ b \\ 1 \end{pmatrix}$. Find a and b.

(3 marks)

General Certificate of Education
Advanced Subsidiary (AS) and Advanced Level

Core Mathematics C4 — Practice Exam One

Time Allowed: 1 hour 30 min

Graphical calculators may be used for this exam.

Give any non-exact numerical answers to an appropriate degree of accuracy.

There are 75 marks available for this paper.

1   a)   Express $\dfrac{(x^2 - 9)(3x^2 - 10x - 8)}{(6x + 4)(x^2 - 7x + 12)}$ as a fraction in its simplest form.

(2 marks)

    b)   Divide $2x^3 - x^2 - 16x + 3$ by $x^2 - 3x - 1$, stating the quotient and remainder.

(4 marks)

2   A comic book was sold for $0.10 on January 1st, 1955. At the beginning of 2010, it was worth $95. The value, V of the comic is modelled by $V = Ak^t$, where t is the time in years since it was first sold and A and k are constants.

    a)   State the value of A.

(1 mark)

    b)   Show that $k = 1.132767$, correct to 6 decimal places.

(3 marks)

    c)   Hence find the year in which the comic will be worth $150.

(3 marks)

3   The graph below shows the curve of $y = \dfrac{1 + \cos x}{2}$:

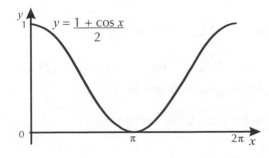

    a)   Use the double angle formula for cos to show that
$$\frac{1 + \cos x}{2} = \cos^2 \frac{x}{2}.$$

(3 marks)

    b)   Hence find the exact values of x for which $\cos^2 \frac{x}{2} = 0.75$ in the interval $0 \le x \le 2\pi$.

(4 marks)

4   The curve C is defined by the parametric equations $x = \dfrac{\sin \theta}{2} - 3$, $y = 5 - \cos 2\theta$.

    a)   (i)   Find an expression for $\dfrac{dy}{dx}$ in terms of θ.

(3 marks)

        (ii)   Hence find the equation of the tangent to C at the point where $\theta = \dfrac{\pi}{6}$.

(3 marks)

    b)   Find a Cartesian equation for C in the form $y = \mathrm{f}(x)$.

(3 marks)

5   a)   Find integers A and B, such that $\dfrac{5x + 4}{(2 - x)(1 + 3x)} \equiv \dfrac{A}{(2 - x)} + \dfrac{B}{(1 + 3x)}$.

(5 marks)

    b)   Hence find the binomial expansion of $\dfrac{5x + 4}{(2 - x)(1 + 3x)}$, up to and including the term in x^3.

(6 marks)

    c)   Find the range of values for which your answer to part b) is valid.

(2 marks)

6   A curve has the equation $x^3 + x^2 y = y^2 - 1$.

    a)   Use implicit differentiation to find an expression for $\dfrac{dy}{dx}$.

(4 marks)

The points P and Q lie on the curve. P has coordinates $(1, a)$ and Q has coordinates $(1, b)$.

    b)   (i)   Find the values of a and b, given that $a > b$.

(2 marks)

        (ii)   Find the equation of the normal to the curve at Q.

(3 marks)

7   Line L_1 has vector equation: $\mathbf{r} = \begin{pmatrix} -1 \\ 0 \\ 3 \end{pmatrix} + \lambda \begin{pmatrix} 2 \\ 2 \\ 1 \end{pmatrix}$.

a)   Show that the line passing through points $P(-2, -2, -1)$ and $Q(-5, -4, 1)$
     intersects with L_1 and find the point at which they meet.

(5 marks)

b)   Given that $\overrightarrow{OT} = 3\overrightarrow{OP}$, show that the distance between Q and T is $\sqrt{21}$.

(3 marks)

c) $\overrightarrow{PV}$ is perpendicular to L_1. If the coordinates of V are $(0, f, g)$, show that $2f + g = -9$.

(3 marks)

d)   The line L_2 is parallel to the vector $\begin{pmatrix} 1 \\ 1 \\ 1 \end{pmatrix}$. Find the acute angle between L_1 and L_2.

(3 marks)

8   a)   An ecologist is monitoring the population of newts in a colony. The rate of increase of the
         population is directly proportional to the square root of the current number of newts in the colony.
         When there were 36 newts in the colony, the rate of change was calculated to be 0.36.

         Formulate a differential equation to model the rate of change, in terms of the variables
         N (number of newts), t (time in weeks).

(3 marks)

    b)   After more research, the ecologist decides that the differential equation
         $$\frac{dN}{dt} = \frac{kN}{\sqrt{t}},$$
         for a positive constant k, is a better model for the population.

         When the ecologist began the survey, the initial population of newts in the colony was 25.

         (i)   Solve the differential equation, leaving your answer in terms of k and t.

(4 marks)

         (ii) Given that the value of k is 0.05, calculate how long (to the nearest week) it will take for the
               population to double.

(3 marks)

General Certificate of Education
Advanced Subsidiary (AS) and Advanced Level

Core Mathematics C4 — Practice Exam Two

Time Allowed: 1 hour 30 min

Graphical calculators may be used for this exam.

Give any non-exact numerical answers to an appropriate degree of accuracy.

There are 75 marks available for this paper.

1   a)   Express $\dfrac{5x^2 + 10x - 13}{(2 - x)^2(1 + 4x)}$ in partial fractions of the form $\dfrac{A}{(2 - x)} + \dfrac{B}{(2 - x)^2} + \dfrac{C}{(1 + 4x)}$,

where A, B and C are constants to be found.

(5 marks)

  b)   Hence find $\displaystyle\int \frac{5x^2 + 10x - 13}{(2 - x)^2(1 + 4x)}\,\mathrm{d}x$.

(4 marks)

2   a)   Write $\sqrt{2}\cos\theta - 3\sin\theta$ in the form $R\cos(\theta + \alpha)$, where $R > 0$ and $0 \le \alpha \le \frac{\pi}{2}$.

(3 marks)

  b)   Hence, or otherwise, solve the equation $\sqrt{2}\cos\theta - 3\sin\theta = 3$ for $0 \le \theta \le 2\pi$.
Give your answers to 3 significant figures.

(4 marks)

  c)   Hence find the maximum and minimum values of $(\sqrt{2}\cos\theta - 3\sin\theta)^4$, and state
where the maximum and minimum points occur in the interval $0 \le \theta \le 2\pi$.

(4 marks)

3   a)   Find the binomial expansion of $(1 - x)^{-\frac{1}{2}}$, up to and including the term in x^3.

(2 marks)

  b)   (i)   Hence show that $(25 - 4x)^{-\frac{1}{2}} \approx \frac{1}{5} + \frac{2}{125}x + \frac{6}{3125}x^2 + \frac{4}{15625}x^3$ for small values of x.

(4 marks)

   (ii)   State the range of values of x for which the expansion from part (i) is valid.

(1 mark)

  c)   Use your expansion from b) with a suitable value of x to show that $\frac{1}{\sqrt{20}} \approx \frac{447}{2000}$.

(3 marks)

4   A curve, C, (shown below) has parametric equations
$$x = t^2 + 2t - 3, \qquad y = 2 - t^3.$$

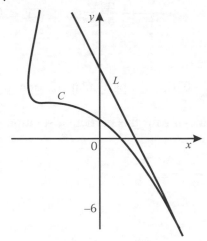

a)   The line L is the tangent to C at $y = -6$. Show that the equation of L is $y = -2x + 4$.

(3 marks)

b) L also meets C at point P.

(i)   Find the coordinates of P.

(3 marks)

(ii)   Find the equation of the normal to the curve at P.

(3 marks)

5   The UK population, P, of an endangered species of bird has been modelled over time, t years, by the function:

$$P = 5700e^{-0.15t} \quad (t \geq 0)$$

The time $t = 0$ is set as the beginning of the year 2010.

a)   State the UK population of the species at the start of 2010.

(1 mark)

b)   Predict the UK population of the species at the start of 2020.

(2 marks)

c)   Predict the year that the population will drop to below 1000.

(2 marks)

d)   Sketch a graph to show the predicted UK population of the species between 2010 and 2025.

(3 marks)

6 a) Find the general solution to the differential equation

$$\frac{e^{2x} + x^2}{e^{2x} + x}\frac{dy}{dx} = 2y, \quad x,y \geq 0.$$

(7 marks)

   b) (i) Given that $y = 3$ when $x = 0$, find the particular solution to the differential equation above.

(2 marks)

       (ii) Hence find the exact value of y for this particular solution when $x = 3$.

(2 marks)

7 A curve is defined by the implicit function $\sin \pi x - \cos \left(\frac{\pi y}{2}\right) = 0.5$, for $0 \leq x \leq 2$, $0 \leq y \leq 2$.

   a) Show that $\dfrac{dy}{dx} = -\dfrac{2\cos \pi x}{\sin \frac{\pi y}{2}}$.

(2 marks)

   b) Hence find:
       (i) the coordinates of the stationary point of the curve,

(4 marks)

       (ii) the equation of the tangent to the curve when $x = \frac{1}{6}$.

(3 marks)

8 Vector **x** is perpendicular to both vector **y** and vector **z**.

$$\mathbf{x} = \begin{pmatrix} p \\ \frac{3}{5} \\ q \end{pmatrix}, \quad \mathbf{y} = \begin{pmatrix} 15 \\ -20 \\ 3 \end{pmatrix}, \quad \mathbf{z} = \begin{pmatrix} \frac{3}{2} \\ -2 \\ 4 \end{pmatrix}.$$

   a) (i) Find the values of p and q.

(3 marks)

       (ii) Find a unit vector in the direction of **y**.

(2 marks)

   b) Given that the scalar product of **y** and **z** is 74.5, show that the angle between these vectors is 51° to the nearest degree.

(3 marks)

Probability Distributions

Hello and welcome to S2. You had a taster of <u>discrete random variables</u> in S1 — now it's time for the juicy stuff.

Getting your head round this **Basic Stuff** is Important

This first bit isn't particularly interesting. But understanding the difference between X and x (bear with me) might make the later stuff a bit less confusing. Might.

1) X (upper case) is just the <u>name</u> of a <u>random variable</u>. So X could be 'score on a dice' — it's <u>just a name</u>.

2) A <u>random variable</u> doesn't have a <u>fixed</u> value. Like with a dice score — the value on any 'roll' is all down to chance.

3) x (lower case) is a <u>particular value</u> that X can take. So for one roll of a dice, x could be 1, 2, 3, 4, 5 or 6.

4) <u>Discrete</u> random variables have only a <u>certain number</u> of possible values. Often these values are whole numbers, but they don't have to be. Usually there are only a few possible values (e.g. the possible scores with one roll of a dice).

5) A <u>probability distribution</u> is a <u>table showing the possible values</u> of x, plus the <u>probability</u> for each one.

6) A <u>probability function</u> is a formula that generates the probabilities for different values of x.

All the Probabilities **Add up to 1**

For a discrete random variable X:

$$\sum_{\text{all} x} P(X=x) = 1$$

This says that if you add up the probabilities of all the possible values of X, you get 1.

EXAMPLE   The random variable X has probability function $P(X = x) = kx$ for $x = 1, 2, 3$. Find the value of k.

So X has three possible values ($x = 1, 2$ and 3), and the probability of each is kx (where you need to find k).

It's easier to understand with a table:

x	1	2	3
$P(X = x)$	$k \times 1 = k$	$k \times 2 = 2k$	$k \times 3 = 3k$

Now just use the formula: $\sum_{\text{all} x} P(X = x) = 1$ Here, this means: $k + 2k + 3k = 6k = 1$

i.e. $k = \dfrac{1}{6}$ Piece of cake.

EXAMPLE   The discrete random variable X has the probability distribution shown below.

x	0	1	2	3	4
$P(X = x)$	0.1	0.2	0.3	0.2	a

Find: (i) the value of a,   (ii) $P(X < 3)$,   (iii) $P(2 \le X < 4)$.

(i)   Use the formula $\sum_{\text{all} x} P(X = x) = 1$ again.

From the table: $0.1 + 0.2 + 0.3 + 0.2 + a = 1$
$0.8 + a = 1$
$a = 0.2$

(ii)   The probability that 'X is less than 3' means the probability that 'X is 0, or X is 1, or X is 2'. So just add up the three probabilities.

$P(X < 3) = P(X = 0) + P(X = 1) + P(X = 2) = 0.1 + 0.2 + 0.3 = \underline{0.6}$

Careful with the inequality signs — you need to include $x = 2$ but not $x = 4$.

(iii)   This is asking for the probability that 'X is greater than or equal to 2, but less than 4'. Easy — just add up the probabilities again.

$P(2 \le X < 4) = P(X = 2) + P(X = 3) = 0.3 + 0.2 = \underline{0.5}$

Probability Distributions

You won't always be given the <u>probability distribution</u> — you'll sometimes have to <u>work it out</u> by calculating probabilities.

EXAMPLE An unbiased six-sided dice has faces marked 1, 1, 1, 2, 2, 3.
The dice is rolled twice. Let X be the random variable "sum of the two scores on the dice".
Show that $P(X = 4) = \frac{5}{18}$. Find the probability distribution of X.

① Make a table showing the 36 possible outcomes.
You can see from the table that 10 of these have the outcome $X = 4$

... so $\boxed{P(X=4)=\frac{10}{36}=\frac{5}{18}}$

Score on roll 1

+	1	1	1	2	2	3
1	2	2	2	3	3	4
1	2	2	2	3	3	4
1	2	2	2	3	3	4
2	3	3	3	4	4	5
2	3	3	3	4	4	5
3	4	4	4	5	5	6

Score on roll 2

Don't forget to change the fractions into their simplest form.

② Use the table to work out the probabilities for the other outcomes and then fill in a table summarising the probability distribution. So...

... $\frac{9}{36}$ of the outcomes are a score of 2

... $\frac{12}{36}$ of the outcomes are a score of 3

... $\frac{4}{36}$ of the outcomes are a score of 5

... $\frac{1}{36}$ of the outcomes are a score of 6

x	2	3	4	5	6
$P(X = x)$	$\frac{1}{4}$	$\frac{1}{3}$	$\frac{5}{18}$	$\frac{1}{9}$	$\frac{1}{36}$

Do Complicated questions Bit by bit

EXAMPLE A game involves rolling two fair dice. If the sum of the scores is greater than 10 then the player wins 50p. If the sum is between 8 and 10 (inclusive) then they win 20p. Otherwise they get nothing. If X is the random variable "amount player wins", find the probability distribution of X.

There are <u>3 possible values</u> for X (0, 20 and 50) and you need the <u>probability</u> of each.
To work these out, you need the probability of getting various totals on the dice.

① You need to know $P(8 \le \text{score} \le 10)$ — the probability that the score is between 8 and 10 <u>inclusive</u> (i.e. including 8 and 10) and $P(11 \le \text{score} \le 12)$ — the probability that the score is <u>greater than</u> 10.

This means working out: $P(\text{score} = 8)$, $P(\text{score} = 9)$, $P(\text{score} = 10)$, $P(\text{score} = 11)$ and $P(\text{score} = 12)$. Use a table...

②

Score on dice 1

+	1	2	3	4	5	6
1	2	3	4	5	6	7
2	3	4	5	6	7	8
3	4	5	6	7	8	9
4	5	6	7	8	9	10
5	6	7	8	9	10	11
6	7	8	9	10	11	12

Score on dice 2

There are 36 possible outcomes...

...5 of these have a total of 8 — so the probability of scoring 8 is $\frac{5}{36}$

...4 have a total of 9 — so the probability of scoring 9 is $\frac{4}{36}$

...the probability of scoring 10 is $\frac{3}{36}$

...the probability of scoring 11 is $\frac{2}{36}$

...the probability of scoring 12 is $\frac{1}{36}$

③ To find the probabilities you need, you just add the right bits together:

$P(X = 20p) = P(8 \le \text{score} \le 10) = \frac{5}{36} + \frac{4}{36} + \frac{3}{36} = \frac{12}{36} = \frac{1}{3}$ $P(X = 50p) = P(11 \le \text{score} \le 12) = \frac{2}{36} + \frac{1}{36} = \frac{3}{36} = \frac{1}{12}$

To find $P(X = 0)$ just take the total of the two probabilities above from 1 (since $X = 0$ is the only other possibility).

$P(X = 0) = 1 - \left[\frac{12}{36} + \frac{3}{36}\right] = 1 - \frac{15}{36} = \frac{21}{36} = \frac{7}{12}$

④ Now just stick all this info in a table (and check that the probabilities all add up to 1):

x	0	20	50
$P(X = x)$	$\frac{7}{12}$	$\frac{1}{3}$	$\frac{1}{12}$

Useful quotes: All you need in life is ignorance and confidence, then success is sure*...

With all this working out of probabilities, you could be forgiven for thinking you're still doing S1. But I can confirm this is S2 alright. And it seems like your probability skills are as in demand as ever — since if you can find the probabilities of the different outcomes, you can find the probability distribution. And remember — ALL THE PROBABILITIES SHOULD ADD UP TO 1.

* Mark Twain

Expected Values, Mean and Variance

This is all about the mean and variance of <u>random variables</u> — <u>not</u> a load of data. It's a tricky concept, but bear with it.

Discrete Random Variables have an 'Expected Value' or 'Mean'

You can work out the <u>expected value</u> (or 'mean') $E(X)$ for a discrete <u>random variable</u> X. $E(X)$ is a kind of 'theoretical mean' — it's what you'd <u>expect</u> the mean of X to be if you took <u>loads</u> of readings. <u>In practice</u>, the mean of your results is unlikely to match the theoretical mean <u>exactly</u>, but it should be pretty near.

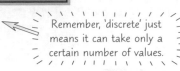
Remember, 'discrete' just means it can take only a certain number of values.

If the possible values of X are x_1, x_2, x_3,... then the expected value of X is:

$$\text{Mean} = \text{Expected Value } E(X) = \sum x_i P(X = x_i) = \sum x_i p_i$$

$p_i = P(X = x_i)$

EXAMPLE The probability distribution of X, the number of daughters in a family of 3 children, is shown in the table. Find the expected number of daughters.

x_i	0	1	2	3
p_i	$\frac{1}{8}$	$\frac{3}{8}$	$\frac{3}{8}$	$\frac{1}{8}$

$$\text{Mean} = \sum x_i p_i = \left[0 \times \tfrac{1}{8}\right] + \left[1 \times \tfrac{3}{8}\right] + \left[2 \times \tfrac{3}{8}\right] + \left[3 \times \tfrac{1}{8}\right] = 0 + \tfrac{3}{8} + \tfrac{6}{8} + \tfrac{3}{8} = \tfrac{12}{8} = 1.5$$

So the <u>expected</u> number of daughters is 1.5 — which sounds a bit weird.
But all it means is that if you check a <u>large number</u> of 3-child families, the <u>mean</u> will be close to 1.5.

The Variance measures how Spread Out the distribution is

You can also find the <u>variance</u> of a random variable. It's the 'expected variance' of a <u>large number</u> of readings.

$$\text{Var}(X) = E(X^2) - [E(X)]^2 = \sum x_i^2 p_i - \left[\sum x_i p_i\right]^2$$

This formula needs $E(X^2) = \sum x_i^2 p_i$ — take each possible value of x, square it, multiply it by its probability and then add up all the results. There's more on this on the next page.

EXAMPLE Work out the variance for the '3 daughters' example above:

First work out $E(X^2)$: $E(X^2) = \sum x_i^2 p_i = \left[0^2 \times \tfrac{1}{8}\right] + \left[1^2 \times \tfrac{3}{8}\right] + \left[2^2 \times \tfrac{3}{8}\right] + \left[3^2 \times \tfrac{1}{8}\right]$
$$= 0 + \tfrac{3}{8} + \tfrac{12}{8} + \tfrac{9}{8} = \tfrac{24}{8} = \underline{3}$$

As always, if you're asked for the standard deviation of X, you just take the square root of Var(X).

Now you take away the mean squared: $\text{Var}(X) = E(X^2) - [E(X)]^2 = 3 - 1.5^2 = 3 - 2.25 = \underline{0.75}$

You can think of this as 'the mean of the squares minus the square of the mean'.

EXAMPLE X has the probability function $P(X = x) = k(x + 1)$ for $x = 0, 1, 2, 3, 4$. Find the mean and variance of X.

① First you need to find k — work out all the probabilities and make sure they add up to 1.

$P(X = 0) = k \times (0 + 1) = k$. Similarly, $P(X = 1) = 2k, P(X = 2) = 3k, P(X = 3) = 4k, P(X = 4) = 5k$.

So $k + 2k + 3k + 4k + 5k = 1$, i.e. $15k = 1$, and so $k = \tfrac{1}{15}$

Now you can work out p_1, p_2, p_3,... where $p_1 = P(X = 1)$ etc.

② Now use the formulas — find the mean $E(X)$ first:

$$E(X) = \sum x_i p_i = \left[0 \times \tfrac{1}{15}\right] + \left[1 \times \tfrac{2}{15}\right] + \left[2 \times \tfrac{3}{15}\right] + \left[3 \times \tfrac{4}{15}\right] + \left[4 \times \tfrac{5}{15}\right] = \tfrac{40}{15} = \tfrac{8}{3}$$

For the variance you need $E(X^2)$:

$$E(X^2) = \sum x_i^2 p_i = \left[0^2 \times \tfrac{1}{15}\right] + \left[1^2 \times \tfrac{2}{15}\right] + \left[2^2 \times \tfrac{3}{15}\right] + \left[3^2 \times \tfrac{4}{15}\right] + \left[4^2 \times \tfrac{5}{15}\right] = \tfrac{130}{15} = \tfrac{26}{3}$$

And finally: $\text{Var}(X) = E(X^2) - [E(X)]^2 = \tfrac{26}{3} - \left[\tfrac{8}{3}\right]^2 = \tfrac{14}{9}$

Expected Values, Mean and Variance

You can find the Expected Value for a Function of X

A <u>function</u> of a random variable X, $g(X)$, is an expression that takes X and does something to it. For example, $g(X) = X^3$, or $g(X) = \frac{12}{X}$, etc. If you're asked to find the <u>expected value</u> of a <u>function</u> of X, just use the following formula:

$$E(g(X)) = \sum g(x_i)p_i$$

EXAMPLE A discrete random variable X has the probability function $P(X = x) = \frac{x}{10}$, for $x = 1, 2, 3, 4$.
Find: a) $E(X^2)$ b) $E\left(\frac{1}{X}\right)$ c) $Var\left(\frac{1}{X}\right)$ You did this on the last page when you found the variance of X. But now you can see the same method works for functions of X in general, not just X².

a) Here $g(X) = X^2$, so $E(X^2) = \sum x_i^2 p_i = \left(1^2 \times \frac{1}{10}\right) + \left(2^2 \times \frac{2}{10}\right) + \left(3^2 \times \frac{3}{10}\right) + \left(4^2 \times \frac{4}{10}\right)$

$$= \frac{1}{10} + \frac{8}{10} + \frac{27}{10} + \frac{64}{10} = \frac{100}{10} = 10$$

b) Now $g(X) = \frac{1}{X}$, so $E\left(\frac{1}{X}\right) = \sum \frac{1}{x_i} \times p_i = \left(\frac{1}{1} \times \frac{1}{10}\right) + \left(\frac{1}{2} \times \frac{2}{10}\right) + \left(\frac{1}{3} \times \frac{3}{10}\right) + \left(\frac{1}{4} \times \frac{4}{10}\right)$

$$= \frac{1}{10} + \frac{1}{10} + \frac{1}{10} + \frac{1}{10} = \frac{4}{10} = \frac{2}{5}$$

c) Replace X with $\frac{1}{X}$ in the variance formula on p.99 to get: A function of X.

$$Var\left(\frac{1}{X}\right) = E\left[\left(\frac{1}{X}\right)^2\right] - \left[E\left(\frac{1}{X}\right)\right]^2 = E\left(\frac{1}{X^2}\right) - \left[E\left(\frac{1}{X}\right)\right]^2 = \sum \frac{1}{x_i^2} \times p_i - \left(\frac{2}{5}\right)^2$$ From part b) above.

$$= \left[\left(\frac{1}{1} \cdot \frac{1}{10}\right) + \left(\frac{1}{4} \cdot \frac{2}{10}\right) + \left(\frac{1}{9} \cdot \frac{3}{10}\right) + \left(\frac{1}{16} \cdot \frac{4}{10}\right)\right] - \frac{4}{25} = \frac{5}{24} - \frac{4}{25} = \frac{29}{600}$$

For Linear Functions of X, there are Two Formulas to Make Life Easier

These formulas really will save you lots of time in the exam, so it's well worth your while learning them.

$$E(aX + b) = aE(X) + b \qquad\qquad Var(aX + b) = a^2Var(X)$$

Here a and b are any numbers.

EXAMPLE If $E(X) = 3$ and $Var(X) = 7$, find $E(2X + 5)$ and $Var(2X + 5)$.

Easy. $E(2X + 5) = 2E(X) + 5 = (2 \times 3) + 5 = 11$

$Var(2X + 5) = 2^2Var(X) = 4 \times 7 = 28$

EXAMPLE The discrete random variable X has the following probability distribution:

x	2	3	4	5	6
$P(X = x)$	0.1	0.2	0.3	0.2	k

Find: a) k, b) $E(X)$, c) $Var(X)$,
d) $E(3X - 1)$, e) $Var(3X - 1)$.

Slowly, slowly — one bit at a time...

a) Remember the probabilities add up to 1 — $0.1 + 0.2 + 0.3 + 0.2 + k = 1$, and so $k = 0.2$

b) Now you can use the formula to find $E(X)$: $E(X) = \sum x_i p_i = (2 \times 0.1) + (3 \times 0.2) + (4 \times 0.3) + (5 \times 0.2) + (6 \times 0.2) = 4.2$

c) Next work out $E(X^2)$: $E(X^2) = \sum x_i^2 p_i = [2^2 \times 0.1] + [3^2 \times 0.2] + [4^2 \times 0.3] + [5^2 \times 0.2] + [6^2 \times 0.2] = 19.2$
and then the variance is easy: $Var(X) = E(X^2) - [E(X)]^2 = 19.2 - 4.2^2 = 1.56$

d) You'd expect the question to get harder but it doesn't: $E(3X - 1) = 3E(X) - 1 = 3 \times 4.2 - 1 = 11.6$

e) And finally: $Var(3X - 1) = 3^2Var(X) = 9 \times 1.56 = 14.04$

Statisticians say: E(Bird in hand) = E(2 Birds in bush)...

The mean and variance here are <u>theoretical</u> values — don't get them confused with the mean and variance of a load of <u>practical observations</u>. And remember, to find $E(g(X))$, you just replace x_i with $g(x_i)$. You can also work out linear functions like this if you want — but since the statistics gods have provided 2 easy-to-learn formulas, it'd be a shame not to use them.

S2 Section 1 — Practice Questions

Probability distribution and probability function are <u>fancy-looking names</u> for things that are actually quite straightforward...ish. Have a go at these to make sure you know who's who in the <u>glitzy world of discrete random variables</u>.

Warm-up Questions

1) The <u>probability distribution</u> of Y is:

y	0	1	2	3
P(Y = y)	0.5	k	k	3k

    a) Find the value of k.   b) Find P($Y < 2$).

2) The discrete random variable X has the <u>probability function</u> P($X = x$) = k for x = 0, 1, 2, 3 and 4. Find the value of k, and then find the <u>mean</u> and <u>variance</u> of X.

3) A <u>discrete random variable</u> X has the probability distribution shown in the table, where k is a constant.

x_i	1	2	3	4
p_i	$\frac{1}{6}$	$\frac{1}{2}$	k	$\frac{5}{24}$

    a)   Find k.
    b)   Find E(X) and show that Var(X) = 63/64.
    c)   Find E($2X - 1$) and Var($2X - 1$).

4) A <u>discrete random variable</u> X has the probability distribution shown in the table.

x_i	1	2	3	4	5	6
p_i	0.1	0.2	0.25	0.2	0.1	0.15

    a)   Find E(X).
    b)   Find Var(X).
    c)   Show that $E\left(\frac{2}{X}\right) = 0.757$, correct to 3 decimal places.
    d)   Show that $Var\left(\frac{2}{X}\right) = 0.221$, correct to 3 decimal places.

Exam Questions

1   In a game a player tosses three fair coins.
    If three heads occur then the player gets 20p; if two heads occur then the player gets 10p.
    For any other outcome, the player gets nothing.

    (a)   If X is the random variable 'amount received', tabulate the probability distribution of X.

(4 marks)

    The player pays 10p to play one game.

    (b)   Use the probability distribution to find the probability that the player wins
         (i.e. gets more money than they pay to play) in one game.

(2 marks)

S2 Section 1 — Practice Questions

There's nothing I enjoy more than pretending I'm in an exam. An eerie silence, sweaty palms, having to be escorted to the toilet by a responsible adult... and all these lovely maths questions too. Just like the real thing.

Exam Questions

2   A discrete random variable X can only take values 0, 1, 2 and 3.
    Its probability distribution is shown below.

x	0	1	2	3
$P(X = x)$	$2k$	$3k$	k	k

   a)   Find the value of k.

(1 mark)

   b)   Find $P(X > 2)$.

(1 mark)

3   The random variable X has the probability function $P(X = x) = k$ for $x = 0, 1, ..., 9$, where k is a constant.

   a)   Write down the probability distribution of X.

(1 mark)

   b)   Find the mean and variance of X.

(3 marks)

   c)   Calculate the probability that X is less than the mean.

(2 marks)

4   A discrete random variable X has the probability function:
    $P(X = x) = ax$ for $x = 1, 2, 3$, where a is a constant.

   a)   Show $a = \frac{1}{6}$.

(1 mark)

   b)   Find $E(X)$.

(2 marks)

   c)   If $Var(X) = \frac{5}{9}$, find $E(X^2)$.

(2 marks)

   d)   Find $E(3X + 4)$ and $Var(3X + 4)$.

(3 marks)

   e)   Find the mean of A, a random variable representing the area of a
        triangle with a base of length X^3 and a height of $\left(\frac{4}{X}\right)$.

(3 marks)

5   The number of points awarded to each contestant in a talent competition is given by
    the discrete random variable X with the following probability distribution:

x	0	1	2	3
$P(X = x)$	0.4	0.3	0.2	0.1

   a)   Find $E(X)$.

(2 marks)

   b)   Find $E(6X + 8)$.

(2 marks)

   c)   Show that $Var(X) = 1$.

(4 marks)

   d)   Find $Var(5 - 3X)$.

(2 marks)

The Poisson Distribution

It's Section 2, and it's the <u>Poisson</u> distribution. If you speak French, you'll know that poisson means fish. I think.

A Poisson Distribution has **Only One Parameter**

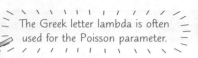

The Greek letter lambda is often used for the Poisson parameter.

A Poisson Distribution has just <u>one parameter</u>: λ.
If the random variable X follows a Poisson distribution, then you can write <u>$X \sim Po(\lambda)$</u>.

Poisson Probability Distribution Po(λ)

If $X \sim Po(\lambda)$, then X can take values 0, 1, 2, 3... with probability:

$$P(X = x) = \frac{e^{-\lambda}\lambda^x}{x!}$$

Random variables following a Poisson distribution are <u>discrete</u> — there are 'gaps' between the possible values.

EXAMPLE If $X \sim Po(2.8)$, find:
   a) $P(X = 0)$, b) $P(X = 1)$, c) $P(X = 2)$, d) $P(X < 3)$, e) $P(X \geq 3)$

Use the formula:

a) $P(X = 0) = \dfrac{e^{-2.8} \times 2.8^0}{0!} = e^{-2.8} = 0.061$ (to 3 d.p.).   *Remember... 0! = 1.*

b) $P(X = 1) = \dfrac{e^{-2.8} \times 2.8^1}{1!} = e^{-2.8} \times 2.8 = 0.170$ (to 3 d.p.).

c) $P(X = 2) = \dfrac{e^{-2.8} \times 2.8^2}{2!} = \dfrac{e^{-2.8} \times 2.8^2}{2 \times 1} = 0.238$ (to 3 d.p.).

If $X \sim Po(\lambda)$, then it can only take whole number values, so $P(X < 3)$ is the same as $P(X \leq 2)$.

d) $P(X < 3) = P(X \leq 2) = P(X = 0) + P(X = 1) + P(X = 2) = 0.061 + 0.170 + 0.238 = 0.469$.

e) $P(X \geq 3) = 1 - P(X < 3) = 1 - 0.469 = 0.531$.   *All the normal probability rules apply.*

For a Poisson Distribution: **Mean = Variance**

For a Poisson distribution, the <u>mean</u> and the <u>variance</u> are <u>the same</u> — and they <u>both</u> equal λ, the <u>Poisson parameter</u>. Remember that and you've probably learnt the most important Poisson fact. Ever.

Poisson Mean and Variance

If $X \sim Po(\lambda)$:   **Mean (μ) of X = E(X) = λ**

Variance (σ^2) of X = Var(X) = λ

So the standard deviation is:
$$\sigma = \sqrt{\lambda}$$

EXAMPLE If $X \sim Po(7)$, find: a) E(X),   b) Var(X).

It's Poisson, so $E(X) = Var(X) = \lambda = 7$.

This is the easiest question ever. So enjoy it while it lasts.

EXAMPLE If $X \sim Po(1)$, find: a) $P(X \leq \mu)$,   b) $P(X \leq \mu - \sigma)$

$E(X) = \mu = 1$, and $Var(X) = \sigma^2 = 1$, and so $\sigma = 1$.

a) $P(X \leq \mu) = P(X \leq 1) = P(0) + P(1) = \dfrac{e^{-1} \times 1^0}{0!} + \dfrac{e^{-1} \times 1^1}{1!} = 0.736$ (to 3 d.p.).

b) $P(X \leq \mu - \sigma) = P(X \leq 0) = P(0) = \dfrac{e^{-1} \times 1^0}{0!} = 0.368$ (to 3 d.p.).

The Poisson distribution is named after its inventor...

...the great French mathematician Monsieur Siméon-Denis Distribution. Boom boom. I always tell that joke at parties (which probably explains why I don't get to go to many parties these days). Most important thing here is that bit about the mean and variance being equal... so if you ever come across a distribution where $\mu = \sigma^2$, think 'Poisson' immediately.

The Poisson Parameter

I know what you're thinking... if only everything could be as accommodating as the Poisson distribution, with only one parameter and most things of interest being equal to it, then life would be so much easier. (Sigh.)

The Poisson Parameter is a *Rate*

The <u>number of events/things</u> that occur/are present <u>in a particular period</u> often follows a Poisson distribution. It could be a period of: <u>time</u> (e.g. minute/hour etc.), or <u>space</u> (e.g. litre/kilometre etc.).

Poisson Probability Distribution: Po(λ)

If X represents the number of events that occur in a particular space or time, then X will follow a Poisson distribution as long as:

1) The events occur <u>randomly</u>, and are all <u>independent</u> of each other.

2) The events happen <u>singly</u> (i.e. "<u>one at a time</u>").

3) The events happen (on average) at a <u>constant rate</u> (either in space or time).

The Poisson parameter λ is then the <u>average rate</u> at which these events occur (i.e. the average number of events in a given interval of space or time).

So the expected number of events that occur is <u>proportional</u> to the length of the period.

EXAMPLE   The random variable X represents the number of a certain type of cell in a particular volume of a blood sample. Assuming that the blood sample has been stirred, and that a given volume of blood always contains the same number of cells, show that X follows a Poisson distribution.

The sample has been stirred, so that should mean the cells of interest <u>aren't all clustered together</u>. This should ensure the 'events' (i.e. the cells you're interested in) occur <u>randomly</u> and <u>singly</u>. And since the total number of cells in a given volume is constant, the cells of interest should occur (on average) at a <u>constant rate</u>. Since X is the total number of 'events' in a given volume, <u>X must follow a Poisson distribution</u>.

The Poisson Parameter is *Additive*

Additive Property of the Poisson Distribution

- If X represents the number of events in <u>1 unit</u> of time/space (e.g. 1 minute / hour / m² / m³), and <u>$X \sim \text{Po}(\lambda)$</u>, then the number of events in x units of time/space follows the distribution <u>$\text{Po}(x\lambda)$</u>.

- If X and Y are <u>independent</u> variables with <u>$X \sim \text{Po}(\lambda)$</u> and <u>$Y \sim \text{Po}(\mu)$</u>, then <u>$X + Y \sim \text{Po}(\lambda + \mu)$</u>.

EXAMPLE   Sunflowers grow singly and randomly in a field with an average of 10 sunflowers per square metre. What is the probability that a randomly chosen area of 0.25 m² contains no sunflowers?

The number of sunflowers in 1 m² follows the distribution Po(10).

So the number of sunflowers in 0.25 m² must follow the distribution $\boxed{\text{Po}(2.5)}$.

This means $\text{P(no sunflowers)} = \dfrac{e^{-2.5} \times 2.5^0}{0!} = e^{-2.5} = 0.082$ (to 3 d.p.) .

$X \sim \text{Po}(10)$

EXAMPLE   The number of radioactive atoms that decay per second follows the Poisson distribution Po(5). If the probability of no atoms decaying in t seconds is 0.5, verify that $t = 0.1386$.

If the random variable X represents the number of radioactive atoms that decay in t seconds, then $\boxed{X \sim \text{Po}(5t)}$.

This means $\text{P}(X = 0) = \dfrac{e^{-5t}(5t)^0}{0!} = e^{-5t} = 0.5$.

This equation is satisfied by $t = 0.1386$, since $\boxed{e^{-5 \times 0.1386} = e^{-0.693} = 0.500 \text{ (to 3 d.p.)}}$.

If events happen randomly, singly and at a constant rate, it's Poisson...

Lots of things follow a Poisson distribution — e.g. the number of radioactive atoms that decay in a given time, the number of sixes in 5 minutes of dice-throwing, the number of raindrops per minute that hit a bit of your tongue as you stare open-mouthed at the sky on a rainy day. Think of a few others... make sure events happen <u>randomly</u>, <u>singly</u> and <u>at a constant rate</u>.

Using Poisson Tables

You've seen <u>statistical tables</u> before — for example, in S1 you saw how great they are for working out probabilities for <u>binomial</u> and <u>normal</u> distributions. So this should all seem <u>eerily familiar</u>.

Look up Probabilities in Poisson Tables

Going back to the <u>sunflowers</u> example near the bottom of the <u>previous page</u>...

EXAMPLE Sunflowers grow singly and randomly in a field with an average of 10 sunflowers per square metre. Find the probability that a randomly chosen square metre contains no more than 8 sunflowers.

If the random variable X represents the number of sunflowers in 1 m², then $X \sim \text{Po}(10)$.
You need to find $P(X \leq 8)$.

① You could do this 'manually': $P(X = 0) + P(X = 1) + \ldots + P(X = 8) = \dfrac{e^{-10} \times 10^0}{0!} + \dfrac{e^{-10} \times 10^1}{1!} + \ldots + \dfrac{e^{-10} \times 10^8}{8!}$

② But it's much quicker and easier to use tables of the Poisson <u>cumulative distribution function</u> (c.d.f.).

These show $P(X \leq x)$ if $X \sim \text{Po}(\lambda)$.

Here's a bit of a Poisson table:

- Find your <u>value of λ</u> (here, 10), and the <u>value of x</u> (here, 8).

- You can quickly see that $P(X \leq 8) = 0.3328$.

Cumulative Poisson Distribution Function
Values show $P(X \leq x)$, where $X \sim \text{Po}(\lambda)$

λ	6.0	6.5	7.0	7.5	8.0	8.5	9.0	9.5	10.0	11.0	12.0	13.0	14.0	15.0
x														
0	0.0025	0.0015	0.0009	0.0006	0.0003	0.0002	0.0001	0.0001	0.0000	0.0000	0.0000	0.0000	0.0000	0.0000
1	0.0174	0.0113	0.0073	0.0047	0.0030	0.0019	0.0012	0.0008	0.0005	0.0002	0.0001	0.0000	0.0000	0.0000
2	0.0620	0.0430	0.0296	0.0203	0.0138	0.0093	0.0062	0.0042	0.0028	0.0012	0.0005	0.0002	0.0001	0.0000
3	0.1512	0.1118	0.0818	0.0591	0.0424	0.0301	0.0212	0.0149	0.0103	0.0049	0.0023	0.0011	0.0005	0.0002
4	0.2851	0.2237	0.1730	0.1321	0.0996	0.0744	0.0550	0.0403	0.0293	0.0151	0.0076	0.0037	0.0018	0.0009
5	0.4457	0.3690	0.3007	0.2414	0.1912	0.1496	0.1157	0.0885	0.0671	0.0375	0.0203	0.0107	0.0055	0.0028
6	0.6063	0.5265	0.4497	0.3782	0.3134	0.2562	0.2068	0.1649	0.1301	0.0786	0.0458	0.0259	0.0142	0.0076
7	0.7440	0.6728	0.5987	0.5246	0.4530	0.3856	0.3239	0.2687	0.2202	0.1432	0.0895	0.0540	0.0316	0.0180
8	0.8472	0.7916	0.7291	0.6620	0.5925	0.5231	0.4557	0.3918	0.3328	0.2320	0.1550	0.0998	0.0621	0.0374
9	0.9161	0.8774	0.8305	0.7764	0.7166	0.6530	0.5874	0.5218	0.4579	0.3405	0.2424	0.1658	0.1094	0.0699
10	0.9574	0.9332	0.9015	0.8622	0.8159	0.7634	0.7060	0.6453	0.5830	0.4599	0.3472	0.2517	0.1757	0.1185

See p139 for the full set of Poisson tables.

You Need to Use Poisson Tables with a Bit of Cunning

This is <u>exactly the same</u> as you've already seen for binomial tables.

EXAMPLE When cloth is manufactured, faults occur randomly in the cloth at a rate of 8 faults per square metre. Use the above Poisson table to find:
   a)   The probability of 7 or fewer faults in a square metre of cloth.
   b)   The probability of more than 4 faults in a square metre of cloth.
   c)   The probability of exactly 10 faults in a square metre of cloth.
   d)   The probability of at least 9 faults in a square metre of cloth.
   e)   The probability of exactly 4 faults in 0.75 m² of cloth.

The faults occur <u>randomly</u>, <u>singly</u> and <u>at a constant rate</u> (= 8 faults per square metre).
So if X represents the number of faults in a square metre, then <u>$X \sim \text{Po}(8)$</u>.

So use the column showing $\lambda = 8$.

a) $P(X \leq 7) = 0.4530$

b) $P(X > 4) = 1 - P(X \leq 4) = 1 - 0.0996 = 0.9004$

c) $P(X = 10) = P(X \leq 10) - P(X \leq 9) = 0.8159 - 0.7166 = 0.0993$

d) $P(X \geq 9) = 1 - P(X < 9) = 1 - P(X \leq 8) = 1 - 0.5925 = 0.4075$

Now use the column showing $\lambda = 6$.

e) Let the random variable Y represent the number of faults in 0.75 m² of cloth. If the number of faults in 1 m² of cloth $\sim \text{Po}(8)$, then $Y \sim \text{Po}(0.75 \times 8) = \text{Po}(6)$.

So P(exactly 4 faults in 0.75 m² of cloth) $= P(Y \leq 4) - P(Y \leq 3) = 0.2851 - 0.1512 = 0.1339$

Poisson tables — the best thing since binomial tables...

Learn the ways of the Poisson tables, and you shall prove your wisdom. In the exam, you'll be given a big booklet of fun containing all the statistical tables you could ever want. You need to think carefully about how to use them though — e.g. you might have to subtract one figure from another, or subtract one of the figures from 1. Or something else similar.

Worked Problems

Make sure you understand what's going on in these examples.

EXAMPLE 1: A breaking-down car

A car randomly breaks down twice a week on average.
The random variable X represents the number of times the car will break down next week.
a)   What probability distribution could be used to model X? Explain your answer.
b)   Find the probability that the car breaks down fewer than 3 times next week.
c)   Find the probability that the car breaks down more than 4 times next week.
d)   Find the probability that the car breaks down exactly 6 times in the next fortnight.

a)   Since the breakdowns occur <u>randomly</u>, <u>singly</u> and (on average) <u>at a constant rate</u>, and X is the <u>total number</u> of breakdowns in one week, X follows a Poisson distribution: $X \sim Po(2)$

b)   Using tables (see p.139) for $\underline{\lambda = 2}$: $P(X < 3) = P(X \le 2) = 0.6767$

c)   Again, using tables for $\underline{\lambda = 2}$: $P(X > 4) = 1 - P(X \le 4) = 1 - 0.9473 = 0.0527$

d)   If the random variable Y represents the number of breakdowns in the next <u>fortnight</u>, then $Y \sim Po(2 \times 2) = Po(4)$.
So using tables for $\underline{\lambda = 4}$: $P(Y = 6) = P(Y \le 6) - P(Y \le 5) = 0.8893 - 0.7851 = 0.1042$

EXAMPLE 2: Bad apples

A restaurant owner needs to buy several crates of apples, so she visits a farm that sells apples by the crate. Each crate contains 150 apples. On average 1.5% of the apples are bad, and these bad apples are randomly distributed between the crates. The restaurant owner opens a random crate and inspects each apple.
•   If there are <u>no</u> bad apples in this crate, then the restaurant owner will <u>buy</u> the apples she needs from this farm.
•   If <u>more than 2 apples</u> in this first crate are bad, then the restaurant owner will <u>not buy</u> from this farm.
•   If <u>only 1 or 2 apples</u> in the first crate are bad, then a <u>second crate</u> is opened.
The restaurant owner will then only buy from this farm if the second crate contains <u>at most 1 bad apple</u>.

a)   Find the probability that none of the apples in the first crate are bad.
b)   Find the probability that more than 2 apples in the first crate are bad.
c)   Find the probability that a second crate is opened.
d)   What is the probability of the restaurant owner buying the apples she needs from this farm?

a)   The <u>average</u> number of bad apples in each crate is $150 \times 0.015 = 2.25$.
So if X represents the number of bad apples in each crate, then $X \sim Po(2.25)$.
$$P(X = 0) = \frac{e^{-2.25} \times 2.25^0}{0!} = e^{-2.25} = 0.1054 \text{ (to 4 d.p.)}.$$

b) $$P(X = 1) = \frac{e^{-2.25} \times 2.25^1}{1!} = e^{-2.25} \times 2.25 = 0.2371 \text{ (to 4 d.p.)}.$$

Definitely Poisson.

$$P(X = 2) = \frac{e^{-2.25} \times 2.25^2}{2!} = \frac{e^{-2.25} \times 2.25^2}{2} = 0.2668 \text{ (to 4 d.p.)}.$$

So $P(X > 2) = 1 - P(X = 0) - P(X = 1) - P(X = 2) = 1 - 0.1054 - 0.2371 - 0.2668 = 0.3907$

c)   A second crate is opened if $X = 1$ or $X = 2$. $P(X = 1 \text{ OR } X = 2) = 0.2371 + 0.2668 = 0.5039$

d)   There are two ways the owner will buy apples from this farm:
•   <u>Either</u> the first crate will contain <u>no</u> bad apples (probability = 0.1054),
•   <u>Or</u> the first crate will contain <u>1 or 2</u> bad apples <u>AND</u> the second crate will contain <u>0 or 1</u> bad apples.
$P(\text{1st crate has 1 or 2 bad AND 2nd crate has 0 or 1 bad}) = 0.5039 \times (0.1054 + 0.2371) = 0.1726$
So $P(\text{restaurant owner buys from this farm}) = 0.1054 + 0.1726 = 0.278$

All it takes is one bad apple question and everything starts to go wrong...

I admit that apple question looks a nightmare at first... but just hold your nerve and take things nice and slowly.
For example, in that last part, ask yourself: "What individual things need to happen before the restaurant owner will buy from this farm?" Work out the individual probabilities, add or multiply them as necessary, and Bob's your uncle.

S2 Section 2 — Practice Questions

Well, that's another section completed, which is as good a reason as most to celebrate. But wait... put that celebratory cup of tea on ice for a few minutes more, because you've still got some questions to answer to prove that you really do know everything. So try the questions... and if you get any wrong, do some more revision and try them again.

Warm-up Questions

1) If $X \sim Po(3.1)$, find (correct to 4 decimal places):
   a) $P(X = 2)$,
   b) $P(X = 1)$,
   c) $P(X = 0)$,
   d) $P(X < 3)$,
   e) $P(X \geq 3)$

2) If $X \sim Po(8.7)$, find (correct to 4 decimal places):
   a) $P(X = 2)$,
   b) $P(X = 1)$,
   c) $P(X = 0)$,
   d) $P(X < 3)$,
   e) $P(X \geq 3)$

3) For the following distributions, find: (i) $E(X)$, (ii) $Var(X)$, and (iii) the standard deviation of X.
   a) $Po(8)$,
   b) $Po(12.11)$
   c) $Po(84.2227)$

4) For the following distributions, find: (i) $P(X \leq \mu)$, (ii) $P(X \leq \mu - \sigma)$
   a) $Po(9)$,
   b) $Po(4)$

5) Which of the following would follow a Poisson distribution? Explain your answers.

   a) The number of defective products coming off a factory's production line in one day if defective products occur at random at an average of 25 per week.

   b) The number of heads thrown using a coin in 25 tosses if the probability of getting a head is always 0.5.

   c) The number of people joining a post-office queue each minute during lunchtime if people arrive at an average rate of 3 every five minutes.

   d) The total number of spelling mistakes in a document if mistakes are randomly made at an average rate of 3 per page.

6) In a radioactive sample, atoms decay at an average rate of 2000 per hour.
   State how the following quantities are distributed, giving as much detail as possible.

   a) The number of atoms decaying per minute.

   b) The number of atoms decaying per day.

7) Atoms in one radioactive sample decay at an average rate of 60 per minute, while in another they decay at an average rate of 90 per minute.

   a) How would the total number of atoms decaying each minute be distributed?

   b) How would the total number of atoms decaying each hour be distributed?

8) If $X \sim Po(8)$, use Poisson tables to find:
   a) $P(X \leq 2)$,
   b) $P(X \leq 7)$,
   c) $P(X \leq 5)$,
   d) $P(X < 9)$,
   e) $P(X \geq 8)$
   f) $P(X > 1)$,
   g) $P(X > 7)$,
   h) $P(X = 6)$,
   i) $P(X = 4)$,
   j) $P(X = 3)$

9) A gaggle of 100 geese is randomly scattered throughout a field measuring 10 m × 10m.
   What is the probability that in a randomly selected square metre of field, I find:
   a) no geese?
   b) 1 goose?
   c) 2 geese?
   d) more than 2 geese?

S2 Section 2 — Practice Questions

Nearly there — just... one... more... page...

1 a) State two conditions needed for a Poisson distribution to be a suitable model for a quantity.
(2 marks)

   b) A birdwatcher knows that the number of chaffinches visiting a particular observation spot per hour follows a Poisson distribution with mean 7.
   Find the probability that in a randomly chosen hour during the day:
   (i) fewer than 4 chaffinches visit the observation spot,
(2 marks)

   (ii) at least 7 chaffinches visit the observation spot,
(2 marks)

   (iii) exactly 9 chaffinches visit the observation spot.
(2 marks)

   c) The number of birds <u>other than</u> chaffinches visiting the same observation spot per hour can be modelled by the Poisson distribution Po(22).
   Find the probability that exactly 3 birds (of any species) visit the observation spot in a random 15-minute period.
(4 marks)

2 The number of calls received at a call centre each hour can be modelled by a Poisson distribution with mean 20.
   a) Find the probability that in a random 30-minute period:
   (i) exactly 8 calls are received,
(3 marks)

   (ii) more than 8 calls are received.
(2 marks)

   b) For a Poisson distribution to be a suitable model, events have to occur independently.
   What is meant by "independently" in this context?
(1 mark)

3 An outdoor equipment store sells a certain type of rucksack at an average rate of 6 a month.
   The number of these rucksacks they sell each month, X, is assumed to follow a Poisson distribution.
   a) Calculate $P(4 < X \leq 7)$
(2 marks)

   b) Calculate the probability that the store sells more than 14 of these rucksacks in a random two-month period.
(3 marks)

   c) Find the probability that the store sells exactly 6 of these rucksacks each month for three consecutive months. Give your answer to one significant figure.
(3 marks)

   d) The number of these rucksacks they sell in each of a random sample of 8 months is shown below.

   1, 12, 8, 3, 6, 6, 2, 10

   Calculate an unbiased estimate of the variance of X. Use your answer to comment on the validity of the assumption that X follows a Poisson distribution.
(4 marks)

Probability Density Functions

A lot of this section should look <u>kinda familiar</u>, but at the same time <u>slightly different</u>. That's because this section covers the same sorts of things as you've seen before with discrete random variables, only now the variables are <u>continuous</u>.

Continuous Random Variables take Any Value in a Range

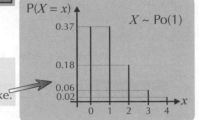

1) With <u>discrete</u> random variables (like the ones in Sections 1 and 2), there are 'gaps' between the <u>possible values</u> the random variable can take. The random variable's <u>probability function</u> tells you the probability of each of these values occurring.

> For example, if $X \sim \text{Po}(1)$, then you know that X can only take the values 0, 1, 2, etc., and you can work out the probability of each of these values using the Poisson probability function on p.103. You could even draw a graph of what this probability function looks like.

2) <u>Continuous</u> random variables are similar, but they can take <u>any</u> value within a <u>certain range</u> (e.g. they represent things like length, height, weight, etc.).

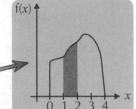

So a continuous random variable X might be able to take <u>any value</u> between 0 and 4, for example. You can still draw a graph showing how likely X is to take values within this range. But instead of a series of <u>bars</u>, it would be a <u>continuous line</u>.

3) These graphs that show how likely continuous random variables are to take various values are called <u>probability density functions</u> (or <u>p.d.f.s</u>). Here, f(x) is a p.d.f.

4) It's actually the <u>area under a p.d.f.</u> that shows probability. For example, the <u>shaded area</u> shows the probability that this continuous random variable will take a value between 1 and 2.

The Total Area under a p.d.f. is 1

Remember... it's the <u>area under a p.d.f.</u> that shows probability, and you find the area under a curve by <u>integrating</u>.

> **EXAMPLE** a) Explain why a p.d.f. can never take negative values.
>   b) Explain why the total area under any p.d.f. must equal 1.
>
> a) A p.d.f. can never be negative, since <u>probabilities can never be negative</u>.
> b) The <u>total area</u> under a p.d.f. must always equal 1 since that's just the <u>total probability</u> of the random variable taking one of its possible values.
>
> In maths-speak, this means $f(x) \geq 0$ for all x, and $\int_{-\infty}^{\infty} f(x)\,dx = 1$.

> Where a formula to do with a <u>discrete</u> random variable involves a <u>summation</u> (Σ), the equivalent formula relating to a <u>continuous</u> random variable involves an <u>integral</u>.

> This is the 'continuous' equivalent of $\sum p_i = 1$.

Find Probabilities by Calculating Areas

Some of the p.d.f.s you'll come across are defined "piecewise" (bit by bit). Don't let that faze you.

> **EXAMPLE** The continuous random variable X has the probability density function below.
>
> $$f(x) = \begin{cases} kx & \text{for } 0 < x < 4 \\ 0 & \text{otherwise} \end{cases}$$
>
> ← This is a piecewise definition — it's in 2 bits.
>
> a) Find the value of k.   b) Find $P(2 < X \leq 3)$.   c) Find $P(X = 2.5)$.
>
> a) The total area under the p.d.f. <u>must equal 1</u>.
>   Using a sketch of f(x), you can tell that $8k = 1$, or $k = 0.125$.
>
> b) You need to find the <u>area under the graph</u> between $x = 2$ and $x = 3$.
>   Using the formula for the area of a trapezium, $P(2 < X \leq 3) = 0.3125$
>
> c) The area under a graph <u>at a single point</u> is <u>zero</u> (since it would be the area of a trapezium with zero width). So $P(X = 2.5) = 0$.
>
> The probability of a continuous random variable equalling <u>any single value</u> is <u>always zero</u> — it only makes sense to find the probability of it taking a value <u>within a particular range</u>. It also means that for a continuous random variable, $P(X < k) = P(X \leq k)$, for any k.

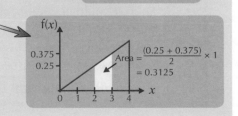

Sometimes, statistics all seems a little bit odd...

That thing about $P(X = x) = 0$ always seems weird to me. I mean... X has to take some value, so it seems peculiar that the probability of it taking any <u>particular</u> value equals zero. But that's the way it is. It makes a bit more sense if you remember that probabilities are represented by <u>areas</u> under a graph. Not many calculations here, but learn the <u>ideas</u> carefully.

Probability Density Functions

It's time to put on your best <u>integrating trousers</u>, because you'll be finding more "areas under curves" on this page.

Some Probabilities Need to be Found by *Integrating*

Remember — <u>probabilities</u> are represented by <u>areas</u>, so if X has p.d.f. f(x):

$$P(a < X < b) = \int_a^b f(x)\,dx$$

EXAMPLE The continuous random variable X has the probability density function below.

$$f(x) = \begin{cases} x^2 + a & \text{for } 0 \le x \le 1 \\ 0 & \text{otherwise} \end{cases}$$

a) Sketch f(x), and find the value of a.

b) Find $P(X > \frac{1}{2})$.

a) The non-zero bit of the p.d.f. is a <u>quadratic</u> function, and so f(x) looks like this:
The area under the graph must equal 1, so <u>integrate</u>.

$$\int_{-\infty}^{\infty} f(x)\,dx = \int_{-\infty}^0 f(x)\,dx + \int_0^1 f(x)\,dx + \int_1^{\infty} f(x)\,dx$$

> Splitting an integral like this is a good trick — remember it.

$$= \int_{-\infty}^0 0\,dx + \int_0^1 (x^2 + a)\,dx + \int_1^{\infty} 0\,dx$$

$$= \left[\frac{x^3}{3} + ax\right]_0^1 = \left(\frac{1}{3} + a\right) = 1, \text{ which means } a = \frac{2}{3}.$$

> Shaded area = P(X > 0.5).

b) Integrate again — this time between $x = \frac{1}{2}$ and $x = 1$.

$$P(X > 0.5) = \int_{\frac{1}{2}}^1 \left(x^2 + \frac{2}{3}\right)dx = \left[\frac{x^3}{3} + \frac{2}{3}x\right]_{\frac{1}{2}}^1 = \left(\frac{1}{3} + \frac{2}{3}\right) - \left(\frac{1}{24} + \frac{1}{3}\right) = \frac{15}{24} = \frac{5}{8}$$

You Might Need to Spot a Function that's *NOT* a p.d.f.

EXAMPLE Which of the following could be probability density functions?

a) $f(x) = \begin{cases} 3x & \text{for } -1 \le x \le 1 \\ 0 & \text{otherwise} \end{cases}$

b) $g(x) = \begin{cases} kx & \text{for } 2 \le x \le 4 \\ 0 & \text{otherwise} \end{cases}$

c) $h(x) = \begin{cases} kx & \text{for } -2 \le x \le 2 \\ 0 & \text{otherwise} \end{cases}$

a) The graph of f(x) looks like this:
But a p.d.f. can <u>never</u> take negative values, so this cannot be a probability density function.

b) Since a p.d.f. can never take a negative value, k <u>cannot</u> be <u>negative</u>.
If k is <u>positive</u>, then the graph of g(x) looks like this,
and the <u>total area</u> under the graph is $\frac{2k + 4k}{2} \times 2 = 6k$.

> The yellow area must equal 1 for g(x) to be a p.d.f.

So g(x) could be a p.d.f. as long as $k = \frac{1}{6}$.

c) If k is <u>positive</u>, then h(x) is negative for $-2 \le x < 0$, so k <u>cannot be positive</u>.
If k is <u>negative</u>, then h(x) is negative for $0 < x \le 2$, so k <u>cannot be negative</u>.

If $k = 0$, then $\int_{-\infty}^{\infty} h(x)\,dx = \int_{-\infty}^{\infty} 0\,dx = 0$, so h(x) cannot be a p.d.f.

> The integral $\int_{-\infty}^{\infty} h(x)\,dx$ must equal 1 for h(x) to be a p.d.f.

Three things you should definitely know about a p.d.f...

There's not really heaps to say about probability density functions. They <u>can't be negative</u>, the <u>total area under a p.d.f. must equal 1</u>, and you can find probabilities by finding areas under the p.d.f. <u>between different limits</u>. If you remember just those facts and can do a bit of integration, then you'll be well on the way to earning a few easy marks come exam time.

Cumulative Distribution Functions

Now it's time for <u>cumulative distribution functions</u> (c.d.f.s). "Cumulative distribution function" sounds pretty complicated, but all it means is "the area under a p.d.f. up to a certain point".

A *Cumulative Distribution Function* shows P(X ≤ x)

> 'Cumulative distribution functions' are sometimes called '<u>distribution functions</u>'. These are exactly the same thing.

Cumulative Distribution Functions

If X is a continuous random variable with p.d.f. f(x), then its <u>cumulative distribution function</u> (c.d.f.) F(x) is given by:

$$F(x) = \int_{-\infty}^{x} f(t)\,dt$$

1) Cumulative distribution functions are usually labelled with <u>capital letters</u>, e.g. **F(*x*)** — unlike p.d.f.s, which are usually labelled with <u>lower case</u> letters, e.g. **f(*x*)**.

2) For any value of x, the c.d.f. shows the probability that X is between $-\infty$ and x.

To <u>find</u> a cumulative distribution function (c.d.f.), you need to <u>integrate the probability density function</u> (p.d.f.).

EXAMPLE A continuous random variable X has probability density function f(x), where
$$f(x) = \begin{cases} 2x - 2 & \text{for } 1 \leq x \leq 2 \\ 0 & \text{otherwise} \end{cases}$$
Find the cumulative distribution function of X.

To find F(x), you need to <u>integrate</u> between $-\infty$ and x (so x actually needs to be the <u>upper limit</u> of your integral). To avoid having x as the <u>limit</u> of the integral <u>and</u> the <u>variable</u> you're integrating with respect to, it helps to use a <u>different</u> variable (e.g. 't') inside the integral.

The t then <u>disappears</u> when you put in the limits.

$$F(x) = \int_{-\infty}^{1} f(t)\,dt + \int_{1}^{x} f(t)\,dt = \int_{-\infty}^{1} 0\,dt + \int_{1}^{x} (2t - 2)\,dt$$

For 1 ≤ x ≤ 2.
$$= [t^2 - 2t]_{1}^{x} = x^2 - 2x - (1 - 2) = x^2 - 2x + 1$$

So $$F(x) = \begin{cases} 0 & \text{for } x < 1 \\ x^2 - 2x + 1 & \text{for } 1 \leq x \leq 2 \\ 1 & \text{for } x > 2 \end{cases}$$

> You <u>must</u> define F(x) for <u>all</u> possible values of x. And the 'pieces' should join together with '<u>no jumps</u>' — the value of the c.d.f. at the end of one 'piece' must equal the value of the c.d.f. at the start of the next 'piece'. Here, F(1) = O using both the first and second 'pieces', and F(2) = 1 using both the second and third.

Now, once you've found F(x), you can use it to find P($X \leq x_0$) for a given value x_0.

EXAMPLE For the continuous random variable X defined in the example above, find P($X \leq 1.5$).

P($X \leq 1.5$) is just F(1.5). You find F(1.5) by substituting 1.5 into the expression for F(x), and since 1.5 lies in the interval $1 \leq x \leq 2$, the expression is $x^2 - 2x + 1$.

$$P(X \leq 1.5) = F(1.5) = 1.5^2 - (2 \times 1.5) + 1 = 2.25 - 3 + 1 = \underline{0.25}$$

Differentiate a c.d.f. to Find a *Probability Density Function*

EXAMPLE Find the p.d.f. of the continuous random variable X if its cumulative distribution function F(x) is
$$F(x) = \begin{cases} 0 & \text{for } x < 0 \\ \frac{1}{2}(3x - x^3) & \text{for } 0 \leq x \leq 1 \\ 1 & \text{for } x > 1 \end{cases}$$
Differentiate the c.d.f. F(x) to find the p.d.f. f(x): $\rightarrow$ $$f(x) = \frac{dF(x)}{dx} = \begin{cases} \frac{3}{2} - \frac{3}{2}x^2 & \text{for } 0 \leq x \leq 1 \\ 0 & \text{otherwise} \end{cases}$$

OMG — too many three-letter abbreviations...

Well that wasn't too bad. That bit about using t instead of x looks odd at first but notice how the t disappears once you've done the integration and put in the limits. And don't forget to define F(x) and f(x) for all x between $-\infty$ and ∞.

Cumulative Distribution Functions

Be Extra Careful if the p.d.f. is in 'Pieces'

If a p.d.f. is defined <u>piecewise</u>, then you have to be careful with the c.d.f. where the 'pieces' join.

EXAMPLE Find the cumulative distribution function of X, whose probability density function is

$$f(x) = \begin{cases} 0.5 & \text{for } 3 \leq x < 4 \\ 1.5 - 0.25x & \text{for } 4 \leq x \leq 6 \\ 0 & \text{otherwise} \end{cases}$$

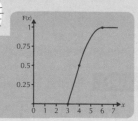

The <u>graph</u> of this p.d.f. is on the right. There'll be <u>4 pieces</u> to your c.d.f. ⟹

- For $x < 3$, $P(X \leq x) = 0$ — i.e. $F(x) = 0.$ ⟸ So to join on from this smoothly, F(3) = 0.

- Then there are <u>two ways</u> to make sure the next piece joins on <u>smoothly</u>.

(i) Always start your integral at $-\infty$:

For $3 \leq x < 4$: $\boxed{= F(3)}$

$$F(x) = \int_{-\infty}^{x} f(t)\,dt = \int_{-\infty}^{3} f(t)\,dt + \int_{3}^{x} f(t)\,dt$$

$$= F(3) + \int_{3}^{x} 0.5\,dt = 0 + [0.5t]_{3}^{x}$$

$$= 0.5x - 1.5 \Longleftarrow \text{So to join on smoothly, F(4) = 0.5.}$$

For $4 \leq x \leq 6$: $\boxed{= F(4)}$

$$F(x) = \int_{-\infty}^{4} f(t)\,dt + \int_{4}^{x} f(t)\,dt = F(4) + \int_{4}^{x} f(t)\,dt$$

$$= 0.5 + \int_{4}^{x} (1.5 - 0.25t)\,dt$$

$$= 0.5 + [1.5t - 0.125t^2]_{4}^{x}$$

$$= 0.5 + (1.5x - 0.125x^2) - (6 - 2)$$

$$= 1.5x - 0.125x^2 - 3.5$$

(ii) Use an <u>indefinite integral</u> and choose the <u>constant of integration</u> so that the join is 'smooth'.

For $3 \leq x < 4$: Use x rather than t in this integral — since there are no limits, the t wouldn't disappear (see p111).

$$F(x) = \int f(x)\,dx = \int 0.5\,dx = 0.5x + k_1$$

But $F(3) = 0$ (to join the first piece of c.d.f. smoothly).
So $k_1 = -1.5$, which gives $F(x) = 0.5x - 1.5$.

For $4 \leq x \leq 6$:

$$F(x) = \int f(x)\,dx = \int (1.5 - 0.25x)\,dx$$

$$= 1.5x - 0.125x^2 + k_2$$

But $F(4) = 0.5$ (using the previous part of the c.d.f.).
So $k_2 = -3.5$, giving $F(x) = 1.5x - 0.125x^2 - 3.5$.

- For $x > 6$, $F(x) = F(6) = 1.$ ⟸ A c.d.f. always ends up at 1, but double-check that this makes a smooth join with the previous part of the c.d.f.

Put the bits together to get: $F(x) = \begin{cases} 0 & \text{for } x < 3 \\ 0.5x - 1.5 & \text{for } 3 \leq x < 4 \\ 1.5x - 0.125x^2 - 3.5 & \text{for } 4 \leq x \leq 6 \\ 1 & \text{for } x > 6 \end{cases}$

Find All Sorts of Probabilities Using a c.d.f.

You can use a <u>c.d.f.</u> to find the probability of a continuous random variable taking a value within a certain range.

EXAMPLE The cumulative distribution function $F(x)$ of the continuous random variable X is given below.

$$F(x) = \begin{cases} 0 & \text{for } x < 0 \\ 0.5(3x - x^3) & \text{for } 0 \leq x \leq 1 \\ 1 & \text{for } x > 1 \end{cases}$$

Find: a) $P(X \leq 0.5)$, b) $P(X > 0.25)$, c) $P(0.1 \leq X \leq 0.2)$, d) $P(X < 0.5)$

a) $P(X \leq 0.5) = F(0.5) = 0.5 \times (3 \times 0.5 - 0.5^3) = 0.6875.$

b) $P(X > 0.25) = 1 - P(X \leq 0.25) = 1 - F(0.25) = 1 - 0.5 \times (3 \times 0.25 - 0.25^3) = 1 - 0.3672 = 0.633$ (to 3 d.p.).

c) $P(0.1 \leq X \leq 0.2) = P(X \leq 0.2) - P(X \leq 0.1) = F(0.2) - F(0.1) = 0.296 - 0.1495 = 0.1465.$

d) $P(X < 0.5) = P(X \leq 0.5) = 0.6875.$ ⟸ For a <u>continuous</u> random variable, $P(X \leq k) = P(X < k)$ — since $P(X = k) = 0$.

Don't fall to pieces now — you've done the hardest bit...

Using a c.d.f. to find the probability of X falling within a particular range is similar to what you saw on p105 with the tables of values of the Poisson c.d.f. — you can work out anything you need, as long as you're prepared to think a bit.

Mean of a Continuous Random Variable

You'll have seen something a bit like this before (in Section 1) — except there, the random variables were <u>discrete</u> and the formulas involved a <u>summation</u> (Σ). Here, they're <u>continuous</u>, and you're going to need to <u>integrate</u>.

*Integrate to Find the **Mean** of a Continuous Random Variable*

Mean of a Continuous Random Variable

If X is a continuous random variable with p.d.f. f(x), then its <u>mean</u> (μ) or expected value (E(X)) is given by:

$$\mu = E(X) = \int_{-\infty}^{\infty} x f(x) dx$$

This is a bit like the formula for the mean (expected value) of a discrete random variable you saw on p.99 — except the sigma (Σ) has been replaced with an integral sign, and p_i with f(x)dx.

EXAMPLE Find the expected value of the continuous random variable X with p.d.f. f (x) given below.

$$f(x) = \begin{cases} \frac{3}{32}(4 - x^2) & \text{for } -2 \le x \le 2 \\ 0 & \text{otherwise} \end{cases}$$

$$E(X) = \int_{-\infty}^{\infty} x f(x) dx = \int_{-2}^{2} x \cdot \frac{3}{32}(4 - x^2) dx$$

$$= \int_{-2}^{2}\left(\frac{3}{8}x - \frac{3x^3}{32}\right) dx = \left[\frac{3x^2}{16} - \frac{3x^4}{128}\right]_{-2}^{2}$$

$$= \left(\frac{3 \times 2^2}{16} - \frac{3 \times 2^4}{128}\right) - \left(\frac{3 \times (-2)^2}{16} - \frac{3 \times (-2)^4}{128}\right) = 0$$

You'd expect a mean of O here, since f(x) is symmetrical about the y-axis. So you didn't actually <u>need</u> to integrate.

$y = f(x)$

*You can find the **Expected Value** for a **Function of X***

A function of X, g(X), is just an expression involving X, like X^2 or $3X + 5$. Finding E(g(X)) is simple — you do the same as if you were finding E(X), but replace x with g(x).

Expected Value of a function of X, g(X)

See — x replaced with g(x).

For a continuous random variable X with p.d.f. f(x), and a <u>function of X, g(X)</u>: $E(g(X)) = \int_{-\infty}^{\infty} g(x) f(x) dx$

And if your function is <u>linear</u> (of the form $aX + b$), it's easier still: $E(aX + b) = aE(X) + b$

EXAMPLE The continuous random variable X has p.d.f. f (x), where $f(x) = \begin{cases} \frac{3}{37}x^2 & \text{for } 3 \le x \le 4 \\ 0 & \text{otherwise} \end{cases}$

Find: a) the expected value of X, μ,
  b) $E(X^2)$,
  c) $E(3X + 2)$.

This p.d.f. isn't symmetrical in the interval [3, 4], so you <u>have</u> to integrate this time.

a) $\mu = E(X) = \int_{-\infty}^{\infty} x f(x) dx = \int_{3}^{4} x \cdot \frac{3}{37}x^2 dx$

$$= \int_{3}^{4} \frac{3}{37}x^3 dx = \frac{3}{37}\left[\frac{x^4}{4}\right]_{3}^{4} = \frac{3}{37 \times 4}(4^4 - 3^4) = \frac{3 \times (256 - 81)}{148} = \frac{525}{148}$$

g(X) = X², so g(x) = x².

b) $E(X^2) = \int_{-\infty}^{\infty} x^2 f(x) dx = \int_{3}^{4} x^2 \cdot \frac{3}{37}x^2 dx = \int_{3}^{4} \frac{3}{37}x^4 dx$

Always check your mean looks sensible. Here, you'd expect the mean to be somewhere between 3 and 4 (so 525 ÷ 148 = 3.547... seems 'about right').

$$= \frac{3}{37}\left[\frac{x^5}{5}\right]_{3}^{4} = \frac{3}{37 \times 5}(4^5 - 3^5) = \frac{2343}{185}$$

c) $E(3X + 2) = 3E(X) + 2 = 3 \times \frac{525}{148} + 2 = \frac{1575 + 296}{148} = \frac{1871}{148}$

Variance of a Continuous Random Variable

More integrating, I'm afraid. But stick with it — it'll soon be over.

Integrate to Find the **Variance** of a Continuous Random Variable

Variance of a Continuous Random Variable

If X is a continuous random variable with p.d.f. f(x), then its variance is given by:

$$\text{Var}(X) = \text{E}(X^2) - [\text{E}(X)]^2 = \text{E}(X^2) - \mu^2$$

This is exactly the same formula that you saw on p.99 for discrete random variables.

$$= \int_{-\infty}^{\infty} x^2 \, \text{f}(x)\text{d}x - \mu^2$$

EXAMPLE The continuous random variable X has p.d.f. f(x) given below, and a mean of 0. Find the variance and standard deviation of X.

$$\text{f}(x) = \begin{cases} \dfrac{3}{32}(4 - x^2) & \text{for } -2 \le x \le 2 \\ 0 & \text{otherwise} \end{cases}$$

You saw on page 113 that the mean of this p.d.f. is O.

$$\text{Var}(X) = \text{E}(X^2) - \mu^2 = \int_{-\infty}^{\infty} x^2 \text{f}(x)\text{d}x - \mu^2 = \int_{-2}^{2} x^2 \cdot \frac{3}{32}(4 - x^2)\text{d}x - 0^2$$

$$= \int_{-2}^{2}\left(\frac{3x^2}{8} - \frac{3x^4}{32}\right)\text{d}x = \left[\frac{x^3}{8} - \frac{3x^5}{160}\right]_{-2}^{2}$$

$$= \left(\frac{2^3}{8} - \frac{3 \times 2^5}{160}\right) - \left(\frac{(-2)^3}{8} - \frac{3 \times (-2)^5}{160}\right) = 0.8.$$

The standard deviation of X is then just $\sqrt{\text{Var}(X)} = \sqrt{0.8} = 0.894$ (3 d.p.)

Find **Var(aX + b)** by **Squaring** *a* and **Getting Rid of** *b*

This is the same formula you saw on page 100 for discrete random variables.

Variance of (aX + b)

For a continuous random variable X with p.d.f. f(x): $\text{Var}(aX + b) = a^2\text{Var}(X)$

EXAMPLE The continuous random variable X has p.d.f. f (x), where $\text{f}(x) = \begin{cases} \dfrac{3}{37}x^2 & \text{for } 3 \le x \le 4 \\ 0 & \text{otherwise} \end{cases}$

If $\text{E}(X) = \dfrac{525}{148}$, find: a) the variance,
  b) Var(3X + 2).

See page 113 for the calculation of the mean of this p.d.f.

a) $\text{Var}(X) = \text{E}(X^2) - \mu^2 = \int_{-\infty}^{\infty} x^2\text{f}(x)\text{d}x - \left(\frac{525}{148}\right)^2 = \int_{3}^{4} x^2 \cdot \frac{3}{37}x^2\text{d}x - \left(\frac{525}{148}\right)^2$

$$= \frac{3}{37}\left[\frac{x^5}{5}\right]_{3}^{4} - \left(\frac{525}{148}\right)^2 = \frac{3}{185}(4^5 - 3^5) - \left(\frac{525}{148}\right)^2 = 0.0815467... = 0.0815 \text{ (to 4 d.p.)}$$

b) $\text{Var}(3X + 2) = 3^2 \times \text{Var}(X) = 9 \times 0.0815467... = 0.734 \text{ (to 3 d.p.)}$.

Don't be fooled by the easy-looking formulas above...

...there are a couple of traps lurking here for the unwary:
1) Remember what goes inside the integral when you're calculating the variance... it's $x^2\text{f}(x)$.
2) Don't obsess so much about getting that integral right that you forget to subtract the square of the mean.

Median and Quartiles

Find the **Median** and **Quartiles** using the **Area Under the p.d.f.**

The <u>median</u>, Q_2, is the value which splits the <u>area under the p.d.f. in half</u>
— i.e. the area to the left of Q_2 = 0.5 and the area to the right of Q_2 = 0.5.

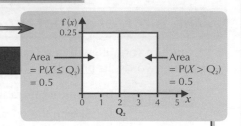

Median and Quartiles of a Continuous Random Variable

If X is a continuous random variable with probability density function $f(x)$, then:

- The <u>median</u> (Q_2) of X is given by $\displaystyle\int_{-\infty}^{Q_2} f(x)\,dx = 0.5.$ ⬅ $P(X \leq Q_2) = 0.5$

- The <u>lower</u> and <u>upper quartiles</u> (Q_1 and Q_3) of X are given by $\displaystyle\int_{-\infty}^{Q_1} f(x)\,dx = 0.25$ and $\displaystyle\int_{-\infty}^{Q_3} f(x)\,dx = 0.75.$

<u>Percentiles</u> are a similar kind of thing, but they divide the distribution into 100 parts, where n% of the total probability is less than the nth percentile.

You find percentiles by integrating as well — for example, to find the 10th percentile, P_{10}, you'd solve $\displaystyle\int_{-\infty}^{P_{10}} f(x)\,dx = 0.1.$

> **EXAMPLE** The continuous random variable X has the p.d.f. shown below. Find the value of the <u>median</u> of X, Q_2.
>
> $$f(x) = \begin{cases} \dfrac{x}{6} & \text{for } 2 \leq x \leq 4 \\ 0 & \text{otherwise} \end{cases}$$
>
> $$\int_{-\infty}^{Q_2} f(x)\,dx = 0.5 \Rightarrow \int_{2}^{Q_2} \frac{x}{6}dx = 0.5 \Rightarrow \frac{1}{6}\int_{2}^{Q_2} x\,dx = 0.5 \Rightarrow \frac{1}{6}\left[\frac{x^2}{2}\right]_{2}^{Q_2} = 0.5$$
>
> *Always check that your answer seems sensible. Here, it has to be between 2 and 4, so $\sqrt{10}$ = 3.16... looks fine.*
>
> $$\Rightarrow \frac{1}{6}\left[\frac{(Q_2)^2}{2} - \frac{4}{2}\right] = 0.5 \Rightarrow \frac{(Q_2)^2 - 4}{12} = 0.5 \Rightarrow (Q_2)^2 - 4 = 6 \Rightarrow Q_2 = \sqrt{10}$$

Find the **Median** and **Quartiles** using the **c.d.f.**

Since the c.d.f. $F(x)$ gives $P(X \leq x)$ for a given value of x, you can <u>easily</u> find the <u>median</u> by substituting Q_2 into $F(x)$ and equating to 0.5. This is a particularly clever move if you've already been asked to find $F(x)$ earlier in the question.

> If X is a continuous random variable with cumulative distribution function $F(x)$, then:
> - The <u>median</u> (Q_2) of X is given by $F(Q_2) = 0.5$.
> - The <u>lower quartile</u> (Q_1) of X is given by $F(Q_1) = 0.25$.
> - The <u>upper quartile</u> (Q_3) of X is given by $F(Q_3) = 0.75$.
>
> *And you use the same method for the <u>percentiles</u>. E.g. the 10th percentile P_{10} is given by $F(P_{10}) = 0.1$.*

> **EXAMPLE**
> The continuous random variable X has p.d.f. $f(x)$, where $f(x) = \begin{cases} 0.4 & \text{for } 1 \leq x < 2 \\ 0.4(x-1) & \text{for } 2 \leq x \leq 3 \\ 0 & \text{otherwise} \end{cases}$
> Find $F(x)$. Then find the interquartile range, $Q_3 - Q_1$.

<u>Integrate</u> to find the c.d.f., making sure the joins are <u>smooth</u> — I used the 'constants of integration' method (p112).

$$F(x) = \begin{cases} 0 & \text{for } x < 1 \\ 0.4x + k_1 & \text{for } 1 \leq x < 2 \\ 0.2x^2 - 0.4x + k_2 & \text{for } 2 \leq x \leq 3 \\ 1 & \text{for } x > 3 \end{cases}$$

➡ *Choose k_1 and k_2 to give 'smooth joins'.* ➡

$$F(x) = \begin{cases} 0 & \text{for } x < 1 \\ 0.4x - 0.4 & \text{for } 1 \leq x < 2 \\ 0.2x^2 - 0.4x + 0.4 & \text{for } 2 \leq x \leq 3 \\ 1 & \text{for } x > 3 \end{cases}$$

- The lower quartile (Q_1) is given by $F(Q_1) = 0.25$
  — and you know Q_1 must be less than 2 (since $F(2)$ = 0.4). ⬅ *Find the value of $F(x)$ where the second and third pieces join to work out which piece contains each quartile.*
  So solve $0.4Q_1 - 0.4 = 0.25$, which gives $Q_1 = 1.625$.

- The upper quartile (Q_3) is given by $F(Q_3) = 0.75$ — and you know x must be greater than 2 (again, as $F(2)$ = 0.4).
  So solve $0.2Q_3^2 - 0.4Q_3 + 0.4 = 0.75$, which gives $Q_3 = \dfrac{0.4 + \sqrt{0.44}}{0.4} = 1 + \dfrac{\sqrt{0.44}}{0.4}$ (using the quadratic formula).

- This means the interquartile range = $Q_3 - Q_1 = 1 + \dfrac{\sqrt{0.44}}{0.4} - 1.625 = 1.033$ (to 3 d.p.).

Median, quartiles — hmmm, that rings a vague bell from S1...

You should know these terms already, but the difference here is that you're finding a <u>theoretical</u> value for, say, the median of a distribution — not the actual median value for a set of data. Remember, the $F(x)$ method will be quicker if you know $F(x)$.

Rectangular Distributions

A <u>continuous random variable</u> X whose value is <u>equally likely</u> to be anywhere within a particular <u>range</u> is said to follow a <u>rectangular</u> distribution. You'll see why they went for 'rectangular' shortly (it's not very imaginative).

The p.d.f. of a Rectangular Distribution is a Rectangle

A random variable with a rectangular distribution takes <u>any value</u> within a given <u>range</u> with <u>equal probability</u>. In other words, its <u>probability density function</u> has the <u>same</u> value over the whole range.

> **EXAMPLE** The continuous random variable X has a rectangular distribution and can take any value from 1 to 5.
> a) Sketch the graph of f(x), the probability density function (p.d.f.) of X.
> b) Define f(x).
>
> a) It's a <u>rectangular</u> distribution, so within its range of possible values, f(x) is <u>constant</u>. Since the <u>total area</u> under the p.d.f. must equal 1 and the width of the rectangle is $5 - 1 = 4$, its height must be $1 \div 4 = 0.25$.
>
>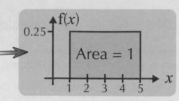
>
> b) So f(x) is given by: $f(x) = \begin{cases} 0.25 & \text{for } 1 \leq x \leq 5 \\ 0 & \text{otherwise} \end{cases}$

You can go through the same process to work out the p.d.f. of <u>any</u> rectangular distribution. But here's the <u>general formula</u> in a big box.

Rectangular Distribution

If X is a random variable with a <u>rectangular distribution</u>, then the p.d.f. of X is:

$$f(x) = \begin{cases} \dfrac{1}{b-a} & \text{for } a \leq x \leq b \\ 0 & \text{otherwise} \end{cases} \qquad \text{for constants } a \text{ and } b.$$

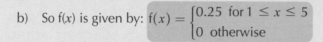

These distributions can also be called 'continuous uniform distributions' and written U[a, b].

Remember... Probability = Area Under a p.d.f.

> **EXAMPLE** The continuous random variable X follows a rectangular distribution with the p.d.f. given below.
>
> $f(x) = \begin{cases} \dfrac{1}{10} & \text{for } 8 \leq x \leq 18 \\ 0 & \text{otherwise} \end{cases}$
>
> Find: a) $P(10 < X < 14.1)$, b) $P(X \leq 14)$, c) $P(X < 14)$, d) $P(X \geq 10.5)$.
>
> It's best to start off by drawing a <u>sketch</u> of the p.d.f.
> It's a <u>rectangle</u> with <u>width</u> $18 - 8 = 10$, and <u>height</u> 0.1.
>
> a) $P(10 < X < 14.1)$ = the area under the p.d.f. between $x = 10$ and $x = 14.1$.
> This is $(14.1 - 10) \times 0.1 = 4.1 \times 0.1 = 0.41$
>
> b) $P(X \leq 14)$ = the area under the p.d.f. for $x \leq 14$.
> This is $(14 - 8) \times 0.1 = 6 \times 0.1 = 0.6$
>
> c) For a <u>continuous</u> distribution, $P(X \leq k) = P(X < k)$ — so $P(X < 14) = P(X \leq 14) = 0.6$
>
> d) $P(X \geq 10.5)$ = the area under the p.d.f. for $x \geq 10.5$.
> This is $(18 - 10.5) \times 0.1 = 7.5 \times 0.1 = 0.75$
>
>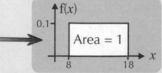

Working out the areas of rectangles — this page really is the limit...

Well, who'd have thought... a page on working out the areas of rectangles in S2. (Best enjoy it while the going's easy, mind.) There's not much more to say about this page really. So I'll keep my mouth shut and let you get on with the next page.

Rectangular Distributions

You'll be working out <u>expected values</u> and <u>variances</u> of <u>continuous random variables</u> on this page — so you can expect a bit of <u>integration</u>. See pages 113-114 for a bit more info if you don't remember why.

You *Might* be Asked to *Prove* these Formulas for *E(X)* and *Var(X)*

You could be asked to show <u>why</u> these formulas are true, so read this section very carefully.

Rectangular Distributions

If X has a rectangular distribution with p.d.f. $f(x) = \begin{cases} \dfrac{1}{b-a} & \text{for } a \leq x \leq b, \\ 0 & \text{otherwise} \end{cases}$

then (i) $E(X) = \dfrac{a+b}{2}$ and (ii) $Var(X) = \dfrac{(b-a)^2}{12}$.

EXAMPLE X follows a rectangular distribution with $f(x) = \begin{cases} \dfrac{1}{b-a} & \text{for } a \leq x \leq b \\ 0 & \text{otherwise} \end{cases}$

Show: (i) $E(X) = \dfrac{a+b}{2}$, (ii) $Var(X) = \dfrac{(b-a)^2}{12}$, and hence that the standard deviation of X is $\dfrac{b-a}{2\sqrt{3}}$.

(i) From the <u>symmetry of the p.d.f.</u>, the expected value of X must be $\dfrac{a+b}{2}$.

<u>OR</u>, using <u>integration</u>: $E(X) = \displaystyle\int_{-\infty}^{\infty} xf(x)dx = \int_a^b \frac{x}{b-a}dx = \frac{1}{b-a}\int_a^b xdx = \frac{1}{b-a}\left[\frac{x^2}{2}\right]_a^b$

$= \dfrac{1}{b-a}\left(\dfrac{b^2}{2} - \dfrac{a^2}{2}\right) = \dfrac{1}{b-a} \times \dfrac{b^2-a^2}{2} = \dfrac{(b+a)(b-a)}{2(b-a)} = \dfrac{a+b}{2}$

(ii) $Var(X) = \displaystyle\int_{-\infty}^{\infty} x^2 f(x)dx - \mu^2 = \int_{-\infty}^{\infty} x^2 f(x)dx - \left(\dfrac{a+b}{2}\right)^2$ | See p114.

But $\displaystyle\int_{-\infty}^{\infty} x^2 f(x)dx = \int_a^b x^2\left(\frac{1}{b-a}\right)dx = \frac{1}{b-a}\int_a^b x^2 dx = \frac{1}{b-a}\left[\frac{x^3}{3}\right]_a^b = \frac{b^3-a^3}{3(b-a)} = \frac{b^2+ab+a^2}{3}$

> $b^3 - a^3 =$ $(b-a)(b^2 + ab + a^2)$

So $Var(X) = \dfrac{b^2+ab+a^2}{3} - \left(\dfrac{a+b}{2}\right)^2 = \dfrac{4b^2 + 4ab + 4a^2 - 3a^2 - 6ab - 3b^2}{12} = \dfrac{b^2 - 2ab + a^2}{12} = \dfrac{(b-a)^2}{12}$

And so, the standard deviation of X is $\sqrt{\dfrac{(b-a)^2}{12}} = \dfrac{b-a}{\sqrt{12}} = \dfrac{b-a}{\sqrt{4}\times\sqrt{3}} = \dfrac{b-a}{2\sqrt{3}}$

And you'll definitely be asked to <u>use</u> these formulas...

EXAMPLE The continuous random variable X has the p.d.f. $f(x) = \begin{cases} \dfrac{1}{29} & \text{for } -7 \leq x \leq 22 \\ 0 & \text{otherwise} \end{cases}$
Find: (i) $E(X)$, (ii) $Var(X)$

> $f(x)$ is a constant, so you know that this is a rectangular distribution.

(i) $E(X) = \dfrac{a+b}{2} = \dfrac{-7+22}{2} = 7.5$ (ii) $Var(X) = \dfrac{(b-a)^2}{12} = \dfrac{(22-(-7))^2}{12} = \dfrac{29^2}{12} = 70.083$ (to 3 d.p.).

Remember you need to *Integrate* to find *F(x)*

> If you're given F(x), you differentiate to find f(x).

EXAMPLE The continuous random variable X has the p.d.f. given in the previous example. Find: (i) $F(x)$, (ii) $F(4)$

(i) $F(x) = \displaystyle\int_{-\infty}^{x} f(t)dt = \int_{-7}^{x}\frac{1}{29}dt = \frac{1}{29}\int_{-7}^{x}1dt$

$= \dfrac{1}{29}[t]_{-7}^{x} = \dfrac{1}{29}[x-(-7)] = \dfrac{x+7}{29}$ So, $F(x) = \begin{cases} 0 & \text{for } x < -7 \\ \dfrac{x+7}{29} & \text{for } -7 \leq x \leq 22 \\ 1 & \text{for } x > 22 \end{cases}$

> You need to write down <u>all</u> of this.

(ii) Now all you have to do is substitute '4' into your expression for $F(x)$. Easy peasy. $F(4) = \dfrac{4+7}{29} = \dfrac{11}{29}$

Applications of Rectangular Distributions

Rectangular distributions describe things that are equally likely to take <u>any</u> value within an interval. So they're good for describing things that are <u>completely random</u>.

Use a **Rectangular** Distribution When All Values are **Equally Likely**

EXAMPLE A runner's times over 100 m are measured to the nearest 0.1 second. Describe the distribution of the errors in the times.

If the times are <u>measured</u> to the <u>nearest 0.1 s</u>, then each recorded time could be anything <u>up to 0.05 s</u> above or below the actual time. These errors are <u>random</u> — there's no reason to think they're likely to be high, low or in the middle. So if the random variable X represents the errors in the timing, then:

X follows a <u>rectangular distribution</u> over the interval [–0.05, 0.05]. The <u>probability density function</u> is given by:

$\boxed{\frac{1}{b-a}}$ $f(x) = \begin{cases} \frac{1}{0.1} & \text{for } -0.05 \leq x \leq 0.05 \\ 0 & \text{otherwise} \end{cases} \Rightarrow f(x) = \begin{cases} 10 & \text{for } -0.05 \leq x \leq 0.05 \\ 0 & \text{otherwise} \end{cases}$

All the Usual **Probability Rules** Still Apply with Rectangular Distributions

EXAMPLE If X has the p.d.f. $f(x) = \begin{cases} \frac{1}{3} & \text{for } 4 \leq x \leq 7 \\ 0 & \text{otherwise} \end{cases}$, and $Y = 8X - 3$, find E(Y) and Var(Y).

$E(X) = \frac{a+b}{2} = \frac{4+7}{2} = 5.5 \Rightarrow E(Y) = E(8X - 3) = 8E(X) - 3 = 8 \times 5.5 - 3 = 41$

> See pages 113-114 for more info.

$Var(X) = \frac{(b-a)^2}{12} = \frac{(7-4)^2}{12} = \frac{9}{12} = 0.75 \Rightarrow Var(Y) = Var(8X - 3) = 8^2 \times Var(X) = 64 \times 0.75 = 48$

EXAMPLE X and Y are independent random variables, with $f(x) = \begin{cases} \frac{1}{2} & \text{for } 1 \leq x \leq 3 \\ 0 & \text{otherwise} \end{cases}$ and $f(y) = \begin{cases} \frac{1}{5} & \text{for } 0 \leq y \leq 5 \\ 0 & \text{otherwise} \end{cases}$.

Find the probability that both X and Y take values greater than 1.2.

X and Y are <u>independent</u>, so $\boxed{P(X > 1.2 \text{ and } Y > 1.2) = P(X > 1.2) \times P(Y > 1.2)}$.
You could find each of these probabilities by <u>integrating</u> — but it's easier to <u>sketch</u> the p.d.f.s of X and Y, and take it from there.

$\boxed{P(X > 1.2) = 0.5 \times 1.8 = 0.9}$ and $\boxed{P(Y > 1.2) = 0.2 \times 3.8 = 0.76}$

So $\boxed{P(X > 1.2 \text{ and } Y > 1.2) = 0.9 \times 0.76 = 0.684}$.

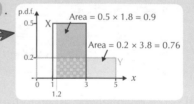

EXAMPLE X has the probability density function $f(x) = \begin{cases} \frac{1}{9} & \text{for } 3 \leq x \leq 12 \\ 0 & \text{otherwise} \end{cases}$

(a) Sketch the probability density function of X.   (b) Find E(X^2).

(a) It's a rectangular distribution, so the p.d.f. is a <u>rectangle</u> with a <u>height</u> of $\frac{1}{9}$ and a <u>width</u> of 9.

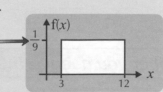

(b) You need to <u>integrate</u> to find E(X^2).

$E(X^2) = \int_{-\infty}^{\infty} x^2 f(x) dx = \int_3^{12} \frac{x^2}{9} dx = \frac{1}{9}\left[\frac{x^3}{3}\right]_3^{12} = \frac{12^3 - 3^3}{27} = \frac{1728 - 27}{27} = \frac{1701}{27} = 63$

Rectangular distributions — the clue's in the name...

Questions on rectangular distributions probably won't involve any really tricky maths, and you won't need to use any of those awkward, fiddly tables. So they're potentially slightly easier marks... as long as you know what you're doing. So learn the stuff above, think carefully before you start pressing loads of buttons on your calculator, and Bob <u>should</u> be your uncle.

S2 Section 3 — Practice Questions

It's the end of Section 3, and I'm going to assume that you know what you're supposed to do by now. And if you get any wrong, well... I'll say no more.

Warm-up Questions

1) Find the value of k for each of the probability density functions below.

   a) $f(x) = \begin{cases} kx & \text{for } 1 \leq x \leq 10 \\ 0 & \text{otherwise} \end{cases}$

   b) $g(x) = \begin{cases} 0.2x + k & \text{for } 0 \leq x \leq 1 \\ 0 & \text{otherwise} \end{cases}$

2) For each of the probability density functions below, find: (i) $P(X < 1)$, (ii) $P(2 \leq X \leq 5)$, (iii) $P(X = 4)$.

   a) $f(x) = \begin{cases} 0.08x & \text{for } 0 \leq x \leq 5 \\ 0 & \text{otherwise} \end{cases}$

   b) $g(x) = \begin{cases} 0.02(10 - x) & \text{for } 0 \leq x \leq 10 \\ 0 & \text{otherwise} \end{cases}$

3) Find the exact value of k for each of the probability density functions below. Then for each p.d.f., find $P(X < 1)$.

   a) $f(x) = \begin{cases} kx^2 & \text{for } 0 \leq x \leq 5 \\ 0 & \text{otherwise} \end{cases}$

   b) $g(x) = \begin{cases} 0.1x^2 + kx & \text{for } 0 \leq x \leq 2 \\ 0 & \text{otherwise} \end{cases}$

4) Say whether the following are probability density functions. Explain your answers.

   a) $f(x) = \begin{cases} 0.1x^2 + 0.2 & \text{for } 0 \leq x \leq 2 \\ 0 & \text{otherwise} \end{cases}$

   b) $g(x) = \begin{cases} x & \text{for } -1 \leq x \leq 1 \\ 0 & \text{otherwise} \end{cases}$

5) Find the cumulative distribution function (c.d.f.) for each of the following p.d.f.s.

   a) $f(x) = \begin{cases} 0.08x & \text{for } 0 \leq x \leq 5 \\ 0 & \text{otherwise} \end{cases}$

   b) $g(x) = \begin{cases} 0.02(10 - x) & \text{for } 0 \leq x \leq 10 \\ 0 & \text{otherwise} \end{cases}$

   c) $h(x) = \begin{cases} 2x & \text{for } 0 \leq x \leq 0.5 \\ 1 & \text{for } 0.5 \leq x \leq 1 \\ 3 - 2x & \text{for } 1 \leq x \leq 1.5 \\ 0 & \text{otherwise} \end{cases}$

   d) $m(x) = \begin{cases} 0.5 - 0.1x & \text{for } 2 \leq x \leq 4 \\ 0.1 & \text{for } 4 \leq x \leq 10 \\ 0 & \text{otherwise} \end{cases}$

6) Find the probability density function (p.d.f.) for each of the following c.d.f.s.

   a) $F(x) = \begin{cases} 0 & \text{for } x < 0 \\ x^4 & \text{for } 0 \leq x \leq 1 \\ 1 & \text{for } x > 1 \end{cases}$

   b) $G(x) = \begin{cases} 0 & \text{for } x < 1 \\ \dfrac{1}{100}(x - 1)^2 & \text{for } 1 \leq x < 6 \\ \dfrac{3}{8}x - 2 & \text{for } 6 \leq x \leq 8 \\ 1 & \text{for } x > 8 \end{cases}$

7) The random variables X and Y have p.d.f.s. $f(x)$ and $g(y)$ respectively, where

   $f(x) = \begin{cases} 0.08x & \text{for } 0 \leq x \leq 5 \\ 0 & \text{otherwise} \end{cases}$ and $g(y) = \begin{cases} 0.02(10 - y) & \text{for } 0 \leq y \leq 10 \\ 0 & \text{otherwise} \end{cases}$

   a) Find the mean and variance of X and Y.

   b) Find the mean and variance of $4X + 2$ and $3Y - 4$.

   c) Find the median and the interquartile range of X.

S2 Section 3 — Practice Questions

Warm-up Questions Continued

8) Sketch the p.d.f. of the continuous random variable Y, where $f(y) = \begin{cases} \frac{1}{22} & \text{for} -4 \leq y \leq 18 \\ 0 & \text{otherwise} \end{cases}$

9) The random variable X has the p.d.f. $f(x) = \begin{cases} \frac{1}{10} & \text{for } 0 \leq x \leq 10 \\ 0 & \text{otherwise} \end{cases}$

Find: a) $P(X < 4)$, b) $P(X \geq 8)$, c) $P(X = 5)$, d) $P(3 < X \leq 7)$.

10) X follows a rectangular distribution with p.d.f. given by $f(x) = \begin{cases} c & \text{for } a \leq x \leq b \\ 0 & \text{otherwise} \end{cases}$.
   a) Write down the formulas for $E(X)$ and $Var(X)$.
   b) Write an expression for c in terms of a and b.
   c) Prove, by integration, that the formula you've written for $E(X)$ is true.

11) X has the probability density function $f(x) = \begin{cases} \frac{1}{15} & \text{for } 4 \leq x \leq 19 \\ 0 & \text{otherwise} \end{cases}$
   a) Calculate $E(X)$, $Var(X)$, and the cumulative distribution function of X, $F(x)$.
   b) Given that $Y = 6X - 3$, calculate $E(Y)$ and $Var(Y)$.

12) X and Y are independent random variables with $f(x) = \begin{cases} \frac{1}{4} & \text{for } 4 \leq x \leq 8 \\ 0 & \text{otherwise} \end{cases}$ and $g(y) = \begin{cases} \frac{1}{20} & \text{for} -8 \leq y \leq 12 \\ 0 & \text{otherwise} \end{cases}$
   Find: a) $P(X < 6 \text{ and } Y > 0)$, b) $P(X < 6 \text{ or } Y > 0)$.

13) I travel by train to work five days per week. The length of time, in minutes, that my morning train is delayed for can be modelled by the random variable X with p.d.f. $f(x) = \begin{cases} \frac{1}{12} & \text{for } 0 \leq x \leq 12 \\ 0 & \text{otherwise} \end{cases}$

   If the delay is any greater than 8 minutes, I arrive late for work.
   a) Find the probability that I am late for work on a randomly chosen day during a particular week.
   b) Find the probability that I am late for work more than once during a single week.

Exam Questions

1   The continuous random variable X has probability density function $f(x)$, as defined below.

$$f(x) = \begin{cases} \frac{1}{k}(x + 4) & \text{for } 0 \leq x \leq 2 \\ 0 & \text{otherwise} \end{cases}$$

   a)   Find the value of k.

(3 marks)

   b)   Find the cumulative distribution function of X, $F(x)$.

(5 marks)

   c)   Calculate $E(X)$.

(3 marks)

   d)   Calculate the variance of:
        (i) X

(3 marks)

        (ii) $4X - 2$

(2 marks)

   e)   Find the median of X.

(4 marks)

S2 Section 3 — Practice Questions

Think of this page as a game. To win the game, you have to get all the answers to the questions right.
I know what you're thinking... it's a terrible game. In fact, it's not a game at all, but a shameless fib.

Exam Questions Continued

2 The continuous random variable X has cumulative distribution function F(x), as defined below.

$$F(x) = \begin{cases} 0 \text{ for } x < 1 \\ k(x - 1) \text{ for } 1 \le x < 3 \\ 0.5(x - 2) \text{ for } 3 \le x \le 4 \\ 1 \text{ for } x > 4 \end{cases}$$

a) Calculate the value of k.

(2 marks)

b) Calculate the interquartile range of X.

(5 marks)

c) (i) Specify the probability density function of X, f(x).

(3 marks)

   (ii) Sketch the graph of f(x).

(1 mark)

d) (i) Find the mean (μ) of X.

(3 marks)

   (ii) Find the variance (σ^2) of X.

(3 marks)

   (iii) Find $P(X < \mu - \sigma)$.

(2 marks)

3 A 40 cm length of ribbon is cut in two at a random point. The length, in cm, of the shorter piece of ribbon can be represented by the random variable X with probability density function

$$f(x) = \begin{cases} \dfrac{1}{20} & \text{for } 0 \le x \le 20 \\ 0 & \text{otherwise} \end{cases}$$

a) Sketch the probability density function of X.

(1 mark)

b) Find:
   (i) $P(X > 5)$,

(1 mark)

   (ii) $P(X = 2)$.

(1 mark)

c) Calculate $E(X)$ and $Var(X)$.

(3 marks)

Given that $Y = X^3$ and $Z = \dfrac{2X^6}{Y}$, find:

d) $E(Y)$

(3 marks)

e) $E(Z)$

(3 marks)

Confidence Intervals

You've met <u>confidence intervals</u> for the <u>mean</u> of a distribution before. Well now they're back.
And they've brought a shiny, new distribution with them...

*Remember, a **Confidence Interval** for the **Mean** should contain the true value of µ*

A <u>confidence interval</u> for the <u>mean</u> of a population modelled by a random variable X is: $\left(\overline{X} - z\dfrac{\sigma}{\sqrt{n}},\ \overline{X} + z\dfrac{\sigma}{\sqrt{n}}\right)$

Here, $\overline{X}$ is the <u>mean of a random sample</u> of n observations of X and <u>σ is the standard deviation</u> of the distribution.
'z' is a value from the <u>standard normal distribution</u> ($Z \sim N(0, 1)$), which depends on the <u>level of confidence</u> required.
For example, for a 95% confidence interval, use $z = 1.96$, since $P(-1.96 < Z < 1.96) = 0.95$.

The above method works <u>fine</u> as long as the following <u>conditions</u> are satisfied:

> 1) $\overline{X}$ follows a <u>normal</u> distribution
> 2) You <u>know</u> σ (or can <u>estimate</u> it pretty well)

- If X follows a <u>normal</u> distribution, then condition 1) is satisfied.
  Or, if <u>n is large</u>, the <u>Central Limit Theorem</u> tells you that condition 1) is satisfied.

- And if σ is unknown, but <u>n is large</u>, $S^2 = \dfrac{n}{n-1}\left[\dfrac{\sum X_i^2}{n} - \left(\dfrac{\sum X_i}{n}\right)^2\right]$

  is a pretty good estimator of the variance σ^2.

> <u>The Central Limit Theorem says...</u>
> If you take a sample of n readings
> from <u>any</u> distribution with mean µ and
> variance σ^2: for <u>large n</u> (n > 30),
> the distribution of the <u>sample mean</u>, $\overline{X}$,
> is <u>approximately normal</u>: $\overline{X} \sim N\left(\mu, \dfrac{\sigma^2}{n}\right)$

But for <u>small n</u>, when you <u>don't know</u> the <u>variance</u>, the situation is a bit more complicated.

*For **Unknown Variance** and **Small n**, you need the **t-Distribution***

1) If the population is normally distributed but the <u>variance is unknown</u> and the sample size is <u>small</u> ($n < 30$),
   you can still estimate σ^2 using s^2, but you <u>can't assume</u> that the quantity $\dfrac{\overline{X} - \mu}{S/\sqrt{n}}$ follows an $N(0, 1)$ distribution.
   Instead, it has a <u>t-distribution</u>.

2) <u>t-distributions</u> are very similar to the standard normal distribution — their graphs are <u>shaped like a bell</u> and
   are <u>symmetrical</u> about a <u>mean of zero</u>. A t-distribution has <u>one parameter</u>, v, called the <u>degrees of freedom</u>,
   and a t-distribution with v degrees of freedom is written $t_{(v)}$.

   > v is the Greek letter 'nu'.

3) So, going back to the quantity $\dfrac{\overline{X} - \mu}{S/\sqrt{n}}$ — this follows a

   t-distribution with $v = (n - 1)$ degrees of freedom.

   In other words: $\dfrac{\overline{X} - \mu}{S/\sqrt{n}} = T$ and $T \sim t_{(n-1)}$

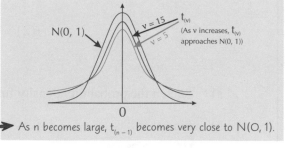

As n becomes large, $t_{(n-1)}$ becomes very close to N(0, 1).

So now you're ready for another big box and a <u>second formula</u> for finding confidence intervals:

Confidence Intervals — Normal Distribution with Unknown Variance

A <u>confidence interval</u> for the <u>population mean</u> when the <u>sample size n is small</u> is: $\left(\overline{X} - \dfrac{S}{\sqrt{n}}t_{(n-1)}\ ,\ \overline{X} + \dfrac{S}{\sqrt{n}}t_{(n-1)}\right)$

> The t-tables give values of t at different <u>percentage points</u> of p for various values of v.
> The value of p you choose depends on the '<u>level of confidence</u>'.
> E.g., for a 95% confidence interval, choose $t_{(n-1)}$ so that: $P(-[t_{(n-1)}] < T < [t_{(n-1)}]) = 0.95$.
>
> But hold your horses... The tables give values of t such that $P(T \le t) = p$. For a 95% C.I. you want
> $P(-t < T < t) = 0.95$, which means $P(T \le t) = 0.975$. So choose the value of $t_{(n-1)}$ for $p = 0.975$.

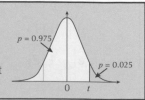

Useful Quote: Tea is liquid wisdom (Anonymous)...

You'll also see t-distributions called <u>Student's</u> t-distributions. William Sealy Gosset, the chap who first studied them, worked
for Guinness at the time and wasn't allowed to publish research papers. So he used the pen name 'Student'. Interesting stuff.

Confidence Intervals

Don't worry, I wouldn't leave you without an example to work through. In fact, here's a whole page of them...

EXAMPLE A shop manager wants to check that the mean weight of the jars of pickled onions she sells is at least 300 g. The weights (x grams) of a random sample of 8 jars from the shop are given below.

$$289, \quad 301, \quad 302, \quad 304, \quad 298, \quad 310, \quad 302, \quad 298$$

a) The manager wishes to construct a confidence interval for the mean weight of the jars of pickled onions she sells. What assumption does she need to make before she can do this?

b) Find a 95% confidence interval for the mean weight of the jars.

a) Because the population variance is unknown and this sample size is small, the manager needs to work out the confidence interval using a t-distribution,

so she needs to make the <u>assumption</u> that the <u>jar weights follow a normal distribution</u> .

b) Start by finding the <u>sample mean</u>: $\bar{x} = \dfrac{\sum x}{n} = \dfrac{2404}{8} = \underline{300.5\ g}$

Next, <u>estimate</u> the <u>variance</u>: $s^2 = \dfrac{n}{n-1}\left[\dfrac{\sum x^2}{n} - \left(\dfrac{\sum x}{n}\right)^2\right] = \dfrac{8}{7}\left[\dfrac{722\,654}{8} - 300.5^2\right] = \dfrac{8}{7} \times 31.5 = \underline{36}$

$n = 8$, so you need to look up $t_{(7)}$ in the <u>t-distribution tables</u> (p.140).
For a 95% C.I., you need $P(T \le t) = 0.975$, so read across to $p = 0.975$ to get $t_{(7)} = \underline{2.365}$.

So, your <u>confidence interval</u> is:

$\left(\bar{x} - \dfrac{s}{\sqrt{n}}t_{(n-1)},\ \bar{x} + \dfrac{s}{\sqrt{n}}t_{(n-1)}\right) = \left(300.5 - \dfrac{6}{\sqrt{8}} \times 2.365,\ 300.5 + \dfrac{6}{\sqrt{8}} \times 2.365\right) = \underline{(295, 306)}$ (3 sig.fig.)

EXAMPLE A random sample of 10 potato plants is selected from a field of potato plants, and the heights, h cm, recorded. The heights are assumed to be normally distributed, and for the 10 plants: $\sum h = 350$ and $\sum h^2 = 12\,528$.
a) Calculate a 99% confidence interval for the mean height of all the potato plants in the field.
b) Comment on the claim that the mean height of all the potato plants is 42 cm.

a) • Start by finding the <u>sample mean</u>, $\bar{x}$, and an <u>estimate</u> of the population <u>variance</u>, s^2.

$\bar{x} = \dfrac{350}{10} = \underline{35}$ cm and $s^2 = \dfrac{10}{9}\left[\dfrac{12\,528}{10} - 35^2\right] = \dfrac{278}{9} = \underline{30.889}$ (3 d.p.)

• $n = 10$, so you need to look up $t_{(9)}$ in the <u>t-distribution tables</u>. It's a 99% C.I., so $p = 0.995$ and $t_{(9)} = \underline{3.250}$.

• So your <u>confidence interval</u> is: $\left(35 - \dfrac{\sqrt{278/9}}{\sqrt{10}} \times 3.25,\ 35 + \dfrac{\sqrt{278/9}}{\sqrt{10}} \times 3.25\right) = \underline{(29.3, 40.7)}$ (3 s.f.)

b) The mean height claimed lies <u>outside the confidence interval</u>, so there is <u>evidence to doubt this claim</u>.

You could also be asked to do some trickier calculations...

EXAMPLE A random sample of 12 observations is taken from a normal distribution with mean μ and variance σ². This data is used to calculate a 95% confidence interval for μ of (8.6, 23.8).

a) Find the sample mean $\bar{x}$.
b) Calculate an estimate of the standard error of the sample mean.

a) The <u>trick</u> here is to use the fact that the confidence interval is <u>symmetrical</u> about the sample mean, which means $\bar{x}$ will be right in the <u>middle</u> of the interval. ⟶ $\bar{x} = \dfrac{8.6 + 23.8}{2} = \underline{16.2}$

b) Remember, the <u>standard error</u> is $\dfrac{\sigma}{\sqrt{n}}$, so its estimate is given by $\dfrac{s}{\sqrt{n}}$, which you can find

by using the formula for a confidence interval and substituting in what you know.

So, using the upper limit: $\bar{x} + \dfrac{s}{\sqrt{n}}t_{(n-1)} = 23.8$.

Substituting in $\bar{x} = 16.2$ and $t_{(11)} = 2.201$ gives: $16.2 + \dfrac{s}{\sqrt{n}} \times 2.201 = 23.8 \Rightarrow \dfrac{s}{\sqrt{n}} = \dfrac{23.8 - 16.2}{2.201} = \underline{3.45}$ (3 s.f.)

Null and Alternative Hypotheses

Hypothesis testing means checking if your theories about a population are consistent with the observations from your sample. The technical stuff on the next two pages might seem hard-going, but stick with it — it'll help later on.

A Hypothesis is a Statement you want to Test

Hypothesis testing is about using sample data to test statements about population parameters. Unfortunately, it comes with a fleet of terms you need to know.

- **Null Hypothesis (H_0)** — a statement about the value of a population parameter. Your data may allow you to reject this hypothesis.

- **Alternative Hypothesis (H_1)** — a statement that describes the value of the population parameter if H_0 is rejected.

- **Hypothesis test** — a statistical test that tests the claim made about a parameter by H_0 against that made by H_1. It tests whether H_0 should be rejected or not, using evidence from sample data.

- **Test Statistic** — a statistic calculated from sample data which is used to decide whether or not to reject H_0.

1) For any hypothesis test, you need to write two hypotheses — a null hypothesis and an alternative hypothesis.

2) You often choose the null hypothesis to be something you actually think is false. This is because hypothesis tests can only show that statements are false — they can't prove that things are true. So, you're aiming to find evidence for what you think is true, by disproving what you think is false.

3) H_0 needs to give a specific value to the parameter, since all your calculations will be based on this value. You assume this value holds true for the test, then see if your data allows you to reject it. H_1 is then a statement that describes how you think the value of the parameter differs from the value given by H_0.

4) The test statistic you choose depends on the parameter you're interested in. It should be a 'summary' of the sample data, and should have a sampling distribution that can be calculated using the parameter value specified by H_0.

> **EXAMPLE** Jemma thinks that the average length of the worms in her worm farm is greater than 8 cm. She measures the lengths of a random sample of 50 of the worms and calculates the sample mean.
> a) Write down a suitable null hypothesis to test Jemma's theory.
> b) Write down a suitable alternative hypothesis.
> c) Describe the test statistic Jemma should use.
>
> a) The parameter Jemma is interested in is the mean length of all the worms, μ. She thinks that μ is greater than 8, so she's looking to find evidence that μ does not equal 8.
> So, $H_0: \mu = 8$ ◄──── H_0 gives μ the specific value of 8. Jemma is then interested in disproving this hypothesis.
>
> b) H_1 says what Jemma actually thinks. So: $H_1: \mu > 8$
>
> c) The test statistic is the sample mean $\overline{X}$ ◄── Assuming H_0 is true, $\overline{X} \sim N\left(8, \frac{\sigma^2}{50}\right)$, where σ^2 = variance.
>
> You actually use the standardised sample mean — you'll see what I mean when you get to page 126.
>
> If the sample size is large enough (like here), the Central Limit Theorem (p122) tells you that $\overline{X}$ will be normally distributed with mean μ variance $\frac{\sigma^2}{n}$.

Hypothesis Tests can be One-Tailed or Two-Tailed

The 'tailed' business is to do with the critical region used by the test — see next page.

For $H_0: \theta = a$, where θ is a parameter and a is a number:

1) The test is one-tailed if H_1 is specific about the value of θ compared to a, i.e. $H_1: \theta > a$, or $H_1: \theta < a$.

2) The test is two-tailed if H_1 specifies only that θ doesn't equal a, i.e. $H_1: \theta \neq a$.

Whether you use a one-tailed or a two-tailed test depends on how you define H_1. And that depends on what you want to find out about the parameter and any suspicions you might have about it.

> E.g. in the example above, Jemma suspects that the average worm length is greater than 8 cm. This is what she wants to test, so it is sensible to define $H_1: \mu > 8$.
>
> If she was unsure whether the length was greater than or less than 8 cm, she could define $H_1: \mu \neq 8$.

A statistician's party game — pin two tails on the donkey...

Or should it be one? Anyway, a very important thing to remember is that the results of a hypothesis test are either 'reject H_0', or 'do not reject H_0' — which means you haven't found enough evidence to disprove H_0, and not that you've proved it.

Significance Levels and Critical Regions

You use the value of your test statistic to decide whether or not to reject your null hypothesis. Poor little unloved H_0.

If your Data is *Significant*, Reject H_0

1) You would <u>reject H_0</u> if the <u>observed value</u> of the test statistic is <u>unlikely</u> under the null hypothesis.

2) The <u>significance level</u> (α) of a test determines <u>how unlikely</u> the value needs to be before H_0 is rejected. It also determines the <u>strength of the evidence</u> that the test has provided — the lower the value of α, the stronger the evidence you have for saying H_0 is false. You'll usually be told what level to use — e.g. 1% ($\alpha = 0.01$), 5% ($\alpha = 0.05$) or 10% ($\alpha = 0.1$). α is also the probability of incorrectly rejecting H_0 — i.e. of getting extreme data by chance.

3) To decide whether your result is <u>significant</u>:
   - Define the <u>sampling distribution</u> of the <u>test statistic</u> under the <u>null hypothesis</u>.
   - Calculate the <u>probability</u> of getting a value that's <u>at least as extreme as the observed value</u> from this distribution.
   - If the probability is <u>less than or equal to the significance level</u>, <u>reject H_0</u> in favour of H_1.

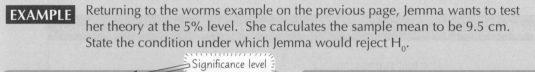

> **EXAMPLE**   Returning to the worms example on the previous page, Jemma wants to test her theory at the 5% level. She calculates the sample mean to be 9.5 cm. State the condition under which Jemma would reject H_0.
>
> Significance level
>
> If $P(\overline{X} \geq 9.5) \leq 0.05$, Jemma would reject H_0.
>
> P(at least as extreme as 9.5) means 9.5 or more.
>
> Since, under H_0, $\overline{X} \sim N\left(8, \frac{\sigma^2}{50}\right)$, this is the same as saying that Jemma would reject H_0 if $P\left(Z \geq \dfrac{9.5 - 8}{\sigma / \sqrt{50}}\right) \leq 0.05$

The *Critical Region* is the *Set of Significant Values*

1) The <u>critical region</u> (CR) is the <u>set of all values of the test statistic</u> that would cause you to <u>reject</u> H_0. And the <u>acceptance region</u> is the set of values that would mean you <u>do not reject</u> H_0. The <u>critical region</u> is chosen so that P(test statistic is in CR, assuming H_0 is true) = α, and the value on the <u>boundary</u> of the critical region is called the <u>critical value</u>.

2) <u>One-tailed tests</u> have a <u>single</u> critical region (and critical value), containing the highest or lowest values. For <u>two-tailed tests</u>, the region is <u>split into two</u> — half at the lower end and half at the upper end, so there are two critical values. Each half of the region has a probability of $\frac{1}{2}\alpha$. ◄ *Or as close to $\frac{1}{2}\alpha$ as you can get — whether you'll be able to make each half <u>exactly</u> $\frac{1}{2}\alpha$ depends on the distribution of the test statistic.*

3) To <u>test</u> whether your result is <u>significant</u>, find the relevant <u>critical value</u> and compare it to the value of your <u>test statistic</u>. If the observed value of the test statistic is '<u>more extreme</u>' than the critical value and so <u>falls in the critical region</u>, reject H_0.

4) Hypothesis tests for the mean of a <u>normal distribution</u> are usually done using this critical region method. You'll see how on the next page.

In Hypothesis Testing, you can *Work Out How Likely Things are to go Wrong*

1) The <u>significance level</u> (α) of a test is the <u>probability of rejecting H_0</u> (assuming H_0 is true). So it's the probability of <u>incorrectly rejecting</u> H_0 — i.e. rejecting H_0 when it's true. Another <u>incorrect decision</u> you can make is to <u>not reject</u> H_0 when it's <u>not true</u>.

> <u>TYPE I ERROR</u> — reject H_0 when H_0 is true
>
> <u>TYPE II ERROR</u> — do not reject H_0 when H_0 is not true

2) So the <u>probability</u> of making a <u>Type I error</u> when doing a hypothesis test is just:

> P(Type I error) = P(value of test statistic is significant, assuming H_0 is true) = significance level (α).

I repeat, X has entered the critical region — we have a significant situation...

Hope you've been following the last two pages closely. Basically, you need two hypotheses and the value of a test statistic calculated from sample data. By assuming H_0 is true, you can find the probabilities of the different values this statistic can take — if the observed value is unlikely enough, reject H_0. But bear in mind there's a chance you might have got it wrong...

Hypothesis Tests and Normal Distributions

If you like normal distributions and you like hypothesis testing, you're going to *love* this page.

If you're hazy on normal distributions, it's time to remind yourself about them. They'll assume you know everything you learnt in S1.

For a *Normal Population* with *Known Variance* — use a *z-Test*

1) Suppose $X \sim N(\mu, \sigma^2)$, where you know the value of σ^2 but μ is unknown. If you take a random sample of n observations from the distribution of X, and calculate the sample mean $\overline{X}$, you can use your observed value $\overline{x}$ to test theories about the population mean μ.

2) You want to test whether your value of $\overline{X}$ is likely enough, under the hypothesised value of μ (remember that $\overline{X} \sim N(\mu, \frac{\sigma^2}{n})$). So that means finding the critical region for an $N(\mu, \frac{\sigma^2}{n})$ distribution.

   If your sample mean lies in this critical region, you should reject H_0.

3) However, the only normal distribution that you can look up the probabilities of different values for is the standard normal distribution Z. So, to get your final test statistic, you need to use the classic 'normal trick' — standardise your sample mean by subtracting the mean (use the value you're assuming for the mean — the one in H_0) and dividing by the standard deviation. Then you can compare this test statistic to a critical value from $N(0, 1)$.

Hypothesis Test for the Mean of a Normal Distribution — Known Variance

The test statistic is: $Z = \dfrac{\overline{X} - \mu}{\sigma/\sqrt{n}} \sim N(0, 1)$

---

4) The critical value(s) depends on the significance level α, and whether it's a one-tailed or a two-tailed test.

   For example, for a two-tailed test at the 5% level of significance, the critical values are $z = -1.96$ and $z = 1.96$, since $P(Z < -1.96) = 0.025$ and $P(Z > 1.96) = 0.025$. So the critical region is: $Z < -1.96$ or $Z > 1.96$.

Example

The times, in minutes, taken by the athletes in a running club to complete a certain run have been found to follow an $N(12, 4)$ distribution. The coach increases the number of training sessions per week, and a random sample of 20 times run since the increase gives a mean time of 11.2 minutes. Assuming that the variance has remained unchanged, test at the 5% significance level whether there is evidence that the average time has decreased.

Let μ = mean time since increase in training sessions. Then $H_0: \mu = 12$, $H_1: \mu < 12$, $\alpha = 0.05$.

You assume that there's been no change in the value of the parameter (μ), so you can give it a value of 12.

This is what you're looking to find evidence for.

Under H_0, $\overline{X} \sim N(12, \frac{4}{20}) \Rightarrow \overline{X} \sim N(12, 0.2)$ and $Z = \dfrac{\overline{X} - 12}{\sqrt{0.2}} \sim N(0, 1)$.

Since $\overline{x} = 11.2$, $z = \dfrac{11.2 - 12}{\sqrt{0.2}} = -1.789$.

This is a one-tailed test and you're interested in the lower end of the distribution. So the critical value is z such that $P(Z < z) = 0.05$. Using the 'normal' tables you find that $P(Z < 1.6449) = 0.95$, which means $P(Z > 1.6449) = 0.05$, and so by symmetry, $P(Z < -1.6449) = 0.05$. So the critical value is -1.6449 and the critical region is $Z < -1.6449$.

If you want, you can instead do the test by working out P(value at least as extreme as observed sample mean) and comparing it to α. So here you'd do: $P(\overline{X} \leq 11.2)$
$= P\left(Z \leq \dfrac{11.2 - 12}{\sqrt{0.2}}\right) = P(Z \leq -1.79) = 1 - P(Z \leq 1.79)$
$= 1 - 0.96327 = 0.03673 < 0.05$, so reject H_0.

Since $z = -1.789 < -1.6449$, the result is significant and there is evidence at the 5% level of significance to reject H_0 and to suggest that the average time has decreased.

Hypothesis Tests and Normal Distributions

If *n is large*, you can always use a *z-Test*

The z-test can also be used in the following situations:

1) The population variance is unknown, but the sample size is large ($n > 30$).

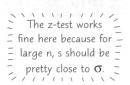

The z-test works fine here because for large n, s should be pretty close to σ.

Use the same test statistic but replace σ with its estimate s, where $s = \sqrt{\frac{n}{n-1}\left[\frac{\sum x^2}{n} - \left(\frac{\sum x}{n}\right)^2\right]}$.

2) The distribution of the population is unknown, but the sample size is large ($n > 30$).

As long as *n is large*, you can use the z-test for any population (since you can use the Central Limit Theorem (see p.122) to approximate the sampling distribution of the mean of any distribution by a normal distribution).

> **EXAMPLE** The average volume of the drinks dispensed by a drinks machine is claimed to be 250 ml. Greg thinks that the machine has developed a fault and wants to test whether the average volume has changed. He measures the volumes, x, of a random sample of 40 drinks from the machine and calculates the following:
>
> $$\sum x = 9800 \quad \text{and} \quad \sum(x - \overline{x})^2 = 3900$$
>
> Carry out Greg's test at the 5% level of significance.
>
> Since n is fairly large, you can apply the Central Limit Theorem and use a z-test with σ estimated by s.
>
> $$\overline{x} = \frac{\sum x}{n} = \frac{9800}{40} = 245\,\text{ml} \quad \text{and} \quad s^2 = \frac{\sum(x - \overline{x})^2}{n-1} = \frac{3900}{39} = 100$$
>
> You can use s² in this form, or in the form shown on p.122. Use whichever is easier with the summary statistics they give you.
>
> The average volume is assumed to be 250 ml, so $H_0: \mu = 250$ and $H_1: \mu \neq 250$. The significance level $\alpha = 0.05$.
>
> Under H_0, $\overline{X} \sim N(250, {}^{100}\!/\!_{40}) \Rightarrow \overline{X} \sim N(250, 2.5)$ and $Z = \frac{\overline{X} - 250}{\sqrt{2.5}} \sim N(0,1)$. $\overline{x} = 245$, so $z = \frac{245 - 250}{\sqrt{2.5}} = -3.16$
>
> This is a two-tailed test at the 5% level. So the critical values are $z = \pm 1.9600$, and the   CR is $Z < -1.96$ or $Z > 1.96$.
>
> Since $z = -3.16 < -1.96$, the result is significant and there is evidence at the 5% level of significance to reject H_0 and to suggest that the average volume has changed.

If the *Variance is Unknown* and the *Sample Size is Small* — use a *t-Test*

If the population variance is unknown and *n is small* (< 30), you can still estimate σ with s, but your test statistic won't follow the standard normal distribution. Instead it'll follow a t-distribution with $(n - 1)$ degrees of freedom.

> ### Hypothesis Test for the Mean of a Normal Distribution — Unknown Variance
> The test statistic, given a small sample size, n, is: $T = \frac{\overline{X} - \mu}{S/\sqrt{n}} \sim t_{(n-1)}$

See p.122 for more on t-distributions.

> **EXAMPLE** A random sample of 8 observations from a normal distribution with mean μ and variance σ^2 produces the following results: $\overline{x} = 9.5$ and $s^2 = 2.25$. Test at the 1% level of significance the claim that $\mu > 9$.
>
> $H_0: \mu = 9, \quad H_1: \mu > 9, \quad \alpha = 0.01$.
>
> σ^2 is unknown and $n = 8$, so you need to use a t-test with 7 degrees of freedom:
>
> Under H_0, $T = \frac{\overline{X} - 9}{1.5/\sqrt{8}} \sim t_{(7)}$. Since $\overline{x} = 9.5$, $t = \frac{9.5 - 9}{1.5/\sqrt{8}} = 0.94$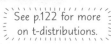
>
> The critical value is t such that $P(T > t) = 0.01$, which means looking up $P(T < t) = 0.99$ in the t-distribution tables. You find that $P(T < 2.998) = 0.99$, and so the critical region is $T > 2.998$.
>
> Since $t = 0.94 < 2.998$, the result is not significant — there is no evidence at this level to support the claim that $\mu > 9$.

My hypothesis is — this is very likely to come up in the exam...

It's really important you know what to look out for when you're faced with questions like the examples above. You'll have to choose whether to do a z-test or a t-test, and that depends on what information about variance and sample size you're given.

Chi-Squared (χ^2) Contingency Table Tests

Another page, another distribution, and another statistical table. But this is the last thing you'll have to learn. Promise.

Contingency Tables show Observed Frequencies for Two Variables

1) Suppose you've got a sample of size n, and you're interested in two different <u>variables</u> for each of the n members — where each variable can be <u>classified</u> into <u>different categories</u>. E.g. eye colour (blue, brown, green, ...), favourite way of cooking potatoes (boiled, roast, baked, ...), etc. You can show this data in a <u>contingency table</u>.

2) You use the <u>columns</u> to show the <u>categories</u> for one of the variables, and the <u>rows</u> to show the other. You then fill in each <u>cell</u> in the table with the <u>number of sample members</u> that fit that particular <u>combination</u> of classes — e.g. 'blue eyes and boiled potatoes'.

3) With the data in this format, you can do a <u>hypothesis test</u> of whether the two variables are <u>independent</u> or <u>linked</u>.

Use a χ^2 Test to test whether Two Variables are Independent

> χ is the lower case Greek letter 'chi'.

The easiest way to see how this test works is to go through an example.

EXAMPLE This table shows soil pH and plant growth for a sample of 100 plants. Test at the 5% level whether there is a link between soil pH and growth for these plants.

	Poor growth	Average growth	Good growth	Total
Acidic soil	12	16	4	32
Neutral soil	3	13	14	30
Alkaline soil	3	10	25	38
Total	18	39	43	100

← Observed frequencies

① As always, the first step is to <u>define the hypotheses</u>:

H_0: the variables are <u>independent</u>, H_1: they're <u>not independent</u>

> Your null hypothesis is always that there is <u>no link</u>.

② Next you need to make a new table — adding the <u>expected frequencies</u> (E), assuming H_0 is true, for each cell in the original table.

Using the formula: $E = \dfrac{\text{(row total)} \times \text{(column total)}}{\text{Overall total } (n)}$, gives you this column:

E.g. for the first observation, 12: (32 × 18) / 100 = 5.76. You get this formula for E by saying that under H_0 the <u>ratio</u> of the growth classes should be the same for each soil category. E.g. (18/100) of each row should have poor growth.

③ Now you can calculate the <u>test statistic</u>: $X^2 = \sum \dfrac{(O_i - E_i)^2}{E_i}$,

> X is the upper case Greek letter 'chi'.

where O_i and E_i are the <u>observed</u> and <u>expected</u> frequencies for cell i.

<u>Add the third column shown</u> to your table and sum the values. $X^2 = 24.3$

Observed frequency (O)	Expected Frequency (E)	$\dfrac{(O - E)^2}{E}$
12	5.76	6.76
3	5.4	1.066...
3	6.84	2.155...
16	12.48	0.992...
13	11.7	0.144...
10	14.82	1.567...
4	13.76	6.922...
14	12.9	0.093...
25	16.34	4.589...
100	100	24.3

④ Under H_0, $X^2 \sim \chi^2_{(\nu)}$ (approx.) — it follows the <u>chi-squared distribution</u> with ν degrees of freedom.

> For this <u>approximation</u> to be valid, all E_i must be <u>greater than 5</u>.

The value of $\underline{\nu}$ depends on how many rows and columns there are in the contingency table.

To work out ν, use this formula: $\nu = [\text{(no. of rows)} - 1] \times [\text{(no. of columns)} - 1] = 2 \times 2 = \underline{4}$

> in original table

⑤ The <u>significance level</u> is <u>5%</u>, so look up the 5% point of $\chi^2_{(4)}$ in the table. The <u>critical value</u> is x where $P(X > x) = 0.05$, which means looking up $P(X \le x) = 0.95$.

Reject H_0 if $X^2 >$ this critical value.

This is just the top right corner of the χ^2 table. The table shows values of x satisfying $P(X \le x) = p$, for $X \sim \chi^2_{(\nu)}$.

0.1	0.9	0.95	0.975	0.99	0.995	p
						ν
0.016	2.706	3.841	5.024	6.635	7.879	1
0.211	4.605	5.991	7.378	9.210	10.597	2
0.584	6.251	7.815	9.348	11.345	12.838	3
1.064	7.779	9.488	11.143	13.277	14.860	4

$P(X \le x) = 0.95$ for $x = 9.488$. $X^2 = 24.3 > 9.488$, so it's <u>significant</u> at this level. There is <u>evidence to reject</u> H_0 and to suggest that there <u>is a link</u> between soil pH and growth for these plants.

Chi-Squared (χ^2) Contingency Table Tests

If your contingency table has <u>two columns</u> and <u>two rows</u>, you have to learn a slightly different test statistic.
This is a bit annoying, but at least it gives us an excuse for another example — hurrah...

2 × 2 Contingency Tables are a Special Case

If your table has <u>2 columns and 2 rows</u>, you can improve the χ^2 approximation by using <u>Yates' continuity correction</u>:

The <u>test statistic for a 2 × 2 table</u> is:

$$X^2 = \sum \frac{(|O_i - E_i| - 0.5)^2}{E_i} \sim \chi^2_{(1)} \text{ (approx.)}$$

EXAMPLE The contingency table on the right was produced after doing an investigation into newts. Carry out a χ^2 test at a 1% level of significance to test whether there is evidence of an association between the variables.

	Red colour	Green colour	Total
Long	12	29	41
Short	29	30	59
Total	41	59	100

① First, <u>define the hypotheses</u>:

H_0: the variables are <u>independent</u>, H_1: they're <u>not independent</u>

② Next, make a new table showing the <u>expected frequencies</u> (E), under H_0:

$\dfrac{41 \times 41}{100} = 16.81$, $\dfrac{59 \times 41}{100} = 24.19$, $\dfrac{41 \times 59}{100} = 24.19$, $\dfrac{59 \times 59}{100} = 34.81$

Observed frequency (O)	Expected Frequency (E)
12	16.81
29	24.19
29	24.19
30	34.81
100	100

③ This is a <u>2 × 2</u> table, so your <u>test statistic</u> includes <u>Yates' continuity correction</u>:

$$X^2 = \sum \frac{(|O_i - E_i| - 0.5)^2}{E_i} \sim \chi^2_{(1)} \text{ (approx.)}$$

Every value of E is greater than 5, so the approximation will be valid.

<u>Add the third column shown</u> to your table and work out the values...

$\dfrac{(|12 - 16.81| - 0.5)^2}{16.81} = 1.105$

$\dfrac{(|29 - 24.19| - 0.5)^2}{24.19} = 0.768$ — This value goes in two of the cells.

$\dfrac{(|30 - 34.81| - 0.5)^2}{34.81} = 0.534$ ...then fill them in.

Observed frequency (O)	Expected Frequency (E)	$\frac{(|O - E| - 0.5)^2}{E}$
12	16.81	1.105
29	24.19	0.768
29	24.19	0.768
30	34.81	0.534
100	100	3.175

Now you can work out the value of the test statistic by adding up the numbers in the 3rd column: $X^2 = 3.175$.

④ Here $\nu = 1$ — i.e. $X^2 \sim \chi^2_{(1)}$ and the <u>significance level</u> is <u>1%</u>. So the <u>critical value</u> is x where $P(X > x) = 0.01$, which means looking up $P(X \le x) = 0.99$ for $\chi^2_{(1)}$.

$P(X \le x) = 0.99$ for $x = 6.635$. $X^2 = 3.175 < 6.635$, so it's <u>not significant</u> at this level. There is <u>no evidence</u> of an association between the variables.

Now you can prove that 'reading this book' and 'exam grade' are linked...

Well, that was a bit heavy going for the last double page of revision — sorry about that. Still, it's really just another hypothesis test with the usual gubbins, plus some tables. The main formula will be given, but Yates' correction needs learning.

S2 Section 4 — Practice Questions

Phew, that section was jam-packed with hypothesis-testing treats.
To make sure you've fully digested them all, finish off with these delicious practice questions.

Warm-up Questions

1) A random sample of size 12 is taken from a population with unknown mean, μ, and unknown variance, σ^2.
   a) Karl wants to construct a confidence interval for μ, using the data from this sample.
      What assumption does he need to make about the population?
   b) Write down the confidence-interval formula that Karl should use.
   c) Find a 95% confidence interval for μ if the sample mean is 50 and $s^2 = 0.7$.

2) A 99% confidence interval for the mean of a normal population is found to be (4.2, 8.7).
   Comment on the claim that the mean value is 9.

3) a) For each of the following, state whether a one-tailed or a two-tailed hypothesis test should be used:
      i) Salma wants to test whether the average height of the students at her college is greater than 160 cm.
      ii) An investigation into the diameter of the metal discs produced by a machine found that the mean diameter was 2.2 cm. Joy wants to test the claim that the mean diameter has changed since the investigation was done.
   b) Define suitable null and alternative hypotheses for each test above.

4) Andrew carries out a hypothesis test concerning the mean of a normal distribution.
   His conclusion is to reject the null hypothesis that $\mu = 10$.
   If it turned out that the mean was actually 10, what type of error would Andrew have made?

5) Explain when you would use a t-test to test the mean of a population.

6) Carry out the following test of the mean, μ, of a normal distribution with variance $\sigma^2 = 9$.
   A random sample of 16 observations from the distribution was taken and the sample mean ($\bar{x}$) calculated.
   Test $H_0: \mu = 45$ against $H_1: \mu < 45$, at the 5% significance level, using $\bar{x} = 42$.

7) A random sample of 10 observations is taken from a normal distribution with unknown mean μ and unknown variance σ^2. The results are shown below.
   $$20.1, \quad 18.5, \quad 19.6, \quad 21.1, \quad 20.7, \quad 20.2, \quad 19.5, \quad 19.7, \quad 20.2, \quad 18.2$$
   a) Calculate the value of the sample mean and an unbiased estimate of the population variance.
   b) Test at the 5% level of significance the claim that $\mu < 20$.

8) A χ^2 contingency table test produces the test statistic $\chi^2 = 8.3$. By comparing this statistic to the $\chi^2_{(4)}$ distribution, test at the 1% level whether there is evidence of an association between the variables.

9) Test at the 5% level of significance whether there is an association between the variables in this table:

	Likes olives	Doesn't like olives	Total
Male	22	18	40
Female	30	30	60
Total	52	48	100

S2 Section 4 — Practice Questions

Aha, some exam-style practice questions to test whether you've got this section sussed. Wasn't expecting that.

Exam Questions

1   Joe claims that, on average, it takes him 15 minutes to walk to work. He records his journey times, x minutes, on 20 randomly selected days and calculates the following:

$$\sum x = 324 \quad \text{and} \quad \sum(x - \overline{x})^2 = 19.2$$

   a)   Find a 95% confidence interval for the mean journey time,
        stating any assumption you make.

(7 marks)

   b)   Comment on Joe's claim that, on average, it takes him 15 minutes to walk to work.

(1 mark)

2   The heights of trees in an area of woodland are known to be normally distributed with a mean of 5.1 m. A random sample of 100 trees from a second area of woodland is selected and the heights, X, of the trees are measured giving the following results:

$$\sum x = 490 \quad \text{and} \quad \sum x^2 = 2421$$

   a)   Calculate unbiased estimates of the population mean, μ, and variance, σ^2, for the trees
        in this second area.

(3 marks)

   b)   Test at the 1% level of significance whether the trees in the second area of woodland have a
        different mean height from the trees in the first area.

(6 marks)

3   A random sample of 100 shoppers is surveyed to determine whether age is associated with favourite flavour of ice cream. The results are shown in the table.

		Age in full years		
		0 – 40	41 +	Total
Flavour of	Vanilla	10	14	24
ice cream	Chocolate	24	26	50
	Strawberry	7	4	11
	Mint choc chip	7	8	15
	Total	48	52	100

   a)   Use a χ^2 test at the 5% level of significance to examine
        whether there is any association between age and favourite flavour of ice cream.

(9 marks)

   b)   Describe what is meant by a Type II error in this context.

(2 marks)

General Certificate of Education
Advanced Subsidiary (AS) and Advanced Level
Statistics S2 — Practice Exam One
Time Allowed: 1 hour 30 min

Graphical calculators may be used for this exam.

Give any non-exact numerical answers to three significant figures.

Statistical tables can be found on page 138.

There are 75 marks available for this paper.

1   The number of houses, X, sold each week by an estate agent in a small town can be modelled
by a Poisson distribution. The estate agent sells houses at an average rate of 2 per week.

   a)   Find the probability that in a randomly selected week, the estate agent will sell:

      (i)   exactly 1 house,

(2 marks)

      (ii)   at least 2 houses but no more than 4 houses.

(3 marks)

   b)   To qualify for a "monthly bonus", the estate agent needs to sell at least 2 houses each week for
4 consecutive weeks. Find the probability that the estate agent qualifies for the "monthly bonus"
over the next 4-week period.

(3 marks)

   c)   The number of houses, Y, sold each week by a second estate agent at the same firm
can be modelled by a Poisson distribution with a mean of 3.

      (i)   Write down the distribution of H, the total number of houses sold by the two estate agents
each week.

(1 mark)

      (ii)   Calculate the probability that in a randomly selected two-week period, the two estate agents
will sell at least 9 houses between them.

(4 marks)

2   The continuous random variable X has the probability density function

$$\mathrm{f}(x) = \begin{cases} \dfrac{kx}{2} & \text{for } 0 \le x < 2 \\[2mm] \dfrac{k}{3}(5 - x) & \text{for } 2 \le x \le 5 \\[2mm] 0 & \text{otherwise} \end{cases}$$

where k is a positive constant.

   a)   Sketch the graph of $\mathrm{f}(x)$.

(2 marks)

   b)   Find the value of k.

(2 marks)

   c)   Specify fully the cumulative distribution function, $\mathrm{F}(x)$, of X.

(6 marks)

   d)   Hence, or otherwise, calculate the median, m, of X.

(3 marks)

3   A racing car driver records his lap time, x seconds, for each lap he does of a particular circuit.
    His times on each of 8 randomly selected laps are given below.

$$176.5, \quad 175.5, \quad 176, \quad 176.2, \quad 176.3, \quad 175.7, \quad 175.8, \quad 176$$

   a)   Calculate a 99% confidence interval for the driver's mean lap time.
        Give your answer to 1 decimal place and state any assumption you make.

(8 marks)

   b)   A second driver claims that, on average, his lap times on this circuit are quicker.
        His mean lap time is 175.4 seconds. Comment on his claim.

(1 mark)

4   Each day, a particular train can arrive at a random time between 2 minutes before its scheduled
    time and 9 minutes after. The continuous random variable X, which represents the number
    of minutes after its scheduled time the train arrives, has probability density function:

$$f(x) = \begin{cases} \frac{1}{11} & \text{for} -2 \le x \le 9 \\ 0 & \text{otherwise} \end{cases}$$

   a)   (i)   Find the probability that the train is more than 6 minutes late.

(1 mark)

        (ii) Find the probability that the train arrives within 1 minute of its scheduled arrival
              time (either early or late).

(1 mark)

   b)   Given that $E(X) = \frac{7}{2}$, prove (using integration) that $Var(X) = \frac{121}{12}$.

(5 marks)

   c)   A commuter catches this same train 5 days a week. If the train is more than 6 minutes late,
        he will miss a connecting train.

        Calculate the probability that the commuter will miss the connecting train at least once during a
        particular week.

(3 marks)

5   Each roll of fabric used by a home furnishings manufacturer should be 5 metres long.
    However, the manager claims that the average length of fabric per roll is less than 5 metres.
    The length of fabric, x cm, on 50 randomly selected rolls is measured, giving the following results:

$$\sum x = 24\,500 \quad \text{and} \quad \sum x^2 = 12\,011\,500$$

Test the manager's claim at the 5% level of significance.

(8 marks)

6   The probability distribution for the cash prizes, x pence, offered by a gambling machine is as follows:

x	0	10	20	50	100
$P(X=x)$	0.2	0.2	0.2	0.2	p

a)   Write down the value of p.

(1 mark)

b)   Find $E(X)$ and $Var(X)$.

(4 marks)

c)   Find $E(3X-4)$ and $Var(3X-4)$.

(4 marks)

d)   The owner of the machine charges 40p per game. Comment on this cost.

(2 marks)

e)   Comment on whether the above distribution is really likely to be used in gambling machines.

(2 marks)

7   Jack wants to know whether there is a link between gender and the foreign language that students at his school choose to study for their GCSEs. He carries out a survey of 50 students and gets the following results:

	French	Spanish	Total
Male	14	6	20
Female	8	22	30
Total	22	28	50

a)   Carry out a χ^2 test at the 5% level of significance to determine whether there is an association between gender and the language chosen.

(8 marks)

b)   Explain what is meant by a Type I error in this context.

(1 mark)

General Certificate of Education
Advanced Subsidiary (AS) and Advanced Level

Statistics S2 — Practice Exam Two

Time Allowed: 1 hour 30 min

Graphical calculators may be used for this exam.

Give any non-exact numerical answers to three significant figures.

Statistical tables can be found on page 138.

There are 75 marks available for this paper.

---

1   A scientist is testing a household cleaning product. She cleans a tile on which bacteria have been grown,
then examines how many bacteria survive. Surviving bacteria are spread randomly on the tile.

    a)   An average of 6 bacteria per square centimetre are initially assumed to survive.

        If the random variable X represents the number of surviving bacteria in a randomly chosen square
centimetre of tile, find:

        (i) $P(X < 10)$

(2 marks)

        (ii) $P(5 \leq X \leq 7)$

(3 marks)

    b)   During one test, the scientist counts the total number of surviving bacteria on 15 randomly chosen
square centimetres of tile.

        The scientist's results can be summarised as: $\Sigma x = 83$ and $\Sigma x^2 = 543$.

        Calculate the mean and the variance of the number of surviving bacteria per square centimetre.
Give your answers to 2 decimal places.

(3 marks)

    c)   Explain why the data in b) support the use of a Poisson distribution to
model the number of surviving bacteria per square centimetre.

(1 mark)

    d)   Use your mean from b) to find $P(X = 5)$.

(2 marks)

---

2   The continuous random variable X has the cumulative distribution function

$$F(x) = \begin{cases} 0 & \text{for } x < 0 \\ 0.5x^4 + 0.2x & \text{for } 0 \leq x \leq 1 \\ 9.2x - 3.5x^2 - k & \text{for } 1 < x \leq 1.2 \\ 1 & \text{for } x > 1.2 \end{cases}$$

for some constant k.

    a)   Find the value of k.

(2 marks)

    b)   Given that the lower quartile (Q_1) of X is 0.688, calculate the interquartile range.

(3 marks)

    c)   Find the probability density function, $f(x)$, of X.

(3 marks)

    d)   Find $P(X < 1.1)$.

(2 marks)

3   The average height of the sunflowers in a particular field is 150 cm.
    The heights (in cm) of 6 randomly selected sunflowers in a second field are given below.

$$142.5, \quad 152, \quad 151.8, \quad 144, \quad 141.4, \quad 144.3$$

   a)   Test at the 5% level of significance whether the average height of the sunflowers
        in the second field is the same as the average height of the sunflowers in the first field,
        stating any assumptions you make.

        (9 marks)

   b)   The heights of the sunflowers in a third field are known to follow a normal distribution, with a
        variance of 20. The heights (in cm) of a random sample of 6 of these sunflowers are:

$$140, \quad 142.5, \quad 137.5, \quad 141, \quad 140, \quad 139$$

   Test at the 1% level of significance whether the average height of the sunflowers
   in this field is the same as for the sunflowers in the first field.

   (6 marks)

4   A machine tool is set up to produce metal cylinders with a diameter of exactly 42 mm. However, the actual
    diameters of the finished cylinders differ randomly by as much as 0.5 mm from the intended value.

   The random variable X, which represents the actual diameter (in mm) of the cylinders produced, has the
   probability density function:

$$f(x) = \begin{cases} 1 & \text{for } 41.5 \leq x \leq 42.5 \\ 0 & \text{otherwise} \end{cases}$$

   a)   (i)   Calculate $E(X)$ and $Var(X)$.

             (2 marks)

        (ii) Find $F(x)$, the cumulative distribution function of X.

             (2 marks)

        (iii) Hence or otherwise find the median, m, of X.

             (1 mark)

   b)   One of the firm's customers says it can only accept cylinders that are within ±0.3 mm of 42 mm.
        No alterations are made to the machine tool.

        Find the probability that a random cylinder is acceptable to the customer.

             (1 mark)

5   A cricketer wants to know how fast, on average, he bowls. The speeds of the balls he bowls are assumed to
    follow a normal distribution. The speeds, x mph, of 20 randomly selected balls result in the following:

$$\sum x = 1700 \quad \text{and} \quad \sum (x - \overline{x})^2 = 60$$

   Find a 95% confidence interval for the bowler's mean bowling speed.

   (6 marks)

6   a)   The discrete random variable X has the probability function shown below:

$$P(X = x) = \begin{cases} \dfrac{kx}{6} & \text{for } x = 1, 2, 3 \\[2mm] \dfrac{k(7 - x)}{6} & \text{for } x = 4, 5, 6 \\[2mm] 0 & \text{otherwise} \end{cases}$$

(i)   Find the value of k.

(3 marks)

(ii)   Find $P(X \leq 3)$.

(2 marks)

(iii)   Show that $E(X) = 3.5$.

(2 marks)

(iv)   Given that $\text{Var}(X) = \dfrac{23}{12}$, find:

$E(2 - 3X)$, $\text{Var}(2 - 3X)$ and $E(X^2)$.

(7 marks)

b)   The random variable Y has the following probability distribution:

y	2	4	6	8	10
$P(Y = y)$	0.1	0.2	p	q	0.2

The mean of the random variable Y is 6.3.

(i)   Write down two independent equations involving p and q.

(2 marks)

(ii)   Solve your equations to find the values of p and q.

(3 marks)

7   The table below shows the results of a study of 100 trees.

	Leaf disease	No leaf disease	Total
Height < 3m	32	38	70
Height ≥ 3m	19	11	30
Total	51	49	100

Test at the 5% level of significance whether there is an association between the variables.

(8 marks)

S2 — STATISTICAL TABLES

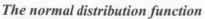
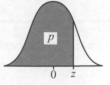

The normal distribution function

This table gives the probability, p, that the random variable $Z \sim N(0, 1)$ is less than or equal to z.

z	0.00	0.01	0.02	0.03	0.04	0.05	0.06	0.07	0.08	0.09	z
0.0	0.50000	0.50399	0.50798	0.51197	0.51595	0.51994	0.52392	0.52790	0.53188	0.53586	0.0
0.1	0.53983	0.54380	0.54776	0.55172	0.55567	0.55962	0.56356	0.56749	0.57142	0.57535	0.1
0.2	0.57926	0.58317	0.58706	0.59095	0.59483	0.59871	0.60257	0.60642	0.61026	0.61409	0.2
0.3	0.61791	0.62172	0.62552	0.62930	0.63307	0.63683	0.64058	0.64431	0.64803	0.65173	0.3
0.4	0.65542	0.65910	0.66276	0.66640	0.67003	0.67364	0.67724	0.68082	0.68439	0.68793	0.4
0.5	0.69146	0.69497	0.69847	0.70194	0.70540	0.70884	0.71226	0.71566	0.71904	0.72240	0.5
0.6	0.72575	0.72907	0.73237	0.73565	0.73891	0.74215	0.74537	0.74857	0.75175	0.75490	0.6
0.7	0.75804	0.76115	0.76424	0.76730	0.77035	0.77337	0.77637	0.77935	0.78230	0.78524	0.7
0.8	0.78814	0.79103	0.79389	0.79673	0.79955	0.80234	0.80511	0.80785	0.81057	0.81327	0.8
0.9	0.81594	0.81859	0.82121	0.82381	0.82639	0.82894	0.83147	0.83398	0.83646	0.83891	0.9
1.0	0.84134	0.84375	0.84614	0.84849	0.85083	0.85314	0.85543	0.85769	0.85993	0.86214	1.0
1.1	0.86433	0.86650	0.86864	0.87076	0.87286	0.87493	0.87698	0.87900	0.88100	0.88298	1.1
1.2	0.88493	0.88686	0.88877	0.89065	0.89251	0.89435	0.89617	0.89796	0.89973	0.90147	1.2
1.3	0.90320	0.90490	0.90658	0.90824	0.90988	0.91149	0.91309	0.91466	0.91621	0.91774	1.3
1.4	0.91924	0.92073	0.92220	0.92364	0.92507	0.92647	0.92785	0.92922	0.93056	0.93189	1.4
1.5	0.93319	0.93448	0.93574	0.93699	0.93822	0.93943	0.94062	0.94179	0.94295	0.94408	1.5
1.6	0.94520	0.94630	0.94738	0.94845	0.94950	0.95053	0.95154	0.95254	0.95352	0.95449	1.6
1.7	0.95543	0.95637	0.95728	0.95818	0.95907	0.95994	0.96080	0.96164	0.96246	0.96327	1.7
1.8	0.96407	0.96485	0.96562	0.96638	0.96712	0.96784	0.96856	0.96926	0.96995	0.97062	1.8
1.9	0.97128	0.97193	0.97257	0.97320	0.97381	0.97441	0.97500	0.97558	0.97615	0.97670	1.9
2.0	0.97725	0.97778	0.97831	0.97882	0.97932	0.97982	0.98030	0.98077	0.98124	0.98169	2.0
2.1	0.98214	0.98257	0.98300	0.98341	0.98382	0.98422	0.98461	0.98500	0.98537	0.98574	2.1
2.2	0.98610	0.98645	0.98679	0.98713	0.98745	0.98778	0.98809	0.98840	0.98870	0.98899	2.2
2.3	0.98928	0.98956	0.98983	0.99010	0.99036	0.99061	0.99086	0.99111	0.99134	0.99158	2.3
2.4	0.99180	0.99202	0.99224	0.99245	0.99266	0.99286	0.99305	0.99324	0.99343	0.99361	2.4
2.5	0.99379	0.99396	0.99413	0.99430	0.99446	0.99461	0.99477	0.99492	0.99506	0.99520	2.5
2.6	0.99534	0.99547	0.99560	0.99573	0.99585	0.99598	0.99609	0.99621	0.99632	0.99643	2.6
2.7	0.99653	0.99664	0.99674	0.99683	0.99693	0.99702	0.99711	0.99720	0.99728	0.99736	2.7
2.8	0.99744	0.99752	0.99760	0.99767	0.99774	0.99781	0.99788	0.99795	0.99801	0.99807	2.8
2.9	0.99813	0.99819	0.99825	0.99831	0.99836	0.99841	0.99846	0.99851	0.99856	0.99861	2.9
3.0	0.99865	0.99869	0.99874	0.99878	0.99882	0.99886	0.99889	0.99893	0.99896	0.99900	3.0
3.1	0.99903	0.99906	0.99910	0.99913	0.99916	0.99918	0.99921	0.99924	0.99926	0.99929	3.1
3.2	0.99931	0.99934	0.99936	0.99938	0.99940	0.99942	0.99944	0.99946	0.99948	0.99950	3.2
3.3	0.99952	0.99953	0.99955	0.99957	0.99958	0.99960	0.99961	0.99962	0.99964	0.99965	3.3
3.4	0.99966	0.99968	0.99969	0.99970	0.99971	0.99972	0.99973	0.99974	0.99975	0.99976	3.4
3.5	0.99977	0.99978	0.99978	0.99979	0.99980	0.99981	0.99981	0.99982	0.99983	0.99983	3.5
3.6	0.99984	0.99985	0.99985	0.99986	0.99986	0.99987	0.99987	0.99988	0.99988	0.99989	3.6
3.7	0.99989	0.99990	0.99990	0.99990	0.99991	0.99991	0.99992	0.99992	0.99992	0.99992	3.7
3.8	0.99993	0.99993	0.99993	0.99994	0.99994	0.99994	0.99994	0.99995	0.99995	0.99995	3.8
3.9	0.99995	0.99995	0.99996	0.99996	0.99996	0.99996	0.99996	0.99996	0.99997	0.99997	3.9

Percentage points of the normal distribution

The table gives the values of z satisfying $P(Z \leq z) = p$, where $Z \sim N(0, 1)$.

p	0.00	0.01	0.02	0.03	0.04	0.05	0.06	0.07	0.08	0.09	p
0.5	0.0000	0.0251	0.0502	0.0753	0.1004	0.1257	0.1510	0.1764	0.2019	0.2275	0.5
0.6	0.2533	0.2793	0.3055	0.3319	0.3585	0.3853	0.4125	0.4399	0.4677	0.4959	0.6
0.7	0.5244	0.5534	0.5828	0.6128	0.6433	0.6745	0.7063	0.7388	0.7722	0.8064	0.7
0.8	0.8416	0.8779	0.9154	0.9542	0.9945	1.0364	1.0803	1.1264	1.1750	1.2265	0.8
0.9	1.2816	1.3408	1.4051	1.4758	1.5548	1.6449	1.7507	1.8808	2.0537	2.3263	0.9

p	0.000	0.001	0.002	0.003	0.004	0.005	0.006	0.007	0.008	0.009	p
0.95	1.6449	1.6546	1.6646	1.6747	1.6849	1.6954	1.7060	1.7169	1.7279	1.7392	0.95
0.96	1.7507	1.7624	1.7744	1.7866	1.7991	1.8119	1.8250	1.8384	1.8522	1.8663	0.96
0.97	1.8808	1.8957	1.9110	1.9268	1.9431	1.9600	1.9774	1.9954	2.0141	2.0335	0.97
0.98	2.0537	2.0749	2.0969	2.1201	2.1444	2.1701	2.1973	2.2262	2.2571	2.2904	0.98
0.99	2.3263	2.3656	2.4089	2.4573	2.5121	2.5758	2.6521	2.7478	2.8782	3.0902	0.99

S2 — STATISTICAL TABLES

The Poisson cumulative distribution function

The table below shows $P(X \le x)$, where $X \sim Po(\lambda)$.

λ	0.10	0.20	0.30	0.40	0.50	0.60	0.70	0.80	0.90	1.0	1.2	1.4	1.6	1.8	λ
x															x
0	0.9048	0.8187	0.7408	0.6703	0.6065	0.5488	0.4966	0.4493	0.4066	0.3679	0.3012	0.2466	0.2019	0.1653	0
1	0.9953	0.9825	0.9631	0.9384	0.9098	0.8781	0.8442	0.8088	0.7725	0.7358	0.6626	0.5918	0.5249	0.4628	1
2	0.9998	0.9989	0.9964	0.9921	0.9856	0.9769	0.9659	0.9526	0.9371	0.9197	0.8795	0.8335	0.7834	0.7306	2
3	1.0000	0.9999	0.9997	0.9992	0.9982	0.9966	0.9942	0.9909	0.9865	0.9810	0.9662	0.9463	0.9212	0.8913	3
4		1.0000	1.0000	0.9999	0.9998	0.9996	0.9992	0.9986	0.9977	0.9963	0.9923	0.9857	0.9763	0.9636	4
5				1.0000	1.0000	1.0000	0.9999	0.9998	0.9997	0.9994	0.9985	0.9968	0.9940	0.9896	5
6							1.0000	1.0000	1.0000	0.9999	0.9997	0.9994	0.9987	0.9974	6
7										1.0000	1.0000	0.9999	0.9997	0.9994	7
8												1.0000	1.0000	0.9999	8
9														1.0000	9

λ	2.0	2.2	2.4	2.6	2.8	3.0	3.2	3.4	3.6	3.8	4.0	4.5	5.0	5.5	λ
x															x
0	0.1353	0.1108	0.0907	0.0743	0.0608	0.0498	0.0408	0.0334	0.0273	0.0224	0.0183	0.0111	0.0067	0.0041	0
1	0.4060	0.3546	0.3084	0.2674	0.2311	0.1991	0.1712	0.1468	0.1257	0.1074	0.0916	0.0611	0.0404	0.0266	1
2	0.6767	0.6227	0.5697	0.5184	0.4695	0.4232	0.3799	0.3397	0.3027	0.2689	0.2381	0.1736	0.1247	0.0884	2
3	0.8571	0.8194	0.7787	0.7360	0.6919	0.6472	0.6025	0.5584	0.5152	0.4735	0.4335	0.3423	0.2650	0.2017	3
4	0.9473	0.9275	0.9041	0.8774	0.8477	0.8153	0.7806	0.7442	0.7064	0.6678	0.6288	0.5321	0.4405	0.3575	4
5	0.9834	0.9751	0.9643	0.9510	0.9349	0.9161	0.8946	0.8705	0.8441	0.8156	0.7851	0.7029	0.6160	0.5289	5
6	0.9955	0.9925	0.9884	0.9828	0.9756	0.9665	0.9554	0.9421	0.9267	0.9091	0.8893	0.8311	0.7622	0.6860	6
7	0.9989	0.9980	0.9967	0.9947	0.9919	0.9881	0.9832	0.9769	0.9692	0.9599	0.9489	0.9134	0.8666	0.8095	7
8	0.9998	0.9995	0.9991	0.9985	0.9976	0.9962	0.9943	0.9917	0.9883	0.9840	0.9786	0.9597	0.9319	0.8944	8
9	1.0000	0.9999	0.9998	0.9996	0.9993	0.9989	0.9982	0.9973	0.9960	0.9942	0.9919	0.9829	0.9682	0.9462	9
10		1.0000	1.0000	0.9999	0.9998	0.9997	0.9995	0.9992	0.9987	0.9981	0.9972	0.9933	0.9863	0.9747	10
11				1.0000	1.0000	0.9999	0.9999	0.9998	0.9996	0.9994	0.9991	0.9976	0.9945	0.9890	11
12						1.0000	1.0000	0.9999	0.9999	0.9998	0.9997	0.9992	0.9980	0.9955	12
13								1.0000	1.0000	1.0000	0.9999	0.9997	0.9993	0.9983	13
14											1.0000	0.9999	0.9998	0.9994	14
15												1.0000	0.9999	0.9998	15
16													1.0000	0.9999	16
17														1.0000	17

λ	6.0	6.5	7.0	7.5	8.0	8.5	9.0	9.5	10.0	11.0	12.0	13.0	14.0	15.0	λ
x															x
0	0.0025	0.0015	0.0009	0.0006	0.0003	0.0002	0.0001	0.0001	0.0000	0.0000	0.0000	0.0000	0.0000	0.0000	0
1	0.0174	0.0113	0.0073	0.0047	0.0030	0.0019	0.0012	0.0008	0.0005	0.0002	0.0001	0.0000	0.0000	0.0000	1
2	0.0620	0.0430	0.0296	0.0203	0.0138	0.0093	0.0062	0.0042	0.0028	0.0012	0.0005	0.0002	0.0001	0.0000	2
3	0.1512	0.1118	0.0818	0.0591	0.0424	0.0301	0.0212	0.0149	0.0103	0.0049	0.0023	0.0011	0.0005	0.0002	3
4	0.2851	0.2237	0.1730	0.1321	0.0996	0.0744	0.0550	0.0403	0.0293	0.0151	0.0076	0.0037	0.0018	0.0009	4
5	0.4457	0.3690	0.3007	0.2414	0.1912	0.1496	0.1157	0.0885	0.0671	0.0375	0.0203	0.0107	0.0055	0.0028	5
6	0.6063	0.5265	0.4497	0.3782	0.3134	0.2562	0.2068	0.1649	0.1301	0.0786	0.0458	0.0259	0.0142	0.0076	6
7	0.7440	0.6728	0.5987	0.5246	0.4530	0.3856	0.3239	0.2687	0.2202	0.1432	0.0895	0.0540	0.0316	0.0180	7
8	0.8472	0.7916	0.7291	0.6620	0.5925	0.5231	0.4557	0.3918	0.3328	0.2320	0.1550	0.0998	0.0621	0.0374	8
9	0.9161	0.8774	0.8305	0.7764	0.7166	0.6530	0.5874	0.5218	0.4579	0.3405	0.2424	0.1658	0.1094	0.0699	9
10	0.9574	0.9332	0.9015	0.8622	0.8159	0.7634	0.7060	0.6453	0.5830	0.4599	0.3472	0.2517	0.1757	0.1185	10
11	0.9799	0.9661	0.9467	0.9208	0.8881	0.8487	0.8030	0.7520	0.6968	0.5793	0.4616	0.3532	0.2600	0.1848	11
12	0.9912	0.9840	0.9730	0.9573	0.9362	0.9091	0.8758	0.8364	0.7916	0.6887	0.5760	0.4631	0.3585	0.2676	12
13	0.9964	0.9929	0.9872	0.9784	0.9658	0.9486	0.9261	0.8981	0.8645	0.7813	0.6815	0.5730	0.4644	0.3632	13
14	0.9986	0.9970	0.9943	0.9897	0.9827	0.9726	0.9585	0.9400	0.9165	0.8540	0.7720	0.6751	0.5704	0.4657	14
15	0.9995	0.9988	0.9976	0.9954	0.9918	0.9862	0.9780	0.9665	0.9513	0.9074	0.8444	0.7636	0.6694	0.5681	15
16	0.9998	0.9996	0.9990	0.9980	0.9963	0.9934	0.9889	0.9823	0.9730	0.9441	0.8987	0.8355	0.7559	0.6641	16
17	0.9999	0.9998	0.9996	0.9992	0.9984	0.9970	0.9947	0.9911	0.9857	0.9678	0.9370	0.8905	0.8272	0.7489	17
18	1.0000	0.9999	0.9999	0.9997	0.9993	0.9987	0.9976	0.9957	0.9928	0.9823	0.9626	0.9302	0.8826	0.8195	18
19		1.0000	1.0000	0.9999	0.9997	0.9995	0.9989	0.9980	0.9965	0.9907	0.9787	0.9573	0.9235	0.8752	19
20				1.0000	0.9999	0.9998	0.9996	0.9991	0.9984	0.9953	0.9884	0.9750	0.9521	0.9170	20
21					1.0000	0.9999	0.9998	0.9996	0.9993	0.9977	0.9939	0.9859	0.9712	0.9469	21
22						1.0000	0.9999	0.9999	0.9997	0.9990	0.9970	0.9924	0.9833	0.9673	22
23							1.0000	0.9999	0.9999	0.9995	0.9985	0.9960	0.9907	0.9805	23
24								1.0000	1.0000	0.9998	0.9993	0.9980	0.9950	0.9888	24
25										0.9999	0.9997	0.9990	0.9974	0.9938	25
26										1.0000	0.9999	0.9995	0.9987	0.9967	26
27											0.9999	0.9998	0.9994	0.9983	27
28											1.0000	0.9999	0.9997	0.9991	28
29												1.0000	0.9999	0.9996	29
30													0.9999	0.9998	30
31													1.0000	0.9999	31
32														1.0000	32

S2 — STATISTICAL TABLES

Percentage points of the χ^2 distribution

The table shows values of x satisfying $P(X \leq x) = p$,
where X has the χ^2 distribution with v degrees of freedom.

p	0.005	0.01	0.025	0.05	0.1	0.9	0.95	0.975	0.99	0.995	p
v											v
1	0.00004	0.0002	0.001	0.004	0.016	2.706	3.841	5.024	6.635	7.879	1
2	0.010	0.020	0.051	0.103	0.211	4.605	5.991	7.378	9.210	10.597	2
3	0.072	0.115	0.216	0.352	0.584	6.251	7.815	9.348	11.345	12.838	3
4	0.207	0.297	0.484	0.711	1.064	7.779	9.488	11.143	13.277	14.860	4

Percentage points of the Student's t-distribution

The table shows values of x satisfying $P(X \leq x) = p$,
where X has the Student's t-distribution with v degrees of freedom.

p	0.9	0.95	0.975	0.99	0.995
v					
1	3.078	6.314	12.706	31.821	63.657
2	1.886	2.920	4.303	6.965	9.925
3	1.638	2.353	3.182	4.541	5.841
4	1.533	2.132	2.776	3.747	4.604
5	1.476	2.015	2.571	3.365	4.032
6	1.440	1.943	2.447	3.143	3.707
7	1.415	1.895	2.365	2.998	3.499
8	1.397	1.860	2.306	2.896	3.355
9	1.383	1.833	2.262	2.821	3.250
10	1.372	1.812	2.228	2.764	3.169
11	1.363	1.796	2.201	2.718	3.106
12	1.356	1.782	2.179	2.681	3.055
13	1.350	1.771	2.160	2.650	3.012
14	1.345	1.761	2.145	2.624	2.977
15	1.341	1.753	2.131	2.602	2.947
16	1.337	1.746	2.120	2.583	2.921
17	1.333	1.740	2.110	2.567	2.898
18	1.330	1.734	2.101	2.552	2.878
19	1.328	1.729	2.093	2.539	2.861
20	1.325	1.725	2.086	2.528	2.845
21	1.323	1.721	2.080	2.518	2.831
22	1.321	1.717	2.074	2.508	2.819
23	1.319	1.714	2.069	2.500	2.807
24	1.318	1.711	2.064	2.492	2.797
25	1.316	1.708	2.060	2.485	2.787
26	1.315	1.706	2.056	2.479	2.779
27	1.314	1.703	2.052	2.473	2.771
28	1.313	1.701	2.048	2.467	2.763

Moments

In this lifetime there are moments — moments of joy and of sorrow, and those moments where you have to answer questions on moments in exams.

Moments are **Clockwise** or **Anticlockwise**

A 'moment' is the turning effect a force has around a point.
The larger the force, and the greater the distance from the point, then the larger the moment.

> Moment = Force × Perpendicular Distance

EXAMPLE A plank 2 m long is attached to a ship at one end, O, as shown. A bird lands on the other end of the plank, applying a force of 15 N. Model the plank as a light rod and find the moment applied by the bird.

$$\begin{aligned}\text{Moment} &= F \times d \\ &= 15 \times 2 \\ &= 30 \text{ Nm}\end{aligned}$$

The units are just newtons × metres = Nm. Couldn't they have thought of a cleverer name?

EXAMPLE A force of 20 N is applied to a spanner, attached to a bolt at a point, O. The force is applied at an angle of 60° to the spanner head, as shown. Find the turning effect of the force upon the bolt.

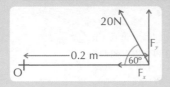

The 20 N force has components F_x and F_y.
F_x goes through O, so its moment is 0.

Resolve vertically: $F_y = 20\sin60°$

$$\begin{aligned}\text{Moment} &= 20\sin60° \times 0.2 \\ &= 3.46 \text{ Nm (to 3 s.f.)}\end{aligned}$$

EXAMPLE A force of 25 N acts upon a point, O, via a light rod 5 m in length connected at an angle of 40°, as shown. What is the turning effect applied to O?

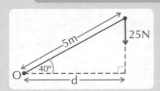

Remember it's got to be perpendicular distance, so you can't just plug in the 5m.

Here d is 5cos40°, so:

$$\begin{aligned}\text{Moment} &= 25 \times 5\cos40° \\ &= 95.8 \text{ Nm}\end{aligned}$$

In **Equilibrium** Moments Total **Zero**...

...and that means that for a body in equilibrium the total moments either way must be equal:

> Total Clockwise Moment = Total Anticlockwise Moment

Also, for a body in equilibrium, the resultant force acting on the body is zero. So:

> Resolving Vertically: Force up = Force down   Resolving horizontally: Force left = Force right

You can resolve the forces acting on a body in any direction — at equilibrium the resultant will always be zero.

EXAMPLE Two weights of 30 N and 45 N are placed on a light 8 m beam. The 30 N weight is at one end of the beam, as shown, whilst the other weight is a distance d from the midpoint M. The beam is in equilibrium held by a single wire with tension T attached at M. Find T and the distance d.

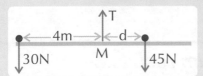

Resolving vertically: $30 + 45 = T = 75$ N

Take moments about M: Clockwise Moment = Anticlockwise Moment
$$45 \times d = 30 \times 4$$
$$d = \frac{120}{45} = 2\tfrac{2}{3} = 2.67 \text{ m}$$

Moments

The **Weight** of a **Uniform Beam** Acts at its **Middle**

The weight of anything always acts at its <u>centre of mass</u>.
For a uniform beam, the centre of mass is always at the exact centre of the beam.

EXAMPLE

A 6 m long uniform beam AB of weight 40 N is supported at A by a vertical reaction R. AB is held horizontal by a vertical wire attached 1 m from the other end. A particle of weight of 30 N is placed 2 m from the support R.

Find the tension T in the wire and the force R.

> Start by taking moments around the point of action of one of the <u>unknown</u> forces.

Take <u>moments about A</u>.

Clockwise Moment = Anticlockwise Moment

$$(30 \times 2) + (40 \times 3) = T \times 5$$
$$T = 36 \text{ N}$$

Resolve vertically: $T + R = 30 + 40$

So: $R = 34 \text{ N}$

> The beam is in equilibrium, so the total force acting upwards equals the total force acting downwards.

EXAMPLE

A Christmas banner, AB, is attached to a ceiling by two pieces of tinsel. One piece of tinsel is attached to A, the other to the point C, where BC = 0.6 m. The banner has mass 8 kg and length 3.6 m and is held in a horizontal position.

Modelling the banner as a uniform rod held in equilibrium and the tinsel as light strings, find the tension in the tinsel at A and C. Take $g = 9.8 \text{ ms}^{-2}$.

Take <u>moments about A</u>.

Clockwise Moment = Anticlockwise Moment

$$8g \times 1.8 = T_C \times 3$$
$$\text{So, } T_C = \frac{141.12}{3} = 47.0 \text{ N (3 s.f.)}$$

Resolve <u>vertically</u>.

$$T_A + T_C = 8g$$
$$\text{So, } T_A = 8g - 47.0 = 31.4 \text{ N (3 s.f.)}$$

The tinsel at A snaps and a downward force is applied at B to keep the banner horizontal. Find the magnitude of the force applied at B and the tension in the tinsel attached at C.

Take <u>moments about C</u>.

$$8g \times 1.2 = F_B \times 0.6$$
$$\text{So, } F_B = \frac{94.08}{0.6} = 157 \text{ N (3 s.f.)}$$

Resolve <u>vertically</u>.

$$T_C = 8g + 157$$
$$\text{So, } T_C = 235 \text{ N (3 s.f.)}$$

Significant moments in life — birthdays, exams, exam results...

Well, there's lots of stuff to learn in this section. I hope you've got your head around it so far, because next up are things that are non-uniform or non-horizontal. Onwards and upwards folks. Well, clockwise, anticlockwise, upwards and downwards...

Moments and Ladder Questions

Beams and rods <u>aren't</u> always uniform (not even in exam questions), so their centre of mass <u>isn't</u> always in the middle. As for ladders, whether they're uniform or not, they always have <u>reaction forces</u> and often <u>frictional forces</u> too.

You can **Calculate** the Centre of Mass for **Non-Uniform** rods

If the weight acts at an <u>unknown</u> point along a rod, the point can be found in the usual way — by taking <u>moments</u>. You might also have to <u>resolve</u> the forces <u>horizontally</u> or <u>vertically</u> to find some missing information.

EXAMPLE
A non-uniform plank of mass 5 kg is supported by a vertical string attached at a point B, as shown. One end of the plank, A, rests upon a pole. The tension in the string is T and the normal reaction at the pole is 70 N. A particle, P, of mass 9 kg rests on the plank 2 m from A, as shown. Find T and the distance, x, between A and the centre of mass of the plank.

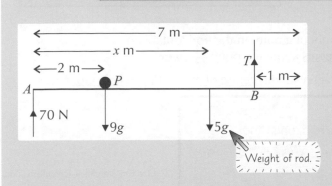

Resolve vertically:
upward forces = downward forces:

$T + 70 = 9g + 5g$
so, $T = 137.2 - 70 = 67.2$ N

These statements are only (and always) true at equilibrium.

Weight of rod.

Moments about A:
clockwise moments = anticlockwise moments:

$(9g \times 2) + (5g \times x) = 67.2 \times 6$
$49x = 403.2 - 176.4$

so $x = \dfrac{226.8}{49} = 4.63$ m (3 s.f.)

Ladder Questions involve **Multiple Reactions** and **Frictional Forces**

'Ladder' questions, where a rod rests at an angle against the ground and a wall, are common in M2 exams. Often, the ground is modelled as <u>rough</u> and the wall as <u>smooth</u>. Can't take these things for granted though...

The 4 possible combinations of surfaces for 'ladder' questions:

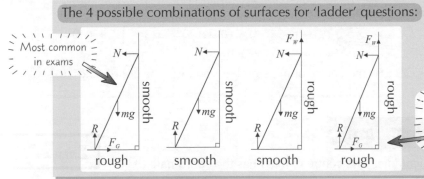

Most common in exams

There are always <u>reaction forces</u> at the wall and the ground. These act <u>perpendicular</u> to the <u>wall</u> and <u>ground</u>, <u>not</u> perpendicular to the ladder.

Friction acts to <u>prevent</u> motion — so think about which way the ladder would slip and draw the frictional force in the opposite direction.

EXAMPLE
A ladder rests against a smooth wall at an angle of 65° to the rough ground, as shown. The ladder has mass 1.3 kg and length $5x$ m. A cat of mass 4.5 kg sits on the ladder at C, $4x$ m from the base. The ladder is in limiting equilibrium. Model the ladder as a uniform rod and the cat as a particle. Find the coefficient of friction between the ground and the ladder.

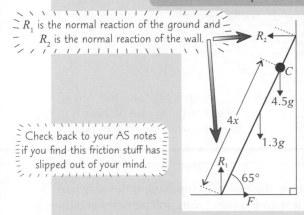

R_1 is the normal reaction of the ground and R_2 is the normal reaction of the wall.

Check back to your AS notes if you find this friction stuff has slipped out of your mind.

Resolving horizontally: $F = R_2$

Take moments about the base of the ladder to find R_2:
$R_2\sin65° \times 5x = (1.3g\cos65° \times 2.5x) + (4.5g\cos65° \times 4x)$
$4.532xR_2 = 13.46x + 74.55x$

so, $R_2 = \dfrac{88.01x}{4.532x} = 19.42$ N

Resolve vertically to find R_1:
$R_1 = 1.3g + 4.5g$
$\Rightarrow R_1 = 56.84$ N

The ladder is in limiting equilibrium, so $F = \mu R_1$:
Resolving horizontally shows $F = R_2$, so, $19.42 = 56.84\mu$
and $\mu = 0.342$ (to 3 s.f.)

Discrete Groups of Particles in 1 Dimension

Welcome to more on the <u>Centre of Mass</u>. And it's got nothing to do with your local Catholic church...

For **Particles in a Line** — Combine **Moments** about the **Origin**

1) As you've seen on the previous two pages, the weight of an object is considered to act at its <u>centre of mass</u>. A <u>group</u> of objects <u>also</u> has a centre of mass, which isn't necessarily in the same position as any one of the objects.

2) It's often convenient to model these objects as <u>particles</u> (point masses) since the position of a particle is the position of its centre of mass. If a group of particles all lie in a <u>horizontal line</u>, then the centre of mass of the <u>group</u> will lie somewhere on the <u>same line</u>.

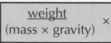

3) The <u>moment</u> (turning effect) of a particle from a fixed point is:
   This is <u>mgx</u> if the fixed point and the particle are
   <u>horizontally aligned</u>.

   | weight (mass × gravity) | × | perpendicular distance from point |

4) The moment of a <u>group</u> of particles in a <u>horizontal line</u> about a point in the horizontal line can be found by <u>adding together</u> all the <u>individual moments</u> about the point — Σmgx.

5) This has the same effect as the <u>combined weight</u> (Σmg) acting at the <u>centre of mass</u> of the <u>whole group</u> ($\overline{x}$).

Writing this as a formula:

$$\Sigma mgx = \overline{x}\Sigma mg$$

e.g. for 3 particles in a horizontal line:

$$m_1 gx_1 + m_2 gx_2 + m_3 gx_3 = \overline{x}(m_1 g + m_2 g + m_3 g)$$

$$\Rightarrow m_1 x_1 + m_2 x_2 + m_3 x_3 = \overline{x}(m_1 + m_2 + m_3)$$

$$\Rightarrow \Sigma mx = \overline{x}\Sigma m$$

The gs cancel out on each side.

Use this simplified formula to find the centre of mass, $\overline{x}$, of a group of objects in a horizontal line.

EXAMPLE Three particles are placed at positions along the *x*-axis as shown. Find the coordinates of the centre of mass of the group of particles.

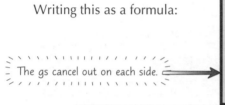

$m_1 = 3$ kg $m_2 = 1.5$ kg $m_3 = 0.5$ kg
(-2, 0)   0   (3, 0)   (5, 0)

Negative coordinates go in the formula just as they are.

1) Use the formula $\Sigma mx = \overline{x}\Sigma m$ and put in what you know:
   $$m_1 x_1 + m_2 x_2 + m_3 x_3 = \overline{x}(m_1 + m_2 + m_3)$$
   $$\Rightarrow (3 \times -2) + (1.5 \times 3) + (0.5 \times 5) = \overline{x}(3 + 1.5 + 0.5)$$
   $$\Rightarrow 1 = 5\overline{x} \quad \Rightarrow \quad \overline{x} = 0.2$$

2) So the centre of mass of the group has the coordinates (0.2, 0)

Use $\overline{y}$ for Particles in a Vertical Line

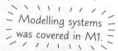

$$\Sigma my = \overline{y}\Sigma m$$

It's the same for particles arranged in a <u>vertical</u> line. The centre of mass has the coordinate (0, $\overline{y}$).

EXAMPLE A light vertical rod AB has particles attached at various positions, as shown. At what height is the centre of mass of the rod?

A light rod has length but no width or depth, and no mass (as it's light).

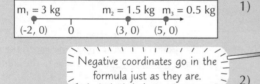

B
$m_4 = 2$ kg   1 m
$m_3 = 1$ kg
                2 m
$m_2 = 4$ kg
$m_1 = 3$ kg   1 m
                1 m
A

1) First, work out the positions of all the particles relative to a <u>single point</u> or 'origin'. Since you're asked for the <u>vertical height</u>, pick point A at the bottom of the rod:
   $y_1 = 1, y_2 = 2, y_3 = 4, y_4 = 5$.

2) Plug the numbers into the formula:
   $\Sigma my = \overline{y}\Sigma m \quad \Rightarrow \quad m_1 y_1 + m_2 y_2 + m_3 y_3 + m_4 y_4 = \overline{y}(m_1 + m_2 + m_3 + m_4)$
   $\Rightarrow (3 \times 1) + (4 \times 2) + (1 \times 4) + (2 \times 5) = \overline{y} \times (3 + 4 + 1 + 2)$
   $\Rightarrow 25 = \overline{y} \times 10 \quad \Rightarrow \quad \overline{y} = 25 \div 10 = 2.5$.

3) Make sure you've answered the question — $\overline{y}$ is the <u>vertical coordinate</u> from the 'origin' which we took as the bottom of the rod. So the vertical height of the centre of mass is <u>2.5 m</u>.

Take a moment to understand the basics...

Once you've got your head around what's going on with a system of particles, the number crunching is the easy part. You'll often have to tackle wordy problems where you first have to model a situation using rods and particles and things — you should be more than familiar with doing this from M1, and there's more practice to come later in the section.

Discrete Groups of Particles in 2 Dimensions

Let's face it, in the 'real world', you'll rarely come across a group in a perfectly orderly line (think of queuing up in the sales — madness). Luckily, the same principles apply in two dimensions — it's no harder than the stuff on the last page.

Use the **Position Vector** $\bar{r}$ for **Centre of Mass** of a **Group** on a **Plane**

There are two ways to find the centre of mass of a group of particles on a plane (i.e. in 2 dimensions, x and y, rather than just in a line). The quickest way uses position vectors, but I'll show you both methods and you can choose.

EXAMPLE Find the coordinates of the centre of mass of the system of particles shown in the diagram.

The Long Way — find the x and y coordinates separately:

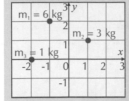

1) Find the x coordinate of the centre of mass first (pretend they're in a horizontal line...)
$x_1 = -1$, $x_2 = 1$, $x_3 = -2$, so:
$m_1x_1 + m_2x_2 + m_3x_3 = \bar{x}(m_1 + m_2 + m_3) \Rightarrow (6 \times -1) + (3 \times 1) + (1 \times -2) = \bar{x}(6 + 3 + 1)$
$\Rightarrow \bar{x} = -\frac{5}{10} = \underline{-0.5}$.

2) Now find the y coordinate in the same way: $y_1 = 2$, $y_2 = 1$, $y_3 = 0$, so:
$m_1y_1 + m_2y_2 + m_3y_3 = \bar{y}(m_1 + m_2 + m_3) \Rightarrow (6 \times 2) + (3 \times 1) + (1 \times 0) = \bar{y}(6 + 3 + 1)$
$\Rightarrow \bar{y} = \frac{15}{10} = \underline{1.5}$.

3) So the centre of mass has the coordinates $\underline{(-0.5, 1.5)}$.

> Column position vectors like these are just like coordinates standing upright — $\mathbf{r} = \binom{x}{y}$.

The Short Way — use position vectors:

1) Write out the position vector ($\mathbf{r}$) for each particle: $\mathbf{r}_1 = \binom{-1}{2}$, $\mathbf{r}_2 = \binom{1}{1}$, $\mathbf{r}_3 = \binom{-2}{0}$.

2) Use the formula, but replace the xs and ys with $\mathbf{r}$s: $\Sigma m\mathbf{r} = \bar{\mathbf{r}}\Sigma m \Rightarrow m_1\mathbf{r}_1 + m_2\mathbf{r}_2 + m_3\mathbf{r}_3 = \bar{\mathbf{r}}(m_1 + m_2 + m_3)$

$\Rightarrow 6\binom{-1}{2} + 3\binom{1}{1} + 1\binom{-2}{0} = \bar{\mathbf{r}}(6 + 3 + 1) \Rightarrow \binom{-6}{12} + \binom{3}{3} + \binom{-2}{0} = 10\bar{\mathbf{r}}$

$\Rightarrow \binom{-5}{15} = 10\bar{\mathbf{r}} \Rightarrow \bar{\mathbf{r}} = \binom{-0.5}{1.5}$. So the centre of mass has position vector $\binom{-0.5}{1.5}$, and coordinates $\underline{(-0.5, 1.5)}$.

> Using this method the formula becomes: $\Sigma m\mathbf{r} = \bar{\mathbf{r}}\Sigma m$

The **Formula** works for finding **Unknown Masses** and **Locations**

You won't always be asked to find the centre of mass of a system. You could be given the position of the centre of mass and asked to work out something else, like the mass or coordinates of a particle in the system. Use the same formula:

EXAMPLE The diagram shows the position of the centre of mass (COM) of a system of three particles attached to the corners of a light rectangular lamina. Find m_2.

> A lamina is just a flat (2D) shape.

1) First of all, pick your origin — bottom left looks as good as anywhere — and define all your positions from this point:
$\mathbf{r}_1 = \binom{0}{4}$, $\mathbf{r}_2 = \binom{6}{4}$, $\mathbf{r}_3 = \binom{6}{0}$. The COM, $\bar{\mathbf{r}}$, is at $\binom{3}{3.5}$.

2) Fill in what you know in the formula:
$\Sigma m\mathbf{r} = \bar{\mathbf{r}}\Sigma m \Rightarrow m_1\mathbf{r}_1 + m_2\mathbf{r}_2 + m_3\mathbf{r}_3 = \bar{\mathbf{r}}(m_1 + m_2 + m_3)$

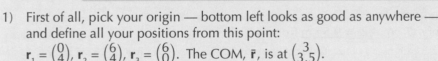

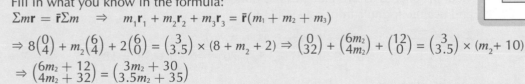

$\Rightarrow 8\binom{0}{4} + m_2\binom{6}{4} + 2\binom{6}{0} = \binom{3}{3.5} \times (8 + m_2 + 2) \Rightarrow \binom{0}{32} + \binom{6m_2}{4m_2} + \binom{12}{0} = \binom{3}{3.5} \times (m_2 + 10)$

$\Rightarrow \binom{6m_2 + 12}{4m_2 + 32} = \binom{3m_2 + 30}{3.5m_2 + 35}$

3) Pick either the top row or bottom row to solve the equation for m_2 (it should be the same in both),
e.g.: Top — $6m_2 + 12 = 3m_2 + 30 \Rightarrow m_2 = \underline{6}$ kg. Bottom — $4m_2 + 32 = 3.5m_2 + 35 \Rightarrow m_2 = \underline{6}$ kg.

2D or not 2D — that is the question...

Well actually the question's more likely to be 'Find the centre of mass of the following system of particles...', but then I doubt that would have made Hamlet quite such a gripping tale. Make sure you can do this stuff with your eyes shut because you'll need it again later on, and there's also a new compulsory blindfolded section to the M2 exam this year...

Laminas and Composite Shapes

Some shapes for you to learn, just like in little school. However, you need to be able to find the centres of mass of these <u>uniform plane laminas</u>, not just colour them in. Even if you <u>can</u> do it neatly inside the lines.

Use Lines of Symmetry with Regular and Standard Shapes

<u>Uniform</u> laminas have <u>evenly spread</u> mass, so the centre of mass is in the centre of the shape, on all the <u>lines of symmetry</u>. So for shapes with more than one line of symmetry, the <u>centre of mass</u> is where the lines of symmetry <u>intersect</u>.

> **EXAMPLE** Find the coordinates of the centre of mass of a uniform rectangular lamina with vertices A(−4, 7), B (2, 7), C(−4, −3) and D(2, −3).
>
> 1) A little sketch never goes amiss...
>
> 2) $\bar{x}$ is the midpoint of AB (or CD), i.e. $(−4 + 2) \div 2 = −1$.
>
> 3) $\bar{y}$ is the midpoint of AC (or BD), i.e. $(7 + −3) \div 2 = 2$.
>
> 4) So the centre of mass is at <u>(−1, 2)</u>. Easy peasy lemon squeezy*.

It's time to combine all the things covered so far in the section into one <u>lamina lump</u>. Yay.

For a Composite Shape — Find each COM Individually then Combine

A <u>composite</u> shape is one that can be broken up into standard <u>parts</u> such as rectangles and circles. Once you've found the COM of a <u>part</u>, imagine replacing it with a <u>particle</u> of the <u>same mass</u> in the <u>position of the COM</u>. Do this for each part, then find the COM of the <u>group</u> of 'particles' — this is the COM of the composite shape.

> **EXAMPLE** A sign for the 'Rising Sun' restaurant is made from a uniform circular lamina attached to a uniform rectangular lamina made from the same material. The dimensions of the two laminas are shown below. Find the location of the centre of mass of the shape in relation to the point O.
>
>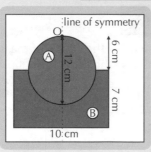
>
>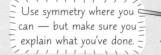
>
> 1) First, split up the shape into a circle (A) and rectangle (B). As both bits are made of the same material, the masses of A and B are in proportion to their areas, so we can say $m_A = \pi r^2 = \pi \times 6^2 = \underline{113.1}$, and $m_B = 10 \times 7 = \underline{70}$.
>
> 2) The shape has a line of symmetry, so the centre of mass <u>must be on that line</u>, directly below the point O.
>
> 3) Next find the vertical position of the centres of mass of both A and B individually:
>
> $y_A = \underline{6 \text{ cm}}$ from O
>
> $y_B = 6 \text{ cm} + (7 \text{ cm} \div 2) = \underline{9.5 \text{ cm}}$ from O
>
> Since A and B each have a horizontal line of symmetry halfway down them (but B is 6 cm below O to start with).
>
> 4) Treat the shapes as two particles positioned at the centres of mass of each shape, and use the formula from page 144:
>
> $\Sigma my = \bar{y} \Sigma m \Rightarrow m_A y_A + m_B y_B = \bar{y}(m_A + m_B)$
>
> $\Rightarrow (113.1 \times 6) + (70 \times 9.5) = \bar{y}(113.1 + 70) \Rightarrow 1343.6 = 183.1\bar{y} \Rightarrow \bar{y} = \underline{7.34 \text{ cm}}$.
>
> 5) Make sure you've answered the question —
>
> The centre of mass of the whole shape is <u>7.34 cm</u> vertically below O on the line of symmetry. Job done.

Use symmetry where you can — but make sure you explain what you've done.

I love a lamina in uniform...

A nice easy page with lots of pretty shapes and colours. Before you start unleashing your inner toddler and demanding sweets and afternoon naps, make sure you fully understand what's been said on this page, because the tough stuff is coming right up. There's plenty of time for sweets and afternoon naps when the exams are over. Trust me...

*Squeezing lemons is actually quite tricky so I'm not sure where this saying comes from.

Frameworks

More pretty shapes, this time made from <u>rods</u> rather than laminas — imagine bending a wire coathanger into something shapely (and infinitely more useful since wire hangers are rubbish). These shapes are called <u>frameworks</u>.

Treat **Each Side** as a **Rod** with its own **Centre of Mass**

In a framework, there's nothing in the middle, so all the mass is within the <u>rods</u> that make up the shape's <u>edges</u>. If the rods are <u>straight</u> and <u>uniform</u>, the centre of mass of each one is at the <u>midpoint</u> of the rod. Try to imagine each side of the shape as a <u>separate rod</u>, even if it's a single wire bent round into a shape.

> **EXAMPLE** Find the coordinates of the centre of mass of the framework shown.
>
> 1) The black dots are the <u>centres of mass</u> of each of the rods that make up the frame — so the position vectors can simply be written down for each one, e.g. $\mathbf{r}_{AB} = \begin{pmatrix} 1 \\ 3.5 \end{pmatrix}$.
>
> 2) The mass of each rod is <u>proportional to its length</u>, so $m_{AB} = 5$ etc.
>
> 3) You've now got the equivalent of a group of 6 particles, so put it all in the formula:
> $$m_{AB}\mathbf{r}_{AB} + m_{BC}\mathbf{r}_{BC} + m_{CD}\mathbf{r}_{CD} + m_{DE}\mathbf{r}_{DE} + m_{EF}\mathbf{r}_{EF} + m_{FA}\mathbf{r}_{FA} = \bar{\mathbf{r}}(m_{AB} + m_{BC} + m_{CD} + m_{DE} + m_{EF} + m_{FA})$$
>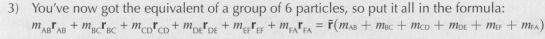
> $$5\begin{pmatrix} 1 \\ 3.5 \end{pmatrix} + 5\begin{pmatrix} 3.5 \\ 6 \end{pmatrix} + 2\begin{pmatrix} 6 \\ 5 \end{pmatrix} + 2\begin{pmatrix} 5 \\ 4 \end{pmatrix} + 3\begin{pmatrix} 4 \\ 2.5 \end{pmatrix} + 3\begin{pmatrix} 2.5 \\ 1 \end{pmatrix} = (5 + 5 + 2 + 2 + 3 + 3)\bar{\mathbf{r}}$$
>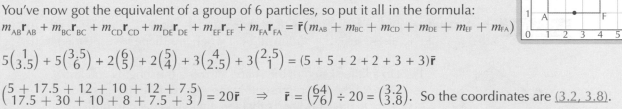
> $$\begin{pmatrix} 5 + 17.5 + 12 + 10 + 12 + 7.5 \\ 17.5 + 30 + 10 + 8 + 7.5 + 3 \end{pmatrix} = 20\bar{\mathbf{r}} \quad \Rightarrow \quad \bar{\mathbf{r}} = \begin{pmatrix} 64 \\ 76 \end{pmatrix} \div 20 = \begin{pmatrix} 3.2 \\ 3.8 \end{pmatrix}.$$ So the coordinates are <u>(3.2, 3.8)</u>.

Frameworks can be **Loaded with Particles**

<u>Loaded frameworks</u> are just frameworks with <u>particles plonked on them</u> — and examiners just love 'em. There are <u>two</u> types of question you could get:

1) Questions where the framework has a <u>mass</u>.

> **EXAMPLE** A particle with the same mass as the whole framework is attached to the frame in the example above at A. Find the new centre of mass of the system.
>
> 1) The system consists of the framework mass which acts at (3.2, 3.8) (from above), plus the mass of a particle at (1, 1). As they're the same mass, you can call each mass '1'.
>
> 2) $1\mathbf{r}_{Frame} + 1\mathbf{r}_{Particle} = 2\bar{\mathbf{r}} \quad \Rightarrow \quad \begin{pmatrix} 3.2 \\ 3.8 \end{pmatrix} + \begin{pmatrix} 1 \\ 1 \end{pmatrix} = 2\bar{\mathbf{r}} \quad \Rightarrow \quad \bar{\mathbf{r}} = \begin{pmatrix} 4.2 \\ 4.8 \end{pmatrix} \div 2 = \begin{pmatrix} 2.1 \\ 2.4 \end{pmatrix}.$
> So the coordinates of the new COM are <u>(2.1, 2.4)</u>.

2) Questions where the framework is <u>light</u>, so its mass can be <u>ignored</u>. This means you've really just got a <u>group of particles</u> in two dimensions.

> **EXAMPLE** A particle is attached to each vertex of a light triangular frame. The masses of the particles and the dimensions of the frame are shown below. Find the distance of the centre of mass of the system from AB.
>
>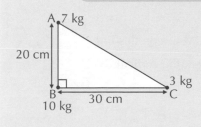
>
> 1) The only masses are the masses of the three particles.
>
> 2) You're only interested in the horizontal distance of the COM from side AB. So you don't need to mess around with column vectors.
>
> 3) Just plonk the masses and their distances from AB in the old $\Sigma mx = \bar{x}\Sigma m$ formula:
> $$(7 \times 0) + (10 \times 0) + (3 \times 30) = \bar{x} \times (7 + 10 + 3)$$
> $$90 = 20\bar{x} \quad \Rightarrow \quad \bar{x} = 4.5 \text{ cm}$$
> So the COM is <u>4.5 cm</u> from AB.

Wire coat hangers make great ferret hang-gliders though...

There's been a lot to take in on the last few pages. You'll notice every 'new' bit needs you to do all the 'old' bits too, and more besides. Maths is kinda like that. Make sure you're astoundingly marvellous at the section so far before you move on.

? >

Laminas in Equilibrium

This is what the whole section's been working up to. The raison d'être for centres of mass, if you'll pardon my French. The position of the centre of mass will tell you what happens when you hang it up or tilt it. Très intéressant, non?

Laminas **Hang** with the Centre of Mass **Directly Below** the Pivot

When you suspend a shape, either from a point on its edge or from a pivot point within the shape, it will hang in equilibrium so that the centre of mass is vertically below the suspension point.

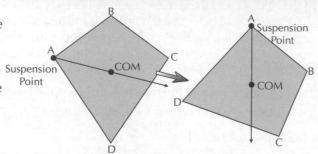

Knowing where the centre of mass lies will let you work out the angle that the shape hangs at.

EXAMPLE In the shape above, A is at (0, 6), C is at (8, 6), and the COM is at (4, 5). Find, in radians to 3 s.f., the angle AC makes with the vertical when the shape is suspended from A.

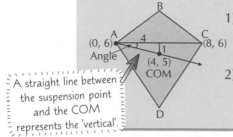

1) Do a little sketch of the shape showing the lengths you know. Draw in the line representing the vertical from the suspension point to the COM and label the angle you need to find.

2) The angle should now be an easy piece of trig away:
   Angle $= \tan^{-1}\frac{1}{4} = $ 0.245 radians to 3 s.f.

A straight line between the suspension point and the COM represents the 'vertical'.

In an exam question, you'll usually have to find the position of the centre of mass first and THEN find the angle that it hangs at to finish off.

EXAMPLE The cardboard mallet below is cut from one piece of cardboard and hung from the ceiling at a DIY enthusiast's birthday party.
a) By modelling the mallet as a uniform lamina, find the distance of the centre of mass from AB.

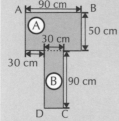

1) First, split up the shape into rectangle A and rectangle B. The masses of A and B are in proportion to their areas, so $m_A = 90 \times 50 = $ 4500, and $m_B = 90 \times 30 = $ 2700.

2) Next find the vertical position of the centres of mass of both A and B individually:
   $y_A = $ 25 cm from AB   and $y_B = 50$ cm $+ (90$ cm $\div 2) = $ 95 cm from AB
   Since A and B each have a horizontal line of symmetry halfway down them (but B is 50 cm below AB to start with).

3) Treat the shapes as two particles: $\Sigma my = \bar{y}\Sigma m \Rightarrow m_A y_A + m_B y_B = \bar{y}(m_A + m_B)$
   $\Rightarrow (4500 \times 25) + (2700 \times 95) = \bar{y}(4500 + 2700) \Rightarrow 369\,000 = 7200\bar{y} \Rightarrow \bar{y} = $ 51.25 cm.

b) The mallet is suspended from corner A and hangs in equilibrium. Find the angle that AB makes with the vertical in degrees to 3 s.f.

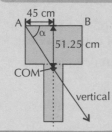

1) The shape has a line of symmetry — so the COM lies on this line.

2) Draw a line through A and the COM to represent the vertical.

3) So, $\alpha = \tan^{-1}\frac{51.25}{45} = $ 48.7° to 3 s.f.

Don't hang around — get practising or you're heading for a fall...

It's a good idea to have a squiz at your answer and check it's sensible — e.g. for the whole mallet, you know the COM will lie somewhere between the COMs of the two rectangles. As for the angle of the dangle, make sure it's not just plain ludicrous. Luckily, there's plenty of practice at doing these sorts of questions on the next few pages... So go on, give 'em a whirl.

M2 Section 1 — Practice Questions

Hurrah and huzzah — it's time to put your <u>slick Section 1 skills</u> (try saying that in a hurry) to the test.
As with all <u>strenuous exercise</u>, you need to <u>warm up</u> properly — and as if by chance, look what we have here...

Warm-up Questions

1) A 60 kg uniform beam AE of length 14 m is in equilibrium, supported by two vertical ropes attached to B and D as shown.

   Find the tensions in the ropes to 1 d.p.

   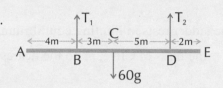

2) What is meant by a 'non-uniform rod'?

3) A uniform ladder, of length l m, is placed on rough horizontal ground and rests against a smooth vertical wall at an angle of 20° to the wall. Draw a diagram illustrating this system with forces labelled. State what assumptions you would make.

4) Three particles have mass $m_1 = 1$ kg, $m_2 = 2$ kg, and $m_3 = 3$ kg. Find the centre of mass of the system of particles if their coordinates are, respectively:
   a) (1, 0), (2, 0), (3, 0)   b) (0, 3), (0, 2), (0, 1)   c) (3, 4), (3, 1), (1, 0)

5) A system of particles located at coordinates A(0, 0), B(0, 4), C(5, 4) and D(5, 0) have masses m kg, $2m$ kg, $3m$ kg and 12 kg respectively. Find m, if the centre of mass of the system is at (3.5, 2).

6) Find the coordinates of the centre of mass of each of these shapes made from uniform laminas:

   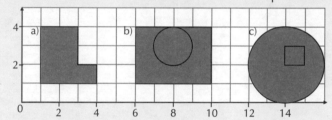

   b) and c) are made up of a small lamina stuck on a larger lamina of the same material.

7) a) A light square framework has side lengths of 5 cm. Masses are attached to the corners as shown on the right. Find the distance of the centre of mass from: i) side AB   ii) side AD.

   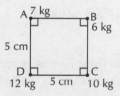

   b) The frame is suspended from corner A and hangs in equilibrium. Find the angle AB makes with the vertical. Give your answer in degrees to the nearest degree.

The universe is full of seemingly <u>unanswerable questions</u> to ponder.
Fortunately for those not particularly inclined towards philosophy there are some perfectly good <u>answerable</u> ones here. Enjoy.

Exam Questions

Whenever a numerical value of g is required in the following questions, take $g = 9.8$ ms⁻².

1 A horizontal uniform beam with length x and weight 18 N is held in equilibrium by 2 vertical strings. One string is attached to one end of the beam and the other at point A, 3 m from the first string. The tension in the string at A is 12 N, and the tension in the other string is T.

   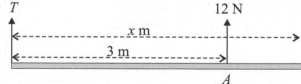

   a) Show that $x = 4$ m.

   (2 marks)

   b) Find T.

   (1 mark)

M2 Section 1 — Practice Questions

2   A uniform ladder, *AB*, is positioned against a smooth vertical wall and rests upon rough horizontal ground at an angle of θ, as shown. Clive stands on the ladder at point *C*, two-thirds of the way along the ladder's length from *A*. The ladder is 4.2 m long and weighs 180 N. The normal reaction at A is 490 N.

The ladder rests in limiting equilibrium. Model Clive as a particle and find:

a)   the mass of Clive, *m*, to the nearest kg.

(4 marks)

b)   the coefficient of friction, μ, between the ground and the ladder. Give your answer to 2 s.f.

(4 marks)

$\tan\theta = \dfrac{8}{11}$

3   The diagram below shows three particles attached to a light rectangular lamina at coordinates A(1, 3), B(5, 1) and C(4, *y*).

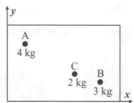

The centre of mass of the system is at $(\overline{x}, 2)$.

(a)   Show that $y = 1.5$.

(3 marks)

(b)   Show that $\overline{x} = 3$.

(3 marks)

The light lamina is replaced with a uniform rectangle PQRS, having a mass of 6 kg and vertices at P(0, 0), Q(0, 5), R(7, 5) and S(7, 0). Particles A, B and C remain at their existing coordinates.

(c)   Find the coordinates of the new centre of mass of the whole system.

(6 marks)

4   A cardboard advertising sign is modelled as two uniform square laminas with a uniform circular lamina attached, as shown. The masses of the small and large squares are 1 kg and 4 kg respectively. The mass of the circle is 5 kg.

(a)   Show that the centre of mass of the sign is 28 cm from AB and 38 cm from AF.

(5 marks)

The sign is suspended from point C, and hangs in equilibrium. A small weight, modelled as a particle, is attached at A, so that the sign hangs with AF horizontal.

(b)   Find the mass of the particle needed to make the sign hang in this way.

(3 marks)

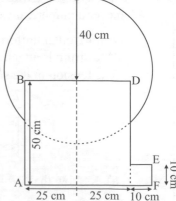

Displacement, Velocity and Acceleration

The "uvast" equations you saw back in M1 are all well and good when you've got a particle with constant acceleration. But when the <u>acceleration</u> of a particle <u>varies with time</u>, you need a few new tricks up your sleeve...

Differentiate to find *Velocity* and *Acceleration* from *Displacement*...

If you've got a particle moving in a <u>straight line</u> with acceleration that varies with time, you need to use <u>calculus</u> to find equations to describe the motion.   (Look back at your C1 and C2 notes for a reminder about calculus.)

1)   To find an equation for <u>velocity</u>, <u>differentiate</u> the equation for <u>displacement</u> with respect to time.

2)   To find an equation for <u>acceleration</u>, <u>differentiate</u> the equation for <u>velocity</u> with respect to time.
      (Or differentiate the equation for displacement with respect to time <u>twice</u>.)

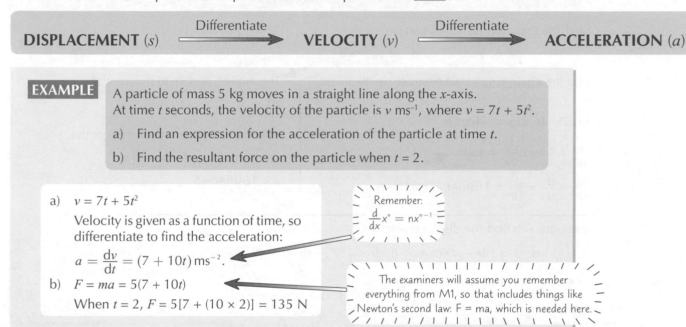

Differentiate

DISPLACEMENT (s) $\longrightarrow$ **VELOCITY** (v) $\longrightarrow$ **ACCELERATION** (a)

Differentiate

EXAMPLE

A particle of mass 5 kg moves in a straight line along the x-axis.
At time t seconds, the velocity of the particle is v ms^{-1}, where $v = 7t + 5t^2$.

a)   Find an expression for the acceleration of the particle at time t.

b)   Find the resultant force on the particle when $t = 2$.

a) $v = 7t + 5t^2$

Velocity is given as a function of time, so differentiate to find the acceleration:

$a = \dfrac{dv}{dt} = (7 + 10t)\,\text{ms}^{-2}$.

Remember:
$\dfrac{d}{dx}x^n = nx^{n-1}$

b) $F = ma = 5(7 + 10t)$

When $t = 2$, $F = 5[7 + (10 \times 2)] = 135$ N

The examiners will assume you remember everything from M1, so that includes things like Newton's second law: F = ma, which is needed here.

...and Integrate to find *Velocity* and *Displacement* from *Acceleration*

It's pretty similar if you're trying to go "back the other way", except you <u>integrate</u> rather than differentiate:

1)   To find an equation for <u>velocity</u>, <u>integrate</u> the equation for <u>acceleration</u> with respect to time.

2)   To find an equation for <u>displacement</u>, <u>integrate</u> the equation for <u>velocity</u> with respect to time.

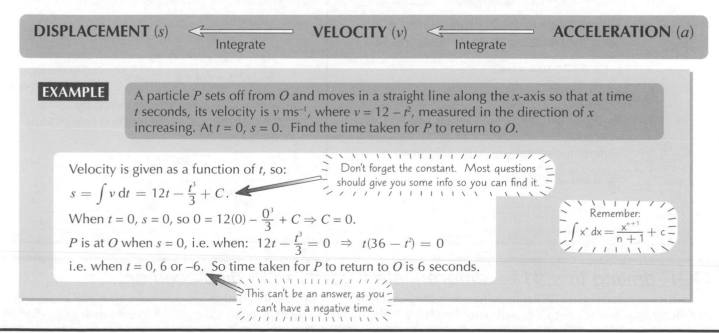

DISPLACEMENT (s) $\longleftarrow$ **VELOCITY** (v) $\longleftarrow$ **ACCELERATION** (a)

Integrate   Integrate

EXAMPLE

A particle P sets off from O and moves in a straight line along the x-axis so that at time t seconds, its velocity is v ms^{-1}, where $v = 12 - t^2$, measured in the direction of x increasing. At $t = 0$, $s = 0$. Find the time taken for P to return to O.

Velocity is given as a function of t, so:

$s = \int v\,dt = 12t - \dfrac{t^3}{3} + C$.

Don't forget the constant. Most questions should give you some info so you can find it.

When $t = 0$, $s = 0$, so $0 = 12(0) - \dfrac{0^3}{3} + C \Rightarrow C = 0$.

Remember:
$\int x^n\,dx = \dfrac{x^{n+1}}{n+1} + c$

P is at O when $s = 0$, i.e. when: $12t - \dfrac{t^3}{3} = 0 \Rightarrow t(36 - t^2) = 0$

i.e. when $t = 0$, 6 or –6. So time taken for P to return to O is 6 seconds.

This can't be an answer, as you can't have a negative time.

Displacement, Velocity and Acceleration

You might get given an equation of motion containing <u>trig</u> or <u>exponential</u> functions. If you've forgotten how to do calculus with these types of functions, you'd better get those C3 and C4 notes out and brush up.

Use the **Chain Rule** for Functions of Functions

Once you've worked through a couple of examples, the Core stuff should all come flooding back to you...

EXAMPLE
A particle sets off from the origin at $t = 0$ and moves along the x-axis.
At time t seconds, the velocity of the particle is $v \; ms^{-1}$, where $v = 5t - 4\cos4t + 8$. Find:

a) an expression for the acceleration of the particle at time t,

b) the displacement of the particle from the origin when $t = \pi$.

a) Split the equation for v into two parts:

$$v = -4\cos4t \quad \text{and} \quad v = 5t + 8$$

If you're struggling with the chain rule have a look at p. 17

Use the <u>chain rule</u> to differentiate the tricky bit — '$v = -4\cos 4t$':

let $u = 4t$, so $v = -4\cos u$

$\dfrac{du}{dt} = 4$ and $\dfrac{dv}{du} = 4\sin u$

Remember: $\dfrac{d}{dx}\cos x = -\sin x$

$\dfrac{dv}{dt} = \dfrac{dv}{du} \times \dfrac{du}{dt} = 16\sin4t$

This bit is a doddle to differentiate:

$\dfrac{dv}{dt} = 5$

Add the two parts together to get the final expression for $a = \dfrac{dv}{dt}$:

$a = 16\sin4t + 5$

b) Integrate v to find the displacement:

$$s = \int v \, dt = \int_0^\pi (5t - 4\cos 4t + 8)\, dt = \left[\frac{5}{2}t^2 - \sin 4t + 8t\right]_0^\pi$$

$$= \frac{5}{2}\pi^2 + 8\pi \text{ m } (= 49.8 \text{ m to 3 s.f.})$$

Doing a <u>definite integral</u> means you don't have to find a constant.

$\int \cos nx \, dx = \dfrac{1}{n}\sin nx$ (see page 27).

EXAMPLE
At time t seconds, a particle moving in a straight line along the x-axis has displacement s m, where $s = 3e^{-2t} + 4t$. Find:

a) an expression for the velocity of the particle at time t seconds,

b) the range of values for the particle's velocity.

a) <u>Differentiate</u> s to get an expression for v, using the <u>chain rule</u> to differentiate '$s = 3e^{-2t}$':

Let $u = -2t$, so $s = 3e^u$,

$\Rightarrow \dfrac{ds}{du} = 3e^u$ and $\dfrac{du}{dt} = -2$

So, $\dfrac{ds}{dt} = \dfrac{ds}{du} \times \dfrac{du}{dt} = 3e^{-2t} \times -2 = -6e^{-2t}$

Differentiating the <u>whole equation</u> for s gives:

$\dfrac{ds}{dt} = v = -6e^{-2t} + 4$

b) t must be ≥ 0.
When $t = 0$, $e^{-2t} = 1$, so $v = -6 + 4 = -2 \text{ ms}^{-1}$.
As $t \to \infty$, $e^{-2t} \to 0$, so $v \to 4$.
So, $-2 \leq v < 4 \text{ ms}^{-1}$.

Remember — '$\to$'means 'tends to'.

You could also answer this question by <u>sketching the graph</u> of the function (see page 8):

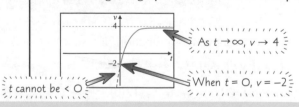

As $t \to \infty$, $v \to 4$

t cannot be < 0

When $t = 0$, $v = -2$

CGP driving tips #1 — differentiate velocity from displacement...

Calculus? In Mechanics? What fresh horror is this? Actually, it's really not that bad at all. Just make sure you know when to differentiate and when to integrate and then bang in the numbers you're given in the question to get the answer. Sorted.

Describing Motion Using Vectors

I can tell that you loved the last two pages, but I know what you're thinking: "That's all fair enough mate, but what about when a particle is moving in two dimensions?" Well, you know I can't ignore a question like that, so here you go...

Differentiate and *Integrate* with *Vector Notation* for Motion on a *Plane*

1) When you've got a particle moving in <u>two dimensions</u> (i.e. on a plane), you can describe its <u>position</u>, <u>velocity</u> and <u>acceleration</u> using the unit vectors **i** and **j** (which you should remember from M1). This "**i** and **j**" notation shows the <u>horizontal</u> and <u>vertical components</u> of displacement, velocity or acceleration <u>separately</u>.

2) The relationship between displacement (position), velocity and acceleration from page 151 still applies to particles moving on a plane:

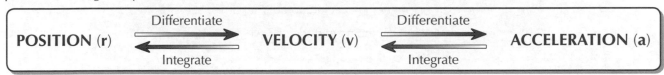

3) This means that you'll have to differentiate and integrate <u>vectors</u> written in **i** and **j** notation. Luckily, doing this is as easy as <u>squeezing lemons</u> — all you have to do is differentiate/integrate <u>each component</u> of the vector <u>separately</u>:

So, if $\mathbf{r} = x\mathbf{i} + y\mathbf{j}$ is a position vector, then:

velocity, $\mathbf{v} = \dfrac{d\mathbf{r}}{dt} = \dfrac{dx}{dt}\mathbf{i} + \dfrac{dy}{dt}\mathbf{j}$

> The shorthand for $\dfrac{d\mathbf{r}}{dt}$ is $\dot{\mathbf{r}}$ (the single dot means differentiate r <u>once</u> with respect to time)...

and acceleration, $\mathbf{a} = \dfrac{d\mathbf{v}}{dt} = \dfrac{d^2\mathbf{r}}{dt^2} = \dfrac{d^2x}{dt^2}\mathbf{i} + \dfrac{d^2y}{dt^2}\mathbf{j}$.

> ...and the shorthand for $\dfrac{d^2\mathbf{r}}{dt^2}$ is $\ddot{\mathbf{r}}$ (the double dots mean differentiate r <u>twice</u> with respect to time).

It's a similar thing for <u>integration</u>:

If $\mathbf{v} = w\mathbf{i} + z\mathbf{j}$ is a velocity vector, then position, $\mathbf{r} = \int \mathbf{v}\,dt = \int (w\mathbf{i} + z\mathbf{j})\,dt = \left[\int w\,dt\right]\mathbf{i} + \left[\int z\,dt\right]\mathbf{j}$

Unfortunately, there's no snazzy shorthand for integration. Ahh well, easy come, easy go.

EXAMPLE A particle is moving on a horizontal plane so that at time t it has velocity v ms⁻¹, where
$$\mathbf{v} = (8 + 2t)\mathbf{i} + (t^3 - 6t)\mathbf{j}$$
At $t = 2$, the particle has a position vector of $(10\mathbf{i} + 3\mathbf{j})$ m with respect to a fixed origin O.
a) Find the acceleration of the particle at time t.
b) Show that the position of the particle relative to O when $t = 4$ is $\mathbf{r} = 38\mathbf{i} + 27\mathbf{j}$.

a) $\mathbf{a} = \dot{\mathbf{v}} = \dfrac{d\mathbf{v}}{dt}$
$= 2\mathbf{i} + (3t^2 - 6)\mathbf{j}$

> Yep, that <u>really is</u> all there is to it.

b) $\mathbf{r} = \int \mathbf{v}\,dt$
$= (8t + t^2)\mathbf{i} + \left(\dfrac{t^4}{4} - 3t^2\right)\mathbf{j} + \mathbf{C}$

> You still need a constant of integration, but it will be a <u>vector</u> with **i** and **j** components.

When $t = 2$, $\mathbf{r} = (10\mathbf{i} + 3\mathbf{j})$, so use this info to find the vector $\mathbf{C}$:

$10\mathbf{i} + 3\mathbf{j} = 20\mathbf{i} - 8\mathbf{j} + \mathbf{C}$

$\Rightarrow \mathbf{C} = (10 - 20)\mathbf{i} + (3 - -8)\mathbf{j} = -10\mathbf{i} + 11\mathbf{j}$

> Collect **i** and **j** terms and add/subtract to simplify.

So, $\mathbf{r} = (8t + t^2 - 10)\mathbf{i} + \left(\dfrac{t^4}{4} - 3t^2 + 11\right)\mathbf{j}$.

When $t = 4$, $\mathbf{r} = (32 + 16 - 10)\mathbf{i} + (64 - 48 + 11)\mathbf{j} = 38\mathbf{i} + 27\mathbf{j}$ — as required.

It's easy enough to extend this to <u>three dimensions</u>. The position vector will be of the form $\mathbf{r} = x\mathbf{i} + y\mathbf{j} + z\mathbf{k}$, so you'll have <u>three components</u> to differentiate or integrate.

> If you're given the vector in column form, just deal with it in exactly the same way — by differentiating or integrating each component separately.

Describing Motion Using Vectors

Watch out for Questions that include **Forces**

When you see "<u>the action of a single force, **F** newtons</u>" in one of these vector questions, you should <u>immediately</u> think **F = ma**, because you're almost certainly going to need it. Here are a couple of examples showing the examiners' faves:

EXAMPLE

A particle P is moving under the action of a single force, **F** newtons. The position vector, **r** m, of P after t seconds is given by

$$\mathbf{r} = (2t^3 - 3)\mathbf{i} + \frac{t^4}{2}\mathbf{j}$$

a) Find an expression for the acceleration of P at time t seconds.

b) P has mass 6 kg. Find the magnitude of **F** when $t = 3$.

---

a) $\mathbf{v} = \dot{\mathbf{r}} = 6t^2\mathbf{i} + 2t^3\mathbf{j}$
   $\mathbf{a} = \dot{\mathbf{v}} = 12t\mathbf{i} + 6t^2\mathbf{j}$

b) At $t = 3$, $\mathbf{a} = 36\mathbf{i} + 54\mathbf{j}$

Using **F** = $m\mathbf{a}$, substitute $m = 6$:

$\mathbf{F} = (6 \times 36)\mathbf{i} + (6 \times 54)\mathbf{j} = 216\mathbf{i} + 324\mathbf{j}$

$|\mathbf{F}| = \sqrt{216^2 + 324^2} = 389$ N (3 s.f.)

*You could find the magnitude of **a** first instead if you wanted, then just multiply by m.*

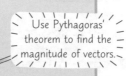
Use Pythagoras' theorem to find the magnitude of vectors.

EXAMPLE

A particle of mass 4 kg moves in a plane under the action of a single force, **F** newtons.

At time t seconds, $\mathbf{F} = (24t\mathbf{i} - 8\mathbf{j})$ N

At time $t = 0$, the velocity of the particle is $(7\mathbf{i} + 22\mathbf{j})$ ms⁻¹.

Here you have to work out the acceleration vector before you can do any integrating.

a) The velocity of the particle at time t is **v** ms⁻¹. Show that

$$\mathbf{v} = (3t^2 + 7)\mathbf{i} + (22 - 2t)\mathbf{j}$$

b) Find the value of t when the particle is moving parallel to the vector **i**.

---

a) Use **F** = $m\mathbf{a}$ to find an expression for the acceleration of the particle at time t:

$(24t\mathbf{i} - 8\mathbf{j}) = 4\mathbf{a} \Rightarrow \mathbf{a} = 6t\mathbf{i} - 2\mathbf{j}$

$\mathbf{v} = \int \mathbf{a}\, dt = \int (6t\mathbf{i} - 2\mathbf{j})\, dt = 3t^2\mathbf{i} - 2t\mathbf{j} + \mathbf{C}$

When $t = 0$, $\mathbf{v} = (7\mathbf{i} + 22\mathbf{j})$ ms⁻¹. Use this information to find **C**:

$7\mathbf{i} + 22\mathbf{j} = 0\mathbf{i} + 0\mathbf{j} + \mathbf{C} \Rightarrow \mathbf{C} = 7\mathbf{i} + 22\mathbf{j}$. So at time t,

$\mathbf{v} = 3t^2\mathbf{i} - 2t\mathbf{j} + 7\mathbf{i} + 22\mathbf{j}$

$= (3t^2 + 7)\mathbf{i} + (22 - 2t)\mathbf{j}$ — as required.

b) When the particle is moving parallel to the vector **i**, the **j** component of **v** is 0, and the **i** component is non-zero, so:

$22 - 2t = 0 \Rightarrow t = 11$

At $t = 11$, the **i** component of velocity is $(3 \times 11^2) + 7 = 370$, i.e. not zero.

So the particle is moving parallel to the vector **i** at 11 s.

Motion in two dimensions — it's plane simple...

Just remember to differentiate and integrate by treating each component separately, and pretty soon you'll be able to differentiate velocity vectors in 11-dimensional hyperspace. Just think how cool that'll look at the next sci-fi convention.

Applying Differential Equations

Often, the hardest thing about M2 is working out which bits of maths you need to dredge up from the darkest recesses of your brain to help you answer a question. Although some people claim that's half the fun of it. Hmmm...

Form **Differential Equations** using **Force = Mass × dv/dt**

You should be pretty familiar with $F = ma$ by now, and on page 151, you were introduced to $a = \dfrac{dv}{dt}$.

Well guess what — you can stick these two equations together to form some super-useful differential equations:

EXAMPLE
The combined mass of a cyclist and her bike is 75 kg. She is cycling along a horizontal road and stops pedalling when her velocity is 10 ms⁻¹. The only horizontal force acting on the cyclist and her bike is a resistive force of $15v$ N, where v is the velocity of the bike.

Show that $\dfrac{dv}{dt} = -\dfrac{v}{5}$.

> The resistive force is the only horizontal force acting on the cyclist, so the resultant force, F, is negative.

Resolving forces horizontally, using $F = ma$:

$$-15v = 75 \times \frac{dv}{dt} \qquad \Rightarrow \qquad \frac{dv}{dt} = -\frac{v}{5}$$

Solve **Differential Equations** by **Separating the Variables**

To make the most of these differential equations, you need to <u>solve</u> them. And that means bringing in another C4 skill — <u>separating variables in differential equations</u>. Head back to page 78 if you've forgotten all about it.

EXAMPLE a) In the example above, how long does it take before the speed of the bike falls to 3 ms⁻¹?

First <u>rearrange</u> the differential equation to get all the v terms on one side, and all the t terms on the other:

$$\frac{dv}{dt} = -\frac{v}{5} \quad \Rightarrow \quad \frac{1}{v}\,dv = -\frac{1}{5}\,dt$$

Next <u>integrate</u> both sides:

$$\int \frac{1}{v}\,dv = \int -\frac{1}{5}\,dt \quad \Rightarrow \quad \left[\ln|v|\right]_{10}^{3} = \left[-\frac{t}{5}\right]_{0}^{T}$$

> Wondering where these limits appeared from? Velocity is 10 ms⁻¹ at $t = 0$, when the cyclist stops pedalling. And velocity is 3 ms⁻¹ at some unknown time, $t = T$. Easy.

So $\ln 3 - \ln 10 = -\dfrac{T}{5} \Rightarrow T = 6.02$ s (3 s.f.)

b) Show that $v = 10e^{-0.2t}$ for the cyclist.

As in part a), separate the variables and integrate both sides:

$$\int \frac{1}{v}\,dv = \int -\frac{1}{5}\,dt \quad \Rightarrow \quad \ln|v| = -\frac{t}{5} + C$$

> An <u>indefinite</u> integral this time.

Take exponentials of both sides to find an expression for v:

$$e^{\ln|v|} = e^{-0.2t + C} \quad \Rightarrow \quad |v| = e^{-0.2t} \times e^{C}. \text{ So } v = ke^{-0.2t}, \text{ for some constant } k.$$

Now find k. At $t = 0$, $v = 10$ ms⁻¹, so:

$$10 = ke^{-(0.2 \times 0)} \quad \Rightarrow \quad k = 10$$

> To do this step, just rewrite the constant e^C as another constant, k — see page 28.

So, $\boxed{v = 10e^{-0.2t}}$ as required.

> If you have a suggestion about what we could use to fill this annoying bit of space, we'd like to hear it. Send us a postcard. Or a carrier pigeon.

dv/dt — I thought you got that from long-haul flights...

The questions you get on this stuff tend to be the same every time — form the <u>differential equation</u>, integrate it to get an equation connecting v and t, then use this equation to find t for a certain value of v. You just need to be able to manipulate yucky equations.

M2 Section 2 — Practice Questions

And so continues the world of M2. Before you crack on with more mechanical delights, I reckon it's time for some practice questions to make sure you've made sense of everything in this section. And because I'm nice, I'll start you off with some nice easy warm-up questions...

Warm-up Questions

1) A particle sets off from the origin at $t = 0$ and moves along the x-axis with velocity $v = 8t^2 - 2t$.
   Find expressions for:
   a) the acceleration of the particle at time t, and   b) the displacement of the particle at time t

2) A particle sets off from the origin at $t = 0$ and moves along in a straight line with velocity $v = 3t^2 - 4\cos 2t + 8$.
   Find expressions for:
   a) the acceleration of the particle at time t, and   b) the displacement of the particle at time t

3) A particle moving in a plane has position vector $\mathbf{r}$, where $\mathbf{r} = x\mathbf{i} + y\mathbf{j}$.
   What quantities are represented by the vectors $\dot{\mathbf{r}}$ and $\ddot{\mathbf{r}}$?

4) A particle with a mass of 3 kg moves off from the origin at $t = 0$, under a force $\mathbf{F}$.
   It moves in a plane with velocity $\mathbf{v} = 4t\mathbf{i} + t^2\mathbf{j}$.
   a) Find the position vector $\mathbf{r}$ and the acceleration vector $\mathbf{a}$ for the particle at time t.
   b) Find an expression for $\mathbf{F}$ at time t.

5) A car's engine is switched off when the car is travelling along a horizontal road at 15 ms⁻¹.
   The only horizontal force acting on the car from this point is a resistive force of $0.025mv$ newtons,
   where m is the mass of the car in kg and v is its velocity in ms⁻¹.
   Show that $\dfrac{dv}{dt} = -0.025v$.

Right, now you're warmed up and there's absolutely no danger of you pulling a maths muscle,
it's time to get down to the serious business of practice exam questions.

Exam Questions

1   A particle moves in a straight line along the x-axis. At time t, the particle has acceleration a, where:
$$a = 8t^2 + 6\sin 2t$$
When $t = 0$, $v = 0$.

   a)   Find an expression for v, the particle's velocity at time t.

   (4 marks)

   b)   Show that when $t = \dfrac{\pi}{2}$, the particle's velocity is $\dfrac{\pi^3}{3} + 6$.

   (2 marks)

2   A particle of mass m kg moves in a straight line from the origin, O.
     Its velocity, v ms⁻¹, at time t seconds is:
$$v = 2t - 3e^{-2t} + 4$$

   a)   Find an expression for the particle's acceleration at time t.

   (2 marks)

   b)   Find the range of values for the particle's acceleration.

   (3 marks)

   c)   The resultant force acting on the particle when $t = 2$ is 6 N.
        Find the value of m.

   (2 marks)

   d)   Find an expression for the particle's displacement from O at time t.

   (4 marks)

M2 Section 2 — Practice Questions

There's more where that came from. Oh yes indeed...

3 A particle P is moving in a horizontal plane under the action of a single force $\mathbf{F}$ newtons. After t seconds, P has position vector:

$$\mathbf{r} = (2t^3 - 7t^2 + 12)\mathbf{i} + (3t^2 - 4t^3 - 7)\mathbf{j} \text{ m}$$

where the unit vectors $\mathbf{i}$ and $\mathbf{j}$ are in the directions of east and north respectively. Find:

a) an expression for the velocity of P after t seconds.

(2 marks)

b) the speed of P when $t = \frac{1}{2}$, and the direction of motion of P at this time.

(3 marks)

At $t = 2$, the magnitude of $\mathbf{F}$ is 170 N. Find:

c) the acceleration of P at $t = 2$,

(3 marks)

d) the mass of the particle,

(3 marks)

e) the value of t when $\mathbf{F}$ is acting due parallel to $\mathbf{j}$.

(3 marks)

4 A particle is moving in a curved path. Its velocity, $\mathbf{v}$, at time t is given by:

$$\mathbf{v} = (2\cos 3t + 5t)\mathbf{i} + (2t - 7)\mathbf{j}$$

where the unit vectors $\mathbf{i}$ and $\mathbf{j}$ are in the directions of east and north respectively. Find:

a) an expression for the particle's acceleration after t seconds.

(2 marks)

b) the magnitude of the particle's maximum acceleration. Give an exact value.

(4 marks)

5 A plane of mass m kg is taxiing along a runway. Its engines exert a horizontal driving force of $10\,000v^{-1}$ N, and it experiences a horizontal resistive force of $0.1mv^2$, where v is the velocity of the plane in ms^{-1}. Assume that these are the only two forces acting horizontally on the plane.

a) Show that the equation of motion of the plane is:

$$\frac{dv}{dt} = \frac{10\,000}{mv} - 0.1v^2$$

(2 marks)

b) The pilot switches the engines off. Write down the new equation of motion for the plane.

(1 mark)

c) If the pilot switched off the engines when the plane was travelling at 20 ms^{-1}, find the time it would take for the plane to slow down to 10 ms^{-1}.

(5 marks)

6 A 2 kg bowling ball moves along a smooth horizontal surface with initial velocity 12 ms^{-1}. The ball experiences a horizontal resistive force of kv N, where v is the velocity of the ball in ms^{-1} and k is a constant. Assuming that this is the only horizontal force experienced by the ball:

a) Show that: $\dfrac{dv}{dt} = -\dfrac{kv}{2}$

(2 marks)

b) Show that: $v = 12\sqrt{e^{-kt}}$

(4 marks)

Work Done

Hello, good evening, welcome to Section 3 — where <u>work</u> and <u>energy</u> are tonight's chef's specials...

You Can Find the **Work Done** by a Force Over a Certain **Distance**

When a force is acting on a particle, you can work out the <u>work done</u> by the force using the formula:

> **Work done = force (F) × distance moved in the direction of the force (s)**

For F in newtons, and s in metres, the unit of work done is joules (J).

E.g. if an object is pushed <u>4 m</u> across a horizontal floor by a force of magnitude <u>12 N</u> acting horizontally, the <u>work done</u> by the force will be $12 × 4 = \underline{48\ J}$

EXAMPLE
A rock is dragged across horizontal ground by a rope attached to the rock at an angle of 25° to the horizontal. Given that the work done by the force is 470 J and the tension in the rope is 120 N, find the distance the rock is moved.

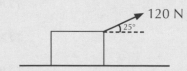
120 N
25°

Work = horizontal component of force × s

$$470 = 120\cos25 × s$$

$$s = 4.32\ m\ (3\ s.f.)$$

Because the force and the distance moved have to be in the same direction.

EXAMPLE
A sack of flour of mass m kg is attached to a vertical rope and raised h m at a constant speed. Show that the work done against gravity by the tension in the rope, T, can be expressed as mgh.

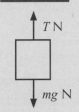
T N
mg N

Resolve vertically:

$F = ma$

$T - mg = m × 0$

$\Rightarrow T = mg$

Work done = Fs

$= T × h$

$= mgh$

Work and gravity

You can always use the formula mgh to find the work done by a force against gravity.

A Particle Moving **Up a Rough Slope** does Work against **Friction and Gravity**

EXAMPLE
A block of mass 3 kg is pulled 9 m up a rough plane inclined at an angle of 20° to the horizontal by a force, T. The block moves at a constant speed. The work done by T against friction is 154 J.

Find: a) the work done by T against gravity
       b) the coefficient of friction between the block and the plane.

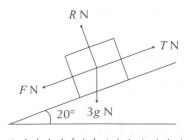
R N
T N
F N
20° $3g$ N

a) Work done against gravity = mgh
$= 3g × 9\sin20$
$= \mathbf{90.5\ J}$ (3 s.f.)

You need to use the <u>vertical</u> height, because it's only vertically that T does work against gravity.

b) Resolve perpendicular to the slope to find R:
$R - 3g\cos20 = m × 0$
$\Rightarrow R = 3g\cos20$

Particle is moving, so:
$F = \mu R$
$= \mu × 3g\cos20$

Remember — for a moving particle, $F = \mu R$, where μ is the coefficient of friction and R is the normal reaction.

Work done by T against friction
$= F × s = 154$
So, $\mu × 3g\cos20 × 9 = 154$
$\mu = \mathbf{0.619}$ (3 s.f.)

The bit of T that is working against friction must be equal to F as the block is moving with constant speed (i.e. a = O), so you can just use F here.

My work done = coffee × flapjack...

The really important thing to remember from this page is that the distance moved must be in the <u>same direction</u> as the force. Also, don't forget that a particle moving at constant velocity has no resultant force acting on it — this makes resolving forces easy.

Kinetic and Potential Energy

Here are a couple of jokers you might remember from GCSE Science. I know, I know — Science. This means we're skirting dangerously close to the <u>real world</u> here. :| Don't be too afraid though — it's not as scary as you might think...

A *Moving Particle* Possesses *Kinetic Energy*

Any particle that is <u>moving</u> has <u>kinetic energy</u> (K.E.). You can find the kinetic energy of a particle using the formula:

$$\text{K.E.} = \frac{1}{2}mv^2$$

You need to learn this formula — you won't be given it in the exam.

If mass, m, is measured in kg and velocity, v, in ms^{-1}, then kinetic energy is measured in joules.

EXAMPLE
An ice skater of mass 60 kg is moving at a constant velocity of 8 ms^{-1}. Find the ice skater's kinetic energy.

Kinetic energy $= \frac{1}{2}mv^2$

$= \frac{1}{2} \times 60 \times 8^2 = 1920$ J

Work Done is the same as the *Change* in a Particle's *Kinetic Energy*

The <u>work done</u> by a force to <u>change the velocity</u> of a particle moving <u>horizontally</u> is equal to the change in that particle's kinetic energy:

Work done = change in kinetic energy

Work done $= \frac{1}{2}mv^2 - \frac{1}{2}mu^2 = \frac{1}{2}m(v^2 - u^2)$

EXAMPLE
A particle P of mass 6 kg is pulled along a rough horizontal plane by a force of 40 N, acting parallel to the plane. The particle travels 4 m in a straight line between two points on the plane, A and B. The coefficient of friction between P and the plane is 0.35.

a) Find the work done against friction in moving P from A to B.

At B, P has a speed of 8 ms^{-1}.

b) Calculate the speed of P at A.

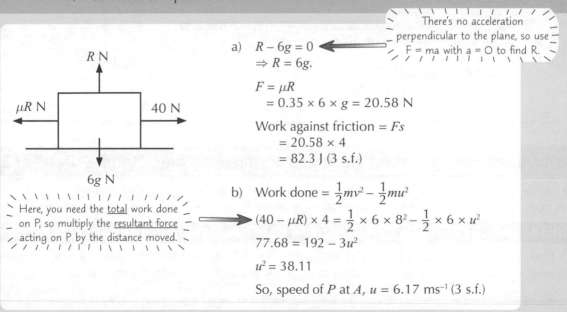

There's no acceleration perpendicular to the plane, so use $F = ma$ with $a = 0$ to find R.

a) $R - 6g = 0$
    $\Rightarrow R = 6g$.

$F = \mu R$
   $= 0.35 \times 6 \times g = 20.58$ N

Work against friction $= Fs$
   $= 20.58 \times 4$
   $= 82.3$ J (3 s.f.)

Here, you need the <u>total</u> work done on P, so multiply the <u>resultant force</u> acting on P by the distance moved.

b) Work done $= \frac{1}{2}mv^2 - \frac{1}{2}mu^2$

$(40 - \mu R) \times 4 = \frac{1}{2} \times 6 \times 8^2 - \frac{1}{2} \times 6 \times u^2$

$77.68 = 192 - 3u^2$

$u^2 = 38.11$

So, speed of P at A, $u = 6.17$ ms^{-1} (3 s.f.)

Kinetic and Potential Energy

Gravitational Potential Energy *is all about a Particle's* Height

The gravitational potential energy (G.P.E.) of a particle can be found using the formula:

$$\text{G.P.E.} = mgh$$

← You need to learn this formula as well.

If mass (*m*) is measured in kg, acceleration due to gravity (*g*) in ms^{-2} and the vertical height above some base level (*h*) in m, then G.P.E. is measured in joules, J.

The greater the height of a particle above the 'base level', the greater that particle's gravitational potential energy.

EXAMPLE

A lift and its occupants have a combined mass of 750 kg. The lift moves vertically from the ground to the first floor of a building, 6.1 m above the ground. After pausing, it moves vertically to the 17th floor, 64.9 m above the ground. Find the gravitational potential energy gained by the lift and its occupants in moving:

a) from the ground floor to the first floor,

b) from the first floor to the 17th floor.

a) G.P.E. gained = mg × increase in height
= 750 × 9.8 × 6.1
= 44 800 J (3 s.f)

b) G.P.E. gained = mg × increase in height
= 750 × 9.8 × (64.9 − 6.1)
= 432 000 J (3 s.f.)

G.P.E. *Always uses the* Vertical Height

When you're working out the gravitational potential energy of a particle, the value of *h* you use should always, always, always be the vertical height above the 'base level'. This means that for a particle moving on a slope, it's only the vertical component of the distance you're interested in:

EXAMPLE

A skateboarder and her board have a combined mass of 65 kg. The skateboarder starts from rest at a point *X* and freewheels down a slope inclined at 15° to the horizontal. She travels 40 m down the line of greatest slope. Find the gravitational potential energy lost by the skateboarder.

The skateboarder has moved a distance of 40 m down the slope, so this is a vertical distance of: 40sin15° m.
G.P.E. = mgh
= 65 × 9.8 × 40sin15°
= 6590 J = 6.59 kJ (both to 3 s.f.)

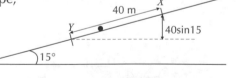

Mechanical Energy *is the* Sum *of a Particle's* Kinetic and Potential Energies

Over the next couple of pages, you're going to see a fair bit about 'mechanical energy'. This is nothing to freak out about — it's just the sum of the kinetic and potential energies of a particle:

Total Mechanical Energy = Kinetic Energy + Gravitational Potential Energy (+ Elastic Potential Energy)

You'll find out all about elastic potential energy on p.163-164. In the calculations on the next couple of pages, you can ignore elasticity, and just use kinetic energy and gravitational potential energy.

Particle P has so much potential — if only he could apply himself...

There shouldn't be anything earth-shattering on these two pages — I'd bet my completed 1994-95 Premier League sticker album that you've seen both of these types of energy before*. Still, it's worth refreshing yourself for what comes next.

*I won't though, it's too dear to me. Ahh, shinies...

The Work-Energy Principle

Those pages refreshing your memory on potential and kinetic energy weren't just for fun and giggles. Behold...

Learn the *Principle of Conservation of Mechanical Energy...*

The <u>principle of conservation of mechanical energy</u> says that:

> **If there are no external forces doing work on an object, the total mechanical energy of the object will remain constant.**

An <u>external force</u> is any force other than the weight of the object, e.g. friction, air resistance, tension in a rope, etc. This means that the sum of <u>potential</u> and <u>kinetic</u> energies remains the <u>same</u> throughout an object's motion. This is a <u>pretty useful</u> bit of knowledge:

EXAMPLE

A BASE jumper with mass 88 kg jumps from a ledge on a building, 150 m above the ground. He falls with an initial velocity of 6 ms⁻¹ towards the ground. He releases his parachute at a point 60 m above the ground.

a) Find the initial kinetic energy of the jumper.

b) Use the principle of conservation of mechanical energy to find the jumper's kinetic energy and speed at the point where he releases his parachute.

c) State one assumption you have made in modelling this situation.

a) Initial K.E. $= \frac{1}{2}mu^2 = \frac{1}{2} \times 88 \times (6)^2$
$= 1584$ J

You can just use the *change* in height here, as it's the change in G.P.E. that you're interested in.

b) Decrease in G.P.E. as he falls:
$mgh = 88 \times 9.8 \times (150 - 60)$
$= 77\,616$ J

Using conservation of mechanical energy: Increase in K.E. = Decrease in G.P.E.

So, K.E. when parachute released – Initial K.E. = Decrease in G.P.E.

$\frac{1}{2}mv^2 =$ Decrease in G.P.E. + Initial K.E.
$= 77\,616 + 1584 = 79\,200$ J

Rearrange $\frac{1}{2}mv^2 = 79\,200$ to find the speed of the jumper when parachute is released:

If you don't assume this, then you can't use the principle of conservation of energy.

$v = \sqrt{\dfrac{79\,200}{\frac{1}{2} \times 88}} = 42.4$ ms⁻¹ (3 s.f.)

c) That the only force acting on the jumper is his weight.

...and the *Work-Energy Principle*

1) As you saw above, if there are <u>no external forces</u> doing work on an object, then the total mechanical energy of the object remains <u>constant</u>.

2) So, if there *is* an <u>external force</u> doing work on an object, then the <u>total mechanical energy</u> of the object must <u>change</u>.

3) This leads to the <u>work-energy principle</u>:

> **The work done on an object by external forces is equal to the change in the <u>total mechanical energy</u> of that object.**

4) The work-energy principle is pretty similar to the result on page 159. It's generally <u>more useful</u> though, because you can use it for objects moving in any direction — not just horizontally.

Turn the page for a **HOT** and **SEXY** example...

The Work-Energy Principle

As promised, a <u>lovely example</u> of the work-energy principle...

Example

A particle of mass 3 kg is projected up a rough plane inclined at an angle θ to the horizontal, where $\tan\theta = \frac{5}{12}$. The particle moves through a point A at a speed of 11 ms⁻¹.

The particle continues to move up the line of greatest slope and comes to rest at a point B before sliding back down the plane. The coefficient of friction between the particle and the slope is $\frac{1}{3}$.

a) Use the work-energy principle to find the distance AB.

b) Find the speed of the particle when it returns to A.

a) Call the distance $AB\ x$.

You're told to use the work-energy principle, so first find the change in total mechanical energy:

Change in K.E. of the particle = Final K.E. – Initial K.E.

$$= \frac{1}{2}mv^2 - \frac{1}{2}mu^2 = 0 - \left(\frac{1}{2} \times 3 \times 11^2\right) = -181.5 \text{ J}$$

Change in G.P.E. of the particle = $mg \times$ (change in height)

$$= 3gx\sin\theta = 3gx \times \frac{5}{13} = \frac{15gx}{13} \text{ J}$$ ← $\tan\theta = \frac{5}{12} \Rightarrow \sin\theta = \frac{5}{13}$

So, change in total mechanical energy

$$= -181.5 + \frac{15gx}{13}$$

The only external force doing work on the particle is the frictional force, F.
So you need to find the work done by F.
First, resolve perpendicular to slope:

$$R - 3g\cos\theta = 0 \Rightarrow R = 3g \times \frac{12}{13} = \frac{36g}{13}$$

$$F = \mu R = \frac{1}{3} \times \frac{36g}{13} = \frac{12g}{13}$$

$\tan\theta = \frac{5}{12} \Rightarrow \cos\theta = \frac{12}{13}$

Displacement is <u>negative</u> because the particle is moving in the <u>opposite direction</u> to F.

Work done by $F = Fs = \frac{12g}{13} \times -x = -\frac{12gx}{13}$

Using the work-energy principle:
Change in total mechanical energy = Work done by F

So: $-181.5 + \frac{15gx}{13} = -\frac{12gx}{13}$

$$\frac{27gx}{13} = 181.5$$

$$x = \frac{181.5 \times 13}{27g} = 8.92 \text{ m (3 s.f.)}$$

b) The particle moves from A, up to B and back down to A, so overall change in G.P.E. = 0

So, the change in total mechanical energy between the first and second time the particle is at A is just the change in Kinetic Energy, i.e. Final K.E. – Initial K.E. = $\frac{1}{2}mv^2 - \frac{1}{2}mu^2$

Work done on the particle = $Fs = F \times -2x$

$$= \frac{12g}{13} \times -2(8.917) = -161.3$$

The particle has travelled the distance AB twice and is always moving in the opposite direction to the frictional force.

Using the work-energy principle:

$$\frac{1}{2} \times 3 \times v^2 - \frac{1}{2} \times 3 \times 11^2 = -161.3$$

u = 11 ms⁻¹, as this is the speed of the particle when it's first at A.

$$\frac{3}{2}v^2 = 181.5 - 161.3 \quad \Rightarrow \quad v = 3.67 \text{ ms⁻¹ (3 s.f.)}$$

Does this mean we can save energy by doing less work...

There are a few different ways you could tackle part b). You could just look at the motion back down the slope and look at the K.E. gained and the G.P.E. lost. Or you could resolve parallel to the slope, work out the acceleration and use $v^2 = u^2 + 2as$. If the question doesn't tell you what method to use, you'll get marks for using any correct method. <u>Correct</u> being the key word.

Elastic Potential Energy

This page is all about stretching stuff. Exciting or what?

Use **Hooke's Law** to find **Tension** in a **String** or **Spring**

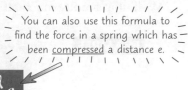

You can also use this formula to find the force in a spring which has been compressed a distance e.

1) Hooke's Law is a formula for finding the <u>tension</u> (T) in a <u>string</u> or <u>spring</u> that has been <u>stretched</u> a distance e. You need to <u>learn</u> this formula — you won't be given it in the exam.

$$T = \frac{\lambda}{l}e$$

2) l is the <u>natural length</u> of the spring or elastic string — i.e. its length when it is not being stretched.

3) The <u>modulus of elasticity</u> (λ) is a measure of <u>how easily</u> something can be <u>stretched</u> in a way that it will return to its original shape afterwards. If T has units of N, then the units of λ will also be N.

> **EXAMPLE** A wooden block is suspended in equilibrium from an elastic string. The string is extended from its natural length of 5 m to a length of 8 m. Given that the modulus of elasticity of the string is 30 N, find the mass of the block.
>
>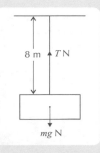
>
> Use <u>Hooke's Law</u> to find the <u>tension</u> in the string: $\quad T = \frac{\lambda}{l}e = \frac{30}{5} \times 8 = 48\,\text{N}.$
>
> The block is in <u>equilibrium</u>, so resolving forces vertically: $\quad T = mg = 48 \Rightarrow m = 48 \div 9.8 = 4.90\,\text{kg (3 s.f.)}.$

Elastic Potential Energy is energy stored in a **Stretched String** or **Spring**

1) When an elastic string (or spring) is stretched, the <u>work done</u> in stretching it is converted into <u>elastic potential energy</u> (E.P.E.), which is <u>stored</u> in the string.

The E.P.E. stored in a compressed spring can be found exactly the same way.

2) You've already seen that W, the work done by a constant force over a distance x m, is given by $W = Fx$. But tension in an elastic string is not constant — it's a <u>variable force</u>.

3) To find the <u>work done</u> by a variable force, you need to <u>integrate the force</u> with respect to <u>distance</u>, i.e. $W = \int F\,\mathrm{d}x$.

4) This can be used to find a <u>formula for E.P.E.</u> It's another formula you need to know I'm afraid. But even worse, you could be asked to <u>derive</u> it in the exam. I know — absolutely shocking.

The formula for Elastic Potential Energy

From Hooke's law, the <u>tension</u> in an elastic string extended a distance of x m is: $\quad T = \frac{\lambda}{l}x$

So, <u>work done against tension</u>:

$$W = \int_0^e T\,\mathrm{d}x = \int_0^e \frac{\lambda}{l}x\,\mathrm{d}x = \left[\frac{\lambda}{2l}x^2\right]_0^e = \frac{\lambda}{2l}e^2.$$

The limits of the integral are chosen to be $[0, e]$ rather than $[0, x]$ to avoid using x, the variable you are integrating, as a limit. Another variable, e, is picked to represent the length of extension.

The <u>potential energy</u> stored in the string is equal to the work done, so $\boxed{\text{E.P.E.} = \frac{\lambda}{2l}e^2}$

This is the baby you've got to learn — there's an example using it on the next page.

Mechanical Energy also includes **Elastic Potential Energy**

We can no longer ignore the E.P.E. term from the equation on page 160. So:

Total Mechanical Energy = Kinetic Energy + Gravitational Potential Energy + Elastic Potential Energy

1) Including the extra term in the equation opens up a whole new <u>array of exciting questions</u> which you could be asked about the <u>principle of conservation of mechanical energy</u> and the <u>work-energy principle</u> from page 161.

2) It's nothing scary — just remember that if the only forces acting on a particle are its <u>weight</u> and <u>tension</u> in an <u>elastic</u> string or spring, then the total mechanical energy will be <u>constant</u>.

3) And if any other forces <u>are</u> acting on a particle, the <u>work done by them</u> is equal to the <u>change in total mechanical energy</u>. Simples.

Turn the page for a **COLD** and **UGLY** example...

Elastic Potential Energy

Well, that's pretty much all the theory on E.P.E. Now it's time to hone your skills with this <u>beast</u> of an example.

EXAMPLE

One end of a light elastic string is attached at point O to a smooth plane inclined at an angle of 30° to the horizontal, as shown. The other end of the string is attached to a particle of mass 8 kg. The string has a natural length of 1 m and modulus of elasticity 40 N.

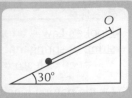

The particle is released from rest at O and slides down the slope.

a) Find the length of the string when the particle's acceleration is zero.

b) The string extends to a total length of x m before the particle first comes to rest. Show that $x^2 - 3.96x + 1 = 0$.

c) Hence find the distance from O at which the particle first comes to rest.

The particle is held at point A, 3 m down the slope from O, where it is released from rest and moves up the slope with speed v ms⁻¹.

> 'Taut' means that the string is stretched to some length greater than its natural length.

d) Show that, while the string is taut, the particle's motion satisfies the equation $v^2 = -5y^2 + 19.8y - 14.4$, where y is the particle's distance from O down the slope.

e) Find the speed of the particle at the point where the string becomes slack.

a) Resolve parallel to the slope to find the <u>tension</u> in the string, T:

$$T - mg\sin30 = 8 \times 0 \Rightarrow T = 8 \times 9.8 \times \sin30 = \textbf{39.2 N}.$$

Now use <u>Hooke's Law</u> to find the <u>length of extension</u> at this point:

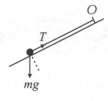

$$T = \frac{\lambda}{l}e \Rightarrow e = \frac{Tl}{\lambda} = \frac{39.2 \times 1}{40} = \textbf{0.98 m}.$$

So the length of the string at this point is $l + e = 1 + 0.98 = 1.98$ m.

b) The particle starts and ends at rest, so the change in the particle's <u>kinetic energy</u> is zero. So, by the <u>conservation of mechanical energy</u>: Change in G.P.E. = Change in E.P.E.

G.P.E. lost $= mgh = 8 \times 9.8 \times x\sin30 = 39.2x$.

E.P.E. gained $= \frac{\lambda}{2l}e^2 = \frac{40}{2 \times 1} \times (x - 1)^2 = 20(x - 1)^2$

> The total length of the extended string is x m, and its natural length is 1 m, so the length of extension is $(x - 1)$ m.

So $20(x - 1)^2 = 39.2x \Rightarrow x^2 - 2x + 1 = 1.96x \Rightarrow x^2 - 3.96x + 1 = 0$.

c) Solving $x^2 - 3.96x + 1 = 0$ using the <u>quadratic formula</u> gives

$x = \textbf{3.69}$ or $\textbf{0.271}$.

0.271 can be ignored as we know that the string is <u>extended</u>, so x must be <u>greater than 1</u> (the natural length of the string). So the particle is first stationary when it is 3.69 m from O (3 s.f.).

d) At point A, the particle has <u>no K.E.</u> and <u>no G.P.E.</u> (if the level of A is taken as the 'base level').

So, total mechanical energy $= 0 + 0 + $ E.P.E. $= \frac{\lambda}{2l}e^2 = \frac{40}{2 \times 1} \times (3 - 1)^2 = \textbf{80 J}$

By the conservation of mechanical energy, during the motion of the particle after release from A:

$$\frac{\lambda}{2l}e^2 + mgh + \frac{1}{2}mv^2 = 80 \Rightarrow 20(y - 1)^2 + 78.4(3 - y)\sin30 + 4v^2 = 80,$$

> The vertical distance between A (3 m from O) and the particle's current position (y m from O).

which rearranges to $v^2 = -5y^2 + 19.8y - 14.4$ — as required.

e) The string becomes <u>slack</u> when it is no longer stretched, i.e. when it is at its <u>natural length</u>. So, substitute $y = 1$ into the equation from part d) and solve for v:

$$v^2 = -5 + 19.8 - 14.4 \Rightarrow v = 0.63 \text{ ms}^{-1} \text{ (2 s.f.)}$$

I'm just Hooked on elastic potential energy...

All in all quite a nice little topic, if you ask me. You need to know the formulas, and the principle of conservation of mechanical energy always crops up somewhere along the way. As long as you're down with that, then it's all good.

Power

Snap! may have had the power in 1990 — but that won't really help you prepare for your M2 exam now, will it?

Power is the Rate at which Work is done on an Object

Power is a measure of the <u>rate a force does work on an object</u>. ◄—————
The unit for power is the <u>watt</u>, where 1 watt (1 W) = 1 joule per second.

So Power = $\dfrac{\text{Work Done}}{\text{Time}}$

For an <u>engine</u> producing a <u>driving force</u> of F newtons, and moving a vehicle at a speed of v ms^{-1}, the power in watts can be found using the formula:

Power = $F \times v$ ◄—————

Power = $\dfrac{\text{Work Done}}{\text{Time}} = \dfrac{\text{Force} \times \text{Distance}}{\text{Time}} = \text{Force} \times \text{Velocity}$

This is the formula you'll end up using most of the time — those examiners can't resist a question about engines.
But don't forget what power means, just in case they throw you a curveball — it's the <u>rate of doing work</u>.

EXAMPLE

A train of mass 500 000 kg is travelling along a straight horizontal track with a constant speed of 20 ms^{-1}. The train experiences a constant resistance to motion of magnitude 275 000 N.

a) Find the rate at which the train's engine is working. Give your answer in kW.

b) The train now moves up a hill inclined at 2° to the horizontal. If the engine continues to work at the same rate and the magnitude of the non-gravitational resistance to motion remains the same, find the new constant speed of the train.

a) Call the driving force of the train T N and the speed of the train u ms^{-1}.
Resolve horizontally to find T:
$T - 275\,000 = m \times 0$
So $T = 275\,000$ N
Power = $T \times u = 275\,000 \times 20 = 5500$ kW.

b) Call the new driving force T' and resolve parallel to the slope:
$T' - 275\,000 - 500\,000g\sin2° = m \times 0$
$\Rightarrow T' = 275\,000 + 500\,000g\sin2°$ N $= 446\,008$ N

Power = $T' \times v$

$5\,500\,000 = 446\,008 \times v \Rightarrow v = \dfrac{5\,500\,000}{446\,008} = 12.3$ ms^{-1} (3 s.f.)

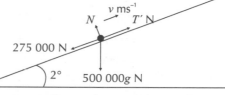

EXAMPLE

A tractor of mass 3000 kg is moving down a hill inclined at an angle of θ to the horizontal, where $\sin\theta = \dfrac{1}{24}$. The acceleration of the tractor is 1.5 ms^{-2} and its engine is working at a constant rate of 30 kW. Find the magnitude of the non-gravitational resistance to motion at the instant when the tractor is travelling at a speed of 8 ms^{-1}.

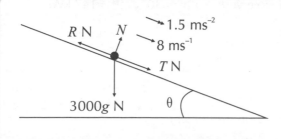

Use Power = $F \times v$ to find T:

$30\,000 = T \times 8 \Rightarrow T = 3750$ N

Add the component of weight, as the tractor is moving <u>down</u> the slope.

Resolve parallel to the slope: $T + mg\sin\theta - R = ma$

$3750 + (3000 \times 9.8 \times \dfrac{1}{24}) - R = 3000 \times 1.5$

$R = 3750 + 1225 - 4500$

$R = 475$ N

There <u>is</u> acceleration here, so this term <u>doesn't disappear</u> for once.

All together now — Watt's the unit for power...

These power questions all revolve around the use of $F = ma$, $P = Fv$ and maybe the occasional Power = Work ÷ Time.
Learn these and you're set for life. Well, maybe not life, but at least your exams. And what is life without exams?

Power

Right, last page of learnin' in this section. It's a good 'un as well. And just think: after this — practice questions. Get in.

Be prepared for a **Variable Resistive Force**

There's a good chance you'll get a power question where the resistive force isn't constant — it'll be <u>dependent on the velocity</u> of whatever's moving. Like the examples on the previous page, these questions require resolving of forces and the careful use of $F = ma$.

> **EXAMPLE**
>
> A van of mass 1500 kg moves up a road inclined at an angle of 5° to the horizontal. The van's engine works at a constant rate of 25 kW and the van experiences a resistive force of magnitude kv N, where k is a constant and v is the van's speed in ms⁻¹. At the point where the van has speed 8 ms⁻¹, its acceleration is 0.5 ms⁻².
>
> a) Show that $k = 137$ to 3 significant figures.
>
> b) Using $k = 137$, show that U, the maximum speed of the van on this road, satisfies the equation: $U^2 + 9.35U - 182 = 0$, where the coefficients are given to 3 s.f.

a) Use Power = $T \times v$, to find T, the driving force of the van's engine:

$$T = \frac{\text{Power}}{v} = \frac{25\,000}{8} = 3125 \text{ N}$$

Resolve forces parallel to the slope: $T - kv - mg\sin 5 = ma$

So: $3125 - 8k - (1500 \times 9.8 \times \sin 5) = 1500 \times 0.5$

And rearrange: $k = \frac{1}{8}(3125 - (1500 \times 9.8 \times \sin 5) - (1500 \times 0.5)) = 137\,(3 \text{ s.f.})$

b) From Power = Fv, the driving force of the van's engine at speed U is $\frac{25\,000}{U}$ N.

Again, resolve forces parallel to the slope: $\frac{25\,000}{U} - 137U - (1500 \times 9.8 \times \sin 5) = 0$

Multiply throughout by U: $25\,000 - 137U^2 - 1281U = 0$

Rearrange and simplify (to 3 s.f.) to give: $U^2 + 9.35U - 182 = 0$ — as required.

The van is travelling at maximum speed, so acceleration is zero.

> **EXAMPLE**
>
> A car of mass 1200 kg travels on a straight horizontal road. It experiences a resistive force of magnitude $30v$ N, where v is the car's speed in ms⁻¹. The maximum speed of the car on this road is 70 ms⁻¹. Find:
>
> a) the car's maximum power,
>
> b) the car's maximum possible acceleration when its speed is 40 ms⁻¹.

a) When the car is travelling at its maximum speed, its acceleration is zero, and so the driving force of the car, T, must be equal to the resistive force, i.e. $T = 30v$.

Now use Power = Force × Velocity to give $P = 30v^2 = 30 \times 70^2 = 147$ kW.

b) Call the new driving force of the car F.

Power = Force × Velocity $\Rightarrow F = \frac{147\,000}{40} = 3675$ N

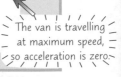

Resolve forces horizontally:

$3675 - 30v = ma$

$3675 - (30 \times 40) = 1200a \Rightarrow a = 2.06 \text{ ms}^{-2}\,(3 \text{ s.f.})$.

Maximum acceleration will only be possible when engine is working at maximum power.

The Power of Love — a Variable Resistive Force from Above...

Well that pretty much wraps up this section on work and energy. Plenty of formulas to learn and plenty of fun force diagrams to draw. If you're itching for some practice at all this then turn over and crack on. Even if you're not, do it anyway.

M2 Section 3 — Practice Questions

I don't know about you, but I enjoyed that section. Lots of <u>engines</u> and <u>energy</u> and <u>blocks</u> moving on <u>slopes</u> and GRRRRR look how manly I am as I do work against <u>friction</u>. *Ahem* sorry about that. Right-oh — practice questions...

Warm-up Questions

1) A crate is pushed across a smooth horizontal floor by a force of 250 N, acting in the direction of motion. Find the work done in pushing the crate 3 m.

2) A crane lifts a concrete block 12 m vertically at constant speed. If the crane does 34 kJ of work against gravity, find the mass of the concrete block. Take $g = 9.8$ ms^{-2}.

3) A horse of mass 450 kg is cantering at a speed of 13 ms^{-1}. Find the horse's kinetic energy.

4) An ice skater of mass 65 kg sets off from rest. After travelling 40 m in a straight line across horizontal ice, she has done 800 J of work. Find the speed of the ice skater at this point.

5) A particle of mass 0.5 kg is projected upwards from ground level and reaches a maximum height of 150 m above the ground. Find the increase in the particle's gravitational potential energy. Take $g = 9.8$ ms^{-2}.

6) State the principle of conservation of mechanical energy.
   Explain why you usually need to model an object as a particle if you are using this principle.

7) A jubilant cowboy throws his hat vertically upwards with a velocity of 5 ms^{-1}. Use conservation of energy to find the maximum height the hat reaches above the point of release. Take $g = 9.8$ ms^{-2}.

8) State the work-energy principle. Explain what is meant by an 'external force'.

9) A spring of natural length 3 m is compressed so that its new length is 1.5 m.
   Given that the modulus of elasticity of the spring is 25 N, find:

   a)   the compression force in the spring,   b)   the elastic potential energy stored in the spring.

10) A car's engine is working at a rate of 350 kW. If the car is moving with speed 22 ms^{-1}, find the driving force of the engine.

11) A bus travels along a straight horizontal road. It experiences a resistive force of magnitude $80v$ N, where v is the speed of the bus in ms^{-1}. The bus's maximum power is 65 kW. Find the maximum speed of the bus.

Well those warm-up questions should have got your maths juices flowing, and you should now be eager to move on to something a bit more <u>exam-like</u>. It's probably best not to ask what maths juice is.

Exam Questions

Whenever a numerical value of g is required in the questions below, take $g = 9.8$ ms^{-2}.

1   A skier is pulled up a sloping plane by a constant force, L, acting parallel to the plane which is inclined at an angle of 30° to the horizontal. The skier and his skis have a combined mass of 90 kg and he experiences a constant frictional force of 66 N as he moves up the slope.

   The skier passes through two gates, which are 28 m apart. His speed at the lower gate is 4 ms^{-1}. At the upper gate, his speed has increased to 6 ms^{-1}. Find:

   a)   the increase in the skier's total mechanical energy as he moves from the lower gate to the upper gate,

   (5 marks)

   b)   the magnitude of the force, L, pulling the skier up the slope.

   (3 marks)

M2 Section 3 — Practice Questions

I hope you've still got the energy left to power through this last bit of work. I don't want to have to force you...

2   A stone of mass 0.3 kg is dropped down a well. The stone hits the surface of the water in the well with a speed of 20 ms⁻¹.

   a)   Calculate the kinetic energy of the stone as it hits the water.

   (2 marks)

   b)   By modelling the stone as a particle and using conservation of energy, find the height above the surface of the water from which the stone was dropped.

   (3 marks)

   c)   When the stone hits the water, it begins to sink vertically and experiences a constant resistive force of 23 N. Use the work-energy principle to find the depth the stone has sunk to when the speed of the stone is reduced to 1 ms⁻¹.

   (5 marks)

3   A van of mass 2700 kg is travelling at a constant speed of 16 ms⁻¹ up a road inclined at an angle of 12° to the horizontal. The non-gravitational resistance to motion is modelled as a single force of magnitude of 800 N.

   a)   Find the power of the engine.

   (4 marks)

   When the van passes a point A, still travelling at 16 ms⁻¹, the engine is switched off and the van comes to rest without braking, a distance *x* m from A. If all resistance to motion remains constant, find:

   b)   the distance *x*,

   (4 marks)

   c)   the time taken for the van to come to rest.

   (4 marks)

4

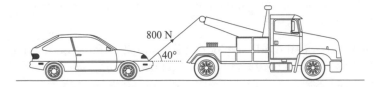

   A car of mass 1500 kg is towed 320 m along a straight horizontal road by a rope attached to a pick-up truck. The rope is attached to the car at an angle of 40° to the horizontal and the tension in the rope is 800 N. The car experiences a constant resistance to motion from friction.

   a)   Find the work done by the towing force.

   (3 marks)

   b)   Over the 320 m, the car increases in speed from 11 ms⁻¹ to 16 ms⁻¹. Assuming that the magnitude of the towing force remains constant at 800 N, find the coefficient of friction between the car and the road.

   (4 marks)

5   A cyclist is riding up a road at a constant speed of 4 ms⁻¹. The road is inclined at an angle α to the horizontal. The cyclist is working at a rate of 250 W and experiences a constant non-gravitational resistance to motion of magnitude 35 N. The cyclist and his bike have a combined mass of 88 kg.

   a)   Find the angle of the slope, α.

   (4 marks)

   b)   The cyclist now increases his work rate to 370 W. If all resistances to motion remain unchanged, find the cyclist's acceleration when his speed is 4 ms⁻¹.

   (4 marks)

M2 Section 3 — Practice Questions

6   A block of mass 3 kg is attached to one end of a light elastic string of natural length 2 m. The other end of the string is attached to a fixed point A. The weight of the block extends the length of the string to 5 m. The system is in equilibrium, with the block hanging directly below A. Find:

    a)   the modulus of elasticity of the string,

(3 marks)

    b)   the elastic potential energy in the string.

(2 marks)

The block is pulled down to a distance of 8 m directly below A, where it is released from rest and begins to move upwards.

    c)   Find the speed of the block when it is a distance of 3 m below A.

(4 marks)

7   A car of mass 1000 kg experiences a resistive force of magnitude kv N, where k is a constant and $v\,\text{ms}^{-1}$ is the car's speed. The car travels up a slope inclined at an angle of $\theta°$ to the horizontal, where $\sin\theta = 0.1$. The power generated by the car is 20 kW and its speed up the slope remains constant at 10 ms^{-1}.

    a)   Show that $k = 102$.

(3 marks)

    b)   The car's maximum power output is 50 kW.

        (i)   Show that, going up this slope, the car's maximum possible speed, u, satisfies the equation

$$102u^2 + 980u - 50\,000 = 0.$$

(4 marks)

        (ii)   Hence find the car's maximum possible speed up this slope.

(2 marks)

The car reaches the top of the slope and begins travelling on a flat horizontal road. The power increases to 21 kW and the resistive force remains at kv N.

    c)   Find the acceleration of the car when its speed is 12 ms^{-1}.

(3 marks)

8   A particle of weight 10 N is attached to one end of a light elastic string, the other end of which is O, a point on a vertical wall.
    The particle is placed on a rough horizontal surface, as shown, where the coefficient of friction between the particle and the surface is $\mu = 0.5$. The string has natural length 5 m and modulus of elasticity 50 N.

    a)   The particle is held a horizontal distance d m from O, where $d > 5$.
    Find an expression for the elastic potential energy of the system in terms of d.

(2 marks)

The particle is released from rest d m from O. The subsequent motion results in the particle coming to rest just as it reaches O.

    b)   Find d.

(7 marks)

Circular Motion

Things often move in <u>circular paths</u> — think satellites in orbits, fairground carousel horses and conkers on strings being twirled dangerously. It's a whole new world of motion to sink your teeth into.

Angular Speed is Measured in Radians per Second

1) You can measure the speed of a particle travelling in a circle in two different ways — <u>linear speed</u> and <u>angular speed</u>: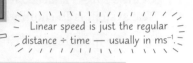
   > Linear speed is just the regular distance ÷ time — usually in ms⁻¹.

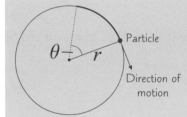

The <u>angular speed</u>, ω, is how quickly the <u>radius</u>, r, is turning — or the <u>rate of change of θ</u>. There's a formula for working it out:

$$\omega = \frac{\theta}{t}$$

> Angle radius has moved through — in radians.

> Angular speed — radians per second.

> Time taken — in seconds.

2) It's really important to measure the angle in <u>RADIANS</u>, or this lovely equation linking <u>angular</u> and <u>linear</u> speed won't work:

Linear speed = radius × angular speed
(ms⁻¹)   (m)   (radians s⁻¹)

$$v = r\omega$$

3) You might have to convert from units such as <u>revolutions per minute</u> to <u>radians per second</u>, so learn these:

$$360° = 2\pi \text{ radians} = 1 \text{ revolution}$$

> **EXAMPLE** A particle moves in a horizontal circle completing 600 revolutions per minute. What is its angular speed?
>
> Find θ: 600 revolutions = $600 \times 2\pi$ radians = 1200π radians.
>
> Now find ω: $\omega = \frac{\theta}{t} = \frac{1200\pi}{60} = 20\pi$ radians s⁻¹
>
> > The time must be in seconds.

Direction is Always Changing so the Velocity is Changing too

1) The <u>direction</u> of something moving in a circle is always <u>parallel to the tangent</u> of the circle — so it's <u>constantly changing</u>. Velocity has magnitude <u>and direction</u>, so changing direction means <u>changing velocity</u>.

2) If something's velocity is changing, it must be <u>accelerating</u>. So even if a particle is moving in a circle with a <u>constant speed</u>, it will still be <u>accelerating</u>.
   > This is a strange one — take a moment to make sure you get it.

3) The <u>acceleration</u> is always directed towards the <u>centre of the circle</u>, perpendicular to the direction of motion. It's called <u>radial acceleration</u> and there are a couple of formulas to learn:

One using <u>angular speed</u>...   ...and one using <u>linear speed</u>.

4) There must be a <u>force</u> acting on the particle to produce the acceleration. And there is. It's called the <u>centripetal force</u>, it <u>always</u> acts towards the <u>centre</u> of the circle, and you just use the old $F = ma$ formula to find it.

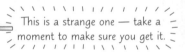

$$a = r\omega^2 \qquad a = \frac{v^2}{r}$$

> **EXAMPLE** A particle moves with an angular speed of 20π rad s⁻¹ around a horizontal circle of radius 0.25 m.
> a) Find the magnitude of its acceleration.
>
> $$a = r\omega^2 = 0.25 \times (20\pi)^2 = 100\pi^2 \text{ ms}^{-2}$$
>
> > In the case of a particle on a string, the centripetal force is provided by the tension in the string.
>
> b) A string connects the particle above to the centre of the circle. Find the tension in the string if the particle's mass is 3 kg.
>
> Resolving horizontally:
> $F = ma \Rightarrow T = mr\omega^2$
> $= 3 \times 100\pi^2 = 300\pi^2 \text{ N}$

I propose the motion that we stop going round in circles and move on...

You need to learn all the formulas on this page — you won't be given them in the exam. Remember that θ should be in <u>radians</u> when you're calculating ω and remember to use the <u>radial</u> acceleration in $F = ma$ to find the centripetal force.

Conical Pendulums

Conical pendulum questions <u>aren't</u> as tricky as they look — they're usually just a case of <u>resolving a force</u> and then plonking things into the equations on the previous page.

Resolve Tension in a Conical Pendulum into Components

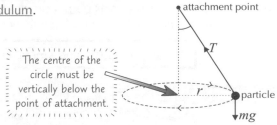

1) If you dangle an object at the end of a string, then <u>twirl</u> it round so the object moves in a <u>horizontal circle</u>, you've made a <u>conical pendulum</u>.

2) There are only <u>two</u> forces acting on the object — its <u>weight</u> and the <u>tension</u> in the string.

The centre of the circle must be vertically below the point of attachment.

3) The <u>vertical component</u> of the tension in the string supports the <u>weight</u> of the object, and the <u>horizontal component</u> is the <u>centripetal force</u> causing the radial acceleration.

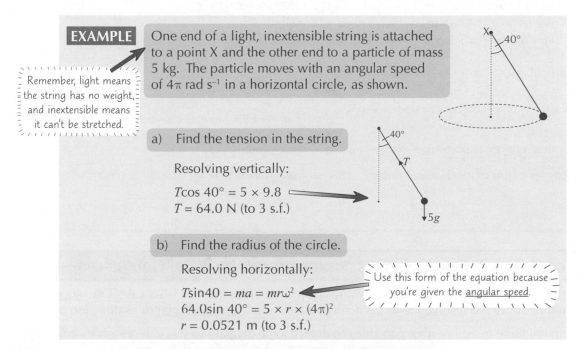

EXAMPLE One end of a light, inextensible string is attached to a point X and the other end to a particle of mass 5 kg. The particle moves with an angular speed of 4π rad s^{-1} in a horizontal circle, as shown.

Remember, light means the string has no weight, and inextensible means it can't be stretched.

a) Find the tension in the string.

Resolving vertically:

$T\cos 40° = 5 \times 9.8$
$T = 64.0$ N (to 3 s.f.)

b) Find the radius of the circle.

Resolving horizontally:

Use this form of the equation because you're given the <u>angular speed</u>.

$T\sin 40 = ma = mr\omega^2$
$64.0\sin 40° = 5 \times r \times (4\pi)^2$
$r = 0.0521$ m (to 3 s.f.)

Don't be Confused by Slight Variations in Questions

The conical pendulums in most exam questions are just like those above.
However, watch out for <u>special pendulums</u> that they sometimes throw in to spice things up:

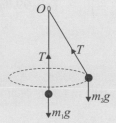

The <u>single string</u> through a ring:

The tension in <u>both</u> parts of the string is <u>the same</u> — and it's equal to the <u>weight</u> of the particle hanging vertically:

$T = m_1g$

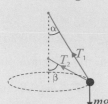

The <u>two-string</u> pendulum:

Each string has a <u>separate tension</u>. You have to include the horizontal or vertical components of <u>both</u> strings when resolving forces,

e.g. Resolving <u>vertically</u>:
$T_1\cos \alpha + T_2\cos \beta = mg$

The second string might be <u>horizontal</u> — that makes life easier, cos there'll be no <u>vertical</u> component of tension. <u>Brilliant</u>.

A big deep breath... And... resolve...

You might have to use radians and degrees in the same question — so stay alert. You'll need angles in radians for finding the angular speed, but in degrees for finding the components of forces. Don't worry — just a few more pages to go and then you'll be entering the CGP holodeck. I've programmed it to simulate M2 questions so beautiful, you'll weep actual tears.

Vertical Circular Motion

So far you've only seen particles moving in horizontal circles — well, you need to know about vertical circles too. The thing with vertical circles is that the speed isn't the same all the way round. It increases on the way down and decreases on the way up. All this on top of the ever-changing acceleration due to the changing direction. AAAH.

Energy is Always Conserved in Vertical Circular Motion

The centripetal force always acts <u>perpendicular</u> to the direction of motion, so does <u>no</u> work in this direction. So, for something moving in a vertical circle, you can use the <u>conservation of mechanical energy</u> — see page 161.

> The <u>sum</u> of <u>G.P.E.</u> and <u>kinetic energy</u> is the <u>same</u> at any point on the circle.

EXAMPLE A particle of mass m kg is attached to a string of length 0.4 m. The other end of the string is attached to a fixed point, O, and the particle moves in a vertical circle. It has speed $v_A = 6$ ms^{-1} when it passes through point A, the lowest point on the circle.
Find v_B, the particle's speed when it reaches point B, shown.

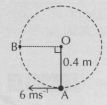

Total mechanical energy at point A: $\frac{1}{2}mv_A^2 = \frac{1}{2}m \times 6^2 = 18m$ ← A is the lowest point, so say that it has no G.P.E. here.

Always use the linear speed to calculate kinetic energy.

Point B is higher, so it has both kinetic energy and G.P.E.

Total mechanical energy at point B: $\frac{1}{2}mv_B^2 + mgh = \frac{1}{2}mv_B^2 + (mg \times 0.4)$

So, by the conservation of mechanical energy: $18m = \frac{1}{2}mv_B^2 + (mg \times 0.4)$

$$18 = \frac{1}{2}v_B^2 + 0.4g \Rightarrow v_B = \sqrt{36 - 0.8g} \Rightarrow v_B = 5.31 \text{ms}^{-1}$$

A Centripetal Force Causes the Acceleration in Vertical Circles too

As with any circular motion, the <u>resultant force</u> towards the centre of the circle is what causes the <u>acceleration</u>. To find the resultant force, you <u>resolve</u> the forces acting on the particle <u>perpendicular</u> to its direction of motion.

With any centripetal force question, it's a good idea to draw a <u>force diagram</u> so you can see what's going on.

EXAMPLE a) Find the tension in the string when the particle in the example above is at point A.

First draw a <u>force diagram</u> — there are only two forces acting on the particle, the <u>tension</u> in the string, T, and the particle's <u>weight</u>.

Now, resolving vertically:

$$T - mg = \frac{mv^2}{r} \Rightarrow T - mg = \frac{m \times 6^2}{0.4} \Rightarrow T = mg + \left(\frac{m \times 6^2}{0.4}\right) \Rightarrow T = 99.8m$$

$\frac{v^2}{r}$ is the formula for radial acceleration from page 170.

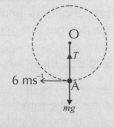

b) Find the tension in the string when it is at an angle of 60° to OA, given that at this point, the particle has a speed of v ms^{-1}. Give your answer in terms of m and v.

Resolve perpendicular to the direction of motion:

$$T - mg\cos 60 = \frac{mv^2}{0.4} \Rightarrow T = m\left(9.8\cos 60 + \frac{v^2}{0.4}\right) \Rightarrow T = m(4.9 + 2.5v^2)$$

Centripetals — in the middle of the flower...

Remember that the speed of a particle moving in a vertical circle <u>changes</u>. Don't start assuming it's moving with constant speed. That would be BAD. Well, not as bad as a meteor crashing into Earth and causing a tsunami which wipes out the entire population, except for the US government, Paris Hilton and her pet chihuahua, who all get to go in the secret bunker.

Vertical Circular Motion

Being attached to a string isn't the only way a particle can get to move in a circle...

A **Bead on a Wire** has a **Reaction Force**

1) Questions often involve a bead sliding around a <u>smooth ring or circular wire</u>.
2) There's no tension in strings here. Instead, the wire exerts a <u>reaction force</u> on the bead.

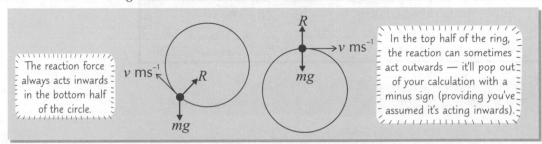

The reaction force always acts inwards in the bottom half of the circle.

R

v ms^{-1}

mg

In the top half of the ring, the reaction can sometimes act outwards — it'll pop out of your calculation with a minus sign (providing you've assumed it's acting inwards).

EXAMPLE A bead of mass m kg moves around a smooth ring of radius 3 m as shown. If its speed at point A is $2v$ ms^{-1} and its speed at point B is v ms^{-1}, find the reaction of the ring on the bead at point B in terms of m and g.

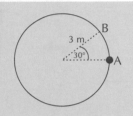

B
3 m.
30°
A

1) Draw a force diagram:

The diagram assumes R is acting outwards.

2) Resolve perpendicular to the direction of motion:

$$mg\sin 30° - R = \frac{mv^2}{r}$$

$$\Rightarrow R = \frac{mg}{2} - \frac{mv^2}{3}$$

You've got a v in your expression, but you need it in terms of m and g only.

3) Find v using conservation of mechanical energy:

$$\frac{1}{2}m(2v)^2 = \frac{1}{2}mv^2 + (mg \times 3\sin 30°)$$

$$4v^2 = v^2 + 3g \Rightarrow v^2 = g$$

At A, the bead has only K.E. — at B it also has G.P.E.

4) You can now eliminate v from the equation for R:

$$R = \frac{mg}{2} - \frac{mg}{3} \Rightarrow R = \frac{mg}{6}$$

Particles can move on **Circular Surfaces**

1) A particle can move in a vertical circle on the <u>inside</u> of a <u>horizontal cylinder</u>.
2) You treat it just like the bead on a ring above — except that the <u>reaction</u> of the surface on the particle always acts <u>inwards</u>.
3) You can also have a particle rolling <u>over</u> the surface of a <u>hemisphere</u> (or over the top half of a <u>horizontal cylinder</u>).
4) Again, treat it just like the bead on a ring — but remember that the <u>reaction</u> of the surface on the particle always acts <u>outwards</u>.

The main difference with these two types of motion is that the particle can leave the circular path here — it obviously can't for a bead on a wire.

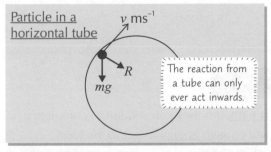

<u>Particle in a horizontal tube</u>

v ms^{-1}

R

mg

The reaction from a tube can only ever act inwards.

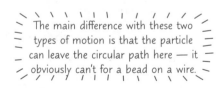

<u>Particle outside a hemisphere</u>

R

v ms^{-1}

mg

The reaction from the surface always acts outwards.

To fall or not to fall — Bard on a wire...

So particles inside cylinders are <u>exactly like</u> particles on strings, except the string tension is replaced by a reaction force. And they're in a cylinder. With no string in sight. Beads on wires are <u>kind of</u> like particles on strings. There's a reaction force instead of a tension, but this isn't always directed towards the centre of the circle. My mind is literally boggled.

More Vertical Circular Motion

As you'll know from swinging conkers round, they'll only do <u>complete circles</u> if you swing 'em hard enough.

Some things can **Leave** the **Circular Path**

Some things, like particles at the ends of <u>strings</u>, or particles on the <u>surfaces</u> of cylinders, will <u>leave</u> the circular path if their speed isn't sufficient. If such a particle is set into vertical circular motion, it'll <u>only complete the circle</u> if:

> 1) It has enough <u>kinetic energy</u> to reach the <u>top</u> of the circle.
>
> 2) When the particle is at the top of the circle, the <u>tension</u> in the string or the reaction from the cylinder wall is <u>positive</u> (or <u>zero</u>).

EXAMPLE A particle hanging at the end of a 0.6 m string is set into motion with a horizontal speed of 5 ms⁻¹. Will it form a complete circle?

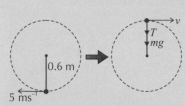

Energy of particle at lowest point: $\frac{1}{2}m \times 5^2 = 12.5m$

Total mechanical energy of particle at the top: $\frac{1}{2}mv^2 + mgh = \frac{1}{2}mv^2 + 1.2mg$

So, assuming that the particle completes a full circle, by the conservation of mechanical energy:

$\frac{1}{2}mv^2 + 1.2mg = 12.5m \Rightarrow v^2 = 25 - (2.4 \times 9.8)$

$\Rightarrow v = \sqrt{25 - (2.4 \times 9.8)} = \textbf{1.217 ms}^{-1}$

If something goes nutty crackers in here and you find yourself trying to take the square root of a negative number, then the particle doesn't have enough energy to complete the circle.

Resolve vertically: $T + mg = \frac{m(1.217^2)}{0.6} \Rightarrow T = m(2.47 - 9.8) \Rightarrow \textbf{T} = \textbf{-7.33}\textbf{\textit{m}}$

The tension is negative, so the particle doesn't make a complete circle.

You Can Find **Where** a Particle **Leaves the Circle**

At the point where a particle <u>leaves</u> the circular path, the tension in the string, or the reaction of the surface, is <u>zero</u>. So the <u>component of the weight acting towards the centre of the circle</u> is <u>just</u> enough to maintain the radial acceleration.

EXAMPLE A particle is set in motion at 3 ms⁻¹ vertically upwards from point A on the inside surface of a smooth pipe of radius 0.5 m. Find the value of θ (shown) when the particle leaves the pipe wall.

First find an expression for the <u>speed</u> of the particle when it leaves the wall. By the conservation of mechanical energy, taking the horizontal line through O as the 'base level':

$\frac{1}{2}m \times 3^2 = \frac{1}{2}mv^2 + (mg \times 0.5\cos\theta) \Rightarrow 4.5 = \frac{1}{2}v^2 + 0.5g\cos\theta \Rightarrow v^2 = 9 - g\cos\theta$

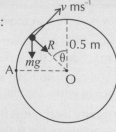

When the particle leaves the wall, $R = 0$. So, resolving perpendicular to the direction of motion, $mg\cos\theta = \frac{mv^2}{r}$:

Leave it as v^2 — you need v^2 in the next step.

$mg\cos\theta = \frac{m(9 - g\cos\theta)}{0.5} \Rightarrow 0.5g\cos\theta = 9 - g\cos\theta$

$1.5g\cos\theta = 9 \Rightarrow \cos\theta = \frac{9}{1.5 \times 9.8} = 0.6122...$

And so $\theta = 52.2°$ (3 s.f.)

But some things **Must** Stay on the **Circular Path**

1) Some particles, like a bead on a wire, <u>can't leave the circular path</u>, but they can still fail to complete a full circle.

2) For particles like these, you only need to check that they've got <u>enough energy</u> to get to the top. You <u>don't</u> need to worry whether any forces are positive or negative.

Me loop de loop didn't quite loop de loop...

So in a question about whether something will manage to complete the circle, always think about whether it can leave the circle or not. It makes a difference to what you have to show. Don't forget tension always acts towards the circle's centre.

M2 Section 4 — Practice Questions

When you design your own fairground, you'll need to know about <u>circular motion</u> — so it really is a vital life skill. It'll also be handy for the M2 exam, in which you're virtually guaranteed one, if not two, questions on it.

Warm-up Questions

Whenever a numerical value of g is required in the following questions, take $g = 9.8$ ms^{-2}.

1) A particle attached to a light, inextensible string moves in a horizontal circle of radius 3 m with constant speed. Find the particle's angular speed and its acceleration if:

 a) the particle takes 1.5 seconds to complete 1 revolution,

 b) the particle completes 15 revolutions in one minute,

 c) the string moves through 160° in one second,

 d) the linear speed of the particle is 10 ms^{-1}.

2) A particle with mass 2 kg moves in a horizontal circle of radius 0.4 m with constant speed. Find the centripetal force acting on the particle if:

 a) the particle's angular speed is 10π radians s^{-1},

 b) the particle's linear speed is 4 ms^{-1}.

3) For the conical pendulum shown on the right, find:

 a) the tension in the string (which is light and inextensible),

 b) the radius of the circle described by the pendulum given that the particle has a speed of v ms^{-1}.

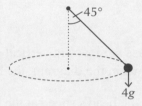

4) A particle of mass m kg is set into vertical circular motion inside a horizontal pipe from point A, vertically above the circle's centre. At point A it has a speed of 2.2 ms^{-1}.

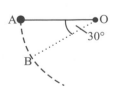

 a) Draw a force diagram for the particle when it is at point B, shown on the right.

 b) Use conservation of mechanical energy to find v_B, the particle's speed at point B.

 c) Find, in terms of m, the normal reaction of the pipe on the particle when it is at point B.

5) A particle is set into vertical circular motion with a horizontal speed of 9 ms^{-1} from the lowest point of the circle. The circular path has a 2 m radius.

 a) Show that the particle will complete the circle if it is a bead on a smooth wire but not if it's a bead at the end of a light inextensible string.

 b) Find the angle the string makes with the vertical when the bead leaves the circular path.

More on the merry-go-round of M2 maths magic...

Exam Questions

Whenever a numerical value of g is required in the following questions, take $g = 9.8$ ms^{-2}.

1 A 2 kg particle is attached to one end of a light inextensible string of length 0.5 m. The other end of the string is attached to a fixed point, O. The particle is released from rest at point A, as shown, and moves in a circular path in a vertical plane. Find, in terms of g:

 a) the particle's speed at point B, where $\angle AOB = 30°$,

 (3 marks)

 b) the tension in the string when the particle is at point B,

 (3 marks)

 c) the angular speed of the particle at point B.

 (2 marks)

M2 Section 4 — Practice Questions

2   Particle P is attached to two light inextensible strings. The other end of each string is attached to a vertical rod XY as shown in the diagram. The tension in string PX is 55 N, and the tension in string PY is 80 N. The particle moves in a horizontal circle about Y with a constant speed of 3 ms⁻¹. Find:

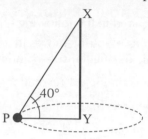

a)   the mass of particle P, correct to three significant figures,

(2 marks)

b)   the length of string PY, correct to three significant figures,

(3 marks)

c)   the number of revolutions the particle will make in one minute.

(3 marks)

3   A bead with mass m moves in vertical circular motion about O on a smooth ring with radius 1 m. At point A, shown in the diagram, the bead has a speed of $\sqrt{20}$ ms⁻¹.

a)   Show that the bead's speed at the highest point of the circle, B, is $\sqrt{0.4}$ ms⁻¹.

(3 marks)

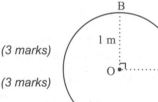

b)   Find the reaction of the ring on the bead at point B in terms of m.

(3 marks)

c)   Find, to three significant figures, the minimum speed at point A that will allow a complete circle to be made.

(3 marks)

4   A quad bike of mass 500 kg is travelling with constant speed around a horizontal circular track with a radius of 30 m. A frictional force acts towards the centre of the track, and there is no resistance to motion.

If the coefficient of friction between the quad bike and the track is 0.5, find the greatest speed the quad bike can go round the track without slipping. Give your answer to 3 significant figures.

(5 marks)

5   A particle at the end of a light, inextensible string of length 5 m is set into vertical circular motion about a point O from position J, the lowest point of the circle. The particle's initial speed is 15 ms⁻¹.

When the particle reaches position K, it has a speed of v ms⁻¹ and the string is at an angle of θ to the vertical.

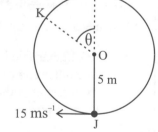

a)   Show that $v^2 = 225 - 10g(1 + \cos\theta)$ ms⁻¹.

(4 marks)

b)   Show that the particle will not complete the circle.

(5 marks)

c)   Find the value of θ when the string first becomes slack.

(5 marks)

General Certificate of Education
Advanced Subsidiary (AS) and Advanced Level

Mechanics M2 — Practice Exam One

Time Allowed: 1 hour 30 min

Graphical calculators may be used for this exam.

Whenever a numerical value of g is required, take $g = 9.8$ ms^{-2}.

Unless told otherwise, give any non-exact numerical answers to 3 significant figures.

There are 75 marks available for this paper.

1 A fireman of mass 80 kg slides down a smooth pole. He sets off at rest from the top of the pole, and reaches the bottom of the pole with a speed of 14 ms^{-1}.

    a) Find the fireman's kinetic energy when he reaches the bottom of the pole.

(2 marks)

    b) Find the height of the pole.

(3 marks)

    c) Now assume that there is a constant resistive force of magnitude 400 N acting on the fireman. Find the speed of the fireman when he is halfway down the pole.

(3 marks)

2 A ball of mass 0.1 kg moves in a vertical circle on the inside of a smooth cylinder of radius 0.2 m and centre O. The ball is set in motion with a speed of 3 ms^{-1} from the lowest point of the cylinder.

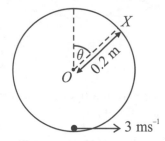

    a) At point X, the reaction of the cylinder on the ball is R N. Show that:

$$R = 4.5 - 0.2g - 0.3g \cos\theta$$

    where θ is the angle that OX makes with the vertical, as shown in the diagram.

(6 marks)

    b) Find the value of θ when the ball leaves the surface of the cylinder.

(3 marks)

3   A car of mass 1300 kg has a maximum speed of 70 ms^{-1}. It travels in a straight line along a horizontal road with speed v ms^{-1}, experiencing a total resistive force of magnitude $40v$ N.

a)   Find the maximum power of the car's engine.

(3 marks)

b)   At time $t = 0$, when the car is travelling at a speed of 25 ms^{-1}, the engine in the car is switched off and the car is allowed to freewheel. The only horizontal force now acting on the car is the resistive force, $40v$ N.

(i)   Show that $\frac{dv}{dt} = -\frac{2}{65}v$.

(2 marks)

(ii)   Hence find an expression for v, the speed of the car at time t.

(6 marks)

(iii)   Use this expression to find the time it takes for the car to slow to a speed of 5 ms^{-1}.

(3 marks)

4   A light uniform wire is bent into a frame shaped as a right-angled triangle, as shown below. Particles of mass 3 kg, 5 kg, and 2 kg are attached to corners O, A and B respectively.

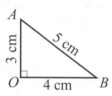

a)   Find the distance of the centre of mass of the system of particles from side OA.

(3 marks)

b)   Show that the centre of mass of the frame is 1.5 cm away from side OB.

(3 marks)

The framework is suspended freely from point O, and it hangs in equilibrium.

c)   Find the angle that side AB makes with the horizontal.
     Give your answer in degrees, to 3 significant figures.

(5 marks)

5   A particle of mass 5 kg is attached to one end of a light elastic string of natural length 4 m. The other end of the string is attached to a fixed point O.

The particle is released from rest at O and begins to move vertically downwards.

a)   Find the speed of the particle when the string first becomes taut.

(3 marks)

When the particle is 7 m below O, it is moving downwards with speed 10 ms^{-1}.

b)   Find the modulus of elasticity of the string.

(3 marks)

c)   Hence find the length of extension of the string when the particle hangs in equilibrium directly below O.

(3 marks)

6   A particle of mass 2 kg moves on a plane with horizontal and vertical unit vectors **i** and **j**, respectively. After t seconds, the particle has velocity **v** ms^{-1}, where:

$$\mathbf{v} = -8(\sin 2t)\mathbf{i} + 8(\cos 2t)\mathbf{j}$$

a)   Show that the particle is moving with constant speed.

(2 marks)

b)   By finding an expression for the particle's acceleration, show that the resultant force acting on the particle at time t is
$$\mathbf{F} = -32(\cos 2t)\mathbf{i} - 32(\sin 2t)\mathbf{j} \text{ N.}$$

(3 marks)

c)   Find the time at which the particle is first moving parallel to **i**.

(3 marks)

d)   Given that the particle has position $\mathbf{r} = 4\mathbf{i} + 0\mathbf{j}$ relative to the origin O at $t = 0$, prove that the particle is moving in a circle.

(5 marks)

e)   Find the particle's angular speed, ω.

(2 marks)

f)   Find the time it takes the particle to complete a full circle.

(2 marks)

7   A particle, A, is attached to one end of a light, inextensible string. The string passes through a smooth, fixed ring, O, and a second particle, B, is attached to the other end of the string. Particle A has mass 6 kg and hangs at rest vertically below the ring. Particle B moves in a horizontal circle with speed v ms^{-1}.

The angle between OB and OA is 30°.

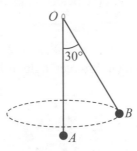

a)   Show that the mass of particle B is 5.20 kg, correct to three significant figures.

(3 marks)

b)   Given that the radius of the horizontal circle is 0.3 m, find v.

(3 marks)

c)   Explain how you have used the fact that the ring is smooth.

(1 mark)

General Certificate of Education
Advanced Subsidiary (AS) and Advanced Level
Mechanics M2 — Practice Exam Two
Time Allowed: 1 hour 30 min

Graphical calculators may be used for this exam.

Whenever a numerical value of g is required, take g = 9.8 ms^{-2}.

Unless told otherwise, give any non-exact numerical answers to 3 significant figures.

There are 75 marks available for this paper.

1   A uniform beam, AB, rests with A on rough horizontal ground and B against a smooth vertical wall
to make a ramp. The beam has length 3 m and mass 8 kg, and makes an angle of θ with the horizontal,
where $\tan\theta$ = 0.45. A woman of mass 60 kg stands at C, a distance of l m from B, as shown.
The woman may be modelled as a particle.

The beam is on the point of slipping, and is prevented from doing so by a frictional force of magnitude 199 N.

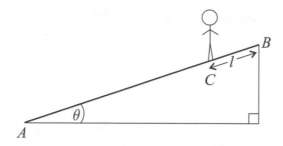

a)   Show that μ, the coefficient of friction between the ground and the beam,
is 0.3 to 1 significant figure.

(4 marks)

b)   Find l.

(5 marks)

c)   Explain how you have used the fact that the beam is uniform.

(1 mark)

2   A piece of jewellery is made by combining a thin rectangle of metal $PQRS$ and a circle of the same material,
as shown:

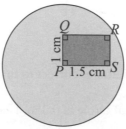

P is attached to the centre of the circle, which has radius 2 cm. The shapes can be modelled as uniform
laminas.

a)   Show that the centre of mass of the shape is 0.0961 cm from P.

(5 marks)

The shape hangs in equilibrium from a pin at point Q, about which it is able to freely rotate.
The pin can be modelled as a smooth peg.

b)   Find the angle that PQ makes with the vertical. Give your answer in degrees.

(3 marks)

3   A bus of mass 13 000 kg is travelling along a straight, horizontal road at a constant speed of 14 ms⁻¹.
    The bus experiences a constant resistance to motion from non-gravitational forces which is modelled as a
    single force of magnitude 4500 N.

    a) Find the rate at which the engine of the bus is working. Give your answer in kW.

        (3 marks)

    The bus now moves up a hill inclined at an angle, α, to the horizontal, where $\sin\alpha = \dfrac{1}{35}$. The engine in the
    bus now works at a rate of 72 kW.

    b) Assuming that the non-gravitational resistance to motion remains constant at 4500 N, find the
        acceleration of the bus when the speed of the bus is 12 ms⁻¹.

        (4 marks)

4   A particle, P, of mass 2 kg is attached to two light, inextensible strings. The other ends of the strings are
    attached to fixed points A and B, where A is vertically above B, as shown. P moves in a horizontal circle
    with uniform speed.

    The tension, T, in the string BP is half the tension in the string AP.

    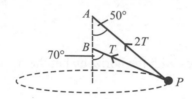

    a) The particle completes 100 revolutions per minute.
        Find the particle's angular speed in terms of π.

        (2 marks)

    b) Draw a diagram showing the forces acting on the particle.

        (1 mark)

    c) Show that $T = 12.0$ N, correct to 3 significant figures.

        (3 marks)

    d) Find the magnitude of the acceleration of P.

        (3 marks)

5   A particle of mass 15 kg is moving in a straight horizontal line. At time $t = 0$, it has speed 10 ms⁻¹.
    The only horizontal force acting on the particle is a resistance force of $5\sqrt{v}$ N, where v ms⁻¹ is the speed of
    the particle at time t.

    Express v in terms of t.

        (7 marks)

6   A particle, P, of mass 2.5 kg is moving in a horizontal plane under the action of a single force, **F** newtons. At t seconds, the position vector of P is **r** m, where **r** is given by:

$$\mathbf{r} = (t^3 - 6t^2 + 4t)\mathbf{i} + (7t - 4t^2 + 3)\mathbf{j}$$

Where **i** and **j** are the unit vectors directed due east and due north respectively.

a)   Show that when $t = 5$, the velocity of P is $19\mathbf{i} - 33\mathbf{j}$.

(3 marks)

b)   Find the value of t when P is moving due south.

(4 marks)

c)   Find the magnitude of the resultant force acting on P when $t = 3$.

(5 marks)

7   A particle of mass m kg is attached to a light, inextensible string of length 0.75 m. The other end of the string is attached to a fixed point, O. The particle moves in a vertical circle and passes through point A, shown below, with speed v ms^{-1}. When it reaches point B it has speed $4v$ ms^{-1}.

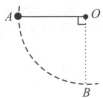

a)   Show that $v = \sqrt{\dfrac{g}{10}}$.

(5 marks)

b)   Find the angle, θ, that the string makes with the horizontal at the point where the particle has speed $2v$ ms^{-1}.

(3 marks)

8   A block of mass 20 kg is attached to a light spring of natural length 3 m and modulus of elasticity 30 N. The other end of the spring is attached to a fixed point O on a vertical wall. The block is placed on a horizontal surface, as shown. Assume that the block can be modelled as a particle.

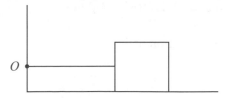

a)   Find the elastic potential energy stored in the spring when the block is held 10 m from O.

(2 marks)

The block is released from rest a distance of 10 m from O.

b)   When the block is x m from O, it is travelling with speed v ms^{-1}. Assuming that the horizontal surface is smooth, show that, while the spring is stretched, the motion of the block satisfies the equation:

$$2v^2 = 6x - x^2 + 40$$

(4 marks)

c)   Now assume that the horizontal surface is rough. The block comes to rest when the spring is compressed by 1 m. Find μ, the coefficient of friction between the block and the surface.

(8 marks)

Answers

C3 Section 1 — Algebra and Functions
Warm-up Questions

1) a) Range f(x) ≥ –16. This is a function, and it's one-to-one (the domain is restricted so every x-value is mapped to only one value of f(x)).

   b) To find the range of this function, you need to find the minimum point of $x^2 - 7x + 10$ — do this by completing the square: $x^2 - 7x + 10 = (x - 3.5)^2 - 12.25 + 10$
   $$= (x - 3.5)^2 - 2.25.$$
   As $(x - 3.5)^2 ≥ 0$ the minimum value of $x^2 - 7x + 10$ is –2.25, so the range is f(x) ≥ –2.25.
   This is a function, and it's many-to-one (as more than one x-value is mapped to the same value of f(x)).

   You could also have found the minimum point by differentiating, setting the derivative equal to O and solving for x.

   c) Range f(x) ≥ 0. Not a function as f(x) doesn't exist for $x < 0$.

   d) Sketch the graph for this one:

   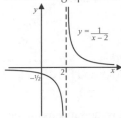

   From the graph, the range is f(x) ∈ ℝ, f(x) ≠ 0.
   This is not a function as it's not defined for $x = 2$.

   If you're not sure about any of the domains or ranges for the other parts, draw the graphs and see if that helps you figure it out.

2) a) fg(2) = f(2(2) + 3) = f(7) = $\frac{3}{7}$.
   gf(1) = g(3/1) = g(3) = 2(3) + 3 = 9.
   fg(x) = f(2x + 3) = $\frac{3}{2x + 3}$.

   b) fg(2) = f(2 + 4) = f(6) = 3(6²) = 3 × 36 = 108.
   gf(1) = g(3(1²)) = g(3) = 3 + 4 = 7.
   fg(x) = f(x + 4) = 3(x + 4)².

3) f is a one-to-one function so it has an inverse. The domain of the inverse is the range of the function and vice versa, so the domain of f⁻¹(x) is $x ≥ 3$ and the range is f⁻¹(x) ∈ ℝ.

4) Let y = f(x). Then $y = \sqrt{2x - 4}$
   $$y^2 = 2x - 4$$
   $$y^2 + 4 = 2x$$
   $$x = \frac{y^2 + 4}{2} = \frac{y^2}{2} + 2$$
   Writing in terms of x and f⁻¹(x) gives the inverse function as
   f⁻¹(x) = $\frac{x^2}{2}$ + 2, which has domain $x ≥ 0$ (as the range of f(x) ≥ 0) and range f⁻¹(x) ≥ 2.

5) a) 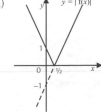   b)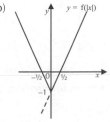

6)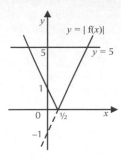

   From the graph, |2x – 1| = 5 has 2 solutions, one where 2x – 1 = 5 (so x = 3) and one where –(2x – 1) = 5 (so x = –2).

7) First, square both sides: $(2x + 1)^2 = (x + 4)^2$
   $$4x^2 + 4x + 1 = x^2 + 8x + 16$$
   $$3x^2 - 4x - 15 = 0$$
   $$(3x + 5)(x - 3) = 0.$$
   So $x = -\frac{5}{3}$ or $x = 3$.
   You could have solved this one by sketching the graphs instead, then solving the equations 2x + 1 = x + 4 and –(2x + 1) = x + 4.

8)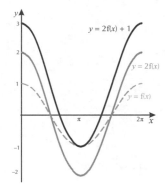

9) a)-d)

   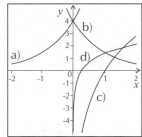

10) a) $e^{2x} = 6 ⇒ 2x = \ln 6 ⇒ x = \ln 6 ÷ 2 = 0.8959$ to 4 d.p.

    b) $\ln(x + 3) = 0.75 ⇒ x + 3 = e^{0.75} ⇒ x = e^{0.75} - 3$
    $= -0.8830$ to 4 d.p.

    c) $3e^{-4x+1} = 5 ⇒ e^{-4x+1} = \frac{5}{3} ⇒ e^{4x-1} = \frac{3}{5} ⇒ 4x - 1 = \ln \frac{3}{5}$
    $⇒ x = (\ln \frac{3}{5} + 1) ÷ 4 = 0.1223$ to 4 d.p.

    d) $\ln x + \ln 5 = \ln 4 ⇒ \ln(5x) = \ln 4 ⇒ 5x = 4$
    $⇒ x = 0.8000$ to 4 d.p.

11) a) $\ln(2x - 7) + \ln 4 = -3 ⇒ \ln(4(2x - 7)) = -3$
    $⇒ 8x - 28 = e^{-3} ⇒ x = \frac{e^{-3} + 28}{8}$ or $\frac{1}{8e^3} + \frac{7}{2}$.

    b) $2e^{2x} + e^x = 3$, so if $y = e^x$, $2y^2 + y - 3 = 0$,
    which will factorise to: $(2y + 3)(y - 1) = 0$,
    so $e^x = -1.5$ (not possible), and $e^x = 1$,
    so $x = 0$ is the only solution.

Answers

12) a) $y = 2 - e^{x+1}$

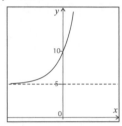

Goes through (0, –0.72) and (–0.31, 0),
with asymptote at $y = 2$.

b) $y = 5e^{0.5x} + 5$

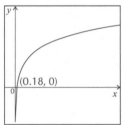

Goes through (0, 10), with asymptote at $y = 5$.

c) $y = \ln (2x) + 1$

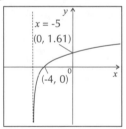

Goes through (0.18, 0), with asymptote at $x = 0$.

d) $y = \ln (x + 5)$

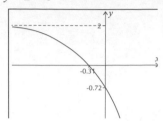

Goes through (0, 1.61) and (–4, 0), with asymptote at $x = –5$.

You can use your 'graph transformation' skills to work out what they'll look like, e.g. d) is just $y = \ln x$ translated 5 to the left.

Exam Questions

1   To transform the curve $y = x^3$ into $y = (x – 1)^3$, translate +1 unit *[1 mark]* along the x-axis *[1 mark]*. To transform this into the curve $y = 2(x – 1)^3$, stretch it in the y-direction *[1 mark]* by a scale factor of 2 *[1 mark]*. Finally, to transform into the curve $y = 2(x – 1)^3 + 4$, the whole curve is translated +4 units *[1 mark]* along the y-axis *[1 mark]*.

2   a) $gf(x) = g(x^2 – 3)$ *[1 mark]* $= \dfrac{1}{x^2 – 3}$ *[1 mark]*

b) $\dfrac{1}{x^2 – 3} = \dfrac{1}{6} \Rightarrow x^2 – 3 = 6 \Rightarrow x^2 = 9 \Rightarrow x = 3, x = – 3$
[3 marks available — 1 mark for rearranging to solve equation, 1 mark for each correct solution]

3   a) $fg(6) = f(\sqrt{(3 \times 6) – 2}) = f(\sqrt{16})$ *[1 mark]*
$= f(4) = 2^4 = 16$ *[1 mark]*

b) $gf(2) = g(2^2) = g(4)$ *[1 mark]*
$= \sqrt{(3 \times 4) – 2} = \sqrt{10}$ *[1 mark]*

c) (i)   First, write $y = g(x)$ and rearrange to make x the subject:
$y = \sqrt{3x – 2}$
$\Rightarrow y^2 = 3x – 2$
$\Rightarrow y^2 + 2 = 3x$
$\Rightarrow \dfrac{y^2 + 2}{3} = x$ *[1 mark]*
Then replace x with $g^{-1}(x)$ and y with x: $g^{-1}(x) = \dfrac{x^2 + 2}{3}$
[1 mark].

(ii) $fg^{-1}(x) = f\left(\dfrac{x^2 + 2}{3}\right)$ *[1 mark]*
$= 2^{\frac{x^2+2}{3}}$ *[1 mark]*

4   a) The range of f is $f(x) > 0$ *[1 mark]*.

b) (i)   Let $y = f(x)$. Then $y = \dfrac{1}{x + 5}$.
Rearrange this to make x the subject:
$y(x + 5) = 1$
$\Rightarrow x + 5 = \dfrac{1}{y}$ *[1 mark]*
$\Rightarrow x = \dfrac{1}{y} – 5$ *[1 mark]*
Finally, write out in terms of x and $f^{-1}(x)$:
$f^{-1}(x) = \dfrac{1}{x} – 5$ *[1 mark]*.

(ii)   The domain of the inverse is the same as the range of the function, so $x > 0$ *[1 mark]*. The range of the inverse is the same as the domain of the function, so $f^{-1}(x) > –5$ *[1 mark]*.

c)

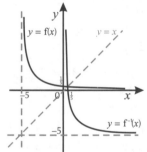

[2 marks available — 1 mark for each correct curve, each with correct intersections and asymptotes as shown]

5   a)

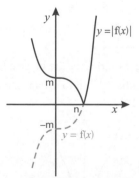

[2 marks available — 1 mark for reflecting in x-axis at $x = n$, 1 mark for crossing y-axis at $y = m$]

b)

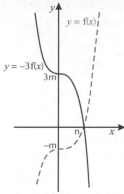

[2 marks available — 1 mark for reflecting in y-axis and 1 mark for crossing y-axis at y = 3m (due to stretch by scale factor 3)]

c)

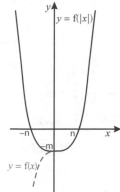

[2 marks available — 1 mark for reflecting in y-axis and 1 mark for crossing the x-axis at −n]

6 a) $6e^x = 3 \Rightarrow e^x = 0.5$ *[1 mark]* $\Rightarrow x = \ln 0.5$ *[1 mark]*.

b) $e^{2x} - 8e^x + 7 = 0$.

(This looks like a quadratic, so use $y = e^x$...)

If $y = e^x$, then $y^2 - 8y + 7 = 0$. This will factorise to give:
$(y - 7)(y - 1) = 0 \Rightarrow y = 7$ and $y = 1$.
So $e^x = 7 \Rightarrow x = \ln 7$, and $e^x = 1 \Rightarrow x = \ln 1 = 0$.

[4 marks available — 1 mark for factorisation of a quadratic, 1 mark for both solutions for e^x, and 1 mark for each correct solution for x.]

c) $4 \ln x = 3 \Rightarrow \ln x = 0.75$ *[1 mark]* $\Rightarrow x = e^{0.75}$ *[1 mark]*.

d) $\ln x + \dfrac{24}{\ln x} = 10$

(You need to get rid of that fraction, so multiply through by $\ln x$...)

$(\ln x)^2 + 24 = 10 \ln x$
$\Rightarrow (\ln x)^2 - 10 \ln x + 24 = 0$

(...which looks like a quadratic, so use $y = \ln x$...)

$y^2 - 10y + 24 = 0 \Rightarrow (y - 6)(y - 4) = 0$
$\Rightarrow y = 6$ or $y = 4$.
So $\ln x = 6 \Rightarrow x = e^6$, or $\ln x = 4 \Rightarrow x = e^4$.

[4 marks available — 1 mark for factorisation of a quadratic, 1 mark for both solutions for ln x, and 1 mark for each correct solution for x.]

7 $y = e^{ax} + b$

The sketch shows that when $x = 0$, $y = -6$, so:
$-6 = e^0 + b$ *[1 mark]*
$-6 = 1 + b \Rightarrow b = -7$ *[1 mark]*.

The sketch also shows that when $y = 0$, $x = \frac{1}{4} \ln 7$, so:
$0 = e^{(\frac{a}{4} \ln 7)} - 7$ *[1 mark]*
$\Rightarrow e^{(\frac{a}{4} \ln 7)} = 7$
$\Rightarrow \frac{a}{4} \ln 7 = \ln 7 \Rightarrow \frac{a}{4} = 1 \Rightarrow a = 4$ *[1 mark]*.
The asymptote occurs as $x \to -\infty$, so $e^{4x} \to 0$,
and since $y = e^{4x} - 7$, $y \to -7$.
So the equation of the asymptote is $y = -7$ *[1 mark]*.

8 a) $y = \ln (4x - 3)$, and $x = a$ when $y = 1$.
$1 = \ln (4a - 3) \Rightarrow e^1 = 4a - 3$ *[1 mark]*
$\Rightarrow a = (e^1 + 3) \div 4 = 1.43$ to 2 d.p. *[1 mark]*.

b) The curve can only exist when $4x - 3 > 0$ *[1 mark]*
so $x > 3 \div 4$, $x > 0.75$. If $x > b$, then $b = 0.75$ *[1 mark]*.

c)

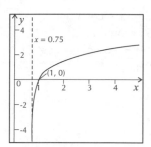

When $y = 0$, $4x - 3 = e^0 = 1$, so $x = 1$.
As $x \to \infty$, $y \to \infty$ gradually.
From (b), there will be an asymptote at $x = 0.75$.

[2 marks available — 1 mark for correct shape including asymptote at x = 0.75, 1 mark for (1, 0) as a point on the graph.]

9 a) $2e^x + 18e^{-x} = 20$

(Multiply through by e^x to remove the e^{-x}, since $e^x \times e^{-x} = 1$)

$2e^{2x} + 18 = 20e^x$
$\Rightarrow 2e^{2x} - 20e^x + 18 = 0 \Rightarrow e^{2x} - 10e^x + 9 = 0$

(This now looks like a quadratic equation, so use $y = e^x$ to simplify...)

$y^2 - 10y + 9 = 0$
$\Rightarrow (y - 1)(y - 9) = 0 \Rightarrow y = 1$ or $y = 9$.

So $e^x = 1 \Rightarrow x = 0$
or $e^x = 9 \Rightarrow x = \ln 9$.

[4 marks available — 1 mark for factorisation of a quadratic, 1 mark for both solutions for e^x, and 1 mark for each correct exact solution for x.]

b) $2 \ln x - \ln 3 = \ln 12$
$\Rightarrow 2 \ln x = \ln 12 + \ln 3$

(Use the log laws to simplify at this point...)

$\Rightarrow \ln x^2 = \ln 36$ *[1 mark]*
$\Rightarrow x^2 = 36$ *[1 mark]*
$\Rightarrow x = 6$ *[1 mark]*

(x must be positive as ln (−6) does not exist.)

Answers

C3 Section 2 — Trigonometry

Warm-up Questions

1) a) $\sin^{-1}\frac{1}{\sqrt{2}} = \frac{\pi}{4}$

   b) $\cos^{-1}0 = \frac{\pi}{2}$

   c) $\tan^{-1}\sqrt{3} = \frac{\pi}{3}$

2) See p13.

3) a) $\operatorname{cosec} 30° = 2$ (since $\sin 30° = 0.5$)

   b) $\sec 30° = \frac{2}{\sqrt{3}}$ (since $\cos 30° = \frac{\sqrt{3}}{2}$)

   c) $\cot 30° = \sqrt{3}$ (since $\tan 30° = \frac{1}{\sqrt{3}}$)

4) See p14.

5) Divide the whole identity by $\cos^2\theta$ to get:
   $$\frac{\cos^2\theta}{\cos^2\theta} + \frac{\sin^2\theta}{\cos^2\theta} \equiv \frac{1}{\cos^2\theta}$$
   $$\Rightarrow 1 + \tan^2\theta \equiv \sec^2\theta$$
   (as sin/cos $\equiv$ tan and 1/cos $\equiv$ sec)

6) Using the identities $\operatorname{cosec}^2\theta \equiv 1 + \cot^2\theta$ and $\sin^2\theta + \cos^2\theta \equiv 1$, the LHS becomes:
   $(\operatorname{cosec}^2\theta - 1) + (1 - \cos^2\theta) \equiv \operatorname{cosec}^2\theta - \cos^2\theta$,
   which is the same as the RHS.

Exam Questions

1 a)

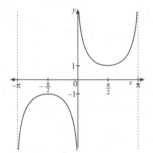

   [3 marks available — 1 mark for n-shaped curve in third quadrant and u-shaped curve in first quadrant, 1 mark for asymptotes at 0 and ±π and 1 mark for max/min points of the curves at −1 and 1]

   b) If $\operatorname{cosec} x = \frac{5}{4} \Rightarrow \frac{1}{\sin x} = \frac{5}{4} \Rightarrow \sin x = \frac{4}{5}$ *[1 mark]*.
   Solving this for x gives $x = 0.927, 2.21$
   [1 mark for each solution, lose a mark if answers aren't given to 3 s.f.].

   The second solution can be found by sketching $y = \sin x$:

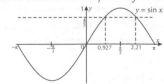

   You can see that there are two solutions, one at 0.927, and the other at $\pi - 0.927 = 2.21$.

   c) $\operatorname{cosec} x = 3\sec x \Rightarrow \frac{1}{\sin x} = \frac{3}{\cos x} \Rightarrow \frac{\cos x}{\sin x} = 3$
   $$\Rightarrow \frac{1}{\tan x} = 3 \text{ so } \tan x = \frac{1}{3}$$
   Solving for x gives $x = -2.82, 0.322$, *[1 mark for appropriate rearranging, 1 mark for each solution.]*.

Again, you need to sketch a graph to find the second solution:

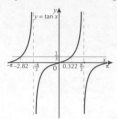

You can see that there are two solutions in the given range, one at 0.322 (this is the one you get from your calculator) and one at $-\pi + 0.322 = -2.82$.

2 a) The start and end points of the cos curve (with restricted domain) are $(0, 1)$ and $(\pi, -1)$, so the coordinates of the start point of $\cos^{-1}$ (point A) are $(-1, \pi)$ *[1 mark]* and the coordinates of the end point (point B) are $(1, 0)$ *[1 mark]*.

   b) $y = \cos^{-1}x$, so $x = \cos y$ *[1 mark]*.

   c) $\cos^{-1}x = 2$, so $x = \cos 2$ *[1 mark]* $\Rightarrow x = -0.416$ *[1 mark]*.

3 a) $\dfrac{2\sin x}{1 - \cos x} - \dfrac{2\cos x}{\sin x} \equiv \dfrac{2\sin^2 x - 2\cos x + 2\cos^2 x}{\sin x(1 - \cos x)}$ *[1 mark]*
   $$\equiv \frac{2 - 2\cos x}{\sin x(1 - \cos x)} \quad \text{[1 mark]}$$
   $$\equiv \frac{2(1 - \cos x)}{\sin x(1 - \cos x)} \quad \text{[1 mark]}$$
   $$\equiv \frac{2}{\sin x} \equiv 2\operatorname{cosec} x \quad \text{[1 mark]}$$

   b) $2\operatorname{cosec} x = 4$
   $\operatorname{cosec} x = 2$ OR $\sin x = \frac{1}{2}$ *[1 mark]*
   $x = \frac{\pi}{6}$ *[1 mark]*, $x = \frac{5\pi}{6}$ *[1 mark]*.

4 a) (i) Rearrange the identity $\sec^2\theta \equiv 1 + \tan^2\theta$ to get $\sec^2\theta - 1 \equiv \tan^2\theta$, then replace $\tan^2\theta$ in the equation:
   $3\tan^2\theta - 2\sec\theta = 5$
   $3(\sec^2\theta - 1) - 2\sec\theta - 5 = 0$ *[1 mark]*
   $3\sec^2\theta - 3 - 2\sec\theta - 5 = 0$
   so $3\sec^2\theta - 2\sec\theta - 8 = 0$ *[1 mark]*

   (ii) To factorise this, let $y = \sec\theta$, so the equation becomes $3y^2 - 2y - 8 = 0$, so $(3y + 4)(y - 2) = 0$ *[1 mark]*. Solving for y gives $y = -\frac{4}{3}$ or $y = 2$. As $y = \sec\theta$, this means that $\sec\theta = -\frac{4}{3}$ or $\sec\theta = 2$ *[1 mark]*. $\sec\theta = \frac{1}{\cos\theta}$, so $\cos\theta = -\frac{3}{4}$ or $\cos\theta = \frac{1}{2}$ *[1 mark]*.

   b) Let $\theta = 2x$. From above, we know that the solutions to $3\tan^2\theta - 2\sec\theta = 5$ satisfy $\cos\theta = -\frac{3}{4}$ or $\cos\theta = \frac{1}{2}$. The range for x is $0 \le x \le 180°$, so as $\theta = 2x$, the range for θ is $0 \le \theta \le 360°$ *[1 mark]*. Solving these equations for θ gives $\theta = 138.59°, 221.41°$ and $\theta = 60°, 300°$ *[1 mark]*. So, as $\theta = 2x$, $x = \frac{1}{2}\theta$, so $x = 69.30°, 110.70°, 30°, 150°$ *[1 mark]*.

   Once you have the values 60° and 138.59°, you can sketch the graph to find the other values:

Answers

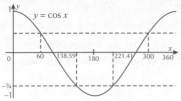

There is a solution at $360 - 60 = 300°$, and another at $360 - 138.59 = 221.41°$.

C3 Section 3 — Differentiation

Warm-up Questions

1) a) $y = u^{\frac{1}{2}} \Rightarrow \frac{dy}{du} = \frac{1}{2}u^{-\frac{1}{2}} = \frac{1}{2\sqrt{u}} = \frac{1}{2\sqrt{x^3 + 2x^2}}$
   $u = x^3 + 2x^2 \Rightarrow \frac{du}{dx} = 3x^2 + 4x$
   $\Rightarrow \frac{dy}{dx} = \frac{3x^2 + 4x}{2\sqrt{x^3 + 2x^2}}.$

   b) $y = u^{-\frac{1}{2}} \Rightarrow \frac{dy}{du} = -\frac{1}{2}u^{-\frac{3}{2}} = -\frac{1}{2(\sqrt{u})^3} = -\frac{1}{2(\sqrt{x^3 + 2x^2})^3}$
   $u = x^3 + 2x^2 \Rightarrow \frac{du}{dx} = 3x^2 + 4x$
   $\Rightarrow \frac{dy}{dx} = -\frac{3x^2 + 4x}{2(\sqrt{x^3 + 2x^2})^3}.$

   c) $y = e^u \Rightarrow \frac{dy}{du} = e^u = e^{5x^2}.$
   $u = 5x^2 \Rightarrow \frac{du}{dx} = 10x$
   $\Rightarrow \frac{dy}{dx} = 10xe^{5x^2}.$

   d) $y = \ln u \Rightarrow \frac{dy}{du} = \frac{1}{u} = \frac{1}{(6 - x^2)}$
   $u = 6 - x^2 \Rightarrow \frac{du}{dx} = -2x$
   $\Rightarrow \frac{dy}{dx} = -\frac{2x}{(6 - x^2)}.$

2) a) $x = 2e^y \Rightarrow \frac{dx}{dy} = 2e^y \Rightarrow \frac{dy}{dx} = \frac{1}{2e^y}.$

   b) $x = \ln u$ where $u = 2y + 3$
   $\frac{dx}{du} = \frac{1}{u} = \frac{1}{2y + 3}$ and $\frac{du}{dy} = 2 \Rightarrow \frac{dx}{dy} = \frac{2}{2y + 3}$
   $\Rightarrow \frac{dy}{dx} = \frac{2y + 3}{2} = y + 1.5.$

3) a) For $f(x) = y = \sin^2 (x + 2)$, use the chain rule twice:
   $y = u^2$, where $u = \sin (x + 2)$
   $\frac{dy}{du} = 2u = 2 \sin (x + 2)$ and $\frac{du}{dx} = \cos (x + 2)\cdot1$ (by chain rule)
   $\Rightarrow \frac{dy}{dx} = f'(x) = 2 \sin (x + 2) \cos (x + 2).$

   b) $f(x) = y = 2 \cos 3x$:
   $y = 2 \cos u$, where $u = 3x$
   $\frac{dy}{du} = -2 \sin u = -2 \sin 3x$ and $\frac{du}{dx} = 3$
   $\Rightarrow \frac{dy}{dx} = f'(x) = -6 \sin 3x.$

   c) $f(x) = y = \sqrt{\tan x} = (\tan x)^{\frac{1}{2}}$:
   $y = u^{\frac{1}{2}}$, where $u = \tan x$
   $\frac{dy}{du} = \frac{1}{2}u^{-\frac{1}{2}} = \frac{1}{2\sqrt{u}} = \frac{1}{2\sqrt{\tan x}}$ and $\frac{du}{dx} = \sec^2 x$
   $\Rightarrow \frac{dy}{dx} = f'(x) = \frac{\sec^2 x}{2\sqrt{\tan x}}.$

4) a) For $y = e^{2x}(x^2 - 3)$, use the product rule:
   $u = e^{2x} \Rightarrow \frac{du}{dx} = 2e^{2x}$ (from the chain rule),
   $v = x^2 - 3 \Rightarrow \frac{dv}{dx} = 2x.$
   $\frac{dy}{dx} = u\frac{dv}{dx} + v\frac{du}{dx} = 2xe^{2x} + 2e^{2x}(x^2 - 3) = 2e^{2x}(x^2 + x - 3).$
   When $x = 0$, $\frac{dy}{dx} = 2e^0(0 + 0 - 3) = 2 \times 1 \times -3 = -6.$

   b) For $y = \ln x \sin x$, use the product rule:
   $u = \ln x \Rightarrow \frac{du}{dx} = \frac{1}{x}$,
   $v = \sin x \Rightarrow \frac{dv}{dx} = \cos x.$
   $\frac{dy}{dx} = u\frac{dv}{dx} + v\frac{du}{dx} = \ln x \cos x + \frac{\sin x}{x}.$
   When $x = 1$, $\frac{dy}{dx} = \ln 1 \cos 1 + \frac{\sin 1}{1} = 0 + \sin 1$
   $= 0.841$ (to 3 s.f.).

5) For $y = \frac{6x^2 + 3}{4x^2 - 1}$, use the quotient rule:
   $u = 6x^2 + 3 \Rightarrow \frac{du}{dx} = 12x$,
   $v = 4x^2 - 1 \Rightarrow \frac{dv}{dx} = 8x.$
   $\frac{dy}{dx} = \frac{v\frac{du}{dx} - u\frac{dv}{dx}}{v^2} = \frac{12x(4x^2 - 1) - 8x(6x^2 + 3)}{(4x^2 - 1)^2}.$
   At $(1, 3)$, $x = 1$ and so gradient $=$
   $\frac{dy}{dx} = \frac{12(4 - 1) - 8(6 + 3)}{(4 - 1)^2} = \frac{36 - 72}{9} = -4.$
   Equation of a straight line is:
   $y - y_1 = m(x - x_1)$, where m is the gradient.
   So the equation of the tangent at $(1, 3)$ is:
   $y - 3 = -4(x - 1) \Rightarrow y = -4x + 7$ (or equivalent).

6) $y = \mathrm{cosec}\, (3x - 2)$, so use chain rule:
   $y = \mathrm{cosec}\, u$ where $u = 3x - 2$
   $\frac{dy}{du} = -\mathrm{cosec}\, u \cot u = -\mathrm{cosec}\, (3x - 2) \cot (3x - 2)$
   and $\frac{du}{dx} = 3$,
   $\Rightarrow \frac{dy}{dx} = -3\, \mathrm{cosec}\, (3x - 2) \cot (3x - 2)$
   $= \frac{-3}{\sin(3x - 2)\tan(3x - 2)}.$
   When $x = 0$, $\frac{dy}{dx} = \frac{-3}{\sin(-2)\tan(-2)} = 1.51$ (to 3 s.f.).

7) For $y = \frac{e^x}{\sqrt{x}}$, use the quotient rule:
   $u = e^x \Rightarrow \frac{du}{dx} = e^x$,
   $v = x^{\frac{1}{2}} \Rightarrow \frac{dv}{dx} = \frac{1}{2}x^{-\frac{1}{2}} = \frac{1}{2\sqrt{x}}.$
   $\frac{dy}{dx} = \frac{v\frac{du}{dx} - u\frac{dv}{dx}}{v^2} = \frac{e^x \sqrt{x} - \frac{e^x}{2\sqrt{x}}}{(\sqrt{x})^2}.$
   Multiplying top and bottom by $2\sqrt{x}$ gives:
   $\frac{dy}{dx} = \frac{2xe^x - e^x}{2x\sqrt{x}} = \frac{e^x(2x - 1)}{2x\sqrt{x}}.$
   At the stationary point, $\frac{dy}{dx} = 0$,
   $\Rightarrow \frac{e^x(2x - 1)}{2x\sqrt{x}} = 0 \Rightarrow e^x(2x - 1) = 0,$
   so either $e^x = 0$ or $2x - 1 = 0$. e^x does not exist at 0, so the
   stationary point must be at $2x - 1 = 0$, $x = \frac{1}{2}$.
   To find out the nature of the stationary point,
   differentiate again: $\frac{dy}{dx} = \frac{e^x(2x - 1)}{2x\sqrt{x}}$, so use quotient rule
   and product rule:
   $u = e^x(2x - 1) \Rightarrow$ using product rule $\frac{du}{dx} = 2e^x + e^x(2x - 1)$
   $= e^x(2x - 1 + 2) = e^x(2x + 1).$
   $v = 2x^{\frac{3}{2}} \Rightarrow \frac{dv}{dx} = 3x^{\frac{1}{2}} = 3\sqrt{x}.$
   $\frac{d^2y}{dx^2} = \frac{v\frac{du}{dx} - u\frac{dv}{dx}}{v^2} = \frac{2x\sqrt{x}\, e^x(2x + 1) - 3\sqrt{x}\, e^x(2x - 1)}{(2x\sqrt{x})^2}$
   $= \frac{\sqrt{x}\, e^x(4x^2 - 4x + 3)}{4x^3}.$

Answers

When $x = \frac{1}{2}$, $\frac{d^2y}{dx^2} > 0$, so it is a minimum point.

Give yourself a big pat on the back if you survived question 7. I told you it was hard...

Exam Questions

1   a)   For $y = \ln(3x + 1)\sin(3x + 1)$,
    use the product rule and the chain rule:
    Product rule: $u = \ln(3x + 1)$ and $v = \sin(3x + 1)$.
    Using the chain rule for $\frac{du}{dx} = \frac{3}{3x+1}$ *[1 mark]*.
    Using the chain rule for $\frac{dv}{dx} = 3\cos(3x + 1)$ *[1 mark]*.

So $\frac{dy}{dx} = u\frac{dv}{dx} + v\frac{du}{dx}$
$= [\ln(3x + 1) \cdot 3\cos(3x + 1)] + [\sin(3x + 1) \cdot \frac{3}{3x+1}]$ *[1 mark]*
$= 3\ln(3x + 1)\cos(3x + 1) + \frac{3\sin(3x + 1)}{3x + 1}$ *[1 mark]*.

b)   For $y = \frac{\sqrt{x^2 + 3}}{\cos 3x}$, use the quotient rule and the chain rule:
    Quotient rule: $u = \sqrt{x^2 + 3}$ and $v = \cos 3x$.
    Using the chain rule for $\frac{du}{dx} = \frac{2x}{2\sqrt{x^2+3}} = \frac{x}{\sqrt{x^2+3}}$ *[1 mark]*.
    Using the chain rule for $\frac{dv}{dx} = -3\sin 3x$ *[1 mark]*.

So $\frac{dy}{dx} = \frac{v\frac{du}{dx} - u\frac{dv}{dx}}{v^2} = \frac{\left[\cos 3x \cdot \frac{x}{\sqrt{x^2+3}}\right] - \left[\sqrt{x^2+3} \cdot -3\sin 3x\right]}{\cos^2 3x}$
[1 mark]. Then multiply top and bottom by $\sqrt{x^2 + 3}$ to get:
$\frac{dy}{dx} = \frac{x\cos 3x + 3(x^2 + 3)\sin 3x}{(\sqrt{x^2+3})\cos^2 3x} = \frac{x + 3(x^2 + 3)\tan 3x}{(\sqrt{x^2+3})\cos 3x}$
[1 mark].

c)   For $y = \sin^3(2x^2)$, use the chain rule twice:
    $y = u^3$ where $u = \sin(2x^2)$.
    $\frac{dy}{du} = 3u^2 = 3\sin^2(2x^2)$ *[1 mark]*.
    $\frac{du}{dx} = 4x\cos(2x^2)$ (using chain rule again) *[1 mark]*.
    So $\frac{dy}{dx} = 12x\sin^2(2x^2)\cos(2x^2)$ *[1 mark]*.

d)   For $y = 2\operatorname{cosec}(3x)$, use the chain rule:
    $y = 2\operatorname{cosec} u$ where $u = 3x$.
    $\frac{dy}{du} = -2\operatorname{cosec} u \cot u = -2\operatorname{cosec} 3x \cot 3x$.
    $\frac{du}{dx} = 3$ *[1 mark for both]*,
    so $\frac{dy}{dx} = -6\operatorname{cosec} 3x \cot 3x$ *[1 mark]*.

2   a)   For $x = \sqrt{y^2 + 3y}$, find $\frac{dx}{dy}$ first (using the chain rule):
    $x = u^{\frac{1}{2}}$ where $u = y^2 + 3y$.
    $\frac{dx}{du} = \frac{1}{2}u^{-\frac{1}{2}} = \frac{1}{2\sqrt{u}} = \frac{1}{2\sqrt{y^2+3y}}$ *[1 mark]*.
    $\frac{du}{dy} = 2y + 3$ *[1 mark]*.
    So $\frac{dx}{dy} = \frac{2y + 3}{2\sqrt{y^2+3y}}$ *[1 mark]*.
    (Now, flip the fraction upside down for dy/dx...)
    $\frac{dy}{dx} = \frac{2\sqrt{y^2+3y}}{2y + 3}$ *[1 mark]*.
    At the point (2, 1), $y = 1$, so:
    $\frac{dy}{dx} = \frac{2\sqrt{1^2+3}}{2+3} = \frac{4}{5} = 0.8$ *[1 mark]*.

b)   Equation of a straight line is:
    $y - y_1 = m(x - x_1)$, where m is the gradient.
    For the tangent at (2, 1), $y_1 = 1$, $x_1 = 2$, and $m = \frac{dy}{dx} = 0.8$.

So the equation is:
$y - 1 = 0.8(x - 2) \Rightarrow y = 0.8x - 0.6$ (or equivalent fractions)
[2 marks available — 1 mark for correct substitution of (2, 1) and gradient from (a), and 1 mark for final answer.]

3   $f(x) = \sec x = \frac{1}{\cos x}$, so using the quotient rule:
    $u = 1 \Rightarrow \frac{du}{dx} = 0$ and $v = \cos x \Rightarrow \frac{dv}{dx} = -\sin x$.
    $\frac{dy}{dx} = \frac{v\frac{du}{dx} - u\frac{dv}{dx}}{v^2} = \frac{(\cos x \cdot 0) - (1 \cdot -\sin x)}{\cos^2 x} = \frac{\sin x}{\cos^2 x}$.
    Since $\tan x = \frac{\sin x}{\cos x}$, and $\sec x = \frac{1}{\cos x}$,
    $f'(x) = \frac{dy}{dx} = \frac{\sin x}{\cos x} \times \frac{1}{\cos x} = \sec x \tan x$.
    [4 marks available — 1 mark for correct identity for sec x, 1 mark for correct entry into quotient rule, 1 mark for correct answer from quotient rule, and 1 mark for correct rearrangement to sec x tan x.]

4   a)   For $y = \sqrt{e^x + e^{2x}}$, use the chain rule:
    $y = u^{\frac{1}{2}}$ where $u = e^x + e^{2x}$.
    $\frac{dy}{du} = \frac{1}{2}u^{-\frac{1}{2}} = \frac{1}{2\sqrt{u}} = \frac{1}{2\sqrt{e^x+e^{2x}}}$ *[1 mark]*.
    $\frac{du}{dx} = e^x + 2e^{2x}$ *[1 mark]*.
    So $\frac{dy}{dx} = \frac{e^x + 2e^{2x}}{2\sqrt{e^x+e^{2x}}}$ *[1 mark]*.

b)   For $y = 3e^{2x+1} - \ln(1 - x^2) + 2x^3$, use the chain rule for the first 2 parts separately:
    For $y = 3e^{2x+1}$, $y = 3e^u$ where $u = 2x + 1$, so $\frac{dy}{du} = 3e^u = 3e^{2x+1}$
    and $\frac{du}{dx} = 2$, so $\frac{dy}{dx} = 6e^{2x+1}$ *[1 mark]*.
    For $y = \ln(1 - x^2)$, $y = \ln u$ where $u = 1 - x^2$,
    so $\frac{dy}{du} = \frac{1}{u} = \frac{1}{(1-x^2)}$ and $\frac{du}{dx} = -2x$, so $\frac{dy}{dx} = -\frac{2x}{(1-x^2)}$
    [1 mark].

So overall: $\frac{dy}{dx} = 6e^{2x+1} + \frac{2x}{(1-x^2)} + 6x^2$ *[1 mark]*.

5   a)   For $f(x) = 4\ln 3x$, use the chain rule:
    $y = 4\ln u$ where $u = 3x$, so $\frac{dy}{du} = \frac{4}{u} = \frac{4}{3x}$, and $\frac{du}{dx} = 3$
    [1 mark for both], so $f'(x) = \frac{dy}{dx} = \frac{12}{3x} = \frac{4}{x}$ *[1 mark]*.
    So for $x = 1$, $f'(1) = 4$ *[1 mark]*.

b)   Equation of a straight line is:
    $y - y_1 = m(x - x_1)$, where m is the gradient.
    For the tangent at $x_1 = 1$, $y_1 = 4\ln 3$, and $m = \frac{dy}{dx} = 4$.
    So the equation is:
    $y - 4\ln 3 = 4(x - 1) \Rightarrow y = 4(x - 1 + \ln 3)$ (or equivalent).
    [3 marks available — 1 mark for finding y = 4ln 3, 1 mark for correct substitution of (1, 4ln3) and gradient from (a), and 1 mark for correct final answer.]

6   For $y = \sin^2 x - 2\cos 2x$, use the chain rule on each part:
    For $y = \sin^2 x$, $y = u^2$ where $u = \sin x$, so $\frac{dy}{du} = 2u = 2\sin x$
    and $\frac{du}{dx} = \cos x$, so $\frac{dy}{dx} = 2\sin x \cos x$ *[1 mark]*.
    For $y = 2\cos 2x$, $y = 2\cos u$ where $u = 2x$, so $\frac{dy}{du} = -2\sin u$
    $= -2\sin 2x$ and $\frac{du}{dx} = 2$, so $\frac{dy}{dx} = -4\sin 2x$ *[1 mark]*.

Overall $\frac{dy}{dx} = 2\sin x \cos x + 4\sin 2x$ *[1 mark]*.

(For gradient of the tangent, put the x value into dy/dx...)

Gradient of the tangent when $x = \frac{\pi}{12}$ is:

$(2 \times \sin\frac{\pi}{12} \times \cos\frac{\pi}{12}) + (4 \times \sin\frac{\pi}{6}) = 2.5$ *[1 mark]*.

7   For $y = \frac{e^x + x}{e^x - x}$, use the quotient rule:

$u = e^x + x \Rightarrow \frac{du}{dx} = e^x + 1$.

$v = e^x - x \Rightarrow \frac{dv}{dx} = e^x - 1$.

$\frac{dy}{dx} = \frac{v\frac{du}{dx} - u\frac{dv}{dx}}{v^2} = \frac{(e^x - x)(e^x + 1) - (e^x + x)(e^x - 1)}{(e^x - x)^2}$.

When $x = 0$, $e^x = 1$, and $\frac{dy}{dx} = \frac{(1-0)(1+1)-(1+0)(1-1)}{(1-0)^2}$

$= \frac{2-0}{1^2} = 2$.

[3 marks available — 1 mark for finding u, v and their derivatives, 1 mark for dy/dx (however rearranged), and 1 mark for dy/dx = 2 when x = 0.]

8   For $x = \sin 4y$, $\frac{dx}{dy} = 4\cos 4y$ *[1 mark]* (using chain rule),

and so $\frac{dy}{dx} = \frac{1}{4\cos 4y}$ *[1 mark]*.

At $(0, \frac{\pi}{4})$, $y = \frac{\pi}{4}$ and so $\frac{dy}{dx} = \frac{1}{4\cos\pi} = -\frac{1}{4}$ *[1 mark]*.

(This is the gradient of the tangent at that point, so to find the gradient of the normal do –1 ÷ gradient of tangent...)

Gradient of normal at $(0, \frac{\pi}{4}) = -1 \div -\frac{1}{4} = 4$ *[1 mark]*.

Equation of a straight line is:

$y - y_1 = m(x - x_1)$, where m is the gradient.

For the normal at $(0, \frac{\pi}{4})$, $x_1 = 0$, $y_1 = \frac{\pi}{4}$, and m = 4.

So the equation is:

$y - \frac{\pi}{4} = 4(x - 0)$ *[1 mark]* $\Rightarrow y = 4x + \frac{\pi}{4}$ (or equivalent) *[1 mark]*.

9   a) For $y = e^x \sin x$, use the product rule:

$u = e^x \Rightarrow \frac{du}{dx} = e^x$

$v = \sin x \Rightarrow \frac{dv}{dx} = \cos x$

So $\frac{dy}{dx} = u\frac{dv}{dx} + v\frac{du}{dx} = (e^x \cdot \cos x) + (\sin x \cdot e^x)$

$= e^x(\cos x + \sin x)$ *[1 mark]*.

At the turning points, $\frac{dy}{dx} = 0$, so:

$e^x(\cos x + \sin x) = 0$ *[1 mark]*

$\Rightarrow$ turning points are when $e^x = 0$ or $\cos x + \sin x = 0$.

e^x cannot be 0, so the turning points are when

$\cos x + \sin x = 0$ *[1 mark]*

$\Rightarrow \sin x = -\cos x \Rightarrow \frac{\sin x}{\cos x} = -1 \Rightarrow \tan x = -1$ *[1 mark]*.

Look back at C2 for the graph of tan x to help you find all the solutions — it repeats itself every π radians...

There are two solutions for $\tan x = -1$ in the

interval $-\pi \leq x \leq \pi$: $x = -\frac{\pi}{4}$ and $x = \pi - \frac{\pi}{4} = \frac{3\pi}{4}$,

so the values of x at each turning point are $-\frac{\pi}{4}$ *[1 mark]*

and $\frac{3\pi}{4}$ *[1 mark]*.

b) To determine the nature of the turning points,

find $\frac{d^2y}{dx^2}$ at the points:

For $\frac{dy}{dx} = e^x(\cos x + \sin x)$, use the product rule:

$u = e^x \Rightarrow \frac{du}{dx} = e^x$

$v = \cos x + \sin x \Rightarrow \frac{dv}{dx} = \cos x - \sin x$, so:

$\frac{d^2y}{dx^2} = u\frac{dv}{dx} + v\frac{du}{dx} = [e^x \cdot (\cos x - \sin x)] + [(\cos x + \sin x) \cdot e^x]$

$= 2e^x \cos x$ *[1 mark]*.

When $x = -\frac{\pi}{4}$, $\frac{d^2y}{dx^2} > 0$ *[1 mark]*, so this is a minimum point *[1 mark]*.

When $x = \frac{3\pi}{4}$, $\frac{d^2y}{dx^2} < 0$ *[1 mark]*, so this is a maximum point *[1 mark]*.

C3 Section 4 — Integration
Warm-up Questions

1) $2e^{2x} + C$

2) $\frac{1}{3}e^{3x-5} + C$

3) $\frac{2}{3}\ln|x| + C$

4) $\ln|2x + 1| + C$

5) a) Just integrate each term separately: $\int \cos 4x \, dx = \frac{1}{4}\sin 4x$,

$\int \sec^2 7x = \frac{1}{7}\tan 7x \, dx$. Putting these bits together

gives: $\frac{1}{4}\sin 4x - \frac{1}{7}\tan 7x + C$.

b) Again, just integrate each term separately:

$\int 6\sec 3x\tan 3x \, dx = 2\sec 3x, \int -\csc^2\frac{x}{5} \, dx = 5\cot\frac{x}{5}$.

Putting these bits together gives: $2\sec 3x + 5\cot\frac{x}{5} + C$.

6) $\ln|\sin x| + C$

7) $e^{x^3} + C$

8) $4\ln|x^5 + x^3 - 3x| + C$

9)   If $u = e^x - 1$, then $\frac{du}{dx} = e^x$ (so $\frac{du}{e^x} = dx$) and $e^x + 1 = u + 2$.

Substituting this into the integral gives:

$\int e^x(u + 2)u^2 \frac{du}{e^x} = \int (u + 2)u^2 du$

$= \int u^3 + 2u^2 du = \frac{1}{4}u^4 + \frac{2}{3}u^3 + C$

$= \frac{1}{4}(e^x - 1)^4 + \frac{2}{3}(e^x - 1)^3 + C$

Make sure you put $u = e^x - 1$ back into your final answer.

10)   If $u = \sec x$, then $\frac{du}{dx} = \sec x \tan x$ (so $\frac{du}{\sec x \tan x} = dx$).

Change the limits: when $x = \frac{\pi}{4}$, $u = \sec\frac{\pi}{4} = \sqrt{2}$ and when

$x = \frac{\pi}{3}$, $u = \sec\frac{\pi}{3} = 2$. Substituting into the integral gives:

$\int_{\sqrt{2}}^{2} \sec x\tan x \, u^3 \frac{du}{\sec x\tan x} = \int_{\sqrt{2}}^{2} u^3 \, du = [\frac{1}{4}u^4]_{\sqrt{2}}^{2}$

$= [\frac{1}{4}(2)^4] - [\frac{1}{4}(\sqrt{2})^4]$

$= \frac{1}{4}(16) - \frac{1}{4}(4) = 4 - 1 = 3$.

11)   Let $u = \ln x$ and let $\frac{dv}{dx} = 3x^2$. So $\frac{du}{dx} = \frac{1}{x}$ and $v = x^3$.

Putting these into the formula gives:

$\int 3x^2\ln x \, dx = [x^3\ln x] - \int \frac{x^3}{x}dx = [x^3\ln x] - \int x^2 dx$

$= x^3\ln x - \frac{1}{3}x^3 + C = x^3(\ln x - \frac{1}{3}) + C$

12)   Let $u = 4x$, and let $\frac{dv}{dx} = \cos 4x$. So $\frac{du}{dx} = 4$ and $v = \frac{1}{4}\sin 4x$.

Putting these into the formula gives:

$\int 4x\cos 4x \, dx = 4x(\frac{1}{4}\sin 4x) - \int 4(\frac{1}{4}\sin 4x)dx$

$= x\sin 4x + \frac{1}{4}\cos 4x + C$

Answers

13) If $y = \frac{1}{x}$ then $y^2 = \frac{1}{x^2}$. Putting this into the integral gives:
$V = \pi \int_2^4 \frac{1}{x^2} \, dx = \pi\left[-\frac{1}{x}\right]_2^4 = \pi\left[\left(-\frac{1}{4}\right) - \left(-\frac{1}{2}\right)\right] = \frac{\pi}{4}$.

14) First, rearrange the equation to get it in terms of x^2:
$y = x^2 + 1 \Rightarrow x^2 = y - 1$. Putting this into the formula:
$V = \pi \int_1^3 y - 1 \, dy = \pi\left[\frac{1}{2}y^2 - y\right]_1^3$
$= \pi\left[\left(\frac{1}{2}(9) - 3\right) - \left(\frac{1}{2}(1) - 1\right)\right] = 2\pi$.

Exam Questions

1   $-\frac{1}{2}e^{(5 - 6x)} + C$

[1 mark for answer in the form $ke^{(5 - 6x)}$, 1 mark for the correct value of k]

2   $V = \pi \int_{\frac{\pi}{4}}^{\frac{\pi}{3}} y^2 \, dx = \pi \int_{\frac{\pi}{4}}^{\frac{\pi}{3}} \text{cosec}^2 x \, dx = \pi[-\cot x]_{\frac{\pi}{4}}^{\frac{\pi}{3}}$
$= \pi[(-\cot\frac{\pi}{3}) - (-\cot\frac{\pi}{4})]$
$= \pi[-\frac{1}{\sqrt{3}} + 1] = 1.328 \text{ (3 d.p.)}.$

[3 marks available — 1 mark for correct function for y^2, 1 mark for integrating, 1 mark for substituting in values of x to obtain correct answer]

Don't forget π here.

3   If $u = \ln x$, then $\frac{du}{dx} = \frac{1}{x}$, so $x \, du = dx$. Changing the limits: when $x = 1$, $u = \ln 1 = 0$. When $x = 2$, $u = \ln 2$. Substituting all this into the integral gives:
$\int_1^2 \frac{8}{x}(\ln x + 2)^3 \, dx = \int_0^{\ln 2} \frac{8}{x}(u + 2)^3 x \, du = \int_0^{\ln 2} 8(u + 2)^3 \, du$
$= [2(u + 2)^4]_0^{\ln 2}$
$= [2(\ln 2 + 2)^4] - [2(0 + 2)^4]$
$= 105.21 - 32 = 73.21 \text{ (4 s.f.)}.$

[6 marks available — 1 mark for finding substitution for dx, 1 mark for finding correct limits, 1 mark for correct integral in terms of u, 2 marks for correct integration (1 for an answer in the form $k(u + 2)^n$, 1 mark for correct values of k and n), 1 mark for final answer (to 4 s.f.)]

4   To find the volume of the solid formed when R is rotated, find the volume for each curve separately then subtract. First, find the volume when the area under the curve $y = \sqrt{\sin x}$ is rotated about the x-axis:
As $y = \sqrt{\sin x}$, $y^2 = \sin x$.
$V = \pi \int_{\frac{\pi}{3}}^{\frac{2\pi}{3}} \sin x \, dx = \pi[-\cos x]_{\frac{\pi}{3}}^{\frac{2\pi}{3}}$ *[1 mark]*
$= \pi\left(-\left(-\frac{1}{2}\right) - -\frac{1}{2}\right) = \pi$ *[1 mark]*.
Now find the volume for $y = e^{-0.5x}$:
$y^2 = (e^{-0.5x})^2 = e^{-x}$ *[1 mark]*.
$V = \pi \int_{\frac{\pi}{3}}^{\frac{2\pi}{3}} e^{-x} \, dx = \pi[-e^{-x}]_{\frac{\pi}{3}}^{\frac{2\pi}{3}}$ *[1 mark]*
$= \pi(-e^{-\frac{2\pi}{3}} - (-e^{-\frac{\pi}{3}})) = 0.7156$ *[1 mark]*.

[1 mark for using correct formula for the volume of revolution for both curves]

To find the volume you want, you need to subtract 0.7156 from π: $\pi - 0.7156 = 2.426 \text{ (4 s.f.)}$ *[1 mark]*.

5   Let $u = x$, so $\frac{du}{dx} = 1$. Let $\frac{dv}{dx} = \sin x$, so $v = -\cos x$ *[1 mark for both parts correct]*. Using integration by parts,
$\int_0^\pi x \sin x \, dx = [-x \cos x]_0^\pi - \int_0^\pi -\cos x \, dx$ *[1 mark]*
$= [-x \cos x]_0^\pi + [\sin x]_0^\pi$ *[1 mark]*
$= (\pi - 0) + (0) = \pi$ *[1 mark]*

If you'd tried to use u = sin x, you'd have ended up with a more complicated function to integrate ($x^2 \cos x$).

6   First, rearrange the equation to get it in terms of x^2:
$y = \frac{1}{x^2} \Rightarrow x^2 = \frac{1}{y}$. Putting this into the formula:
$V = \pi \int_1^3 \frac{1}{y} \, dy = \pi[\ln y]_1^3$
$= \pi[(\ln 3) - (\ln 1)] = \pi \ln 3$.

[5 marks available — 1 mark for rearranging equation, 1 mark for correct formula for volume, 1 mark for correct integration, 1 mark for substituting in limits, 1 mark for final answer (in terms of π and ln)]

C3 Section 5 — Numerical Methods
Warm-up Questions

1) There are 2 roots (graph crosses the x-axis twice in this interval).

2) a) $\sin (2 \times 3) = -0.2794...$ and $\sin (2 \times 4) = 0.9893...$
Since $\sin(2x)$ is a continuous function, the change of sign means there is a root between 3 and 4.

   b) $\ln (2.1 - 2) + 2 = -0.3025...$
   and $\ln (2.2 - 2) + 2 = 0.3905...$
   Since the function is continuous for $x > 2$, the change of sign means there is a root between 2.1 and 2.2.

   c) Rearrange first to give $x^3 - 4x^2 - 7 = 0$, then:
   $4.3^3 - 4 \times (4.3^2) - 7 = -1.453$ and
   $4.5^3 - 4 \times (4.5^2) - 7 = 3.125$.
   The function is continuous, so the change of sign means there is a root between 4.3 and 4.5.

3) If 1.2 is a root to 1 d.p. then there should be a sign change for f(x) between the upper and lower bounds:
$f(1.15) = 1.15^3 + 1.15 - 3 = -0.3291...$
$f(1.25) = 1.25^3 + 1.25 - 3 = 0.2031...$
There is a change of sign, and the function is continuous, so the root must lie between 1.15 and 1.25, so to 1 d.p. the root is at $x = 1.2$.

4) $x_1 = -\frac{1}{2} \cos (-1) = -0.2701...$
$x_2 = -\frac{1}{2} \cos (-0.2701...) = -0.4818...$
$x_3 = -\frac{1}{2} \cos (-0.4818...) = -0.4430...$
$x_4 = -\frac{1}{2} \cos (-0.4430...) = -0.4517...$
$x_5 = -\frac{1}{2} \cos (-0.4517...) = -0.4498...$
$x_6 = -\frac{1}{2} \cos (-0.4498...) = -0.4502...$
x_4, x_5 and x_6 all round to -0.45, so to 2 d.p. $x = -0.45$.

5) $x_1 = \sqrt{\ln 2 + 4} = 2.1663...$

$x_2 = \sqrt{\ln 2.1663... + 4} = 2.1847...$

$x_3 = \sqrt{\ln 2.1847... + 4} = 2.1866...$

$x_4 = \sqrt{\ln 2.1866... + 4} = 2.1868...$

$x_5 = \sqrt{\ln 2.1868... + 4} = 2.1868...$

x_3, x_4 and x_5 all round to 2.187, so to 3 d.p. $x = 2.187$.

6) a) i) $2x^2 - x^3 + 1 = 0 \Rightarrow 2x^2 - x^3 = -1$

$\Rightarrow x^2(2 - x) = -1 \Rightarrow x^2 = \dfrac{-1}{2 - x} \Rightarrow x = \sqrt{\dfrac{-1}{2 - x}}$.

ii) $2x^2 - x^3 + 1 = 0 \Rightarrow x^3 = 2x^2 + 1$

$\Rightarrow x = \sqrt[3]{2x^2 + 1}$.

iii) $2x^2 - x^3 + 1 = 0 \Rightarrow 2x^2 = x^3 - 1$

$\Rightarrow x^2 = \dfrac{x^3 - 1}{2} \Rightarrow x = \sqrt{\dfrac{x^3 - 1}{2}}$.

b) Using $x_{n+1} = \sqrt{\dfrac{-1}{2 - x_n}}$ with $x_0 = 2.3$ gives:

$x_1 = \sqrt{\dfrac{-1}{2 - 2.3}} = 1.8257...$

$x_2 = \sqrt{\dfrac{-1}{2 - 1.8257...}}$ has no real solution

so this formula does not converge to a root.

Using $x_{n+1} = \sqrt[3]{2x_n^2 + 1}$ with $x_0 = 2.3$ gives:

$x_1 = \sqrt[3]{2 \times (2.3)^2 + 1} = 2.2624...$

$x_2 = \sqrt[3]{2 \times (2.2624...)^2 + 1} = 2.2398...$

$x_3 = \sqrt[3]{2 \times (2.2398...)^2 + 1} = 2.2262...$

$x_4 = \sqrt[3]{2 \times (2.2262...)^2 + 1} = 2.2180...$

$x_5 = \sqrt[3]{2 \times (2.2180...)^2 + 1} = 2.2131...$

$x_6 = \sqrt[3]{2 \times (2.2131...)^2 + 1} = 2.2101...$

$x_7 = \sqrt[3]{2 \times (2.2101...)^2 + 1} = 2.2083...$

x_5, x_6 and x_7 all round to 2.21,

so to 2 d.p. $x = 2.21$ is a root.

Using $x_{n+1} = \sqrt{\dfrac{x_n^3 - 1}{2}}$ with $x_0 = 2.3$ gives:

$x_1 = \sqrt{\dfrac{2.3^3 - 1}{2}} = 2.3629...$

$x_2 = \sqrt{\dfrac{2.3629...^3 - 1}{2}} = 2.4691...$

$x_3 = \sqrt{\dfrac{2.4691...^3 - 1}{2}} = 2.6508...$

$x_4 = \sqrt{\dfrac{2.6508...^3 - 1}{2}} = 2.9687...$

This sequence is diverging so does not converge to a root.
The only formula that converges to a root is
$x_{n+1} = \sqrt[3]{2x_n^2 + 1}$.

7)

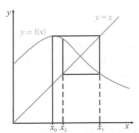

8) a) The width of each strip is $\dfrac{4 - 1}{6} = 0.5$, so you need
y-values for $x = 1, 1.5, 2, 2.5, 3, 3.5$ and 4:

$x_0 = 1, y_0 = 1.0986, x_1 = 1.5, y_1 = 1.1709, x_2 = 2, y_2 = 1.2279,$

$x_3 = 2.5, y_3 = 1.2757, x_4 = 3, y_4 = 1.3170, x_5 = 3.5,$

$y_5 = 1.3535, x_6 = 4, y_6 = 1.3863$. Putting these values into
the formula gives:

$A \approx \frac{1}{3}0.5[(1.0986 + 1.3863) + 4(1.1709 + 1.2757 +$
$1.3535) + 2(1.2279 + 1.3170)] = 3.7959$ (4 d.p.).

If you'd had a go at this using the Mid-Ordinate Rule,
you'd have ended up with A ≈ 3.797 (to 3 d.p.).

b) Simpson's Rule only works with an even number of strips.

9) The width of each strip is $\dfrac{4 - 2}{4} = 0.5$, so $x_0 = 2$, $x_1 = 2.5$,
$x_2 = 3$, $x_3 = 3.5$ and $x_4 = 4$. You need y-values for the
midpoints of these strips, i.e. $x = 2.25, 2.75, 3.25$ and 3.75:

$x_{0.5} = 2.25$, $y_{0.5} = 6.5004$, $x_{1.5} = 2.75$, $y_{1.5} = 16.0098$,

$x_{2.5} = 3.25$, $y_{2.5} = 36.8667$, $x_{3.5} = 3.75$, $y_{3.5} = 80.9241$.

Putting these values into the formula gives:

$A \approx 0.5[6.5004 + 16.0098 + 36.8667 + 80.9241]$

$= 70.1505$ (4 d.p.).

Using Simpson's Rule, you'd have got A ≈ 71.996 (3 d.p.).

Exam Questions

1 a) There will be a change of sign between f(0.7) and f(0.8) if
p lies between 0.7 and 0.8.

$f(0.7) = (2 \times 0.7 \times e^{0.7}) - 3 = -0.1807...$ *[1 mark]*

$f(0.8) = (2 \times 0.8 \times e^{0.8}) - 3 = 0.5608...$ *[1 mark]*

$f(x)$ is continuous, and there is a change of sign,
so $0.7 < p < 0.8$ *[1 mark]*.

b) If $2xe^x - 3 = 0$, then $2xe^x = 3 \Rightarrow xe^x = \dfrac{3}{2}$

$\Rightarrow x = \dfrac{3}{2e^x} \Rightarrow x = \dfrac{3}{2}e^{-x}$.

[2 marks available — 1 mark for partial
rearrangement, 1 mark for correct final answer.]

c) $x_{n+1} = \dfrac{3}{2}e^{-x_n}$ and $x_0 = 0.7$, so:

$x_1 = \dfrac{3}{2}e^{-0.7} = 0.74487... = 0.7449$ to 4 d.p.

$x_2 = \dfrac{3}{2}e^{-0.74487...} = 0.71218... = 0.7122$ to 4 d.p.

$x_3 = \dfrac{3}{2}e^{-0.71218...} = 0.73585... = 0.7359$ to 4 d.p.

$x_4 = \dfrac{3}{2}e^{-0.73585...} = 0.71864... = 0.7186$ to 4 d.p.

[3 marks available — 1 mark for x_1 correct,
1 mark for x_2 correct, 1 mark for all 4 correct.]

d) If the root of f(x) = 0, p, is 0.726 to 3 d.p. then there must
be a change of sign in f(x) between the upper and lower
bounds of p.

Lower bound = 0.7255.

$f(0.7255) = (2 \times 0.7255 \times e^{0.7255}) - 3 = -0.0025...$

Upper bound = 0.7265.

$f(0.7265) = (2 \times 0.7265 \times e^{0.7265}) - 3 = 0.0045...$

f(x) is continuous, and there's a change of sign,
so $p = 0.726$ to 3 d.p.

[3 marks available — 1 mark for identifying upper and
lower bounds, 1 mark for finding value of the function
at both bounds, 1 mark for indicating that the change
in sign and the fact that it's a continuous function
shows the root is correct to the given accuracy.]

2 a) Where $y = \sin 3x + 3x$ and $y = 1$ meet,

$\sin 3x + 3x = 1 \Rightarrow \sin 3x + 3x - 1 = 0$ *[1 mark]*.

$x = a$ is a root of this equation, so if $x = 0.1$ and $x = 0.2$
produce different signs, then a lies between them. So for
the continuous function $f(x) = \sin 3x + 3x - 1$:

$f(0.1) = \sin (3 \times 0.1) + (3 \times 0.1) - 1 = -0.4044...$ *[1 mark]*

$f(0.2) = \sin (3 \times 0.2) + (3 \times 0.2) - 1 = 0.1646...$ *[1 mark]*

There is a change of sign, so $0.1 < a < 0.2$ *[1 mark]*.

Answers

b) $\sin 3x + 3x = 1 \Rightarrow 3x = 1 - \sin 3x \Rightarrow x = \frac{1}{3}(1 - \sin 3x)$.

[2 marks available — 1 mark for partial rearrangement, 1 mark for correct final answer.]

c) $x_{n+1} = \frac{1}{3}(1 - \sin 3x_n)$ and $x_0 = 0.2$:

$x_1 = \frac{1}{3}(1 - \sin(3 \times 0.2)) = 0.1451...$ *[1 mark]*

$x_2 = \frac{1}{3}(1 - \sin(3 \times 0.1451...)) = 0.1927...$

$x_3 = \frac{1}{3}(1 - \sin(3 \times 0.1927...)) = 0.1511...$

$x_4 = \frac{1}{3}(1 - \sin(3 \times 0.1511...)) = 0.1873...$

So $x_4 = 0.187$ to 3 d.p. *[1 mark]*.

3 a) $x_{n+1} = \sqrt[3]{x_n^2 - 4}$, $x_0 = -1$:

$x_1 = \sqrt[3]{(-1)^2 - 4} = -1.44224... = -1.4422$ to 4 d.p.

$x_2 = \sqrt[3]{(-1.4422...)^2 - 4} = -1.24287... = -1.2429$ to 4 d.p.

$x_3 = \sqrt[3]{(-1.2428...)^2 - 4} = -1.34906... = -1.3491$ to 4 d.p.

$x_4 = \sqrt[3]{(-1.3490...)^2 - 4} = -1.29664... = -1.2966$ to 4 d.p.

[3 marks available — 1 mark for x_1 correct, 1 mark for x_2 correct, 1 mark for all 4 correct.]

b) If b is a root of $x^3 - x^2 + 4 = 0$, then $x^3 - x^2 + 4 = 0$ will rearrange to form $x = \sqrt[3]{x^2 - 4}$, the iteration formula used in (a). *(This is like finding the iteration formula in reverse...)*

$x^3 - x^2 + 4 = 0 \Rightarrow x^3 = x^2 - 4 \Rightarrow x = \sqrt[3]{x^2 - 4}$, and so b must be a root of $x^3 - x^2 + 4 = 0$.

[2 marks available — 1 mark for stating that b is a root if one equation can be rearranged into the other, 1 mark for correct demonstration of rearrangement.]

c) If the root of $f(x) = x^3 - x^2 + 4 = 0$, b, is -1.315 to 3 d.p. then there must be a change of sign in $f(x)$ between the upper and lower bounds of b, which are -1.3145 and -1.3155.

$f(-1.3145) = (-1.3145)^3 - (-1.3145)^2 + 4 = 0.00075...$

$f(-1.3155) = (-1.3155)^3 - (-1.3155)^2 + 4 = -0.00706...$

$f(x)$ is continuous, and there's a change of sign, so $b = -1.315$ to 3 d.p.

[3 marks available — 1 mark for identifying upper and lower bounds, 1 mark for finding value of the function at both bounds, 1 mark for indicating that the change in sign and the fact that it's a continuous function shows the root is correct to the given accuracy.]

4 a) For $f(x) = \ln(x + 3) - x + 2$, there will be a change in sign between $f(3)$ and $f(4)$ if the root lies between those values.

$f(3) = \ln(3 + 3) - 3 + 2 = 0.7917...$ *[1 mark]*

$f(4) = \ln(4 + 3) - 4 + 2 = -0.0540...$ *[1 mark]*

There is a change of sign, and the function is continuous for $x > -3$, so the root, m, must lie between 3 and 4 *[1 mark]*.

b) $x_{n+1} = \ln(x_n + 3) + 2$, and $x_0 = 3$, so:

$x_1 = \ln(3 + 3) + 2 = 3.7917...$

$x_2 = \ln(3.7917... + 3) + 2 = 3.9157...$

$x_3 = \ln(3.9157... + 3) + 2 = 3.9337...$

$x_4 = \ln(3.9337... + 3) + 2 = 3.9364...$

$x_5 = \ln(3.9364... + 3) + 2 = 3.9367...$

So $m = 3.94$ to 2 d.p.

[3 marks available — 1 mark for correct substitution of x_0 to find x_1, 1 mark for evidence of correct iterations up to x_5, 1 mark for correct final answer to correct accuracy.]

c) From b), $m = 3.94$ to 2 d.p. If this is correct then there will be a change of sign in $f(x)$ between the upper and lower bounds of m, which are 3.935 and 3.945.

$f(3.935) = \ln(3.935 + 3) - 3.935 + 2 = 0.00158...$

$f(3.945) = \ln(3.945 + 3) - 3.945 + 2 = -0.00697...$

$f(x)$ is continuous for $x > -3$, and there's a change of sign, so $m = 3.94$ is correct to 2 d.p.

[3 marks available — 1 mark for identifying upper and lower bounds, 1 mark for finding value of the function at both bounds, 1 mark for indicating that the change in sign and the fact that it's a continuous function shows the root is correct to the given accuracy.]

d)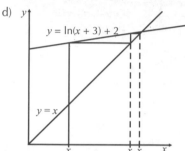

[2 marks available — 1 mark for converging staircase, 1 mark for correct positions of x_1 and x_2]

5 The width of each strip is $\frac{5-1}{4} = 1$, so you need y-values for $x = 1, 2, 3, 4$ and 5:

$x_0 = 1, y_0 = 0.25, x_1 = 2, y_1 = 0.1, x_2 = 3, y_2 = 0.0556,$
$x_3 = 4, y_3 = 0.0357, x_4 = 5, y_4 = 0.025.$

Putting these values into the formula gives:

$A \approx \frac{1}{3}1[(0.25 + 0.025) + 4(0.1 + 0.0357) + 2(0.0556)]$
$= 0.310$ (3 s.f.).

[4 marks available — 1 mark for correct x-values, 1 mark for correct y-values, 1 mark for correct use of formula, 1 mark for final answer]

6 The width of each strip is $\frac{3-1}{4} = 0.5$, so $x_0 = 1, x_1 = 1.5, x_2 = 2, x_3 = 2.5$ and $x_4 = 3$. You need y-values for the midpoints of these strips, i.e. $x = 1.25, 1.75, 2.25$ and 2.75:

$x_{0.5} = 1.25, y_{0.5} = 2.3784, x_{1.5} = 1.75, y_{1.5} = 3.3636,$
$x_{2.5} = 2.25, y_{2.5} = 4.7568, x_{3.5} = 2.75, y_{3.5} = 6.7272.$

Putting these values into the formula gives:

$A \approx 0.5[2.3784 + 3.3636 + 4.7568 + 6.7272]$
$= 8.613$ (4 s.f.).

[3 marks available — 1 mark for calculating y-values for the midpoint of each strip, 1 mark for correct use of formula, 1 mark for correct answer]

C3 Practice Exam One

1 a) For $3\ln x - \ln 3x = 0$, use the log laws to simplify to:

$\ln x^3 - \ln 3x = 0 \Rightarrow \ln \frac{x^3}{3x} = 0 \Rightarrow \ln \frac{x^2}{3} = 0$ *[1 mark]*.

Taking e to the power of both sides gives:

$\frac{x^2}{3} = e^0 = 1 \Rightarrow x^2 = 3 \Rightarrow x = \sqrt{3}$ (ignore the negative solution as $x > 0$) *[1 mark]*.

Answers

b) Let $y = f(x)$. Now, to find the inverse of $y = 3\ln x - \ln 3x$, make x the subject then swap x and y:

$y = \ln \frac{x^2}{3}$ (from (a)) $\Rightarrow e^y = \frac{x^2}{3} \Rightarrow x^2 = 3e^y$

$\Rightarrow x = \sqrt{3e^y}$ *[1 mark]*.

So $f^{-1}(x) = \sqrt{3e^x}$ *[1 mark]*.

c) When $\sqrt{3e^x} = 1$, squaring both sides gives:

$3e^x = 1 \Rightarrow e^x = \frac{1}{3}$ *[1 mark]*.

Taking ln of both sides gives:

$x = \ln \frac{1}{3}$ *[1 mark]*.

d) $f(x) = 3\ln x - \ln 3x$, so differentiating gives:

$f'(x) = \frac{3}{x} - \frac{3}{3x} = \frac{3}{x} - \frac{1}{x} = \frac{2}{x}$ *[1 mark]*.

So when $x = 1$, $f'(x) = \frac{2}{1} = 2$ *[1 mark]*.

2 a) (i)

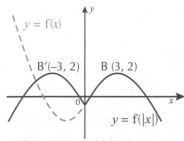

[3 marks available — 1 mark for reflection in the y-axis, 1 mark for each coordinate of B' after transformation]

(ii)

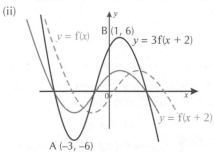

[3 marks available — 1 mark for shape (stretch and translation), 1 mark each for coordinates of A and B after transformation]

The solid grey line shows the graph of $y = f(x + 2)$ — it's easier to do the transformation in two stages, instead of doing it all at once.

b) (i) $gh(4) = g(h(4)) = g\left(\frac{6}{4^2 - 4}\right) = g(0.5)$ *[1 mark]*

$= \sqrt{(2 \cdot 0.5) + 3} = \sqrt{1 + 3} = \sqrt{4} = 2.$ *[1 mark]*

(ii) $hg(3) = h(g(3)) = h(\sqrt{(2 \cdot 3) + 3}) = h(3)$ *[1 mark]*

$= \frac{6}{3^2 - 4} = \frac{6}{9 - 4} = \frac{6}{5} = 1.2$ *[1 mark]*.

(iii) $hg(x) = h(g(x)) = h(\sqrt{2x + 3})$

$\frac{6}{(\sqrt{2x + 3})^2 - 4} = \frac{6}{2x + 3 - 4} = \frac{6}{2x - 1}$.

[3 marks available — 1 mark for functions in the correct order, 1 mark for substituting g(x) into formula for h, 1 mark for simplifying].

3 If $x = \sin\theta$, then $\frac{dx}{d\theta} = \cos\theta$, so $dx = d\theta \cos\theta$ *[1 mark]*.
Change the limits: as $x = \sin\theta$, $\theta = \sin^{-1}x$,
so when $x = 0$, $\theta = 0$ and when $x = 0.5$, $\theta = \frac{\pi}{6}$ *[1 mark]*.
Putting all this into the integral gives:

$\int_0^{\frac{1}{2}} \frac{x}{1 - x^2}\,dx = \int_0^{\frac{\pi}{6}} \frac{\sin\theta}{1 - \sin^2\theta}\cos\theta\,d\theta$ *[1 mark]*

Using the identity $\sin^2\theta + \cos^2\theta = 1$, replace $1 - \sin^2\theta$:

$\int_0^{\frac{\pi}{6}} \frac{\sin\theta\cos\theta}{\cos^2\theta}\,d\theta = \int_0^{\frac{\pi}{6}} \frac{\sin\theta}{\cos\theta}\,d\theta = \int_0^{\frac{\pi}{6}} \tan\theta\,d\theta$ *[1 mark]*

$= [-\ln|\cos\theta|]_0^{\frac{\pi}{6}}$ *[1 mark]*

$= -\ln|\cos\frac{\pi}{6}| + \ln|\cos 0| = -\ln\frac{\sqrt{3}}{2} + \ln 1$

$= -\ln\sqrt{3} + \ln 2$

$= \ln 2 - \ln\sqrt{3} \left(= \ln\frac{2}{\sqrt{3}}\right)$ *[1 mark]*

Be careful when the substitution is of the form $x = f(\theta)$ rather than $\theta = f(x)$ — when you change the limits, you need to find the inverse of $f(\theta)$ then put in the given values of x.

4 $y = \frac{4x - 1}{\tan x}$, so use quotient rule:

$u = 4x - 1 \Rightarrow \frac{du}{dx} = 4$

$v = \tan x \Rightarrow \frac{dv}{dx} = \sec^2 x$

$\frac{dy}{dx} = \frac{v\frac{du}{dx} - u\frac{dv}{dx}}{v^2} = \frac{4\tan x - (4x - 1)\sec^2 x}{\tan^2 x}$

$= \frac{4}{\tan x} - \frac{(4x - 1)\sec^2 x}{\tan^2 x}$.

Since $\frac{1}{\tan x} = \cot x$, $\sec^2 x = \frac{1}{\cos^2 x}$, and $\tan^2 x = \frac{\sin^2 x}{\cos^2 x}$:

$\frac{dy}{dx} = 4\cot x - \frac{(4x - 1)}{\cos^2 x\left(\frac{\sin^2 x}{\cos^2 x}\right)} = 4\cot x - \frac{(4x - 1)}{\sin^2 x}$.

Since $\frac{1}{\sin^2 x} = \text{cosec}^2 x$:

$\frac{dy}{dx} = 4\cot x - (4x - 1)\text{cosec}^2 x$.

[3 marks available — 1 mark for correct expressions for du/dx and dv/dx, 1 mark for correct use of the quotient rule, and 1 mark for reaching the correct expression for dy/dx.]

You could also use the product rule with $y = (4x - 1)\cot x$.

5 a)

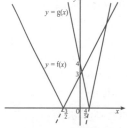

[3 marks available — 1 mark for $y = |2x + 3|$ (with reflection in the x-axis and y-intercept at 3), 1 mark for $y = |5x - 4|$ (with reflection in the x-axis and y-intercept at 4), 1 mark for showing graphs cross twice]

Make sure you draw enough of the graph to show where the lines cross — you'll need it for the next bit of the question.

b) From the graph, it is clear that there are two points where the graphs intersect. One is in the range $-\frac{3}{2} < x < \frac{4}{5}$, where $(2x + 3) > 0$ but $(5x - 4) < 0$. This gives $2x + 3 = -(5x - 4)$ *[1 mark]*.

Answers

The other one is in the range $x > \frac{4}{5}$, where $(2x + 3) > 0$ and $(5x - 4) > 0$, so $2x + 3 = 5x - 4$ *[1 mark]*. Solving the first equation gives: $2x + 3 = -5x + 4 \Rightarrow 7x = 1$, so $x = \frac{1}{7}$ *[1 mark]*. Solving the second equation gives:

$2x + 3 = 5x - 4 \Rightarrow 7 = 3x$, so $x = \frac{7}{3}$ *[1 mark]*.

You could also have solved this one by squaring both sides of the equation — you'd have ended up with the equation $21x^2 - 52x + 7$ which factorises to give $(3x - 7)(7x - 1)$ so you'd have got the same solutions as above.

c) For $|2x + 3| \geq |5x - 4|$, you need the region where the graph of $|2x + 3|$ is above the graph of $|5x - 4|$ *[1 mark]*. From the sketch from part a) and the values of x from part b), this occurs when $\frac{1}{7} \leq x \leq \frac{7}{3}$ *[1 mark]*.

6　As $y = \sqrt{\sin x}$, $y^2 = \sin x$. Putting this into the formula:
$V = \pi \int_0^\pi \sin x\, dx = \pi[-\cos x]_0^\pi = -\pi[(-1) - 1] = 2\pi$.

[4 marks available — 1 mark for correct expression for y^2, 1 mark for formula for volume of revolution, 1 mark for correct integration of sin x, 1 mark for correct answer]

7　a)　$\operatorname{cosec}\theta = \frac{5}{3} \Rightarrow \sin\theta = \frac{3}{5}$. Solving for θ gives $\theta = 0.644$, $\pi - 0.644 = 2.50$ (3 s.f.) *[1 mark for each correct answer]*.

Sketch the graph of y = sin x to help you find the second solution.

b)　(i)　The identity $\operatorname{cosec}^2\theta \equiv 1 + \cot^2\theta$ rearranges to give $\operatorname{cosec}^2\theta - 1 \equiv \cot^2\theta$. Putting this into the equation:
$3\operatorname{cosec}\theta = (\operatorname{cosec}^2\theta - 1) - 17$
$17 + 3\operatorname{cosec}\theta - (\operatorname{cosec}^2\theta - 1) = 0$
$18 + 3\operatorname{cosec}\theta - \operatorname{cosec}^2\theta = 0$
as required.

[2 marks available — 1 mark for using correct identity, 1 mark for rearranging into required form]

(ii)　To factorise the expression above, let $x = \operatorname{cosec}\theta$. Then $18 + 3x - x^2 = 0$, so $(6 - x)(3 + x) = 0$ *[1 mark]*. The roots of this quadratic occur at $x = 6$ and $x = -3$, so $\operatorname{cosec}\theta = 6$ and $\operatorname{cosec}\theta = -3$ *[1 mark]*.
$\operatorname{cosec}\theta = 1/\sin\theta$, so $\sin\theta = \frac{1}{6}$ and $\sin\theta = -\frac{1}{3}$.
Solving these equations for θ gives $\theta = 0.167, 2.97$ *[1 mark]* and $\theta = 3.48, 5.94$ *[1 mark]*.

You don't have to use x = cosec θ — it's just a little easier to factorise without all those pesky cosecs flying around. Have a look back at Section 2 for stuff on cosec etc.

8　a)　For $6^x = x + 2$, take ln of both sides:
$\ln 6^x = \ln(x + 2)$ *[1 mark]*, and using log laws,
$x\ln 6 = \ln(x + 2) \Rightarrow x = \frac{\ln(x + 2)}{\ln 6}$ *[1 mark]*.

b)　Using $x_{n+1} = \frac{\ln(x_n + 2)}{\ln 6}$ and $x_0 = 0.5$ gives:
$x_1 = \frac{\ln(0.5 + 2)}{\ln 6} = 0.51139... = 0.5114$ to 4 d.p. *[1 mark]*
$x_2 = \frac{\ln(0.51139... + 2)}{\ln 6} = 0.51392... = 0.5139$ to 4 d.p. *[1 mark]*
$x_3 = \frac{\ln(0.51392... + 2)}{\ln 6} = 0.51449... = 0.5145$ to 4 d.p. *[1 mark]*

c)　If $x = 0.515$ to 3 d.p., the upper and lower bounds are 0.5155 and 0.5145 *[1 mark]* — any value in this range would be rounded to 0.515. $f(x) = 6^x - x - 2$, and at point P, $f(x) = 0$. $f(0.5145) = -0.000537$ and $f(0.5155) = 0.00297$ *[1 mark for both f(0.5145) negative and f(0.5155) positive]*. There is a change of sign, and since $f(x)$ is continuous there must be a root in this interval *[1 mark]*.

9　a)　For $x = \frac{e^y + 2y}{e^y - 2y}$, use the quotient rule to find $\frac{dx}{dy}$:

$u = e^y + 2y \Rightarrow \frac{du}{dy} = e^y + 2$
$v = e^y - 2y \Rightarrow \frac{dv}{dy} = e^y - 2$

$\frac{dx}{dy} = \frac{v\frac{du}{dy} - u\frac{dv}{dy}}{v^2} = \frac{(e^y - 2y)(e^y + 2) - (e^y + 2y)(e^y - 2)}{(e^y - 2y)^2}$

$= \frac{(e^{2y} + 2e^y - 2ye^y - 4y) - (e^{2y} - 2e^y + 2ye^y - 4y)}{(e^y - 2y)^2}$

$= \frac{4e^y - 4ye^y}{(e^y - 2y)^2} = \frac{4e^y(1 - y)}{(e^y - 2y)^2}$.

$\frac{dy}{dx} = \frac{1}{\frac{dx}{dy}} = \frac{(e^y - 2y)^2}{4e^y(1 - y)}$.

[3 marks available — 1 mark for correct expressions for du/dy and dv/dy, 1 mark for finding expression for dx/dy using the quotient rule, and 1 mark for correct (or equivalent) expression for dy/dx]

b)　At the point (1, 0), $y = 0$ and so $e^y = e^0 = 1$. So the gradient at that point is:
$\frac{dy}{dx} = \frac{(1 - 0)^2}{4(1 - 0)} = \frac{1}{4}$.
The gradient of the normal at that point is $-1 \div \frac{1}{4} = -4$.
Equation of a straight line is $y - y_1 = m(x - x_1)$, so at (1, 0) with m = -4, the equation of the normal is:
$y - 0 = -4(x - 1) \Rightarrow y = -4x + 4$.

[3 marks available — 1 mark for finding gradient of the normal, 1 mark for correct substitution of -4 and (1, 0) into equation, and 1 mark for rearrangement into the correct form.]

10　a)　When $x = 1.5$, $y = \frac{3\ln 1.5}{(1.5)^2} = 0.54062$ *[1 mark]*, and when $x = 3$, $y = \frac{3\ln 3}{3^2} = 0.36620$ *[1 mark]*.

b)　$h = 0.5$. Putting h and the values from the table into the formula for Simpson's Rule:
$A \approx \frac{0.5}{3}[0 + 0.36620 + 4(0.54062 + 0.43982) + 2(0.51986)]$
$= \frac{1}{6}[0.36620 + 3.92176 + 1.03972] = 0.88795$ (5 d.p.).

[3 marks available — 1 mark for putting the correct numbers into the formula for Simpson's Rule, 1 mark for some correct working and 1 mark for correct answer]

c) Let $u = \ln x$, so $\dfrac{du}{dx} = \dfrac{1}{x}$. Let $\dfrac{dv}{dx} = \dfrac{3}{x^2}$, so $v = -\dfrac{3}{x}$.

Putting this into the formula for integration by parts gives:

$3\displaystyle\int_1^3 \dfrac{\ln x}{x^2}\,dx = 3\left[-\dfrac{\ln x}{x}\right]_1^3 - 3\int_1^3 -\dfrac{1}{x}\dfrac{1}{x}\,dx$

$= 3\left[-\dfrac{\ln x}{x}\right]_1^3 + 3\displaystyle\int_1^3 \dfrac{1}{x^2}\,dx = 3\left[-\dfrac{\ln x}{x}\right]_1^3 + 3\left[-\dfrac{1}{x}\right]_1^3$

$= \dfrac{-3\ln 3}{3} + \dfrac{3\ln 1}{1} - \dfrac{3}{3} + \dfrac{3}{1}$

$= -\ln 3 - 1 + 3 = 2 - \ln 3 = 0.90139$

[5 marks available — 1 mark for correct expression for du/dx, 1 mark for correct expression for v, 1 mark for correct formula for integration by parts, 1 mark for correct working and 1 mark for correct answer]

If the question asked for the exact value, you'd leave your answer as 2 − ln 3.

C3 Practice Exam Two

1 a) Let $u = 4x$, so $\dfrac{du}{dx} = 4$. Let $\dfrac{dv}{dx} = e^{-2x}$, so $v = -\tfrac{1}{2}e^{-2x}$.

Putting this into the integral gives:

$\displaystyle\int 4xe^{-2x}\,dx = [4x(-\tfrac{1}{2}e^{-2x})] - \int 4(-\tfrac{1}{2}e^{-2x})\,dx$

$= -2xe^{-2x} + \displaystyle\int 2e^{-2x}\,dx$

$= -2xe^{-2x} - e^{-2x} + C \;(= -e^{-2x}(2x + 1) + C)$

[4 marks available — 1 mark for correct choice of u and dv/dx, 1 mark for correct differentiation and integration to obtain du/dx and v, 1 mark for correct integration by parts method, 1 mark for answer]

b) As $u = \ln x$, $\dfrac{du}{dx} = \dfrac{1}{x}$, so $x\,du = dx$ **[1 mark]**. The limits $x = 1$ and $x = 2$ become $u = \ln 1 = 0$ and $u = \ln 2$ **[1 mark]**. $\left(\dfrac{\ln x}{\sqrt{x}}\right)^2 = \dfrac{(\ln x)^2}{x}$ **[1 mark]**. So the integral is:

$\displaystyle\int_0^{\ln 2} \dfrac{u^2}{x} x\,du = \int_0^{\ln 2} u^2\,du$ **[1 mark]**

$= \left[\dfrac{u^3}{3}\right]_0^{\ln 2} = \dfrac{(\ln 2)^3}{3} = 0.111\ (3\,s.f.)$ **[1 mark]**.

2 a) g has range $g(x) \ge -9$ **[1 mark]**, as the minimum value of g is −9.

b) Neither f nor g are one-to-one functions, so they don't have inverses **[1 mark]**.

f and g are many-to-one not one-to-one, as more than one value of x is mapped to the same f(x) or g(x) value, e.g. x = 1 and x = −1 are both mapped to f(x) = 1 and g(x)= −8.

c) (i) $fg(4) = f(4^2 - 9) = f(7)$ **[1 mark]** $= \dfrac{1}{7^2} = \dfrac{1}{49}$ **[1 mark]**.

(ii) $gf(1) = g(1/1^2) = g(1)$ **[1 mark]** $= 1^2 - 9 = -8$ **[1 mark]**.

d) (i) $fg(x) = f(x^2 - 9)$ **[1 mark]** $= \dfrac{1}{(x^2 - 9)^2}$ **[1 mark]**.
The domain of fg is $x \in \mathbb{R},\ x \ne \pm 3$ **[1 mark]**, as the denominator of the function can't be 0.

(ii) From part (i), you know that $fg(x) = \dfrac{1}{(x^2 - 9)^2}$, so

$\dfrac{1}{(x^2 - 9)^2} = \dfrac{1}{256} \Rightarrow (x^2 - 9)^2 = 256$ **[1 mark]**

$x^2 - 9 = \pm\sqrt{256} = \pm 16$ **[1 mark]**

$x^2 = 9 \pm 16 = 25, -7$ **[1 mark]**

$x = \sqrt{25} = \pm 5$ **[1 mark]**

You can ignore $x^2 = -7$, as this has no solutions in $x \in \mathbb{R}$.

3 a) $\sec x = \dfrac{1}{\cos x}$, so as $\cos x = \dfrac{8}{9}$, $\sec x = \dfrac{9}{8}$ **[1 mark]**.

b) The right-angled triangle with angle x, hypotenuse of length 9 and the adjacent side of length 8 (which gives the cos x value as stated) has the opposite side of length $\sqrt{9^2 - 8^2} = \sqrt{81 - 64} = \sqrt{17}$ **[1 mark]**. It looks like this:

So the value of $\sin x = \dfrac{\sqrt{17}}{9}$ (opposite / hypotenuse).

$\operatorname{cosec} x = \dfrac{1}{\sin x}$, so $\operatorname{cosec} x = \dfrac{9}{\sqrt{17}}$ **[1 mark]**.

c) For the triangle described in part (b), the value of $\tan x$ is given by opposite / adjacent $= \dfrac{\sqrt{17}}{8}$ **[1 mark]**.

So $\tan^2 x = \left(\dfrac{\sqrt{17}}{8}\right)^2 = \dfrac{17}{64}$ **[1 mark]**.

4 a) $f(x) = (\sqrt{x + 2})\ln(x + 2)$,
so $f(7) = (\sqrt{7 + 2})\ln(7 + 2) = (\sqrt{9})\ln 9 = 3\ln 9$ **[1 mark]**.

Using the log laws:
$f(7) = 3\ln(3^2) = 2 \times 3\ln 3 = 6\ln 3$ **[1 mark]**.

b) For $y = (\sqrt{x + 2})\ln(x + 2)$, use the product rule:

$u = \sqrt{x + 2} = (x + 2)^{\frac{1}{2}} \Rightarrow \dfrac{du}{dx} = \dfrac{1}{2}(x + 2)^{-\frac{1}{2}} = \dfrac{1}{2\sqrt{x + 2}}$

$v = \ln(x + 2) \Rightarrow \dfrac{dv}{dx} = \dfrac{1}{x + 2}$.

$f'(x) = \dfrac{dy}{dx} = u\dfrac{dv}{dx} + v\dfrac{du}{dx} = \dfrac{\sqrt{x + 2}}{x + 2} + \dfrac{\ln(x + 2)}{2\sqrt{x + 2}}$.

So $f'(7) = \dfrac{\sqrt{7 + 2}}{7 + 2} + \dfrac{\ln(7 + 2)}{2\sqrt{7 + 2}} = \dfrac{3}{9} + \dfrac{\ln 9}{2 \times 3}$.

Since, using log laws, $\ln 9 = \ln 3^2 = 2\ln 3$,

$f'(7) = \dfrac{1}{3} + \dfrac{2\ln 3}{2 \times 3} = \dfrac{1}{3} + \dfrac{\ln 3}{3} = \dfrac{1}{3}(1 + \ln 3)$.

[4 marks available — 1 mark for correct expressions for du/dx and dv/dx, 1 mark for correct use of product rule formula, 1 mark for correct substitution of x = 7, and 1 mark for correct rearrangement using the log laws]

c) Equation of a straight line is $y - y_1 = m(x - x_1)$. For the tangent at $x = 7$, $y = 6\ln 3$ (from (a)) and $m = \dfrac{1}{3}(1 + \ln 3)$ (from (b)), so the equation of the tangent is:

$y - 6\ln 3 = \dfrac{1}{3}(1 + \ln 3)(x - 7)$

$\Rightarrow y = \dfrac{1}{3}(1 + \ln 3)(x - 7) + 6\ln 3$

$\Rightarrow 3y = (1 + \ln 3)(x - 7) + 18\ln 3$

$\Rightarrow 3y = x + x\ln 3 - 7 - 7\ln 3 + 18\ln 3$

$\Rightarrow 3y = x + x\ln 3 + 11\ln 3 - 7$.

[2 marks available — 1 mark for correct substitution of m, y_1 and x_1 into equation, 1 mark for correct rearrangement to give final answer]

5 First, rearrange the equation to get x^2 on its own:
$e^y = x^2 - 1$, so $x^2 = e^y + 1$. Now put this into the formula for a volume of revolution:

$V = \pi \displaystyle\int_1^3 e^y + 1\,dy = \pi[e^y + y]_1^3$

$= \pi[(e^3 + 3) - (e^1 + 1)] = 60.84$

Answers

[5 marks available —1 mark for taking exponentials of both sides of the equation, 1 mark for getting x^2 on its own, 1 mark for using the correct formula for the volume of revolution, 1 mark for correct integration and 1 mark for substituting the values to get the final answer]

6 a) (i) The width of each strip is $(1 - 0)/4 = 0.25$. For 4 strips, the x-values are $x_0 = 0$, $x_1 = 0.25$, $x_2 = 0.5$, $x_3 = 0.75$ and $x_4 = 1$. This means the mid-points of each strip are $x_{0.5} = 0.125$, $x_{1.5} = 0.375$, $x_{2.5} = 0.625$ and $x_{3.5} = 0.875$ *[1 mark]*. Calculating the y-values at these points gives:
$x_{0.5} = 0.125$, $y_{0.5} = 1.1243$; $x_{1.5} = 0.375$, $y_{1.5} = 1.3539$;
$x_{2.5} = 0.625$, $y_{2.5} = 1.5151$; $x_{3.5} = 0.875$, $y_{3.5} = 1.5377$
[1 mark for all 4 values correct]. Putting these values into the formula for the Mid-Ordinate Rule gives:
$A \approx 0.25(1.1243 + 1.3539 + 1.5151 + 1.5377)$ *[1 mark]*
$= 1.383$ (4 s.f.) *[1 mark]*

   (ii) To improve the approximation, increase n (i.e. use more strips) *[1 mark]*.

   b) First, differentiate $e^x \sin x$ using the product rule:
let $u = e^x$ so $\frac{du}{dx} = e^x$ and $v = \sin x$ so $\frac{dv}{dx} = \cos x$ *[1 mark]*.
This means that $\frac{d}{dx} = e^x \cos x + e^x \sin x$ *[1 mark]*.
Now differentiate $e^x \cos x$ using the product rule:
let $u = e^x$ so $\frac{du}{dx} = e^x$ and $v = \cos x$ so $\frac{dv}{dx} = -\sin x$.
This means that $\frac{d}{dx} = -e^x \sin x + e^x \cos x$ *[1 mark]*.
Putting all this together: $\frac{d}{dx} \frac{1}{2}(e^x \sin x + e^x \cos x)$
$= \frac{1}{2}[(e^x \cos x + e^x \sin x) + (-e^x \sin x + e^x \cos x)$
$= \frac{1}{2}[2 e^x \cos x] = e^x \cos x$ *[1 mark]*.

   c) As $\frac{1}{2}(e^x \sin x + e^x \cos x)$ differentiates to give $e^x \cos x$, so $e^x \cos x$ integrates to give $\frac{1}{2}(e^x \sin x + e^x \cos x)$.
So $\int_0^1 e^x \cos x \, dx = [\frac{1}{2}(e^x \sin x + e^x \cos x)]_0^1$ *[1 mark]*
$= [\frac{1}{2}((e^1 \sin 1 + e^1 \cos 1) - (e^0 \sin 0 + e^0 \cos 0))]$
$= \frac{1}{2}(3.756 - 1) = 1.378 \,(4 \, s.f.)$ *[1 mark]*

7 a) $y = e^{2x} - 5e^x + 3x$, so, using chain rule:
$\frac{dy}{dx} = 2e^{2x} - 5e^x + 3$.
[2 marks available — 1 mark for $2e^{2x}$, 1 mark for rest of answer.]

   b) Differentiating again gives: $\frac{d^2y}{dx^2} = 4e^{2x} - 5e^x$.
[2 marks available — 1 mark for $4e^{2x}$, 1 mark for $-5e^x$]

   c) Stationary points occur when $\frac{dy}{dx} = 0$, so:
$2e^{2x} - 5e^x + 3 = 0$ *[1 mark]*.
(This looks like a quadratic, so substitute $y = e^x$ and factorise...)
$2y^2 - 5y + 3 = 0 \Rightarrow (2y - 3)(y - 1) = 0$ *[1 mark]*.
So the solutions are:
$2y - 3 = 0 \Rightarrow y = \frac{3}{2} \Rightarrow e^x = \frac{3}{2} \Rightarrow x = \ln \frac{3}{2}$ *[1 mark]*, and
$y - 1 = 0 \Rightarrow y = 1 \Rightarrow e^x = 1 \Rightarrow x = \ln 1 = 0$ *[1 mark]*.

   d) To determine the nature of the stationary points, find $\frac{d^2y}{dx^2}$ at $x = 0$ and $x = \ln \frac{3}{2}$:
$\frac{d^2y}{dx^2} = 4e^{2x} - 5e^x$ (from (b)), so when $x = 0$:

$\frac{d^2y}{dx^2} = 4e^0 - 5e^0 = 4 - 5 = -1$ *[1 mark]*,
so $\frac{d^2y}{dx^2} < 0$, which means the point is a maximum *[1 mark]*.
When $x = \ln \frac{3}{2}$:
$\frac{d^2y}{dx^2} = 4e^{2\ln \frac{3}{2}} - 5e^{\ln \frac{3}{2}} = 4(\frac{3}{2})^2 - 5(\frac{3}{2}) = \frac{3}{2}$ *[1 mark]*,
so $\frac{d^2y}{dx^2} > 0$, which means the point is a minimum *[1 mark]*.

8 a) To find the inverse, let $y = f(x)$, so $y = 4(x^2 - 1)$. Now make x the subject: $y = 4(x^2 - 1) \Rightarrow \frac{y}{4} = x^2 - 1 \Rightarrow \frac{y}{4} + 1 = x^2$
so $x = \sqrt{\frac{y}{4} + 1}$ *[1 mark]* (you can ignore the negative square root, as the domain of $f(x)$ is $x \geq 0$). Finally, replace y with x and x with $f^{-1}(x)$: $f^{-1}(x) = \sqrt{\frac{x}{4} + 1}$ *[1 mark]*.
$f^{-1}(x)$ is a reflection of $f(x)$ in the line $y = x$ *[1 mark]*,
so the point at which the lines $f(x)$ and $f^{-1}(x)$ meet is also the point where $f^{-1}(x)$ meets the line $y = x$. At this point,
$x = \sqrt{\frac{x}{4} + 1}$ *[1 mark]*.

   b) Let $g(x) = \sqrt{\frac{x}{4} + 1} - x$ *[1 mark]*.
If there is a root in the interval $1 < x < 2$ then there will be a change of sign for $g(x)$ between 1 and 2:
$g(1) = \sqrt{\frac{1}{4} + 1} - 1 = 0.1180...$
$g(2) = \sqrt{\frac{2}{4} + 1} - 2 = -0.7752...$ *[1 mark for both]*
There is a change of sign, so there is a root in the interval $1 < x < 2$ *[1 mark]*.

   c) $x_{n+1} = \sqrt{\frac{x_n}{4} + 1}$, and $x_0 = 0.5$, so:
$x_1 = \sqrt{\frac{0.5}{4} + 1} = 1.0606...$
$x_2 = \sqrt{\frac{1.0606...}{4} + 1} = 1.1247...$ *[1 mark]*
$x_3 = \sqrt{\frac{1.1247...}{4} + 1} = 1.1319...$
$x_4 = \sqrt{\frac{1.1319...}{4} + 1} = 1.1326...$ *[1 mark]*
So $x = 1.13$ to 3 s.f. *[1 mark]*.

   d)
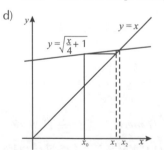

[2 marks available — 1 mark for convergent staircase diagram, 1 mark for positions of x_1 and x_2]

Answers

C4 Section 1 — Algebra and Functions
Warm-up Questions

1) a) $\dfrac{4x^2-25}{6x-15}=\dfrac{(2x+5)(2x-5)}{3(2x-5)}=\dfrac{2x+5}{3}$

b) $\dfrac{2x+3}{x-2}\times\dfrac{4x-8}{2x^2-3x-9}$

$=\dfrac{2x+3}{x-2}\times\dfrac{4(x-2)}{(2x+3)(x-3)}$

$=\dfrac{4}{x-3}$

c) $\dfrac{x^2-3x}{x+1}\div\dfrac{x}{2}=\dfrac{x(x-3)}{x+1}\times\dfrac{2}{x}$

$=\dfrac{x-3}{x+1}\times 2=\dfrac{2(x-3)}{x+1}$

2) a) $\dfrac{x}{2x+1}+\dfrac{3}{x^2}+\dfrac{1}{x}=\dfrac{x\cdot x^2}{x^2(2x+1)}+\dfrac{3(2x+1)}{x^2(2x+1)}+\dfrac{x(2x+1)}{x^2(2x+1)}$

$=\dfrac{x^3+6x+3+2x^2+x}{x^2(2x+1)}=\dfrac{x^3+2x^2+7x+3}{x^2(2x+1)}$

b) $\dfrac{2}{x^2-1}-\dfrac{3x}{x-1}+\dfrac{x}{x+1}$

$=\dfrac{2}{(x+1)(x-1)}-\dfrac{3x(x+1)}{(x+1)(x-1)}+\dfrac{x(x-1)}{(x+1)(x-1)}$

$=\dfrac{2-3x^2-3x+x^2-x}{(x+1)(x-1)}=\dfrac{2-2x^2-4x}{(x+1)(x-1)}$

$=\dfrac{2(1-x^2-2x)}{(x+1)(x-1)}$

3)
$$\begin{array}{r}x^2-2x+7\ \ r-9\\ x+4\overline{\smash{\big)}\,x^3+2x^2-x+19}\\ -\ \underline{x^3+4x^2}\\ -2x^2-x\\ -\ \underline{-2x^2-8x}\\ 7x+19\\ -\ \underline{7x+28}\\ -9\end{array}$$

so $(x^3+2x^2-x+19)\div(x+4)=x^2-2x+7$ remainder -9.

4) $2x^3+8x^2+7x+8\equiv(Ax^2+Bx+C)(x+3)+D$.

Set $x=-3$: $2(-3)^3+8(-3)^2+7(-3)+8=0+D\Rightarrow D=5$.

Set $x=0$: $0+8=C(0+3)+D\Rightarrow C=1$.

Equating the coefficients of x^3 gives $2=A$.

Finally, equating the coefficients of x^2 gives $8=3A+B$

$\Rightarrow 8=(3\times2)+B$, so $B=2$.

So $2x^3+8x^2+7x+8=(2x^2+2x+1)(x+3)+5$. The result when $2x^3+8x^2+7x+8$ is divided by $(x+3)$ is $2x^2+2x+1$ remainder 5.

For these questions, you can use the substitution method or the equating coefficients method. I've just shown one method for each.

5) a) $\dfrac{4x+5}{(x+4)(2x-3)}\equiv\dfrac{A}{(x+4)}+\dfrac{B}{(2x-3)}$

$4x+5\equiv A(2x-3)+B(x+4)$

Using substitution method:

substitute $x=-4$: $-11=-11A\Rightarrow A=1$

substitute $x=1.5$: $11=5.5B\Rightarrow B=2$

$\dfrac{4x+5}{(x+4)(2x-3)}\equiv\dfrac{1}{(x+4)}+\dfrac{2}{(2x-3)}$

b) $\dfrac{-7x-7}{(3x+1)(x-2)}\equiv\dfrac{A}{(3x+1)}+\dfrac{B}{(x-2)}$

$-7x-7\equiv A(x-2)+B(3x+1)$

Using equating coefficients method:

coefficients of x: $-7=A+3B$

constants: $-7=-2A+B$

Solving simultaneously: $A=2,\ B=-3$

$\dfrac{-7x-7}{(3x+1)(x-2)}\equiv\dfrac{2}{(3x+1)}-\dfrac{3}{(x-2)}$

c) $\dfrac{x-18}{(x+4)(3x-4)}\equiv\dfrac{A}{(x+4)}+\dfrac{B}{(3x-4)}$

$x-18\equiv A(3x-4)+B(x+4)$

Using substitution method:

substitute $x=-4$: $-22=-16A\Rightarrow A=\dfrac{11}{8}$.

And using equating coefficients method:

coefficients of x: $1=3A+B$

Substituting $A=\dfrac{11}{8}$: $1=3A+B\Rightarrow B=1-\dfrac{33}{8}=-\dfrac{25}{8}$.

$\dfrac{x-18}{(x+4)(3x-4)}\equiv\dfrac{11}{8(x+4)}-\dfrac{25}{8(3x-4)}$

Don't worry if you get fractions for your coefficients — just put the numerator on the top and the denominator on the bottom.

d) Factorise the denominator:

$\dfrac{5x}{x^2+x-6}\equiv\dfrac{5x}{(x+3)(x-2)}\equiv\dfrac{A}{(x+3)}+\dfrac{B}{(x-2)}$

$5x\equiv A(x-2)+B(x+3)$

Using substitution method:

substitute $x=-3$: $-15=-5A\Rightarrow A=3$

substitute $x=2$: $10=5B\Rightarrow B=2$

$\dfrac{5x}{x^2+x-6}\equiv\dfrac{3}{(x+3)}+\dfrac{2}{(x-2)}$

e) Factorise the denominator:

$\dfrac{6+4y}{9-y^2}\equiv\dfrac{6+4y}{(3-y)(3+y)}\equiv\dfrac{A}{(3-y)}+\dfrac{B}{(3+y)}$

$6+4y\equiv A(3+y)+B(3-y)$

Using substitution method:

substitute $y=3$: $18=6A\Rightarrow A=3$

substitute $y=-3$: $-6=6B\Rightarrow B=-1$

$\dfrac{6+4y}{9-y^2}\equiv\dfrac{3}{(3-y)}-\dfrac{1}{(3+y)}$

f) $\dfrac{10x^2+32x+16}{(x+3)(2x+4)(x-2)}\equiv\dfrac{A}{(x+3)}+\dfrac{B}{(2x+4)}+\dfrac{C}{(x-2)}$

$10x^2+32x+16$
$\equiv A(2x+4)(x-2)+B(x+3)(x-2)+C(x+3)(2x+4)$

Using substitution method:

substitute $x=2$: $120=40C\Rightarrow C=3$

substitute $x=-3$: $10=10A\Rightarrow A=1$

substitute $x=-2$: $-8=-4B\Rightarrow B=2$

$\dfrac{10x^2+32x+16}{(x+3)(2x+4)(x-2)}\equiv\dfrac{1}{(x+3)}+\dfrac{2}{(2x+4)}+\dfrac{3}{(x-2)}$

g) Factorise the denominator:

$\dfrac{4x^2+12x+6}{x^3+3x^2+2x}=\dfrac{4x^2+12x+6}{x(x^2+3x+2)}=\dfrac{4x^2+12x+6}{x(x+1)(x+2)}$

$\equiv\dfrac{A}{x}+\dfrac{B}{(x+1)}+\dfrac{C}{(x+2)}$

$4x^2+12x+6\equiv A(x+1)(x+2)+Bx(x+2)+Cx(x+1)$

Answers

Using substitution method:

substitute $x = -1$: $-2 = -B \Rightarrow B = 2$

substitute $x = 0$: $6 = 2A \Rightarrow A = 3$

substitute $x = -2$: $-2 = 2C \Rightarrow C = -1$

$$\frac{4x^2 + 12x + 6}{x^3 + 3x^2 + 2x} \equiv \frac{3}{x} + \frac{2}{(x+1)} - \frac{1}{(x+2)}$$

h) $\dfrac{-11x^2 + 6x + 11}{(2x+1)(3-x)(x+2)} \equiv \dfrac{A}{(2x+1)} + \dfrac{B}{(3-x)} + \dfrac{C}{(x+2)}$

$-11x^2 + 6x + 11$
$\equiv A(3-x)(x+2) + B(2x+1)(x+2) + C(2x+1)(3-x)$

Using substitution method:

substitute $x = 3$: $-70 = 35B \Rightarrow B = -2$

substitute $x = -2$: $-45 = -15C \Rightarrow C = 3$

substitute $x = -0.5$: $5.25 = 5.25A \Rightarrow A = 1$

$$\frac{-11x^2 + 6x + 11}{(2x+1)(3-x)(x+2)} \equiv \frac{1}{(2x+1)} - \frac{2}{(3-x)} + \frac{3}{(x+2)}$$

6) a) $\dfrac{2x+2}{(x+3)^2} \equiv \dfrac{A}{(x+3)} + \dfrac{B}{(x+3)^2}$

$2x + 2 \equiv A(x+3) + B$

Using substitution method:

substitute $x = -3$: $-4 = B$

substitute $x = 0$: $2 = 3A - 4 \Rightarrow A = 2$

$$\frac{2x+2}{(x+3)^2} \equiv \frac{2}{(x+3)} - \frac{4}{(x+3)^2}$$

b) $\dfrac{6x^2 + 17x + 5}{x(x+2)^2} \equiv \dfrac{A}{x} + \dfrac{B}{(x+2)} + \dfrac{C}{(x+2)^2}$

$6x^2 + 17x + 5 \equiv A(x+2)^2 + Bx(x+2) + Cx$

substitute $x = -2$: $-5 = -2C \Rightarrow C = \dfrac{5}{2}$

substitute $x = 0$: $5 = 4A \Rightarrow A = \dfrac{5}{4}$

coefficients of x^2: $6 = A + B$

substitute $A = \dfrac{5}{4}$: $6 = \dfrac{5}{4} + B \Rightarrow B = \dfrac{19}{4}$

$$\frac{6x^2 + 19x + 8}{x(x+2)^2} \equiv \frac{5}{4x} + \frac{19}{4(x+2)} + \frac{5}{2(x+2)^2}$$

c) $\dfrac{-18x + 14}{(2x-1)^2(x+2)} \equiv \dfrac{A}{(2x-1)} + \dfrac{B}{(2x-1)^2} + \dfrac{C}{(x+2)}$

$-18x + 14 \equiv A(2x-1)(x+2) + B(x+2) + C(2x-1)^2$

substitute $x = -2$: $50 = 25C \Rightarrow C = 2$

substitute $x = 0.5$: $5 = 2.5B \Rightarrow B = 2$

coefficients of x^2: $0 = 2A + 4C$

substitute $C = 2$: $0 = 2A + 8 \Rightarrow A = -4$

$$\frac{-18x + 14}{(2x-1)^2(x+2)} \equiv \frac{-4}{(2x-1)} + \frac{2}{(2x-1)^2} + \frac{2}{(x+2)}$$

d) Factorise the denominator:

$\dfrac{8x^2 - x - 5}{x^3 - x^2} \equiv \dfrac{8x^2 - x - 5}{x^2(x-1)} \equiv \dfrac{A}{x} + \dfrac{B}{x^2} + \dfrac{C}{(x-1)}$

$8x^2 - x - 5 \equiv Ax(x-1) + B(x-1) + Cx^2$

coefficients of x^2: $8 = A + C$ (eq. 1)

coefficients of x: $-1 = -A + B$ (eq. 2)

constants: $-5 = -B \Rightarrow B = 5$

substitute $B = 5$ in eq. 2: $-1 = -A + 5 \Rightarrow A = 6$

substitute $A = 6$ in eq. 1: $8 = 6 + C \Rightarrow C = 2$

$$\frac{8x^2 - x - 5}{x^3 - x^2} \equiv \frac{6}{x} + \frac{5}{x^2} + \frac{2}{(x-1)}$$

7) a) Expand the denominator:

$\dfrac{2x^2 + 18x + 26}{(x+2)(x+4)} \equiv \dfrac{2x^2 + 18x + 26}{x^2 + 6x + 8}$

Divide the fraction:

$$x^2 + 6x + 8 \overline{\smash{\big)}\ \begin{array}{l} 2 \\ 2x^2 + 18x + 26 \\ \underline{2x^2 + 12x + 16} \\ 6x + 10 \end{array}}$$

$\dfrac{2x^2 + 18x + 26}{(x+2)(x+4)} \equiv 2 + \dfrac{6x + 10}{(x+2)(x+4)}$

Now express $\dfrac{6x+10}{(x+2)(x+4)}$ as partial fractions:

$\dfrac{6x+10}{(x+2)(x+4)} \equiv \dfrac{A}{(x+2)} + \dfrac{B}{(x+4)}$

$6x + 10 \equiv A(x+4) + B(x+2)$

substitute $x = -4$: $-14 = -2B \Rightarrow B = 7$

substitute $x = -2$: $-2 = 2A \Rightarrow A = -1$

So overall $\dfrac{2x^2 + 18x + 26}{(x+2)(x+4)} \equiv 2 - \dfrac{1}{(x+2)} + \dfrac{7}{(x+4)}$

b) Expand the denominator:

$\dfrac{3x^2 + 9x + 2}{x(x+1)} \equiv \dfrac{3x^2 + 9x + 2}{x^2 + x}$

Divide the fraction:

$$x^2 + x \overline{\smash{\big)}\ \begin{array}{l} 3 \\ 3x^2 + 9x + 2 \\ \underline{3x^2 + 3x} \\ 6x + 2 \end{array}}$$

$\dfrac{3x^2 + 9x + 2}{x(x+1)} \equiv 3 + \dfrac{6x + 2}{x(x+1)}$

Now express $\dfrac{6x+2}{x(x+1)}$ as partial fractions:

$\dfrac{6x+2}{x(x+1)} \equiv \dfrac{A}{x} + \dfrac{B}{(x+1)}$

$6x + 2 \equiv A(x+1) + Bx$

substitute $x = -1$: $-4 = -B \Rightarrow B = 4$

substitute $x = 0$: $2 = A$

So overall $\dfrac{3x^2 + 9x + 2}{x(x+1)} \equiv 3 + \dfrac{2}{x} + \dfrac{4}{(x+1)}$

c) Expand the denominator:

$\dfrac{24x^2 - 70x + 53}{(2x-3)^2} \equiv \dfrac{24x^2 - 70x + 53}{4x^2 - 12x + 9}$

Divide the fraction:

$$4x^2 - 12x + 9 \overline{\smash{\big)}\ \begin{array}{l} 6 \\ 24x^2 - 70x + 53 \\ \underline{24x^2 - 72x + 54} \\ 2x - 1 \end{array}}$$

$\dfrac{24x^2 - 70x + 53}{(2x-3)^2} \equiv 6 + \dfrac{2x - 1}{(2x-3)^2}$

Now express $\dfrac{2x-1}{(2x-3)^2}$ as partial fractions:

$\dfrac{2x-1}{(2x-3)^2} \equiv \dfrac{A}{(2x-3)} + \dfrac{B}{(2x-3)^2}$

$2x - 1 \equiv A(2x-3) + B$

substitute $x = 1.5$: $2 = B$

substitute $x = 0$, and $B = 2$: $-1 = -3A + 2 \Rightarrow A = 1$

So overall $\dfrac{24x^2 - 70x + 53}{(2x-3)^2} \equiv 6 + \dfrac{1}{(2x-3)} + \dfrac{2}{(2x-3)^2}$

d) Expand the denominator:

$\frac{3x^3 - 2x^2 - 2x - 3}{(x+1)(x-2)} \equiv \frac{3x^3 - 2x^2 - 2x - 3}{x^2 - x - 2}$

Divide the fraction using $f(x) = q(x)d(x) + r(x)$:

$3x^3 - 2x^2 - 2x - 3 = (Ax + B)(x^2 - x - 2) + Cx + D$

coefficients of x^3: $\ 3 = A$

coefficients of x^2: $\ -2 = -A + B$

substitute $A = 3$: $\ -2 = -3 + B \Rightarrow B = 1$

coefficients of x: $\ -2 = -2A - B + C$

substitute $A = 3$ and $B = 1$: $\ -2 = -6 - 1 + C \Rightarrow C = 5$

constants: $\ -3 = -2B + D$

substitute $B = 1$: $\ -3 = -2 + D \Rightarrow D = -1$

$\frac{3x^3 - 2x^2 - 2x - 3}{(x+1)(x-2)} \equiv 3x + 1 + \frac{5x-1}{(x+1)(x-2)}$

Now express $\frac{5x-1}{(x+1)(x-2)}$ as partial fractions:

$\frac{5x-1}{(x+1)(x-2)} \equiv \frac{M}{(x+1)} + \frac{N}{(x-2)}$

$5x - 1 \equiv M(x-2) + N(x+1)$

substitute $x = 2$: $\ 9 = 3N \Rightarrow N = 3$

substitute $x = -1$: $\ -6 = -3M \Rightarrow M = 2$

So overall $\frac{3x^3 - 2x^2 - 2x - 3}{(x+1)(x-2)} \equiv 3x + 1 + \frac{2}{(x+1)} + \frac{3}{(x-2)}$

I used the remainder theorem to divide this fraction, because it's a bit trickier than the rest have been. You could have used the remainder theorem in 7)a)-c) too, but I reckon they were easier to do with long division.

8) a) $V = 7500k^{-0.2t}$, so when $t = 0$, $V = 7500 \times k^0 = £7500$.

   b) $3000 = 7500k^{-0.2 \times 5} \Rightarrow 0.4 = k^{-1} \Rightarrow k = 2.5$.

   c) $V = 7500 \times 2.5^{(-0.2 \times 10)} = £1200$.

   d) When $V = 500$, $500 = 7500(2.5)^{-0.2t}$

   $\Rightarrow 2.5^{-0.2t} = \frac{500}{7500} \Rightarrow 2.5^{0.2t} = \frac{7500}{500} = 15$

   $\Rightarrow 0.2t\ln 2.5 = \ln 15$

   $\Rightarrow t = 2.9554... \div 0.2 = 14.777...$ years.

   So it will be 14.8 years old before the value falls below £500.

Exam Questions

1 $5x^2 + 3x + 6 \equiv A(2x-1)^2 + B(3+x) + C(2x-1)(3-x)$

   [1 mark]

   Using substitution method:

   substitute $x = 3$: $\ 60 = 25A \Rightarrow A = \frac{12}{5}$ *[1 mark]*

   substitute $x = \frac{1}{2}$: $\ \frac{35}{4} = \frac{5}{2}B \Rightarrow B = \frac{7}{2}$ *[1 mark]*

   coefficients of x^2: $\ 5 = 4A - 2C$

   substitute $A = \frac{12}{5}$: $\ 5 = \frac{48}{5} - 2C$

   $-\frac{23}{5} = -2C \Rightarrow C = \frac{23}{10}$ *[1 mark]*

2 First put $x = -6$ into both sides of the identity

   $x^3 + 15x^2 + 43x - 30 \equiv (Ax^2 + Bx + C)(x+6) + D$:

   $(-6)^3 + 15(-6)^2 + 43(-6) - 30 = D \Rightarrow 36 = D$ *[1 mark]*.

   Now set $x = 0$ to get $-30 = 6C + D$, so $C = -11$ *[1 mark]*.

   Equating the coefficients of x^3 gives $1 = A$. Equating the coefficients of x^2 gives $15 = 6A + B$, so $B = 9$ *[1 mark]*.

So $x^3 + 15x^2 + 43x - 30 = (x^2 + 9x - 11)(x+6) + 36$.

You could also do this question by algebraic long division — you just have to use your answer to work out A, B, C and D.

3 $\frac{2x^2 - 9x - 35}{x^2 - 49} = \frac{(2x+5)(x-7)}{(x+7)(x-7)} = \frac{2x+5}{x+7}$

   [3 marks available — 1 mark for factorising the numerator, 1 mark for factorising the denominator and 1 mark for correct answer (after cancelling)]

4 Add the partial fractions and equate the numerators:

   $5 + 9x \equiv A + B(1 + 3x)$ *[1 mark]*

   Using substitution method:

   substitute $x = -\frac{1}{3}$: $\ 2 = A \Rightarrow A = 2$ *[1 mark]*

   substitute $x = 0$: $\ 5 = 2 + B \Rightarrow B = 3$ *[1 mark]*

5 Expand the denominator:

   $\frac{18x^2 - 15x - 62}{(3x+4)(x-2)} \equiv \frac{18x^2 - 15x - 62}{3x^2 - 2x - 8}$

   Divide the fraction:

   $\begin{array}{r} 6 \\ 3x^2 - 2x - 8 \overline{)18x^2 - 15x - 62} \\ -\ \underline{18x^2 - 12x - 48} \\ -\ -3x - 14 \end{array}$

   Watch out for the negative signs here. You're subtracting the bottom line from the top, so be sure to get it right.

   You could use alternative methods — e.g. the remainder theorem for the division. You'll still get the marks, so use the one you're happiest with unless they tell you otherwise.

   $\frac{18x^2 - 15x - 62}{(3x+4)(x-2)} \equiv 6 + \frac{-3x - 14}{(3x+4)(x-2)}$

   $A = 6$ *[1 mark]*

   $\frac{-3x - 14}{(3x+4)(x-2)} \equiv \frac{B}{(3x+4)} + \frac{C}{(x-2)}$

   $-3x - 14 \equiv B(x-2) + C(3x+4)$ *[1 mark]*

   substitute $x = 2$: $\ -20 = 10C \Rightarrow C = -2$ *[1 mark]*

   coefficients of x: $\ -3 = B + 3C$

   $\qquad\qquad -3 = B - 6 \Rightarrow B = 3$ *[1 mark]*

   I used the equating coefficients method for the last bit, because I realised that I'd need to substitute $-\frac{4}{3}$ in for x, and I really couldn't be bothered.

6 a) When $t = 0$ (i.e. when the mink were introduced to the habitat) $M = 74 \times e^0 = 74$, so there were 74 mink originally *[1 mark]*.

   b) After 3 years, $M = 74 \times e^{0.6 \times 3}$ *[1 mark]* $= 447.6739...$ $= 447$ mink *[1 mark]*.

   You can't round up here as there are only 447 whole mink.

   c) For $M = 10\ 000$:

   $10\ 000 = 74e^{0.6t}$

   $\Rightarrow e^{0.6t} = 10\ 000 \div 74 = 135.1351$

   $\Rightarrow 0.6t = \ln 135.1351 = 4.9063$ *[1 mark]*

   $\Rightarrow t = 4.9063 \div 0.6 = 8.2$ years to reach 10 000, so it would take 9 complete years for the population to exceed 10 000 *[1 mark]*.

Answers

d)

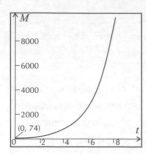

[2 marks available — 1 mark for correct shape of graph, 1 mark for (0, 74) as a point on the graph.]

7   Expand the denominator:

$$\frac{-80x^2 + 49x - 9}{(5x-1)(2-4x)} \equiv \frac{-80x^2 + 49x - 9}{-20x^2 + 14x - 2}$$

Divide the fraction:

$$-20x^2 + 14x - 2 \overline{) \begin{array}{l} 4 \\ -80x^2 + 49x - 9 \end{array}}$$
$$\underline{-80x^2 + 56x - 8}$$
$$-7x - 1$$

$$\frac{-80x^2 + 49x - 9}{(5x-1)(2-4x)} \equiv 4 + \frac{-7x - 1}{(5x-1)(2-4x)} \text{ } \textbf{[1 mark]}$$

$$\frac{-7x-1}{(5x-1)(2-4x)} \equiv \frac{A}{(5x-1)} + \frac{B}{(2-4x)}$$

$-7x - 1 \equiv A(2 - 4x) + B(5x - 1)$ **[1 mark]**

substitute $x = 0.5$: $-4.5 = 1.5B \Rightarrow B = -3$ **[1 mark]**

coefficients of x: $-7 = -4A + 5B$

substitute $B = -3$: $-7 = -4A - 15$

$ 8 = -4A \Rightarrow A = -2$ **[1 mark]**

8 a) Expand the denominator:

$$\frac{3x^2 + 12x - 11}{(x+3)(x-1)} \equiv \frac{3x^2 + 12x - 11}{x^2 + 2x - 3}$$

Divide the fraction:

$$x^2 + 2x - 3 \overline{) \begin{array}{l} 3 \\ 3x^2 + 12x - 11 \end{array}}$$
$$\underline{3x^2 + 6x - 9}$$
$$6x - 2 \Rightarrow -2 + 6x \text{ } \textbf{[1 mark]}$$

$$\frac{3x^2 + 12x - 11}{(x+3)(x-1)} \equiv 3 + \frac{-2 + 6x}{(x+3)(x-1)}$$

$A = 3$ **[1 mark]**, $B = -2$ **[1 mark]**, $C = 6$ **[1 mark]**

   b) $\frac{3x^2 + 12x - 11}{(x+3)(x-1)} \equiv 3 + \frac{-2 + 6x}{(x+3)(x-1)} \equiv 3 + \frac{M}{(x+3)} + \frac{N}{(x-1)}$

$-2 + 6x \equiv M(x - 1) + N(x + 3)$

substitute $x = 1$: $4 = 4N \Rightarrow N = 1$ **[1 mark]**

substitute $x = -3$: $-20 = -4M \Rightarrow M = 5$ **[1 mark]**

So overall $\frac{3x^2 + 12x - 11}{(x+3)(x-1)} \equiv 3 + \frac{5}{(x+3)} + \frac{1}{(x-1)}$ **[1 mark]**

9 a) B is the value of A when $t = 0$.
From the table, $B = 50$ **[1 mark]**.

   b) Substitute $t = 5$ and $A = 42$ into $A = 50e^{-kt}$:

$42 = 50e^{-5k} \Rightarrow e^{-5k} = \frac{42}{50} \Rightarrow e^{5k} = \frac{50}{42}$ **[1 mark]**

$\Rightarrow 5k = \ln\left(\frac{50}{42}\right) = 0.17435$

$\Rightarrow k = 0.17435 \div 5 = 0.0349$ to 3 s.f. **[1 mark]**.

c) $A = 50e^{-0.0349t}$ (using values from (a) and (b)),
so when $t = 10$, $A = 50 \times e^{-0.0349 \times 10}$ **[1 mark]**
$= 35$ to the nearest whole **[1 mark]**.

d) The half-life will be the value of t when A reaches half of the original value of 50, i.e. when $A = 25$.

$25 = 50e^{-0.0349t}$

$\Rightarrow \frac{25}{50} = e^{-0.0349t} \Rightarrow \frac{50}{25} = e^{0.0349t} \Rightarrow e^{0.0349t} = 2$ **[1 mark]**.

$0.0349t = \ln 2$ **[1 mark]**

$\Rightarrow t = \ln 2 \div 0.0349 = 20$ days to the nearest day **[1 mark]**.

C4 Section 2 — Trigonometry

Warm-up Questions

1) $\cos 2\theta \equiv \cos^2\theta - \sin^2\theta$
    $\cos 2\theta \equiv 2\cos^2\theta - 1$
    $\cos 2\theta \equiv 1 - 2\sin^2\theta$

2) $\sin 2\theta = -\sqrt{3}\sin\theta \Rightarrow \sin 2\theta + \sqrt{3}\sin\theta = 0$
    $2\sin\theta\cos\theta + \sqrt{3}\sin\theta = 0$
    $\sin\theta(2\cos\theta + \sqrt{3}) = 0$
    So either $\sin\theta = 0$, so $\theta = 0°$, $180°$, $360°$ or
    $2\cos\theta + \sqrt{3} = 0 \Rightarrow \cos\theta = -\frac{\sqrt{3}}{2}$
    so $\theta = 150°$ or $210°$. The set of values for θ is $0°$, $150°$, $180°$, $210°$, $360°$.

    If you don't know where the 180°, 360°, 210° etc. came from, you need to go back over your C2 notes...

3) $\frac{\pi}{12} = \frac{\pi}{3} - \frac{\pi}{4}$, so use the addition formula for $\cos(A - B)$:

    $\cos\frac{\pi}{12} = \cos\left(\frac{\pi}{3} - \frac{\pi}{4}\right) = \cos\frac{\pi}{3}\cos\frac{\pi}{4} + \sin\frac{\pi}{3}\sin\frac{\pi}{4}$

    As $\cos\frac{\pi}{3} = \frac{1}{2}$, $\cos\frac{\pi}{4} = \frac{1}{\sqrt{2}}$, $\sin\frac{\pi}{3} = \frac{\sqrt{3}}{2}$ and $\sin\frac{\pi}{4} = \frac{1}{\sqrt{2}}$, putting these values into the equation gives:

    $\cos\frac{\pi}{3}\cos\frac{\pi}{4} + \sin\frac{\pi}{3}\sin\frac{\pi}{4} = \left(\frac{1}{2} \cdot \frac{1}{\sqrt{2}}\right) + \left(\frac{\sqrt{3}}{2} \cdot \frac{1}{\sqrt{2}}\right)$

    $= \frac{1}{2\sqrt{2}} + \frac{\sqrt{3}}{2\sqrt{2}} = \frac{1 + \sqrt{3}}{2\sqrt{2}} = \frac{\sqrt{2}(1 + \sqrt{3})}{4} = \frac{\sqrt{2} + \sqrt{6}}{4}$

    You could also have used $\frac{\pi}{12} = \frac{\pi}{4} - \frac{\pi}{6}$ in your answer.

4) $\sin(A + B) \equiv \sin A \cos B + \cos A \sin B$.
    As $\sin A = \frac{4}{5}$, $\cos A = \frac{3}{5}$ (from the right-angled triangle with sides of length 3, 4 and 5) and as
    $\sin B = \frac{7}{25}$, $\cos B = \frac{24}{25}$ (from the right-angled triangle with sides of length 7, 24 and 25). Putting these values into the equation gives:

    $\sin A \cos B + \cos A \sin B = \left(\frac{4}{5} \cdot \frac{24}{25}\right) + \left(\frac{3}{5} \cdot \frac{7}{25}\right)$

    $= \frac{96}{125} + \frac{21}{125} = \frac{117}{125}$ $(= 0.936)$

5) $a\cos\theta + b\sin\theta \equiv R\cos(\theta - \alpha)$ or
    $b\sin\theta + a\cos\theta \equiv R\sin(\theta + \alpha)$

6) $5\sin\theta - 6\cos\theta \equiv R\sin(\theta - \alpha)$
    $ \equiv R\sin\theta\cos\alpha - R\cos\theta\sin\alpha$ (using the addition rule for sin).
    Equating coefficients of $\sin\theta$ and $\cos\theta$ gives:
    1. $R\cos\alpha = 5$ and 2. $R\sin\alpha = 6$.
    Dividing 2. by 1. to find α: $\frac{R\sin\alpha}{R\cos\alpha} = \tan\alpha$, so $\frac{6}{5} = \tan\alpha$

Solving this gives α = 50.19°.

To find R, square equations 1. and 2., then square root:

$R = \sqrt{5^2 + 6^2} = \sqrt{25 + 36} = \sqrt{61}$, so
$5\sin\theta - 6\cos\theta \equiv \sqrt{61}\sin(\theta - 50.19°)$.

7) Use the sin addition formulas:
$\sin(x + y) \equiv \sin x \cos y + \cos x \sin y$
$\sin(x - y) \equiv \sin x \cos y - \cos x \sin y$
Take the second away from the first:
$\sin(x + y) - \sin(x - y) \equiv 2\cos x \sin y$.
Let $A = x + y$ and $B = x - y$, so that $x = \frac{1}{2}(A + B)$ and
$y = \frac{1}{2}(A - B)$. Then
$\sin A - \sin B \equiv 2\cos\left(\frac{A + B}{2}\right)\sin\left(\frac{A - B}{2}\right)$.
Hint: to get the formulas for x and y in terms of A and B,
you need to treat A = x + y and B = x − y as a pair of
simultaneous equations.

8) Start by putting the LHS over a common denominator:
$\frac{\cos\theta}{\sin\theta} + \frac{\sin\theta}{\cos\theta} \equiv \frac{\cos\theta\cos\theta}{\sin\theta\cos\theta} + \frac{\sin\theta\sin\theta}{\sin\theta\cos\theta}$
$\equiv \frac{\cos^2\theta + \sin^2\theta}{\sin\theta\cos\theta} \equiv \frac{1}{\sin\theta\cos\theta}$
(using the identity $\sin^2\theta + \cos^2\theta \equiv 1$).
Now, $\sin 2\theta \equiv 2\sin\theta\cos\theta$, so $\sin\theta\cos\theta = \frac{1}{2}\sin 2\theta$.
So $\frac{1}{\sin\theta\cos\theta} \equiv \frac{1}{\frac{1}{2}\sin 2\theta} \equiv 2\operatorname{cosec} 2\theta$, which is the
same as the RHS.

Exam Questions

1 a) $9\sin\theta + 12\cos\theta \equiv R\sin(\theta + \alpha)$. Using the sin addition formula, $9\sin\theta + 12\cos\theta \equiv R\sin\theta\cos\alpha + R\cos\theta\sin\alpha$.
Equating coefficients of $\sin\theta$ and $\cos\theta$ gives:
$R\cos\alpha = 9$ and $R\sin\alpha = 12$ *[1 mark]*.
$\frac{R\sin\alpha}{R\cos\alpha} = \tan\alpha$, so $\tan\alpha = \frac{12}{9} = \frac{4}{3}$
Solving this gives $\alpha = 0.927$
[1 mark — no other solutions in given range].
$R = \sqrt{9^2 + 12^2} = \sqrt{81 + 144} = \sqrt{225} = 15$ *[1 mark]*,
so $9\sin\theta + 12\cos\theta = 15\sin(\theta + 0.927)$.

b) If $9\sin\theta + 12\cos\theta = 3$, then from part a),
$15\sin(\theta + 0.927) = 3$, so $\sin(\theta + 0.927) = 0.2$. The range for
θ is $0 \le \theta \le 2\pi$, which becomes $0.927 \le \theta + 0.927 \le 7.210$.
Solving the equation gives $(\theta + 0.927) = 0.201$ *[1 mark]*.
As this is outside the range, use a sketch to find values that
are in the range:

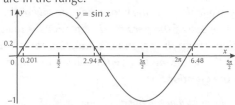

From the graph, it is clear that there are solutions at
$\pi - 0.201 = 2.94$ and at $2\pi + 0.201 = 6.48$, so
$(\theta + 0.927) = 2.940, 6.48$ *[1 mark for each value]*,
so $\theta = 2.01, 5.56$ *[1 mark for each solution]*.
Be careful with the range — if you hadn't extended the range
to 2π + 0.927, you would have missed one of the solutions.

2 $\sin 3x \equiv \sin(2x + x) \equiv \sin 2x \cos x + \cos 2x \sin x$ *[1 mark]*
$\equiv (2\sin x \cos x)\cos x + (1 - 2\sin^2 x)\sin x$ *[1 mark]*
$\equiv 2\sin x \cos^2 x + \sin x - 2\sin^3 x$
$\equiv 2\sin x(1 - \sin^2 x) + \sin x - 2\sin^3 x$ *[1 mark]*
$\equiv 2\sin x - 2\sin^3 x + \sin x - 2\sin^3 x$
$\equiv 3\sin x - 4\sin^3 x$ *[1 mark]*

3 a) $5\cos\theta + 12\sin\theta \equiv R\cos(\theta - \alpha)$. Using the cos addition
formula, $5\cos\theta + 12\sin\theta \equiv R\cos\theta\cos\alpha + R\sin\theta\sin\alpha$.
Equating coefficients gives:
$R\cos\alpha = 5$ and $R\sin\alpha = 12$ *[1 mark]*.
$\frac{R\sin\alpha}{R\cos\alpha} = \tan\alpha$, so $\tan\alpha = \frac{12}{5}$ *[1 mark]*.
Solving this gives $\alpha = 67.38°$ *[1 mark]*.
$R = \sqrt{5^2 + 12^2} = \sqrt{25 + 144} = \sqrt{169} = 13$ *[1 mark]*,
so $5\cos\theta + 12\sin\theta = 13\cos(\theta - 67.38°)$.

b) From part (a), if $5\cos\theta + 12\sin\theta = 2$, that means
$13\cos(\theta - 67.38°) = 2$, so $\cos(\theta - 67.38°) = \frac{2}{13}$
[1 mark]. The range for θ is $0 \le \theta \le 360°$, which becomes
$-67.38° \le \theta - 67.38° \le 292.62°$ *[1 mark]*. Solving the
equation gives $\theta - 67.38 = 81.15, 278.85$ *[1 mark]*,
so $\theta = 148.53°, 346.23°$ *[1 mark for each value]*.
Look at the cos graph to get the second solution of θ − 67.38°:

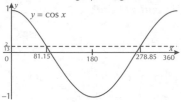

There are two solutions, one at 81.15°, and the other
at 360 − 81.15 = 278.85°.

c) The minimum points of the cos curve have a value of -1,
so as $5\cos\theta + 12\sin\theta = 13\cos(\theta - 67.38°)$, the minimum
value of $5\cos\theta + 12\sin\theta$ is -13 *[1 mark]*. Hence the
minimum value of $(5\cos\theta + 12\sin\theta)^3$ is $(-13)^3 = -2197$
[1 mark].

C4 Section 3
— Coordinate Geometry in the (x, y) Plane
Warm-up Questions

1) a) Substitute the values of t into the parametric equations to
find the corresponding values of x and y:
$t = 0 \Rightarrow x = \frac{6 - 0}{2} = 3, y = 2(0)^2 + 0 + 4 = 4$
$t = 1 \Rightarrow x = \frac{6 - 1}{2} = 2.5, y = 2(1)^2 + 1 + 4 = 7$
$t = 2 \Rightarrow x = \frac{6 - 2}{2} = 2, y = 2(2)^2 + 2 + 4 = 14$
$t = 3 \Rightarrow x = \frac{6 - 3}{2} = 1.5, y = 2(3)^2 + 3 + 4 = 25$

b) Use the given values in the parametric equations and solve
for t:
(i) $\frac{6 - t}{2} = -7 \Rightarrow t = 20$
(ii) $2t^2 + t + 4 = 19$
$\Rightarrow 2t^2 + t - 15 = 0$

Answers

$\Rightarrow (2t - 5)(t + 3) = 0$

$\Rightarrow t = 2.5, t = -3$

c) Rearrange the parametric equation for x to make t the subject:

$x = \frac{6 - t}{2} \Rightarrow 2x = 6 - t \Rightarrow t = 6 - 2x$

Now substitute this into the parametric equation for y:

$y = 2t^2 + t + 4$

$= 2(6 - 2x)^2 + (6 - 2x) + 4$

$= 2(36 - 24x + 4x^2) + 10 - 2x$

$y = 8x^2 - 50x + 82.$

2) a) Substitute the values of θ into the parametric equations to find the corresponding values of x and y:

(i) $x = 2\sin\frac{\pi}{4} = \frac{2}{\sqrt{2}} = \sqrt{2}$

$y = \cos^2\frac{\pi}{4} + 4 = \left(\cos\frac{\pi}{4}\right)^2 + 4 = \left(\frac{1}{\sqrt{2}}\right)^2 + 4 = \frac{1}{2} + 4 = \frac{9}{2}$

So the coordinates are $\left(\sqrt{2}, \frac{9}{2}\right)$.

(ii) $x = 2\sin\frac{\pi}{6} = 2 \times \frac{1}{2} = 1$

$y = \cos^2\frac{\pi}{6} + 4 = \left(\cos\frac{\pi}{6}\right)^2 + 4 = \left(\frac{\sqrt{3}}{2}\right)^2 + 4 = \frac{3}{4} + 4 = \frac{19}{4}$

So the coordinates are $\left(1, \frac{19}{4}\right)$.

b) Use the identity $\cos^2\theta = 1 - \sin^2\theta$ in the equation for y so both equations are in terms of $\sin\theta$:

$y = \cos^2\theta + 4$

$= 1 - \sin^2\theta + 4$

$= 5 - \sin^2\theta$

Rearrange the equation for x to get $\sin^2\theta$ in terms of x:

$x = 2\sin\theta \Rightarrow \frac{x}{2} = \sin\theta \Rightarrow \sin^2\theta = \frac{x^2}{4}$

So $y = 5 - \sin^2\theta \Rightarrow y = 5 - \frac{x^2}{4}$

c) $x = 2\sin\theta$, and $-1 \le \sin\theta \le 1$ so $-2 \le x \le 2$.

I know what you're thinking — this answer section would be brightened up immensely by a cheery song-and-dance number. Sorry, no such luck I'm afraid. Here's the next answer instead...

3) Use the identity $\cos2\theta = 1 - 2\sin^2\theta$ in the equation for y:

$y = 3 + 2\cos2\theta$

$= 3 + 2(1 - 2\sin^2\theta)$

$= 5 - 4\sin^2\theta$

Rearrange the equation for x to get $\sin^2\theta$ in terms of x:

$x = \frac{\sin\theta}{3} \Rightarrow 3x = \sin\theta \Rightarrow \sin^2\theta = 9x^2$

So $y = 5 - 4\sin^2\theta$

$\Rightarrow y = 5 - 4(9x^2)$

$\Rightarrow y = 5 - 36x^2$

4) a) On the y-axis:

$x = 0 \Rightarrow t^2 - 1 = 0 \Rightarrow t = \pm1$

If $t = 1$, $y = 4 + \frac{3}{1} = 7$

If $t = -1$, $y = 4 + \frac{3}{-1} = 1$

So the curve crosses the y-axis at $(0, 1)$ and $(0, 7)$.

b) Substitute the parametric equations into the equation of the line:

$x + 2y = 14$

$\Rightarrow (t^2 - 1) + 2(4 + \frac{3}{t}) = 14$

$\Rightarrow t^2 - 1 + 8 + \frac{6}{t} = 14$

$\Rightarrow t^2 - 7 + \frac{6}{t} = 0$

$\Rightarrow t^3 - 7t + 6 = 0$

$\Rightarrow (t - 1)(t^2 + t - 6) = 0$

$\Rightarrow (t - 1)(t - 2)(t + 3) = 0$

$\Rightarrow t = 1, t = 2, t = -3$

When $t = 1$, $x = 0$, $y = 7$ (from part (i))

When $t = 2$, $x = 2^2 - 1 = 3$, $y = 4 + \frac{3}{2} = 5.5$

When $t = -3$, $x = (-3)^2 - 1 = 8$, $y = 4 + \frac{3}{-3} = 3$

So the curve crosses the line $x + 2y = 14$ at $(0, 7)$, $(3, 5.5)$ and $(8, 3)$.

Exam Questions

1 a) Substitute the given value of θ into the parametric equations:

$\theta = \frac{\pi}{3} \Rightarrow x = 1 - \tan\frac{\pi}{3} = 1 - \sqrt{3}$

$y = \frac{1}{2}\sin\left(\frac{2\pi}{3}\right) = \frac{1}{2}\left(\frac{\sqrt{3}}{2}\right) = \frac{\sqrt{3}}{4}$

So $P = \left(1 - \sqrt{3}, \frac{\sqrt{3}}{4}\right)$

[2 marks available — 1 mark for substituting $\theta = \frac{\pi}{3}$ into the parametric equations, 1 mark for both coordinates of P correct.]

b) Use $y = -\frac{1}{2}$ to find the value of θ:

$-\frac{1}{2} = \frac{1}{2}\sin2\theta \Rightarrow \sin2\theta = -1$

$\Rightarrow 2\theta = -\frac{\pi}{2}$

$\Rightarrow \theta = -\frac{\pi}{4}$

You can also find θ using the parametric equation for x, with x = 2.

[2 marks available — 1 mark for substituting given x- or y-value into the correct parametric equation, 1 mark for finding the correct value of θ.]

c) $x = 1 - \tan\theta \Rightarrow \tan\theta = 1 - x$

$y = \frac{1}{2}\sin2\theta$

$= \frac{1}{2}\left(\frac{2\tan\theta}{1 + \tan^2\theta}\right)$

$= \frac{\tan\theta}{1 + \tan^2\theta}$

$= \frac{(1 - x)}{1 + (1 - x)^2}$

$= \frac{1 - x}{1 + 1 - 2x + x^2}$

$= \frac{1 - x}{x^2 - 2x + 2}$

[3 marks available — 1 mark for using the given identity to rearrange one of the parametric equations, 1 mark for eliminating θ from the parametric equation for y, 1 mark for correctly expanding to give the Cartesian equation given in the question.]

Just think, if you lived in the Bahamas, you could be doing this revision on the beach. (Please ignore that comment if you actually do live in the Bahamas. Or anywhere else where you can revise on the beach.)

2 a) Substitute $y = 1$ into the parametric equation for y:

$t^2 - 2t + 2 = 1$

$\Rightarrow t^2 - 2t + 1 = 0$

$\Rightarrow (t-1)^2 = 0$

$\Rightarrow t = 1$ *[1 mark]*

So a is the value of x when $t = 1$.

$a = t^3 + t = 1^3 + 1 = 2$ *[1 mark]*

b) Substitute the parametric equations for x and y into the equation of the line:

$8y = x + 6$

$\Rightarrow 8(t^2 - 2t + 2) = (t^3 + t) + 6$ *[1 mark]*

$\Rightarrow 8t^2 - 16t + 16 = t^3 + t + 6$

$\Rightarrow t^3 - 8t^2 + 17t - 10 = 0$

We know that this line passes through K, and from a) we know that $t = 1$ at K, so $t = 1$ is a solution of this equation, and $(t - 1)$ is a factor:

$\Rightarrow (t - 1)(t^2 - 7t + 10) = 0$ *[1 mark]*

$\Rightarrow (t - 1)(t - 2)(t - 5) = 0$

So $t = 2$ at L and $t = 5$ at M.   *[1 mark]*

If you got stuck on this bit, go back and look up 'factorising cubics' in your AS notes.

Substitute $t = 2$ and $t = 5$ back into the parametric equations: *[1 mark]*

If $t = 2$, then $x = 2^3 + 2 = 10$

and $y = 2^2 - 2(2) + 2 = 2$

If $t = 5$, then $x = 5^3 + 5 = 130$

and $y = 5^2 - 2(5) + 2 = 17$

So $L = (10, 2)$ *[1 mark]*

and $M = (130, 17)$ *[1 mark]*

3 a) Substitute $t = 0.5$ into the parametric equations for x and y:

$x = t^3 = 0.5^3 = 0.125$ *[1 mark]*

$y = t^2 - 4 = 0.5^2 - 4 = -3.75$ *[1 mark]*.

So the coordinates of F are $(0.125, -3.75)$.

b) First, put the parametric equations into the equation of the line and rearrange: $3(t^2 - 4) = 2(t^3) - 11$

$3t^2 - 12 = 2t^3 - 11 \Rightarrow 2t^3 - 3t^2 + 1 = 0$. *[1 mark]* Now solve for t: Putting $t = 1$ into the equation gives 0, so 1 is a root. This means that $(t - 1)$ is a factor *[1 mark]*.

$(t - 1)(2t^2 - t - 1) = 0 \Rightarrow (t - 1)(2t + 1)(t - 1) = 0$.

So $t = 1$ *[1 mark]* and $t = -\frac{1}{2}$ *[1 mark]* (ignore the repeated root). Putting these values of t back into the parametric equations gives the coordinates $(1, -3)$ *[1 mark]* and $(-0.125, -3.75)$ *[1 mark]*.

4 a) Use the x- or y-coordinate of H in the relevant parametric equation to find θ:

At H, $3 + 4\sin\theta = 5$

$\Rightarrow 4\sin\theta = 2$

$\Rightarrow \sin\theta = \frac{1}{2}$

$\Rightarrow \theta = \frac{\pi}{6}$

OR

At H, $\frac{1 + \cos 2\theta}{3} = \frac{1}{2}$

$\Rightarrow 1 + \cos 2\theta = \frac{3}{2}$

$\Rightarrow \cos 2\theta = \frac{1}{2}$

$\Rightarrow 2\theta = \frac{\pi}{3}$

$\Rightarrow \theta = \frac{\pi}{6}$

[2 marks available — 1 mark for substituting one coordinate of H into the correct parametric equation, 1 mark finding the correct value of θ.]

b) Rearrange the parametric equation for x to make $\sin\theta$ the subject:

$x = 3 + 4\sin\theta \Rightarrow \sin\theta = \frac{x - 3}{4}$ *[1 mark]*

Use the identity $\cos 2\theta = 1 - 2\sin^2\theta$ to rewrite the parametric equation for y in terms of $\sin\theta$:

$y = \frac{1 + \cos 2\theta}{3}$

$= \frac{1 + (1 - 2\sin^2\theta)}{3}$ *[1 mark]*

$= \frac{2 - 2\sin^2\theta}{3}$

$= \frac{2}{3}(1 - \sin^2\theta)$

$= \frac{2}{3}\left(1 - \left(\frac{x-3}{4}\right)^2\right)$ *[1 mark]*

$= \frac{2}{3}\left(1 - \frac{(x-3)^2}{16}\right)$

$= \frac{2}{3}\left(\frac{16 - (x^2 - 6x + 9)}{16}\right)$

$= \frac{2}{3}\left(\frac{-x^2 + 6x + 7}{16}\right)$

$= \frac{-x^2 + 6x + 7}{24}$ *[1 mark]*

c) $-\frac{\pi}{2} \leq \theta \leq \frac{\pi}{2} \Rightarrow -1 \leq \sin\theta \leq 1$ *[1 mark]*

$\Rightarrow -4 \leq 4\sin\theta \leq 4$

$\Rightarrow -1 \leq 3 + 4\sin\theta \leq 7$

$\Rightarrow -1 \leq x \leq 7$ *[1 mark]*

As Shakespeare* himself might have put it "That section was a ruddy pain in the backside, but at least it's finished."
*Arnold Shakespeare (1948–)

C4 Section 4 — Sequences and Series
Warm-up Questions

1) a) $(1 + 2x)^3 = 1 + 3(2x) + \frac{3 \times 2}{1 \times 2}(2x)^2 + \frac{3 \times 2 \times 1}{1 \times 2 \times 3}(2x)^3$

$= 1 + 6x + 12x^2 + 8x^3$

You could have used Pascal's Triangle to get the coefficients here. I've done it the long way because I like to show off.

b) $(1 - x)^4 = 1 + 4(-x) + \frac{4 \times 3}{1 \times 2}(-x)^2$

$+ \frac{4 \times 3 \times 2}{1 \times 2 \times 3}(-x)^3 + \frac{4 \times 3 \times 2 \times 1}{1 \times 2 \times 3 \times 4}(-x)^4$

$= 1 - 4x + 6x^2 - 4x^3 + x^4$

c) $(1 - 4x)^4 = 1 + 4(-4x) + \frac{4 \times 3}{1 \times 2}(-4x)^2$

$+ \frac{4 \times 3 \times 2}{1 \times 2 \times 3}(-4x)^3 + \frac{4 \times 3 \times 2 \times 1}{1 \times 2 \times 3 \times 4}(-4x)^4$

$= 1 - 16x + 96x^2 - 256x^3 + 256x^4$

Be extra careful with terms like (−4x)²... remember to square <u>everything</u> in the brackets — the x, the 4 <u>and</u> the minus.

2) Positive integer values (and zero).

3) a) $(1 + x)^{-4}$

$\approx 1 + (-4)x + \frac{-4 \times -5}{1 \times 2}x^2 + \frac{-4 \times -5 \times -6}{1 \times 2 \times 3}x^3$

$= 1 - 4x + 10x^2 - 20x^3$

Answers

b) $(1 - 3x)^{-3} \approx 1 + (-3)(-3x) + \frac{-3 \times -4}{1 \times 2}(-3x)^2$

$\qquad + \frac{-3 \times -4 \times -5}{1 \times 2 \times 3}(-3x)^3$

$\qquad = 1 + 9x + 54x^2 + 270x^3$

c) $(1 - 5x)^{\frac{1}{2}}$

$\approx 1 + \frac{1}{2}(-5x) + \frac{\frac{1}{2} \times -\frac{1}{2}}{1 \times 2}(-5x)^2 + \frac{\frac{1}{2} \times -\frac{1}{2} \times -\frac{3}{2}}{1 \times 2 \times 3}(-5x)^3$

$= 1 - \frac{5}{2}x - \frac{25}{8}x^2 - \frac{125}{16}x^3$

4) a) $\left|\frac{dx}{c}\right| < 1$ (or $|x| < |\frac{c}{d}|$)

b) 3) a): expansion valid for $|x| < 1$

3) b): expansion valid for $|-3x| < 1 \Rightarrow |-3||x| < 1 \Rightarrow |x| < \frac{1}{3}$

3) c): expansion valid for $|-5x| < 1 \Rightarrow |-5||x| < 1 \Rightarrow |x| < \frac{1}{5}$

5) a) $(3 + 2x)^{-2} = \left(3\left(1 + \frac{2}{3}x\right)\right)^{-2} = \frac{1}{9}\left(1 + \frac{2}{3}x\right)^{-2}$

$\approx \frac{1}{9}\left(1 + (-2)\left(\frac{2}{3}x\right) + \frac{-2 \times -3}{1 \times 2}\left(\frac{2}{3}x\right)^2\right)$

$= \frac{1}{9}\left(1 - \frac{4}{3}x + \frac{4}{3}x^2\right)$

$= \frac{1}{9} - \frac{4}{27}x + \frac{4}{27}x^2$

This expansion is valid for $\left|\frac{2x}{3}\right| < 1 \Rightarrow \frac{2}{3}|x| < 1 \Rightarrow |x| < \frac{3}{2}$.

b) $(8 - x)^{\frac{1}{3}} = \left(8\left(1 - \frac{1}{8}x\right)\right)^{\frac{1}{3}} = 2\left(1 - \frac{1}{8}x\right)^{\frac{1}{3}}$

$\approx 2\left(1 + \frac{1}{3}\left(-\frac{1}{8}x\right) + \frac{\frac{1}{3} \times -\frac{2}{3}}{1 \times 2}\left(-\frac{1}{8}x\right)^2\right)$

$= 2\left(1 - \frac{1}{24}x - \frac{1}{576}x^2\right)$

$= 2 - \frac{1}{12}x - \frac{1}{288}x^2$

This expansion is valid for $\left|\frac{-x}{8}\right| < 1 \Rightarrow \frac{|-1||x|}{8} < 1$
$\Rightarrow |x| < 8$.

Exam Questions

1 a) $f(x) = (9 - 4x)^{-\frac{1}{2}} = (9)^{-\frac{1}{2}}\left(1 - \frac{4}{9}x\right)^{-\frac{1}{2}} = \frac{1}{3}\left(1 - \frac{4}{9}x\right)^{-\frac{1}{2}}$

$= \frac{1}{3}\begin{bmatrix} 1 + \left(-\frac{1}{2}\right)\left(-\frac{4}{9}x\right) + \frac{\left(-\frac{1}{2}\right) \times \left(-\frac{3}{2}\right)}{1 \times 2}\left(-\frac{4}{9}x\right)^2 \\ + \frac{\left(-\frac{1}{2}\right) \times \left(-\frac{3}{2}\right) \times \left(-\frac{5}{2}\right)}{1 \times 2 \times 3}\left(-\frac{4}{9}x\right)^3 + ... \end{bmatrix}$

$= \frac{1}{3}\left(1 + \left(-\frac{1}{2}\right)\left(-\frac{4}{9}x\right) + \frac{\left(\frac{3}{4}\right)}{2}\left(-\frac{4}{9}x\right)^2 + \frac{\left(-\frac{15}{8}\right)}{6}\left(-\frac{4}{9}x\right)^3 + ...\right)$

$= \frac{1}{3}\left(1 + \left(-\frac{1}{2}\right)\left(-\frac{4}{9}x\right) + \frac{3}{8}\left(-\frac{4}{9}x\right)^2 + \left(-\frac{5}{16}\right)\left(-\frac{4}{9}x\right)^3 + ...\right)$

$= \frac{1}{3}\left(1 + \frac{2}{9}x + \frac{2}{27}x^2 + \frac{20}{729}x^3 + ...\right)$

$= \frac{1}{3} + \frac{2}{27}x + \frac{2}{81}x^2 + \frac{20}{2187}x^3 + ...$

[5 marks available in total:
• 1 mark for factorising out $(9)^{-\frac{1}{2}}$ or $\frac{1}{3}$
• 1 mark for expansion of an expression of the form
$(1 + ax)^{-\frac{1}{2}}$
• 2 marks for the penultimate line of working — 1 for the
first two terms in brackets correct, 1 for the 3rd and 4th
terms in brackets correct.
• 1 mark for the final answer correct]

Multiplying out those coefficients can be pretty tricky. Don't try
to do things all in one go — you won't be penalised for writing an
extra line of working, but you probably will lose marks if your final
answer's wrong.

b) $(2 - x)\left(\frac{1}{3} + \frac{2}{27}x + \frac{2}{81}x^2 + \frac{20}{2187}x^3 + ...\right)$

You only need the first three terms of the expansion, so just
write the terms up to x^2 when you multiply out the brackets:

$= \frac{2}{3} + \frac{4}{27}x + \frac{4}{81}x^2 + ...$

$\qquad - \frac{1}{3}x - \frac{2}{27}x^2 + ...$

$= \frac{2}{3} - \frac{5}{27}x - \frac{2}{81}x^2 + ...$

[4 marks available in total:
• 1 mark for multiplying your answer to part (a) by (2 – x)
• 1 mark for multiplying out brackets to find
constant term, two x-terms and two x²-terms.
• 1 mark for correct constant and x-terms in final answer
• 1 mark for correct x²-term in final answer]

2 a) $36x^2 + 3x - 10 \equiv A(1 - 3x)^2 + B(4 + 3x)(1 - 3x) + C(4 + 3x)$
[1 mark]
Let $x = \frac{1}{3}$, then $4 + 1 - 10 = 5C \Rightarrow -5 = 5C \Rightarrow C = -1$
[1 mark]
Let $x = -\frac{4}{3}$, then $64 - 4 - 10 = 25A \Rightarrow 50 = 25A \Rightarrow A = 2$
[1 mark]
Equate the terms in x^2:
$36 = 9A - 9B = 18 - 9B \Rightarrow -18 = 9B \Rightarrow B = -2$ *[1 mark]*

b) $f(x) = \frac{2}{(4 + 3x)} - \frac{2}{(1 - 3x)} - \frac{1}{(1 - 3x)^2}$

Expand each term separately:

$2(4 + 3x)^{-1} = 2\left(4\left(1 + \frac{3}{4}x\right)\right)^{-1} = \frac{1}{2}\left(1 + \frac{3}{4}x\right)^{-1}$

$= \frac{1}{2}\left(1 + (-1)\left(\frac{3}{4}x\right) + \frac{(-1) \times (-2)}{1 \times 2}\left(\frac{3}{4}x\right)^2 + ...\right)$

$= \frac{1}{2}\left(1 - \frac{3}{4}x + \frac{9}{16}x^2 + ...\right) = \frac{1}{2} - \frac{3}{8}x + \frac{9}{32}x^2 + ...$

Now the second term: $-2(1 - 3x)^{-1} =$

$-2\left(1 + (-1)(-3x) + \frac{(-1) \times (-2)}{1 \times 2}(-3x)^2 + ...\right)$

$= -2(1 + 3x + 9x^2 + ...) = -2 - 6x - 18x^2 + ...$

And the final term: $-(1 - 3x)^{-2} =$

$-\left(1 + (-2)(-3x) + \frac{(-2) \times (-3)}{1 \times 2}(-3x)^2 + ...\right)$

$= -(1 + 6x + 27x^2 + ...) = -1 - 6x - 27x^2 + ...$

Putting it all together gives

$\frac{1}{2} - \frac{3}{8}x + \frac{9}{32}x^2 - 2 - 6x - 18x^2 - 1 - 6x - 27x^2$

$= -\frac{5}{2} - \frac{99}{8}x - \frac{1431}{32}x^2 + ...$

[6 marks available in total:
• 1 mark for rewriting f(x) in the form
$A(4 + 3x)^{-1} + B(1 - 3x)^{-1} + C(1 - 3x)^{-2}$
• 1 mark for correct binomial expansion of $(4 + 3x)^{-1}$
• 1 mark for correct binomial expansion of $(1 - 3x)^{-1}$
• 1 mark for correct binomial expansion of $(1 - 3x)^{-2}$
• 1 mark for correct constant and x-terms in final answer
• 1 mark for correct x²-term in final answer]

You know what, I can't think of anything else remotely useful, witty or interesting to say about binomials... Seriously, I'm going to have to resort to slightly weird jokes in a minute... You've been warned...

c) Expansion of $(4 + 3x)^{-1}$ is valid for $\left|\frac{3x}{4}\right| < 1 \Rightarrow \frac{3|x|}{4} < 1$
$\Rightarrow |x| < \frac{4}{3}$

Expansions of $(1 - 3x)^{-1}$ and $(1 - 3x)^{-2}$ are valid for
$\left|\frac{-3x}{1}\right| < 1 \Rightarrow \frac{|-3\|x|}{1} < 1 \Rightarrow |x| < \frac{1}{3}$

The combined expansion is valid for the narrower of these two ranges. So the expansion of f(x) is valid for $|x| < \frac{1}{3}$.

[2 marks available in total:
• 1 mark for identifying the valid range of the expansion of f(x) as being the narrower of the two valid ranges shown
• 1 mark for correct answer]

3 a) $(16 + 3x)^{\frac{1}{4}} = 16^{\frac{1}{4}}\left(1 + \frac{3}{16}x\right)^{\frac{1}{4}} = 2\left(1 + \frac{3}{16}x\right)^{\frac{1}{4}}$
$\approx 2\left(1 + \left(\frac{1}{4}\right)\left(\frac{3}{16}x\right) + \frac{\frac{1}{4} \times -\frac{3}{4}}{1 \times 2}\left(\frac{3}{16}x\right)^2\right)$
$= 2\left(1 + \left(\frac{1}{4}\right)\left(\frac{3}{16}x\right) + \left(-\frac{3}{32}\right)\left(\frac{9}{256}x^2\right)\right)$
$= 2\left(1 + \frac{3}{64}x - \frac{27}{8192}x^2\right)$
$= 2 + \frac{3}{32}x - \frac{27}{4096}x^2$

[5 marks available in total:
• 1 mark for factorising out $16^{\frac{1}{4}}$ or 2
• 1 mark for expansion of an expression of the form $(1 + ax)^{\frac{1}{4}}$
• 2 marks for the penultimate line of working — 1 for the first two terms in brackets correct, 1 for the 3rd term in brackets correct.
• 1 mark for the final answer correct]

b) (i) $16 + 3x = 12.4 \Rightarrow x = -1.2$
So $(12.4)^{\frac{1}{4}} \approx 2 + \frac{3}{32}(-1.2) - \frac{27}{4096}(-1.2)^2$
$= 2 - 0.1125 - 0.0094921875$
$= 1.878008$ (to 6 d.p.)

[2 marks available in total:
• 1 mark for substituting x = -1.2 into the expansion from part (a)
• 1 mark for correct answer]

(ii) Percentage error
$= \left|\frac{\text{real value} - \text{estimate}}{\text{real value}}\right| \times 100$ *[1 mark]*
$= \left|\frac{\sqrt[4]{12.4} - 1.878008}{\sqrt[4]{12.4}}\right| \times 100$
$= \frac{|1.876529... - 1.878008|}{1.876529...} \times 100$
$= 0.0788\%$ (to 3 s.f.) *[1 mark]*

Why did the binomial expansion cross the road?
Don't be silly, binomial expansions can't move independently...
...can they?

4 a) $\left(1 - \frac{4}{3}x\right)^{-\frac{1}{2}}$
$\approx 1 + \left(-\frac{1}{2}\right)\left(-\frac{4}{3}x\right) + \frac{\left(-\frac{1}{2}\right) \times \left(-\frac{3}{2}\right)}{1 \times 2}\left(-\frac{4}{3}x\right)^2$
$\quad + \frac{\left(-\frac{1}{2}\right) \times \left(-\frac{3}{2}\right) \times \left(-\frac{5}{2}\right)}{1 \times 2 \times 3}\left(-\frac{4}{3}x\right)^3$
$= 1 + \left(-\frac{1}{2}\right)\left(-\frac{4}{3}x\right) + \frac{\left(\frac{3}{4}\right)}{2}\left(-\frac{4}{3}x\right)^2 + \frac{\left(-\frac{15}{8}\right)}{6}\left(-\frac{4}{3}x\right)^3$
$= 1 + \left(-\frac{1}{2}\right)\left(-\frac{4}{3}x\right) + \frac{3}{8}\left(\frac{16}{9}x^2\right) + \left(-\frac{15}{48}\right)\left(-\frac{64}{27}x^3\right)$
$= 1 + \frac{2}{3}x + \frac{2}{3}x^2 + \frac{20}{27}x^3$

[4 marks available in total:
• 1 mark for writing out binomial expansion formula with $n = -\frac{1}{2}$
• 1 mark for writing out binomial expansion formula substituting $-\frac{4}{3}x$ for x
• 1 mark for correct constant and x-terms in final answer
• 1 mark for correct x^2- and x^3-terms in final answer]

b) $\sqrt{\frac{27}{(3 - 4x)}} = \sqrt{\frac{27}{3\left(1 - \frac{4}{3}x\right)}} = \sqrt{\frac{9}{\left(1 - \frac{4}{3}x\right)}} = \frac{3}{\sqrt{\left(1 - \frac{4}{3}x\right)}}$
$= 3\left(1 - \frac{4}{3}x\right)^{-\frac{1}{2}}$
$\approx 3\left(1 + \frac{2}{3}x + \frac{2}{3}x^2\right)$
$= 3 + 2x + 2x^2$

So $a = 3$, $b = 2$, $c = 2$.

Expansion is valid for $\left|-\frac{4}{3}x\right| < 1 \Rightarrow \left|-\frac{4}{3}\right\|x| < 1 \Rightarrow |x| < \frac{3}{4}$

[3 marks available in total:
• 1 mark for showing expression is equal to $3\left(1 - \frac{4}{3}x\right)^{-\frac{1}{2}}$
• 1 mark for using expansion from part (b) to find the correct values of a, b and c.
• 1 mark for correct valid range]

Doctor, doctor, I keep thinking I'm a binomial expansion...
I'm sorry, I don't think I can help you, I'm a cardiologist.

5 a) (i) $\sqrt{\frac{1 + 2x}{1 - 3x}} = \frac{\sqrt{1 + 2x}}{\sqrt{1 - 3x}} = (1 + 2x)^{\frac{1}{2}}(1 - 3x)^{-\frac{1}{2}}$ *[1 mark]*
$(1 + 2x)^{\frac{1}{2}} \approx 1 + \frac{1}{2}(2x) + \frac{\left(\frac{1}{2}\right) \times \left(-\frac{1}{2}\right)}{1 \times 2}(2x)^2$
$= 1 + x - \frac{1}{2}x^2$ *[1 mark]*

$(1 - 3x)^{-\frac{1}{2}} \approx 1 + \left(-\frac{1}{2}\right)(-3x) + \frac{\left(-\frac{1}{2}\right) \times \left(-\frac{3}{2}\right)}{1 \times 2}(-3x)^2$
$= 1 + \frac{3}{2}x + \frac{27}{8}x^2$ *[1 mark]*

$\sqrt{\frac{1 + 2x}{1 - 3x}} \approx \left(1 + x - \frac{1}{2}x^2\right)\left(1 + \frac{3}{2}x + \frac{27}{8}x^2\right)$ *[1 mark]*
$\approx 1 + \frac{3}{2}x + \frac{27}{8}x^2 + x + \frac{3}{2}x^2 - \frac{1}{2}x^2$
(ignoring any terms in x^3 or above)
$= 1 + \frac{5}{2}x + \frac{35}{8}x^2$ *[1 mark]*

(ii) Expansion of $(1 + 2x)^{\frac{1}{2}}$ is valid for $|2x| < 1 \Rightarrow |x| < \frac{1}{2}$
Expansion of $(1 - 3x)^{-\frac{1}{2}}$ is valid for $|-3x| < 1$
$\Rightarrow |-3\|x| < 1 \Rightarrow |x| < \frac{1}{3}$
The combined expansion is valid for the narrower of these two ranges.

Answers

So the expansion of $\sqrt{\dfrac{1+2x}{1-3x}}$ is valid for $|x| < \dfrac{1}{3}$.

[2 marks available in total:
• 1 mark for identifying the valid range of the
expansion as being the narrower of the two valid
ranges shown
• 1 mark for correct answer]

b) $x = \dfrac{2}{15} \Rightarrow \sqrt{\dfrac{1+2x}{1-3x}} = \sqrt{\dfrac{1+\frac{4}{15}}{1-\frac{6}{15}}} = \sqrt{\dfrac{\frac{19}{15}}{\frac{9}{15}}} = \sqrt{\dfrac{19}{9}} = \dfrac{1}{3}\sqrt{19}$

[1 mark]

$\Rightarrow \sqrt{19} \approx 3\left(1 + \dfrac{5}{2}\left(\dfrac{2}{15}\right) + \dfrac{35}{8}\left(\dfrac{2}{15}\right)^2\right)$

$= 3\left(1 + \dfrac{1}{3} + \dfrac{7}{90}\right)$

$= 3\left(\dfrac{127}{90}\right)$

$= \dfrac{127}{30}$ *[1 mark]*

The binomial expansion walks into a bar and asks for a pint.
The barman says, "I'm sorry, I can't serve alcohol in a joke that may
be read by under-18s."

6 a) $13x - 17 \equiv A(2x - 1) + B(5 - 3x)$ *[1 mark]*

Let $x = \dfrac{1}{2}$, then $\dfrac{13}{2} - 17 = B(5 - \dfrac{3}{2}) \Rightarrow -\dfrac{21}{2} = \dfrac{7}{2}B \Rightarrow B = -3$

[1 mark]

Let $x = \dfrac{5}{3}$, then $\dfrac{65}{3} - 17 = A(\dfrac{10}{3} - 1) \Rightarrow \dfrac{14}{3} = \dfrac{7}{3}A \Rightarrow A = 2$

[1 mark]

b) (i) $(2x - 1)^{-1} = -(1 - 2x)^{-1}$ *[1 mark]*

$\approx -\left(1 + (-1)(-2x) + \dfrac{(-1)\times(-2)}{1\times 2}(-2x)^2\right)$

$= -(1 + 2x + 4x^2)$

$= -1 - 2x - 4x^2$ *[1 mark]*

(ii) $(5 - 3x)^{-1} = 5^{-1}\left(1 - \dfrac{3}{5}x\right)^{-1} = \dfrac{1}{5}\left(1 - \dfrac{3}{5}x\right)^{-1}$

$\approx \dfrac{1}{5}\left(1 + (-1)\left(-\dfrac{3}{5}x\right) + \dfrac{(-1)\times(-2)}{1\times 2}\left(-\dfrac{3}{5}x\right)^2\right)$

$= \dfrac{1}{5}\left(1 + \dfrac{3}{5}x + \dfrac{9}{25}x^2\right)$

$= \dfrac{1}{5} + \dfrac{3}{25}x + \dfrac{9}{125}x^2$

[5 marks available in total:
• 1 mark for factorising out 5^{-1} or $\dfrac{1}{5}$
• 1 mark for expansion of an expression of the form
$(1 + ax)^{-1}$
• 2 marks for the penultimate line of working —
1 mark for the first two terms in brackets correct,
1 mark for the 3rd term in brackets correct.
• 1 mark for the final answer correct]

c) $\dfrac{13x - 17}{(5 - 3x)(2x - 1)} = \dfrac{2}{(5 - 3x)} - \dfrac{3}{(2x - 1)}$

$= 2(5 - 3x)^{-1} - 3(2x - 1)^{-1}$ *[1 mark]*

$\approx 2\left(\dfrac{1}{5} + \dfrac{3}{25}x + \dfrac{9}{125}x^2\right) - 3(-1 - 2x - 4x^2)$

$= \dfrac{2}{5} + \dfrac{6}{25}x + \dfrac{18}{125}x^2 + 3 + 6x + 12x^2$

$= \dfrac{17}{5} + \dfrac{156}{25}x + \dfrac{1518}{125}x^2$

[1 mark]

C4 Section 5 — Differentiation and Integration

Warm-up Questions

1) a) $\dfrac{dx}{dt} = 2t$, $\dfrac{dy}{dt} = 9t^2 - 4$, so $\dfrac{dy}{dx} = \dfrac{dy}{dt} \div \dfrac{dx}{dt} = \dfrac{9t^2 - 4}{2t}$

b) The stationary points are when $\dfrac{9t^2 - 4}{2t} = 0$

$\Rightarrow 9t^2 = 4 \Rightarrow t = \pm\dfrac{2}{3}$

$t = \dfrac{2}{3} \Rightarrow x = \left(\dfrac{2}{3}\right)^2 = \dfrac{4}{9}$, $y = 3\left(\dfrac{2}{3}\right)^3 - 4\left(\dfrac{2}{3}\right) = \dfrac{8}{9} - \dfrac{8}{3} = -\dfrac{16}{9}$

$t = -\dfrac{2}{3} \Rightarrow x = \left(-\dfrac{2}{3}\right)^2 = \dfrac{4}{9}$,

$y = 3\left(-\dfrac{2}{3}\right)^3 - 4\left(-\dfrac{2}{3}\right) = -\dfrac{8}{9} + \dfrac{8}{3} = \dfrac{16}{9}$

So the stationary points are $\left(\dfrac{4}{9}, -\dfrac{16}{9}\right)$ and $\left(\dfrac{4}{9}, \dfrac{16}{9}\right)$.

2) a) Differentiate each term separately with respect to x:

$\dfrac{d}{dx}4x^2 - \dfrac{d}{dx}2y^2 = \dfrac{d}{dx}7x^2y$

Differentiate $4x^2$ first:

$\Rightarrow 8x - \dfrac{d}{dx}2y^2 = \dfrac{d}{dx}7x^2y$

Differentiate $2y^2$ using chain rule:

$\Rightarrow 8x - \dfrac{d}{dy}2y^2\dfrac{dy}{dx} = \dfrac{d}{dx}7x^2y$

$\Rightarrow 8x - 4y\dfrac{dy}{dx} = \dfrac{d}{dx}7x^2y$

Differentiate $7x^2y$ using product rule:

$\Rightarrow 8x - 4y\dfrac{dy}{dx} = 7x^2\dfrac{d}{dx}y + y\dfrac{d}{dx}7x^2$

$\Rightarrow 8x - 4y\dfrac{dy}{dx} = 7x^2\dfrac{dy}{dx} + 14xy$

Rearrange to make $\dfrac{dy}{dx}$ the subject:

$\Rightarrow (4y + 7x^2)\dfrac{dy}{dx} = 8x - 14xy$

$\Rightarrow \dfrac{dy}{dx} = \dfrac{8x - 14xy}{4y + 7x^2}$

For implicit differentiation questions, you need to know what you're
doing with the chain rule and product rule. If you're struggling to
keep up with what's going on here, go back to C3 and refresh your
memory.

b) Differentiate each term separately with respect to x:

$\dfrac{d}{dx}3x^4 - \dfrac{d}{dx}2xy^2 = \dfrac{d}{dx}y$

Differentiate $3x^4$ first:

$\Rightarrow 12x^3 - \dfrac{d}{dx}2xy^2 = \dfrac{dy}{dx}$

Differentiate $2xy^2$ using product rule:

$\Rightarrow 12x^3 - \left(y^2\dfrac{d}{dx}2x + 2x\dfrac{d}{dy}y^2\dfrac{dy}{dx}\right) = \dfrac{dy}{dx}$

$\Rightarrow 12x^3 - 2y^2 - 4xy\dfrac{dy}{dx} = \dfrac{dy}{dx}$

Rearrange to make $\dfrac{dy}{dx}$ the subject:

$\Rightarrow (1 + 4xy)\dfrac{dy}{dx} = 12x^3 - 2y^2$

$\Rightarrow \dfrac{dy}{dx} = \dfrac{12x^3 - 2y^2}{1 + 4xy}$

c) Use the product rule to differentiate each term separately with respect to x:

$\dfrac{d}{dx}\cos x\sin y = \dfrac{d}{dx}xy$

Answers

$\Rightarrow \cos x \frac{\mathrm{d}}{\mathrm{d}x}(\sin y) + \sin y \frac{\mathrm{d}}{\mathrm{d}x}(\cos x) = x\frac{\mathrm{d}}{\mathrm{d}x}y + y\frac{\mathrm{d}}{\mathrm{d}x}x$

Use the chain rule on $\frac{\mathrm{d}}{\mathrm{d}x}(\sin y)$:

$\Rightarrow \cos x \frac{\mathrm{d}}{\mathrm{d}y}(\sin y)\frac{\mathrm{d}y}{\mathrm{d}x} + \sin y \frac{\mathrm{d}}{\mathrm{d}x}(\cos x) = x\frac{\mathrm{d}}{\mathrm{d}x}y + y\frac{\mathrm{d}}{\mathrm{d}x}x$

$\Rightarrow (\cos x \cos y)\frac{\mathrm{d}y}{\mathrm{d}x} - \sin y \sin x = x\frac{\mathrm{d}y}{\mathrm{d}x} + y$

Rearrange to make $\frac{\mathrm{d}y}{\mathrm{d}x}$ the subject:

$\Rightarrow (\cos x \cos y - x)\frac{\mathrm{d}y}{\mathrm{d}x} = y + \sin x \sin y$

$\Rightarrow \frac{\mathrm{d}y}{\mathrm{d}x} = \frac{\sin x \sin y + y}{\cos x \cos y - x}$

Make sure you learn how to differentiate trig functions — if they pop up in the exam you need to be able to do them. And even if they don't, that sort of skill will make you a hit at parties. Trust me.

3) a) At $(1, -4)$, $\frac{\mathrm{d}y}{\mathrm{d}x} = \frac{8x - 14xy}{4y + 7x^2}$

$= \frac{8(1) - 14(1)(-4)}{4(-4) + 7(1)^2} = \frac{8 + 56}{-16 + 7} = -\frac{64}{9}$

b) At $(1, 1)$, $\frac{\mathrm{d}y}{\mathrm{d}x} = \frac{12x^3 - 2y^2}{1 + 4xy}$

$= \frac{12(1)^3 - 2(1)^2}{1 + 4(1)^2(1)} = \frac{12 - 2}{1 + 4} = \frac{10}{5} = 2$

So the gradient of the normal is $-\frac{1}{2}$.

4) Use the double angle formula for $\tan 2x$ to write

$\frac{2\tan 3x}{1 - \tan^2 3x}$ as $\tan 6x$. The integral becomes

$\int \tan 6x\,\mathrm{d}x = \int \frac{\sin 6x}{\cos 6x}\,\mathrm{d}x = -\frac{1}{6}\ln|\cos 6x| + C$.

Don't forget to double the coefficient of x when you use the double angle formula.

5) From the identity $\sec^2 x \equiv 1 + \tan^2 x$, write $2\tan^2 3x$ as $2\sec^2 3x - 2$. The integral becomes:

$\int 2\sec^2 3x - 2 + 2\,\mathrm{d}x$

$= \int 2\sec^2 3x\,\mathrm{d}x = \frac{2}{3}\tan 3x + C$.

6) First, find the partial fractions: If

$\frac{3x + 10}{(2x + 3)(x - 4)} \equiv \frac{A}{2x + 3} + \frac{B}{x - 4}$,

then $3x + 10 \equiv A(x - 4) + B(2x + 3)$.

From this, you get the simultaneous equations $3 = A + 2B$ and $10 = -4A + 3B$. Solving these gives $A = -1$ and $B = 2$:

$\frac{3x + 10}{(2x + 3)(x - 4)} = \frac{-1}{2x + 3} + \frac{2}{x - 4}$.

Now putting this into the integral gives:

$\int \frac{-1}{2x + 3} + \frac{2}{x - 4}\,\mathrm{d}x = -\frac{1}{2}\ln|2x + 3| + 2\ln|x - 4| + C$

7) $\frac{\mathrm{d}y}{\mathrm{d}x} = \frac{1}{y}\cos x \Rightarrow y\,\mathrm{d}y = \cos x\,\mathrm{d}x$

so $\int y\,\mathrm{d}y = \int \cos x\,\mathrm{d}x \Rightarrow \frac{y^2}{2} = \sin x + C_0$

$\Rightarrow y^2 = 2\sin x + C_1$ (where $C_1 = 2C_0$)

8) a) $\frac{\mathrm{d}S}{\mathrm{d}t} = kS$

b) Solving the differential equation above gives:

$\frac{\mathrm{d}S}{\mathrm{d}t} = kS \Rightarrow \int \frac{1}{S}\,\mathrm{d}S = \int k\,\mathrm{d}t$

$\ln|S| = kt + C$

$S = Ae^{kt}$ where $A = e^c$

For the initial population, $t = 0$. Put $S = 30$ and $t = 0$ into the equation to find the value of A: $30 = Ae^0 \Rightarrow A = 30$.

Now, use $S = 150$, $k = 0.2$ and $A = 30$ to find t:

$150 = 30e^{0.2t} \Rightarrow 5 = e^{0.2t} \Rightarrow \ln 5 = 0.2t$, so $t = 8.047$.

It will take the squirrels 8 weeks before they can take over the forest.

Go squirrels go!

Exam Questions

1 a) Start by differentiating x and y with respect to θ:

$\frac{\mathrm{d}y}{\mathrm{d}\theta} = 2\cos\theta$ **[1 mark]**

$\frac{\mathrm{d}x}{\mathrm{d}\theta} = 3 + 3\sin 3\theta$ **[1 mark]**

$\frac{\mathrm{d}y}{\mathrm{d}x} = \frac{\mathrm{d}y}{\mathrm{d}\theta} \div \frac{\mathrm{d}x}{\mathrm{d}\theta} = \frac{2\cos\theta}{3 + 3\sin 3\theta}$ **[1 mark]**

b) (i) We need the value of θ at $(\pi + 1, \sqrt{3})$:

$y = 2\sin\theta = \sqrt{3}$, for $-\pi \le \theta \le \pi \Rightarrow \theta = \frac{\pi}{3}$ or $\frac{2\pi}{3}$
[1 mark]

If $\theta = \frac{\pi}{3}$, then $x = 3\theta - \cos 3\theta = \pi - \cos\pi = \pi + 1$.

If $\theta = \frac{2\pi}{3}$, then $x = 3\theta - \cos 3\theta = 2\pi - \cos 2\pi = 2\pi - 1$.

So at $(\pi + 1, \sqrt{3})$, $\theta = \frac{\pi}{3}$ **[1 mark]**

$\theta = \frac{\pi}{3} \Rightarrow \frac{\mathrm{d}y}{\mathrm{d}x} = \frac{2\cos\frac{\pi}{3}}{3 + 3\sin\pi} = \frac{2\left(\frac{1}{2}\right)}{3 + 0} = \frac{1}{3}$ **[1 mark]**

(ii) $\theta = \frac{\pi}{6} \Rightarrow x = \frac{\pi}{2} - \cos\frac{\pi}{2} = \frac{\pi}{2} - 0 = \frac{\pi}{2}$

$\theta = \frac{\pi}{6} \Rightarrow y = 2\sin\frac{\pi}{6} = 2 \times \frac{1}{2} = 1$

So $\theta = \frac{\pi}{6}$ at the point $(\frac{\pi}{2}, 1)$ **[1 mark]**

$\theta = \frac{\pi}{6} \Rightarrow \frac{\mathrm{d}y}{\mathrm{d}x} = \frac{2\cos\frac{\pi}{6}}{3 + 3\sin\frac{\pi}{2}} = \frac{2\left(\frac{\sqrt{3}}{2}\right)}{3 + 3(1)} = \frac{\sqrt{3}}{6}$ **[1 mark]**

Gradient of normal $= -\frac{1}{\left(\frac{\mathrm{d}y}{\mathrm{d}x}\right)} = -\frac{6}{\sqrt{3}} = -\frac{6\sqrt{3}}{3}$

$= -2\sqrt{3}$ **[1 mark]**

So the normal is $y = -2\sqrt{3}x + c$ for some c.

$\Rightarrow 1 = -2\sqrt{3} \times \frac{\pi}{2} + c = -\pi\sqrt{3} + c$

$\Rightarrow c = 1 + \pi\sqrt{3}$

The equation of the normal is $y = -2\sqrt{3}x + 1 + \pi\sqrt{3}$
[1 mark]

2 Use the identity $\mathrm{cosec}^2 x \equiv 1 + \cot^2 x$ to write $2\cot^2 x$ as $2\,\mathrm{cosec}^2 x - 2$ **[1 mark]**. The integral becomes:

$\int 2\,\mathrm{cosec}^2 x - 2\,\mathrm{d}x = -2\cot x - 2x + C$
[1 mark for −2cot x, 1 mark for −2x + C].

3 a) c is the value of y when $x = 2$. If $x = 2$, then

$6x^2y - 7 = 5x - 4y^2 - x^2 \Rightarrow 6(2)^2y - 7 = 5(2) - 4y^2 - (2)^2$

$\Rightarrow 24y - 7 = 6 - 4y^2$

$\Rightarrow 4y^2 + 24y - 13 = 0$

$\Rightarrow (2y + 13)(2y - 1) = 0$

$\Rightarrow y = -6.5$ or $y = 0.5$ **[1 mark]**

$c > 0$, so $c = 0.5$ **[1 mark]**

Answers

b) (i) Q is another point on C where $y = 0.5$.
   If $y = 0.5$, then $6x^2y - 7 = 5x - 4y^2 - x^2$
   $\Rightarrow 6x^2(0.5) - 7 = 5x - 4(0.5)^2 - x^2$ *[1 mark]*
   $\Rightarrow 3x^2 - 7 = 5x - 1 - x^2$
   $\Rightarrow 4x^2 - 5x - 6 = 0$
   $\Rightarrow (x - 2)(4x + 3)$
   $\Rightarrow x = 2$ or $x = -0.75$
   $x \neq 2$, as $x = 2$ at the other point where T crosses C.
   So the coordinates of Q are $(-0.75, 0.5)$. *[1 mark]*

(ii) To find the gradient of C, use implicit differentiation.
   Differentiate each term separately with respect to x:
   $\frac{d}{dx}6x^2y - \frac{d}{dx}7 = \frac{d}{dx}5x - \frac{d}{dx}4y^2 - \frac{d}{dx}x^2$ *[1 mark]*
   Differentiate x-terms and constant terms:
   $\Rightarrow \frac{d}{dx}6x^2y - 0 = 5 - \frac{d}{dx}4y^2 - 2x$ *[1 mark]*
   Differentiate y-terms using chain rule:
   $\Rightarrow \frac{d}{dx}6x^2y = 5 - \frac{d}{dy}4y^2\frac{dy}{dx} - 2x$
   $\Rightarrow \frac{d}{dx}6x^2y = 5 - 8y\frac{dy}{dx} - 2x$ *[1 mark]*
   Differentiate xy-terms using product rule:
   $\Rightarrow 6x^2\frac{dy}{dx} + y\frac{d}{dx}6x^2 = 5 - 8y\frac{dy}{dx} - 2x$
   $\Rightarrow 6x^2\frac{dy}{dx} + 12xy = 5 - 8y\frac{dy}{dx} - 2x$ *[1 mark]*
   Rearrange to make $\frac{dy}{dx}$ the subject:
   $\Rightarrow 6x^2\frac{dy}{dx} + 8y\frac{dy}{dx} = 5 - 2x - 12xy$
   $\Rightarrow \frac{dy}{dx} = \frac{5 - 2x - 12xy}{6x^2 + 8y}$ *[1 mark]*
   So at $Q = (-0.75, 0.5)$,
   $\frac{dy}{dx} = \frac{5 - 2\left(-\frac{3}{4}\right) - 12\left(-\frac{3}{4}\right)\left(\frac{1}{2}\right)}{6\left(-\frac{3}{4}\right)^2 + 8\left(\frac{1}{2}\right)} = \frac{5 + \frac{3}{2} + \frac{9}{2}}{\frac{27}{8} + 4}$
   $= \frac{11}{\left(\frac{59}{8}\right)} = 11 \times \frac{8}{59} = \frac{88}{59}$ *[1 mark]*

4 a) $\frac{dy}{dx} = \frac{\cos x \cos^2 y}{\sin x} \Rightarrow \frac{1}{\cos^2 y}dy = \frac{\cos x}{\sin x}dx$
   $\Rightarrow \int \sec^2 y \, dy = \int \frac{\cos x}{\sin x}dx$
   $\Rightarrow \tan y = \ln|\sin x| + C$
   [4 marks available — 1 mark for separating the variables into functions of x and y, 1 mark for correct integration of RHS, 1 mark for correct integration of LHS, 1 mark for general solution]

b) If $y = \pi$ when $x = \frac{\pi}{6}$, that means that
   $\tan \pi = \ln|\sin\frac{\pi}{6}| + C$
   $0 = \ln|\frac{1}{2}| + C$ *[1 mark]*
   As $\ln \frac{1}{2} = \ln 1 - \ln 2 = -\ln 2$ (as $\ln 1 = 0$), it follows that $C = \ln 2$.
   So $\tan y = \ln|\sin x| + \ln 2$ or $\tan y = \ln |2 \sin x|$ *[1 mark]*.
   This is the particular solution — you found the general solution in part a).

5 a) (i) Using implicit differentiation:
   $3e^x + 6y = 2x^2y \Rightarrow \frac{d}{dx}3e^x + \frac{d}{dx}6y = \frac{d}{dx}2x^2y$ *[1 mark]*

$\Rightarrow 3e^x + 6\frac{dy}{dx} = 2x^2\frac{dy}{dx} + y\frac{d}{dx}2x^2$
$\Rightarrow 3e^x + 6\frac{dy}{dx} = 2x^2\frac{dy}{dx} + 4xy$ *[1 mark]*
$\Rightarrow 2x^2\frac{dy}{dx} - 6\frac{dy}{dx} = 3e^x - 4xy$
$\Rightarrow \frac{dy}{dx} = \frac{3e^x - 4xy}{2x^2 - 6}$ *[1 mark]*

(ii) At the stationary points of C, $\frac{dy}{dx} = 0$
$\Rightarrow \frac{3e^x - 4xy}{2x^2 - 6} = 0$ *[1 mark]*
$\Rightarrow 3e^x - 4xy = 0$
$\Rightarrow y = \frac{3e^x}{4x}$ *[1 mark]*

b) Substitute $y = \frac{3e^x}{4x}$ into the original equation of curve C:
$3e^x + 6y = 2x^2y \Rightarrow 3e^x + 6\frac{3e^x}{4x} = 2x^2\frac{3e^x}{4x}$ *[1 mark]*
$\Rightarrow 3e^x(1 + \frac{3}{2x} - \frac{x}{2}) = 0$
$3e^x = 0$ has no solutions, so $(1 + \frac{3}{2x} - \frac{x}{2}) = 0$ *[1 mark]*
$\Rightarrow x^2 - 2x - 3 = 0$
$\Rightarrow (x + 1)(x - 3) = 0$
$\Rightarrow x = -1$ or $x = 3$
$x = -1 \Rightarrow y = \frac{3e^{-1}}{4(-1)} = -\frac{3}{4e}$
$x = 3 \Rightarrow y = \frac{3e^3}{4(3)} = \frac{1}{4}e^3$
So the stationary points of C are $(-1, -\frac{3}{4e})$ and $(3, \frac{1}{4}e^3)$
[2 marks — 1 mark for each correct pair of coordinates]
Don't forget — if the question asks you for an exact answer, that usually means leaving it in terms of something like π or $\ln$ or, in this case, e.

6 a) $\frac{dm}{dt} = k\sqrt{m}$, $k > 0$ *[1 mark for RHS, 1 mark for LHS]*
b) First solve the differential equation to find m:
   $\frac{dm}{dt} = k\sqrt{m} \Rightarrow \frac{1}{\sqrt{m}}dm = k \, dt$
   $\Rightarrow \int m^{-\frac{1}{2}} dm = \int k \, dt$ *[1 mark]*
   $\Rightarrow 2m^{\frac{1}{2}} = kt + C$
   $\Rightarrow m = \left(\frac{1}{2}(kt + C)\right)^2 = \frac{1}{4}(kt + C)^2$ *[1 mark]*
   At the start of the campaign, $t = 0$. Putting $t = 0$ and $m = 900$ into the equation gives: $900 = \frac{1}{4}(0 + C)^2 \Rightarrow 3600 = C^2 \Rightarrow C = 60$ (C must be positive, otherwise the sales would be decreasing). *[1 mark]*. This gives the equation $m = \frac{1}{4}(kt + 60)^2$ *[1 mark]*.
c) Substituting $t = 5$ and $k = 2$ into the equation gives:
   $m = \frac{1}{4}((2 \times 5) + 60)^2 = 1225$ tubs sold.
   [3 marks available — 2 marks for substituting correct values of t and k, 1 mark for answer]

Answers

C4 Section 6 — Vectors

Warm-up Questions

1) Any multiples of the vectors will do:

   a) e.g. **a** and 4**a**

   b) e.g. 6**i** + 8**j** – 4**k** and 9**i** + 12**j** – 6**k**

   c) e.g. $\begin{pmatrix} 2 \\ 4 \\ -2 \end{pmatrix}$ and $\begin{pmatrix} 4 \\ 8 \\ -4 \end{pmatrix}$

2) a) **b** – **a** b) **a** – **b** c) **b** – **c** d) **c** – **a**

3) 2**i** – 4**j** + 5**k**

4) a) $\sqrt{3^2 + 4^2 + (-2)^2} = \sqrt{29}$

   b) $\sqrt{1^2 + 2^2 + (-1)^2} = \sqrt{6}$

5) a) $\sqrt{(3-1)^2 + (-1-2)^2 + (-2-3)^2} = \sqrt{38}$

   b) $\sqrt{1^2 + 2^2 + 3^2} = \sqrt{14}$

   c) $\sqrt{3^2 + (-1)^2 + (-2)^2} = \sqrt{14}$

6) a) **r** = (4**i** + **j** + 2**k**) + t(3**i** + **j** – **k**) or **r** = $\begin{pmatrix} 4 \\ 1 \\ 2 \end{pmatrix}$ + t$\begin{pmatrix} 3 \\ 1 \\ -1 \end{pmatrix}$

   b) **r** = (2**i** – **j** + **k**) + t((2**j** + 3**k**) – (2**i** – **j** + **k**))
   $\Rightarrow$ **r** = (2**i** – **j** + **k**) + t(–2**i** + 3**j** + 2**k**)

   or **r** = $\begin{pmatrix} 2 \\ -1 \\ 1 \end{pmatrix}$ + t$\begin{pmatrix} -2 \\ 3 \\ 2 \end{pmatrix}$

7) E.g. If t = 1, ((3 + 1(–1)), (2 + 1(3)), (4 + 1(0))) = (2, 5, 4)

   If t = 2, ((3 + 2(–1)), (2 + 2(3)), (4 + 2(0))) = (1, 8, 4)

   If t = –1, ((3 + –1(–1)), (2 + –1(3)), (4 + –1(0))) = (4, –1, 4)

8) a) (3**i** + 4**j**).(**i** – 2**j** + 3**k**) = 3 – 8 + 0 = –5

   b) $\begin{pmatrix} 4 \\ 2 \\ 1 \end{pmatrix} \cdot \begin{pmatrix} 3 \\ -4 \\ -3 \end{pmatrix}$ = (4 × 3) + (2 × –4) + (1 × –3) = 1

9) a) $\begin{pmatrix} 2 \\ -1 \\ 2 \end{pmatrix} + t\begin{pmatrix} -4 \\ 6 \\ -2 \end{pmatrix} = \begin{pmatrix} 3 \\ 2 \\ 4 \end{pmatrix} + u\begin{pmatrix} -1 \\ 3 \\ 0 \end{pmatrix}$

   Where the lines intersect, these 3 equations are true:

   2 – 4t = 3 – u

   –1 + 6t = 2 + 3u

   2 – 2t = 4

   Solve the third equation to give t = –1.
   Substituting t = –1 in either of the other equations gives u = –3.
   Substituting t = –1 and u = –3 in the remaining equation gives a true result, so the lines intersect.
   Substituting t = –1 in the first vector equation gives the position vector of the intersection point:

   $\begin{pmatrix} 6 \\ -7 \\ 4 \end{pmatrix}$

   You'll often have to solve a pair of equations simultaneously (both variables will usually be in all three equations).

b) To find the angle between the lines, only consider the direction components of the vector equations:

$\begin{pmatrix} -4 \\ 6 \\ -2 \end{pmatrix} \cdot \begin{pmatrix} -1 \\ 3 \\ 0 \end{pmatrix}$ = 4 + 18 + 0 = 22

magnitude of 1st vector: $\sqrt{(-4)^2 + 6^2 + (-2)^2} = \sqrt{56}$

magnitude of 2nd vector: $\sqrt{(-1)^2 + 3^2 + (0)^2} = \sqrt{10}$

$\cos\theta = \frac{22}{\sqrt{56}\sqrt{10}} = \Rightarrow \theta = 21.6°$

10) Find values for a, b and c that give a scalar product of 0 when the two vectors are multiplied together.

   (3**i** + 4**j** – 2**k**).(a**i** + b**j** + c**k**) = 3a + 4b – 2c = 0

   E.g. a = 2, b = 1, c = 5

   Perpendicular vector = (2**i** + **j** + 5**k**)

   Just pick values for a and b, then see what value of c is needed to make the scalar product zero.

Exam Questions

1 a) $\overrightarrow{AB} = \mathbf{b} - \mathbf{a} = \begin{pmatrix} 3 \\ 2 \\ 1 \end{pmatrix} - \begin{pmatrix} 1 \\ 5 \\ 9 \end{pmatrix} = \begin{pmatrix} 2 \\ -3 \\ -8 \end{pmatrix}$

   [2 marks available — 1 mark for attempting to subtract position vector a from position vector b, 1 mark for correct answer.]

   b) $l_1: \mathbf{r} = \mathbf{c} + \mu(\mathbf{d} - \mathbf{c}) = \begin{pmatrix} -2 \\ 4 \\ 3 \end{pmatrix} + \mu\left(\begin{pmatrix} 5 \\ -1 \\ -7 \end{pmatrix} - \begin{pmatrix} -2 \\ 4 \\ 3 \end{pmatrix}\right)$ *[1 mark]*

   $\mathbf{r} = \begin{pmatrix} -2 \\ 4 \\ 3 \end{pmatrix} + \mu\begin{pmatrix} 7 \\ -5 \\ -10 \end{pmatrix}$ *[1 mark]*

   c) Equation of line through AB:

   $\overrightarrow{AB}: \mathbf{r} = \mathbf{a} + t(\mathbf{b} - \mathbf{a}) = \begin{pmatrix} 1 \\ 5 \\ 9 \end{pmatrix} + t\begin{pmatrix} 2 \\ -3 \\ -8 \end{pmatrix}$ *[1 mark]*

   At intersection of lines:

   $\begin{pmatrix} 1 \\ 5 \\ 9 \end{pmatrix} + t\begin{pmatrix} 2 \\ -3 \\ -8 \end{pmatrix} = \begin{pmatrix} -2 \\ 4 \\ 3 \end{pmatrix} + \mu\begin{pmatrix} 7 \\ -5 \\ -10 \end{pmatrix}$ *[1 mark]*

   Any two of: $1 + 2t = -2 + 7\mu$

   $5 - 3t = 4 - 5\mu$

   $9 - 8t = 3 - 10\mu$ *[1 mark]*

   Solving any two equations simultaneously gives

   t = 2 or μ = 1 *[1 mark]*

   Substituting t = 2 in the equation of the line through AB (or μ = 1 in the equation for l_1) gives: (5, –1, –7) *[1 mark]*

   d) i) Vectors needed: $\begin{pmatrix} 2 \\ -3 \\ -8 \end{pmatrix}$ and $\begin{pmatrix} 7 \\ -5 \\ -10 \end{pmatrix}$ (direction vector of l_1).

   $\begin{pmatrix} 2 \\ -3 \\ -8 \end{pmatrix} \cdot \begin{pmatrix} 7 \\ -5 \\ -10 \end{pmatrix}$ = 14 + 15 + 80 = 109 *[1 mark]*

Answers

magnitude of 1st vector: $\sqrt{2^2 + (-3)^2 + (-8)^2} = \sqrt{77}$

magnitude of 2nd vector:

$\sqrt{7^2 + (-5)^2 + (-10)^2} = \sqrt{174}$ *[1 mark]*

$\cos\theta = \dfrac{109}{\sqrt{77}\sqrt{174}}$ *[1 mark]*

$\Rightarrow \theta = 19.7°$ *[1 mark]*

ii) Draw a diagram:

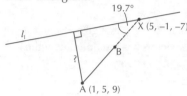

[1 mark for showing that the shortest distance is perpendicular to l_1]

X is the intersection point found in part c)

— (5, −1, −7)

Distance from A to X =

$\sqrt{(5-1)^2 + (-1-5)^2 + (-7-9)^2} = \sqrt{308}$

[1 mark]

Now you've got a right-angled triangle, so just use trig to find the side you want:

Shortest distance from A to l_1

$= \sqrt{308} \times \sin 19.7° $ *[1 mark]* $= 5.9$ units *[1 mark]*

The tricky thing here is figuring out how to go about it. Drawing a diagram definitely helps you see what you know and what you need to work out. Often, you'll be meant to use something you worked out in a previous part of the question.

2   a)

$-3\begin{pmatrix}1\\-4\\2\end{pmatrix} = \begin{pmatrix}-3\\12\\-6\end{pmatrix}$ *[1 mark]*

b) **i** component: $3 + (\mu \times 1) = 2$ gives $\mu = -1$ *[1 mark]*

$\mathbf{r} = \begin{pmatrix}3\\-3\\-2\end{pmatrix} - 1\begin{pmatrix}1\\-4\\2\end{pmatrix} = \begin{pmatrix}2\\1\\-4\end{pmatrix}$ *[1 mark]*

This is the position vector of the point A(2, 1, −4)

c) B lies on l_2 so it has position vector

$\mathbf{b} = \begin{pmatrix}10\\-21\\11\end{pmatrix} + \lambda\begin{pmatrix}-3\\12\\-6\end{pmatrix}$ *[1 mark]*

So $\overrightarrow{AB} = \mathbf{b} - \mathbf{a}$

$= \begin{pmatrix}10\\-21\\11\end{pmatrix} + \lambda\begin{pmatrix}-3\\12\\-6\end{pmatrix} - \begin{pmatrix}2\\1\\-4\end{pmatrix}$

$= \begin{pmatrix}8-3\lambda\\-22+12\lambda\\15-6\lambda\end{pmatrix}$ *[1 mark]*

You know the scalar product of the direction vector of l_1 and $\overrightarrow{AB}$ must equal zero as they're perpendicular:

$\begin{pmatrix}1\\-4\\2\end{pmatrix} \cdot \begin{pmatrix}8-3\lambda\\-22+12\lambda\\15-6\lambda\end{pmatrix}$ *[1 mark]*

$= (8 - 3\lambda) + (88 - 48\lambda) + (30 - 12\lambda)$

$= 126 - 63\lambda = 0$

$\Rightarrow \lambda = 2$ *[1 mark]*

Substitute in $\lambda = 2$ to find the position vector **b**:

$\mathbf{b} = \begin{pmatrix}10\\-21\\11\end{pmatrix} + 2\begin{pmatrix}-3\\12\\-6\end{pmatrix}$ *[1 mark]*

$= \begin{pmatrix}4\\3\\-1\end{pmatrix}$

Position vector of B $= \begin{pmatrix}4\\3\\-1\end{pmatrix}$ *[1 mark]*

You could have multiplied $\overrightarrow{AB}$ by the direction bit of the l_2 vector equation, as $\overrightarrow{AB}$ is perpendicular to both l_1 and l_2. But the numbers for the l_1 vector are smaller, making your calculations easier.

d) $\overrightarrow{AB} = \mathbf{b} - \mathbf{a}$

$= \begin{pmatrix}4\\3\\-1\end{pmatrix} - \begin{pmatrix}2\\1\\-4\end{pmatrix} = \begin{pmatrix}2\\2\\3\end{pmatrix}$ *[1 mark]*

$|\overrightarrow{AB}| = \sqrt{2^2 + 2^2 + 3^2} = \sqrt{17} = 4.1$ *[1 mark]*

3   a) At an intersection point: $\begin{pmatrix}3\\0\\-2\end{pmatrix} + \lambda\begin{pmatrix}1\\3\\-2\end{pmatrix} = \begin{pmatrix}0\\2\\1\end{pmatrix} + \mu\begin{pmatrix}2\\-5\\-3\end{pmatrix}$

[1 mark]

This gives equations: $3 + \lambda = 2\mu$

$3\lambda = 2 - 5\mu$

$-2 - 2\lambda = 1 - 3\mu$ *[1 mark]*

Solving the first two equations simultaneously gives:

$\lambda = -1, \mu = 1$ *[1 mark]*

Substituting these values in the third equation gives:

$-2 - 2(-1) = 1 - 3(1) \Rightarrow 0 \neq -2$ *[1 mark]*

So the lines don't intersect.

You could have solved any two of the equations simultaneously, then substituted the results in the remaining equation to show that they don't work and there's no intersection point.

b) (i) At the intersection point of PQ and l_1:

$\begin{pmatrix}3\\0\\-2\end{pmatrix} + \lambda\begin{pmatrix}1\\3\\-2\end{pmatrix} = \begin{pmatrix}5\\4\\-9\end{pmatrix} + t\begin{pmatrix}0\\2\\3\end{pmatrix}$ *[1 mark]*

This gives equations: $3 + \lambda = 5$

$3\lambda = 4 + 2t$

$-2 - 2\lambda = -9 + 3t$

[1 mark for any two equations]

Solving two of these equations gives: $\lambda = 2, t = 1$

[1 mark]

Intersection point $= \begin{pmatrix}5\\4\\-9\end{pmatrix} + 1\begin{pmatrix}0\\2\\3\end{pmatrix} = \begin{pmatrix}5\\6\\-6\end{pmatrix} = (5, 6, -6)$

[1 mark]

(ii) If perpendicular, the scalar product of direction vectors of lines will equal 0:

Answers

$$\begin{pmatrix} 0 \\ 2 \\ 3 \end{pmatrix} \cdot \begin{pmatrix} 1 \\ 3 \\ -2 \end{pmatrix} \; \textbf{[1 mark]}$$

$$= (0 \times 1) + (2 \times 3) + (3 \times -2) = 0 \; \textbf{[1 mark]}$$

(iii) Call intersection point X.

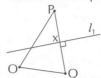

$$\vec{PX} = \mathbf{x} - \mathbf{p}$$

$$= \begin{pmatrix} 5 \\ 6 \\ -6 \end{pmatrix} - \begin{pmatrix} 5 \\ 8 \\ -3 \end{pmatrix} = \begin{pmatrix} 0 \\ -2 \\ -3 \end{pmatrix} \; \textbf{[1 mark]}$$

$$\vec{OQ} = \vec{OP} + 2\vec{PX} = \begin{pmatrix} 5 \\ 8 \\ -3 \end{pmatrix} + 2\begin{pmatrix} 0 \\ -2 \\ -3 \end{pmatrix} \; \textbf{[1 mark]}$$

$$= \begin{pmatrix} 5 \\ 4 \\ -9 \end{pmatrix} \; \textbf{[1 mark]}$$

The trick with this one is to realise that point Q lies the same distance from the intersection point as P does — drawing a quick sketch will definitely help.

4 a) $(\vec{OA}).(\vec{OB})$ *[1 mark]*

$$= \begin{pmatrix} 3 \\ 2 \\ 1 \end{pmatrix} \cdot \begin{pmatrix} 3 \\ -4 \\ -1 \end{pmatrix} = 9 - 8 - 1 = 0 \; \textbf{[1 mark]}$$

Therefore, side OA is perpendicular to side OB, and the triangle has a right angle. *[1 mark]*

You could also have found the lengths |OA|, |OB| and |AB| and shown by Pythagoras that AOB is a right-angled triangle (|AB|² = |OA|² + |OB|²).

b) $\vec{BA} = \mathbf{a} - \mathbf{b}$

$$= \begin{pmatrix} 3 \\ 2 \\ 1 \end{pmatrix} - \begin{pmatrix} 3 \\ -4 \\ -1 \end{pmatrix} = \begin{pmatrix} 0 \\ 6 \\ 2 \end{pmatrix} \; \textbf{[1 mark]}$$

$$\vec{BO} = \begin{pmatrix} -3 \\ 4 \\ 1 \end{pmatrix}$$

$$\vec{BA}.\vec{BO} = 24 + 2 = 26 \; \textbf{[1 mark]}$$

$$|\vec{BA}| = \sqrt{6^2 + 2^2} = \sqrt{40}$$

$$|\vec{BO}| = \sqrt{(-3)^2 + 4^2 + 1^2} = \sqrt{26} \; \textbf{[1 mark]}$$

$$\cos \angle ABO = \frac{\vec{BA} \cdot \vec{BO}}{|\vec{BA}| \cdot |\vec{BO}|} = \frac{26}{\sqrt{40}\sqrt{26}} \; \textbf{[1 mark]}$$

$$\angle ABO = 36.3° \; \textbf{[1 mark]}$$

c) (i) $\vec{AC} = \mathbf{c} - \mathbf{a}$

$$= \begin{pmatrix} 3 \\ -1 \\ 0 \end{pmatrix} - \begin{pmatrix} 3 \\ 2 \\ 1 \end{pmatrix} = \begin{pmatrix} 0 \\ -3 \\ -1 \end{pmatrix} \; \textbf{[1 mark]}$$

$$|\vec{AC}| = \sqrt{(-3)^2 + (-1)^2} = \sqrt{10}$$

$$|\vec{OC}| = \sqrt{3^2 + (-1)^2} = \sqrt{10} \; \textbf{[1 mark]}$$

Sides AC and OC are the same length, so the triangle is isosceles. *[1 mark]*

(ii) You know side lengths AC and OC from part c)(i). Calculate length of OA:

$$|\vec{OA}| = \sqrt{3^2 + 2^2 + 1^2} = \sqrt{14} \; \textbf{[1 mark]}$$

Now find the height of the triangle, x, using Pythagoras:

$$x = \sqrt{(\sqrt{10})^2 - \left(\frac{\sqrt{14}}{2}\right)^2} = \sqrt{6.5} \; \textbf{[1 mark]}$$

Area $= \frac{1}{2}(\text{base} \times \text{height})$
$= \frac{1}{2}(\sqrt{14} \times \sqrt{6.5})$ *[1 mark]*
$= 4.77$ square units *[1 mark]*

d) (i) $\mathbf{r} = \mathbf{a} + t(\mathbf{b} - \mathbf{a})$

$$= \begin{pmatrix} 3 \\ 2 \\ 1 \end{pmatrix} + t\left(\begin{pmatrix} 3 \\ -4 \\ -1 \end{pmatrix} - \begin{pmatrix} 3 \\ 2 \\ 1 \end{pmatrix}\right) \; \textbf{[1 mark]}$$

$$= \begin{pmatrix} 3 \\ 2 \\ 1 \end{pmatrix} + t\begin{pmatrix} 0 \\ -6 \\ -2 \end{pmatrix} \; \textbf{[1 mark]}$$

(ii) **k** component: $1 - 2t = 1$, $t = 0$ *[1 mark]*

$$\begin{pmatrix} 3 \\ 2 \\ 1 \end{pmatrix} + 0\begin{pmatrix} 0 \\ 6 \\ 2 \end{pmatrix} = \begin{pmatrix} 3 \\ 2 \\ 1 \end{pmatrix}$$

$a = 3$ *[1 mark]*, $b = 2$ *[1 mark]*

C4 Practice Exam One

1 a) $\dfrac{(x^2 - 9)(3x^2 - 10x - 8)}{(6x + 4)(x^2 - 7x + 12)} = \dfrac{(x + 3)(x - 3)(3x + 2)(x - 4)}{2(3x + 2)(x - 3)(x - 4)}$
$= \dfrac{x + 3}{2}$

[2 marks available — 1 mark for correctly factorising numerator __or__ denominator, 1 mark for correct final answer]

b)
$$\begin{array}{r} 2x + 5 \quad\quad r\, x + 8 \\ x^2 - 3x - 1 \overline{)2x^3 - x^2 - 16x + 3} \\ \underline{-\;2x^3 - 6x^2 - 2x} \\ 5x^2 - 14x + 3 \\ \underline{-\;5x^2 - 15x - 5} \\ x + 8 \end{array}$$

so the quotient is $(2x + 5)$ and the remainder is $(x + 8)$.

[4 marks available — up to 2 marks for correct working, 1 mark for quotient and 1 mark for remainder]

If you'd tried to use the remainder theorem formula for this question, you'd have found it a bit tricky as the divisor doesn't factorise easily. Instead, you'd need to equate coefficients of x^3, x^2 and x, as well as putting in $x = 0$.

2 a) $0.1 = Ak^0 \Rightarrow A = 0.1$ *[1 mark]*.

b) $t = 2010 - 1955 = 55$. So $95 = 0.1k^{55}$ *[1 mark]*.
$\Rightarrow \ln 950 = 55\ln k$
$\Rightarrow \dfrac{\ln 950}{55} = \ln k \Rightarrow \exp\left(\dfrac{\ln 950}{55}\right) = k$ *[1 mark]*
So $k = 1.132767$ (6 d.p.) *[1 mark]*.

You could have solved this one like this:
$950 = k^{55} \Rightarrow k = 950^{\frac{1}{55}} = 1.132....$

Answers

c) Using the values of A and k from above,
$150 = 0.1(1.1326766)^t$ *[1 mark]*
$\Rightarrow \ln 1500 = t\ln 1.132766$
$\Rightarrow \dfrac{\ln 1500}{\ln 1.132766} = t$, so $t = 58.664...$ *[1 mark]*
$1955 + 58 = 2013$, so the comic will be worth
$150 in 2013 *[1 mark]*.

3 a) $\dfrac{1 + \cos x}{2} = \dfrac{1}{2}\left(1 + \cos 2\left(\dfrac{x}{2}\right)\right)$ *[1 mark]*
$= \dfrac{1}{2}\left(1 + \left(2\cos^2 \dfrac{x}{2} - 1\right)\right)$ *[1 mark]*
$= \dfrac{1}{2}\left(2\cos^2 \dfrac{x}{2}\right) = \cos^2 \dfrac{x}{2}$ *[1 mark]*

b) As $\cos^2 \dfrac{x}{2} = 0.75$, then $\dfrac{1 + \cos x}{2} = 0.75$.
So $1 + \cos x = 1.5$
$\cos x = 0.5 \Rightarrow x = \dfrac{\pi}{3}, \dfrac{5\pi}{3}$.
[4 marks available — 2 marks for rearranging equation
to get in terms of cos x, 1 mark for each correct answer]

4 a) (i) $\dfrac{dx}{d\theta} = \dfrac{\cos\theta}{2}$, $\dfrac{dy}{d\theta} = 2\sin 2\theta$ *[1 mark]*
So $\dfrac{dy}{dx} = \dfrac{dy}{d\theta} \times \dfrac{d\theta}{dx} = \dfrac{dy}{d\theta} \div \dfrac{dx}{d\theta}$ *[1 mark]*
$= 2\sin 2\theta \div \dfrac{\cos\theta}{2} = \dfrac{4\sin 2\theta}{\cos\theta}$ *[1 mark]*

(ii) $\theta = \dfrac{\pi}{6} \Rightarrow \dfrac{dy}{dx} = \dfrac{4\sin(\frac{\pi}{3})}{\cos(\frac{\pi}{6})} = \dfrac{4\left(\frac{\sqrt{3}}{2}\right)}{\left(\frac{\sqrt{3}}{2}\right)} = 4$ *[1 mark]*
$x = \dfrac{1}{2}\sin\dfrac{\pi}{6} - 3 = \dfrac{1}{2} \times \dfrac{1}{2} - 3 = \dfrac{1}{4} - 3 = -\dfrac{11}{4}$
$y = 5 - \cos\dfrac{\pi}{3} = 5 - \dfrac{1}{2} = \dfrac{9}{2}$
[1 mark for x and y values both correct]
So $y = mx + c$
$\Rightarrow \dfrac{9}{2} = 4 \times -\dfrac{11}{4} + c = -11 + c$
$\Rightarrow c = 11 + \dfrac{9}{2} = \dfrac{31}{2}$
The equation of the tangent when $\theta = \dfrac{\pi}{6}$ is $y = 4x + \dfrac{31}{2}$
[1 mark]

b) Rewrite the equation for y using the identity
$\cos 2\theta \equiv 1 - 2\sin^2\theta$:
$y = 5 - \cos 2\theta = 5 - (1 - 2\sin^2\theta) = 4 + 2\sin^2\theta$ *[1 mark]*
Now rearrange the equation for x to make $\sin\theta$ the subject:
$x = \dfrac{\sin\theta}{2} - 3 \Rightarrow 2x + 6 = \sin\theta$ *[1 mark]*
Sub this into the equation for y:
$y = 4 + 2\sin^2\theta = 4 + 2(2x + 6)^2$
$\Rightarrow y = 4 + 2(4x^2 + 24x + 36)$
$\Rightarrow y = 8x^2 + 48x + 76$ *[1 mark]*

5 a) $5x + 4 \equiv A(1 + 3x) + B(2 - x)$ *[1 mark]*
let $x = 2$: $14 = 7A$ *[1 mark]* $\Rightarrow A = 2$ *[1 mark]*.
Equating coefficients of x: $5 = 3A - B$ *[1 mark]* $\Rightarrow B = 1$
[1 mark].

b) As $\dfrac{5x + 4}{(2 - x)(1 + 3x)} \equiv \dfrac{2}{(2 - x)} + \dfrac{1}{(1 + 3x)}$,
you want the binomial expansion of $\dfrac{2}{(2 - x)} + \dfrac{1}{(1 + 3x)}$
This can be written as $2(2 - x)^{-1} + (1 + 3x)^{-1}$.

Taking each term in turn,
$2(2 - x)^{-1} = 2\left(2\left(1 - \dfrac{1}{2}x\right)\right)^{-1} = 2\left(\dfrac{1}{2}\left(1 - \dfrac{1}{2}x\right)^{-1}\right)$
$= \left(1 - \dfrac{1}{2}x\right)^{-1}$
$= 1 + (-1)\left(-\dfrac{1}{2}x\right) + \dfrac{(-1)(-2)}{1 \times 2}\left(-\dfrac{1}{2}x\right)^2$
$\quad + \dfrac{(-1)(-2)(-3)}{1 \times 2 \times 3}\left(-\dfrac{1}{2}x\right)^3$
$= 1 + \dfrac{1}{2}x + \dfrac{1}{4}x^2 + \dfrac{1}{8}x^3$
and $(1 + 3x)^{-1} =$
$1 + (-1)(3x) + \dfrac{(-1)(-2)}{1 \times 2}(3x)^2 + \dfrac{(-1)(-2)(-3)}{1 \times 2 \times 3}(3x)^3$
$= 1 - 3x + 9x^2 - 27x^3$
So $2(2 - x)^{-1} + (1 + 3x)^{-1} = 1 + \dfrac{1}{2}x + \dfrac{1}{4}x^2 + \dfrac{1}{8}x^3 + 1 - 3x +$
$9x^2 - 27x^3 = 2 - \dfrac{5}{2}x + \dfrac{37}{4}x^2 - \dfrac{215}{8}x^3$.

[6 marks available in total:
• 1 mark for rewriting f(x) in partial fractions
• 1 mark for correct binomial expansion of (2 – x)⁻¹
• 1 mark for correct binomial expansion of (1 + 3x)⁻¹
• 1 mark for correct constant and x-terms in final answer
• 1 mark for correct x²-term in final answer
• 1 mark for correct x³-term in final answer]

c) Expansion of $(1 + 3x)^{-1}$ is valid for $\left|\dfrac{3x}{1}\right| < 1 \Rightarrow \dfrac{3|x|}{1} < 1$
$\Rightarrow |x| < \dfrac{1}{3}$
Expansion of $(2 - x)^{-1}$ is valid for $\left|\dfrac{-x}{2}\right| < 1 \Rightarrow \dfrac{|-1||x|}{2} < 1$
$\Rightarrow |x| < 2$
The combined expansion is valid for the narrower of these
two ranges. So the expansion in part b) is valid for $|x| < \dfrac{1}{3}$.
[2 marks available in total:
• 1 mark for identifying the valid range
of one of the expansions.
• 1 mark for correct answer]

6 a) Differentiate each term with respect to x:
$x^3 + x^2y = y^2 - 1$
$\Rightarrow \dfrac{d}{dx}x^3 + \dfrac{d}{dx}x^2y = \dfrac{d}{dx}y^2 - \dfrac{d}{dx}1$
Differentiate x^3 and 1 first:
$\Rightarrow 3x^2 + \dfrac{d}{dx}x^2y = \dfrac{d}{dx}y^2 - 0$ *[1 mark]*
Differentiate y^2 using the chain rule:
$\Rightarrow 3x^2 + \dfrac{d}{dx}x^2y = \dfrac{d}{dy}y^2\dfrac{dy}{dx}$ *[1 mark]*
$\Rightarrow 3x^2 + \dfrac{d}{dx}x^2y = 2y\dfrac{dy}{dx}$
Differentiate x^2y using the product rule:
$\Rightarrow 3x^2 + x^2\dfrac{d}{dx}y + y\dfrac{d}{dx}x^2 = 2y\dfrac{dy}{dx}$
$\Rightarrow 3x^2 + x^2\dfrac{dy}{dx} + 2xy = 2y\dfrac{dy}{dx}$ *[1 mark]*
Rearrange to make $\dfrac{dy}{dx}$ the subject:
$\Rightarrow (2y - x^2)\dfrac{dy}{dx} = 3x^2 + 2xy$
$\Rightarrow \dfrac{dy}{dx} = \dfrac{3x^2 + 2xy}{2y - x^2}$ *[1 mark]*

b) (i) Substitute $x = 1$ into the original equation:
$x = 1 \Rightarrow (1)^3 + (1)^2 y = y^2 - 1$ *[1 mark]*
$\Rightarrow y^2 - y - 2 = 0$
$\Rightarrow (y - 2)(y + 1) = 0$
$\Rightarrow y = 2$ or $y = -1$
$a > b$, so $a = 2$, $b = -1$ *[1 mark]*

(ii) At $Q = (1, -1)$,
$\frac{dy}{dx} = \frac{3(1)^2 + 2(1)(-1)}{2(-1) - (1)^2} = \frac{3 - 2}{-2 - 1} = -\frac{1}{3}$ *[1 mark]*
So the gradient of the normal at $Q = 3$. *[1 mark]*
$(y - y_1) = m(x - x_1)$
$\Rightarrow (y + 1) = 3(x - 1)$
$\Rightarrow y = 3x - 4$ *[1 mark]*

7 a) Vector equation of line through P and Q:
$r = \begin{pmatrix} -2 \\ -2 \\ -1 \end{pmatrix} + \mu\left(\begin{pmatrix} -5 \\ -4 \\ 1 \end{pmatrix} - \begin{pmatrix} -2 \\ -2 \\ -1 \end{pmatrix}\right)$

$r = \begin{pmatrix} -2 \\ -2 \\ -1 \end{pmatrix} + \mu\begin{pmatrix} -3 \\ -2 \\ 2 \end{pmatrix}$ *[1 mark]*

Where lines intersect:
$-1 + 2\lambda = -2 - 3\mu$
$2\lambda = -2 - 2\mu$
$3 + \lambda = -1 + 2\mu$ *[1 mark]*
Solving any pair of equations simultaneously gives $\lambda = -2$ and $\mu = 1$. *[1 mark]*
Substitute these values into the remaining equation to show that the lines intersect. E.g. $3 + \lambda = -1 + 2\mu$
$\Rightarrow 3 + -2 = -1 + 2(1) \Rightarrow 1 = 1$ *[1 mark]*
Intersection point:
$r = \begin{pmatrix} -2 \\ -2 \\ -1 \end{pmatrix} + \mu\begin{pmatrix} -3 \\ -2 \\ 2 \end{pmatrix} \Rightarrow r = \begin{pmatrix} -2 \\ -2 \\ -1 \end{pmatrix} + 1\begin{pmatrix} -3 \\ -2 \\ 2 \end{pmatrix} = \begin{pmatrix} -5 \\ -4 \\ 1 \end{pmatrix}$
$\Rightarrow (-5, -4, 1)$ *[1 mark]*

b) $\overrightarrow{OT} = 3\begin{pmatrix} -2 \\ -2 \\ -1 \end{pmatrix} = \begin{pmatrix} -6 \\ -6 \\ -3 \end{pmatrix}$ *[1 mark]*

$\overrightarrow{QT} = \begin{pmatrix} -6 \\ -6 \\ -3 \end{pmatrix} - \begin{pmatrix} -5 \\ -4 \\ 1 \end{pmatrix} = \begin{pmatrix} -1 \\ -2 \\ -4 \end{pmatrix}$ *[1 mark]*

$|\overrightarrow{QT}| = \sqrt{(-1)^2 + (-2)^2 + (-4)^2} = \sqrt{21}$ *[1 mark]*

c) $\overrightarrow{PV} = \begin{pmatrix} 0 \\ f \\ g \end{pmatrix} - \begin{pmatrix} -2 \\ -2 \\ -1 \end{pmatrix} = \begin{pmatrix} 2 \\ f + 2 \\ g + 1 \end{pmatrix}$ *[1 mark]*

The scalar product of $\overrightarrow{PV}$ and the direction vector of L_1 must be zero as they're perpendicular.
$(2 \times 2) + (2 \times (f + 2)) + (1 \times (g + 1)) = 0$ *[1 mark]*
$4 + 2f + 4 + g + 1 = 0 \Rightarrow 2f + g = -9$ *[1 mark]*

d) $\cos\alpha = \frac{(2 \times 1) + (2 \times 1) + (1 \times 1)}{(\sqrt{2^2 + 2^2 + 1^2}) \times (\sqrt{1^2 + 1^2 + 1^2})}$ *[1 mark]*
$\cos\alpha = \frac{5}{(\sqrt{9}) \times (\sqrt{3})} = 0.962$ *[1 mark]*
$\alpha = 15.8°$ (3 s.f.) *[1 mark]*

8 a) $\frac{dN}{dt} = k\sqrt{N}$, $k > 0$ *[1 mark for LHS, 1 mark for RHS]*
When $N = 36$, $\frac{dN}{dt} = 0.36$. Putting these values into the equation gives $0.36 = k\sqrt{36} = 6k \Rightarrow k = 0.06$ *[1 mark]* (the population is increasing so ignore the negative square root).
So the differential equation is $\frac{dN}{dt} = 0.06\sqrt{N}$.

b) (i) $\frac{dN}{dt} = \frac{kN}{\sqrt{t}} \Rightarrow \int \frac{1}{N}\, dN = \int \frac{k}{\sqrt{t}}\, dt$ *[1 mark]*
$\ln|N| = 2k\sqrt{t} + C$ *[1 mark]*
$\Rightarrow N = e^{2k\sqrt{t} + C} = Ae^{2k\sqrt{t}}$, where $A = e^C$ *[1 mark]*
For the initial population, $t = 0$, so $N = 25$ when $t = 0$. Putting these values into the equation:
$25 = Ae^0 \Rightarrow 25 = A$, so the equation for N is:
$N = 25e^{2k\sqrt{t}}$ *[1 mark]*.

(ii) When initial population has doubled, $N = 50$ *[1 mark]*. Put this value and the value for k into the equation and solve for t:
$50 = 25e^{2(0.05)\sqrt{t}} \Rightarrow 2 = e^{0.1\sqrt{t}} \Rightarrow \ln 2 = 0.1\sqrt{t}$ *[1 mark]*
$10\ln 2 = \sqrt{t} \Rightarrow (10\ln 2)^2 = t \Rightarrow t = 48.045$
So it will take 48 weeks *[1 mark]* (to the nearest week) for the population to double.

C4 Practice Exam Two

1 a) $5x^2 + 10x - 13 \equiv A(2 - x)(1 + 4x) + B(1 + 4x) + C(2 - x)^2$
[1 mark]
Substitute values of x to make the brackets on the RHS equal to zero: *[1 mark]*
Let $x = 2$, then $5(2)^2 + 10(2) - 13 = B(1 + 4(2))$
$\Rightarrow 27 = 9B \Rightarrow B = 3$ *[1 mark]*
Let $x = -\frac{1}{4}$, then $5\left(-\frac{1}{4}\right)^2 + 10\left(-\frac{1}{4}\right) - 13 = C\left(2 - \left(-\frac{1}{4}\right)\right)^2$
$\Rightarrow \frac{5}{16} - \frac{5}{2} - 13 = C\frac{81}{16} \Rightarrow -\frac{243}{16} = \frac{81}{16}C \Rightarrow C = -3$ *[1 mark]*
Equate the terms in x^2:
$5 = -4A + C = -4A - 3 \Rightarrow 8 = -4A \Rightarrow A = -2$ *[1 mark]*
so $\frac{5x^2 + 10x - 13}{(2 - x)^2(1 + 4x)} = \frac{-2}{2 - x} + \frac{3}{(2 - x)^2} - \frac{3}{1 + 4x}$.

b) $\int \frac{5x^2 + 10x - 13}{(2 - x)^2(1 + 4x)}\, dx \equiv \int \frac{-2}{2 - x} + \frac{3}{(2 - x)^2} - \frac{3}{1 + 4x}\, dx$
$= 2\ln|2 - x| + \frac{3}{2 - x} - \frac{3}{4}\ln|1 + 4x| + C$
[4 marks available — 1 mark for using partial fractions from part a), 1 mark for each correct term of the answer (not including C)]

2 a) $\sqrt{2}\cos\theta - 3\sin\theta \equiv R\cos(\theta + \alpha)$. Using the cos addition rule, $R\cos(\theta + \alpha) \equiv R\cos\theta\cos\alpha - R\sin\theta\sin\alpha$,
so $R\cos\alpha = \sqrt{2}$ and $R\sin\alpha = 3$ *[1 mark]*.
$\frac{R\sin\alpha}{R\cos\alpha} = \tan\alpha$, so $\tan\alpha = \frac{3}{\sqrt{2}}$
Solving this gives $\alpha = 1.13$ (3 s.f.) *[1 mark]*.
$R = \sqrt{(\sqrt{2})^2 + 3^2} = \sqrt{2 + 9} = \sqrt{11}$ *[1 mark]*,
$\sqrt{2}\cos\theta - 3\sin\theta = \sqrt{11}\cos(\theta + 1.13)$.

Answers

b) If $\sqrt{2}\cos\theta - 3\sin\theta = 3$, then $\sqrt{11}\cos(\theta + 1.13) = 3$.
So $\cos(\theta + 1.13) = \frac{3}{\sqrt{11}}$. Solving this gives
$\theta + 1.13 = 0.441$ (3 s.f.) *[1 mark]*. The range of solutions
becomes $1.13 \leq \theta + 1.13 \leq 7.41$ $(2\pi + 1.13)$. To find the
other values of θ within the new range, $2\pi - 0.441 = 5.84$,
$2\pi + 0.441 = 6.72$ *[1 mark]*. Subtracting 1.13 gives
$\theta = 4.71, 5.59$ *[1 mark for each correct value]*.

You can sketch the graph to help you find all the values of θ.

c) $(\sqrt{2}\cos\theta - 3\sin\theta)^4 = (\sqrt{11}\cos(\theta + 1.13))^4$. The maximum
values occurs when $\cos(\theta + 1.13) = 1$. This value is
$(\sqrt{11})^4 = 121$ *[1 mark]*. Solving $\cos(\theta + 1.13) = 1$ gives
the location of the maximum as $2\pi - 1.13 = 5.15$ *[1 mark]*.
Since $(\sqrt{11}\cos(\theta + 1.13))^4 \geq 0$, the minimum value is 0
[1 mark] and it occurs when $\cos(\theta + 1.13) = 0$. Solving
this gives the locations of the minimums at $\frac{\pi}{2} - 1.13 = 0.44$
and $\frac{3\pi}{2} - 1.13 = 3.58$ *[1 mark]*.

This one was a bit nasty — if you didn't realise that
$(\sqrt{11}\cos(\theta + 1.13))^4$ *is never negative, you'd have got*
the minimum values wrong.

3 a) $(1-x)^{-\frac{1}{2}} \approx 1 + \left(-\frac{1}{2}\right)(-x) + \frac{\left(-\frac{1}{2}\right)\times\left(-\frac{3}{2}\right)}{1\times 2}(-x)^2$
$\qquad + \frac{\left(-\frac{1}{2}\right)\times\left(-\frac{3}{2}\right)\times\left(-\frac{5}{2}\right)}{1\times 2\times 3}(-x)^3$ *[1 mark]*
$= 1 + \frac{x}{2} + \frac{3}{8}x^2 + \frac{5}{16}x^3$ *[1 mark]*

b) (i) $(25 - 4x)^{-\frac{1}{2}}$
$= (25)^{-\frac{1}{2}}\left(1 - \frac{4}{25}x\right)^{-\frac{1}{2}} = \frac{1}{5}\left(1 - \frac{4}{25}x\right)^{-\frac{1}{2}}$ *[1 mark]*
$= \frac{1}{5}\left(1 + \frac{1}{2}\left(\frac{4}{25}x\right) + \frac{3}{8}\left(\frac{4}{25}x\right)^2 + \frac{5}{16}\left(\frac{4}{25}x\right)^3\right)$ *[1 mark]*
$= \frac{1}{5}\left(1 + \frac{1}{2}\left(\frac{4}{25}x\right) + \frac{3}{8}\left(\frac{16}{625}x^2\right) + \frac{5}{16}\left(\frac{64}{15625}x^3\right)\right)$
$= \frac{1}{5}\left(1 + \frac{2}{25}x + \frac{6}{625}x^2 + \frac{4}{3125}x^3\right)$
$= \frac{1}{5} + \frac{2}{125}x$ *[1 mark]* $+ \frac{6}{3125}x^2 + \frac{4}{15625}x^3$ *[1 mark]*

(ii) The expansion is valid for $\left|\frac{-4x}{25}\right| < 1 \Rightarrow \frac{|-4\|x\|}{25} < 1$
$\Rightarrow |x| < \frac{25}{4}$ *[1 mark]*

c) $25 - 4x = 20 \Rightarrow x = \frac{5}{4}$ *[1 mark]*
So $\frac{1}{\sqrt{20}} = \left(25 - 4\left(\frac{5}{4}\right)\right)^{-\frac{1}{2}}$
$\approx \frac{1}{5} + \frac{2}{125}\left(\frac{5}{4}\right) + \frac{6}{3125}\left(\frac{5}{4}\right)^2 + \frac{4}{15625}\left(\frac{5}{4}\right)^3$ *[1 mark]*
$= \frac{1}{5} + \frac{2}{125}\left(\frac{5}{4}\right) + \frac{6}{3125}\left(\frac{25}{16}\right) + \frac{4}{15625}\left(\frac{125}{64}\right)$
$= \frac{1}{5} + \frac{1}{50} + \frac{3}{1000} + \frac{1}{2000}$
$= \frac{447}{2000}$ *[1 mark]*

4 a) First find the value of t when $y = -6$:
$y = 2 - t^3 = -6 \Rightarrow t^3 = 8 \Rightarrow t = 2$ *[1 mark]*
$\Rightarrow x = 2^2 + 2(2) - 3 = 5$
Now find the gradient of the curve:
$\frac{dy}{dt} = -3t^2$, $\frac{dx}{dt} = 2t + 2$
So $\frac{dy}{dx} = \frac{dy}{dt} \div \frac{dx}{dt} = \frac{-3t^2}{2t + 2}$ *[1 mark]*
So when $t = 2$, $\frac{dy}{dx} = \frac{-3(2)^2}{2(2) + 2} = \frac{-12}{6} = -2$

So the tangent at $y = -6$ is
$y = -2x + c \Rightarrow -6 = -2(5) + c \Rightarrow c = 4$
The equation of L is $y = -2x + 4$ *[1 mark]*

b) (i) Sub $y = 2 - t^3$ and $x = t^2 + 2t - 3$ into the equation of L:
$y = -2x + 4$
$\Rightarrow 2 - t^3 = -2(t^2 + 2t - 3) + 4$ *[1 mark]*
$\Rightarrow 2 - t^3 = -2t^2 - 4t + 10$
$\Rightarrow t^3 - 2t^2 - 4t + 8 = 0$
We know from part (a) that $t = 2$ is a root, so take out
$(t - 2)$ as a factor:
$\Rightarrow (t - 2)(t^2 - 4) = 0$
$\Rightarrow (t - 2)(t + 2)(t - 2) = 0$
$\Rightarrow t = 2$ or $t = -2$ *[1 mark]*
So t must be -2 at P.
$t = -2 \Rightarrow x = (-2)^2 + 2(-2) - 3 = -3$, $y = 2 - (-2)^3 = 10$.
The coordinates of P are $(-3, 10)$. *[1 mark]*

(ii) At P, $t = -2$, so $\frac{dy}{dx} = \frac{-3(-2)^2}{2(-2) + 2} = \frac{-12}{-2} = 6$.
[1 mark]
So the gradient of the normal at P is
$-\frac{1}{\left(\frac{dy}{dx}\right)} = -\frac{1}{6}$ *[1 mark]*
The equation of the normal at P is
$y = -\frac{1}{6}x + c \Rightarrow 10 = -\frac{(-3)}{6} + c \Rightarrow c = \frac{19}{2}$
So the normal to the curve at point P is
$y = -\frac{1}{6}x + \frac{19}{2}$ *[1 mark]*

5 a) $P = 5700e^{-0.15t}$, so when $t = 0$, $P = 5700e^0 = 5700$ *[1 mark]*.

b) At the start of 2020, $t = 10$,
so $P = 5700e^{-0.15 \times 10}$ $= 1271.8419...$
$= 1271$
[2 marks available — 1 mark for correct substitution of
$t = 10$, 1 mark for correct final answer]

Remember — round down as there are only 1271 whole birds.

c) When $P = 1000$: $1000 = 5700e^{-0.15t} \Rightarrow 1000 = \frac{5700}{e^{0.15t}}$
$\Rightarrow e^{0.15t} = \frac{5700}{1000} = 5.7$ *[1 mark]*. Take ln of both sides:
$0.15t = \ln 5.7 \Rightarrow t = \frac{\ln 5.7}{0.15} = 11.6031...$ years.
So the population will drop below 1000 in the
year 2021 *[1 mark]*.

d)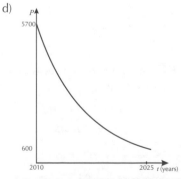

[3 marks available — 1 mark for correct shape of graph,
1 mark for (0, 5700) labelled, 1 mark for calculating P
when t = 15 (the population $\approx$ 600 in 2025)]

Answers

6 a) First, rearrange the equation into the form $\frac{dy}{dx} = f(x)g(y)$:

$\frac{dy}{dx} = 2y\frac{e^{2x} + x}{e^{2x} + x^2}$.

Then separate out the variables and integrate:

$\frac{1}{y}dy = \frac{2(e^{2x} + x)}{e^{2x} + x^2}dx \Rightarrow \int \frac{1}{y}dy = \int \frac{2(e^{2x} + x)}{e^{2x} + x^2}dx$

$\Rightarrow \ln|y| = \ln|e^{2x} + x^2| + C$

$\Rightarrow y = A(e^{2x} + x^2)$.

[7 marks available — 1 mark for separating variables, 1 mark for integrating LHS correctly, 1 mark for spotting that RHS is of the form f'(x)/f(x), 1 mark for integrating this correctly, 1 mark for adding C, 1 mark for simplifying to remove ln, 1 mark for rearranging to get in terms of y]

For this one, you need to spot that $2(e^{2x} + x)$ is the derivative of $e^{2x} + x^2$. A is just a constant (= e^C). You don't need the modulus signs around y as you're told that y ≥ O.

b) (i) Substitute $y = 3$ and $x = 0$ *[1 mark]* into the equation above to find the value of A:

$3 = A(e^0 + 0^2) \Rightarrow 3 = A \cdot 1 \Rightarrow A = 3$.

So the particular solution is $y = 3(e^{2x} + x^2)$. *[1 mark]*

(ii) When $x = 3$, $y = 3(e^{2\cdot3} + 3^2) = 3e^6 + 27$. *[1 mark]*

So $y = 3e^6 + 27$ *[1 mark]*.

You have to leave the e^6 in your answer because you're asked for the exact value.

7 a) Differentiate each term with respect to x:

$\sin \pi x - \cos \frac{\pi y}{2} = 0.5$

$\Rightarrow \frac{d}{dx}(\sin \pi x) - \frac{d}{dx}\left(\cos \frac{\pi y}{2}\right) = \frac{d}{dx}(0.5)$

Differentiate $\sin \pi x$ and 0.5 first:

$\Rightarrow \pi \cos \pi x - \frac{d}{dx}\left(\cos \frac{\pi y}{2}\right) = 0$

Differentiate $\cos \frac{\pi y}{2}$ using the chain rule:

$\Rightarrow \pi \cos \pi x - \frac{d}{dy}\left(\cos \frac{\pi y}{2}\right)\frac{dy}{dx} = 0$ *[1 mark]*

$\Rightarrow \pi \cos \pi x + \left(\frac{\pi}{2}\sin \frac{\pi y}{2}\right)\frac{dy}{dx} = 0$

Rearrange to make $\frac{dy}{dx}$ the subject:

$\Rightarrow \frac{dy}{dx} = -\frac{\pi \cos \pi x}{\frac{\pi}{2}\sin \frac{\pi y}{2}} = -\frac{2\cos \pi x}{\sin \frac{\pi y}{2}}$ *[1 mark]*

b) (i) The stationary point is where the gradient is zero.

$\frac{dy}{dx} = 0 \Rightarrow -\frac{2\cos \pi x}{\sin \frac{\pi y}{2}} = 0 \Rightarrow \cos \pi x = 0$ *[1 mark]*

$\Rightarrow x = \frac{1}{2}$ or $x = \frac{3}{2}$ *[1 mark]*

$x = \frac{3}{2} \Rightarrow \sin \frac{3\pi}{2} - \cos \frac{\pi y}{2} = 0.5$

$\Rightarrow -1 - \cos \frac{\pi y}{2} = 0.5$

$\Rightarrow \cos \frac{\pi y}{2} = -1.5$

So y has no solutions when $x = \frac{3}{2}$ *[1 mark]*

$x = \frac{1}{2} \Rightarrow \sin \frac{\pi}{2} - \cos \frac{\pi y}{2} = 0.5$

$\Rightarrow 1 - \cos \frac{\pi y}{2} = 0.5$

$\Rightarrow \cos \frac{\pi y}{2} = 0.5$

$\Rightarrow \frac{\pi y}{2} = \frac{\pi}{3}$

$\Rightarrow y = \frac{2}{3}$

So the only stationary point of the graph of $\sin \pi x - \cos \frac{\pi y}{2} = 0.5$ for the given ranges of x and y is at $\left(\frac{1}{2}, \frac{2}{3}\right)$.   *[1 mark]*

(ii) $x = \frac{1}{6} \Rightarrow \sin \frac{\pi}{6} - \cos \frac{\pi y}{2} = 0.5$

$\Rightarrow 0.5 - \cos \frac{\pi y}{2} = 0.5$

$\Rightarrow \cos \frac{\pi y}{2} = 0$

$\Rightarrow \frac{\pi y}{2} = \frac{\pi}{2}$

$\Rightarrow y = 1$ *[1 mark]*

At $\left(\frac{1}{6}, 1\right)$, $\frac{dy}{dx} = -\frac{2\cos \frac{\pi}{6}}{\sin \frac{\pi}{2}} = \frac{-2\left(\frac{\sqrt{3}}{2}\right)}{1} = -\sqrt{3}$ *[1 mark]*

so the equation of the tangent to the curve is:

$y - 1 = -\sqrt{3}\left(x - \frac{1}{6}\right)$ *[1 mark]* (or $y = -\sqrt{3}x + \frac{6 + \sqrt{3}}{6}$).

8 a) (i) The scalar product of perpendicular lines is 0.

So $\mathbf{x.y} = 15p - 12 + 3q = 0$

So $\mathbf{x.z} = \frac{3}{2}p - \frac{6}{5} + 4q = 0$ *[1 mark]*

Solving simultaneously gives $p = \frac{4}{5}$ *[1 mark]*, $q = 0$ *[1 mark]*

(ii) $|\mathbf{y}| = \sqrt{15^2 + (-20)^2 + 3^2} = \sqrt{634}$ *[1 mark]*

Unit vector in the direction of $\mathbf{y}$

$= \frac{1}{\sqrt{634}}\begin{pmatrix}15\\-20\\3\end{pmatrix}$ *[1 mark]*

Unit vectors have a magnitude of 1 — that's all there is to it.

b) $\cos \alpha = \frac{\mathbf{y.z}}{|\mathbf{y}||\mathbf{z}|} = \frac{74.5}{(\sqrt{634}) \times \left(\sqrt{\left(\frac{3}{2}\right)^2 + (-2)^2 + 4^2}\right)}$ *[1 mark]*

$= \frac{74.5}{118.77} = 0.627$ *[1 mark]* $\Rightarrow \alpha = 51°$ *[1 mark]*

Answers

S2 Section 1 — Discrete Random Variables

Warm-up Questions

1) a) All the probabilities have to add up to 1.
So $0.5 + k + k + 3k = 0.5 + 5k = 1$, i.e. $5k = 0.5$, i.e. $k = 0.1$.

b) $P(Y < 2) = P(Y = 0) + P(Y = 1) = 0.5 + 0.1 = 0.6$.

2) There are 5 possible outcomes, and the probability of each of them is k. That means $5k = 1$, so $k = 1 \div 5 = 0.2$.
Mean of $X = (0 \times 0.2) + (1 \times 0.2) + (2 \times 0.2) + (3 \times 0.2) + (4 \times 0.2) = 2$.
$E(X^2) = (0 \times 0.2) + (1 \times 0.2) + (4 \times 0.2) + (9 \times 0.2) + (16 \times 0.2) = 6$, so variance of $X = E(X^2) - [E(X)]^2 = 6 - 4 = 2$.

3) a) As always, the probabilities have to add up to 1, so
$k = 1 - \left(\frac{1}{6} + \frac{1}{2} + \frac{5}{24}\right) = 1 - \frac{21}{24} = \frac{3}{24} = \frac{1}{8}$

b) $E(X) = \left(1 \times \frac{1}{6}\right) + \left(2 \times \frac{1}{2}\right) + \left(3 \times \frac{1}{8}\right) + \left(4 \times \frac{5}{24}\right)$
$= \frac{4 + 24 + 9 + 20}{24} = \frac{57}{24} = \frac{19}{8}$

$E(X^2) = \left(1^2 \times \frac{1}{6}\right) + \left(2^2 \times \frac{1}{2}\right) + \left(3^2 \times \frac{1}{8}\right) + \left(4^2 \times \frac{5}{24}\right)$
$= \frac{4 + 48 + 27 + 80}{24} = \frac{159}{24} = \frac{53}{8}$

$Var(X) = E(X^2) - [E(X)]^2 = \frac{53}{8} - \left(\frac{19}{8}\right)^2$
$= \frac{424 - 361}{64} = \frac{63}{64}$

c) $E(2X - 1) = 2E(X) - 1 = 2 \times \frac{19}{8} - 1 = \frac{30}{8} = \frac{15}{4}$

$Var(2X - 1) = 2^2 Var(X) = 4 \times \frac{63}{64} = \frac{63}{16}$

4) a) $E(X) = (1 \times 0.1) + (2 \times 0.2) + (3 \times 0.25) + (4 \times 0.2)$
$+ (5 \times 0.1) + (6 \times 0.15) = 3.45$

b) $Var(X) = E(X^2) - (E(X))^2$
$E(X^2) = (1 \times 0.1) + (4 \times 0.2) + (9 \times 0.25) + (16 \times 0.2)$
$+ (25 \times 0.1) + (36 \times 0.15) = 14.25$
So $Var(X) = 14.25 - 3.45^2 = 2.3475$

c) $E\left(\frac{2}{X}\right) = \sum\left(\frac{2}{x_i} \times p_i\right) = \left(\frac{2}{1} \times 0.1\right) + \left(\frac{2}{2} \times 0.2\right) + \left(\frac{2}{3} \times 0.25\right)$
$+ \left(\frac{2}{4} \times 0.2\right) + \left(\frac{2}{5} \times 0.1\right) + \left(\frac{2}{6} \times 0.15\right) = 0.757 \, (3 \text{ d.p.})$

You could have calculated part c) by doing 2[E(1/X)] instead — if you'd wanted to show off your ability to deal with linear functions too.

d) $Var\left(\frac{2}{X}\right) = E\left[\left(\frac{2}{X}\right)^2\right] - \left[E\left(\frac{2}{X}\right)\right]^2$
$E\left[\left(\frac{2}{X}\right)^2\right] = E\left[\left(\frac{4}{X^2}\right)\right] = \sum\left(\frac{4}{x_i^2} \times p_i\right)$
$= \left(\frac{4}{1} \cdot \frac{1}{10}\right) + \left(\frac{4}{4} \cdot \frac{2}{10}\right) + \left(\frac{4}{9} \cdot \frac{1}{4}\right) + \left(\frac{4}{16} \cdot \frac{2}{10}\right) + \left(\frac{4}{25} \cdot \frac{1}{10}\right) + \left(\frac{4}{36} \cdot \frac{15}{100}\right)$
$= \frac{2}{5} + \frac{1}{5} + \frac{1}{9} + \frac{1}{20} + \frac{2}{125} + \frac{1}{60}$
$= \frac{893}{1125}$

$Var\left(\frac{2}{X}\right) = \frac{893}{1125} - 0.757^2 = 0.221 \, (3 \text{ d.p.})$

Exam Questions

1 a) The probability of getting 3 heads is: $\frac{1}{2} \times \frac{1}{2} \times \frac{1}{2} = \frac{1}{8}$
[1 mark]

The probability of getting 2 heads is: $3 \times \frac{1}{2} \times \frac{1}{2} \times \frac{1}{2} = \frac{3}{8}$
(multiply by 3 because any of the three coins could be the tail — the order in which the heads and the tail occur isn't important).
[1 mark]

Similarly the probability of getting 1 head is:
$3 \times \frac{1}{2} \times \frac{1}{2} \times \frac{1}{2} = \frac{3}{8}$
And the probability of getting no heads is $\frac{1}{2} \times \frac{1}{2} \times \frac{1}{2} = \frac{1}{8}$

So the probability of 1 or no heads $= \frac{3}{8} + \frac{1}{8} = \frac{1}{2}$ *[1 mark]*

Hence the probability distribution of X is:

x	20p	10p	nothing
P(X = x)	$\frac{1}{8}$	$\frac{3}{8}$	$\frac{1}{2}$

[1 mark]

b) You need the probability that X >10p *[1 mark]*

This is just $P(X = 20p) = \frac{1}{8}$ *[1 mark]*

Easy peasy. The difficult question is — why would anyone play such a rubbish game?

2 a) All the probabilities must add up to 1, so
$2k + 3k + k + k = 1$, i.e. $7k = 1$, and so $k = \frac{1}{7}$. *[1 mark]*

b) $P(X > 2) = P(X = 3) = \frac{1}{7}$, using part a) *[1 mark]*

All probabilities add up to one! OK, that's the last time I'm going to say it. Scout's honour.

3 a) There are 10 possible values,
so $10k = 1$ and $k = 1 \div 10 = 0.1$.

x	0	1	2	3	4	5	6	7	8	9
P(X = x)	0.1	0.1	0.1	0.1	0.1	0.1	0.1	0.1	0.1	0.1

[1 mark]

b) Mean $= 0 + 0.1 + 0.2 + 0.3 + 0.4 + 0.5 + 0.6 + 0.7 + 0.8 + 0.9 = 4.5$ *[1 mark]*
Variance $= E(X^2) - [E(X)]^2$
$E(X^2) = 0 + 0.1 + 0.4 + 0.9 + 1.6 + 2.5 + 3.6 + 4.9 + 6.4 + 8.1 = 28.5$ *[1 mark]*
So variance $= 28.5 - 4.5^2 = 8.25$ *[1 mark]*

c) $P(X < 4.5) = P(X = 0) + P(X = 1)$
$+ P(X = 2) + P(X = 3) + P(X = 4)$ *[1 mark]*
$= 0.5$ *[1 mark]*

4 a) $P(X = 1) = a$, $P(X = 2) = 2a$, $P(X = 3) = 3a$.
Therefore the total probability is $3a + 2a + a = 6a$.
This must equal 1, so $a = \frac{1}{6}$. *[1 mark]*

b) $E(X) = \left(1 \times \frac{1}{6}\right) + \left(2 \times \frac{2}{6}\right) + \left(3 \times \frac{3}{6}\right) = \frac{1 + 4 + 9}{6}$ *[1 mark]*
$= \frac{7}{3}$ *[1 mark]*

c) $E(X^2) = Var(X) + [E(X)]^2 = \frac{5}{9} + \left(\frac{7}{3}\right)^2 = \frac{5 + 49}{9}$ *[1 mark]*
$= \frac{54}{9} = 6$ *[1 mark]*

d) $E(3X + 4) = 3E(X) + 4 = 3 \times \frac{7}{3} + 4 = 11$ *[1 mark]*
$Var(3X + 4) = 3^2 Var(X) = 9 \times \frac{5}{9}$ *[1 mark]*
$= 5$ *[1 mark]*

Answers

e) $A = \frac{1}{2} \times X^3 \times \frac{4}{X} = 2X^2$ *[1 mark]*
So E(A) = E($2X^2$) = 2E(X^2) *[1 mark]*
Using your value of E(X^2) from part c), E(A) = 2 × 6 = 12
[1 mark]

5 a) E(X) = $(0 \times 0.4) + (1 \times 0.3) + (2 \times 0.2) + (3 \times 0.1)$
= $0 + 0.3 + 0.4 + 0.3$ *[1 mark]*
= 1 *[1 mark]*

b) E(6X + 8) = 6E(X) + 8 = 6 + 8 *[1 mark]*
= 14 *[1 mark]*

c) The formula for variance is Var(X) = E(X^2) − [E(X)^2]
So first work out E(X^2):
E(X^2) = $(0^2 \times 0.4) + (1^2 \times 0.3) + (2^2 \times 0.2) + (3^2 \times 0.1)$
= $0.3 + 0.8 + 0.9$ *[1 mark]*
= 2 *[1 mark]*

Then complete the formula also using your answer to part a):
E(X^2) − [E(X)^2] = 2 − (1^2) *[1 mark]*
= 1 *[1 mark]*

d) Var(aX + b) = a^2Var(X)
Var(5 − 3X) = (− 3)^{2}Var(X) = 9Var(X) = 9 × 1
[1 mark]
= 9 *[1 mark]*

S2 Section 2 — The Poisson Distribution
Warm-up Questions

1) a) P($X = 2$) = $\frac{e^{-3.1} \times 3.1^2}{2!}$ = 0.2165 (to 4 d.p.).

b) P($X = 1$) = $\frac{e^{-3.1} \times 3.1}{1!}$ = 0.1397 (to 4 d.p.).

c) P($X = 0$) = $\frac{e^{-3.1} \times 3.1^0}{0!}$ = 0.0450 (to 4 d.p.).

d) P($X < 3$) = P($X = 0$) + P($X = 1$) + P($X = 2$)
= $0.0450 + 0.1397 + 0.2165 = 0.4012$

e) P($X \geq 3$) = 1 − P($X < 3$)
= $1 − 0.4012 = 0.5988$ (to 4 d.p.).

2) a) P($X = 2$) = $\frac{e^{-8.7} \times 8.7^2}{2!}$ = 0.0063 (to 4 d.p.).

b) P($X = 1$) = $\frac{e^{-8.7} \times 8.7}{1!}$ = 0.0014 (to 4 d.p.).

c) P($X = 0$) = $\frac{e^{-8.7} \times 8.7^0}{0!}$ = 0.0002 (to 4 d.p.).

d) P($X < 3$) = P($X = 0$) + P($X = 1$) + P($X = 2$)
= $0.0002 + 0.0014 + 0.0063 = 0.0079$

e) P($X \geq 3$) = 1 − P($X < 3$)
= $1 − 0.0079 = 0.9921$ (to 4 d.p.).

3) a) E(X) = Var(X) = 8
standard deviation = $\sigma = \sqrt{8} = 2.828$ (to 3 d.p.).

b) E(X) = Var(X) = 12.11
standard deviation = $\sigma = \sqrt{12.11} = 3.480$ (to 3 d.p.).

c) E(X) = Var(X) = 84.2227
standard deviation = $\sigma = \sqrt{84.2227} = 9.177$ (to 3 d.p.).

4) Using tables:
a) P($X \leq \mu$) = P($X \leq 9$) = 0.5874
P($X \leq \mu - \sigma$) = P($X \leq 6$) = 0.2068

b) P($X \leq \mu$) = P($X \leq 4$) = 0.6288
P($X \leq \mu - \sigma$) = P($X \leq 2$) = 0.2381

5) a) The defective products occur randomly, singly and (on average) at a constant rate, and the random variable represents the number of 'events' (i.e. defective products) within a fixed period, so this would follow a Poisson distribution.

b) There is a fixed number of trials in this situation, and so this situation would be modelled by a binomial distribution. (Or you could say it won't follow a Poisson distribution, as the events don't occur at a constant rate over the 25 trials.)

c) If the random variable represents the number of people joining the queue within a fixed period, and assuming that the people join the queue randomly, singly and (on average) at a constant rate, then this would follow a Poisson distribution.

You do need to make a couple of assumptions here — the Poisson model wouldn't work if you had, say, big groups of factory workers all coming in together a couple of minutes after the lunchtime hooter sounds.

d) The mistakes occur randomly, singly and (on average) at a constant rate, and the random variable represents the number of mistakes within a fixed 'period' (i.e. the number of pages in the document), so this would follow a Poisson distribution.

6) a) The number of atoms decaying in an hour would follow the Poisson distribution Po(2000). So the number decaying in a minute would follow Po(2000 ÷ 60) = Po(33.3).

b) The number of atoms decaying in a day would follow Po(2000 × 24) = Po(48 000).

7) a) If X represents the number of atoms from the first sample decaying per minute, then X ~ Po(60). And if Y represents the number of atoms from the second sample decaying per minute, then Y ~ Po(90). So $X + Y$ (the total number of atoms decaying per minute) ~ Po(60 + 90) = Po(150).

b) The total number of atoms decaying per hour would be distributed as Po(150 × 60) = Po(9000).

8) a) P($X \leq 2$) = 0.0138

b) P($X \leq 7$) = 0.4530

c) P($X \leq 5$) = 0.1912

d) P($X < 9$) = P($X \leq 8$) = 0.5925

e) P($X \geq 8$) = 1 − P($X < 8$) = 1 − P($X \leq 7$)
= 1 − 0.4530 = 0.5470

f) P($X > 1$) = 1 − P($X \leq 1$) = 1 − 0.0030 = 0.9970

g) P($X > 7$) = 1 − P($X \leq 7$) = 1 − 0.4530 = 0.5470

h) P($X = 6$) = P($X \leq 6$) − P($X \leq 5$) = 0.3134 − 0.1912 = 0.1222

i) P($X = 4$) = P($X \leq 4$) − P($X \leq 3$) = 0.0996 − 0.0424 = 0.0572

j) P($X = 3$) = P($X \leq 3$) − P($X \leq 2$) = 0.0424 − 0.0138 = 0.0286

Answers

9)   If X represents the number of geese in a random square metre of field, then $X \sim \text{Po}(1)$ — since the 'rate' at which geese occur is constant, they're randomly scattered, and geese only occur singly.

a) $P(X = 0) = \dfrac{e^{-1} \times 1^0}{0!} = 0.3679$

b) $P(X = 1) = \dfrac{e^{-1} \times 1^1}{1!} = 0.3679$

c) $P(X = 2) = \dfrac{e^{-1} \times 1^2}{2!} = 0.1839$

d) $P(X > 2) = 1 - P(X \leq 2) = 1 - (0.3679 + 0.3679 + 0.1839)$
     $= 1 - 0.9197 = 0.0803$

This is one of those questions where you could use either your Poisson tables or the probability function.

Exam Questions

1   a)   Events need to happen at a constant average rate *[1 mark]* and singly ("one at a time") *[1 mark]*.

You could also have had "events occur randomly" or "independently".

b)   (i)   If X represents the number of chaffinches visiting the observation spot, then $X \sim \text{Po}(7)$ *[1 mark]*.
Using tables, $P(X < 4) = P(X \leq 3) = 0.0818$ *[1 mark]*.

(ii) $P(X \geq 7) = 1 - P(X < 7) = 1 - P(X \leq 6)$ *[1 mark]*
$= 1 - 0.4497 = 0.5503$ *[1 mark]*

(iii) $P(X = 9) = P(X \leq 9) - P(X \leq 8)$ *[1 mark]*
$= 0.8305 - 0.7291 = 0.1014$ *[1 mark]*

Or you could work this last one out using the formula:
$P(X = 9) = \dfrac{e^{-7}7^9}{9!} = 0.1014$

— you get the same answer either way, obviously.

c)   The number of birds of any species visiting per hour would follow the distribution $\text{Po}(22 + 7) = \text{Po}(29)$ *[1 mark]*. So the total number of birds visiting in a random 15-minute period will follow $\text{Po}(29 \div 4) = \text{Po}(7.25)$ *[1 mark]*.

$P(X = 3) = \dfrac{e^{-7.25} \times 7.25^3}{3!}$ *[1 mark]*
$= 0.045$ (to 3 d.p.) *[1 mark]*.

2   a)   (i)   If the mean is 20, then the number of calls per hour follows $\text{Po}(20)$. So the number of calls in a random 30-minute period follows $\text{Po}(20 \div 2) = \text{Po}(10)$ *[1 mark]*.
Using tables for $\lambda = 10$:
$P(X = 8) = P(X \leq 8) - P(X \leq 7)$ *[1 mark]*
$= 0.3328 - 0.2202 = 0.1126$ *[1 mark]*

Or you could work this out using the formula:
$P(X = 8) = \dfrac{e^{-10}10^8}{8!} = 0.1126$.

(ii) $P(X > 8) = 1 - P(X \leq 8)$ *[1 mark]*
$= 1 - 0.3328 = 0.6672$ *[1 mark]*

b)   In this context, independently means that receiving a phone call at one particular instant does not affect whether or not a call will be received at a different instant.   *[1 mark]*.

3   a)   It's assumed that $X \sim \text{Po}(6)$.
$P(4 < X \leq 7) = P(X \leq 7) - P(X \leq 4)$ *[1 mark]*
$= 0.7440 - 0.2851 = 0.4589$ *[1 mark]*

b)   Let Y be the number of rucksacks sold in a random two-month period. Then $Y \sim \text{Po}(12)$ *[1 mark]*.
$P(Y > 14) = 1 - P(Y \leq 14)$ *[1 mark]*
$= 1 - 0.7720 = 0.2280$ *[1 mark]*

c) $P(X = 6) = \dfrac{e^{-6} \times 6^6}{6!}$ *[1 mark]* $= 0.1606$ (4 d.p.), so the probability they sell 6 rucksacks in one month is 0.1606.

Assuming each month's sales are independent, the probability they sell 6 in each of 3 consecutive months is $0.1606^3 = 0.00414...$ *[1 mark]* $= 0.004$ (1 s.f.) *[1 mark]*.

d)   Unbiased estimate of $\text{Var}(X)$ is:

$s^2 = \dfrac{n}{n-1}\left[\dfrac{\sum x^2}{n} - \left(\dfrac{\sum x}{n}\right)^2\right] = \dfrac{8}{7}\left[\dfrac{394}{8} - \left(\dfrac{48}{8}\right)^2\right]$ *[1 mark]*

$= \dfrac{8}{7} \times \left(\dfrac{394}{8} - 36\right) = \dfrac{8}{7} \times \left(\dfrac{394}{8} - \dfrac{288}{8}\right)$

$= \dfrac{8}{7} \times \dfrac{106}{8} = \dfrac{106}{7} = 15.1$ (3 s.f.) *[1 mark]*

Remember to use this formula for the variance, rather than $\dfrac{\sum x^2}{n} - \left(\dfrac{\sum x}{n}\right)^2$ — you're estimating the population variance from the sample.

You already know that $\mu = E(X) = 6$ *[1 mark]*, and so, since the mean and variance of the distribution are very different, the assumption that X follows a Poisson distribution seems to be invalid. *[1 mark]*

S2 Section 3 —
Continuous Random Variables
Warm-up Questions

1)   a)   Sketch the p.d.f.:

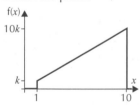

Area under p.d.f. $= \dfrac{10k + k}{2} \times (10 - 1) = \dfrac{99k}{2} = 1$.

So $k = \dfrac{2}{99}$.

b)   Sketch the p.d.f.:

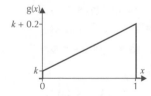

Area under p.d.f. $= \dfrac{2k + 0.2}{2} \times 1 = k + 0.1 = 1$.

So $k = 0.9$.

2 a) Sketch the p.d.f.:

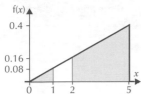

    (i)   Area under p.d.f. between $x = 0$ and $x = 1$ is:

        $1 \times 0.08 \div 2 = 0.04$, so $P(X < 1) = 0.04$.

    (ii) Area under p.d.f. between $x = 2$ and $x = 5$ is:

        $\dfrac{0.16 + 0.4}{2} \times 3 = 0.84$, so $P(2 \leq X \leq 5) = 0.84$.

    (iii) Area under p.d.f. at the point $x = 4$ is 0.

        So $P(X = 4) = 0$.

b) Sketch the p.d.f.:

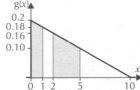

    (i)   Area under p.d.f. between $x = 0$ and $x = 1$ is:

        $\dfrac{0.2 + 0.18}{2} \times 1 = 0.19$, so $P(X < 1) = 0.19$.

    (ii) Area under p.d.f. between $x = 2$ and $x = 5$ is:

        $\dfrac{0.16 + 0.1}{2} \times 3 = 0.39$, so $P(2 \leq X \leq 5) = 0.39$.

    (iii) Area under p.d.f. at the point $x = 4$ is 0.

        So $P(X = 4) = 0$.

3 a) $\displaystyle\int_{-\infty}^{\infty} f(x)\,dx = k\int_0^5 x^2\,dx = k\left[\dfrac{x^3}{3}\right]_0^5 = \dfrac{125k}{3} = 1$, so $k = \dfrac{3}{125}$.

   $P(X < 1) = \displaystyle\int_0^1 \dfrac{3}{125}x^2\,dx = \dfrac{3}{125}\left[\dfrac{x^3}{3}\right]_0^1 = \dfrac{1}{125}$.

b) $\displaystyle\int_{-\infty}^{\infty} g(x)\,dx = \int_0^2 (0.1x^2 + kx)\,dx$

        $= \left[\dfrac{0.1x^3}{3} + \dfrac{kx^2}{2}\right]_0^2 = \dfrac{0.8}{3} + 2k = 1$.

   So $k = \dfrac{1}{2} - \dfrac{0.4}{3} = \dfrac{15 - 4}{30} = \dfrac{11}{30}$

   $P(X < 1) = \displaystyle\int_0^1 \left(0.1x^2 + \dfrac{11}{30}x\right)\,dx = \left[\dfrac{0.1x^3}{3} + \dfrac{11x^2}{60}\right]_0^1$

        $= \dfrac{0.1}{3} + \dfrac{11}{60} = \dfrac{13}{60}$

4 a) $\displaystyle\int_{-\infty}^{\infty} f(x)\,dx = \int_0^2 (0.1x^2 + 0.2)\,dx$

        $= \left[\dfrac{0.1x^3}{3} + 0.2x\right]_0^2 = \dfrac{0.8}{3} + 0.4 \neq 1$

   So $f(x)$ is not a p.d.f.

b) $g(x) < 0$ for $-1 \leq x < 0$, so $g(x)$ is not a p.d.f.

5 a) Integrate the pieces of the p.d.f., and then make sure the 'joins' are smooth using a suitable constant of integration (k).

$$F(x) = \begin{cases} 0 & \text{for } x < 0 \\ 0.04x^2 + k & \text{for } 0 \leq x \leq 5 \\ 1 & \text{for } x > 5 \end{cases}$$

Since $F(0) = 0$ and $F(5) = 1$, the pieces of this function join smoothly with $\underline{k = 0}$.

b) Integrate the pieces of the p.d.f., and then make sure the 'joins' are smooth using a suitable constant of integration (k).

$$G(x) = \begin{cases} 0 & \text{for } x < 0 \\ 0.2x - 0.01x^2 + k & \text{for } 0 \leq x \leq 10 \\ 1 & \text{for } x > 10 \end{cases}$$

Since $G(0) = 0$ and $G(10) = 1$, the pieces of this function join smoothly with $\underline{k = 0}$.

c) Integrate the pieces of the p.d.f., and then make sure the 'joins' are smooth using suitable constants of integration ($k_1 \text{-} k_3$).

$$H(x) = \begin{cases} 0 & \text{for } x < 0 \\ x^2 + k_1 & \text{for } 0 \leq x \leq 0.5 \\ x + k_2 & \text{for } 0.5 \leq x \leq 1 \\ 3x - x^2 + k_3 & \text{for } 1 \leq x \leq 1.5 \\ 1 & \text{for } x > 1.5 \end{cases}$$

$H(0) = 0$ means that $\underline{k_1 = 0}$, which then gives $H(0.5) = 0.25$.
$H(0.5) = 0.25$ means that $\underline{k_2 = -0.25}$, giving $H(1) = 0.75$.
$H(1) = 0.75$ means that $\underline{k_3 = -1.25}$, giving $H(1.5) = 1$.
This means all the joins are now 'smooth'.

d) Integrate the pieces of the p.d.f., and then make sure the 'joins' are smooth using suitable constants of integration (k_1 and k_2).

$$M(x) = \begin{cases} 0 & \text{for } x < 2 \\ 0.5x - 0.05x^2 + k_1 & \text{for } 2 \leq x \leq 4 \\ 0.1x + k_2 & \text{for } 4 \leq x \leq 10 \\ 1 & \text{for } x > 10 \end{cases}$$

$M(2) = 0$ means that $\underline{k_1 = -0.8}$, which gives $M(4) = 0.4$.
$M(4) = 0.4$ means that $\underline{k_2 = 0}$, which gives $M(10) = 1$.
This means all the joins are now 'smooth'.

6 a) Differentiate the different parts of the c.d.f.:

$$f(x) = \begin{cases} 4x^3 & \text{for } 0 \leq x \leq 1 \\ 0 & \text{otherwise} \end{cases}$$

b)

$$g(x) = \begin{cases} \dfrac{1}{50}(x - 1) & \text{for } 1 \leq x < 6 \\ \dfrac{3}{8} & \text{for } 6 \leq x \leq 8 \\ 0 & \text{otherwise} \end{cases}$$

7 a) $E(X) = \displaystyle\int_{-\infty}^{\infty} xf(x)\,dx = \int_0^5 0.08x^2\,dx = 0.08\left[\dfrac{x^3}{3}\right]_0^5$

       $= \dfrac{125 \times 0.08}{3} = \dfrac{10}{3}$

   $Var(X) = \displaystyle\int_{-\infty}^{\infty} x^2 f(x)\,dx - \mu^2 = \int_0^5 0.08x^3\,dx - \left(\dfrac{10}{3}\right)^2$

       $= 0.08\left[\dfrac{x^4}{4}\right]_0^5 - \left(\dfrac{10}{3}\right)^2 = \dfrac{625 \times 0.08}{4} - \left(\dfrac{10}{3}\right)^2$

       $= \dfrac{25}{2} - \left(\dfrac{10}{3}\right)^2 = \dfrac{25}{18} = 1.39$ (to 2 d.p.).

   $E(Y) = \displaystyle\int_{-\infty}^{\infty} yg(y)\,dy = \int_0^{10} 0.02y(10 - y)\,dy$

       $= 0.02\left[5y^2 - \dfrac{y^3}{3}\right]_0^{10}$

       $= 0.02\left(500 - \dfrac{1000}{3}\right) = 10 - \dfrac{20}{3} = \dfrac{10}{3}$

Answers

$\text{Var}(Y) = \int_{-\infty}^{\infty} y^2 g(y) dy - \mu^2$

$= \int_{0}^{10} 0.02y^2(10-y)dy - \left(\frac{10}{3}\right)^2$

$= 0.02\left[\frac{10y^3}{3} - \frac{y^4}{4}\right]_0^{10} - \left(\frac{10}{3}\right)^2$

$= 0.02 \times \left(\frac{10\,000}{3} - \frac{10\,000}{4}\right) - \left(\frac{10}{3}\right)^2$

$= \frac{50}{3} - \left(\frac{10}{3}\right)^2 = \frac{50}{9} = 5.56 \text{ (to 2 d.p.).}$

b) $E(4X+2) = 4E(X) + 2 = 4 \times \frac{10}{3} + 2 = \frac{46}{3}$

$E(3Y-4) = 3E(Y) - 4 = 3 \times \frac{10}{3} - 4 = 6$

$\text{Var}(4X+2) = 16 \times \text{Var}(X)$

$\quad = 16 \times \frac{25}{18} = \frac{200}{9} = 22.22 \text{ (to 2 d.p.).}$

$\text{Var}(3Y-4) = 9 \times \text{Var}(Y) = 9 \times \frac{50}{9} = 50$

c) Sketch the p.d.f.:

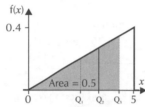

The median is Q_2, where:

$\int_0^{Q_2} 0.08x dx = 0.08\left[\frac{x^2}{2}\right]_0^{Q_2} = 0.04Q_2^2 = 0.5$

So the median $= \sqrt{12.5} = 3.54$ (to 2 d.p.).

The lower quartile is Q_1, where:

$\int_0^{Q_1} 0.08x dx = 0.08\left[\frac{x^2}{2}\right]_0^{Q_1} = 0.04Q_1^2 = 0.25$

So $Q_1 = \sqrt{6.25} = 2.5$.

The upper quartile is Q_3, where:

$\int_0^{Q_3} 0.08x dx = 0.08\left[\frac{x^2}{2}\right]_0^{Q_3} = 0.04Q_3^2 = 0.75$

So $Q_3 = \sqrt{18.75}$.

This means the interquartile range is:

$\sqrt{18.75} - 2.5 = 1.83$ (to 2 d.p.).

Or you could work these out by finding F(x), and then solving $F(Q_2) = 0.5$, $F(Q_1) = 0.25$ and $F(Q_3) = 0.75$.

8)

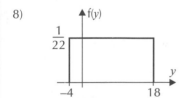

9) a) First sketch the p.d.f.:

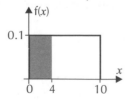

The shaded area represents $P(X < 4)$.
This is $4 \times 0.1 = 0.4$.

b) Similarly, $P(X \geq 8) = 2 \times 0.1 = 0.2$.

c) $P(X = 5) = 0$ [$P(X = k) = 0$ for any k and any continuous random variable X.]

d) $P(3 < X \leq 7) = 4 \times 0.1 = 0.4$.

10) a) $E(X) = \frac{a+b}{2}$, $\text{Var}(X) = \frac{(b-a)^2}{12}$

b) $c = \frac{1}{b-a}$

c) $E(X) = \int_{-\infty}^{\infty} xf(x)dx = c\int_a^b x\,dx = c\left[\frac{x^2}{2}\right]_a^b = c\left[\frac{b^2}{2} - \frac{a^2}{2}\right]$

$= \frac{1}{b-a}\left(\frac{b^2-a^2}{2}\right) = \frac{(b-a)(b+a)}{2(b-a)} = \frac{b+a}{2}$

Which is the same as $E(X) = \frac{a+b}{2}$.

11) a) $E(X) = \frac{a+b}{2} = \frac{4+19}{2} = \frac{23}{2} = 11.5$

$\text{Var}(X) = \frac{(b-a)^2}{12} = \frac{(19-4)^2}{12} = \frac{225}{12} = \frac{75}{4} = 18.75$

$F(x) = \int_{-\infty}^{x} f(t)dt = \int_4^x \frac{1}{15}dt = \frac{1}{15}\int_4^x 1\,dt$

$= \frac{1}{15}\left[t\right]_4^x = \frac{1}{15}(x-4) = \frac{x-4}{15}$

So, $F(x) = \begin{cases} 0 & \text{for } x < 4 \\ \frac{x-4}{15} & \text{for } 4 \leq x \leq 19 \\ 1 & \text{for } x > 19 \end{cases}$

b) $E(Y) = E(6X-3) = 6E(X) - 3 = 6 \times 11.5 - 3 = 66$
$\text{Var}(Y) = \text{Var}(6X-3) = 6^2\text{Var}(X) = 36 \times 18.75 = 675$

12) a) The p.d.f. of X is a rectangle of height 0.25, while the p.d.f. of Y is a rectangle of height 0.05.
$P(X < 6) = (6-4) \times 0.25 = 0.5$.
$P(Y > 0) = (12-0) \times 0.05 = 0.6$.
So $P(X < 6 \text{ and } Y > 0) = 0.5 \times 0.6 = 0.3$.

b) $P(X < 6 \text{ or } Y > 0) = P(X < 6) + P(Y > 0) - P(X < 6 \text{ and } Y > 0)$
$= 0.5 + 0.6 - 0.3 = 0.8$

13) X follows a rectangular distribution with $a = 0$ and $b = 12$. So its p.d.f. is a rectangle of width 12 and height $\frac{1}{12}$.

a) P(late for work) $= P(X > 8) = 4 \times \frac{1}{12} = \frac{1}{3}$

b) P(late more than once) $= 1 - $ P(never late) $-$ P(late once).
So P(late more than once)

$= 1 - \left(\frac{2}{3}\right)^5 - 5\left(\frac{2}{3}\right)^4 \times \frac{1}{3} = \frac{243 - 32 - 80}{243} = \frac{131}{243}$

Exam Questions

1 a) $\int_{-\infty}^{\infty} f(x)dx = \frac{1}{k}\int_0^2 (x+4)dx = \frac{1}{k}\left[\frac{x^2}{2} + 4x\right]_0^2 = \frac{10}{k}$ *[1 mark]*

This must be equal to 1 *[1 mark]*.

So $k = 10$ *[1 mark]*.

There aren't many certainties in life, but "Your S2 exam will test if you know that the total area under a p.d.f. = 1" is one of them.

Answers

b) Integrate the pieces of the p.d.f., and then make sure the 'joins' are smooth using a constant of integration (k). *[1 mark]*.

$$F(x) = \begin{cases} 0 \text{ for } x < 0 \\ 0.05x^2 + 0.4x + k \text{ for } 0 \le x \le 2 \\ 1 \text{ for } x > 2 \end{cases}$$

[1 mark for each part correctly found]

All the joins are 'smooth' if $k = 0$, so the c.d.f. is:

$$F(x) = \begin{cases} 0 \text{ for } x < 0 \\ 0.05x^2 + 0.4x \text{ for } 0 \le x \le 2 \\ 1 \text{ for } x > 2 \end{cases}$$

[1 mark for final answer]

You must define a c.d.f. for all values of x. Don't just do the tricky bits in the middle and assume you're finished.

c) $E(X) = \int_{-\infty}^{\infty} xf(x)dx = \int_0^2 0.1(x^2 + 4x)dx$ *[1 mark]*

$= 0.1\left[\frac{x^3}{3} + 2x^2\right]_0^2$ *[1 mark]*

$= 0.1\left(\frac{8}{3} + 8\right) = \frac{32}{30} = \frac{16}{15} = 1.07$ (to 2 d.p.) *[1 mark]*

d) (i) $Var(X) = \int_{-\infty}^{\infty} x^2f(x)dx - \mu^2$

$= 0.1\int_0^2(x^3 + 4x^2)dx - \left(\frac{16}{15}\right)^2$ *[1 mark]*

$= 0.1\left[\frac{x^4}{4} + \frac{4x^3}{3}\right]_0^2 - \left(\frac{16}{15}\right)^2$ *[1 mark]*

$= 0.1\left(4 + \frac{32}{3}\right) - \left(\frac{16}{15}\right)^2$

$= \frac{44}{30} - \left(\frac{16}{15}\right)^2 = \frac{74}{225}$

$= 0.329$ (to 3 d.p.). *[1 mark]*

If you worked out the integral but forgot to subtract the square of the mean, then you've just thrown a few marks away — at least, you would have done if that had been a real exam.

(ii) $Var(4X - 2) = 16 \times Var(X)$ *[1 mark]*

$= 16 \times \frac{74}{225} = \frac{1184}{225} = 5.262$ (to 3 d.p.). *[1 mark]*

e) Use the c.d.f. from part b) to find the median.
The median is m, where $0.05m^2 + 0.4m = 0.5$ *[1 mark]*.
This simplifies to: $m^2 + 8m - 10 = 0$ *[1 mark]*.
Using the quadratic formula (and choosing the positive answer *[1 mark]*) gives

$m = \frac{-8 + \sqrt{104}}{2} = 1.099$ (to 3 d.p.) *[1 mark]*.

2 a) Using the third part of the c.d.f., $F(3) = 0.5$ *[1 mark]*.
So $F(3)$ must also equal 0.5 using the second part of the c.d.f., which means that $2k = 0.5$, or $k = 0.25$ *[1 mark]*.

Make sure the bits of a cumulative distribution function join together smoothly.

b) Q_1 is given by $F(Q_1) = 0.25$ *[1 mark]*. Since $F(3) = 0.5$, the lower quartile must lie in the region described by the second part of the c.d.f., so solve $0.25(Q_1 - 1) = 0.25$, or $Q_1 = 2$ *[1 mark]*.

Q_3 is given by $F(Q_3) = 0.75$ *[1 mark]*. Since $F(3) = 0.5$, the upper quartile must lie in the region described by the third part of the c.d.f., so solve $0.5(Q_3 - 2) = 0.75$, or $Q_3 = 3.5$ *[1 mark]*.

So the interquartile range is $3.5 - 2 = 1.5$ *[1 mark]*.

c) (i) Differentiate to find the p.d.f.:

$$f(x) = \begin{cases} 0.25 \text{ for } 1 \le x < 3 \text{ [1 mark]} \\ 0.5 \text{ for } 3 \le x \le 4 \text{ [1 mark]} \\ 0 \text{ otherwise [1 mark]} \end{cases}$$

(ii)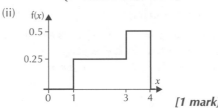

[1 mark]

I always draw a graph of the p.d.f. whether the question asks me to or not. You should too. It not only makes questions easier, but you'll often get marks for doing something that you were going to do anyway. It's like free marks.

d) (i) $\mu = \int_{-\infty}^{\infty} xf(x)dx$

$= \int_1^3 0.25x\,dx + \int_3^4 0.5x\,dx$ *[1 mark]*

$= [0.125x^2]_1^3 + [0.25x^2]_3^4$ *[1 mark]*

$= 1 + \frac{7}{4} = \frac{11}{4} = 2.75$ *[1 mark]*

(ii) $Var(X) = \sigma^2 = \int_{-\infty}^{\infty} x^2f(x)dx - \mu^2$

$= \int_1^3 0.25x^2\,dx + \int_3^4 0.5x^2\,dx - 2.75^2$ *[1 mark]*

$= \left[\frac{0.25x^3}{3}\right]_1^3 + \left[\frac{0.5x^3}{3}\right]_3^4 - 2.75^2$ *[1 mark]*

$= \frac{13}{6} + \frac{37}{6} - \left(\frac{11}{4}\right)^2 = \frac{25}{3} - \frac{121}{16}$

$= \frac{37}{48} = 0.771$ (to 3 d.p.) *[1 mark]*.

I hope you remembered to subtract the square of the mean.

(iii) $P(X < \mu - \sigma) = P(X < 2.75 - \sqrt{0.771}) = P(X < 1.87)$ *[1 mark]*. Using the above sketch, the area under the p.d.f. between $x = 1$ and $x = 1.87$ is:
$(1.87 - 1) \times 0.25 = 0.218$ (to 3 d.p.) *[1 mark]*.

3 a)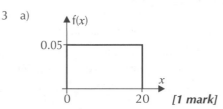

[1 mark]

You probably haven't earned many marks for drawing rectangles since you were about 6 years old and in primary school. So it's nice that the skill you learnt way back then is now helping you pass S2.

b) (i) $P(X > 5) = (20 - 5) \times 0.05 = 0.75$ *[1 mark]*

(ii) $P(X = 2) = 0$ *[1 mark]*

c) $E(X) = \frac{0 + 20}{2} = 10$ *[1 mark]*

$Var(X) = \frac{(20 - 0)^2}{12}$ *[1 mark]*

$= \frac{400}{12} = 33.3$ (to 3 sig. fig.) *[1 mark]*.

Answers

d) $E(Y) = E(X^3) = \int_{-\infty}^{\infty} x^3 f(x) \, dx$ *[1 mark]*

$= \int_0^{20} x^3 \times \frac{1}{20} \, dx = \frac{1}{20} \int_0^{20} x^3 \, dx = \frac{1}{20}\left[\frac{x^4}{4}\right]_0^{20}$ *[1 mark]*

$= \frac{1}{20} \times \frac{20^4}{4} = \frac{20^3}{4} = 2000$ *[1 mark]*

e) $E(Z) = E\left(\frac{2X^6}{Y}\right) = E\left(\frac{2X^6}{X^3}\right)$

$= E(2X^3)$ *[1 mark]* $= E(2Y) = 2E(Y)$ *[1 mark]*

$= 2 \times 2000 = 4000$ *[1 mark]*

Part e) looks tricky, but it's really not so bad as long as you take your time and work out how you can rearrange the expression to make use of what you already know. And that, as they say, is that.

S2 Section 4
— Estimation and Hypothesis Tests
Warm-up Questions

1) a) He needs to make the assumption that the population follows a normal distribution.

b) $\left(\overline{X} - \frac{S}{\sqrt{n}}t_{(n-1)}, \ \overline{X} + \frac{S}{\sqrt{n}}t_{(n-1)}\right)$

c) $n = 12$, so for $p = 0.975$, $t_{(11)} = 2.201$.
So 95% confidence interval
$= \left(50 - \frac{\sqrt{0.7}}{\sqrt{12}} \times 2.201, 50 + \frac{\sqrt{0.7}}{\sqrt{12}} \times 2.201\right)$
$= (49.5, 50.5)$ (to 3 sig.fig.)

2) 9 lies outside this confidence interval, so there is evidence to doubt the claim.

3) a) i) One-tailed — Salma is only interested in whether the average height is greater than 160 cm.

ii) Two-tailed — Joy is interested in either an increase or a decrease in the mean diameter.

b) i) H_0: $\mu = 160$ and H_1: $\mu > 160$

ii) H_0: $\mu = 2.2$ and H_1: $\mu \neq 2.2$

4) A type I error — he rejects H_0 when it's actually true.

5) You'd use a t-test when the population follows a normal distribution, the population variance is unknown and the sample size is small.

6) H_0: $\mu = 45$, H_1: $\mu < 45$, $\alpha = 0.05$ and $\sigma^2 = 9$.
Under H_0, $\overline{X} \sim N\left(45, \frac{9}{16}\right)$ and $Z = \frac{42 - 45}{\frac{3}{4}} = -4$
Critical region is $Z < -1.6449$.
$-4 < -1.6449$, so there is evidence to reject H_0 at the 5% level.

7) a) $\overline{x} = \frac{\sum x}{n} = \frac{197.8}{10} = 19.78$

$s^2 = \frac{n}{n-1}\left[\frac{\sum x^2}{n} - \left(\frac{\sum x}{n}\right)^2\right]$

$= \frac{10}{9}\left[\frac{3919.78}{10} - 19.78^2\right] = \frac{10}{9} \times 0.7296 = 0.811 \text{(3 s.f.)}$

b) H_0: $\mu = 20$ and H_1: $\mu < 20$. $\alpha = 0.05$.
The variance is unknown and $n = 10$, so you need to use a t-test with 9 degrees of freedom.
Under H_0, $T = \frac{\overline{X} - 20}{\sqrt{\frac{0.811}{10}}} \sim t_{(9)}$

$\overline{x} = 19.78 \Rightarrow t = \frac{19.78 - 20}{\sqrt{\frac{0.811}{10}}} = -0.773$

The critical value is t such that $P(T < t) = 0.05$.
By symmetry, it's $-t$, where $P(T > t) = 0.05$, i.e. where $P(T < t) = 0.95$. $P(T < 1.833) = 0.95$, so the critical value is -1.833, and the critical region is $T < -1.833$.
$-0.733 > -1.833$, so the result is not significant at this level. There is no evidence at the 5% level to suggest that $\mu < 20$.

8) The 1% point of $\chi^2_{(4)}$ = value of x where $P(X \leq x) = 0.99$. So critical value = 13.277. $8.3 < 13.277$, so there is no evidence at the 1% level of an association between the variables.

9) H_0: no association between the variables 'gender' and 'likes/dislikes olives',
H_1: there is an association.
It's a 2 × 2 table, so your test statistic is $\sum \frac{(|O - E| - 0.5)^2}{E}$.

Make a table showing the observed frequencies; the expected frequencies, $\frac{\text{(row total)} \times \text{(column total)}}{n}$; and the values of $\frac{(|O - E| - 0.5)^2}{E}$.

Observed frequency (O)	Expected Frequency (E)	$\frac{(|O-E|-0.5)^2}{E}$
22	20.8	0.0236
30	31.2	0.0157
18	19.2	0.0255
30	28.8	0.0170
100	100	**0.0818**

So $\chi^2 = 0.082$ (to 3 d.p.).
Under H_0, $X^2 \sim \chi^2_{(\nu)}$ where $\nu = 1$.
So the critical value at the 5% level is 3.841.
$0.082 < 3.841$, so do not reject H_0.
There is no evidence at the 5% level of an association between a person's gender and whether or not they like olives.

Answers

Exam Questions

1 a) You need to make the assumption that the journey times
       follow a normal distribution *[1 mark]*.

$$\bar{x} = \frac{\sum x}{n} = \frac{324}{20} = 16.2 \text{ mins } \textbf{[1 mark]}$$

$$s^2 = \frac{\sum(x - \bar{x})^2}{n - 1} = \frac{19.2}{19} \Rightarrow s = 1.005 \textbf{ [1 mark]}$$

$n = 20$, so you need to look up $t_{(19)}$ in the tables.
And it's a 95% confidence interval, so read across to
$p = 0.975$ to get $t_{(19)} = 2.093$ *[1 mark]*.
The interval is given by:

$$\left(\bar{x} - \frac{s}{\sqrt{n}} t_{(n-1)} , \; \bar{x} + \frac{s}{\sqrt{n}} t_{(n-1)} \right)$$

$$= \left(16.2 - \frac{1.005}{\sqrt{20}} \times 2.093 , \; 16.2 + \frac{1.005}{\sqrt{20}} \times 2.093 \right) \textbf{[1 mark]}$$

$$= (16.2 - 0.47, 16.2 + 0.47) \textbf{ [1 mark]}$$

$$= (15.7, 16.7) \text{ (to 3 s.f.) } \textbf{[1 mark]}$$

   b) Joe's claimed time of 15 minutes lies outside the 95%
       confidence interval, so there is evidence to doubt this
       claim. *[1 mark]*

2 a) $\bar{x} = \frac{\sum x}{n} = \frac{490}{100} = 4.9 \, m$ *[1 mark]*

$$s^2 = \frac{n}{n-1} \left[\frac{\sum x^2}{n} - \left(\frac{\sum x}{n} \right)^2 \right]$$

$$= \frac{100}{99} \left[\frac{2421}{100} - 4.9^2 \right] \textbf{[1 mark]}$$

$$= \frac{20}{99} = 0.202 \text{ (to 3 d.p.) } \textbf{[1 mark]}$$

   b) Let μ = mean height of trees in 2nd area.
       H_0: $\mu = 5.1$ and H_1: $\mu \neq 5.1$ *[1 mark]*

       Under H_0, $\bar{X} \sim N\left(5.1, \frac{20/99}{100}\right)$ *[1 mark]* $= N\left(5.1, \frac{1}{495}\right)$

$$Z = \frac{4.9 - 5.1}{\sqrt{1/495}} \textbf{ [1 mark]} = -4.45 \textbf{ [1 mark]}$$

       This is a two-tailed test at the 1% level, so the critical
       values you need are z such that $P(Z < z) = 0.005$ and
       $P(Z > z) = 0.005$. Looking these up in the normal tables
       you get critical values of -2.5758 and 2.5758 *[1 mark]*.
       Since $-4.45 < -2.576$, the result is significant. There is
       evidence to reject H_0 and to suggest that the trees have a
       different mean height *[1 mark]*.

3 a) H_0: no association between age and favourite flavour of ice
       cream *[1 mark]*, H_1: there is an association.
       Make a table showing the observed frequencies, the
       expected frequencies and the values of $(O - E)^2 / E$:

Observed frequency (O)	Expected Frequency (E)	$\frac{(O - E)^2}{E}$
10	11.52	0.200...
24	24	0
7	5.28	0.560...
7	7.2	0.005...
14	12.48	0.185...
26	26	0
4	5.72	0.517...
8	7.8	0.005...
100	100	**1.47**

   *[1 mark for calculating the expected frequencies, 1 mark
   for all values of E correct, 1 mark for calculating values of
   (O – E)² / E, 1 mark for all values of (O – E)² / E correct.]*
   So $\chi^2 = 1.47$ *[1 mark]*
   Under H_0, $X^2 \sim \chi^2_{(\nu)}$ where $\nu = (4 - 1) \times (2 - 1) = 3$ *[1 mark]*.
   So the critical value at the 5% level is 7.815 *[1 mark]*.
   $1.47 < 7.815$, so do not reject H_0.
   There is no evidence of association between age and
   favourite flavour of ice cream *[1 mark]*.

   b) Not rejecting H_0 when H_0 is not true *[1 mark]*. Stating that
       there is no association between age and favourite flavour of
       ice cream when there is an association *[1 mark]*.

S2 Practice Exam One

1 a) (i) Since the average number of houses sold per week is 2,
            $X \sim Po(2)$ *[1 mark]*.

$$P(X = 1) = \frac{e^{-2} 2^1}{1!} = \frac{2}{e^2} = 0.271 \text{(to 3 sig. fig.) } \textbf{[1 mark]}$$

            *You can do this with tables, but here it's quicker just to use the
            formula.*

       (ii) $P(2 \leq X \leq 4) = P(X \leq 4) - P(X < 2)$
             $= P(X \leq 4) - P(X \leq 1)$ *[1 mark]*
             $= 0.9473 - 0.4060$ *[1 mark]*
             $= 0.5413$ *[1 mark]*.

            *And you could do this one by working out P(X = 2), P(X = 3) and
            P(X = 4) using the formula, and then adding the results. Do it the
            way that seems to involve less work, that's my (obvious) advice.*

   b) $P(X \geq 2) = 1 - P(X < 2) = 1 - P(X \leq 1)$
       $= 1 - 0.4060 = 0.5940$ *[1 mark]*.
       Since the sales can be modelled by a Poisson distribution,
       the individual events (i.e. house sales) are independent,
       meaning that total sales in each week are also independent.
       This allows you to multiply probabilities for individual
       weeks.

       So P(qualify for "monthly bonus") $= 0.5940^4$ *[1 mark]*
       $= 0.124$ (to 3 sig. fig.) *[1 mark]*.

Answers

c) (i) $X \sim Po(2)$ and $Y \sim Po(3)$, so $H \sim Po(5)$ *[1 mark]*

(ii) Let J be the total number of houses sold between them in a two-week period. Then $J \sim Po(10)$ *[1 mark]*.
$P(J \geq 9) = 1 - P(J < 9) = 1 - P(J \leq 8)$ *[1 mark]*
$= 1 - 0.3328$ *[1 mark]* $= 0.6672$ *[1 mark]*

2 a)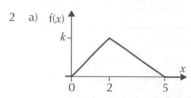

[1 mark for each sloping part of the graph correct]

b) The total area under the p.d.f. must equal 1.
So $\frac{2k}{2} + \frac{3k}{2} = \frac{5k}{2} = 1$ *[1 mark]*.
This means $k = \frac{2}{5}$ *[1 mark]*.

c) $F(x)$ will be in 4 parts.
First part: $F(x) = 0$ for $x < 0$ *[1 mark]*.

Second part: integrate $f(x) = \frac{1}{5}x$ to get $F(x) = \frac{1}{10}x^2 + c_1$, where c_1 is a constant of integration *[1 mark]*, chosen so that $F(0) = 0$. This means $c_1 = 0$, which then gives
$F(2) = \frac{2}{5}$. *[1 mark if this part of the c.d.f. is correct]*

Third part: integrate $f(x) = \frac{2}{15}(5-x) = \frac{2}{3} - \frac{2}{15}x$ to get
$F(x) = \frac{2}{3}x - \frac{1}{15}x^2 + c_2$, where c_2 is a constant of integration *[1 mark]*, chosen so that $F(2) = \frac{2}{5}$.
This means $c_2 = \frac{2}{5} - \frac{4}{3} + \frac{4}{15} = \frac{6 - 20 + 4}{15} = -\frac{10}{15} = -\frac{2}{3}$.
[1 mark if this part of the c.d.f. is correct]

This then gives $F(5) = 1$.
Fourth part: $F(x) = 1$ for $x > 5$ *[1 mark]*.

So overall, the c.d.f. is:
$$F(x) = \begin{cases} 0 & \text{for } x < 0 \\ \frac{1}{10}x^2 & \text{for } 0 \leq x < 2 \\ \frac{2}{3}x - \frac{1}{15}x^2 - \frac{2}{3} & \text{for } 2 \leq x \leq 5 \\ 1 & \text{for } x > 5 \end{cases}$$

Forgetting the constants of integration is a common problem with this kind of question. Remember... the different parts of a c.d.f. must join together smoothly — you can't have 'jumps'.

d) The median, m, of X is given by $F(m) = 0.5$.
From above, you can see that $2 < m < 5$ (since $F(2) = 0.4$).
So solve:
$\frac{2}{3}m - \frac{1}{15}m^2 - \frac{2}{3} = 0.5$, or $2m^2 - 20m + 35 = 0$
[1 mark for either quadratic].

Using the quadratic formula, this gives $m = \frac{20 \pm \sqrt{120}}{4}$,

i.e. $m = 5 \pm \frac{\sqrt{120}}{4}$ *[1 mark]*).

But $m < 5$, so $m = 5 - \frac{\sqrt{120}}{4} = 2.26$ (to 3 s.f.) *[1 mark]*.

Don't forget to use the right part of your c.d.f. to find the median. If you use the wrong bit, you might arrive at something that looks vaguely sensible, but it'll be completely wrong and you'll have egg all over your face. And you won't want that.

3 a) To calculate a confidence interval using this data, you need to make the assumption that the lap times follow a normal distribution *[1 mark]*.
$\bar{x} = \frac{\sum x}{n} = \frac{1408}{8} = 176$ seconds *[1 mark]*
$s^2 = \frac{n}{n-1}\left[\frac{\sum x^2}{n} - \left(\frac{\sum x}{n}\right)^2\right]$
$= \frac{8}{7} \times \left(\frac{247808.76}{8} - 176^2\right)$ *[1 mark]*
$= 0.10857... \Rightarrow s = 0.330$ *[1 mark]*
The 99% confidence interval is given by:
$\left(\bar{x} - \frac{s}{\sqrt{n}}t_{(7)},\ \bar{x} + \frac{s}{\sqrt{n}}t_{(7)}\right)$, where $t_{(7)}$ is 3.499 *[1 mark]*.
So it's: $176 \pm \frac{0.330}{\sqrt{8}} \times 3.499$ *[1 mark]*
$= 176 \pm 0.408$ *[1 mark]*
$= (175.6, 176.4)$ (to 1 d.p.) *[1 mark]*

b) The second driver's mean lap time lies below the 99% confidence interval for the first driver's mean lap time, so there is evidence to support this claim. *[1 mark]*

4 a) (i) *If it helps to draw a sketch, then you should draw one:*

So P(train more than 6 minutes late) $= P(X > 6)$
$= (9 - 6) \times \frac{1}{11}$
$= \frac{3}{11} = 0.273$ (to 3 sig. fig.) *[1 mark]*.

(ii) P(train within 1 minute of scheduled arrival time)
$= P(-1 < X < 1) = (1 - (-1)) \times \frac{1}{11} = \frac{2}{11}$
$= 0.182$ (to 3 sig. fig.) *[1 mark]*.

b) $Var(X) = \int_{-\infty}^{\infty} x^2 f(x)\,dx - [E(X)]^2$
$= \int_{-2}^{9} \frac{x^2}{11}\,dx - \left(\frac{7}{2}\right)^2$ *[1 mark]*
$= \frac{1}{11}\int_{-2}^{9} x^2\,dx - \frac{49}{4}$
$= \frac{1}{11}\left[\frac{x^3}{3}\right]_{-2}^{9} - \frac{49}{4}$ *[1 mark]*
$= \frac{1}{11}\left[\frac{9^3 - (-2)^3}{3}\right] - \frac{49}{4}$ *[1 mark]*
$= \frac{1}{11} \times \frac{737}{3} - \frac{49}{4}$
$= \frac{737}{33} - \frac{49}{4} = \frac{2948 - 1617}{132}$ *[1 mark]*
$= \frac{1331}{132} = \frac{121}{12}$ *[1 mark]*

c) From a), the probability of the train being more than 6 minutes late is $\frac{3}{11}$. Let the random variable Y represent the number of times in 5 days that the train is more than 6 minutes late.
Then, you want to find $P(Y \geq 1)$, which is:
$1 - P(Y < 1) = 1 - P(Y = 0)$ *[1 mark]*.
$P(Y = 0) = \left(1 - \frac{3}{11}\right)^5 = \left(\frac{8}{11}\right)^5$ *[1 mark]*
So, $P(Y \geq 1) = 1 - \left(\frac{8}{11}\right)^5 = 0.797$ (to 3 s.f.) *[1 mark]*
Don't forget that probability rules can come up in these questions. You need to be ready for anything.

Answers

5 Since n is fairly large, you can apply the Central Limit Theorem and carry out a z-test with σ^2 estimated by s^2.
H_0: $\mu = 500$ and H_1: $\mu < 500$. *[1 mark]* $\alpha = 0.05$.

$$\bar{x} = \frac{\sum x}{n} = \frac{24\,500}{50} = 490 \text{ cm } \textbf{[1 mark]}$$

$$s^2 = \frac{n}{n-1}\left[\frac{\sum x^2}{n} - \left(\frac{\sum x}{n}\right)^2\right]$$
$$= \frac{50}{49} \times \left(\frac{12\,011\,500}{50} - 490^2\right)$$
$$= \frac{50}{49} \times 130 = \frac{6500}{49} \textbf{ [1 mark]}$$

Under H_0:
$$\bar{X} \sim N\left(500, \frac{s^2}{n}\right) = N\left(500, \frac{6500}{49 \times 50}\right) = N\left(500, \frac{130}{49}\right)$$
Since $\bar{x} = 490$,

$$z = \frac{490 - 500}{\sqrt{\frac{130}{49}}} \textbf{ [1 mark]} = -6.14 \textbf{ [1 mark]}$$

This is a one-tailed test at the 5% level, so the critical value is z where $P(Z < z) = 0.05$. This is $-z$ where $P(Z > z) = 0.05$, or $P(Z < z) = 0.95$. $P(Z < 1.6449) = 0.95$, so the critical value is -1.6449 *[1 mark]* and the critical region is $Z < -1.6449$.
Since $-6.14 < -1.6449$, you should reject H_0 *[1 mark]*.
There is evidence to support the manager's claim at the 5% level. *[1 mark]*

6 a) $p = 0.2$, since the probabilities have to add up to 1 *[1 mark]*.

Easy.

b) $E(X) = \sum x P(X = x)$
$= 0.2 \times (0 + 10 + 20 + 50 + 100)$ *[1 mark]*
$= 36$ *[1 mark]*
$Var(X) = \sum x^2 P(X = x) - \{E(X)\}^2$
$= 0.2 \times (0 + 100 + 400 + 2500 + 10\,000) - 36^2$ *[1 mark]*
$= 1304$ *[1 mark]*

A bit harder.

c) $E(3X - 4) = 3E(X) - 4$ *[1 mark]*
$= 3 \times 36 - 4 = 104$ *[1 mark]*
$Var(3X - 4) = 3^2 \times Var(X)$ *[1 mark]*
$= 9 \times 1304 = 11\,736$ *[1 mark]*

Trickier — especially the variance bit.

d) X is a random variable that shows what's paid out. The expected value of X is 36p, so a charge of 40p will average a profit of 4p per game *[1 mark]*. This is unlikely to be sufficient to cover the owner's costs *[1 mark for any sensible comment]*.

Ooh — easy again.

e) Probably not. It would be usual for small prizes to have high probabilities and big prizes to have low probabilities.
[1 mark for saying that this model is unlikely, and 1 mark for any sensible explanation as to why.]

Sigh of relief — wasn't as bad as I thought.

7 a) H_0: no association between the variables 'gender' and 'foreign language studied' *[1 mark]*,
H_1: there is an association.

It's a 2 × 2 table, so your test statistic is $\sum \frac{(|O - E| - 0.5)^2}{E}$.

Make a table showing the observed frequencies; the expected frequencies, $\frac{(\text{row total}) \times (\text{column total})}{n}$; and the values of $\frac{(|O - E| - 0.5)^2}{E}$.

Observed frequency (O)	Expected Frequency (E)	$\frac{(|O - E| - 0.5)^2}{E}$
14	8.8	2.510
8	13.2	1.673
6	11.2	1.972
22	16.8	1.315
50	50	7.47

[1 mark for calculating the expected frequencies, 1 mark for all values of E correct, 1 mark for calculating values of $(|O - E| - 0.5)^2 / E$, 1 mark for all values of $(|O - E| - 0.5)^2 / E$ correct.]
So $\chi^2 = 7.47$ *[1 mark]*.
Under H_0, $X^2 \sim \chi^2_{(\nu)}$ where $\nu = 1$.
So the critical value at the 5% level is 3.841 **[1 mark]**.
$7.47 > 3.841$, so reject H_0.
There is evidence of an association between gender and the language chosen. *[1 mark]*

b) Saying that there is an association between gender and language chosen when there isn't one. *[1 mark]*

S2 Practice Exam Two

1 a) (i) The surviving bacteria are spread randomly, singly and are assumed to occur at a constant average rate, which would give rise to a Poisson distribution:
$X \sim Po(6)$ *[1 mark]*.

Using tables:
$P(X < 10) = P(X \leq 9) = 0.9161$ *[1 mark]*

(ii) $P(5 \leq X \leq 7) = P(X \leq 7) - P(X < 5)$
$= P(X \leq 7) - P(X \leq 4)$ *[1 mark]*
$= 0.7440 - 0.2851$ *[1 mark]*
$= 0.4589$ *[1 mark]*

Careful with the step: "$P(5 \leq X \leq 7) = P(X \leq 7) - P(X \leq 4)$" — it's easy to make a mistake there, because that '5' has somehow become a '4'. Think of it as subtracting the 'values of X you want to exclude'. So $P(5 \leq X \leq 7)$ means X can be 5, 6 or 7 — that means you want all the values of X less than or equal to 7 ($= P(X \leq 7)$), and then you want to subtract all the values of 4 or less ($= P(X \leq 4)$).

b) mean $= \frac{\sum x}{n} = \frac{83}{15} = 5.53$ (to 3 sig. fig.) *[1 mark]*

variance $= \frac{\sum x^2}{n} - \left(\frac{\sum x}{n}\right)^2$
$= \frac{543}{15} - \left(\frac{83}{15}\right)^2$ *[1 mark]*
$= 5.58$ (to 3 sig.fig.) *[1 mark]*

Answers

c) The mean and variance are approximately equal, which is a characteristic of a Poisson distribution *[1 mark]*.

Whenever you see a mean and a variance that are roughly equal, the little bell in your head marked 'Poisson' should start ringing.

d) $P(X = 5) = \dfrac{e^{-\lambda}\lambda^x}{x!}$

$= \dfrac{e^{-5.53} \times 5.53^5}{5!}$ *[1 mark]*

$= 0.171$ (to 3 sig. fig.) *[1 mark]*.

2 a) Using the definition of F(x) for $0 \le x \le 1$,
$F(1) = 0.5 + 0.2 = 0.7$ *[1 mark]*.
This means that $9.2 \times 1 - 3.5 \times 1^2 - k = 0.7$.
So $k = 9.2 - 3.5 - 0.7 = 5$ *[1 mark]*.

Remember... the different pieces of a c.d.f. have to join together smoothly for a continuous random variable.

b) You need to find Q_3, which is given by $F(Q_3) = 0.75$.
Since $F(1) = 0.7$, you know that Q_3 must be between 1 and 1.2, so solve $9.2x - 3.5x^2 - 5 = 0.75$,
or $3.5x^2 - 9.2x + 5.75 = 0$ *[1 mark for either quadratic]*.

Using the quadratic formula:

$x = \dfrac{9.2 \pm \sqrt{9.2^2 - 4 \times 3.5 \times 5.75}}{2 \times 3.5} = \dfrac{9.2 \pm \sqrt{4.14}}{7}$

You need to take the smaller of these two solutions (since the other one is greater than 1.2), which means that:

$Q_3 = \dfrac{9.2 - \sqrt{4.14}}{7} = 1.024$ *[1 mark]*.

So the interquartile range $= Q_3 - Q_1$
$= 1.024 - 0.688 = 0.336$ (to 3 sig. fig.) *[1 mark]*.

c) To find f(x), you need to differentiate F(x).

$f(x) = \begin{cases} 0 & \text{for } x < 0 \\ 2x^3 + 0.2 & \text{for } 0 \le x \le 1 \\ 9.2 - 7x & \text{for } 1 < x \le 1.2 \\ 0 & \text{for } x > 1.2 \end{cases}$

or

$f(x) = \begin{cases} 2x^3 + 0.2 & \text{for } 0 \le x \le 1 \\ 9.2 - 7x & \text{for } 1 < x \le 1.2 \\ 0 & \text{otherwise} \end{cases}$

[1 mark for each correct part of the p.d.f. (max. 3 marks)]

d) $P(X < 1.1)$ is just $F(1.1)$
$= (9.2 \times 1.1) - (3.5 \times 1.1^2) - 5$ *[1 mark]*
$= 10.12 - 4.235 - 5 = 0.885$ *[1 mark]*.

You could also work this out by integrating the p.d.f. between 0 and 1.1 if you wanted, but this way is a lot easier.

3 a) The sample size is small, so to carry out a hypothesis test you need to make the assumption that the heights follow a normal distribution *[1 mark]*.
H_0: $\mu = 150$ and H_1: $\mu \ne 150$ *[1 mark]*. $\alpha = 0.05$.
The variance is unknown and n is small, so you need to use a t-test, and estimate σ^2 with s^2.

$\bar{x} = \dfrac{\sum x}{n} = \dfrac{876}{6} = 146$ cm *[1 mark]*

$s^2 = \dfrac{n}{n-1}\left[\dfrac{\sum x^2}{n} - \left(\dfrac{\sum x}{n}\right)^2\right]$

$= \dfrac{6}{5} \times \left(\dfrac{128\,005.94}{6} - 146^2\right)$ *[1 mark]*

$= \dfrac{6}{5} \times 18.323... = 21.988$ *[1 mark]*

$t = \dfrac{146 - 150}{\sqrt{\dfrac{21.988}{6}}}$ *[1 mark]* $= -2.09$ *[1 mark]*

$n = 6$, so under H_0, $t \sim t_{(5)}$.
It's a two-tailed test at the 5% level, so the critical values are $\pm t$ such that $P(T > t) = 0.025$. By looking up $P(T < t) = 0.975$ for the $t_{(5)}$ distribution, you get critical values of ± 2.571 *[1 mark]*, and so the critical region is $T < -2.571$ and $T > 2.571$.
Since $t = -2.09$ is not in the critical region, do not reject H_0. There is no evidence at the 5% level to suggest that the average height isn't the same. *[1 mark]*

b) Let Y represent the height of a sunflower in the third field, then $Y \sim N(\mu, 20)$. The distribution is normal and the variance is known, so you can do a z-test.
H_0: $\mu = 150$ and H_1: $\mu \ne 150$ *[1 mark]*. $\alpha = 0.01$.

$\bar{x} = \dfrac{\sum x}{n} = \dfrac{840}{6} = 140$ cm *[1 mark]*

$z = \dfrac{140 - 150}{\sqrt{\dfrac{20}{6}}}$ *[1 mark]* $= -5.48$ *[1 mark]*,

where $Z \sim N(0, 1)$
It's a two-tailed test at the 1% level, so the critical values are $\pm z$ such that $P(Z > z) = 0.005$. By looking up $P(Z < z) = 0.995$ in the normal tables, you get critical values of ± 2.5758 *[1 mark]*, and so the critical region is $Z < -2.5758$ and $Z > 2.5758$.
Since $z = -5.48$ is in the critical region, reject H_0. There is evidence at the 1% level to suggest that the average height is different. *[1 mark]*

4 a) (i) This is a rectangular distribution with $a = 41.5$ and $b = 42.5$. So:

$E(X) = \dfrac{a + b}{2} = \dfrac{41.5 + 42.5}{2} = 42$ *[1 mark]*

$Var(X) = \dfrac{(b - a)^2}{12} = \dfrac{(42.5 - 41.5)^2}{12} = \dfrac{1}{12}$ *[1 mark]*

These formulas are in your formula booklet. But if you learn them off by heart so you can reel them off without having to look at the formula booklet, then so much the better.

(ii) For $x < 41.5$, $F(x) = 0$ and for $x > 42.5$, $F(x) = 1$.
For $41.5 \le x \le 42.5$, you need to integrate:

$F(x) = \displaystyle\int_{-\infty}^{x} f(t)\,dt = \int_{-\infty}^{41.5} 0\,dt + \int_{41.5}^{x} 1\,dt$

$= 0 + [t]_{41.5}^{x} = x - 41.5$

Putting that all together:

$F(x) = \begin{cases} 0 & \text{for } x < 41.5 \\ x - 41.5 & \text{for } 41.5 \le x \le 42.5 \\ 1 & \text{for } x > 42.5 \end{cases}$

[1 mark for 'x – 41.5' for x between 41.5 and 42.5; 1 mark for a definition of F(x) for all values of x.]

Answers

(iii) The median is given by $F(m) = 0.5$.

So solve $m - 41.5 = 0.5$, giving $m = 42$ *[1 mark]*.

You didn't really need to solve an equation in that last bit — you could have just stated the answer if you'd preferred. For a rectangular distribution, the mean and the median are right in the middle of the distribution.

b) This is the probability that $41.7 < X < 42.3$.

You <u>could</u> sketch the p.d.f. to find the area under the graph between 41.7 and 42.3. Alternatively you can just find the width of this interval ($= 42.3 - 41.7 = 0.6$) and multiply by the height of the p.d.f. ($= 1$) to find that the probability of a random cylinder being acceptable is 0.6 *[1 mark]*.

If in any doubt at all, draw a sketch — that's what I always say.

5 $\bar{x} = \dfrac{\sum x}{n} = \dfrac{1700}{20} = 85$ mph *[1 mark]*

$s^2 = \dfrac{\sum(x - \bar{x})^2}{n-1} = \dfrac{60}{19} \Rightarrow s = 1.777$ *[1 mark]*

The 95% confidence interval is given by:

$\left(\bar{x} - \dfrac{s}{\sqrt{n}}t_{(19)}, \ \bar{x} + \dfrac{s}{\sqrt{n}}t_{(19)}\right)$, where $t_{(19)}$ is 2.093 *[1 mark]*.

So it's: $85 \pm \dfrac{1.777}{\sqrt{20}} \times 2.093$ *[1 mark]*

$= 85 \pm 0.832$ *[1 mark]*

$= (84.2, 85.8)$ (to 3 sig. fig.) *[1 mark]*

6 a) (i) The total probability must be 1, so go through all the possible values of x and add the probabilities *[1 mark]*:

$\dfrac{k}{6} + \dfrac{2k}{6} + \dfrac{3k}{6} + \dfrac{3k}{6} + \dfrac{2k}{6} + \dfrac{k}{6} = \dfrac{12k}{6} = 2k$ *[1 mark]*.

This must equal 1, so k must be $\dfrac{1}{2}$ *[1 mark]*.

(ii) $P(X \le 3)$ is the probability that X takes a value less than or equal to 3. Which is:

$P(X = 1) + P(X = 2) + P(X = 3)$ *[1 mark]*

$= \dfrac{1}{12} + \dfrac{2}{12} + \dfrac{3}{12}$

$= \dfrac{6}{12} = \dfrac{1}{2}$ *[1 mark]*

(iii) $E(X) = \sum x P(X = x)$

$= \left(1 \times \dfrac{1}{12}\right) + \left(2 \times \dfrac{2}{12}\right) + \left(3 \times \dfrac{3}{12}\right)$

$+ \left(4 \times \dfrac{3}{12}\right) + \left(5 \times \dfrac{2}{12}\right) + \left(6 \times \dfrac{1}{12}\right)$ *[1 mark]*

$= \dfrac{1 + 4 + 9 + 12 + 10 + 6}{12} = \dfrac{42}{12}$

$= 3.5$ *[1 mark]*

(iv) $E(2 - 3X) = 2 - 3E(X)$ *[1 mark]*

$= 2 - (3 \times 3.5) = -8.5$ *[1 mark]*

$Var(2 - 3X) = (-3)^2 Var(X)$ *[1 mark]*

$= 9 \times \dfrac{23}{12} = \dfrac{69}{4} = 17.25$ *[1 mark]*

The expected value formula is kind of what you'd expect. But be careful with the variance formula — it's a bit weird.

$Var(X) = E(X^2) - \{E(X)\}^2$

(i.e. the variance is the 'mean of the squares minus the square of the mean').

Rearranging you get: $E(X^2) = Var(X) + \{E(X)\}^2$ *[1 mark]*.

So $E(X^2) = \dfrac{23}{12} + (3.5)^2 = \dfrac{23}{12} + \left(\dfrac{7}{2}\right)^2$ *[1 mark]*

$- \dfrac{23 + 147}{12} = \dfrac{170}{12} = \dfrac{85}{6}$ *[1 mark]*.

b) (i) The probabilities must sum to 1, so:

$0.1 + 0.2 + p + q + 0.2 = 1$, or $p + q = 0.5$ *[1 mark]*.

$E(Y) = 6.3$, so $(0.1 \times 2) + (0.2 \times 4) +$

$(p \times 6) + (q \times 8) + (0.2 \times 10) = 6.3$,

or $6p + 8q = 3.3$ *[1 mark]*.

(ii) Rearrange the first equation to give an expression for p, then substitute this into the second equation.

$p = 0.5 - q$, so

$6 \times (0.5 - q) + 8q = 3.3$ *[1 mark]*,

which gives $2q = 0.3$. This means $q = 0.15$ *[1 mark]*.

Then $p = 0.5 - q = 0.5 - 0.15$, i.e. $p = 0.35$ *[1 mark]*.

Even though simultaneous equations aren't part of S2, you're still expected to know how to solve them.

7 H_0: no association between the variables 'height' and 'presence of disease' *[1 mark]*,

H_1: there is an association.

It's a 2×2 table, so your test statistic is $\sum \dfrac{(|O - E| - 0.5)^2}{E}$.

Make a table showing the observed frequencies; the expected frequencies, $\dfrac{(\text{row total}) \times (\text{column total})}{n}$; and the values of $\dfrac{(|O - E| - 0.5)^2}{E}$.

Observed frequency (O)	Expected Frequency (E)	$\dfrac{(|O - E| - 0.5)^2}{E}$
32	35.7	0.287
19	15.3	0.669
38	34.3	0.299
11	14.7	0.697
100	100	1.952

[1 mark for calculating the expected frequencies, 1 mark for all values of E correct, 1 mark for calculating values of (|O − E| − 0.5)² / E, 1 mark for all values of (|O − E| − 0.5)² / E correct.]

So $\chi^2 = 1.952$ *[1 mark]*.

Under H_0, $X^2 \sim \chi^2_{(v)}$ where $v = 1$.

So the critical value at the 5% level is 3.841 **[1 mark]**.

$1.952 < 3.841$, so do not reject H_0.

There is no evidence at the 5% level to suggest an association between the variables 'height' and 'presence of disease'. *[1 mark]*

Answers

M2 Section 1

— Moments and Centres of Mass

Warm-up Questions

1) Moments about B: $60g \times 3 = T_2 \times 8$

So $T_2 = \dfrac{180g}{8} = 220.5\,\text{N}$

Vertically balanced forces, so $T_1 + T_2 = 60g$

$T_1 = 367.5\,\text{N}$

Ah, I remember my first moments question, it was a very memorable moment...

2) A rod (a long, inextensible particle) where the centre of mass is not at the central point of the rod.

Think of rods as really simple sticks. They don't bend, don't stretch or compress, and have no width.

3) 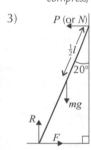 Where:

mg = weight of the ladder

F = friction between ground and ladder

R = normal reaction of the ground

P / N = normal reaction of the wall

As the rod is uniform the weight of the ladder acts at the centre of the rod (i.e. at half of l).

Assumptions: e.g. the ladder can be modelled as a rod, the ladder is rigid, friction is sufficient to keep the ladder in equilibrium, the ladder is perpendicular to the wall when viewed from above.

'Perpendicular' and 'normal' are both used in M2 (as are 'P' and 'N' to label the forces). No need to panic — they mean the same thing in all you'll do here.

4) a) Particles in a horizontal line so use $\Sigma mx = \overline{x}\Sigma m$

$m_1 x_1 + m_2 x_2 + m_3 x_3 = \overline{x}(m_1 + m_2 + m_3)$

$\Rightarrow (1 \times 1) + (2 \times 2) + (3 \times 3) = \overline{x}(1 + 2 + 3)$

$\Rightarrow 14 = 6\overline{x} \Rightarrow \overline{x} = 14 \div 6 = 2\frac{1}{3}$.

So coordinates are $(2\frac{1}{3}, 0)$.

b) Particles in a vertical line so use $\Sigma my = \overline{y}\Sigma m$

$m_1 y_1 + m_2 y_2 + m_3 y_3 = \overline{y}(m_1 + m_2 + m_3)$

$\Rightarrow (1 \times 3) + (2 \times 2) + (3 \times 1) = \overline{y}(1 + 2 + 3)$

$\Rightarrow 10 = 6\overline{y} \Rightarrow \overline{y} = 10 \div 6 = 1\frac{2}{3}$.

So coordinates are $(0, 1\frac{2}{3})$.

c) Particles in 2D so use $\Sigma m\mathbf{r} = \overline{\mathbf{r}}\Sigma m$

$m_1 \mathbf{r}_1 + m_2 \mathbf{r}_2 + m_3 \mathbf{r}_3 = \overline{\mathbf{r}}(m_1 + m_2 + m_3)$

$\Rightarrow 1\binom{3}{4} + 2\binom{3}{1} + 3\binom{1}{0} = \overline{\mathbf{r}}(1 + 2 + 3)$

$\Rightarrow \binom{12}{6} = 6\overline{\mathbf{r}} \Rightarrow \overline{\mathbf{r}} = \binom{12}{6} \div 6 = \binom{2}{1}$.

So coordinates are $(2, 1)$.

5) Use $\Sigma m\mathbf{r} = \overline{\mathbf{r}}\Sigma m$

$m\binom{0}{0} + 2m\binom{0}{4} + 3m\binom{5}{4} + 12\binom{5}{0} = (m + 2m + 3m + 12)\binom{3.5}{2}$

$\Rightarrow \binom{15m + 60}{20m} = \binom{21m + 42}{12m + 24}$

$\Rightarrow 20m = 12m + 24 \Rightarrow 8m = 24 \Rightarrow m = 24 \div 8 = 3\,\text{kg}$.

6) a) Large rectangle (1) has area $2 \times 3 = 6$, so $m_1 = 6$.

$x_1 = 2$ and $y_1 = 2.5$ (symmetry).

Square (2) has area $1 \times 1 = 1$, so $m_2 = 1$.

$x_2 = 3.5$ and $y_2 = 1.5$ (symmetry).

Combined shape has:

$m_1 x_1 + m_2 x_2 = \overline{x}(m_1 + m_2)$

$(6 \times 2) + (1 \times 3.5) = (6 + 1)\overline{x}$

$\Rightarrow 15.5 = 7\overline{x} \Rightarrow \overline{x} = 15.5 \div 7 = 2.21$ (3 s.f.).

and:

$m_1 y_1 + m_2 y_2 = \overline{y}(m_1 + m_2)$

$\Rightarrow (6 \times 2.5) + (1 \times 1.5) = (6 + 1)\overline{y}$

$\Rightarrow 16.5 = 7\overline{y} \Rightarrow \overline{y} = 16.5 \div 7 = 2.36$ (3 s.f.).

So coordinates are $(2.21, 2.36)$.

You could also have used the formula in 2D to find this, but sometimes it's nice to find each coordinate separately.

b) Circle (1) has area $\pi \times 1^2 = \pi$, so $m_1 = \pi$.

$x_1 = 8$ and $y_1 = 3$ (symmetry)

Rectangle (2) has area $4 \times 3 = 12$, so $m_2 = 12$.

$x_2 = 8$ and $y_2 = 2.5$ (symmetry)

Combined shape has $\overline{x} = 8$ (symmetry) and:

$m_1 y_1 + m_2 y_2 = \overline{y}(m_1 + m_2)$

$\Rightarrow (\pi \times 3) + (12 \times 2.5) = (\pi + 12)\overline{y}$

$\Rightarrow 39.42 = 15.14\overline{y}$

$\Rightarrow \overline{y} = 2.60$ (3 s.f.).

So coordinates are $(8, 2.60)$.

c) Circle (1) has area $\pi \times 2^2 = 4\pi$, so $m_1 = 4\pi$.

$x_1 = 14$ and $y_1 = 2$ (symmetry).

Square (2) has area $1 \times 1 = 1$, so $m_2 = 1$.

$x_2 = 14.5$ and $y_2 = 2.5$ (symmetry).

Use the formula to find $\overline{\mathbf{r}}$, the centre of mass of the whole shape:

$m_1 \mathbf{r}_1 + m_2 \mathbf{r}_2 = \overline{\mathbf{r}}(m_1 + m_2)$

$4\pi\binom{14}{2} + 1\binom{14.5}{2.5} = \overline{\mathbf{r}}(4\pi + 1)$

$\binom{56\pi + 14.5}{8\pi + 2.5} = \overline{\mathbf{r}}(4\pi + 1)$

So $\overline{\mathbf{r}} = (14.0, 2.04)$ (to 3 s.f.)

7) a) i) $m_1 y_1 + m_2 y_2 + m_3 y_3 + m_4 y_4 = \overline{y}(m_1 + m_2 + m_3 + m_4)$

$(7 \times 0) + (6 \times 0) + (10 \times 5) + (12 \times 5)$

$= \overline{y}(7 + 6 + 10 + 12)$

$110 = 35\overline{y} \Rightarrow \overline{y} = 3.14\,\text{cm}$ (3 s.f.).

The framework is 'light' so it has no mass.

ii) $m_1 x_1 + m_2 x_2 + m_3 x_3 + m_4 x_4 = \overline{y}(m_1 + m_2 + m_3 + m_4)$

$(7 \times 0) + (6 \times 5) + (10 \times 5) + (12 \times 0)$

$= \overline{x}(7 + 6 + 10 + 12)$

$80 = 35\overline{x} \Rightarrow \overline{x} = 2.29\,\text{cm}$ (3 s.f.).

b)

Angle $= \tan^{-1} \dfrac{3.14}{2.29} = 54°$ to the nearest degree.

Answers

Exam Questions

1 a) Taking moments about end string:

$12 \times 3 = 18 \times \frac{x}{2}$ so, $36 = 9x$ *[1 mark]*

$x = 4$ m *[1 mark]*

It's a uniform beam, so the weight acts exactly in the centre.

  b) Resolving horizontally:

$T + 12 = 18 \Rightarrow T = 6$ N *[1 mark]*

I've got to admit, that was a pretty easy Q to get you started. Hold tight though — it's about to get trickier.

2 a) Taking moments about B:

$(mg\cos\theta \times 1.4) + (180\cos\theta \times 2.1)$

$= (490\sin\theta \times 4.2)$

Dividing by $\cos\theta$ gives:

$1.4mg + 378 = 2058\tan\theta = 2058 \times \frac{8}{11}$

so, $1.4mg = 1496.73 - 378 = 1118.73$

so $m = \dfrac{1118.73}{13.72} = 81.54$

$= 82$ kg (nearest kg)

$AB = 4.2$ m
$AC = 2.8$ m
$BC = 1.4$ m

[4 marks available in total]:
  • *1 mark for taking moments about B*
  • *1 mark for forming a correct equation involving m*
  • *1 mark for correct workings*
  • *1 mark for the correct value of m*

  b) Resolving horizontally:

$F = 490$ N

Resolving vertically:

$R = 180 + 81.54g = 979.1$ N

As equilibrium is limiting, $F = \mu R$

so $979.1\mu = 490$ N and $\mu = 0.50$ (2 s.f.)

[4 marks available in total]:
  • *1 mark for resolving horizontally to find F*
  • *1 mark for resolving vertically to find R*
  • *1 mark for using F = μR*
  • *1 mark for correct value of μ*

3) a) Using the formula $\Sigma my = \bar{y}\Sigma m$

$m_1 y_1 + m_2 y_2 + m_3 y_3 = \bar{y}(m_1 + m_2 + m_3)$

$\Rightarrow (4 \times 3) + (3 \times 1) + (2 \times y) = 2 \times (4 + 3 + 2)$ *[1 mark]*

$\Rightarrow 15 + 2y = 18$ *[1 mark]*

$\Rightarrow y = (18 - 15) \div 2 = 1.5$ *[1 mark]*.

  b) Using the formula $\Sigma mx = \bar{x}\Sigma m$

$m_1 x_1 + m_2 x_2 + m_3 x_3 = \bar{x}(m_1 + m_2 + m_3)$

$\Rightarrow (4 \times 1) + (3 \times 5) + (2 \times 4) = \bar{x}(4 + 3 + 2)$ *[1 mark]*

$\Rightarrow 27 = 9\bar{x}$ *[1 mark]*

$\Rightarrow \bar{x} = 27 \div 9 = 3$ *[1 mark]*.

  c) Centre of mass of the lamina is at (3.5, 2.5), due to the symmetry of the shape, and $m_{lamina} = 6$ kg.
Centre of mass of the group of particles is (3, 2) (from (b)) and $m_{particles} = 4 + 3 + 2 = 9$ kg. Using $\Sigma m\mathbf{r} = \bar{\mathbf{r}}\Sigma m$:

$m_{lamina}\mathbf{r}_{lamina} + m_{particles}\mathbf{r}_{particles} = \bar{\mathbf{r}}(m_{lamina} + m_{particles})$

$\Rightarrow 6\binom{3.5}{2.5} + 9\binom{3}{2} = \bar{\mathbf{r}}(6 + 9)$

$\Rightarrow \binom{21 + 27}{15 + 18} = 15\bar{\mathbf{r}}$

$\Rightarrow \bar{\mathbf{r}} = \binom{48}{33} \div 15 = \binom{3.2}{2.2}$,

so the coordinates are (3.2, 2.2).

[6 marks available — 1 mark for the correct x_{lamina}, 1 mark for the correct y_{lamina}, 1 mark for correct entry of horizontal positions in the formula, 1 mark for correct entry of vertical positions in the formula, 1 mark for x coordinate of 3.2, 1 mark for y coordinate of 2.2.]

4 a) Splitting up the shape into a circle (1), large square (2) and small square (3) and taking the point A as the origin, the position vectors of the centres of mass of each shape are as follows:

Circle:

$x_1 = 25$ and $y_1 = 50 + (40 - 35) = 55$ (symmetry)

so $\mathbf{r}_1 = \binom{25}{55}$.

Large Square:

$x_2 = 25$ and $y_2 = 25$ (symmetry)

so $\mathbf{r}_2 = \binom{25}{25}$.

Small Square:

$x_3 = 50 + 5 = 55$ and $y_3 = 5$ (symmetry)

so $\mathbf{r}_3 = \binom{55}{5}$.

Using the formula $\Sigma m\mathbf{r} = \bar{\mathbf{r}}\Sigma m$

$m_1\mathbf{r}_1 + m_2\mathbf{r}_2 + m_3\mathbf{r}_3 = \bar{\mathbf{r}}(m_1 + m_2 + m_3) \Rightarrow$

$5\binom{25}{55} + 4\binom{25}{25} + 1\binom{55}{5} = \bar{\mathbf{r}}(5 + 4 + 1)$

$\Rightarrow \binom{125 + 100 + 55}{275 + 100 + 5} = 10\bar{\mathbf{r}}$

$\Rightarrow \bar{\mathbf{r}} = \binom{280}{380} \div 10 = \binom{28}{38}$.

The centre of mass of the sign is 28 cm from AB and 38 cm from AF.

[5 marks available — 1 mark for each individual centre of mass entered correctly into the formula, 1 mark for correct distance from AB, 1 mark for correct distance from AF.]

  b) For the sign to hang with AF horizontal, the centre of mass of the whole system (sign + particle) must be vertically below C, i.e. $\bar{x}$ must be 25 (taking A as the origin again).

Given that $m_{sign} = 10$ kg and $x_{sign} = 28$ (from part a)), and $x_{particle} = 0$ (since it's attached at the origin):

$m_{sign}x_{sign} + m_{particle}x_{particle} = \bar{x}(m_{sign} + m_{particle})$

$(10 \times 28) + 0 = 25(10 + m_{particle})$

$\Rightarrow 280 \div 25 = 10 + m_{particle}$

$\Rightarrow 11.2 - 10 = m_{particle}$

$\Rightarrow m_{particle} = 1.2$ kg

[3 marks available — 1 mark for stating the correct required value of $\bar{x}$, 1 mark for correct entry of values into the formula, 1 mark for correct final answer.]

Answers

M2 Section 2 — Kinematics
Warm-up Questions

1) a) $a = \frac{dv}{dt} = 16t - 2$

   b) $s = \int v\,dt = \frac{8t^3}{3} - t^2 + c$

   When $t = 0$, the particle is at the origin, i.e. $s = 0 \Rightarrow c = 0$

   So, $s = \frac{8t^3}{3} - t^2$

2) a) $a = \frac{dv}{dt} = 6t + 8\sin 2t$

   b) $s = \int v\,dt = t^3 - 2\sin 2t + 8t + c$

   When $t = 0$, the particle is at the origin, i.e. $s = 0 \Rightarrow c = 0$
   So, $s = t^3 - 2\sin 2t + 8t$

3) $\dot{\mathbf{r}} = \frac{d\mathbf{r}}{dt}$, which represents the velocity of the particle, and

   $\ddot{\mathbf{r}} = \frac{d^2\mathbf{r}}{dt^2}$, which represents the acceleration of the particle.

4) a) $\mathbf{r} = \int \mathbf{v}\,dt = 2t^2\mathbf{i} + \frac{t^3}{3}\mathbf{j} + \mathbf{C}$

   When $t = 0$, the particle is at the origin $\Rightarrow \mathbf{C} = 0\mathbf{i} + 0\mathbf{j}$.

   So, $\mathbf{r} = 2t^2\mathbf{i} + \frac{t^3}{3}\mathbf{j}$

   $\mathbf{a} = \frac{d\mathbf{v}}{dt} = 4\mathbf{i} + 2t\mathbf{j}$

   b) $\mathbf{F} = m\mathbf{a} = 3 \times (4\mathbf{i} + 2t\mathbf{j}) = 12\mathbf{i} + 6t\mathbf{j}$

5) Use $F = ma$ with $F = -0.025mv$ and $a = \frac{dv}{dt}$:

   $-0.025mv = m \times \frac{dv}{dt} \Rightarrow \frac{dv}{dt} = -0.025v$

Exam Questions

1 a) Find v by integrating a with respect to t:

   $v = \int a\,dt = \int (8t^2 + 6\sin 2t)\,dt$ *[1 mark]*

   $= \frac{8}{3}t^3 - \frac{6}{2}\cos 2t + c = \frac{8}{3}t^3 - 3\cos 2t + c$ *[1 mark]*

   When $t = 0$, $v = 0$:

   $0 = \frac{8}{3}(0)^3 - 3\cos(2 \times 0) + c \Rightarrow 0 = 0 - 3 + c$

   $\Rightarrow c = 3$ *[1 mark]*

   $\therefore v = \frac{8}{3}t^3 - 3\cos 2t + 3$ *[1 mark]*

   b) $v = \frac{8}{3}\left(\frac{\pi}{2}\right)^3 - 3\cos 2\left(\frac{\pi}{2}\right) + 3$ *[1 mark]*

   $v = \frac{\pi^3}{3} - 3(-1) + 3 = \frac{\pi^3}{3} + 6$ *[1 mark]*

2 a) $a = \frac{dv}{dt}$ *[1 mark]*

   $a = 2 - 3(-2)e^{-2t} = 2 + 6e^{-2t}$ *[1 mark]*

   b) t must be greater than or equal to 0.

   When $t = 0$, $a = 2 + 6e^{-2 \times 0} = 8$ *[1 mark]*

   As $t \to \infty$, $6e^{-2t} \to 0$, so $a \to 2$ *[1 mark]*

   So, 2 ms$^{-2} < a \le 8$ ms^{-2} *[1 mark]*

   c) $F = ma \Rightarrow 6 = m \times (2 + 6e^{-2 \times 2})$ *[1 mark]*

   $m = 2.84$ kg (3 s.f.) *[1 mark]*

d) $s = \int v\,dt$ *[1 mark]*

   $s = t^2 + \frac{3}{2}e^{-2t} + 4t + c$ *[1 mark]*

   When $t = 0$, the particle is at the origin (i.e. $s = 0$):

   $0 = 0 + \frac{3}{2} + c \Rightarrow c = -\frac{3}{2}$ *[1 mark]*

   So, $s = t^2 + \frac{3}{2}e^{-2t} + 4t - \frac{3}{2}$ *[1 mark]*

3 a) $\mathbf{v} = \dot{\mathbf{r}} = (6t^2 - 14t)\mathbf{i} + (6t - 12t^2)\mathbf{j}$

   [2 marks in total — 1 mark for attempting to differentiate the position vector, 1 mark for correctly differentiating both components]

   b) $\mathbf{v} = \left(\frac{6}{4} - \frac{14}{2}\right)\mathbf{i} + \left(\frac{6}{2} - \frac{12}{4}\right)\mathbf{j}$ *[1 mark]*

   $= -5.5\mathbf{i} + 0\mathbf{j}$

   Speed $= \sqrt{(-5.5)^2 + 0^2} = 5.5$ ms^{-1} *[1 mark]*

   The component of velocity in the direction of north is zero, and the component in the direction of east is negative, so the particle is moving due west *[1 mark]*

   c) $\mathbf{a} = \dot{\mathbf{v}}$ *[1 mark]*

   $= (12t - 14)\mathbf{i} + (6 - 24t)\mathbf{j}$ *[1 mark]*

   At $t = 2$, $\mathbf{a} = 10\mathbf{i} - 42\mathbf{j}$ *[1 mark]*

   d) Use $\mathbf{F} = m\mathbf{a}$ to find the force at $t = 2$:

   $\mathbf{F} = 10m\mathbf{i} - 42m\mathbf{j}$ *[1 mark]*

   At $t = 2$, $|\mathbf{F}| = \sqrt{(10m)^2 + (-42m)^2} = 43.17m$ *[1 mark]*

   Magnitude of $\mathbf{F}$ at $t = 2$ is 170, so: $43.17m = 170$

   $\Rightarrow m = 3.94$ kg (3 s.f.) *[1 mark]*

   e) The vectors $\mathbf{F}$ and $\mathbf{a}$ always act in the same direction, so when $\mathbf{F}$ is acting parallel to $\mathbf{j}$, so is $\mathbf{a}$. *[1 mark]*

   So, when $\mathbf{F}$ is acting parallel to $\mathbf{j}$, the component of $\mathbf{a}$ in direction of $\mathbf{i}$ will be zero *[1 mark]*, i.e.

   $12t - 14 = 0 \Rightarrow t = 1.17$ s (3 s.f.) *[1 mark]*

4 a) $\mathbf{a} = \dot{\mathbf{v}} = (-6\sin 3t + 5)\mathbf{i} + 2\mathbf{j}$

   [2 marks in total — 1 mark for attempting to differentiate the velocity vector, 1 mark for correctly differentiating both components]

   b) The $\mathbf{j}$-component of the acceleration is constant, so the $\mathbf{i}$-component is the only one which can be maximised. To do this, set $\sin 3t = -1$. *[1 mark]*

   The minimum value of sin(anything) is −1

   $\mathbf{a} = ((-6 \times -1) + 5)\mathbf{i} + 2\mathbf{j} = 11\mathbf{i} + 2\mathbf{j}$ *[1 mark]*

   Magnitude $= a = \sqrt{11^2 + 2^2} = \sqrt{121 + 4}$ *[1 mark]*

   $a = \sqrt{125}$ ms$^{-2} = 5\sqrt{5}$ ms^{-2} *[1 mark]*

5 a) Using $F = ma$,

   $\frac{10\,000}{v} - 0.1mv^2 = m\frac{dv}{dt}$ *[1 mark]*

   Rearranging: $\frac{dv}{dt} = \frac{10\,000}{mv} - 0.1v^2$ *[1 mark]*

   b) $\frac{dv}{dt} = -0.1v^2$ *[1 mark]*

   Once the engines are switched off, the only force acting horizontally on the plane will be the resistive force.

c) Separate the variables and integrate:

$\int \frac{1}{v^2} dv = \int -0.1 dt$ *[1 mark]*

$\Rightarrow -\frac{1}{v} = -0.1t + c$ *[1 mark]*

When $t = 0$, $v = 20$, so

$-\frac{1}{20} = -0.1(0) + c$ *[1 mark]* $\Rightarrow c = -\frac{1}{20}$ *[1 mark]*

So, when $v = 10$, $-\frac{1}{10} - -0.1t - \frac{1}{20}$

$\Rightarrow t = 0.5$ seconds *[1 mark]*

6 a) Using $F = ma$:

$-kv = 2 \times \frac{dv}{dt}$ *[1 mark]*

So, $\frac{dv}{dt} = \frac{-kv}{2}$ *[1 mark]*

b) Separate the variables and integrate:

$\frac{dv}{dt} = \frac{-kv}{2} \Rightarrow \frac{1}{v} dv = -\frac{k}{2} dt$

So $\int \frac{1}{v} dv = \int -\frac{k}{2} dt \Rightarrow \ln v = -\frac{kt}{2} + c$ *[1 mark]*

When $t = 0$, $v = 12$, so:

$\ln 12 = 0 + c \Rightarrow c = \ln 12$ *[1 mark]*

Take exponentials of both sides to get an equation for v:

$v = e^{-\frac{kt}{2} + \ln 12} = e^{-\frac{kt}{2}} \times e^{\ln 12}$ *[1 mark]*

So, $v = 12 e^{-\frac{kt}{2}} = 12\sqrt{e^{-kt}}$ *[1 mark]*

M2 Section 3 — Work and Energy
Warm-up Questions

1) Work done = $F \times s$
   $= 250 \times 3 = 750$ J

2) Work done against gravity = mgh
   $34\,000 = m \times 9.8 \times 12$
   $m = 289$ kg (3 s.f.)

3) Kinetic Energy = $\frac{1}{2}mv^2$
   $= \frac{1}{2} \times 450 \times 13^2$
   $= 38\,025$ J $= 38.0$ kJ (3 s.f.)

4) Work done = Change in Kinetic Energy
   $800 = \frac{1}{2}m(v^2 - u^2)$
   $u = 0$ and $m = 65$, so:
   $v^2 = \frac{1600}{65} \Rightarrow v = 4.96$ ms^{-1} (3 s.f.)

5) Increase in Potential Energy = mg × increase in height
   $= 0.5 \times 9.8 \times 150$
   $= 735$ J

6) "If there are no external forces doing work on an object, the total mechanical energy of the object will remain constant." You usually need to model the object as a particle, because you have to assume that the object is not acted on by any external forces such as air resistance.

7) When the hat reaches its maximum height, its velocity will be zero. Using conservation of energy:
   Change in potential energy = change in kinetic energy
   $mgh = \frac{1}{2}m(u^2 - v^2)$

Cancel m from both sides, and substitute $u = 5$, $v = 0$ and $g = 9.8$:

$9.8h = \frac{1}{2} \times 25 \Rightarrow h = 1.28$ m (3 s.f.)

8) "The work done on an object by external forces is equal to the change in the total mechanical energy of that object." An external force is any force other than an object's weight.

9) a) $T = \frac{\lambda}{l}e = \frac{25}{3} \times (3 - 1.5) = 12.5$ N

   b) E.P.E. $= \frac{\lambda}{2l}e^2 = \frac{25}{2 \times 3}(1.5)^2 = 9.38$ J (3 s.f.)

10) Power of engine = driving force × velocity
    $350\,000 = F \times 22 \Rightarrow F = 15\,900$ N (3 s.f.)

11) When the bus is travelling at its maximum speed, $a = 0$, so the driving force of the engine = $80v$.
    Power = driving force × velocity
    $65\,000 = 80v \times v$
    $\Rightarrow v^2 = 812.5 \Rightarrow v = 28.5$ ms^{-1} (3 s.f.)

Exam Questions

1 a) Increase in Kinetic Energy $= \frac{1}{2}m(v^2 - u^2)$ *[1 mark]*
   $= \frac{1}{2} \times 90 \times (6^2 - 4^2) = 900$ J *[1 mark]*
   Increase in Gravitational Potential Energy = mgh *[1 mark]*
   $= 90 \times 9.8 \times 28\sin 30° = 12\,348$ J *[1 mark]*
   Increase in total Energy = Increase in K.E. + Increase in P.E.
   $= 900 + 12\,348 = 13\,248$ J $= 13.2$ kJ (3 s.f.) *[1 mark]*

   b) Using the work-energy principle:
   Work done on skier = Change in total energy *[1 mark]*
   $(L - 66) \times 28 = 13\,248$ *[1 mark]*
   $L = \frac{13\,248}{28} + 66 = 539$ N (3 s.f.) *[1 mark]*

2 a) K.E. $= \frac{1}{2}mv^2 = \frac{1}{2} \times 0.3 \times 20^2$ *[1 mark]*
   $= 60$ J *[1 mark]*

   b) Only force acting on the stone is its weight, so use conservation of mechanical energy:
   Change in K.E. = Change in P.E. *[1 mark]*
   $60 - 0 = 0.3 \times 9.8 \times h$ *[1 mark]*
   $h = 20.4$ m (3 s.f.) *[1 mark]*

   c) Stone's change in K.E. after hitting the water:
   $\frac{1}{2} \times 0.3 \times 1^2 - 60 = -59.85$ J *[1 mark]*
   Call the depth the stone has sunk x m.
   Change in P.E. after hitting the water:
   $-mgx = -2.94x$ *[1 mark]*
   Work done on the stone by resistive force
   $= Fs = -23x$ *[1 mark]*
   By the work-energy principle:
   Work done on the stone = Change in total energy *[1 mark]*
   $-23x = -59.85 - 2.94x$
   Rearrange to find x:
   $x = 2.98$ m (3 s.f) *[1 mark]*

Answers

3 a)

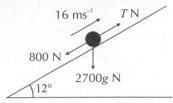

Resolving parallel to the slope using $F = ma$ with $a = 0$:
$T - 800 - 2700g\sin12° = 0$ *[1 mark]*
So, $T = 6301$ N *[1 mark]*
Power of engine = Driving Force × Velocity *[1 mark]*
$= 6301 × 16 = 101$ kW (3 s.f.) *[1 mark]*

b) Work done by resistive force to stop van $= -800x$ *[1 mark]*
Change in total energy = Change in P.E. + Change in K.E.
$= (2700 × g × x\sin12°) - \left(\frac{1}{2} × 2700 × 16^2\right)$ *[1 mark]*
By work-energy principle,
$-800x = 2700gx\sin12° - 345\,600$ *[1 mark]*
Rearrange to find x:
$x = \frac{345\,600}{2700g\sin12° + 800} = 54.8$ m (3 s.f.) *[1 mark]*

c) Resolve parallel to the slope using $F = ma$ to find a:
$-800 - 2700g\sin12° = 2700a$ *[1 mark]*
$a = -2.334$ ms^{-2} *[1 mark]*
Use $v = u + at$ to find the time taken to come to rest:
$0 = 16 - 2.334t$ *[1 mark]*
$t = \frac{16}{2.334} = 6.86$ s (3 s.f.) *[1 mark]*

4 a) Work done = Force × distance moved
$= 800\cos40° × 320 = 196$ kJ (3 s.f.)

[3 marks available in total]:
- *1 mark for using the horizontal component of the force*
- *1 mark for correct use of formula for work done*
- *1 mark for correct final answer.*

b)

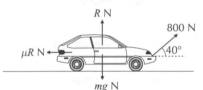

No acceleration vertically, so:
$R + 800\sin40° = mg$
$R = 1500g - 800\sin40° = 14\,190$ N *[1 mark]*
Car is moving only horizontally, so:
Work done = change in kinetic energy *[1 mark]*
$(800\cos40° - \mu R) × 320 = \frac{1}{2} × 1500 × (16^2 - 11^2)$ *[1 mark]*
Rearrange to find μ:
$\mu = \frac{196\,107 - 101\,250}{4\,541\,000} = 0.0209$ (3 s.f.) *[1 mark]*

5 a) Use the work rate to find the 'driving' force, F of the cyclist:
$250 = F × 4$ *[1 mark]*
$F = 62.5$ N
Resolve parallel to the slope: *[1 mark]*
$62.5 - 35 - 88g\sin\alpha = 0$ *[1 mark]*
$\alpha = \sin^{-1}\frac{27.5}{88g} = 1.83°$ (3 s.f.) *[1 mark]*

b) Use the new work rate to find the new 'driving' force, F':
$370 = F' × 4$ *[1 mark]*
$F' = 92.5$ N
Resolve parallel to the slope to find a: *[1 mark]*
$92.5 - 35 - 88g\sin\alpha = 88a$ *[1 mark]*
$a = 0.341$ ms^{-2} (3 s.f.) *[1 mark]*

6 a) The system is in equilibrium, so resolving forces vertically
gives $T = mg$, where T is tension in the string. *[1 mark]*
So, using Hooke's Law:
$T = \frac{\lambda}{l}e = mg$ *[1 mark]*
$\Rightarrow \lambda = \frac{mgl}{e} = \frac{3 × 9.8 × 2}{(5 - 2)} = 19.6$ N *[1 mark]*

b) E.P.E. $= \frac{\lambda}{2l}e^2$ *[1 mark]*
So $\frac{19.6}{2 × 2} × 3^2 = 44.1$ J *[1 mark]*

c) By the Principle of Conservation of Mechanical Energy:
E.P.E. lost = G.P.E. gained + K.E. gained *[1 mark]*
Assuming that block starts with no K.E. or G.P.E.,
$\frac{\lambda}{2l}(8 - 2)^2 - \frac{\lambda}{2l}(3 - 2)^2 = mg(8 - 3) + \frac{1}{2}mv^2$ *[1 mark]*
$\frac{19.6}{4}(36) - \frac{19.6}{4}(1) = (3 × 9.8 × 5) + \left(\frac{1}{2} × 3 × v^2\right)$

[1 mark]
$v^2 = \frac{2}{3}(171.5 - 147) = 16.33$
$v = 4.04$ ms^{-1} (3 s.f.) *[1 mark]*

7 a) Find T, the driving force of the car, using Power = Tv:
$T = $ Power $\div v = 20\,000 \div 10 = 2000$ N. *[1 mark]*
Resolve forces parallel to the slope:
$T - mg\sin\theta - kv = 0$ *[1 mark]*.
$\Rightarrow 2000 - (1000 × 9.8 × 0.1) - 10k = 0$
$\Rightarrow 10k = 1020$
$\Rightarrow k = 102$ *[1 mark]*

b) (i) Call the new driving force F. Using Power = Fv:
$F = \frac{50\,000}{u}$ *[1 mark]*
Resolve forces parallel to the slope:
$\frac{50\,000}{u} - mg\sin\theta - 102u = 0$. *[1 mark]*
Rearranging and substituting known values gives:
$50\,000 - (1000 × 9.8 × 0.1)u - 102u^2 = 0$ *[1 mark]*.
This rearranges to:
$102u^2 + 980u - 50\,000 = 0$ — as required *[1 mark]*.

(ii) Solve for u using the quadratic formula:
$u = \frac{-980 + \sqrt{980^2 - (4 × 102 × -50\,000)}}{2 × 102}$
$u = 17.9$ ms^{-1} (3 s.f.)

[2 marks available in total]:
- *1 mark for correctly using quadratic formula*
- *1 mark for correct value for u*
You don't need to worry about the negative part of ± in the
formula, as you're after a speed — which is always positive.

c) Using $F = ma$ gives $T - 102v = ma$. *[1 mark]*
This time, $T = P \div v = 21000 \div 12$, and so:
$(21000 \div 12) - (102 × 12) = 1000a$ *[1 mark]*
$\Rightarrow a = 0.526$ ms^{-2}. *[1 mark]*

8   a)   E.P.E. $= \frac{\lambda}{2l}e^2$ **[1 mark]**

$= \frac{50}{2 \times 5} \times (d-5)^2 = 5(d-5)^2$ **[1 mark]**

b)

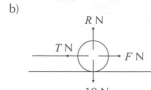

R N

T N   F N

10 N

There is no motion vertically, so $R = 10$ N **[1 mark]**
Particle is moving, so friction is limiting $\Rightarrow$
frictional force, $F = \mu R = 0.5 \times 10 = 5$ N **[1 mark]**
Work done by $F = F \times$ distance moved $= -5d$ **[1 mark]**.
There is no change in K.E. or G.P.E. between the start and
end of motion, so the only change in mechanical energy is
the loss of E.P.E. **[1 mark]**
So, by the work-energy principle:
Change in E.P.E. = Work done on particle by friction
$\Rightarrow -5(d-5)^2 = -5d$ **[1 mark]**
The change in E.P.E. is negative because E.P.E. is lost
Rearranging: $d = d^2 - 10d + 25 \Rightarrow d^2 - 11d + 25 = 0$.
Solve using the quadratic formula: **[1 mark]**
$d = 7.79$ or $d = 3.21$ (each to 3 s.f.)
Question says that $d > 5$, so take $d = 7.79$ m. **[1 mark]**

M2 Section 4 — Uniform Circular Motion
Warm-up Questions

1) a) $\omega = \frac{\theta}{t} = \frac{2\pi}{1.5} = \frac{4\pi}{3}$ radians s^{-1}

$a = r\omega^2 = 3 \times \left(\frac{4\pi}{3}\right)^2 = \frac{16\pi^2}{3}$ ms^{-2}

Don't forget the units — it's radians per second for angular speed.

b) $\omega = \frac{\theta}{t} = \frac{15 \times 2\pi}{60} = \frac{\pi}{2}$ radians s^{-1}

$a = r\omega^2 = 3 \times \left(\frac{\pi}{2}\right)^2 = \frac{3\pi^2}{4}$ ms^{-2}

c) $\omega = \frac{\theta}{t} = \frac{\frac{160}{360} \times 2\pi}{1} = \frac{8}{9}\pi$ radians s^{-1}

$a = r\omega^2 = 3 \times \left(\frac{8}{9}\pi\right)^2 = \frac{64\pi^2}{27}$ ms^{-2}

d) $\omega = \frac{v}{r} = \frac{10}{3}$ radians s^{-1}

$a = \frac{v^2}{r} = \frac{10^2}{3} = \frac{100}{3}$ ms^{-2}

2   a) $F = mr\omega^2 = 2 \times 0.4 \times (10\pi)^2 = 80\pi^2$ N

b) $F = \frac{mv^2}{r} = \frac{2 \times 4^2}{0.4} = 80$ N

*This formula is just the old F = ma in disguise. Just make sure you
know the circular motion acceleration formulas.*

---

3   a) Resolving vertically:

$T\cos 45° = 4g \Rightarrow T = 55.4$ N (3 s.f.)

b) Resolving horizontally:

$T\sin 45° = \frac{mv^2}{r} \Rightarrow 55.4\sin 45° = \frac{4v^2}{r}$

$r = 0.102v^2$ m

4   a)

R

mg

b) Using conservation of mechanical energy
(between points A and B):

$\frac{1}{2}m(2.2)^2 + mg(0.2 - 0.2\cos45°) = \frac{1}{2}mv_B^2$

$4.84 + 2(0.05858g) = v_B^2$

$v_B = \sqrt{4.84 + 0.1172g} = 2.447... = 2.45$ ms^{-1} (3 s.f.)

c) Resolving perpendicular to direction of motion:

$R + mg\cos45° = \frac{mv^2}{r}$

$R + mg\cos45° = \frac{m(2.447^2)}{0.2}$

$R = \frac{m(2.447^2)}{0.2} - mg\cos45° = 23.0m$ N (3 s.f.)

5   a) Find the particle's speed, v, at the highest point:

Using conservation of mechanical energy
(between the lowest and highest points on the circle):

$\frac{1}{2}m(9)^2 = \frac{1}{2}mv^2 + 4mg$

$81 = v^2 + 8g$

$v^2 = 2.6 \Rightarrow v = \sqrt{2.6} = 1.61$ms^{-1}

The particle's still moving, so the bead on the wire will
complete the circle.

Find the tension in the string at the highest point:

mg

T

Resolving perpendicular to motion:

$T + mg = \frac{mv^2}{r} \Rightarrow T = \frac{2.6m}{2} - 9.8m$

$T = 1.3m - 9.8m = -8.5m$

The tension is negative, so the particle on the string
won't complete the circle.

*That's the difference between things that can leave the circle and
things that can't. If something's stuck on the circle (like a bead on
a wire) it only needs enough energy to get to the top. If something
can leave the circle (like a particle on a string), it also needs a
positive (or zero) tension or reaction at the top.*

Answers

b)

Find an expression for the speed, v, when the particle leaves the circle using conservation of mechanical energy (between the lowest point and the point where particle leaves the circle):

$$\frac{1}{2}m(9)^2 = \frac{1}{2}mv^2 + mg(2 + 2\cos\theta)$$
$$81 = v^2 + 4g(1 + \cos\theta)$$
$$v^2 = 81 - 4g(1 + \cos\theta)$$

When the bead leaves the circular path, $T = 0$, so resolving perpendicular to motion:

$$mg\cos\theta = \frac{mv^2}{r} \Rightarrow 2g\cos\theta = 81 - 4g(1 + \cos\theta)$$
$$2g\cos\theta = 81 - 4g - 4g\cos\theta$$
$$\cos\theta = \frac{81 - 4g}{6g} = 0.711 \Rightarrow \theta = 44.7° \text{ (3 s.f.)}$$

Exam Questions

1 a) Using conservation of mechanical energy (between points A and B):

$$\frac{1}{2}m(0)^2 + mg(0.5\sin 30°) = \frac{1}{2}mv^2 \text{ [1 mark]}$$
$$\frac{1}{2}(0)^2 + g(0.5 \times 0.5) = \frac{1}{2}v^2$$
$$\frac{1}{4}g = \frac{1}{2}v^2 \text{ [1 mark]}$$
$$\frac{1}{2}g = v^2 \Rightarrow v = \sqrt{\frac{g}{2}} \text{ ms}^{-1} \text{[1 mark]}$$

b) Resolving perpendicular to motion:

$$T - mg\sin 30° = \frac{mv^2}{r} \text{ [1 mark]}$$
$$T - 2g\left(\frac{1}{2}\right) = \frac{2\left(\frac{g}{2}\right)}{0.5} \text{ [1 mark]}$$
$$T - g = 2g$$
$$\Rightarrow T = 3g \text{ N [1 mark]}$$

c) Using v from part a):

$$v = r\omega \Rightarrow \omega = \frac{v}{r} = \frac{\sqrt{\frac{g}{2}}}{0.5} \text{ [1 mark]}$$
$$\omega = \frac{2\sqrt{g}}{\sqrt{2}} = \sqrt{2g} \text{ radians s}^{-1} \text{ [1 mark]}$$

Don't be put off if you're not shown the whole of the circle.
The particle's started moving in a circular path, so you can use the
circular motion rules.

2 a)

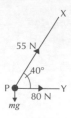

Resolving vertically: $mg = 55\sin 40°$ *[1 mark]*
$\Rightarrow m = 3.61$ kg *[1 mark]*

b) Resolving horizontally:

$$F = \frac{mv^2}{r} \text{ [1 mark]}$$
$$55\cos 40° + 80 = \frac{3.607 \times 3^2}{r} \text{ [1 mark]}$$
$$\Rightarrow r = \frac{3.607 \times 3^2}{55\cos 40° + 80} = 0.266 \text{ m [1 mark]}$$

The radius is the same as the length of the horizontal string.

$$\omega = \frac{v}{r} = \frac{3}{0.2658} = 11.29 \text{ radians s}^{-1} \text{ [1 mark]}$$

c) 2π radians $= 1$ revolution

$$\frac{11.29}{2\pi} = 1.796 \text{ revolutions per second [1 mark]}$$

$1.796 \times 60 = 108$ revolutions per minute (3 s.f.) *[1 mark]*

3 a) Using conservation of mechanical energy (between points A and B):

$$\frac{1}{2}m(\sqrt{20})^2 = \frac{1}{2}mv^2 + mg \text{ [1 mark]}$$
$$20 = v^2 + 2g \text{ [1 mark]}$$
$$v = \sqrt{0.4} \text{ ms}^{-1} \text{ [1 mark]}$$

b) Resolving perpendicular to motion at point B:

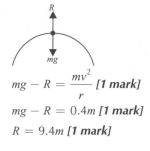

$$mg - R = \frac{mv^2}{r} \text{ [1 mark]}$$
$$mg - R = 0.4m \text{ [1 mark]}$$
$$R = 9.4m \text{ [1 mark]}$$

c) Using conservation of mechanical energy (between points A and B):

$$\frac{1}{2}mv_A^2 = \frac{1}{2}mv_B^2 + mg \text{ [1 mark]}$$

v_B must be greater than or equal to zero.

If $v_B = 0$: $\frac{1}{2}mv_A^2 = mg$ *[1 mark]*

$$\Rightarrow v_A = \sqrt{2g} = 4.43 \text{ ms}^{-1} \text{ [1 mark]}$$

So the minimum speed at A for the circle to be completed is 4.43 ms^{-1} (3 s.f.).

4

Resolving vertically: $R = 500g$ *[1 mark]*

Resolving horizontally: $\mu R = \dfrac{mv^2}{r}$ *[1 mark]*

$0.5 \times 500g = \dfrac{500v^2}{30}$ *[1 mark]*

$0.5g = \dfrac{v^2}{30}$

$v^2 = 15g$ *[1 mark]* $\Rightarrow$ $v = 12.1\text{ms}^{-1}$ *[1 mark]*

5 a) Using conservation of mechanical energy

(between points J and K):

$\dfrac{1}{2}m(15)^2 = \dfrac{1}{2}mv^2 + mg(5 + 5\cos\theta)$

$225 = v^2 + 10g(1 + \cos\theta)$

$v^2 = 225 - 10g(1 + \cos\theta)$

[4 marks available in total]:
* *1 mark for total mechanical energy at J*
* *1 mark for total mechanical energy at K*
* *1 mark for using conservation of mechanical energy*
* *1 mark for correct expression for v^2*

'Show that' questions are quite nice and friendly. You know when you've got the right answer. Don't make any crazy leaps in logic though — the examiners aren't that daft.

b) Use the formula from part a) with $\theta = 0$:

$v^2 = 225 - 10g(2) = 29$

$\Rightarrow v = \sqrt{29}$ ms^{-1} *[1 mark]*

So, it has enough energy to get to the top,

so now find the tension, T, in the string at the top:

$T + mg = \dfrac{mv^2}{r}$ *[1 mark]*

$\Rightarrow T + mg = \dfrac{29m}{5}$ *[1 mark]*

$\Rightarrow T = \dfrac{29m}{5} - 9.8m = -4m$ *[1 mark]*

The tension in the string is negative, so the string is no longer taut and the circle isn't completed *[1 mark]*.

You have to find the speed first here — you need it to work out the tension. Don't forget, if it was something that couldn't leave the circle — like a bead on a ring — you would only need to show that it had enough energy to reach the top.

c) When the string first becomes slack, the tension in the string is zero.
So resolving perpendicular to the direction of motion:

$mg\cos\theta = \dfrac{mv^2}{r}$ *[1 mark]*

$mg\cos\theta = \dfrac{m(225 - 10g(1 + \cos\theta))}{5}$ *[1 mark]*

$5g\cos\theta = 225 - 10g(1 + \cos\theta)$

$15g\cos\theta = 225 - 10g$ *[1 mark]*

$\cos\theta = \dfrac{127}{147}$ *[1 mark]* $\Rightarrow$ $\theta = 30.2°$ (3 s.f.) *[1 mark]*

M2 Practice Exam One

1 a) Kinetic energy $= \dfrac{1}{2}mv^2$ *[1 mark]*

$= \dfrac{1}{2} \times 80 \times 14^2 = 7840$ J *[1 mark]*

b) The only force acting on the fireman is his weight, so, by conservation of mechanical energy:
G.P.E. lost = K.E. gained *[1 mark]*
i.e. $mgh = 7840$ J *[1 mark]*
$\Rightarrow h = 7840 \div (80 \times 9.8) = 10$ m *[1 mark]*.

c) There is now an external force acting on the fireman (call it F), so by the work-energy principle:
Change in K.E. + Change in G.P.E. = W.D. by F *[1 mark]*
$\dfrac{1}{2}mv^2 - mg \times 5 = F \times -5$ *[1 mark]*
Change in G.P.E. is negative, as G.P.E. is lost. Work done by F is negative, as it's done in the opposite direction to motion.
$mv^2 = 10(mg - 400)$
$\Rightarrow v = \sqrt{48} = 6.93$ ms^{-1} (3 s.f.) *[1 mark]*

2 a) Using conservation of mechanical energy (between the lowest point and point X):

$\dfrac{1}{2} \times 0.1 \times 3^2$ *[1 mark]*

$= (\dfrac{1}{2} \times 0.1 \times v^2) + (0.1 \times g \times (0.2 + 0.2\cos\theta))$ *[1 mark]*

(where v = speed at X)

$0.45 = 0.05v^2 + 0.02g(1 + \cos\theta)$ $\Rightarrow$

$v^2 = \dfrac{0.45 - 0.02g(1 + \cos\theta)}{0.05}$

$= 9 - 0.4g(1 + \cos\theta)$ *[1 mark]*

Resolving perpendicular to direction of motion at X:

$R + 0.1g\cos\theta = \dfrac{mv^2}{r}$ *[1 mark]*

$R + 0.1g\cos\theta = \dfrac{0.1(9 - 0.4g(1 + \cos\theta))}{0.2}$ *[1 mark]*

$R = 4.5 - 0.2g(1 + \cos\theta) - 0.1g\cos\theta$

$R = 4.5 - 0.2g - 0.3g\cos\theta$ *[1 mark]*

b) At the point when the ball leaves the surface, $R = 0$, so, using the formula from part a):

$0 = 4.5 - 0.2g - 0.3g\cos\theta$ *[1 mark]*

$\Rightarrow 0.3g\cos\theta = 4.5 - 0.2g$

$\Rightarrow \cos\theta = (4.5 - (0.2 \times 9.8)) \div (0.3 \times 9.8)$

$= 0.864$ *[1 mark]*

$\Rightarrow \theta = 30.2°$ (3 s.f.) *[1 mark]*

Answers

3 a) Call the driving force of the engine F.
Car will be travelling at maximum speed when engine is working at maximum power; i.e. acceleration will be zero.
So, resolving horizontally:
$F - 40v = 0 \Rightarrow F = 40v$ *[1 mark]*
Find the maximum power of the engine using $P = Fv$:
$P = 40v \times v$ *[1 mark]*
$= 40 \times 70 \times 70 = 196$ kW *[1 mark]*.

b) (i) Resolve horizontally with $a = \dfrac{dv}{dt}$:

$-40v = m\dfrac{dv}{dt}$ *[1 mark]*

So $\dfrac{dv}{dt} = -\dfrac{40v}{1300} = -\dfrac{2}{65}v$ — as required. *[1 mark]*

(ii) Separate the variables and integrate both sides:

$\dfrac{dv}{dt} = -\dfrac{2}{65}v \Rightarrow \int \dfrac{1}{v}dv = -\dfrac{2}{65}\int dt$

$\Rightarrow \ln v = -\dfrac{2}{65}t + c.$

Use the initial conditions $v = 25$ when $t = 0$ to find c:
$\ln 25 = 0 + c \Rightarrow c = \ln 25$, and so:
$\ln v = -\dfrac{2}{65}t + \ln 25.$

Take exponents of both sides:
$\Rightarrow v = e^{-\frac{2}{65}t + \ln 25}$

$\Rightarrow v = 25e^{-\frac{2}{65}t}.$

[6 marks available — 1 mark for attempting to separate variables, 1 mark for correct separation of variables, 1 mark for correctly integrating, 1 mark for finding c correctly, 1 mark for taking exponential of both sides, 1 mark for correct final answer]

(iii) $v = 5 \Rightarrow 5 = 25e^{-\frac{2}{65}t}$ *[1 mark]*

$\Rightarrow \dfrac{1}{5} = e^{-\frac{2}{65}t} \Rightarrow \ln\dfrac{1}{5} = -\dfrac{2}{65}t$ *[1 mark]*

$\Rightarrow t = -\dfrac{65}{2}\ln\dfrac{1}{5} = 52.3$ s (3 s.f.) *[1 mark]*.

4 a) Setting point O as the origin, the distance of the centre of mass from OA is the horizontal distance $\overline{x}$.
So, using the formula $\Sigma mx = \overline{x}\Sigma m$:
$m_O x_O + m_A x_A + m_B x_B = \overline{x}(m_O + m_A + m_B)$
$\Rightarrow (3 \times 0) + (5 \times 0) + (2 \times 4) = \overline{x}(3 + 5 + 2)$
$\Rightarrow 8 = 10\overline{x} = \Rightarrow \overline{x} = 0.8$
So the centre of mass of the frame is 0.8 cm from OA.

[3 marks available — 1 mark for correct formula used, 1 mark for correct masses and distances entered, 1 mark for correct final answer]

b) Again, setting O as the origin, the distance of the centre of mass from OB is the vertical distance $\overline{y}$.
So using the formula $\Sigma my = \overline{y}\Sigma m$:
$m_O y_O + m_A y_A + m_B y_B = \overline{y}(m_O + m_A + m_B)$
$\Rightarrow (3 \times 0) + (5 \times 3) + (2 \times 0) = \overline{y}(3 + 5 + 2)$
$\Rightarrow 15 = 10\overline{y} = \Rightarrow \overline{y} = 1.5.$
So the centre of mass of the frame is 1.5 cm from OB.

[3 marks available — 1 mark for correct formula used, 1 mark for correct entry into formula, 1 mark for correct final answer]

c) You'll need to find some other angles first before you get the one asked for in the question.
They say a picture paints a thousand words, so...

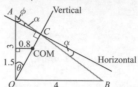

In the diagram, the angles in triangle OAC must add up to $180°$, so:
$\theta + \phi + \alpha + 90 = 180 \Rightarrow \alpha = 90 - (\theta + \phi)$ *[1 mark]*,
where α is the angle that AB makes with the horizontal, as asked for in the question.

The other angles can be found using basic trigonometry. From the right-angled triangle formed between O and the centre of mass: $\theta = \tan^{-1}(\frac{0.8}{1.5})$ *[1 mark]* $= 28.072...°$
[1 mark]

From the right-angled triangle OBA:
$\phi = \tan^{-1}(\frac{4}{3}) = 53.130...°$ *[1 mark]*
So the angle with the horizontal, $\alpha = 90 - (\theta + \phi)$
$= 90 - (28.072... + 53.130...) = 8.80°$ to 3 s.f. *[1 mark]*

5 a) There are no external forces acting on the particle, so by the conservation of mechanical energy,
G.P.E. lost = K.E. gained
i.e. $mgh = \frac{1}{2}mv^2$ *[1 mark]*.
$gh = \frac{1}{2}v^2$
The string first becomes taut when the particle has fallen 4 m (i.e. the natural length of the string). So $h = 4$.
$\Rightarrow v = \sqrt{2gh} = \sqrt{2 \times 9.8 \times 4}$ *[1 mark]*
$= 8.85$ ms^{-1} (3 s.f.) *[1 mark]*.

b) Again, using conservation of mechanical energy,
G.P.E. lost = K.E. gained + E.P.E. gained
i.e. $mgh = \frac{1}{2}mv^2 + \frac{\lambda}{2l}e^2$ *[1 mark]*
$\Rightarrow \lambda = \dfrac{2l}{e^2}(mgh - \frac{1}{2}mv^2)$
$= \left(\dfrac{2 \times 4}{3^2}\right) \times (5 \times 9.8 \times 7 - \frac{1}{2} \times 5 \times 10^2)$ *[1 mark]*
$= 82.7$ N (3 s.f.). *[1 mark]*

c) Resolving vertically:
$mg - T = 0 \Rightarrow mg = T.$ *[1 mark]*
By Hooke's Law, $T = \frac{\lambda}{l}e$, and so $mg = \frac{\lambda}{l}e$ *[1 mark]*
$\Rightarrow e = \dfrac{mgl}{\lambda} = \dfrac{5 \times 9.8 \times 4}{82.67} = 2.37$ m (3 s.f.) *[1 mark]*.

6 a) Speed, $v = |\mathbf{v}| = \sqrt{(-8\sin 2t)^2 + (8\cos 2t)^2}$ *[1 mark]*
$= \sqrt{64(\sin^2 2t + \cos^2 2t)} = 8$ ms^{-1} *[1 mark]*

b) $\mathbf{a} = \dot{\mathbf{v}}$ *[1 mark]*
$= -16(\cos 2t)\mathbf{i} - 16(\sin 2t)\mathbf{j}$ *[1 mark]*
$\mathbf{F} = 2 \times \mathbf{a} = -32(\cos 2t)\mathbf{i} - 32(\sin 2t)\mathbf{j}$ N *[1 mark]*

c) When the particle is moving parallel to **i**, the **j** component of its velocity is zero.

$\Rightarrow 8\cos 2t = 0$ *[1 mark]* $\Rightarrow \cos 2t = 0$

$\Rightarrow 2t = \frac{\pi}{2}$ *[1 mark]* $\Rightarrow t = \frac{\pi}{4}$ s *[1 mark]*.

*Remember to check that the particle is moving — i.e. that the **i** component of velocity isn't O as well: $-8\sin\left(\frac{\pi}{2}\right) = -8$. Hurrah.*

d) First find the position vector of the particle at time t:

$\mathbf{r} = \int \mathbf{v}\, dt$ *[1 mark]*

$= 4(\cos 2t)\mathbf{i} + 4(\sin 2t)\mathbf{j} + \mathbf{C}$ *[1 mark]*

At $t = 0$ $\mathbf{r} = 4\mathbf{i} + 0\mathbf{i} \Rightarrow \mathbf{C} = 0\mathbf{i} + 0\mathbf{j}$ *[1 mark]*

Distance from origin at time $t =$

$|\mathbf{r}| = \sqrt{(4\cos 2t)^2 + (4\sin 2t)^2}$

$= \sqrt{16(\cos^2 2t + \sin^2 2t)} = 4$ *[1 mark]*

So the particle is 4 m from the origin for all t, i.e. it moves in a circle of radius 4 m *[1 mark]*

e) Use $v = r\omega$ to find the angular speed:

$\Rightarrow \omega = \frac{v}{r}$ *[1 mark]*.

$\omega = 8 \div 4 = 2$ rad s^{-1} *[1 mark]*

f) Use $\omega = \frac{\theta}{t}$ to find the time taken for a complete circle:

$\Rightarrow t = \frac{\theta}{\omega}$ *[1 mark]*.

$t = 2\pi \div 2 = \pi$ s *[1 mark]*.

Remember, there's 2π radians in a complete circle.

7 a)

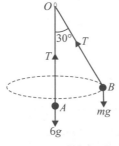

Resolving vertically for particle A:

$T = 6g$ *[1 mark]*

Resolving vertically for particle B:

$T\cos 30 = mg \Rightarrow 6g\cos 30 = mg$ *[1 mark]*

$\Rightarrow m = 6\cos 30 = 5.20$ kg (3 s.f.) *[1 mark]*

b) Resolving horizontally for particle B, perpendicular to the direction of motion:

$6g\sin 30 = \frac{mv^2}{r}$ *[1 mark]*

$3g = \frac{5.196v^2}{0.3}$ *[1 mark]*

$v^2 = 1.697$

$v = 1.30$ ms^{-1} (3 s.f.) *[1 mark]*

c) The fact that the ring is smooth means that the tension is the same throughout the string *[1 mark]*.

M2 Practice Exam Two

1 a)

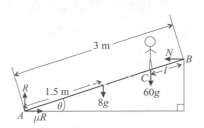

Resolving vertically:

$R = 8g + 60g = 68g$ *[1 mark]*

Beam is in limiting equilibrium so $F = \mu R$ *[1 mark]*:

$199 = \mu \times 68g$ *[1 mark]*

$\mu = 0.298... = 0.3$ to 1 significant figure *[1 mark]*

Adding all the forces to the diagram is always the best way of starting one of these questions.

b) Resolving horizontally: $N = \mu R = 199$ N *[1 mark]*

Taking moments about A:

$((3 - l) \times 60g\cos\theta) + (1.5 \times 8g\cos\theta)$ *[1 mark]*

$= 3 \times 199\sin\theta$ *[1 mark]*

Divide through by $\cos\theta$.

$((3 - l) \times 60g) + (1.5 \times 8g) = 3 \times 199\tan\theta$ *[1 mark]*

$\Rightarrow 180g - 60gl + 12g = 597\tan\theta$

$\tan\theta = 0.45$ (from question),

so $180g + 12g - 268.65 = 60gl$

$l = 2.74$ m *[1 mark]*

You could have taken moments about B instead. This'd mean one extra moment, but you wouldn't have had to resolve horizontally first. It's swings and roundabouts (or ramps and reactions).

c) As the beam is uniform, you can assume that its weight acts at its centre when taking moments *[1 mark]*.

2 a) Since both the circle and the rectangle are made from the same uniform material, their masses are in proportion to their areas:

Circle $m_1 = \pi r^2 = \pi \times 2^2 = 4\pi$

Rectangle $m_2 = 1.5 \times 1 = 1.5$

Taking the point P as the origin, the centre of mass of the circle, $\mathbf{r}_1 = \binom{0}{0}$, since P is the centre of the circle.

The centre of mass of the rectangle is on both the horizontal and vertical lines of symmetry of the rectangle:

$\mathbf{r}_2 = \binom{0.75}{0.5}$.

Use the formula:

$m_1\mathbf{r}_1 + m_2\mathbf{r}_2 = \bar{\mathbf{r}}(m_1 + m_2)$

$\Rightarrow 4\pi\binom{0}{0} + 1.5\binom{0.75}{0.5} = \bar{\mathbf{r}}(4\pi + 1.5)$

$\Rightarrow \binom{1.125}{0.75} = 14.07\bar{\mathbf{r}}$

$\Rightarrow \bar{\mathbf{r}} = \binom{1.125 \div 14.07}{0.75 \div 14.07} = \binom{0.07998}{0.05332}$.

The distance of the COM from P is the magnitude of the position vector:

Answers

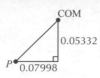

Distance = $\sqrt{0.07998^2 + 0.05332^2}$ = 0.0961 cm (3 s.f.)

[5 marks available — 1 mark for correct relative masses of both shapes, 1 mark for individual centre of mass for both shapes, 1 mark for correct use of formula, 1 mark for correct position vector or coordinates of centre of mass, 1 mark for correct distance from P]

b) The shape is being hung from Q. Drawing a sketch will make it easier to see what's going on:

θ is the angle that PQ makes with the vertical.
Using basic trigonometry:

$\theta = \tan^{-1}(\dfrac{0.07998}{1 - 0.05332}) = 4.83°$ (3 s.f.)

[3 marks available — 1 mark for correct sides of the right-angled triangle, 1 mark for correct working, 1 mark for correct final answer]

3 a) Bus is travelling at constant speed, so resolve horizontally with $F = ma$ to find the driving force of the engine, T:

$T - 4500 = 0 \Rightarrow T = 4500$ N *[1 mark]*

Power of engine = Driving force × velocity *[1 mark]*
$= 4500 × 14 = 63$ kW *[1 mark]*

b) Call the new driving force of the engine T':

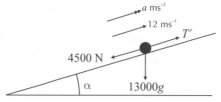

Use Power = Fv to find T':
$72\,000 = T' × 12 \Rightarrow T' = 6000$ N
Resolve parallel to the slope with $F = ma$ to find a:
$T' - (4500 + 13\,000g\sin\alpha) = 13\,000a$
Substitute known values and rearrange:
$a = \dfrac{6000 - 4500 - 3640}{13\,000} = -0.165$ ms^{-2} (3 s.f.)

[4 marks available — 1 mark for using Power = Fv, 1 mark for finding the new driving force of the engine, 1 mark for resolving parallel to the slope and 1 mark for correct final answer]

4 a) $\omega = \dfrac{\theta}{t} = \dfrac{2\pi × 100}{60}$ *[1 mark]*

$\omega = \dfrac{10\pi}{3}$ radians s^{-1} *[1 mark]*

b)
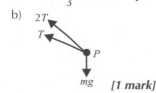
[1 mark]

c) Resolving vertically:
$2T\cos 50 + T\cos 70 = 2g$ *[1 mark]*
$T × (2\cos50 + \cos70) = 2g$
$T × 1.628 = 19.6$ *[1 mark]*
$T = 12.0$ N (3 s.f.) — as required *[1 mark]*

d) Resolving horizontally:
$2T\sin50 + T\sin70 = 2a$ *[1 mark]*
$\Rightarrow (2 × 12.04\sin50) + (12.04\sin70) = 2a$ *[1 mark]*
$\Rightarrow a = 14.9$ ms^{-2} (3 s.f.) *[1 mark]*

5 Resolve horizontally with $a = \dfrac{dv}{dt}$ to give: *[1 mark]*
$-5\sqrt{v} = 15\dfrac{dv}{dt}$ *[1 mark]*
Separate variables:
$-\dfrac{5}{15} dt = v^{-\frac{1}{2}} dv$ *[1 mark]*
Integrate both sides:
$-\int \dfrac{5}{15} dt = \int v^{-\frac{1}{2}} dv$ *[1 mark]*
$-\dfrac{1}{3}t + c = 2v^{\frac{1}{2}}$ *[1 mark]*
When $t = 0$, $v = 10$ ms^{-1}, so:
$-\dfrac{1}{3}(0) + c = 2\sqrt{10}$
$\Rightarrow c = 2\sqrt{10}$ *[1 mark]*
Plug this back into your equation, then rearrange to make v the subject:
$-\dfrac{1}{3}t + 2\sqrt{10} = 2v^{\frac{1}{2}}$
$v = \left(\dfrac{1}{2}(-\dfrac{1}{3}t + 2\sqrt{10})\right)^2$
$v = \left(-\dfrac{1}{6}t + \sqrt{10}\right)^2$ *[1 mark]*

6 a) $\mathbf{v} = \dot{\mathbf{r}} = (3t^2 - 12t + 4)\mathbf{i} + (7 - 8t)\mathbf{j}$
At $t = 5$:
$\mathbf{v} = (3(5^2) - 12(5) + 4)\mathbf{i} + (7 - 8(5))\mathbf{j} = 19\mathbf{i} - 33\mathbf{j}$ as required.

[3 marks available — 1 mark for attempting to differentiate the position vector, 1 mark for a correct expression for velocity at time t, and 1 mark for correct velocity at t = 5]

b) When P is moving south, component of velocity in direction of $\mathbf{i}$ will be zero, i.e.
$3t^2 - 12t + 4 = 0$ *[1 mark]*
Solving using the quadratic formula gives
$t = 0.3670$ or 3.633 *[1 mark]*
When P is moving south, the component of velocity in the direction of $\mathbf{j}$ will be –ve, so find the velocity of P at the two values of t above, and see which is negative: *[1 mark]*
$\mathbf{v}(0.367) = (7 - 8(0.367))\mathbf{j} = 4.06\mathbf{j}$ (so P is moving due north)
$\mathbf{v}(3.633) = (7 - 8(3.633))\mathbf{j} = -22.1\mathbf{j}$
So, P is moving due south when $t = 3.63$ s (3 s.f.) *[1 mark]*
Read through that bit about the components of velocity in the j direction a couple of times, until you're sure it makes sense to you. It can be a little bit confusing.

c) To find force on P, will need to use $\mathbf{F} = m\mathbf{a}$, so first find $\mathbf{a}$:
$\mathbf{a} = \dot{\mathbf{v}} = (6t - 12)\mathbf{i} - 8\mathbf{j}$ *[1 mark]*
When $t = 3$, $\mathbf{a} = (18 - 12)\mathbf{i} - 8\mathbf{j} = 6\mathbf{i} - 8\mathbf{j}$ *[1 mark]*
So, $\mathbf{F} = m\mathbf{a} = 2.5(6\mathbf{i} - 8\mathbf{j}) = 15\mathbf{i} - 20\mathbf{j}$ *[1 mark]*
Magnitude of $\mathbf{F} = \sqrt{15^2 + (-20)^2}$ *[1 mark]*
$= 25$ N *[1 mark]*

Answers

7   a)   Use conservation of mechanical energy between A and B:

$\frac{1}{2}mv^2 + 0.75mg = \frac{1}{2}m(4v)^2$

$v^2 + 1.5g = 16v^2$

$15v^2 = 1.5g$

$v^2 = \dfrac{g}{10}$

$v = \sqrt{\dfrac{g}{10}}$

[5 marks available — 1 mark for using conservation of energy, 1 mark for each side of conservation of energy equation correct, 1 mark for correctly simplifying, 1 mark for correct final answer]

   b)

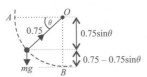

Use conservation of mechanical energy:

$\frac{1}{2}m(2v)^2 + mg(0.75 - 0.75\sin\theta) = \frac{1}{2}m(4v)^2$ *[1 mark]*

$2v^2 + g(0.75 - 0.75\sin\theta) = 8v^2$

$g(0.75 - 0.75\sin\theta) = 6v^2$

$g(0.75 - 0.75\sin\theta) = \dfrac{6g}{10}$ *[1 mark]*

$0.75\sin\theta = 0.15$

$\theta = \sin^{-1}\left(\dfrac{0.15}{0.75}\right) = 11.5°$ (3 s.f.)   *[1 mark]*

8   a)   E.P.E. $= \dfrac{\lambda}{2l}e^2$ *[1 mark]* $= \dfrac{30}{2 \times 3}(10 - 3)^2$

$= 245$ J *[1 mark]*.

   b)   Using conservation of mechanical energy:

Change in K.E. = Change in E.P.E. *[1 mark]*

There is no change in G.P.E., so it can just be ignored.

So, $\frac{1}{2}mv^2 = 245 - \dfrac{\lambda}{2l}e^2$ *[1 mark]*

$10v^2 = 245 - 5(x - 3)^2$ *[1 mark]*

$10v^2 = 245 - 5(x^2 - 6x + 9)$

Which rearranges to $2v^2 = 6x - x^2 + 40$ *[1 mark]*

   c)   Change in K.E. = Change in G.P.E. = 0

E.P.E. in spring when compressed by 1 m $= \dfrac{\lambda}{2l}e^2$ *[1 mark]*

$= \dfrac{30}{2 \times 3}(1)^2 = 5$ J *[1 mark]*

So change in E.P.E. $= 245 - 5 = 240$ J *[1 mark]*

Resolving vertically, $R = mg$ *[1 mark]*

The frictional force, F, is given by $F = \mu R = \mu mg$ *[1 mark]*.

By the work-energy principle:

Work done by frictional force = change in E.P.E. *[1 mark]*

$\mu mg \times (10 - 2) = 240$ *[1 mark]*

$8\mu mg = 240$

$\Rightarrow \mu = 240 \div (8 \times 20 \times 9.8)$

$= 0.153$ (3 s.f.) *[1 mark]*.

Don't forget that the spring has E.P.E. stored in it when it is compressed, as well as when it is stretched. Luckily though, the formula is the same for both.

Index

Index

Index

Index